D1599040

GALICIA

A HISTORICAL SURVEY AND BIBLIOGRAPHIC GUIDE

Other books by Paul Robert Magocsi

Let's Speak Rusyn, 2 vols
The Shaping of a National Identity
The Ukrainian Experience in the United States
Wooden Churches in the Carpathians
The Rusyn-Ukrainians of Czechoslovakia

The symbol that appears on the cover represents the coat of arms of Galicia-Rus', devised in 1642 and the official emblem until 1918.

PAUL ROBERT MAGOCSI

Galicia: A Historical Survey and Bibliographic Guide

Published in association with the Canadian Institute of Ukrainian Studies and the Harvard Ukrainian Research Institute by University of Toronto Press
Toronto Buffalo London

Toronto Buffalo London
Printed in Canada
Reprinted 1985, 1990

ISBN 0-8020-2482-3

Canadian Cataloguing in Publication Data

Magocsi, Paul R.

Galicia : a historical survey and bibliographic guide

Includes index.
ISBN 0-8020-2482-3

1. Galicia (Poland and Ukraine) — History — Bibliography. 2. Ukrainians — Galicia (Poland and Ukraine) — History — Bibliography. I. Canadian Institute of Ukrainian Studies. II. Harvard Ukrainian Research Institute. III. Title.

Z2514.G34M34 016.947'718 C82-094956-6

This book has been published with the help of a grant from the Canadian Federation for the Humanities, using funds provided by the Social Sciences and Humanities Research Council of Canada.

To my mother
ANNA LENGYEL MAGOCSI
whose ancestors probably
came from north of the Carpathians

Contents

Introduction xiii
Abbreviations xix

1: Bibliographical and archival aids 1
Historiographical studies
National bibliographies
Subject bibliographies
Archives
Libraries and other cultural institutions

2: General studies 21
Scholarly journals
Reference works
Historical surveys
Church history
Cultural history
Regional and urban history

3: Early history to 1340 46
Archeological studies
Background
Sources
General histories of Galicia-Volhynia
Specific periods and problems
Galician-Hungarian relations
Church history
Cultural and urban history

4: 1340–1772 65
Background
General surveys and sources
Period of transition, 1340–1387
The establishment and impact of Polish rule
Urban and economic history
Church history
Cultural history: the brotherhoods
Cultural history: book culture, art, and architecture
Cossacks in Galicia and the brigand movement

5: 1772–1848 92
Background
Historical surveys and descriptive works
Establishment of Austrian rule and foreign affairs
Socioeconomic developments
Cultural history: background
Cultural history: sources and surveys
Cultural history: education, church, theater, press
Cultural history: literature (Rusyn Triad)
Cultural history: the language question
Relations with other Slavs

6: 1848–1918 116
Background
Historical surveys, memoirs, reference works
Revolutionary years, 1848–1849
Political developments, 1850–1914
Socioeconomic developments
Cultural history: national identity and national organizations
Cultural history: the press and the language question
Cultural history: education
Cultural history: literary history surveys
Cultural history: individual writers and national leaders
Church history
Relations with other Slavs
World War I

7: 1919–1939 174
Background
General surveys
Establishment of Polish rule, 1918–1923
Polish-Ukrainian war and the Ukrainian Galician Army, 1918–1919
Galicia and the international scene, 1918–1923
Political developments, 1923–1939
Socioeconomic developments and the Communist party
Cultural history: education
Cultural history: the church, national identity, literature

8: 1939–1944 205
Background
Historical surveys and sources
Soviet rule, 1939–1941
Political developments
Military developments

9: 1945 to the present 217
Background
Ukrainian resistance movement
Establishment of Soviet rule

10: Minorities 224
Poles
- Background
- Studies

Jews
- Background
- Bibliographies
- Historical surveys and documentary collections
- Specific periods and problems
- Cultural history
- Interwar Poland and the holocaust

Armenians
- Background

Historiography, archives, general surveys
Cultural history, the church, other specific problems
Germans
Background
Bibliographies, historical surveys, specific problems
Karaites
Background
General surveys

Table of Place Names 256

Index 257

Maps

Ethnogeographic setting xii

Medieval Galicia 51

Galicia in the Polish-Lithuanian Commonwealth 66

Galicia in the Austro-Hungarian Empire 93

Interwar Galicia 177

Galicia since 1939 206

ETHNOGEOGRAPHIC SETTING
International borders, 1980
Galicia before 1918
Galicia (Rus') before 1772
Approximate ethnolinguistic boundary between Poles and Ukrainians, 1930
0 50 MILES
0 50 KILOMETERS
N
POLAND
UKRAINIAN S.S.R.
CZECHOSLOVAKIA
HUNGARY
ROMANIA
CARPATHIAN MOUNTAINS
LEMKIAN REGION
BOIKIAN REGION
HUTSUL REGION
Cracow
Sandomierz
Tarnów
Nowy Sącz
Jasło
Krosno
Brzozów
Rzeszów
Jarosław
Radymno
Przemyśl
Sanok
Chełm
Zamość
Volodymyr Volyns'kyi
Luts'k
Sokal'
Belz
Uhniv
Rava Rus'ka
Kaminka Strumylova
Iavoriv
Nesterov (Zhovkva)
Sudova Vyshnia
Horodok
L'viv
Brody
Zolochiv
Zboriv
Zbarazh
Ternopil'
Terebovlia
Chortkiv
Sambir
Drohobych
Boryslav
Stryi
Turka
Berezhany
Pidhaitsi
Halych
Zhovten' (Iezupil')
Ivano-Frankivs'k (Stanyslaviv)
Buchach
Horodenka
Kolomyia
Sniatyn
Chernivtsi
Kam''ianets' Podil's'kyi
Prešov
Košice
Uzhhorod
Miskolc
Tylyč Pass
Dukla Pass
Laborec Pass
Rus'-Pass
Uzhok Pass
Verets'kyi Pass
Tatar Pass
Vistula
Dunajec
Wisłoka
Wisłok
San
Wieprz
Buh
Styr
Horyn
Seret
Zbruch
Dniester
Stryi
Poprad
Torysa
Laborec
Uzh
Latorytsia
Tysa
Cheremosh
Prut

Introduction

Despite its relatively small size, Galicia has played an important and often crucial role in east-central European and, in particular, Ukrainian historical development. It was in Galicia that the medieval traditions of Kievan Rus' were preserved after the Dnieper region had lost its historical significance in the thirteenth century. Again it was in Galicia where the Orthodox cultural revival and general renaissance in Ukrainian cultural life began in the late sixteenth century–movements that later were carried out in the political sphere with the establishment of a Cossack state in the Dnieper Ukraine. Finally, it was in Galicia where during the late nineteenth century the Ukrainian national idea was kept alive through scholarship and political activity at a time when it was forbidden any normal advancement within the Russian-controlled Dnieper Ukraine. And all of this occurred in a territory that represented no more than 6 percent of the Ukrainian ethnographic land mass and that, in 1910, contained only 9.5 percent of the total Ukrainian population. Galicia was also a meeting ground for Ukrainian and Polish cultures and, at least during the nineteenth century, was a region of crucial importance to the Polish national revival. At the same time, the Jews of Galicia made many contributions to Jewish developments in east-central Europe.

Because of its historical significance, an enormous literature has developed about Galicia. However, as chapter 1 of this study reveals, there is no adequate guide or even comprehensive bibliography of the many writings covering various chronological and thematic aspects of this area. It is for this reason that the present study was undertaken.

The guide has ten chapters and the arrangement is basically chronological. Two introductory chapters deal with bibliographic and archival aids and with general studies, followed by chapters on specific periods: early history to 1340, 1340–1772, 1772–1848, 1848–1918, 1919–1939, 1939–1944, and 1945–present. A final chapter deals with the literature on minorities who inhabited

Galicia–Poles, Jews, Armenians, Germans, and Karaites–most of whom played an important and, in the case of the Poles, a dominant role in the history of the region. Each chronological chapter begins with a brief history of events during the period in question. This makes it possible for the reader to understand better the discussion about the historical literature that follows.

It should be remembered that this book is not a history of Galicia. Nor does it pretend to provide an exhaustive bibliography of the subject. Rather, it is intended to serve as an introduction to the basic historical problems of Galicia and to direct the reader to the major published primary and secondary sources dealing with those problems. The vast majority of the material consists of works in political, socioeconomic, and cultural (in particular literary) history. Works dealing with linguistic and ethnographic problems are, with few exceptions, not to be found here. Even with these limitations, the guide contains 1003 notes with more than 3000 references. It is hoped that these will provide a good starting point for those interested in knowing more about the contributions of Galicia to Ukrainian, to Polish, to Jewish, and to east-central European culture as a whole.

The concept of Galicia is problematic. Most writings generally understand Galicia to be synonymous with the province obtained by the Austrian Empire in 1772–within the boundaries that were finally stabilized in 1815 and which, excepting the addition of the Free City of Cracow in 1847, remained unchanged at least until the outbreak of World War I in 1914.[1] However, as a political entity, Galicia derives from a principality of that name already founded in the mid-twelfth century, whose borders were substantially different from those of post-1772 Austrian Galicia. Although Galicia as a distinct principality existed only for about 200 years (1141–1340), it lasted for more than another four centuries as a historical and territorial concept known as the Rus' palatinate (*Województwo Ruskie*) within the Polish-Lithuanian Commonwealth.

The core territory of historic Galicia lay along both banks of the upper Dniester River. Its southern boundary was defined by the crests of the Carpathian Mountains, and although the peaks were high enough (over 2000 meters in the southeastern corner) to provide a natural historico-geographic frontier with the Hungarian Kingdom, there were nonetheless several passes that have traditionally permitted access to the Danube Basin in the south. The western boundary of historic Galicia lay near the Wisłok River, a tributary of the San. The eastern boundary was formed by the Zbruch and the Cheremosh rivers. The northern boundary had no natural frontier, but followed more or less the boundary of the

1 For a survey of how Galicia's boundaries change after 1772, see Leo J. Haczynski, "Two Contributions to the Problem of Galicia," *East European Quarterly*, IV, 1 (Boulder, Colo. 1970), pp. 94–104.

medieval principality of Galicia and later Rus' palatinate. Within the confines of this core area were the cities of Jarosław and Przemyśl in the west, L'viv in the north, Ternopil' and Terebovlia in the east, and the old capital of Halych near the center. This understanding of the concept of Galicia was best summed up by the leading Ukrainian historian, Mykhailo Hrushevs'kyi: "The term 'Galicia' is very complex and in essence of rather fortuitous origin. Basically, it reflects the tradition of the 'Galician principality', founded in the mid-twelfth century, and which generally is equated with what in the nineteenth century was called 'eastern Galicia'."[2]

Thus, in this study, the concept of Galicia (*Halychyna* in Ukrainian)[3] is used in its long-term historical sense, and this refers basically to the eastern half of the former Austrian province of Galicia (*Galizien*). However, because in Austrian, Polish, Jewish, and other western literature the term Galicia often refers to the old Austrian province as a whole, it may be necessary to use the formulations eastern Galicia or Ukrainian Galicia in order to make a distinction from the western, largely Polish-inhabited half of the former Austrian province. Although Ukrainians always formed the majority of the population in "eastern" Galicia (62 percent in 1910 and even higher in earlier centuries), there were also substantial numbers of Poles and Jews, especially in urban areas, where Polish or Jewish culture dominated city life. Therefore, much of the historic literature discussed in this study, even that which focuses on "eastern," "Ukrainian" Galicia may in fact deal with the Polish or Jewish aspects of the region.

Not surprisingly, the literature under discussion reflects the political fortunes of the territory in question. Consequently, many different names are encountered, all of which are basically synonymous with the historic concept of Galicia as described above. These names include during the medieval period: Galicia (*Halychyna/Galitsiia*), or Red Rus' (*Chervona Rus'/Chervonaia Rus'/Ruś Czerwona*), or Galician Rus' (*Halyts'ka Rus'/Galitskaia Rus'*); during the Polish-Lithuanian era: Rus' palatinate (*Województwo Ruskie*), or Red Rus' (*Ruś Czerwona*); during the Austrian period, 1772–1918: East Galicia (*Ost-Galizien/Skhidna Halychyna/*

2 M. Grushevskii, "Galitsiia: istoricheskii ocherk," *Bol'shaia sovetskaia éntsiklopediia*, vol. XIV (Moscow 1929), p. 368.

3 On the etymology of the term Galicia, see Iaroslav Pasternak, "Zvidkilia nazva Halych," *Students'kyi prapor*, II (L'viv 1944), pp. 9–15; and Iaroslav B. Rudnyts'kyi, *Nazvy 'Halychyna' i 'Volyn''*, Onomastica Ukraïns'koï Vil'noï Akademiï Nauk, no. 3 (Winnipeg 1952), pp. 9–16. Of the many theories, Pasternak favors Galicia as derivative from the Indo-European word for salt (**hal*), mined in significant amounts near the territory's first medieval capital, Halych. Rudnyts'kyi favors the "heraldic hypothesis," whereby Halych is the collective noun derived from the Ukrainian word *halychchia*, meaning jackdaw, a crow-like bird similar to the symbol used on the ancient coat-of-arms of Halych.

Galicja Wschodnia); during the revolutionary years, 1918–1919: Western Ukrainian People's Republic (*Zakhidno-Ukraïns'ka Narodna Respublyka*); during the interwar years: Eastern Little Poland (*Małopolska Wschodnia*), or Southeastern Poland (*Polska Południowo-Wschodnia*); during World War II, 1941–1944; Galician district of the Generalgouvernement (*Distrikt Galizien Generalgouvernement*); and during the Soviet period, 1939–1941 and 1945–present: Western Ukraine (*Zakhidna Ukraïna*–a term that frequently encompasses neighboring northern Bukovina and Transcarpathia as well). In this study, all of the above names will be rendered simply as Galicia, and whenever the context requires it, as eastern Galicia or Ukrainian Galicia.

There has also been more than one name used to describe the Ukrainian inhabitants, and again the historical literature reflects the several known variants. Until the first quarter of the twentieth century, the vast majority of Ukrainians in Galicia called themselves Rusyns (*rusyny*). After 1772, the Austrian government used for official purposes the German term *Ruthenen,* which has often been translated into English as Ruthenians. Old Ruthenian, local Russophile, and Russian writers described the group as Russians (*russkie*) or Little Russians (*malorossy/malorossiiane*). Ukrainophiles described the population as Rusyns and later Ukrainians (*rusyny/ukraïntsi*).[4] There are also several regional names like Lemkian (*Lemko*), Boikian (*Boiko*), and Hutsul. Finally, some Soviet literature uses the term western Ukrainians (*zakhidnoukraïntsi*). In this study, we will only use the term Ukrainian to refer to the Ukrainian inhabitants of Galicia.

Of a more technical nature is the question of place names and the transliteration system. Geographic names are given according to the dominant (sometimes official) language of the country where the place is located today. Thus, places within the Ukrainian Soviet Socialist Republic are in Ukrainian, places within Poland are rendered in Polish. A few names–Cracow, Dnieper, Kiev, Warsaw–are given in their commonly used English form. The justification for such a decision is simple: it is easier for the reader to find these places on modern-day maps. However, because some place names in Galicia differ substantially from one locally used language to another, a table of major places and their linguistic equivalents is provided at the end of this study.

With regard to transliteration, the Library of Congress system has been used to render titles in the Cyrillic alphabet. This system was chosen because most libraries in the United States and Canada have adopted that system; hence, it will be easier for the reader to find a work cited in this study. It should also be noted

4 The Ukrainophile view of the nomenclature problem is found in B. Barvins'kyi, *Istorychnyi rozvii imeny ukraïns'ko-rus'koho narodu* (L'viv 1909). The Russophile view is in F.I. Svistun, "Dlia chego galitskii rusiny nazvany Ruthen'ami?" *Viestnik 'Narodnogo Doma'*, XXIV [II], 11 (L'viv 1906), pp. 220–222.

that the footnote references reproduce names of authors and titles as they appear on the original title page[5] although places of publication have been standardized according to the principles on place names outlined above. Names of political and cultural activists in Galicia, notwithstanding their national orientation (Old Ruthenian, Russophile, Ukrainophile) are given in Ukrainian. This is again a practical matter and in no way casts aspersions on the beliefs of a given individual. Transliterations from Hebrew and Yiddish follow the system adopted by the *Association for Jewish Studies Review*. Names of Jewish authors mentioned in the text are given according to the form used in the *Encyclopedia Judaica*. Dates are provided for historical figures the first time they are mentioned; they are not given for authors unless, of course, the latter were participants in the historical process.

Finally, all references appear in as complete a form as possible, including full names of author(s) or editor(s), title and subtitle, series where applicable, journal volume and number, place of publication of books and journals, publisher, and page numbers for articles. The research needed to supply some of these elements has often been tedious and enormously time consuming, but it has been my experience that full bibliographical references can often make the difference between finding a given item or not. Reviews are generally not mentioned except in those cases where they have contributed substantially to further knowledge about a given subject.

I viewed more than 90 percent of the items mentioned in this study. This has been possible because I was privileged to work in some of the world's leading repositories of Slavic and east-central European materials. Among the collections surveyed were Widener and other affiliated libraries in the Harvard University Library System (Cambridge, Massachusetts); the Library of Congress (Washington, DC); the University of Toronto Library (Toronto, Ontario); the Österreichische Nationalbibliothek, the Parliamentsbibliothek, and Institut für Geschichte Osteuropas und Südostforschungen (Vienna); and the Slovanská knihovna and Národní Muzeum (Prague). The author is particularly grateful for the assistance rendered him by the staffs of the Slavic Division and Judaica Division at Harvard's Widener Library and to Maria Razumovsky of the Österreichische Nationalbibliothek and Dr. Rudolf Stöhr of the Parliamentsbibliothek in Vienna.

5 This means that names of authors as they appear in the footnote references (which reflect the language of the original publication) may differ from the form found in the text (which reflects the nationality of the author). Also, old orthography has been maintained in Polish titles and in transliterating from Russian and Ukrainian. Cyrillic titles by Old Ruthenian authors (written in an uncodified Galician recension of Church Slavonic or Russian) are transliterated according to the Library of Congress system for Ukrainian with the following additions: ѣ = î; ы = ŷ.

The initial research and writing of this volume was undertaken during the academic years 1978–1979 and 1979–1980 while I was resident Senior Research Fellow at the Harvard Ukrainian Research Institute. Further funding was provided by the Canadian Institute of Ukrainian Studies at the University of Alberta to work in Vienna for six weeks during the summer of 1979 and by the Kennan Institute for Advanced Russian Studies at the Woodrow Wilson Center in Washington, DC to survey the Library of Congress collection during the fall of 1980. To all these institutions I am very grateful.

Finally, while any sins of omission or error that still remain are mine alone, it must be said that whatever value the manuscript has is due in no small part to the insights and suggestions of several readers. These have included Mykola Andrusiak (Ukrainian Free University), Kevork B. Bardakjian (Harvard University), Bohdan Budurowycz (University of Toronto), Patricia Kennedy Grimsted (Harvard University), John-Paul Himka (University of Alberta), Robert A. Kann (University of Vienna), Edward Kasinec (University of California at Berkeley), Joseph Kermisz (Yad Vashem, Jerusalem), Julius Krämer (Hilfskomittee der Galiziendeutschen), Ezra Mendelsohn (Hebrew University), Moshé Mishkinsky (Hebrew University), Alexander Motyl (Columbia University), Omeljan Pritsak (Harvard University), Ivan L. Rudnytsky (University of Alberta), and Frank E. Sysyn (Harvard University).

There are also several other individuals who have helped in the technical preparation of the manuscript and in the publication process. Brenda Sens and Patricia Bennett typed varying versions of the manuscript, while Olga Kavochka Mayo and Nadia Odette Diakun worked on additional references, the eternal bane of all bibliographic projects. The crucial job of proofreading several thousand references in sixteen languages was graciously carried out by Dr. Bohdan Budurowycz, Pawel Depta, Dr. Libby Garshowitz, Helga Haynes, Dr. Patricia A. Krafcik, Maria Magocsi, and Josef Staša. The comprehensive index was prepared by Ruth C. Cross in her usual meticulous manner, and the accompanying maps drawn under the direction of Geoff Matthews at the Cartography Office of the University of Toronto's Department of Geography. Finally, I am grateful to the editorial staff of the University of Toronto Press who admirably oversaw the publication process and to the bibliographical commission of Harvard University's Ukrainian Research Institute, which awarded the book the 1982 Cenko Prize for the best work in Ukrainian bibliography.

Abbreviations

AN URSR	Akademiia Nauk Ukraïns'koï Radians'koï Sotsialistychnoï Respubliky
ChSVV	Chyn Sviatoho Vasyliia Velykoho
LDU	L'vivs'kyi Derzhavnyi Universytet
LNBS	L'vivs'ka Naukova Biblioteka imeni Vasylia Stefanyka
LU	L'vivs'kyi Universytet
NTSh	Naukove Tovarystvo imeni Shevchenka
OSBM	Ordino Sancti Basilii Magni
PAN	Polska Akademia Nauk
PWN	Państwowe Wydawnictwo Naukowe
UAN	Ukraïns'ka Akademiia Nauk
URSR	Ukraïns'ka Radians'ka Sotsialistychna Respublika
TP	Tovarystvo 'Prosvita'
VUAN	Vse-ukraïns'ka Akademiia Nauk
YIVO	Yidisher Visenshaftlikher Institut
ZNIO	Zakład Narodowy imienia Ossolińskich

Of making many books there is no end,
And much study is weariness of the flesh.

Ecclesiastes 12: 12

Chapter 1

Bibliographical and archival aids

Historiographical studies

The literature dealing with the historiography of Galicia as a whole is underdeveloped, and only in general studies of Ukrainian historiography can a discussion of works by Galician historians (and usually about Galicia) be found.[1] Historiographical works on specific periods in Galician history are available, however. The best of these focus on medieval and early modern times, as in the extensive sections in several Russian and Ukrainian historiographical works that deal with the Galician-Volhynian principality[2] and in two studies by Ivan Kryp''iakevych that

1 Dmytro Doroshenko, *A Survey of Ukrainian Historiography,* and Olexander Ohloblyn, *Ukrainian Historiography, 1917–1956,* in *Annals of the Ukrainian Academy of Arts and Sciences in the U.S.*, vols V–VI (New York 1957), especially pp. 254–286 and 372–391. Two general bibliographies of Ukrainian bibliographies also include separate sections on Galicia: Ievhen Iu. Pelens'kyi, *Bibliohrafiia ukraïns'koï bibliohrafiï,* Vydannia 'Bohosloviï', no. 18 (L'viv 1934), especially entries 149–165, 190–193, 348–356a, 614a–617, 2061–2063; and R. Kats and F. Maksymenko, *Bibliohrafiia ukraïns'koï i rosiis'koï bibliohrafiï po istoriï URSR* (Kiev: Ministerstvo kul'tury URSR, Derzhavna istorychna biblioteka URSR 1960), especially pp. 89–93.

On the conceptual problem of Galicia as an entity for historical research, see for the medieval period Günther Stökl, ''Die Geschichte des Fürstentums Galizien-Wolhynien als Forschungsproblem,'' in *Forschungen zur osteuropäischen Geschichte,* vol. XXVII (Berlin and Wiesbaden: Otto Harrassowitz for the Osteuropa-Institut an der Freien Universität Berlin 1980), pp. 9–17; and for the Austrian era (1772–1918): Henryk Wereszycki, ''Dzieje Galicji jako problem historyczny,'' *Małopolskie Studia Historyczne,* I, 1 (Cracow 1958), pp. 4–16; and Józef Buszko, ''Jeszcze o Galicji jako o problemie historycznym,'' *ibid.*, II, 2–3 (Cracow 1959), pp. 84–95.

2 See the studies of Ivan Linnichenko, Mykhailo Hrushevs'kyi, Vladimir Ikonnikov, Dmytro Bahalii, and Vladimir Pashuto, chapter 3, n. 18.

analyze in detail the sources available for the study of Galicia before 1772.[3] Polish scholarship that appeared during the interwar period on all periods of Galician history is surveyed in four short essays.[4] Soviet researchers, especially Iaroslav Isaievych and Mykola Koval's'kyi, have prepared extensive analyses of the source materials and secondary literature available for the history of the brotherhoods, education, and printing in the Ukraine during the sixteenth to eighteenth centuries, and much of their discussion focuses on Galicia, in particular L'viv.[5] The majority of Soviet historiographical writing, however, concentrates on more modern periods, and the aim of these works is often to debunk most non-Soviet works for their lack of a Marxist perspective and instead to emphasize the achievements of recent Soviet scholarship. Several brief studies dealing with ''Western Ukrainian'' historiography as a whole or focusing on specific periods have appeared.[6] Refreshingly non-polemical, even if limited in scope, is the

3 Ivan P. Kryp''iakevych, *Dzherela z istoriï Halychyny periodu feodalizmu (do 1772 r.): ohliad publikatsii* (Kiev: AN URSR 1962); idem, ''Litopysy XVI–XVIII st. v Halychyni,'' in *Istorychni dzherela ta ïkh vykorystannia*, vol. I (Kiev 1964), pp. 63–80.

See also the recent discussion of published and unpublished sources on Ukrainian history with references to materials on Galicia in N.P. Koval'skii, *Istochnikovedenie istorii Ukrainy XVI–pervoi poloviny XVII v.*, 5 pts (Dnipropetrovs'k: Dnipropetrovs'kyi derzhavnyi universytet, 1977–79), and his more specific ''Istochniki po istorii Ukrainy s XVI–pervoi poloviny XVII v. vo lvovskikh arkheograficheskikh izdaniiakh XIX–nachala XX v.,'' in *Analiz publikatsii istochnikov po otechestvennoi istorii* (Dnipropetrovs'k 1978), pp. 20–48.

4 Bronisław Włodarski, Ewa Maleczyńska, Kazimierz Lewicki, and Marjan Tyrowicz, ''Przegląd literatury do dziejów politycznych Ziemi Czerwieńskiej,'' *Ziemia Czerwieńska*, I, 1 (L'viv 1935), pp. 106–133.

5 Iaroslav D. Isaievych, *Dzherela z istoriï ukraïns'koï kul'tury doby feodalizmu XVI-XVIII st.* (Kiev: Naukova dumka 1972); M[ykola] P. Koval's'kyi, *Dzherela pro pochatkovyi etap drukarstva na Ukraïni (diial'nist' pershodrukaria Ivana Fedorova v 70-kh–na pochatku 80-kh rr. XVI st.)* (Dnipropetrovs'k: Dnipropetrovs'kyi derzhavnyi universytet 1972).

6 M.N. Leshchenko and L.V. Oliinyk, ''Rozvytok doslidzhen' z istoriï zakhidnoukraïns'kykh zemel','' *Ukraïns'kyi istorychnyi zhurnal*, XXIII, 9 (Kiev 1979), pp. 136–145; M.I. Marchenko, *Ukraïns'ka istoriohrafiia (z davnikh chasiv do seredyny XIX st.)* (Kiev: Vyd-vo Kyïvs'koho universytetu 1959); Iu.M. Grossman, ''Vysvitlennia v istoriohrafiï pytannia pro eksport khliba zakhidnoukraïns'kymy zemliamy v XVI–XVII st.,'' *Visnyk LDU: Seriia istorychna*, no. 6 (L'viv 1970), pp. 72–79; N.M. Pashaeva, ''Russkie uchenye i publitsisty o natsional'nom vozrozhdenii v Galitsii,'' in V.I. Freidzon, ed., *Razvitie kapitalizma i natsional'nye dvizheniia v slavianskikh stranakh* (Moscow: Nauka 1970), pp. 310–321; V.K. Osechyns'kyi ''Do pytannia istoriohrafiï zakhidnoukraïns'kykh zemel' v dobu imperializmu,'' *Visnyk LDU: Seriia istorychna*, no. 5 (L'viv 1969), pp. 3–11; V.K. Osechinskii, ''K voprosu ob istoriografii zapadnoukrainskikh zemel' v period pervoi mirovoi imperialisticheskoi voiny,'' *Naukovi zapysky LDU*, XVII: *Seriia istorychna*, 4 (L'viv 1949), pp. 23–40.

See also the survey of Marxist writings on the Ukrainian Insurgent Army (UPA) in Lew Shankowsky, ''Soviet and Satellite Sources on the Ukrainian Insurgent Army,'' *Annals of the*

valuable description by Iaroslav Dashkevych of sources for Galician history that are available in lexicons and other geographical reference works.[7] Less constrained by dogmatic Marxist historiographical guidelines are Polish historians. Two recent surveys discuss post-1945 publications from Poland dealing with Galicia between 1772 and 1918 and with Polish-Ukrainian relations just after World War II.[8]

Several Galician-Ukrainian scholars, most of whose work dealt with their native province, have been the focus of attention. As might be expected, the largest amount of literature is on Ivan Franko, the prolific belletrist and scholar. The Soviets have virtually transformed Franko into a west Ukrainian (Galician) national institution with writings about all aspects of his career.[9] Mykhailo Moroz has compiled a comprehensive bibliography of Franko's writings (4919 entries), which includes sections listing his scholarly works, social commentary, and published correspondence.[10] Several articles and a monograph by Mykhailo Kravets' focus on Franko as a historian.[11]

Second to Franko in the attention received by a Galician historian is Ivan Kryp''iakevych. Both a bibliography of his writings and studies of his scholarly development have appeared, although these emphasize primarily his activity under Soviet rule, i.e. after 1945.[12] Other Galicians whose historical scholarship

---

Ukrainian Academy of Arts and Sciences in the United States, IX, 1–2 (New York 1961), pp. 234–261; and Wasyl Veryha, ''The 'Galicia' Ukrainian Division in Polish and Soviet Literature,'' *Ukrainian Quarterly,* XXXVI, 3 (New York 1980), pp. 253-270.

7 Iaroslav Dashkevych, ''Skhidna Halychyna v istoryko-heohrafichnykh slovnykakh kintsia XVIII–70-kh rr. XIX st.,'' *Naukovo-informatsiinyi biuleten' Arkhivnoho upravlinnia URSR,* XVII, 2 [58] (Kiev 1963), pp. 10–25.

8 Lawrence D. Orton, ''Polish Publications since 1945 on Austrian and Galician History, 1772–1918,'' *Austrian History Yearbook,* XII–XIII, pt 2 (Houston 1976–77), pp. 315–358; John Basarab, ''Post-War Writings in Poland on Polish-Ukrainian Relations, 1945–1975,'' in Peter J. Potichnyj, ed., *Poland and Ukraine: Past and Present* (Edmonton and Toronto: Canadian Institute of Ukrainian Studies 1980), pp. 247–270.

9 See chapter 6, notes 144–156.

10 M.O. Moroz, *Ivan Franko: bibliohrafiia tvoriv 1874–1964* (Kiev: L'vivs'ka derzhavna biblioteka-Instytut literatury im. Shevchenka AN URSR 1966).

11 M.M. Kravets', *Ivan Franko–istoryk Ukraïny* (L'viv: LU 1971); *I.Ia. Franko iak istoryk,* in *Naukovi zapysky Instytutu istoriï AN URSR,* vol. VIII (Kiev: AN URSR 1956); L.A. Kovalenko, ''Ivan Franko pro istoriiu feodal'no-kriposnyts'koï epokhy na Ukraïni,'' *Naukovi zapysky Uzhhorods'koho derzhavnoho universytetu,* XXV (Uzhhorod 1957), pp. 75–95; idem, ''I.Ia. Franko–istoryk-slavist,'' *Ukraïns'kyi istorychnyi zhurnal,* X, 8 (Kiev 1966), pp. 53–61; I. Hurzhii, ''Ivan Franko iak istoryk: do 110-richchia z dnia narodzhennia I.Ia. Franka,'' *Komunist Ukraïny,* no. 8 (Kiev 1966), pp. 61–70.

12 O.D. Kizlyk, *Ivan Petrovych Kryp''iakevych: bibliohrafichnyi pokazhchyk* (L'viv 1966); M.K. Ivasiuta, 'Ivan Petrovych Kryp''iakevych,'' *Ukraïns'kyi istorychnyi zhurnal,* X, 6 (Kiev

has been analyzed include Denys Zubryts'kyi (1777–1862),[13] Antin Petrushevych (1821–1913),[14] Izydor Sharanevych (1829–1901),[15] Iuliian Tselevych (1843–1892),[16] Iuliian Pelesh (1843–1896),[17] Ostap Terlets'kyi (1850–1902),[18] Kyrylo Studyns'kyi (1868–1941),[19] Volodymyr Hnatiuk (1871–1926),[20] Vasyl'

1966), pp. 127–133; Ia. Isaievych, ''Arkhivoznavstvo i dzhereloznavstvo v pratsiakh I.P. Kryp''iakevycha,'' *Arkhivy Ukraïny*, XX, 3 [77] (Kiev 1966), pp. 20–26. See also the lengthy obituary, which stresses the scholar's pre-Soviet career as well: Omeljan Pritsak, ''Ivan Krypiakevych (1886–1967),'' *Annals of the Ukrainian Academy of Arts and Sciences in the United States,* XI, 1–2 (New York 1964–68), pp. 264–268.

13 Ia. Isaievych, ''D.I. Zubryts'kyi i ioho diial'nist' v haluzi spetsial'nykh istorychnykh dystsyplin,'' *Naukovo-informatsiinyi biuleten' Arkhivnoho upravlinnia URSR,* XVII, 1 [57] (Kiev 1963), pp. 48–57; H.Iu. Herbil's'kyi, ''Do pytannia pro istorychni pohliady D. Zubryts'koho,'' *Visnyk LDU: Seriia istorychna,* no. 4 (L'viv 1967), pp. 63–70. On the impact of Zubryts'kyi's *History of the Galician-Volhynian Principality,* see Mykhailo Tershakovets', ''Rolia Stavropyhiï u vydaniu Denysa Zubryts'koho 'Istorii drevniago galichsko-russkago kniazhestva' I–III. ch. ta ioho broshury p. z. 'Anonim Gneznenskii i Ioann Dlugosh','' in *Zbirnyk L'vivs'koï Stavropyhiï: mynule i suchasne,* vol. I, ed. K. Studyns'kyi (L'viv 1921), pp. 185–246.

14 M.M. Kravets', ''A.S. Petrushevych–vydavets' 'Zvedenoho halyts'ko-rus'koho litopysu 1600–1800 rr.','' *Istoriohrafichni doslidzhennia v Ukraïns'kii RSR,* vol. IV (Kiev: Naukova dumka 1971), pp. 193–198.

15 F.F. Aristov, ''Isidor Ivanovich Sharanevich,'' *Vremennik Stavropigiiskogo Instituta na 1930 god,* pt 2 (L'viv 1929), pp. 8–18; A.V. Kopystianskii, ''Istoricheskie trudy Isidora Iv. Sharanevicha,'' *Vremennik Stavropigiiskogo Instituta na 1930 god,* pt 2 (L'viv 1929), pp. 19–29; V.R. Vavrik, ''Osnovnye cherty literaturnoi deiatel'nosti Isidora Ivanovicha Sharanevicha,'' *ibid.*, pp. 33–121; O. Pavlyk, ''Izydor Sharanevych i ioho istorychne dilo (z nahody 100-littia narodzhennia),'' *Ukraïna*, VI [35] (Kiev 1929), pp. 144–120; M.M. Kravets', ''S.I. Sharanevych,'' *Arkhivy Ukraïny,* XXIII, 4 (Kiev 1969), pp. 52–54.

16 Bohdan Barvins'kyi, *Dr. Iuliian Tselevych i ioho naukova diial'nist' na poli ukraïns'koï istoriohrafiï i etnohrafiï v svitli davnishykh ta novishykh doslidiv* (L'viv: NTSh 1927).

17 Irynei Nazarko, ''Iepyskop Iu. Pelesh–istoryk tserkvy,'' *Ukraïns'kyi istoryk*, XVIII, 1–4 (New York, Toronto, and Munich 1981), pp. 118–127.

18 V.A. Tkachenko, ''Ahrarno-selians'ke pytannia v Halychyni v otsintsi Ostapa Terlets'koho,'' *Sotsial'no-ekonomichni nauky: zbirnyk robit aspirantiv kafedr suspil'nykh nauk* (L'viv: LU 1961), pp. 197–228.

19 Mykhailo Tershakovets', ''Akad. Studyns'kyi iak doslidnyk halytsko-ukraïns'koho vidrodzhennia,'' *Zapysky NTSh,* XCIX (L'viv 1930), pp. 95–112.

20 ''Pam''iati akad. Volod. Hnatiuka,'' *Zapysky istorychno-filolohichnoho viddilu,* X (Kiev 1927), pp. 215–259. On Hnatiuk as a dialectologist and as ethnographer and folklorist on Rusyns living in Subcarpathian Rus' (especially the Prešov Region) and the Bačka, see the studies by Mykola Mushynka, Iosyf Shelepets', Ivan Reboshapka, and František Tichý in *Naukovyi zbirnyk Muzeiu ukraïns'koï kul'tury v Svydnyku,* III: *prysviachenyi pam''iati Volodymyra Hnatiuka* (Bratislava and Prešov 1967), pp. 51–126 and 215–220; Mykola Mushynka, *Volodymyr Hnatiuk: pershyi doslidnyk zhyttia i narodnoï kul'tury rusyniv-ukraïntsiv*

Shchurat (1871–1948),[21] Iuliian Iavors'kyi (1873–1937),[22] Stepan Tomashivs'kyi (1875–1930),[23] Ilarion Svientsits'kyi (1876–1956),[24] Iaroslav Pasternak (1892–1969),[25] and Iaroslav Isaievych (b. 1935).[26] Mykhailo Humeniuk has singled out the bibliographical scholarship of several Galicians, devoting particular attention to Ivan E. Levyts'kyi (1850–1913).[27]

National bibliographies

Much better developed than historiographic studies about Galicia are unannotated and annotated bibliographies. These may be divided into two groups, those which in the tradition of national bibliography try to list all publications that appeared in Galicia or that were written by Galician-Ukrainian authors, and those which list works about a specific subject or historical period.

To the first group belong the bibliographies of Iakiv Holovats'kyi and Ivan E.

Iugoslavii (Ruski Krstur: Ruske slovo 1967); and idem, *Volodymyr Hnatiuk–doslidnyk folkl'oru Zakarpattia,* in *Zapysky NTSh,* CXC (Paris and Munich 1975).

21 See the biography by Stepan V. Shchurat and bibliography by M.O. Moroz in Vasyl' Shchurat, *Vybrani pratsi z istorii literatury* (Kiev: AN URSR 1963), pp. 3–26 and 391–432.

22 F.F. Aristov, "Iul'ian Andreevich Iavorskii (k 40-lietiiu ego literaturno-nauchnoi dieiatel'nosti, 1892–1932)," *Vremennik ... lvovskago Stavropigiona na 1933 god,* LXIX (L'viv 1932).

23 I. Kryp''iakevych, "Stepan Tomashivs'kyi," *Zapysky NTSh,* CLI (L'viv 1931), pp. 225–230; *S. Tomashivs'kyi: istoryk, polityk, publitsyst* (L'viv: Ukraïns'ka Katolyts'ka Narodna Partiia 1932).

24 O.D. Kizlyk and R.Ia. Lutsyk, *I.S. Svientsits'kyi: korotkyi bibliohrafichnyi pokazhchyk* (Kiev: AN URSR 1956); U.Ia. Iedlins'ka, "Ilarion Semenovych Svientsits'kyi (1876–1956)," *Ukraïns'kyi istorychnyi zhurnal,* X, 4 (Kiev 1966), pp. 133–135.

25 Ivan Luchkiv, "Iaroslav Pasternak: bibliohrafichnyi pokazhchyk," *Iuvileinyi zbirnyk naukovykh prats' z nahody 100-richchia NTSh i 25-richchia NTSh u Kanadi,* Kanads'ke NTSh, vol. XIX (Toronto 1977), pp. 162–222. For other bibliographical data and autobiographical material, see Iaroslav Pasternak, *Ranni slov''iany v istorychnykh, arkheolohichnykh ta lingvistychnykh doslidzhenniakh,* in *Zapysky NTSh,* CLXXXIX (New York, Toronto, Paris, and Munich 1976), especially pp. 113–128.

26 Edward Kasinec, "Jaroslav Isajevyč as Historian of the Ukrainian Book," *Recenzija,* V, 1 (Cambridge 1974), pp. 12–24.

27 See the chapters on Ia. Holovats'kyi, I. Franko, M. Pavlyk, V. Lukych-Levyts'kyi, and I.E. Levyts'kyi in Mykhailo P. Humeniuk, *Ukraïns'ki bibliohrafy XIX-pochatku XX stolittia: narysy pro zhyttia ta diial'nist'* (Kharkiv: Knyzhkova palata URSR 1969). See also M. Humeniuk, "Ia.F. Holovats'kyi iak bibliohraf i knyhoznavets'," *Radians'ke literaturoznavstvo,* XIII, 8 (Kiev 1969), pp 60–66; Mykhailo P. Humeniuk, "Bibliohrafichna diial'nist' I.O. Levyts'koho," *Arkhivy Ukraïny,* XXII, 6 (Kiev 1968), pp. 30–36; idem, "Levitskii – vydaiushchiisia ukrainskii bibliograf XIX stoletiia," *Sovetskaia bibliografiia,* no. 41 (Moscow 1955), pp. 45–52; and Paul R. Magocsi, "Nationalism and National Bibliography: Ivan E.

Levyts'kyi. Holovats'kyi has provided a chronological list of over 650 Church-Slavonic imprints from Galicia between the years 1614 and 1865; it is basically a supplement to an earlier work by Vukol M. Undol'skii.[28] Levyts'kyi, the greatest bibliographer in Galicia, if not the Ukraine in general, set out to create a chronologically arranged bibliography for nineteenth-century Galicia. The result was a monumental, two-volume work with several supplements that listed a total of 7303 entries for the years 1801 through 1893. This work also includes invaluable analytics of newspapers, journals, almanacs, and collective works.[29] Although Levyts'kyi did not quite provide complete coverage for the nineteenth century, he did prepare a comprehensive bibliographical listing (99 entries) of works that appeared in Galicia during the first three decades of Austrian rule (1772–1800).[30] The Polish bibliographer Karol Estreicher did complete an eleven-volume Polish national bibliography for the nineteenth century that is arranged according to author and which includes several Galician Ukrainian writers as well. Estreicher is much less reliable than Levyts'kyi, however, although his work contains works

---

Bibliography: Ivan E. Levyts'kyi and Nineteenth-Century Galicia,'' *Harvard Library Bulletin,* XXVIII, 1 (Cambridge, Mass. 1980), pp. 81–109.

28 Ia. Golovatskii, *Dopolnenie k ocherku slaviano-russkoi bibliografii V.M. Undol'skago, soderzhashchee knigi i stat'i propushchennyia v pervom vypuskie khronologicheskago ukazatelia slaviano-russkikh knig tserkovnoi pechati s 1491-go po 1864 god, v osobennosti zhe perechen' galitsko-russkikh izdanii tserkovnoi pechati,* in *Zapiski Imperatorskoi Akademii Nauk,* XXIV, *prilozhenie* no. 3 (St Petersburg 1874). The work that Holovats'kyi supplemented and which also contained some Galician imprints is V.M. Undol'skii, *Ocherk slaviano-russkoi bibliografii* (Moscow: Moskovskii publichnyi i Rumiantsevskii Muzei 1871).

See also A.S. Petrushevych, ''Khronolohycheskaia rospys' tserkovnŷkh i mirskykh russkoslovenskykh knyh, napechatannykh kyryllovskymy bukvamy v horodî L'vovî, nachynaia s 1574 do 1800 hoda,'' *Vremennyk Stavropihiiskaho Instytuta na 1885 hod* (L'viv 1884), pp. 113–133.

29 Ivan E. Levyts'kii, *Halytsko-ruskaia bybliohrafiia XIX stolîtiia s uvzhliadneniem yzdanii poiavyvshykhsia v Uhorshchynî y Bukovynî 1801–1886,* 2 vols (L'viv: p.a. 1888–95), reprinted in *Kraus Slavonic Reference Series,* series II, vol. 2 (Vaduz, Liechtenstein: Kraus Reprint Ltd 1963). Continued for the years 1887 through 1893 as *Halytsko-russkaia bybliohrafiia za 1887, 1888, 1889,* 3 vols (L'viv: p.a. 1888–90; reprinted with subsequent years as *Materiialy do ukraïns'koï bibliografiï: Ukraïns'ka bibliografiia Avstro-Uhorshchyny za roky 1887–1900,* 3 vols [1887–1893], L'viv: Bibliografichna Komisiia NTSh 1909–11). A comprehensive supplement to Levyts'kyi is the list of Galician-Ukrainian publications compiled by Ivan Franko that appeared in a Polish-based Latin alphabet between 1821 and 1859: *Azbuchna viina v Halychynï 1859 r.: novi materiialy,* in *Ukraïns'ko-rus'kyi arkhyv,* vol. VIII (L'viv 1912), pp. iv–xiv.

30 Ivan Em. Levyts'kyi, ''Halyts'ko-rus'ka bibliografiia za roky 1772–1800,'' *Zapysky NTSh,* XII, 2 [vol. LII] (L'viv 1903), 44 pp.

by some Galician Ukrainian authors that appeared between 1894 and 1900 that are missing in Levyts'kyi's unfinished opus.[31]

Systematic coverage of Galician-Ukrainian publications for the twentieth century is at best haphazard. For the years 1901 through 1918 there is no coverage at all. With regard to the interwar period, there are bibliographies of Galician publications by Iuliian Iavors'kyi and Vasilii R. Vavrik done according to the model of Levyts'kyi; unfortunately, these list only works by Russophile authors or institutions.[32] More comprehensive is the current national bibliography for Poland (1929–39). Each issue (i.e. every three months, then two weeks, then monthly) contains a section on "non-Polish publications," including many Galician-Ukrainian titles.[33] An annual bibliography of works on national minorities in Poland also provided systematic coverage for the years 1929 through 1937, with over 450 entries on Ukrainians.[34] For the years after 1958, an annual Soviet publication

31 Karol Estreicher, *Bibliografia polska XIX. stólecia,* 7 vols [vols. I–V: 1800–1870; vols. VI–VII: dopełnienia, 1870–1880] (Cracow: Wyd. Uniwersytetu Jagiellońskiego, 1872–82) and *Bibliografia polska XIX stulecia lata 1881–1900,* 4 vols (Cracow: Spółka Księgarzy Polskich 1906–16; reprinted New York: Johnson Reprint Corporation and Warsaw: PWN 1964–65). A revised second edition under the editorship of the author's grandson, also named Karol Estreicher, that combines the above and adds much new data is presently being published: Karol Estreicher, *Bibliografia polska XIX stulecia,* vols. I–XII [A through J] 2nd rev. ed. (Cracow: Wyd. Uniwersytetu Jagiellońskiego 1959–79).

Estreicher's original *Bibliografia Polska* was continued by him and his son Stanisław Estreicher to include all books published between the fifteenth and eighteenth centuries, vols XII–XXXIII [A through Y] (Cracow: Wyd. Uniwersytetu Jagiellońskiego 1891–1939; reprinted New York: Johnson Reprint Corporation and Warsaw: PWN 1964–65), although these volumes contain few Ukrainian or Old Slavonic titles.

32 Iul'ian Iavorskii, *Materialy po galitsko-russkoi bibliografii* (L'viv: Izd. 'Zhivoe Slovo' 1924); V.R. Vavrik, "Spravka o russkom dvizhenii na Galitskoi Rusi s bibliografioi za 1929 god," *Vremennik: nauchno-literaturnye zapiski L'vovskogo Stavropigiona na 1931 god* (L'viv 1931), pp. 96–112; idem, "Galitsko-russkaia bibliografiia za 1930 god," *ibid.* (1932), pp. 94–96; "za 1931 god," *ibid.* (1933), pp. 97–101; "za 1932 god," *ibid.* (1934), pp. 76–80; "za 1933 god," *ibid.* (1935), pp. 114–117.

For Ukrainian-language works published in 1937 and 1938, see Bohdan Romanenchuk, "Bibliohrafiia," *Ukraïns'ka knyha,* I, 2–5, 7–10 (L'viv 1937), pp. 62–64, 87–90, 119–128, 183–193, 210–218; II, 2, 4, 9–10 (1938), pp. 46–53, 75–80, 130–148; and III, 1 (1939), pp. 16–26.

33 *Urzędowy wykaz druków wydanych w Rzeczpospolitej Polskiej i druków polskich lub Polski dotyczących, wydanych zagranicą,* 12 vols (Warsaw: Ministerstwo Wyznań Religijnych i Oświecenia Publicznego and Biblioteka Narodowa Józefa Piłsudskiego 1929–39).

34 See the sections "Ukraińcy" and "Starorusini" in Piotr Grzegorczyk. "Bibljografija dotycząca mniejszości narodowych w Polsce za 1929 r.," *Sprawy Narodowościowe,* IV, 1 (Warsaw 1930), pp. 141–156; "za 1930," V, 1 (1931), pp. 165–187; "za 1931," VI, 1 (1932), pp. 145–165; "za 1932," VII, 1 (1933), pp. 151–165; "za 1933," VIII, 2–3

lists all books appearing in the Ukrainian SSR and arranges them according to publishing houses, including those in the Galician cities of L'viv and Ivano-Frankivs'k (formerly Stanyslaviv).[35]

Periodicals were first published by Ukrainians in Galicia in 1848, and there are some bibliographies for this important historical source. Besides the annotated listings for all Galician serials before 1893 found in Levyts'kyi's bibliography,[36] Varfolomii Ihnatiienko has prepared a bibliography for the first century of the Ukrainian press (1816 to 1916), most of whose 579 chronologically arranged titles orginate from Galicia or Vienna (i.e. for Galicia).[37] Communist periodicals from the interwar years and the post-1945 period are listed in a study by Iaroslav Dashkevych and in a bibliography of the Soviet Ukrainian press.[38]

Subject bibliographies

The second group of bibliographies comprises those that list works about a specific subject or historical period, such as the Ukrainian Sich Riflemen Organi-

---

(1934), pp. 325–336; "za 1934," IX, 3–4 (1935), pp. 362–373; "za 1935," X, 3 (1936), pp. 329–340; and Maks Berżyński, "Bibliografia prac z zakresu zagadnień narodowościowych drukowanych w Polsce w roku 1936," *Sprawy Narodowościowe,* XI, 4–5 (Warsaw 1937) pp. 547–566; "w roku 1937," XII, 4–5 (1938); pp. 539–554. Each year these bibliographies were also published separately at the same time that they appeared in the journal.

35 These include the L'vivs'ke and Stanislavs'ke, later Ivano-Frankivs'ke oblasne knyzhkovo-hazetne vydavnytstvo; Vydavnytstvo L'vivs'koho derzhavnoho universytetu im. Ivana Franka (later Vyshcha shkola); and Kameniar. *Spysok literatury, vypushchenoï vydavnytstvamy Ukraïny* [1958–1960] (Kharkiv: Knyzhkova Palata URSR 1959–61); *Knyhy vydavnytstv Ukraïny* [1961–present] (Kharkiv: Knyzhkova Palata URSR 1962–present).

36 See above, n. 29.

37 Varfolomii Ihnatiienko, *Bibliohrafiia ukraïns'koï presy, 1816–1916,* in *Trudy Ukraïns'koho naukovo-doslidchoho instytuta knyhoznavstva,* vol. IV (Kharkiv 1930; reprinted State College, Pa.: Wasyl O. Luciw 1968). See also Ivan Krevets'kyi, "Chasopysy Halyts'koho Podillia," in Mykola Bilins'kyi, Nina Spivachevs'ka, and Ivan Krevets'kyi, *Chasopysy Podillia,* Kabinet vyuchuvannia Podillia, vol. XX (Vinnytsia: Vinnyts'ka filiia Vsenarodn'oï biblioteky Ukraïny pry UAN 1927–28), pp. 1–21.

38 Ia. Dashkevych, "Bibliohrafichnyi pokazhchyk komunistychnoï ta prohresyvnoï presy L'vova (1918–1939 rr.)," in *Z istoriï revoliutsiinoho rukhu u L'vovi 1917–1939 rr.* (L'viv 1957), pp. 721–739; *Periodychni vydannia URSR, 1918–1950, zhurnaly: bibliohrafichnyi dovidnyk* (Kharkiv: Knyzhkova palata URSR 1956); *Periodychni vydannia URSR, 1951–1960, zhurnaly: bibliohrafichnyi dovidnyk* (Kharkiv: Knyzhkova palata URSR 1964). The listings in these last two works are alphabetical, although one index is arranged according to place of publication allowing the reader to determine Galician periodicals. See also several studies by Dashkevych and Ts'okh on the interwar communist and left-wing press in chapter 7, n. 80.

zation active during World War I;[39] the publications of the influential Galician cultural society Prosvita;[40] the Lemkian region;[41] and the cities and regions of L'viv, Stanyslaviv, and Przemyśl.[42] The bibliographies on Ukrainian church history by Isydor Patrylo and on the monastic order of St Basil the Great each include several sections devoted largely or wholly to Galicia.[43] There are also two bibliographies of Ukrainian memoirs, many of which are by Galician authors or are about the region.[44]

There are also bibliographies representing certain historical schools. For older Polish writings, the multivolume guide by Ludwik Finkel has some sections dealing with eastern Galicia,[45] but the most comprehensive coverage is given by

39 Petro Zlenko, *Zymovyi pokhid: materiialy dlia bibliohrafichnoho pokazhchyka* (Prague 1935); idem, *Ukraïns'ki Sichovi Stril'tsi: materiialy dlia bibliografichnoho pokazhchyka* (Warsaw: Ukraïns'ke voienno-istorychne tov. 1935); Stepan Ripets'kyi, *Bibliohrafiia dzherel do istoriï Ukraïns'kykh Sichovykh Stril'tsiv* (New York: Vydavnycha Komisiia Bratstva USS 1965).

40 Ivan Kalynovych, *Spys vydan' Tovarystva 'Prosvita' u L'vovi 1868–1924* (L'viv: TP 1926).

41 Marian Jurkowski, "Łemkowszczyzna (materiały do bibliografii)," *Slavia Orientalis*, XI, 4 (Warsaw 1962), pp. 525–536, reprinted as J. Kozłowski, "Lemkowszczyzna," *Annals of the World Lemkos' Federation*, II (Camillus, NY 1975), pp. 240–254.

42 There is an excellent historiographical analysis of the earlier literature on L'viv in Łucja Charewiczowa, *Historiografia i miłośnictwo Lwowa*, Biblioteka Lwowska, vol. XXXVII (L'viv 1938). For Soviet literature, see E.M. Lazeba and T.O. Vorobiova, *700 rokiv m. L'vova: bibliohrafichnyi pokazhchyk literatury* (L'viv: L'vivs'ka biblioteka AN URSR, viddil bibliohrafiï 1956), and the annual *Sotsialistychna L'vivshchyna: bibliohrafichnyi pokazhchyk literatury* [1951–1958?] (L'viv: L'vivs'ka biblioteka AN URSR, viddil bibliohrafiï 1953–56) and Iu.M. Hraidans, ed., *Radians'ka L'vivshchyna: rekomendatsiinyi pokazhchyk literatury* [for 1945 through 1958] (L'viv: L'vivs'ka derzhavna oblasna biblioteka im. Ia. Halana 1971), followed by the annual with the subtitle: *bibliohrafichnyi pokazhchyk literatury pro oblast'* [for 1969 through 1977] (L'viv 1972–79).

On Stanyslaviv and Przemyśl, see *Stanislavshchyna v mynulomu i teper: korotkyi spisok literatury* (Stanislav 1957); and Zdzisław Konieczny and Jerzy Motylewicz, *Materiały do bibliografii dziejów Przemyśla (1944–1974)* (Przemyśl: Polskie Towarzystwo Historyczne, Oddział w Przemyślu 1976).

43 Isydor I. Patrylo, *Dzherela i bibliohrafiia istoriia ukraïns'koï tserkvy*, Analecta OSBM, series II, sectio I: Opera, vol. XXXIII (Rome 1975), first published in *Analecta OSBM*, series II, sectio II, vols VIII and IX (Rome 1973–74), pp. 305–434 and 325–549; Mykhailo Vavryk, "Bibliohrafichnyi ohliad istoriï Vasyliians'koho Chyna za 1935–1950 rr.," *Analecta OSBM*, series II, sectio II, vol. III, 1–2 (Rome 1958), pp. 237–276; idem, "Bibliohrafichnyi ohliad istoriï Vasyliians'koho Chyna za 1950–1970 rr.," *Analecta OSBM*, series II, sectio II, vol. VII, 1–4 (Rome 1971), pp. 334–424.

44 Ivan Kalynovych, "Ukraïns'ka memuarystyka 1914–1924 r.: bibliografichnyi reiester," *Stara Ukraïna*, IX–X (L'viv 1924), pp. 145–150; I. Chaikovs'kyi, "Nasha memuarystyka," *Naukovi zapysky Ukraïns'koho tekhnichno-hospodars'koho institutu*, XI (XIV) (Munich 1966), pp. 63–94, also separately.

45 Ludwik Finkel, *Bibliografia historyi polskiej*, 3 vols (Cracow: Komisyia Historyczna Akademii

Edmund Kołodziejczyk, who lists 1004 Polish studies on all aspects of Galician "Rusini."[46] More recent Polish bibliographies contain works in all languages about Ukrainian Galicia between the years 1795 and 1945.[47] Czech-language writings on Galicia are listed in a meticulous bibliography of Czech-Ukrainian relations by Orest Zilyns'kyj.[48]

Imperial Russian and most especially Soviet literature on Galicia has been given much bibliographic attention. Nina Pashaeva has compiled a comprehensive bibliography of pre-Soviet and Soviet writings on all aspects of eastern Galicia during the Austrian period (1772–1918).[49] The most detailed coverage of Soviet literature for any period is Iurko Nykyforchuk's unannotated bibliography on the western Ukraine in the 1920s, which devotes more than 100 pages to Galicia.[50] The initial entry into eastern Galicia by the Red Army in September 1939 prompted the publication of four bibliographies listing Soviet and pre-Soviet works on the newly acquired regions.[51] There are also sections on Galicia in M.P.

Umiejętności, 1904–06), *Dodatek (obejmujący druki po koniec r. 1900)* (Cracow 1906), and *Dodatek II (lata 1901–1910 obejmujący)* (Cracow 1914); 2nd rev. ed., vol. I (L'viv: Polskie Towarzystwo Historyczne 1937).

46 Edmund Kołodziejczyk, *Bibliografia słowianoznawstwa polskiego* (Cracow: Akademija Umiejętności 1911), pp. 196–252.

47 Helena Madurowicz-Urbańska, ed., *Bibliografia historii Polski,* vol. II: *1795–1918,* 2 pts (Warsaw: PAN 1967), especially the sections dealing with "lands under Austrian rule"; Wiesław Bieńkowski, ed., *Bibliografiia historii Polski,* vol. III: *1918–1945,* 2 pts (Warsaw: PAN 1974), which includes sections on Ukrainian political parties and Ukrainians as a minority.

48 Orest Zilynskyj, ed., *Sto padesát let česko-ukrajinských literárních styků 1814–1964: vědecko-bibliografický sborník* (Prague: Svět Sovětů 1968).

See also the survey of writings by and about Ukrainians, especially in Galicia, that appeared in the journal of the Czech National Museum: Pavlo Bohats'kyi, "Ucrainica z zhurnalu 'Časopis Českého Museum' vid pochatku ioho isnuvannia po 1926 rik (1827–1925)," *Zapysky NTSh,* CXLVI (L'viv 1927), pp. 203–214.

49 N.M. Pashaeva, "Galitsiia pod vlast'iu Avstrii v russkoi i sovetskoi istoricheskoi literature (1772–1918 gg.): bibliografiia," in V.D. Koroliuk et al., eds, *Mezhdunarodnye sviazi stran tsentral'noi, vostochnoi i iugo-vostochnoi Evropy i slaviano-germanskie otnosheniia* (Moscow: Nauka 1968), pp. 295–324.

50 Iurko Nykyforchuk, *Zakhidna Ukraïna, materialy do bibliohrafiï: spys literatury opublikovanoï na tereni URSR, 1917–1929 rr* (Kharkiv and Kiev: Proletar 1932). This work can be supplemented by O. Pavlyk, "Radians'ka istoriohrafiia Zakhidnoï Ukraïny: bibliohrafichnyi ohliad za 1930–1932 rr.," *Ukraïna,* no. 3 (Kiev 1932), pp. 162–168.

51 S. Bruskin, E. Zhilina, and V. Maikov, *Zapadnaia Ukraina i Zapadnaia Belorussiia: spisok literatury* (Leningrad: Gos. publichnaia biblioteka im. Saltykova-Shchedrina 1940); *Novye sovetskie respubliki i oblasti: ukazatel' literatury* (Moscow: Vsesoiuznaia knizhnaia palata 1940); B. Zlatoustovskii and L. Fedorov, "Literatura o zapadnykh oblastiakh Ukrainy i

Rud's general bibliography of the Ukrainian SSR and in a bibliography of documentary collections,[52] as well as in specialized bibliographies of Soviet literature on the western Ukraine for the years 1917 to 1945,[53] 1939 to 1959,[54] World War II,[55] and on the local Communist party.[56] Galicia is also well represented in the outstanding bibliography of Fedir P. Maksymenko, which lists over 1300 works of a statistical and descriptive nature on towns, cities, and regions throughout the Ukraine.[57]

Archives

Archives with material on Galicia are to be found within and beyond the borders of the region. There does not exist a survey of all archives that contain material on

---

Belorussii,'' *Istoricheskii zhurnal,* X, 3 (Moscow 1940), pp. 144–156; *Do pershoï richnytsi vyzvolennia Zakhidnoï Ukraïny vid hnitu pans'koï Pol'shchi: bibliohrafichnyi pokazhchyk* (L'viv: L'vivs'kyi filial biblioteky AN URSR 1940).

52 M.P. Rud', *Ukraïns'ka Radians'ka Sotsialistychna Respublika 1917–1967: bibliohrafichnyi pokazhchyk literatury* (Kiev: Naukova dumka 1969), especially pp. 144–147, 198–200, 241–245, and 269–278; *Radians'ki vydannia dokumental'nykh materialiv z istoriï Ukraïny (1917–1968): bibliohrafichnyi pokazhchyk* (Kiev: Naukova dumka 1970).

53 O.D. Kizlyk and N.H. Terebeichyk, *Vplyv Velykoï Zhovtnevoï sotsialistychnoï revoliutsiï na rozvytok revoliutsiino-vyzvol'noho rukhu na zakhidnoukraïns'kykh zemliakh: bibliohrafichnyi pokazhchyk* (L'viv: AN URSR-LNBS 1977).

54 *Vozz''iednannia ukraïns'kykh zemel' v iedynii ukraïns'kii radians'kii derzhavi (1939–1959 rr.): bibliohrafichnyi pokazhchyk* (Kiev: AN URSR 1959); F.I. Steblii, ''Materialy do bibliohrafiï istoriï zakhidnykh oblastei URSR u periodi sotsializmu,'' in *Z istoriï zakhidnoukraïns'kykh zemel',* vol. IV, ed. I.P. Kryp''iakevych (L'viv: AN URSR 1960), pp. 145–153.

55 *Zakhidni oblasti Ukraïns'koï RSR u Velykii Vitchyznianii viini Radians'koho Soiuzu 1941–1945 rr.: bibliohrafichnyi pokazhchyk* (L'viv: AN URSR-LNBS 1972).

56 *Materialy do bibliohrafiï istoriï Komunistychnoï partiï Zakhidnoï Ukraïny: bibliohrafichnyi pokazhchyk* (L'viv: L'vivs'ka biblioteka URSR 1958); Volodymyr V. Mashotas, *Komunistychna Partiia Zakhidnoï Ukraïny: bibliohrafichnyi pokazhchyk materialiv i publikatsiï za 1919–1967 rr.* (L'viv: Kameniar 1969).

See also Jurij Lawrynenko, *Ukrainian Communism and Soviet Russian Policy toward the Ukraine: An Annotated Bibliography, 1917–1953* (New York: Research Program on the USSR 1953), especially chapter 8, which lists both western and Soviet studies on Galicia.

57 F.P. Maksymenko, ''Zbirka istorychnykh vidomostei pro naseleni punkty Ukraïns'koï RSR: bibliohrafichnyi pokazhchyk,'' *Naukovo-informatsiinyi biulieten' Arkhivnoho upravlinnia URSR,* XVII, 4, 5, and 6 (Kiev 1963), pp. 79–86, 79–84, and 76–85; and XVIII, 1, 2, 3, 4, 5 (1964), pp. 88–98, 92–99, 89–101, 64–71, and 95–105; see especially the sections on the Ivano-Frankivs'k (items 678–705), L'viv (items 858–987), and Ternopil' (items 1130–1177) oblasts. An earlier version of this work–*Materialy do kraieznavchoï bibliohrafiï Ukraïny, 1848–1929* (Kiev: Vsenarodna biblioteka Ukraïny pry VUAN 1930)–did not include any sections on Galicia, at the time outside the borders of the Ukrainian SSR.

Galicia, although for some of them there are useful descriptions. The most important archives have been located in the administrative center of L'viv. After the Austrian government was established in the late eighteenth century, court registers and other documents that had previously been held in various local offices under Polish rule were brought to L'viv and consolidated in the main building of the Bernardine Monastery. From that time, the institution became generally known as the Bernardine Archive, although after 1878 it was officially designated the Galician Central Archive of Early Castle and Land Court Records (Galizisches Haupt-Archiv der alten Grod- und Land Gerichtsakten/Archiwum Krajowe Aktów Grodzkich i Ziemskich we Lwowie). Following World War I and the establishment of a Polish administration, it was known as the L'viv Land Court Archive (Archiwum Ziemskie we Lwowie). Then in 1933, the Land Archive was merged with the Polish State Archive in L'viv (Archiwum Państwowe we Lwowie), which had come into existence in 1919 on the basis of an earlier repository that housed records from the period of Austrian rule (1772–1918).

Besides these centralized provincial archives, L'viv as well as each of the major cities and towns had their own archives with municipal records going back in some cases to the thirteenth century. Each of the churches–Roman Catholic, Greek Catholic, and Armenian Catholic–also had its own archive. Finally, in 1939, during the first Soviet administration of Galicia, the archival system was reorganized. The Polish State Archive became the basis for what, after various name changes and mergers, has been known since 1958 as the Central State Historical Archive (Tsentral'nyi Derzhavnyi Istorychnyi Arkhiv URSR u L'vovi). Besides this centralized repository, there are also regional (oblast) archives located in L'viv, Ivano-Frankivs'k (formerly Stanyslaviv), and Ternopil', as well as branches of these regional archives located in several smaller cities and towns.[58]

As is evident from the above sketch, the fate of archives in Galicia has been deeply affected by the several political changes that have taken place in the twentieth century. The archival system under Austrian rule is described in B. Dudik's extensive survey of all archives in Galicia;[59] in Aleksander Czołowski's study of archives in L'viv;[60] and in more detail analyses of holdings in the

58 On the reorganization of Galician archives under Soviet rule, see O.H. Vainbaun and P.V. Zamkovyi, "Arkhivne budivnytstvo v zakhidnykh oblastiakh Ukraïns'koï RSR," in *Z istoriï arkhivnoho budivnytstva na Ukraïni* (Kharkiv 1958), pp. 93–103; and especially the studies by Grimsted, notes 70, 73, and 84 below.

59 B. Dudik, "Archive im Königreiche Galizien und Lodomerien," *Archiv für österreichische Geschichte,* XXXIX, 1 (Vienna 1868), pp. 1–222.

60 Aleksander Czołowski, *Archiwa rządowe we Lwowie, ich obecna zawartość i znaczenie dla historii Galicyi* (L'viv 1905).

Bernardine Archive,[61] the Archive of the Galician Viceroys (now both part of the Central State Historical Archive in L'viv),[62] and the Archive of the L'viv City Magistracy (whose holdings are now split between the Central Historical and L'viv Oblast Archives).[63] Galician archives in interwar Poland are described by Eugeniusz Barwiński and Edward Chwalewik[64] and there are also specific descriptions and catalogs for collections in the Polish State Archive and City Archive in L'viv,[65] as well as for the municipal archives in Przemyśl and Jaro-

61 The introduction to the initial volume of *Akta grodzkie i ziemskie z czasów Rzeczypospolitej Polskiej z archiwum tak zwanego Bernardyńskiego we Lwowie,* vol. I (L'viv 1868), pp.v–xxii, contains a history and survey of the holdings, supplemented in the introductions to vols XI–XXIII (L'viv 1886–1928), and in Oktaw Liske and Xawery Liske, *Spis oblat zawartych w aktach grodu i ziemstwa lwowskiego,* in vol. X (L'viv 1884). See also Stefan Sochaniewicz, "Archiwum krajowe aktów grodzkich i ziemskich we Lwowie," *Przewodnik Naukowy i Literacki,* XL (L'viv 1912), pp. 835–848, 927–944, and 1024–1046–and separately (L'viv 1912); Przemysław Dąbkowski, "Krajowe Archiwum Akt Grodzkich i Ziemskich we Lwowie" and "Archiwum Krajowe Akt Grodzkich i Ziemskich," in his *Pokłosie z dwudziestu lat pracy naukowej zebrane 1897–1916* (L'viv: p.a. 1917); and Eugeniusz Barwiński, *Repertorium znajdujących się w Bibliotece Universyteckiej we Lwowie aktów zajęcia i sprzedaży dóbr królewskich i kościelnych* (L'viv 1909)– transferred to Bernardine Archive.

62 Alojzy Winiarz, "Z dziejów archiwum Namiestnictwa we Lwowie," *Przewodnik Naukowy i Literacki,* XXXVIII (L'viv 1910) pp. 55–61, 145–163; and idem," Archiwum Namiestnictwa we Lwowie," *ibid.*, XXXVII (L'viv 1909), pp. 566–576, 659–672.

63 Karol Widmann, "Wiadomość o Archiwum miasta Lwowa," *Przegląd Archeologiczny,* I (L'viv 1882), pp. 44–72; II (1883), pp. 73–107; III (1883), pp. 66–101–and separately (L'viv: p.a. 1882).

64 Eugene Barwiński, "Les archives en Petite Pologne orientale," *Bulletin de l'Union des sociétés savantes polonaises de Léopol,* no. 11–12 (L'viv 1931), pp. 1–32–also separately (L'viv 1932); Edward Chwalewik, *Zbiory polskie: archiwa, bibljoteki, gabinety, galerje, muzea i inne zbiory pamiątek przeszłości w ojczyźnie i na obczyźnie,* 2 vols (Warsaw: J. Mortkowicz 1926–27), especially vol. I, pp. 367–376.

See also the comprehensive directory to the varying kinds of archival records produced in pre-partition Poland with data on their location during the interwar years in Stanisław Kutrzeba, *Historia źródeł dawnego prawa polskiego,* 2 vols (L'viv, Warsaw, and Cracow: ZNIO 1925–26). On the early municipal records of L'viv, see Karol Badecki, "Zaginione księgi średniowiecznego Lwowa: studjum rekonstrukcyjne," *Kwartalnik Historyczny,* XLI (L'viv 1927), pp. 519–579–also separately (L'viv: Gmina miasta 1927).

65 On the State Archive, see Przemysław Dąbkowski, *Katalog dawnych aktów sądowych polskich województwa ruskiego i bełskiego przechowywanych w Archiwum Państwowem we Lwowie,* pt 1 (L'viv: Towarzystwo Naukowe 1937). On the City Archive, see Karol Badecki, "Archiwum miasta Lwowa: jego stan obecny oraz potrzeby reorganizacyjne, inwentaryzacyjne i wydawnicze," *Archeion,* XII (Warsaw 1934), pp. 77–200–and separately (Warsaw 1934); and two volumes of a planned eight-volume catalog: Karol Badecki, ed., *Archiwum Akt Dawnych miasta Lwowa: A. Oddział staropolski,* vol. III: *Księgi i akta administracyjno-sądowe, 1382–*

sław.[66] Also, the archives of the Roman Catholic church (the Archdiocese and Cathedral Chapter in L'viv) and the Armenian Catholic church–both now part of the Central State Historical Archive in L'viv–are described in studies from the early 1930s.[67]

The Soviets have prepared guides to the present-day L'viv Oblast State Archive and its formerly separate branch in Sambir.[68] There is no guide for the important Central State Historical Archive, only brief general descriptions and a catalog of its parchment collection.[69] Invaluable introductions to all archives in Galicia, describing their historical development and present-day composition, are provided by Patricia K. Grimsted in an extensive article on L'viv archives and in a forthcoming book on archives in the Ukrainian SSR.[70]

1787 (L'viv: Gmina Królestwej Stoł. miasta Lwowa 1935); and vol. IV: *Księgi rachunkowe (Lonhersie), 1404–1788* (L'viv 1936).

66 Jan Smołka, *Katalog Archiwum Aktów Dawnych miasta Przemyśla* (Przemyśl: Gmina miasta Przemyśla 1927); idem, *Katalog starożytnego Archiwum Miejskiego i Towarzystwa Przyjaciół Nauk w Przemyślu*, pt 1: *Dyplomy pergaminowe* (Przemyśl: Towarzystwo Przyjaciół Nauk 1921); idem, *Katalog Archiwum Aktów Dawnych miasta Jarosławia* (Jarosław: Gmina miasta Jarosławia 1928). The archives of Przemyśl and Jarosław are today in the Polish State Provincial Archives in each of those cities.

67 On the Roman Catholic archives, see three studies by S. Zajączkowski: *Archiwum Archidiecezjalne Obrządu Łacińskiego we Lwowie* (L'viv 1932); ''Archiwum Kapituły Łacińskiej we Lwowie,'' *Archiwum Towarzystwa Naukowego we Lwowie*, pt 2: *historyczno-filozoficzny*, I, 7 (L'viv 1923), pp. 301–428, and ''Archiwum kapitulne we Lwowie,'' *Archeion*, V (Warsaw 1929), pp. 31–36. On the Armenian Catholic archives, see chapter 10, n. 76.

68 V.I. Kotel'nykova, P.B. Plotkina, and O.M. Ruzanov, comps, *L'vivs'kyi oblasnyi derzhavnyi arkhiv: putivnyk* (L'viv: Kameniar 1965); E.A. Dubilevs'kyi, I.M. Rozenblit, and H.V. Tiulina, comps, *Filial L'vivs'koho oblasnoho derzhavnoho arkhivu v Sambori: putivnyk* (L'viv: Knyzhkovo-zhurnal'ne vyd-vo 1962). The Sambir branch archive was abolished and is now within the L'viv Oblast State Archive.

69 N.F. Vradii, ''Tsentral'nyi derzhavnyi istorychnyi arkhiv URSR u m. L'vovi,'' in *Tretia ukraïns'ka respublikans'ka naukova konferentsiia z arkhivoznavstva ta inshykh spetsial'nykh istorychnykh dystsyplin*, vol. I (Kiev 1968), pp. 22–41; Michał Wąsowicz, ''Materiały do dziejów Polski w Centralnych Historycznych Archiwach Państwowych we Lwowie i Kijowie,'' *Archeion*, XXXIII (Warsaw 1960), pp. 99–110; O.A. Kripchyns'kyi and E.I. Ruzhyts'kyi, eds, *Kataloh perhamentnykh dokumentiv Tsentral'noho derzhavnoho istorychnoho arkhivu URSR u L'vovi, 1233–1799* (Kiev 1972).

See also the brief description of the archive of the Greek Catholic Metropolitanate: E.M. Humeniuk, ''Arkhiv stolovykh maietkiv halyts'koï mytropoliï,'' *Arkhivy Ukraïny*, XXIV, 1 (Kiev 1970), pp. 68–72; and the several studies of Armenian materials in the Central State Historical Archive, chapter 10, n. 76.

70 Patricia Kennedy Grimsted, ''The Fate of Early Records in L'viv Archives: Documentation from Western Ukraine Under Polish Rule (Fifteenth Century to 1772),'' *Slavonic and East*

The other great repository for the history of Galicia is Vienna, the former imperial capital of Austria-Hungary. Materials on political, economic, religious, and cultural developments in the province, most especially between 1772 and 1918, are found in the Haus- Hof- und Staatsarchiv in Vienna. General descriptions of the Viennese holdings on Galicia are to be found in the appropriate sections of Ludwig Bittner's multivolume survey of the Haus- Hof- und Staatsarchiv and in an article by Janusz Woliński and Zbigniew Wójcik.[71] Warsaw, Cracow, Kiev, Budapest, and the Vatican also have much archival material, although there are no published descriptions relating specifically to Galician materials. Many documents from these archives have been published, however, as indicated below.[72]

Libraries and other cultural institutions

There are also many libraries, museums, monasteries, and cultural organizations that have held archives, manuscripts, and old imprints important for the study of Galician history. Most of these were located in L'viv, where by the first half of the twentieth century more than twenty such institutions were in existence. However, like the archives, most of the older libraries and cultural institutions have been dismantled and their holdings redistributed after the establishment of Soviet rule. For the most part, institutional archival records have been placed in the Central State Historical Archive, while manuscript collections and printed books are now in the Stefanyk Library of the Academy of Sciences in L'viv (L'vivs'ka Naukova Biblioteka im. V. Stefanyka AN URSR), the Ivan Franko L'viv State University Library (Naukova Biblioteka L'vivs'koho Derzhavnoho Universytetu im. Ivana Franka), and the L'viv State Museum of Ukrainian Art (L'vivs'kyi Derzhavnyi Muzei Ukraïns'koho Mystetstva–formerly the Ukrainian National Museum). Finally, a substantive portion of the collection from the Ossolineum Library was transferred to that institution's successors of the same name in Wrocław, Poland. With regard to these institutional changes, Patricia K. Grimsted has provided a general description of L'viv's libraries and cultural institutions both before and

---

European Review, LX, 3 (London 1982), pp. 321–346; idem, *Archives and Manuscript Repositories in the USSR: Ukraine and Moldavia* (Princeton, NJ: Princeton University Press, forthcoming).

71 Ludwig Bittner, *Gesamtinventar des Wiener Haus-, Hof- und Staatsarchivs,* 8 vols (Vienna: Adolf Holzhausens Nachfolger 1936–40); Janusz Woliński and Zbigniew Wójcik. "Źródła do historii Polski w Haus- Hof- und Staatsarchiv w Wiedniu," *Archeion,* XXVIII (Warsaw 1958), pp. 131–157.

72 See chapter 2, notes 47–55; chapter 3, n. 38; and chapter 4, notes 50, 52, 66, 89.

after Soviet rule, with particular emphasis on the fate of manuscript collections.[73]

With regard to the pre-Soviet period, the best-described collections are those of the Ossolineum, or Ossoliński National Institute (Zakład Narodowy im. Ossolińskich), a major repository especially for Polish materials since its establishment in L'viv in 1823, and the National Home (Narodnyi Dom), which existed in L'viv from 1864 to 1945, primarily as a resource for Old Rus' and Ukrainian materials. As for the Ossoliński Institute, six volumes listing manuscripts and other materials were published.[74] Also, special catalogs appeared describing the archives and manuscripts of the Lubomirski Museum and Pawlikowski Library, two of the many collections that found their way into the Ossoliński Institute.[75] With regard to the National Home, Ilarion Svientsits'kyi prepared detailed catalogs of its manuscript holdings.[76] The Petrushevych Museum, which was part of the National Home, was also accorded special attention in four works.[77]

73 Patricia Kennedy Grimsted, ''L'viv Manuscript Collections and Their Fate,'' in *Eucharisterion: Essays Presented to Omeljan Pritsak*, in *Harvard Ukrainian Studies*, III–IV, pt 1 (Cambridge, Mass. 1979–80), pp. 348–375.

One Polish scholar has also described briefly the manuscript materials on Galicia that he used in L'viv libraries during research trips in 1966 and 1969: Stanisław Franciszek Gajerski, ''Źródła do dziejów południowo-wschodniej Polski w bibliotekach i archiwach Lwowa,'' *Studia Historyczne*, XX, 2 (Cracow 1977), pp. 295–302.

74 Wojciech Kętrzyński, *Katalog rękopisów Biblioteki Zakładu Nar[odowego] im. Ossolińskich*, 3 vols (L'viv: ZNIO 1881–98); *Inwentarz rękopisów Biblioteki Zakładu Narodowego im. Ossolińskich we Lwowie*, 2 vols (L'viv: ZNIO 1926–34); Felix Pohorecki, *Catalogus diplomatum Bibliothecae Instituti Ossoliniani nec non Bibliothecae Pawlikowianae inde ab anno 1227 usque ad annum 1506* (L'viv 1937). See also F. Pohorecki, ''O średniowiecznych dyplomach Zakładu Narodowego im. Ossolińskich, *Ziemia Czerwieńska*, I, 1 (L'viv 1935), pp. 90–98.

75 S. Inglot, *Inwentarz Archiwum XX Lubomirskich (linia Dąbrowieńska)* (Warsaw 1937); M. Gębarowicz, *Katalog rękopisów Biblioteki im. Gwalberta Pawlikowskiego* (L'viv 1929).

76 I.S. Svientsitskii, ''Tserkovno- i russko-slavianskiia rukopisi publichnoi biblioteki Narodnago Doma vo L'vovie,'' *Izviestiia otdeleniia russkago iazyka i slovesnosti Imp. Akademii Nauk*, IX, 3 (St Petersburg 1904), pp. 350–414; idem, ''Rukopisi biblioteki 'Narodnago Doma' vo L'vovie,'' *Nauchno-literaturnyi sbornik 'Galitsko-russkoi Matitsy'*, III, 4 (L'viv 1904), pp. 81–104 and IV, 1 (1905), pp. 108–149, published separately as *Opisanie inoiazychnykh i novieishikh karpato-russkikh rukopisei biblioteki 'Narodnago Doma' vo L'vovie* (L'viv 1905).

See also F.I. Svistun, ''Tserkovno- i slavianorusskie rukopisi biblioteki 'Narodnogo Doma','' *Viestnik 'Narodnogo Doma'*, XXIII (I), 6 (L'viv 1905), pp. 94–96.

77 Iliarion Svientsitskyi, *Opys rukopysiv Narodnoho Domu z kolektsiï Ant. Petrushevycha*, 3 pts in *Ukraïns'ko-rus'kyi arkhyv*, vols I, VI, VII (L'viv 1906–11), and the supplement by O.O. Markov, ''Opisanie rukopisei XIX v. sobraniia A.S. Petrushevicha (v bibl. 'Narodnago Doma' v L'vovie),'' *Viestnik 'Narodnogo Doma'*, XXX (VIII), 1–3 (L'viv 1912), pp. 6–11, 26–32, 34–40; F.I. Svistun, ''Pergaminnyi dokumenty muzeia o. pral. Petrushevicha,'' *Viestnik 'Narodnogo Doma'*, XXX (IV), 1–3 (L'viv 1908), pp. 1–2, 22, 55–56; idem, ''Bumazhnyi

Among other pre-Soviet institutions, the Stauropegial Institute's rich collection of Old Slavonic manuscripts was described in three catalogs.[78] Other collections for which catalogs or descriptions of pre-World War II holdings were prepared include the University of L'viv,[79] the L'viv Historical Museum,[80] the Ukrainian National Museum,[81] and the St Onufrius Basilian Monastery Library.[82]

As for the status of library collections since their reorganization under Soviet rule, Fedir Maksymenko has published a catalog of Old Slavonic books found in L'viv.[83] Most attention has been devoted to the Stefanyk Library of the Academy of Sciences in L'viv, which took over the holdings (among others) of the former Shevchenko Scientific Society, the National Home, the Central Library of the Basilian Order, the L'viv Theological Academy Library, the Baworowski Library, and a large portion of the Ossolineum Library. Patricia K. Grimsted has provided a detailed description of the Stefanyk Library's manuscript collection,[84] while Soviet scholars have prepared catalogs of its incunabula and old imprints,[85] as well as catalogs and descriptions of some of its manuscript collections.[86]

---

dokumenty Muzeia o. pral. A.S. Petrushevicha,'' *Viestnik 'Narodnogo Doma'*, XXVI (IV), 3–6 (L'viv 1908), pp. 57–58, 91–92, 111–112, 130–131.

78 A.S. Petrushevich, *Katalog tserkovno-slovenskikh rukopisei i staropechatannykh knig kirillovskogo pis'ma, nakhodiashchikhsia na arkheologichesko-bibliograficheskoi vystavtsie v stavropigiiskom zavedenii* (L'viv: Stavropigiiskii Institut 1888); I. Sharanevich, *Katalog arkheologichesko-artisticheskikh predmetov, tserkovno-slovenskikh rukopisei i staropechatannykh knig kirillovskogo pis'ma, nakhodiashchikhsia v Muzeie Stavropigiiskogo Instituta na dni 1/13 marta 1890* (L'viv: Stavropigiiskii institut 1890); I.S. Svientsitskii, *Opis' muzeia Stavopigiiskogo Instituta vo L'vovie* (L'viv 1908).

79 Ludwik Finkel, *Inwentarz Archiwum Universitetu Lwowskiego* (L'viv 1917).

80 Łucja Charewiczowa, *Muzeum Historyczne miasta Lwowa: przewodnik po zbiorach* (L'viv 1936).

81 I.S. Svientsits'kyi, *Opys rukopisiv*, pt 1: *kyrylychni perhaminy XII–XV vv.* (L'viv 1933).

82 L. Skruten', ''Biblioteka l'vivs'kykh Vasyliian,'' *Zapysky ChSVV*, I (Zhovkva 1924), pp. 161–176 and III (1928), pp. 65–73; Iaroslav Hordyns'kyi, *Rukopysy Biblioteky monastyria sv. Onufriia ChSVV u L'vovi*, vol. I (Zhovkva 1927), vol. I originally published in *Zapysky ChSVV*, I, 2–3 (Zhovkva 1925) and 4 (1927); vol. II in *Zapysky ChSVV*, III, 1–2 (Zhovkva, 1928), pp. 40–64 and 3–4 (Zhovkva 1930), pp. 345–376.

83 F.P. Maksymenko, *Kyrylychni starodruky ukraïns'kykh drukaren', shcho zberihaiut'sia v l'vivs'kykh zbirkakh (1574–1800)* (L'viv: Vyshcha shkola 1975).

84 Patricia Kennedy Grimsted, ''The Stefanyk Library of the Ukrainian Academy of Sciences–A Treasury of Manuscript Collections in L'viv,'' *Harvard Ukrainian Studies*, V, 2 (Cambridge, Mass. 1981), pp. 195–229.

85 F.P. Maksymenko, *Pershodruky (inkunabuly) Naukovoï biblioteky L'vivs'koho universytetu: kataloh* (L'viv 1958); R.Ia. Lutsyk, *Inkunabuly L'vivs'koï naukovoï biblioteky im. V. Stefanyka AN URSR: kataloh* (L'viv: AN URSR-LNBS 1974). See also the Maksymenko catalog, n. 83 above.

86 These include the catalog of individual manuscript collections: Ie.M. Humeniuk, P.H.

There are also several general descriptions and histories of the major Galician libraries.[87] These include libraries in pre-Soviet institutions: the L'viv Brotherhood (later Stauropegial Institute),[88] the Ossolineum,[89] National Home,[90] Shevchenko Scientific Society,[91] Przemyśl Eparchy,[92] and the Ukrainian National Museum;[93] as well as the present-day Stefanyk Library,[94] Ivan Franko University

---

Bab''iak, and O.O. Dz'oban, *Osobysti arkhivni fondy viddilu rukopysiv: anotovanyi pokazhchyk* (L'viv: AN URSR–LNBS 1977); catalogs of materials on certain historical themes: T.Iu. Kozachuk et al., *Vyzvol'na viina ukraïns'koho narodu v 1648–1654 rr. za vozz''iednaniia Ukraïny z Rosiieiu: anotovanyi pokazhchyk rukopysnykh materialiv biblioteky* (L'viv: L'vivs'ka biblioteka AN URSR 1954) and V.F. Bandura et al., *1848 rik v Halychyni: anotovanyi pokazhchyk rukopysnykh materialiv biblioteky* (L'viv: L'vivs'ka biblioteka AN URSR 1953); a catalog of Ukrainian and Russian autograph literary manuscripts and letters (only a few of Galician origin): P.H. Bab''iak, *Avtohrafy ukraïns'kykh i rosiis'kykh pys'mennykiv: anotovanyi pokazhchyk* (L'viv: AN URSR–LNBS 1976); and descriptions of certain collections: S. Piskovyi [Ia.R. Dashkevych], ''L'vivs'ki 'teky' A. Shneidera iak istoryko-kraieznavche dzherelo,'' *Arkhivy Ukraïny,* XIX, 4 (Kiev 1965), pp. 73–76; S.P. Kostiuk and P.K. Medvedyk, *Denys Sichyns'kyi: materialy po bio-bibliohrafiï diiachiv ukraïns'koï kul'tury* (L'viv 1966); and on the papers of Denys Zubryts'kyi and Ivan E. Levyts'kyi, see the studies of Ia. Isaievych and Ia.R. Dashkevych, n. 13 above, and in chapter 2, n. 6. For its holdings on the L'viv Stauropegial Brotherhood, see the study of Iaroslav Isaievych in chapter 4, n. 65.

87 Studies discussed here concern libraries only. For works on the institutions as a whole in which these libraries are found, see chapter 2, notes 67–75, 82–83.

88 Ia.D. Isaievych, ''Biblioteka L'vivs'koho bratstva,'' in *Bibliotekoznavstvo ta bibliohrafiia,* vol. III (Kharkiv: Redaktsiino-vyd. viddil Knyzhkovoï palaty URSR), pp. 126–132.

89 The literature on the Ossolineum Library is extensive. See the introductory historical surveys and comprehensive bibliography in chapter 2, notes 69–70.

90 Bohdan Barvins'kyi, *Biblioteka i muzei Narodn'oho Domu u L'vovi, 1849–1919* (L'viv 1920), first published in *Viestnik 'Narodnago Doma'*, XXXIII (L'viv 1918–19), supplemented by ''Biblioteka i muzeï 'Narod'noho doma' s 1 ianuaria 1920 h. po 1 iuliia 1921 h.,'' *ibid.*, XXXIV, 1 (L'viv 1921), pp. 26–32; F.I. Svistun, ''Staropechatnyi slaviano-russkii knigi biblioteki 'Narodnago Doma' vo L'vovie i rozvitie knigopechataniia na Rusi,'' *ibid.*, XXV (III), 1–10 (L'viv 1907), pp. 12–16, 21–25, 40–43, 63–65, 76–82, 94–99, 132–136, 167–168, 189–191; XXVI (IV), 1 (1908), pp. 17–18.

91 Volodymyr Doroshenko, *Ukraïns'ka Natsional'na Biblioteka (Biblioteka Naukovoho Tovarystva im. Shevchenka u L'vovi)* (L'viv: NTSh 1936); idem, ''Biblioteka Naukovoho Tovarystva im. Shevchenka u L'vovi,'' *Zapysky NTSh*. CLXXI (New York and Paris 1961), pp. 7–58.

92 Mykhailo Zubryts'kyi, ''Dekanal'ni i parokhiial'ni bibliïoteky peremys'koï eparkhiï, *Zapysky NTSh,* XC (L'viv 1909), pp. 119–136.

93 I. Svientsits'kyi, ''Biblioteka Natsional'noho Muzeiu u L'vovi,'' *Knyhar'*, no. 6 (Kiev 1918), pp. 308–314.

94 *L'vivs'ka naukova biblioteka im. V. Stefanyka AN URSR: putivnyk* (Kiev: AN URSR 1979).

Library,[95] the L'viv Historical Museum,[96] and Ukrainian Art Museum.[97]

Outside of Galicia, there are several libraries with valuable manuscript collections and publications originating from and/or about eastern Galicia. Perhaps the richest of these is the Ossolineum in Wrocław, Poland, which in 1946 and 1947 received much of the material held in the L'viv predecessor of the same name. The Wrocław Ossolineum's manuscript collection, especially rich in material on the early history and Polish aspects of Galicia, has been cataloged in several volumes.[98]

There are also rich collections of publications (and some manuscripts) dealing with Galicia in the Biblioteka Narodowa (Warsaw); the Národní Museum and Slovanská knihovna (Prague); the Österreichische Nationalbibliothek (Vienna); the Institutum Pontificum Orientale (Rome); Library of Congress (Washington, DC); New York Public Library; Harvard University Library (Cambridge, Massachusetts); the Hoover Institution on War, Revolution, and Peace (Stanford, California); the Public Archives of Canada (Ottawa); the Basilian Fathers' Library and Museum (Mundare, Alberta); and the University of Toronto Library. The Galician collections in several of these institutions have been singled out for description in whole or in part.[99]

95 I.M. Kyrylov, *Naukova biblioteka L'vivs'koho derzhavnoho universytetu im. Ivana Franka: korotkyi dovidnyk* (L'viv 1959).

96 R.S. Bahrii et al., *L'vivs'kyi istorychnyi muzei: putivnyk* (L'viv 1976). See also the catalog of its exposition on the late nineteenth and early twentieth centuries: *L'vivs'kyi istorychnyi muzei, viddil istoriï kapitalizmu: putivnyk po ekspozytsiï* (L'viv 1960).

97 Ia.I. Nanovs'kyi et al., *L'vivs'kyi muzei ukraïns'koho mystetstva: putivnyk* (L'viv 1978).

98 *Inwentarz rękopisów Biblioteki Zakładu Narodowego im. Ossolińskich we Wrocławiu*, 6 vols and index vol. (Wrocław: ZNIO 1948–79). The first two volumes, edited by Jadwiga Turska, list the manuscripts transferred from L'viv, especially those dated before 1506. See also the supplement to the catalog of the Pawlikowski collection (n. 74 above) now almost entirely in Wrocław: Adam Fastnacht, *Catalogus diplomaticum Bibliothecae Instituti Ossoliniani, Supplementum I: inde ab anno 1279 usque ad annum 1506* (Wrocław: ZNIO 1951). For documents from 1506 to 1939, see idem, *Katalog dokumentów Biblioteki Zakładu Narodowego im. Ossolińskich*, 2 vols (Wrocław: ZNIO 1953–69). For a description of how the collections were divided between L'viv and Wrocław, see the Grimsted study, n. 73 above.

99 "Rukopysy peremys'koï hreko-katolyts'koï kapituly v Narodovii bibliotetsi u Varshavi," *Bohosloviia*, XXXVII, 1–4 (Rome 1973), pp. 193–213 and XXXVIII, 1–4 (1974),

pp. 237–243; Paul R. Magocsi, ''Vienna as a Resource for Ukrainian Studies: With Special Reference to Galicia,'' in *Eucharisterion: Essays Presented to Omeljan Pritsak on his Sixtieth Birthday by his Colleagues and Students,* in *Harvard Ukrainian Studies,* III–IV, pt 2 (Cambridge, Mass. 1979–80), pp. 609–626. Holdings of the materials at Harvard on the Lemkian region are singled out in Paul R. Magocsi and Olga K. Mayo, *Carpatho-Ruthenica at Harvard: A Catalog of Holdings* (Fairview, NJ: Carpatho-Rusyn Research Center 1983). Two collections at the University of Toronto that contain primarily Galician materials are described in Paul R. Magocsi, *The Peter Jacyk Collection of Ukrainian Serials: A Guide to Newspapers and Periodicals* (Toronto: Chair of Ukrainian Studies 1983); and Edward Kasinec and Bohdan Struminskyj, *The Millennium Collection of Old Ukrainian Books at the University of Toronto Library: A Catalogue* (Toronto: Chair of Ukrainian Studies 1984).

The heading Galicia also appears in the subject catalogs of three major repositories: The New York Public Library, The Research Libraries, *Dictionary Catalog of the Slavonic Collection,* 44 vols, 2nd rev. ed. (Boston: G.K. Hall 1974), especially vol. XIV, pp. 126–138; *The Library Catalogs of the Hoover Institution on War, Revolution, and Peace–Stanford University: Catalog of the Western Language Collections* [including Slavic languages], 63 vols and 2 supplements [11 vols] (Boston: G.K. Hall 1969–77), especially vol. XIX, pp. 60–66; and the several series published on acquisitions from 1950 to the present in the *Library of Congress Catalog, Books: Subjects.*

Chapter 2

General studies

This chapter will first discuss historical journals and reference works that deal in whole or in part with Galician-Ukrainian topics. Then will follow sections devoted to surveys of Galician-Ukrainian political, religious, and cultural history, as well as studies dealing with regions and individual cities. Only works of a more general nature covering most or all of Galician historical development will be treated here. For works dealing with one or two specific periods, it is necessary to consult the appropriate chapter in this volume.

Scholarly journals

A few scholarly journals emanating both from within and beyond the borders of the province are devoted in whole or in part to the history of Ukrainian Galicia. Some of these focus primarily on Galician developments: the *Halyts'kii ystorycheskii sbornyk* (L'viv 1853–54, 1860), *Naukovŷi* (later *Lyteraturnŷi*) *sbornyk* (L'viv 1865–73, 1885–90, 1896–97), and *Nauchno-literaturnyi sbornik* (L'viv 1901–02, 1904–06, 1908, 1930–34) of the Galician Rus' Matytsia; *Halychanyn* (L'viv 1862–63); the *Vremennyk* (L'viv, 1864–1915, 1923–39) of the Stauropegial Institute;[1] the *Vîstnyk* (L'viv 1882–1914, 1918–19, 1921, 1924) of the National Home; and *Ziemia Czerwieńska* (L'viv 1935–38) of the L'viv branch of the Polish Historical Society. Also in the largely Galician-oriented subject category are *Zoria* (L'viv 1880-97), *Literaturno-naukovyi vistnyk* (L'viv and Kiev 1898–1914, 1917–19, 1922–32), and *Zhytie i slovo* (L'viv 1894–97),[2] all of

1 A history and list of contents of the *Vremennyk* is provided in S.Iu. Bendasiuk, ''Vremennik Stavropigiiskogo Instituta: istoriko-bibliograficheskii ocherk k 70-letiiu izdaniia,'' *Vremennik: nauchno-literaturnye zapiski L'vovskago Stavropigiona na 1934 god* (L'viv 1933), pp. 13–67.

2 For commentary on one journal's history, see Volodymyr Doroshenko, *Literaturno-naukovyi*

which emphasize cultural developments; *Ruthenische Revue* (Vienna, 1903–05) and *Ukrainische Rundschau* (Vienna, 1906–10), whose purpose was to inform the Austrian public about contemporary conditions in the province; *Rocznik Przemyski* (Przemyśl, 1909–present), *Litopys Boikivshchyny* (Sambir 1931–39), and *Annaly Svitovoï Federatsiï Lemkiv* (Camilus 1974–present), which have a regional profile; *Litopys Natsional'noho muzeiu* (L'viv 1933–39), mainly on art history; and *Litopys Chervonoï Kalyny* (L'viv 1926–38), which specializes in military history during World War I and the Galician struggle for independence. Finally, there are the more recent Soviet series, *Z istoriï zakhidnoukraïns'kykh zemel'*, later *Z istoriï Ukraïns'koï RSR* (L'viv 1957–62), on all aspects of western Ukrainian history, and *Ukraïns'ke literaturoznavstvo* (L'viv 1966–present), which focuses on the life and work of Ivan Franko.

Some other scholarly journals dealing with Ukrainian or Polish historical problems in general also contain much material on Galicia. The most outstanding of these is the *Zapysky Naukovoho tovarystva im. Shevchenka* (L'viv 1892–1937; Paris, New York, Munich 1948–present), which at least in its pre-1914 volumes, still contains the best work on Galicia. The results of important research on Galicia undertaken by Polish (and some Ukrainian) scholars are found in *Przewodnik Naukowy i Literacki* (L'viv 1873–1913), *Kwartalnik Historyczny* (L'viv 1887–1939; Cracow 1946–49; Warsaw, 1950–present), and *Sprawy Narodowościowe* (Warsaw, 1927–39).[3] Also rich in material on Galicia is *Stara Ukraïna* (L'viv 1924–25), a semi-popular historical journal; *Zapysky Chynu Sv. Vasylia Velykoho* (Zhovkva 1924–42)[4] and its successor *Analecta Ordinis S. Basilii Magni* (Rome 1949–present), with emphasis on church history; *Ukraïns'kyi istorychnyi zhurnal* (Kiev 1957–present), which contains the results of recent Soviet Marxist scholarship;[5] and *Nauchno-informatsionnyi biulleten'*, later re-

---

vistnyk (Augsburg: UVAN 1948). Another has a subject index: P.H. Bab''iak, *Zhytie i slovo, 1894–1897: systematychnyi pokazhchyk zmistu* (L'viv: LNBS 1968).

3 A comprehensive index for the first forty-five years of *Kwartalnik Historyczny* is available: Mieczysław Rutkowski and Karol Maleczyński, *Indeks do Kwartalnika Historycznego (1887–1922)* (L'viv: Polske Towarystwo Historycznego 1925). A brief index of *Sprawy Narodowościowe* was prepared by Witold Sworakowski, *Skorowidz rzeczowy artykułów i kroniki 'Spraw Narodowościowych' ... za okres 1929–1931 (roczniki I–V)* and Maks Berżyński, *Skorowidz ... za okres 1932–1936 (roczniki VI–X)* (Warsaw: Instytut Badań Spraw Narodowościowych 1933 and 1937).

4 An index is available: *Index 'Analectorum O.S.B.M.': Series prima, vol. I–VI,* in Analecta OSBM, series II, sectio II, vol. I, 1 (Rome 1949).

5 A subject index for the first decade of this journal with a specific section on Galicia exists: *Ukraïns'kyi istorychnyi zhurnal (1957–1966): systematychnyi pokazhchyk* (Kiev: Naukova dumka 1968), especially pp. 53–57.

named *Arkhivy Ukraïny* (Kiev 1947–present), which is especially valuable for its descriptions of present-day archives and the publication of some archival documents from Galicia.

Reference works

With regard to reference tools, there have been attempts to produce biographical dictionaries for all or part of Galicia, but none have been brought to a successful conclusion. The outstanding bibliographer Ivan E. Levyts'kyi undertook a comprehensive Galician biographical dictionary, but despite an excellent beginning, he never even completed the letter B.[6] More recently, the Soviet scholar V. Poliek undertook a similar effort just for the Ivano-Frankivs'k oblast, but after completing the letter V (the third Ukrainian letter), his serialized work stopped appearing in 1970.[7] Galician-Ukrainian political and cultural leaders active during the late nineteenth and early twentieth centuries have been the focus of attention in two biographical compilations.[8] While no general Galician biographical dictionary has been completed, there are nonetheless numerous brief biographies of Galician-Ukrainian leaders in the interwar Ukrainian encyclopedia, in the alphabetical edition of the emigré Ukrainian encyclopedia, and some as well in the Soviet Ukrainian encyclopedia.[9] Polish encyclopedias and the Polish and Austrian na-

6 Yvan Em. Levytskii, *Prykarpatska Rus' v XIX-m vîtsî v biohrafiiakh y portretakh iey dîiatelei s uvzhliadnen'em zamîchatel'nŷkh liudei, kotrŷkh 1772 r. zastav pry zhyzny,* vol. I, 4 pts (L'viv 1898–1901). The proposed contents for the rest of this work and the archival material that remains are analyzed by Ia.R. Dashkevych, "Materialy I.O. Levyts'koho iak dzherelo dlia biohrafichnoho slovnyka," in *Istorychni dzherela ta ikh vykorystannia,* vol. II (Kiev: Naukova dumka 1966), pp. 35–53.

7 V. Poliek, "Materialy do ukraïns'koho biohrafichnoho slovnyka: literaturno-mystets'ka i naukova Ivano-Frankivshchyna," *Arkhivy Ukraïny,* XXIII, 4 and 6 (Kiev 1969), pp. 105–112 and 101–107; XXIV, 4 and 6 (1970), 102–111 and 102–106.

8 Kost Levyts'kyi, *Ukraïns'ki polityky: syl'vety nashykh davnikh posliv i politychnykh diiachiv,* 2 vols (L'viv: Dilo 1936–37); Stepan Volynets', ed., *Peredvisnyky i tvortsi lystopadovoho zryvu: zakhidn'o-ukraïns'ki hromads'ki i politychni diiachi* (Winnipeg: Spilka Tryzub 1965). See also the nine biographies by Izydor Sokhots'kyi in *Istorychni postati Halychyny XIX–XX st.,* NTSh, Biblioteka ukraïnoznavstva, vol. VIII (New York, Paris, Sydney, and Toronto 1961), pp. 78–125.

9 *Ukraïnska zahal'na entsyklopediia,* 3 vols, ed. Ivan Rakovs'kyi (L'viv, Stanyslaviv, and Kolomyia: Ridna shkola 1930–35); *Entsyklopediia ukraïnoznavstva: slovnykova chastyna,* vols I–VIII, ed. Volodymyr Kubiiovych (Paris and New York: Molode zhyttia for the NTSh 1955–79). Two volumes remain to be published. *Ukraïns'ka radians'ka entsyklopediia,* 17 vols (Kiev: AN URSR 1959–65). A second revised edition of this work is presently appearing: vols I–V (Kiev: Holovna redaktsiia Ukraïns'koï radians'koï entsyklopediia 1977–80). Seven volumes remain to be published.

tional biographical dictionaries include material on activists in eastern as well as western Galicia, although the coverage of Galician Ukrainians is very limited;[10] in contrast, the excellent Czech-language *Ottův slovník naučný* includes much data on Galician-Ukrainian leaders and organizations.[11] The four-volume Soviet encyclopedia of Ukrainian history also contains information on Galicia, especially concerning Communist developments during the twentieth century.[12]

Writers from the region have received special attention in dictionary-like works. Fedor F. Aristov began a biobibliographic dictionary of Galician writers of the Old Ruthenian and Russophile orientations, although only one volume of this valuable work appeared.[13] Vasilii Vavrik has produced a much briefer, though chronologically more encompassing dictionary on writers of similar orientation.[14] Many Galicians are also treated in the five-volume Soviet biobibliographical dictionary of Ukrainian writers, and in the emigré literary dictionary by Bohdan Romanenchuk, only the first two volumes of which have appeared to date (through the Ukrainian letter H).[15] There are a few biographical dictionaries of

10 The most important of the several Polish encyclopedias from the standpoint of Galicia are the nineteenth-century *Encyklopedja powszechna*, 28 vols, ed. Samuel Orgelbrand (Warsaw 1859–68); 2nd ed., 14 vols (Warsaw 1883–4); 3rd rev. ed., 18 vols (Warsaw 1898–1912) and the post-World War II *Wielka encyclopedia powszechna PWN*, 13 vols, Bogdan Suchodolski et al., eds (Warsaw: PWN 1962–70). The standard biographical dictionary is *Polski słownik biograficzny* (Cracow, Wrocław and Warsaw: Polska Akademija Umiejętności and ZNIO–PAN 1935–present). By 1979, 24 volumes [A–P] had appeared.

The Austrian biographical dictionaries with entries on figures from Galicia are Constant von Wurzbach, *Biographisches Lexikon des Kaiserthums Oesterreich*, 60 vols (Vienna: L.C. Zamarsti and Vlg. der K.K. Hof- und Staatsdruckerei 1856–91), which includes 742 biographies of Galicians; *Österreichisches biographisches Lexikon 1815–1950*, 6 vols [A–M], ed. Leo Santifaller and Eva Obermayer-Marnach (Graz and Köln: Hermann Böhlaus, 1957–73), still in preparation. The Galician entries in the latter work are discussed by Wiesław Bieńkowski, "Galizien und das 'Österreichische Biographische Lexikon': zur Geschichte der polnischen biographischen Arbeiten im 19. und 20. Jahrhundert," *Anzeiger der Österreichischen Akademie der Wissenschaften, philosophisch-historische Klasse*, CV (Vienna 1968), pp. 41–57.

11 *Ottův slovník naučný*, 28 vols (Prague: J. Otto 1888–1909), and the almost complete [A–U] supplement: *Ottův slovník naučný nové doby*, ed. B. Němec, 6 vols in 12 (Prague: J. Otto 1930–43).

12 A.D. Skaba et al., eds, *Radians'ka entsyklopediia istoriï Ukraïny*, 4 vols (Kiev: AN URSR 1969–72).

13 Fedor F. Aristov, *Karpato-russkie pisateli: izsliedovanie po neizdannym istochnikam*, vol. I (Moscow: Galitsko-russkoe obshchestvo, 1916); 2nd rev. ed. (Bridgeport, Conn.: Carpatho-Russian Literary Association 1977). The second edition contains a description of the two following volumes proposed.

14 Vasilii R. Vavrik, *Kratkii ocherk galitsko-russkoi pis'mennosti* (Louvain 1973).

15 *Ukraïns'ki pys'mennyky: bio-bibliohrafichnyi slovnyk*, 5 vols (Kiev: Khudozhnia literatura

Galician writers from specific periods and regions.[16] Finally, Irynei Nazarko has written biographies of all Galician metropolitans.[17]

With regard to the geographic composition of Galicia, comprehensive lists of all villages, towns, and cities are found in statistical surveys compiled under the Austrian and Polish regimes.[18] These can also be supplemented by the *schematisma* produced periodically by each of the Greek Catholic (L'viv, Przemyśl, Stanyslaviv) and Roman (L'viv, Przemyśl) dioceses covering eastern Galicia.[19]

1963–65); Bohdan Romanenchuk, *Azbukovnyk: korotka entsyklopediia ukraïns'koï literatury*, vols I–II (Philadelphia: Kyïv 1966–73).

16 For guides to Soviet and pre-Soviet writers, see chapter 7, n. 100. For the Lemkian region, see T. Kuryllo, "Kratkaia svodka pisatelei i zhurnalistov na Lemkovshchine," *Sbornik Galitsko-russkoi Matitsy*, VIII (L'viv 1934), pp. 22–50.

17 Irynei I. Nazarko, *Kyïvs'ki i halyts'ki mytropolyty: biohrafichni narysy (1590–1960)*, Analecta OSBM, series II, sectio I: Opera, vol. XIII (Rome 1962).

18 *Alphabetisch geordnetes Ortschafts-Verzeichnis der Königreiche Galizien und Lodomerien und das Herzogthum Bukowina* (L'viv 1855); *Bevölkerung und Viehstand von Ost- und West-Galizien nach der Zählung vom 31. Oktober 1857* (Vienna 1859); *Bevölkerung und Viehstand von Galizien nach der Zählung vom 31. Dezember 1869* (Vienna 1871); *Orts-Repertorium des Königreiches Galizien und Lodomerien mit dem Grossherzogthume Krakau* [based on the 1869 census] (Vienna: Carl Gerold's Sohn 1874); *Spezial-Orts-Repertorium der im österreichischen Reichsrate vertretenen Königreiche und Länder*, vol. XII: *Galizien* (Vienna 1886); J. Bigo, *Najnowszy skorowidz wszystkich miejscowości z przysiołkami w Królestwie Galicyi i Bukowinie* (Zolochiv 1886), 5th ed. (L'viv 1914); *Spezial-Orts-Repertorium der im österreichischen Reichsrate vertretenen Königreiche und Länder* [based on 1890 census], vol. XII: *Galizien* (Vienna: Alfred Hölder 1893); *Gemeindelexikon der im Reichsrate vertretenen Königreiche und Länder* [based on 1900 census], vol. XII: *Galizien* (Vienna: K.K. Hof- und Staatsdruckerei 1906); Szymon Chanderys, *Kompletny skorowidz miejscowości w Galicyi i Bukowinie* (L'viv 1909); *Skorowidz miejscowości Rzeczypospolitej Polskiej* [based on 1921 census], vol. VIII: *Województwo Polskie;* vol. XIII: *Województwo Lwowskie;* vol. XIV: *Województwo Stanisławowskie;* vol. XV: *Województwo Tarnopolskie* (Warsaw: Główny Urząd Statystyczny Rzeczypospolitej Polskiej 1923–24).

19 The Greek Catholic *schematisma* include *Shematyzm vsechesnoho klyra arkhidiietseziï mytropolitans'koï hreko-katolyts'koï L'vivs'koï* [1882–1914, 1918, 1924, 1922–28, 1930, 1931/32, 1932/33, 1935/36, 1938] (L'viv 1882–1938); *Shematyzm vseho klyra katolyts'koho obriada hrechesko-russkoho eparkhyy Peremys'koï, Sambirs'koï i Sianots'koï* (Przemyśl 1868–1936); *Shematyzm vseho klyra Hreko-katolyts'koï eparkhiï Stanyslavivs'koï na rik Bozhyi* [1886–1938], vols I-XXXVII (Stanyslaviv 1886–1938); *Schematismus universi cleri Graeco-Catholicae Dioeceseos Stanislaopoliensis pro anno Domini [1886–1938]* (Stanyslaviv 1886–1934).

See also the schematism of the monastic order of St Basil the Great: M.N. Kossak, *Shematyzm provyntsiy sv. spasytelia Chyna sv. Vasyliia Velykoho v Halytsiy ... y korotkii pohliad na monastŷri y monashestvo ruske ôt zavedeniia na Rusy vîrŷ Khrystovoy azh do nŷnîshnoe vremia* (L'viv 1867).

The Roman Catholic *schematisma* include *Schematismus Archidioecesis Leopoliensis ritus latini* [1814–1915, 1917–1939], original titles: *Schematizmus universi* ... [1814–1830];

Systematic descriptions of the province as a whole with emphasis on geography, demography, and economic life are found in nineteenth-century works by Hipolit Stupnicki and Iakiv Holovats'kyi.[20] There is also a mine of geographical, historical, and statistical information on individual Galician towns and villages in the multivolume geographical dictionary of Poland and neighboring Slavic lands completed on the eve of World War I.[21] For the status of the province during the first half of the twentieth century, it is necessary to consult works by Franciszek Bujak and Ivan Shymonovych, and a Polish encyclopedia that appeared just after World War I.[22] During the interwar period, plans were made to produce a Polish regional encyclopedia for eastern Galicia (the L'viv, Ternopil' and Stanyslaviv provinces), but only one volume dealing with geography, archeology, structural

---

Catalogus cleri ... [1832–1913]; *Elenchus cleri* ... [1916–1925] (L'viv 1814–1939); *Schematismus Universi cleri dioecesis Premysliensis ritus latini* [1819–1914, 1916–1935]. Some were published in *Directorium officii divini pro dioecesi Premisliensi ritus latini 1831, 1843, 1844, 1846, 1848–54, 1858–59, 1861, 1877* (Przemyśl 1819–1935).

20 Hippolit Stupnicki, *Galicya pod względem geograficzno-topograficzno-historycznym* (L'viv 1849), 2nd rev. ed. (L'viv 1869); Hippolit Stupnicki, *Das Königreich Galizien und Lodomerien sammt dem Grossherzogthume Krakau und dem Herzogthume Bukowina in geographisch-historisch-statistischer Beziehung* (L'viv: J. Milikowski 1853); H. Stupnicki, *Geograficzno-statystyczny opis Królestwa Galicyi i Lodomeryi* (L'viv 1864); Iakov Golovatskii, ''Karpatskaia Rus': istoriko-étnograficheskii ocherk,'' *Zhurnal MNP,* CLXXIX, 6 (St Petersburg 1875), pp. 349–369, reprinted in his *Narodnyia piesni Galitskoi i Ugorskoi Rusi,* vol. III, pt 2 (Moscow 1878), pp. 616–670; idem, ''Karpatskaia Rus': geograficheskostatisticheskie i istorichesko-étnograficheskie ocherki Galichiny, sievero-vostochnoi Ugrii i Bukoviny,'' *Slavianskii sbornik,* I (St Petersburg 1875), pp. 1–30 and II (1877), pp. 55–84, reprinted in his *Narodnyia piesni,* vol. III, pt 2, pp. 557–615.

See also K. Shmedes, *Geograficheskoe i statisticheskoe obozrenie Galitsii i Bukoviny* (St Petersburg 1870); J. Jandaurek, *Das Königreich Galizien und Lodomerien und das Herzogthum Bukowina,* Die Länder Oesterreich-Ungarns in Wort and Bild (Vienna: K. Graeser 1884); Roman Zaklyns'kyi, *Geografiia Rusy,* pt 1: *Rus' Halyts'ka, Bukovyns'ka i Uhors'ka* (L'viv: TP 1887); and the incomplete encyclopedia: Antoni Schneider, *Encyklopedya do krajoznawstwa Galicyi pod względem historycznym, statystycznym, topograficznym, orograficznym, handlowym, przemysłowym, sfragistycznym, etc.,* 2 vols [A–Balin] (L'viv 1868–74).

An excellent description of geographic works and lexicons published before the 1870s that contain data on eastern Galicia is found in the historiographical study of Iaroslav Dashkevych (see chapter 1, n. 7).

21 Filip Sulimierski et al., eds, *Słownik geograficzny Królestwa Polskiego i innych krajów słowianskich,* 15 vols (Warsaw: Filip Sulimierski and Władisław Wałewski 1880–1900).

22 Fr. Bujak, *Galicya,* 2 vols (L'viv: H. Altenberg 1908); I. Shymonovych, *Halychyna: ekonomichno-statystychna rozvidka* (Kiev: Derzhavne vyd. Ukraïny 1928); *Encyclopédie polonaise,* 3 vols (Fribourg and Lausanne 1920), in English as *Polish Encyclopedia,* 3 vols (Geneva and Fribourg: Committee for the Polish Encyclopedia Publications 1922–6), especially vol. II, which has a section on ''East Galicia.''

anthropology, and ethnography was completed.[23] Soviet writers have prepared works dealing with the geography of certain areas in Galicia,[24] and several members of the L'viv Central State Historical Archive have prepared a very useful guide describing the administrative, judicial, financial, and economic structure of Galicia from the fourteenth century to 1939.[25] There are also several guidebooks with valuable factual data on all aspects of the province.[26]

Historical surveys

The first attempt to present a survey of Galician-Ukrainian history occurred already in 1792, when Johann Christian von Engel (1770–1814) published his *History of Galicia-Volhynia*. Four years later the work reappeared together with Engel's history of the Cossacks as volume 48 in the first multivolume history of the world undertaken in the universalist spirit of the Enlightenment by a group of scholars in Germany and England.[27] Engel was uniquely prepared for his task: he was born in Levoče (Leutschau), a largely German town within the Slovak-inhabited area of northern Hungary–a territory that for several centuries before 1772 had belonged to Poland. The young Engel became an official in Transylvania and was a loyal Habsburg servant.

His history of Galicia presented the Austrian, or more properly, the imperial Austro-Hungarian interpretation of that region's past. In essence, his work was basically a history of the Hungarians in Galicia. Engel distinguished four periods: 980–1130, which began with Hungary's initial interest in the area and ended with

23 Zygmunt Czerny, ed., *Polska Południowo-Wschodnia*, vol. I: *Geografia* [Julian Czyzewski], *Prehistoria* [Leon Kozłowski], *Antropologia* [Jan Czekanowski], *Etnologia* [Adam Fischer] (L'viv: Związek Polskich Towarzystw Naukowych 1939).

24 T.M. Kovalevs'ka, *L'vivs'ka oblast' [heohrafichnyi narys]* (Kiev: Radians'ka shkola 1961); V.V. Onikiienko and Ia.I. Zhupans'kyi, *Pryroda i hospodarstvo Stanislavs'koï oblasti URSR* (Chernivtsi 1960); A.M. Hryhor'iev, *Stanislavs'ka oblast' (heohrafichnyi narys)* (Kiev: Radians'ka shkola 1957); P.V. Voloboi, *Ternopil's'ka oblast': heohrafichnyi narys* (Kiev: Radians'ka shkola 1959).

25 I.L. Butych and V.I. Strel'skii, eds, *Uchrezhdeniia Zapadnoi Ukrainy do vossoedineniia ee v edinom ukrainskom sovetskom sotsialisticheskom gosudarstve: spravochnik* (L'viv: LU 1955).

26 Mieczysław Orłowicz, *Illustrowany przewodnik po Galicyi, Bukowinie, Spiszu, Orawie i Śląsku Cieszyńskim* (L'viv: K. Kwieciński 1914); Mieczysław Orłowicz and Roman Kordys, *Illustrierter Führer durch Galizien* (Vienna and Leipzig: A. Hartlebens Vlg. 1914). For guidebooks and other studies on individual regions, cities, and towns in eastern Galicia, see notes 85–143 below.

27 Johann Christian von Engel, *Geschichte von Halitsch und Vladimir* (1792–93), Fortsetzung der Algemeine Welthistorie durch eine Gesellschaft von Gelehrten in Teutschland und England, vol. XLVIII (Halle: Johann Jacob Gebauer 1796), pp. 407–710.

the unification of Galicia and Volhynia under one prince; 1130–1230, the height of the Galician-Volhynian state under princes András II and his son Kálmán; 1230–1572, the period of Polish-Lithuanian struggle for the region; and 1572–1772, the era of Polish domination until Galicia's "reunification" with Hungary. This Austro-Hungarian view, which started from the premise that Galicia was most naturally a part of Hungary and that it was only temporarily separated from that country, remained for some years the accepted interpretation as revealed in the entry on Galicia in the first Austrian national encyclopedia (1835) and in an essay (1863) by Hermann Bidermann, at the time Austria's leading scholar on nationality problems, who had reacted to Polish and Russian claims upon the area's historical past and political future.[28] The interpretation first put forth by Engel did not, however, enter the framework of the late nineteenth-century encyclopedia of Austria-Hungary begun under the auspices of Crown Prince Rudolf; instead, Polish and Ukrainian scholars were invited to present their views in the large volume treating all aspects of Galicia.[29]

The Austro-Hungarian interpretation had been already challenged in the early nineteenth century, first by Greek Catholic clergymen like Mykhailo Harasevych, who wanted to justify his church's status by revealing its long-standing historico-legal position, then by secular writers like Denys Zubryts'kyi, Iakiv Holovats'kyi, and Izydor Sharanevych, who were anxious to depict the independent status of the medieval Galician-Volhynian Rus' state and its integral relationship to other eastern Slavic developments.[30]

Reacting both to the Austro-Hungarian and eastern orientations, Polish writers, especially during the revolutionary upheavals of 1848, argued that all of Galicia had always been an integral part of Polish cultural and historical development. Antoni Dąbczański best represents these views and argued further that the so-called newly created "Ruthenian" nationality enjoyed religious toleration and freedom only because of its earlier union with Poland.[31] Although the polemical tone of Dąbczański is less strident in most subsequent writings, the general

28 "Galizien und Lodomerien, Königreich," *Oesterreichische National-Encyklopaedie,* vol. II (Vienna 1835), pp. 263–266; Hermann Bidermann, *Die ruthenische Nationalität und ihre Bedeutung für Oesterreich* (Vienna: Vlg. der Donau-Zeitung 1863).

29 *Die österreichisch-ungarische Monarchie in Wort und Bild* [vol. XI]: *Galizien* (Vienna: K.K. Hof- und Staatsdruckerei 1898). See also A. Von Guttry, *Galizien: Land und Leute* (Munich and Leipzig: Georg Müller 1916).

30 See n. 57 below, and chapter 3, notes 19–22.

31 Antoni Dąbczański, *Die ruthenische Frage in Galizien* (L'viv 1848); Antoni Dąbczański, *Wyjaśnienie sprawy ruskiej* (L'viv 1848; reprinted L'viv: L. Piller 1885).

See also the pamphlet by Venceslas Mejbaum, *Étude sur l'ucrainisme* (L'viv: Publications du Bureau des archives de la Commission gouvernante à Lwów 1919).

tendency in Polish scholarship on Galicia is to discuss the province primarily in terms of its western, Polish half.[32] This is also evident in three general encyclopedic surveys on all aspects of Galicia[33] and in essays on Polish-Ukrainian relations by Stanisław Tarnowski and Stanisław Smolka,[34] all of which begin with the premise that eastern as well as western Galicia is part of the Polish political and cultural sphere. Perhaps the best analyses of Polish-Ukrainian relations are found in four studies by Leon Wasilewski, who provides historical surveys of eastern Galicia. While accepting the Ukrainian nature of the region, he still argues for its remaining politically united with Poland.[35]

In contrast to the Austro-Hungarian and Polish views on eastern Galicia are the writings of Old Ruthenians, Russians, and Ukrainians. Although there are differences of emphasis and interpretation between each of these three groups, they all agree with the premise, first elaborated by Zubryts'kyi, that eastern Galicia is historically and culturally part of an eastern Slavic world that traces its roots back to medieval Kievan Rus'. Further, they all agree that the region's apogee was reached during the period of the Galician-Volhynian principality, when Galicia was politically independent but culturally integrated with other eastern Rus' lands. They disagree, however, about the fate of the area under subsequent Polish and Austrian rule and about its specific relationship with eastern Slavdom.

The Old Ruthenian position was expressed by natives of eastern Galicia or northern Bukovina, who consider these lands to be eastern Slavic, but who basically accept Austrian rule as a positive phenomenon. Their writings reflect a strong local patriotism that rejects what is considered long-term Polish domination and late nineteenth-century Ukrainian ethnonational separatism. Surveys of

32 A general history of Galicia is given by Bobrzyński in ''Geschichte [Galiziens] seit der Vereinigung [1386],'' in *Die österreichisch-ungarische Monarchie in Wort und Bild* [vol. XI]: *Galizien* (Vienna: K.K. Hof- und Staatsdruckerei 1898), pp. 180–238.

33 Josef Szujski, *Die Polen und Ruthenen in Galizien* (Vienna and Těšín: Vlg. Karl Prochaska 1882); Bolesław Limanowski, *Galicya przedstawiona słowem i ołówkiem* (Warsaw: Wyd. Przeglądu Tygodniowego 1892); Karol Maleczyński, Tadeusz Mańkowski, Feliks Pohorecki, and Marian Tyrowicz, *Lwów i Ziemia Czerwieńska* (L'viv: Pánstwowe Wyd. Książek Szkolnych 1938).

34 Stanisław Tarnowski, *O Rusi i Rusinach* (Cracow: Księgarnia Spółki Wydawniczej Polskiej 1891); Stanislas Smolka, *Les ruthènes et les problèmes religieux du monde russien* (Bern: Ferdinand Wyss 1917).

35 Leon Wasilewski, *Ukraina i sprawa ukraińska* (Cracow: Książka 1911); idem, *Die Ostprovinzen des alten Polenreichs (Lithauen u. Weissruthenien die Landschaft Chełm–Ost-Galizien–Die Ukraina)* (Cracow: Polnisches Oberstes Nationalkomitee 1916); idem, *Ukraińska sprawa narodowa w jej rozwoju historycznym* (Warsaw and Cracow: J. Mortkowicz 1925); idem, *Kwestja ukraińska jako zagadnienie międzynarodowe*, Pratsi Ukraïns'koho Naukovoho Institutu, vol. 28 (Warsaw 1934).

eastern Galician history that best represent the Old Ruthenian view are provided by Hryhorii Kupchanko and Fedir Ripets'kyi.[36]

The Russian position is represented by writers from the former Russian Empire as well as by Russophile Galicians who identified nationally and culturally with Russia. Basically they consider that eastern Galicia is a ''Russian'' land, and that its unity with Kievan ''Russia'' in the medieval period had only been interrupted temporarily by Polish and Austrian occupation until its eventual ''reunification'' with ''mother Russia'' would take place.

These views were put forth already in 1860 in a French essay by Prince Aleksander Trubetskoi, and later in historical surveys by the Galician Russophiles Osyp Monchalovs'kyi, Dmytro Markov, Dmitrii Vergun, and Adriian Kopystians'kyi.[37] The first years of the twentieth century brought increased tension between the Russian and Austro-Hungarian empires, and Russian publicists produced a spate of general histories and descriptions about ''Russian'' Galicia as background information for the Russian public (and in some cases for the military itself), especially after the tsarist army's occupation of the area in late 1914 and early 1915.[38]

36 Gregor Kupczanko, *Die Schicksale der Ruthenen* (Leipzig: Wilhelm Friedrich 1887). The forgoing is less favorable to Austrian rule than Hryhorii Kupchanko, *Nasha rodyna: ylliustrovannyi sbornyk dlia prostonarodnoho chytan'ia* (Vienna: p.a. 1897; reprinted New York and Berlin: Minkus 1924); F.I.R. [Fedir I. Ripets'kyi], *Yliustrovannaia narodnaia ystoriia Rusy ôt nachala do nainovîishykh vremen,* 2nd rev. ed. (L'viv: S.A. Duda 1905).

37 Prince Alexandre Troubetzkoy, *La Russie rouge* (Paris: E. Dentu 1860); O.A. Monchalovskii, *Sviataia Rus'* (L'viv: p.a. 1903); Dmitrij Markow, *Die russische und ukrainische Idee in Oesterreich* (Vienna and Leipzig: C.W. Stern 1908), 2nd rev. ed. (Vienna and Leipzig: Rosner und Stern 1912), revised and translated into Russian as *Russkaia i ukrainskaia ideia v Avstrii,* Biblioteka karpato-russkikh pisatelei (Moscow: F.F. Aristov 1915); Dmitrii Vergun, *Chto takoe Galitsiia?* 2nd rev. ed. (Petrograd: Lukomor'e 1915); A.V. Kopystianskii, *Iz proshlogo Galitskoi Rusi* (L'viv 1905); idem, *Istoriia Rusi,* 3 vols (L'viv 1931–33).

38 [Adriian Kopystians'kyi?], *Galitskaia Rus' prezhde i nyne: istoricheskii ocherk i vzgliad na sovremennoe sostoianie ochevidtsa* (St Petersburg 1907); M.V. Rapoport, *Chervonaia Rus' (Galitsiia): istoricheskii ocherk* (St Petersburg 1912); L. Burchak, *Galitsiia: eia proshloe i nastoiashchee* (Moscow: Chitatel', 1914)–this work is an exception among others in this note because it argues that eastern Galicia is a Ukrainian land; E. Turaeva-Tserteli, ''Galitskaia Rus' ot drevnosti do nashikh dnei: istoricheskii ocherk,'' in *Ékskursionyi viestnik,* book 4 (St Petersburg 1914), pp. 44–85; Anton Iarinovich, *Galichina v eia proshlom i nastoiashchem: ocherk istorii natsional'noi zhizni rusin v Avstro-Vengrii* (Moscow: Zadruga 1915); I. Murinov, *Istoriia Galitsii* (Moscow 1915), 2nd rev. ed. under the title *Galichina: istoricheskii ocherk* (Moscow 1915); E.F. Turaeva-Tserteli and E.I. de Vitte, *Galitskaia Rus' v ee proshlem i nastoiashchem* (Moscow 1915); A. Morskoi [V.I. Shtein], *Sud'by Galichiny* (Petrograd 1918).

There are also several works from the period dealing with all Austria-Hungary's ''Russians'' (in eastern Galicia, northern Bukovina, and Hungarian Subcarpathia) and including much information on Galicia: T.D. Florinskii, *Zarubezhnaia Rus' i eia gor'kaia dolia* (Kiev 1900);

The Ukrainian position is represented almost exclusively by natives of the province who consider eastern Galicia to be an integral part of a Ukrainian culture that is distinct from both Russian and Polish cultures. Like the Russian interpretation, Ukrainian writers stress the importance of the medieval Galician-Volhynian state, but they do not reject categorically the historical interdependence of the region with Poland and are generally favorably inclined toward the era of Austrian rule (1772–1918). Although Ukrainian scholars achieved much in the way of detailed historical research on certain aspects of Galicia, they did not produce any large-scale syntheses of Galician history. This is perhaps because they generally viewed the region as but part of a larger Ukrainian whole.

In fact, the only extensive histories of Ukrainian Galicia are the popular history of the Ukraine by Oleksander Barvins'kyi, which was written for a Galician audience and hence dwells largely on "local" developments, and the more recent, popular, and overly patriotic book by Michael Yaremko.[39] Galicia's greatest scholars limited their general histories of the region to brief encyclopedic articles. Among the best of these are a Russian-language encyclopedia on Galicia, Bukovina, and Subcarpathian Rus' prepared by the editors of *Ukrainskaia zhizn'* and an article in the first Soviet encyclopedia by Mykhailo Hrushevs'kyi, a native of the Dnieper Ukraine who was the first holder of the chair in Ukrainian history established in 1892 at the University of L'viv.[40] Both of these historical surveys end in 1914. Bohdan Barvins'kyi wrote a brief general history that ends with the German "liberation" in 1941,[41] while several other Galician scholars and nation-

---

I.I. Gumetskii, *Znachenie russkago Prikarpat'ia dlia Rossii* (St Petersburg 1914); P.E. Kazanskii, *Prisoedinenie Galichiny, Bukoviny i ugorskoi Rusi* (Odessa 1914); S. Troitskii, *Kak zhivut i stradaiut pravoslavnye uniaty v Avstro-Vengrii* (St Petersburg 1914); G.A. Voskresenskii, *Pravoslavnye slaviane v Avstro-Vengrii* (St Petersburg 1914); V.P. Ponomarev, *Avstro-Vengriia i eia slavianskie narody* (Baku 1915); Ia. Spanovskii, *Russkii narod v Karpatakh* (Kiev 1915); A.F. Vasil'ev, *Zarubezhnaia Rus'* (Petrograd 1915); L.V. Pokos, *Slavianskie narody Avstro-Vengrii: kratkii ocherk ikh proshlogo byta i sovremennogo polozhenia* (Kiev 1913), especially pp. 44–86; Aleksander L. Pogodin, *Slavianskii mir: politicheskoe i ékonomicheskoe polozhenie slavianskikh narodov pered voinoi 1914 goda* (Moscow, 1915), especially pp. 141–197.

For the numerous other Russian works generated during this period, see the bibliography by Nina Pashaeva, chapter 1, n. 49, especially entries 616–654.

39 Oleksander Barvîn'skii, *Yliustrovana ystoriia Rusy vôd naidavnîishykh do nŷnîshnykh châsov pôslia ruskykh y chuzhykh ystorykôv* (L'viv: NTSh 1890); Michael Yaremko, *Galicia-Halychyna (A Part of Ukraine): From Separation to Unity,* Ukrainian Studies, vol. XVIII: English section, vol. III (Toronto, New York, and Paris: NTSh 1967).

40 *Galichina, Bukovina, Ugorskaia Rus'* (Moscow: Zadruga 1915); M. Grushevskii, "Galitsiia: istoricheskii ocherk," *Bol'shaia sovetskaia éntsiklopediia,* vol. XIV (Moscow 1929), pp. 368–380.

41 Bohdan Barvins'kyi, *Korotka istoriia Halychyny* (L'viv: Ukraïns'ke vyd-vo 1941).

al activists–Ivan Kryp''iakevych, Kost' Levyts'kyi, Ivan Kedryn-Rudnyts'kyi, Mykola Chubatyi, Illia Vytanovych, Stepan Baran, Stepan Vytvyts'kyi, Oleksa Horbach, and Volodymyr Kubiiovych–have contributed to encyclopedic surveys that bring the story closer to more recent times.[42]

The outbreak of World War I also prompted several general historical essays by Ukrainian authors on the problem of Galicia that were intended primarily for Austrian readers.[43] Later, the post-war Peace Conference prompted Mykhailo Lozyns'kyi to write memoranda containing general histories of Galicia that praised the region's rich past and suggested the need for an independent future.[44]

Soviet Marxist writers have set out to revise all previous historiography about Galicia. They accept the view that the region has been from earliest times part of the eastern Slavic world and that it should be treated within that general context. Their view of historical development is determined, however, by the theory of class conflict, so that descriptions of the past dwell largely on that theme. With regard to the particularities of Galicia, the Soviet Marxists see the medieval Galician-Volhynian principality as an eastern Slavic Rus' land under the hegemony of Kiev, which was forcibly occupied by Poland and then Austria; only during the twentieth century were its desires for ''reunification'' with the Soviet homeland (ostensibly the modern version of the medieval eastern Slav entity) realized briefly in 1920, then again in 1939–41, and finally in 1944–45.

The first elaboration of these views was put forth in 1940, just after the Red Army's occupation of eastern Galicia, in historical surveys by Volodymyr Picheta, Serhii Bielousov, and Oleksander Ohloblyn.[45] More recently, a lengthy synthesis on all the western Ukrainian lands has outlined in great detail the present acceptable Soviet Marxist interpretations and periodization for Galician history:

42 *Ukraïns'ka zahal'na entsyklopediia,* 3 vols (L'viv, Stanyslaviv, and Kolomyia: Ridna Shkola 1930–35), especially vol. III (1935), pp. 641–668 and 823–831; Volodymyr Kubijovyč, ed., *Ukraine: A Concise Encyclopedia,* vol. I (Toronto: University of Toronto Press for the Ukrainian National Association 1963), pp. 604–612, 698–707, 714–724, 770–787, 833–850, 871–876, 886–890.

43 S. Tomashivs'kyi, *Halychyna: politychno-istorychnyi narys z pryvodu svitovoï viiny,* 2nd ed. (n.p. 1915), German edition: Stephan Tomaschiwskyj, *Die weltpolitische Bedeutung Galiziens* (Munich: F. Bruckmann 1915).

44 Michael Lozynsky, *L'Ukraine occidentale (Galicie): l'invasion polonaise en Ukraine occidentale est un crime contre le Droit* (Paris 1919); Michael Lozynsky, *Les 'droits' de la Pologne sur la Galicie: exposé des faits historiques sur lesquels les Polonais basent leurs prétentions sur la Galicie* (Lausanne 1917). See also Eugène Levitsky, *La guerre polono-ukrainienne en Galicie et l'avenir de la République ukrainienne de l'Oeust* (Berne 1919).

45 Vladimir Picheta, *Osnovnye momenty istoricheskogo razvitiia Zapadnoi Ukrainy i zapadnoi Belorussii* (Moscow: Gosudarstvennoe sotsial'no-ékonomicheskoe izd. 1940); S.M. Bielousov and O.P. Ohloblin, eds, *Zakhidna Ukraïna: zbirnyk* (Kiev: AN URSR 1940).

the pre-Kievan era; the feudal era (11th century to 1848); the capitalist and imperialist period (1848–1917); the Great October Bolshevik Revolution and its subsequent influence on Galician desires for reunification with the Ukrainian SSR (1917–1939); the reunification (1939–1941); the great patriotic war (1941–1945); and the Soviet era (1945–present).[46]

Church history

Religious history in Galicia has received much attention through published documentary collections and general histories. The Basilian Order in Rome has sponsored the publication of a large number of documents from the archives of the Vatican and the Propaganda Fidei (Missionary Congregation). Although dealing with all Ukrainian (and sometimes Belorussian) religious problems, each volume is carefully indexed and contains numerous documents dealing solely with Galicia. There exist to date one general series[47] and eight other specialized series, each multivolumed and some still in the process of completion. The specialized series, all edited by Athanasius Welykyj, contain papal decrees and letters dealing with Ukrainian matters (1075–1953);[48] papal dispensations and privileges (1650–1862);[49] minutes of the Missionary Congregation (1622–1862);[50] letters and decrees of the Missionary Congregation to Ukrainian bishops (1622–1862);[51] minutes of special meetings of the Missionary Congregation (1622–1862);[52] episcopal letters sent to Rome (1600–);[53] diplomatic dispatches of papal emissaries (1550–);[54] and letters of papal nuncios and Ukrainian bishops to the Vatican

46 M.M. Oleksiuk, et al., *Torzhestvo istorychnoï spravedlyvosti* (L'viv: LU 1968).

47 Andrei Sheptyts'kyi, comp., *Monumenta Ucrainae Historica*, 14 vols (Rome: Vydannia Ukraïns'koho Katolyts'koho Universytetu 1964–77).

48 Athanasius Welykyj, ed., *Documenta Pontificum Romanorum Historiam Ucrainae Illustrantia (1075–1953)*, 2 vols, Analecta OSBM, series II, sectio III (Rome 1953–54).

49 Athanasius Welykyj, ed., *Audientiae Sanctissimi de Rebus Ucrainae et Bielarusjae (1650–1850)*, 2 vols, Analecta OSBM, series II, sectio III (Rome 1963–65).

50 Athanasius Welykyj, ed., *Acta S.C. de Propaganda Fide Ecclesiam Catholicam Ucrainae et Bielarusjae spectantia*, 5 vols, Analecta OSBM, series II, sectio III (Rome 1953–55).

51 Athanasius G. Welykyj, ed., *Litterae S.C. de Propaganda Fide Ecclesiam Catholicam Ucrainae et Bielarusjae spectantes*, 7 vols, Analecta OSBM, series II, sectio III (Rome 1954–57).

52 Athanasius G. Welykyj, ed., *Congregationes Particulares Ecclesiam Catholicam Ucrainae et Bielarusjae spectantes*, 2 vols, Analecta OSBM, series II, sectio III (Rome 1956–57).

53 Athanasius G. Welykyj, ed., *Litterae Episcoporum Historiam Ucrainae Illustrantes (1600–1900)*, 4 vols, Analecta OSBM, series II, sectio III (Rome 1972–76).

54 Athanasius G. Welykyj, ed., *Litterae Nuntiorum Apostolicorum Historiam Ucrainae Illustrantes (1550–1850)*, 14 vols, Analecta OSBM, series II, sectio III (Rome 1959–77).

(1600–1769).[55] The Soviets have also compiled a collection of documents on the church from earliest times to the present, all of which are designed to reveal the "truth about the union," that is, the supposed negative historical role of the Greek Catholic church in Galicia.[56]

The earliest history of the Galician church arose at the beginning of the nineteenth century, when local Greek Catholic churchmen were anxious to provide a historical basis for their demands that the Galician metropolitanate be restored. Among these clerical historians was Mykhailo Harasevych, who produced a heavily documented chronological survey of Ruthenian (i.e. Galician and other Rus' lands in the Polish-Lithuanian Commonwealth) church history.[57] The first scholarly synthesis of Ukrainian church history came in the late 1870s with the appearance of Iuliian Pelesh's two-volume history. Although Pelesh dealt with Ukrainian church history as a whole, he was particularly interested in the efforts toward church union that led to the creation of the Greek Catholic church and in particular its development in Galicia.[58] The evolution of the church in Galicia has also been treated in some detail in more recent general histories of the Greek Catholic church, whether in negative accounts by Soviet authors or in the more sympathetic survey by the German scholar Johannes Maday.[59] Histories focusing specifically on Galicia have been written by Antin Dobrians'kyi, Ivan Rudovych, and Petro Isaïv from the Greek Catholic perspective and by Ievhen Vorobkevych from the Orthodox side.[60] There are also studies on the centuries-long efforts to revive the Galician metropolitanate.[61]

55 Athanasius G. Welykyj, ed., *Supplicationes Ecclesiae Unitae Ucrainae et Bielarusjae*, 3 vols, Analecta OSBM, series II, sectio III (Rome 1960–65).

56 *Pravda pro uniiu: dokumenty i materialy*, 2nd rev. ed. (L'viv: Kameniar 1968).

57 Michael Harasiewicz, *Annales ecclesiae ruthenae* (L'viv: [M. Malynovs'kyi] 1862).

58 Julian Pelesz, *Geschichte der Union der ruthenischen Kirche mit Rom von den aeltesten Zeiten bis auf die Gegenwart*, 2 vols (Vienna: Vlg. der Mechitharisten 1878–80).

59 Vladimir Dobrychev, *V teni sviatogo Iura* (Moscow: Izd. politicheskoi literatury 1971); Sergii T. Danilenko, *Uniaty* (Moscow: Izd. politicheskoi literatury 1972); Johannes Madey, *Kirche zwischen Ost und West: Beiträge zur Geschichte der Ukrainischen und Weissruthenischen Kirche*, Ukrainische Freie Universität, Monographien, vol. XV (Munich 1969).

60 Antonii Dobrianskii, *Istoriia episkopov trekh soedinennykh eparkhii, Peremyshl'skoi, Samborskoi i Sanotskoi, ot naidavnieishikh vremen do 1794 g.* (L'viv: Ivan A. Dobrianskii 1894), Ivan Rudovych, *Ystoriia halytsko-l'vovs'koi ieparkhii* (Zhovkva 1902); Petro Isaïv, *Istoriia peremys'koho iepyskopstva skhidn'oho obriadu* (Philadelphia, Pa.: Vyd-vo 'Ameryka' 1970); Emmanuel-Eugen Worobkiewicz, *Die orthodox-orientalische Kirche in Lemberg und ihre Gemeinde in Lemberg und ganz Galizien* (L'viv 1896).

61 Isidorus I. Patrylo, *Archiepiscopi-Metropolitani Kievo-Haliciensis*, 2nd ed., Analecta OSBM, series II, sectio I, vol. XVI (Rome 1962); I. Nazarko, "Halyts'ka mytropoliia," *Analecta OSBM*, series II, sectio II, vol. III, 1–2 (Rome 1958), pp. 173–189.

Cultural history

With regard to cultural history, the only general surveys devoted exclusively to Ukrainian Galicia are short encyclopedic essays by Omelian Terlets'kyi and Omelian Ohonovs'kyi, both of which dwell primarily on developments since the early nineteenth century.[62] Culture in Galicia is usually seen within the context of Ukrainian developments in general, and as such, western Ukrainian lands, including Galicia, are often given less attention than events in the Dnieper, or eastern Ukraine. Ukrainian literary histories written by Galician authors, however, do dwell extensively on local developments, as in the multivolume work by Omelian Ohonovs'kyi and the shorter more interpretive study by Ivan Franko.[63] Soviet Marxist scholarship has also dealt with Galician cultural history in the larger Ukrainian context, although the eight-volume Soviet history of Ukrainian literature includes several sections devoted exclusively to Galician-Ukrainian writers and movements, especially between the 1830s and 1945.[64] The history of printing in Galicia has also been the subject of attention, from the 1838 history of Galician printing houses by Denys Zubryts'kyi to later surveys and studies on individual printing houses by Ivan Ohiienko, Ilarion Svientsits'kyi, and several Soviet writers.[65]

Literature dealing with the history of cultural and educational institutions in Galicia is much better developed. The oldest of these was the Stauropegial Brotherhood, later Stauropegial Institute, founded in L'viv in the late sixteenth century. There exist several collections of documents dealing with its earliest years,[66] as well as a popular history by Bohdan Didyts'kyi, a scholarly monograph by A. Krylovskii, and two collections of essays on various aspects of the institute's activity.[67] L'viv was also the home of the Ossoliński National Institute,

62 Omelian Terlets'kyi, "Osvita i kul'tura XIX–XX vv.: Halychyna," *Ukraïns'ka zahal'na entsyklopediia*, vol. III (L'viv, Stanyslaviv, and Kolomyia 1935), pp. 823–831; Emil Ohonowskij, "Ruthenische Literatur," in *Die österreichisch-ungarische Monarchie in Wort und Bild* [vol. XII]: *Galizien* (Vienna: K.K. Hof- und Staatsdruckerei 1898), pp. 649–664.

63 Omelian Ohonovskii, *Ystoriia lyteraturŷ ruskoy*, 4 vols in 6 (L'viv: NTSh, 1887–94), first published serially in *Zoria*, VIII–XV (L'viv 1887–94); Ivan Franko, *Narys istoriï ukraïns'ko-rus'koï lïteratury*, Pysania Ivana Franka, I (L'viv: Ukraïns'ko-rus'ka vydavnycha spilka 1910). See also the extensive critique of Ohonovs'kyi's work by Aleksander Pypin, "Osobaia istoriia russkoi literatury," *Viestnik Evropy*, no. 9 (St Petersburg 1890), pp. 241–274. 241–274.

64 *Istoriia ukraïns'koï literatury*, 8 vols (Kiev: Naukova dumka 1967–71), especially volumes II–VII.

65 See chapter 4, notes 76–80.

66 See chapter 4, n. 66.

67 Bohdan A. Dîdyts'kyi, *L'vovskaia Stavropyhiia y 300-lîtnii prazdnyk ey sushchestvovan'ia*,

or Ossolineum as it was best known, which was the main center of Polish cultural life in the province from its establishment in 1817 until its transfer westward to Wrocław in 1945. There is a collection of documents concerning the Ossolineum,[68] a bibliography of works on the activity of the institution before 1939,[69] and general introductory histories by Adam Fischer and Jan Trzynadłowski.[70]

The second half of the nineteenth century witnessed the establishment of several cultural organizations representing the Ukrainian population in Galicia. The first of these were the Galician Rus' Matytsia (est. 1848) and the National Home (est. 1864), each of which have descriptions of their founding and subsequent activity.[71] Among the most influential of organizations was the Shevchenko Scientific Society (est. 1873), whose wide range of scholarly activity made it an unofficial Ukrainian Academy of Sciences. Despite its importance, there are not yet any scholarly histories of the Shevchenko Scientific Society, only several surveys, the most comprehensive of which are by Volodymyr Doroshenko.[72]

Yzdaniia Ob-va ym. M. Kachkovskoho, no. 121–122 (L'viv 1885); A. Krylovskii, *L'vovskoe Stavropigiiskoe Bratstvo: opyt tserkovno-istoricheskago izsliedovaniia* (Kiev 1904); Isidor Sharanevich, ed., *Iubileinoe izdanie v pamiat' 300-lietniago osnovaniia l'vovskogo Stavropigiiskogo Bratstva*, vol. I (L'viv 1886); Kyrylo Studyns'kyi, ed., *Zbirnyk l'vivs'koï Stavropyhiï: mynule i suchasne*, vol. I (L'viv 1921); S.Iu. Bendasiuk, "Stavropigiiskii muzei v nastoiashchee vremia," *Vremennik ... lvovskago Stavropigiona na 1933 god*, LXIX (L'viv 1932). On the early history of the Stauropegial Brotherhood, see chapter 4, notes 70–72.

68 W. Bruchnalski, ed., *Zakładu Narodowego im. Ossolińskich: ustawy, przywileje i rzeczy dziejów jego dotyczące* (L'viv: ZNIO 1928).

69 M. Górkiewicz, "Bibliografia dotycząca Zakładu Narodowego im. Ossolińskich do r. 1939," *Rocznik ZNIO*, IV (Wrocław 1953), pp. 293–327.

70 Adam Fischer, *Zakład Narodowy imienia Ossolińskich: zarys dziejów* (L'viv: ZNIO 1927); Jan Trzynadłowski, *Zakład Narodowy imienia Ossolińskich 1817–1967: zarys dziejów* (Wrocław, Warsaw, and Cracow: ZNIO 1967), translated into French as *Institut National Ossoliński 1817–1967: précis d'histoire* (Wrocław, Warsaw, and Cracow: Institut National Ossoliński 1967).

71 S.Iu. Bendasiuk, "Ucheno-literaturnoe obshchestvo Galitsko-russkaia Matitsa vo L'vove (proshloe i nastoiashchee)," *Nauchno-literaturnyi sbornik Galitsko-russkoi Matitsy*, VII [LXV] (L'viv 1930), pp. 85–109; N.M. Pashaeva and L.N. Klimkova, "Galitsko-russkaia Matitsa vo L'vove i ee izdatel'skaia deiatel'nost'," *Kniga*, XXXIV (Moscow 1977), pp. 61–77; Oleksander Barvins'kyi, *Istorychnyi ohliad zasnovyn Narodnoho Domu u L'vovi* (L'viv 1908). For a contemporary but still-useful description of these and other organizations, see O.P. Drahomanova-Kosach and M.P. Drahomanov, "Russkie literaturnye obshchestva v Galitsii" (1875), in Mykhailo Petrovych Drahomanov, *Literaturno-publitsystychni pratsi*, vol. I (Kiev: Naukova dumka 1970), pp. 221–246. On the establishment and early history of the Galician Rus' Matitsa, see chapter 6, n. 40.

72 Volodymyr Doroshenko, *Ohnyshche ukraïns'koï nauky: Naukove tovarystvo imeny T. Shevchenka* (New York and Philadelphia 1951); and his shorter *Naukove tovarystvo imeny Shevchenka u L'vovi (1873–1892–1912 rr.)* (Kiev and L'viv: NTSh 1913).

Even more important at the popular level were the Prosvita Society (est. 1868) and the Kachkovs'kyi Society (est. 1874), both of which worked directly with the peasantry to disseminate literacy and culture as well as to assist in economic and social matters. Literature on the Kachkovskii Society is limited to one general article.[73] Although there are no scholarly histories of the Prosvita Society, there are several popular histories; the most important are by Mykhailo Lozyns'kyi and Volodymyr Doroshenko.[74] Ilarion Svientsits'kyi has provided a history of one of the last organizations to be founded and of which he was director–the Ukrainian National Museum (est. 1906).[75]

While there are excellent studies on certain periods,[76] a general history of education in Ukrainian Galicia remains to be written. The Polish scholar Mieczysław Baranowski surveyed briefly the development of elementary education for

---

See also the briefer general histories by Volodymyr Hnatiuk, *Naukove Tovarystvo imeny Shevchenka z nahody 50-littia ioho zasnovannia (1873–1923)* (L'viv: NTSh 1923); *Istoriia Naukovoho tovarystva im. Shevchenka* (New York and Munich: NTSh 1949); Vasyl' Lev, *Sto rokiv pratsi dlia nauky i natsiï: korotka istoriia Naukovoho Tovarystva im. Shevchenka* (New York: NTSh 1972); Stephen M. Horak, "The Shevchenko Scientific Society (1873–1973): Contributor to the Birth of a Nation," *East European Quarterly*, VII, 3 (Boulder, Colo. 1973), pp. 249–264; and studies on certain periods by Kyrylo Studyns'kyi, "Naukove Tovarystvo im. Shevchenka u L'vovi (1873–1928 rr.)," *Zapysky NTSh*, CL (L'viv 1929), pp. ix–xviii; Vasyl' Veryha, "Naukove tovarystvo im. Shevchenka v dobi Hrushevs'koho," in *Iuvileinyi zbirnyk naukovykh prats' z nahody 100-richchia NTSh i 25-richchia NTSh u Kanadi*, Kanads'ke NTSh, vol. XIX (Toronto 1977), pp. 15–30; Aleksander S. Grushevskii, "Naukove tovaristvo imena T. Shevchenka i ego izdaniia 1905–1909 gg.," *Izviestiia Otdieleniia russkago iazyka i slovesnosti Imp. Akademii Nauk*, XVI, 3 (St Petersburg 1911), pp. 66–132; and Omelian Pritsak, "Naukove Tovarystvo im. Shevchenka u L'vovi pomizh dvoma viinamy," *Ukraïns'kyi istoryk*, XVIII. 1–4 (New York, Toronto, and Munich, 1981), pp. 147–152.

73 J. Hejret, "Spolek Michaila Kačkovského," *Česká osvěta*, 10 (1909?).

74 Mykhailo Lozyns'kyi, *Sorok lït dïial'nosty 'Pros'vity'* (L'viv: TP 1908); Volodymyr Doroshenko, *'Prosvita' ïï zasnuvannia i pratsia* (Philadelphia: 'Moloda Prosvita' im. Sheptyts'koho 1959).

See also the popular histories by Yvan Belei, *Dvatsiat' y piat' lït ystoriy Tovarystva 'Prosvïty'* (L'viv 1894); Vasyl' Mudryi, *Rolia 'Prosvity' v ukraïns'komu zhytti*, Vyd. Tovarystva 'Prosvita', no. 742 (L'viv 1928); Andrii Kachor, *Rolia 'Prosvity' v ekonomichnomu rozvytku Zakhidnoï Ukraïny*, Litopys UVAN, no. 18 (Winnipeg, 1960); Stepan Pers'kyi [Stepan Shakh], *Populiarna istoriia tovarystva 'Prosvita' u L'vovi*, Vyd. TP, no. 780 (L'viv 1932), reprinted in *Narys istoriï matirnoho tovarystva Prosvity i ohliad prosvitnykh tovarystv u Kanadi* (Winnipeg: Ukraïns'ke tovarystvo chytal'ni "Prosvita" 1968), pp. 1–268. This last book also includes a supplement (pp. 269–288) covering the years 1932 to 1939 written by Stepan Volynets'.

75 Ilarion Svientsits'kyi, *Dvatsiat'piat'-littia Natsional'noho Muzeiu u L'vovi* (L'viv: Dilo 1931).

76 See chapter 5, notes 34–36; chapter 6, notes 110–118; chapter 7, notes 81–89; and chapter 8, n. 20.

the whole province of Galicia.[77] As for specifically Ukrainian educational developments, there are only general encyclopedic articles covering the period since 1772,[78] as well as studies on certain periods in the history of Ukrainian elementary schools,[79] on church-sponsored seminaries and other educational centers,[80] and on specific schools.[81]

The most important educational institution in Galicia was the University of L'viv, which in the second half of the nineteenth century established several chairs for Ukrainian studies. A monumental two-volume history of the university was written by Ludwik Finkel and Stanisław Starzyński; it contains valuable data on Ukrainian as well as Polish faculty members.[82] The Soviets have more recently published a history that stresses the Ukrainian aspect of the institution and in particular its development since 1945.[83]

Regional and urban history

Interest in regional and urban history has produced a rich literature for various parts of eastern Galicia.[84] Beginning already in the nineteenth century, Polish writers prepared histories and encyclopedic-type guides for the regions (*powiat,*

77 Mieczysław Baranowski, *Pogląd na rozwój szkolnictwa ludowego w Galicyi od 1772 do 1895* (Cracow: Redakcya Sprawozdania Powszechnej Wystawy Kraj. we Lwowie 1897).

78 Ivan Herasymovych and Vasyl' Mudryi, ''Ukraïna: Shkil'nytstvo-Halychyna,'' *Ukraïns'ka zahal'na entsyklopediia,* vol. III (L'viv, Stanyslaviv, and Kolomyia 1935), pp. 860–874, 879–882; I. Herasymovych, O. Terletsky, V. Kubijovyč, and M. Terletsky, ''Education in Galicia'' and ''Ukrainian Lands Under Poland,'' in *Ukraine: A Concise Encyclopedia,* vol. II, ed. Volodymyr Kubijovyč (Toronto: University of Toronto Press for the Ukrainian National Association 1971), pp. 327–337 and 371–381.

79 Antin Pavents'kyi, *Pochatok i rozvii shkil'nytstva na Rusy* (L'viv 1900); Lev Iasinchuk, *50 lit Ridnoï Shkoly 1881–1931* (L'viv: Tovarystvo Ridna shkola 1931?); Ivan Fylypchak, *Z istoriï shkil'nytstva na zakhidnii Boikivshchyni (vid 1772–1930)* (Sambir 1931).

80 See the sections on Greek Catholic educational institutions described in Hermann Zschokke, *Die theologischen Studien und Anstalten der katholischen Kirche in Österreich* (Vienna and Leipzig: Wilhelm Braumüller 1894), especially pp. 546–558 and 977–1048.

81 Most of the Ukrainian *gymnasia* issued annual yearbook/reports known as *zvity,* and some contained general histories of the given institution. See also chapter 6, n. 109.

82 Ludwik Finkel and Stanisław Starzyński, *Historya Uniwersytetu Lwowskiego* (L'viv: Senat Akademickiego C.K. Uniwersytetu Lwowskiego 1894).

83 Ie.K. Lazarenko, *300 rokiv L'vivs'koho universytetu* (L'viv: LU 1961).

84 Fedir Maksymenko has compiled a comprehensive bibliography of works on individual regions, cities, and towns in eastern Galicia. See chapter 1, n. 57.

województwo) of Kaminka Strumylova,[85] Krosno,[86] L'viv,[87] Sanok,[88] Sniatyn,[89] Sokal',[90] Stanyslaviv,[91] Ternopil',[92] Terebovlia,[93] and Turka.[94] The Carpathian area along the southern border of Galicia has also been the focus of much scholarly attention, although mainly for its linguistic and ethnographic aspects. The Hutsul region is described in the now classic multivolume ethnographic study by Volodymyr Shukhevych and in a history of the region still being published in the West.[95] Past research on the Boikian region is outlined in a monograph by the Soviet scholar Roman Kyrchiv, while two encyclopedic works on all aspects of

85 Bronisław Faliński, *Powiat Kamionka Strumiłłowa* (Kaminka Strumylova: Koło T-wa Rozwoju Ziem Wschodnich 1935).

86 *Monografia powiatu Krośnieńskiego* (Przemyśl 1938); *Illustrowana monografia powiatu krośnieńskiego* (Krosno: Polskie Towarzystwo Turystyczno-krajoznawcze 1957).

87 Fr. Jaworski, *Przewodnik po Lwowie i okolicy z Żółkwią i Podhorcami* (L'viv: B. Połoniecki [1907]); Marceli Prószyński, *Powiat lwowski* (L'viv: Towarzystwo Szkoły Ludowej 1911); J. Piotrowski, *Lemberg und Umgebung (Żółkiew, Podhorce, Brzeżany u.a.): Handbuch für die Kunstliebhaber und Reisende* (L'viv 1916).

88 A. Bożemski, *Powiat Sanocki w cyfrach: studium statystyczne* (Sanok 1904). See also the yearbook, *Rocznik Sanocki* (Cracow 1963–present), irregular.

89 Ksawery Mroczko, "Śniatyńszczyzna (przyczynek do etnografii krajowej)," *Przewodnik Naukowy i Literacki*, XXV (L'viv 1897), pp. 193–207, 290–304, 385–402, 481–498, 577–595.

90 Bronisław Sokalski, *Powiat Sokalski pod względem geograficznym, etnograficznym, historycznym i ekonomicznym* (L'viv: Wł. Dzieduszycki 1899).

91 A. Szarłowski, *Stanisławów i powiat Stanisławowski pod względem historycznym i geograficzno-statystycznym* (Stanyslaviv: Wł. Dobuszyński 1887); *Przewodnik ilustrowany po województwie Stanisławowskiem*, ed. R. Dąbrowski (Stanyslaviv 1930).

92 Władysław Satke, *Powiat Tarnopolski pod względem geograficzno-statystycznym* (Ternopil' 1895); Aleksander Czołowski and Bohdan Janusz, *Przeszłość i zabytki województwa Tarnopolskiego* (Ternopil': Powiatowa Organizacija Narodowa 1926); *Województwo Tarnopolskie: monografia zbiorowa* (Ternopil': Komitet Wojewódzkiej Wystawy Rolniczej i Regionalnej 1931); T. Kunzek, *Przewodnik po województwie Tarnopolskim: Monografja krajoznawcza* (Ternopil': Podolskie T-wo Krajoznawcze [1936]).

93 J. A. Bayger, *Powiat Trembowelski: szkic geograficzno-historyczny i etnograficzny* (L'viv 1899).

94 Wł. Pulnarowicz, *U zródeł Sanu, Stryja i Dniestru: historja powiatu Turczańskiego* (Turka 1929).

95 Volodymyr Shukhevych, *Hutsul'shchyna*, 5 vols, Materiialy do ukraïns'koï etnolohiï, vols I–V (L'viv: Etnohrafichna komisiia NTSh 1899–1908), in Polish translation as Włodzimierz Szuchiewicz, *Huculszczyzna*, 4 vols (Cracow: Muzeum im. Dzieduszyckich we Lwowie 1902–08); Mykola Domashevs'kyi, ed., *Istoriia Hutsul'shchyny*, vol. I (Chicago: Hutsul's'kyi doslidnyi instytut 1975). See also Jan Falkowski, *Zachodnie pogranicze Huculszczyzny*, Prace Etnograficzne Towarzystwa Ludoznawczego, vol. III (L'viv 1937); idem, *Północno-wschodnie pogranicze Huculszczyzny*, Prace Etnograficzne Towarzystwa Ludoznawczego, vol. IV (L'viv 1938).

that area have been recently published.[96] The westernmost extension of Ukrainian territory–the Lemkian region–has been accorded the most attention, however, and there are histories representing the Ukrainian, Polish, and local Russophile orientations.[97] There is also a history of the San region and a solid historico-demographic study of the whole Galician Carpathian region by Stepan Kopchak.[98]

Ukrainian emigré scholars from Galicia living in the West have in the past two decades published a series of multiauthorized memorial books devoted to their native regions. Although these vary in quality, all of them nonetheless contain a vast quantity of factual information. Their formats are for the most part similar: histories of the region, followed by chapters on political, cultural, and economic organizations, schools, literature, music, sports, biographies of famous sons, and memoirs. Among the best in this genre are the volumes on the Stanyslaviv, Buchach, Terebovlia, Zbarazh, Berezhany, and Pidhaitsi regions.[99] Others have

96 R.F. Kyrchiv, *Etnohrafichne doslidzhennia Boikivshchyny* (Kiev: Naukova dumka 1978); Myron Utrysko, ed., *Boikivshchyna: monohrafichnyi zbirnyk materiialiv pro Boikivshchynu z heohrafiï, istoriï, etnohrafiï i pobutu*, NTSh, Ukraïns'kyi arkhiv, vol. XXIV (Philadelphia and New York 1980); Iurii H. Hoshko, ed., *Boikivshchyna: istoryko-etnohrafichne doslidzhennia* (Kiev: Naukova dumka 1983).

97 The best introduction to the Lemkian problem is Mykola Andrusjak, ''Der westukrainische Stamm der Lemken,'' *Südost-Forschungen*, VI, 3–4 (Leipzig, 1941), pp. 536–575.

The Ukrainian view is best represented in the popular history of Iuliian Tarnovych, *Iliustrovana istoriia Lemkivshchyny*, Biblioteka Lemkivshchyny, no. 1 (L'viv: Na storozhi 1936; reprinted New York: Kul'tura 1964) and in the historical memoirs of Stepan Shakh, *Mizh Sianom i Dunaitsem: spomyny* (Munich: 'Khrystyians'kyi holos' 1960).

The Polish view is in Krystyna Pieradzka, *Na szlakach Łemkowszczyzny* (Cracow: Nakładem Komitetu do Spraw Szlachty Zagrodowej na Wschodzie Polski 1939). See also the more scholarly ethnographic work of Jan Falkowski and Bazyli Pasznycki, *Na pograniczu łemkowsko-bojkowskiem: zarys etnograficzny*, Prace Etnograficzne Towarzystwa Ludoznawczego, vol. II (L'viv 1935).

The local Russophile view is in Y.F. Lemkyn, *Ystoryia Lemkovyny* (Yonkers, NY: Lemko Soiuz 1969).

See also chapter 9, notes 8–10.

98 Petro Oryshkevych, *Ukraïntsi Zasiannia: heohrafichno-istorychnyi narys* (Munich and Philadelphia: Ukraïns'kyi Vil'nyi Universytet 1962), reprinted from B. Zahaikevych, *Peremyshl': zakhidnyi bastion Ukraïny* (New York and Philadelphia: Peremys'kyi vydavnychyi komitet 1961), pp. 110–150; Stepan I. Kopchak, *Naselennia ukraïns'koho Prykarpattia: istoryko-demohrafichnyi narys* (L'viv: Vyshcha shkola 1974).

99 Bohdan Kravtsiv, ed., *Al'manakh stanyslavivs'koï zemli*, NTSh Ukraïns'kyi arkhiv, vol. XXVIII (New York, Toronto, and Munich 1975); *Buchach i Buchachchyna: istorychno-memuarnyi zbirnyk*, NTSh Ukraïns'kyi arkhiv, vol. XXVII (New York, London, Paris, Sidney, and Toronto 1972); Ivan Vynnyts'kyi et al., eds, *Terebovel's'ka zemlia: istorychno-memuarnyi zbirnyk*, NTSh Ukraïns'kyi arkhiv, vol. XX (New York, Paris, Sydney, and Toronto 1968); *Zbarazhchyna: zbirnyk spomyniv, stattei i materiialiv*, NTSh Ukraïns'kyi

also been completed for the Drohobych, Uhniv, Horodenka, and Chortkiv regions as well as for several individual villages.[100]

The Soviets have also produced regional encyclopedias as part of the twenty-six volume history of all the oblasts of the Ukrainian SSR. Three of these (L'viv, Ivano-Frankivs'k, and Ternopil') cover most of what was former eastern Galicia. These volumes are extremely useful for more recent data and all follow the same format: a history of the oblast as a whole followed by histories of each of the districts (*raiony*) with briefer histories and descriptions of the major towns and villages.[101] For those Ukrainian-inhabited areas of Galicia that are today part of Poland, there exists a smaller scale encyclopedic coverage for the region around Przemyśl.[102]

There also exist several studies devoted to the general history of individual cities in eastern Galicia. As might be expected, the most extensive research has been devoted to the cultural and administrative capital of the province–L'viv. In fact, some of the first historical writings emanating from Galicia were actually devoted to L'viv, as in the early nineteenth-century works by the Pole Ignacy

---

arkhiv, vol. XVII (Toronto: Zbarazh Society of the USA and Canada, n.d.); Volodymyr Zhyla and Iar Slavutych, eds, *Zbarazhchyna: zbirnyk stattei, materiialiv i spomyniv,* vol. I, NTSh Ukraïns'kyi arkhiv, vol. XXX (New York, Paris, Sydney, and Toronto 1980); *Berezhans'ka zemlia: istorychno-memuarnyi zbirnyk,* NTSh Ukraïns'kyi arkhiv, vol. XIX (New York: Berezhany Regional Committee 1970); Taras Hunchak, ed., *Pidhaiets'ka zemlia: istorychno-memuarnyi zbirnyk,* NTSh Ukraïns'kyi arkhiv, vol. XXIV (New York, Paris, Sydney, and Toronto 1980).

100 Luka Lutsiv, ed., *Drohobychchyna–zemlia Ivana Franka,* 2 vols. NTSh Ukraïns'kyi arkhiv, vols XXV and XXXII (New York, Paris, Sidney, and Toronto 1973–78); Vasyl' Lev, *Uhniv ta Uhnivshchyna: istorychno-memuarnyi zbirnyk,* NTSh Ukraïns'kyi arkhiv, vol. XVI (New York, Paris, Sydney, and Toronto 1960); Mykhailo H. Marunchak, *Horodenshchyna: istorychno-memuarnyi zbirnyk,* NTSh Ukraïns'kyi arkhiv, vol. XXXIII (New York, Toronto, and Winnipeg 1978); *Istorychno-memuarnyi zbirnyk chortkivs'koï okruhy: povity Chortkiv, Kopychyntsi, Borshchiv, Zalishchyky,* NTSh Ukraïns'kyi arkhiv, vol. XXVI (New York, Paris, Sydney, and Toronto 1974); Mykhailo Blokh, *Vynnyky, Zvenyhorod, Univ ta dovkil'ni sela: istorychno-memuarnyi zbirnyk* (Chicago: p.a. 1970); Ivan Martyniuk, *Moie ridne selo Tseniv u Berezhanshchyni,* NTSh Etnohrafichnyi zbirnyk, vol. XLI (New York, Paris, Sydney, and Toronto 1976).

101 V.Iu. Malanchuk et al., eds, *Istoriia mist i sil Ukraïns'koï RSR: L'vivs'ka oblast'* (Kiev: AN URSR 1968), O.O. Chernov et al., eds, *Istoriia mist i sil Ukraïns'koï RSR: Ivano-Frankivs'ka oblast'* (Kiev: AN URSR 1971); S.P. Nechai et al., eds, *Istoriia mist i sil Ukraïns'koï RSR: Ternopil's'ka oblast'* (Kiev: AN URSR 1973). See also Ie. Iatskevych and V. Kolisnyk, *Dovidnyk po istorychnykh mistsiakh L'vivs'koï oblasti* (L'viv: Knyzhkovo-zhurnal'no vyd-vo 1954).

102 Anton Kunysz, ed., *Miasto i powiat Przemyśl w Polsce ludowej (zarys monograficzny)* (Przemyśl: Towarzystwo Przyjaciół Nauk w Przemyślu 1973).

Chodynicki and the Ukrainian Denys Zubryts'kyi.[103] These works and the subsequent rich literature about the city have been analyzed in a historiographic study by Łucja Charewiczowa.[104]

There are several detailed scholarly monographs and collections of documents dealing with specific periods in L'viv's history (to be discussed in the appropriate sections below),[105] and there are also a few general histories as well. The latter have been written by Ukrainian or Polish authors, each of whom see L'viv as part of their own national and cultural patrimonies. As a result, they dwell almost exclusively on the Ukrainian or Polish aspects of the city's past. The Ukrainian interpretation is best represented in a short history by Ivan Kryp''iakevych and in two collections of essays devoted to varied aspects of the city.[106] Historically oriented descriptions by Kryp''iakevych and Olena Stepaniv are also useful for understanding the ''Ukrainian sections'' of L'viv, especially in the twentieth century.[107] The Polish view is outlined in a comprehensive history by Fryderyk Papée and in shorter more recent studies by Józef Rudnicki and Stefan Mękarski.[108] Soviet writers reject for the most part what they consider to be ''bour-

103 X. Ignacy Chodynicki, *Historya stołecznego królestw Galicyi i Lodomeryi miasta Lwowa od założenia jego aż do czasów teraźnieyszych* (L'viv: Karól Bogusława Pfaff 1829); Dyonizji Zubrzycki, *Kronika miasta Lwowa* (L'viv: p.a. 1844).

104 See chapter 1, n. 42.

105 See chapter 3, n. 50; chapter 4, notes 29–37, 88; chapter 5, notes 15–17, 26; chapter 6, notes 22, 228–229, 239, 242; chapter 7, n. 17; chapter 8, n. 11; chapter 10, notes 16–17, 45, 63, 88.

106 Ivan P. Kryp''iakevych, *L'viv: ioho mynuvshyna i teperishnist'* (L'viv: L'vivs'ka Rus' 1910); *Nash L'viv: iubileinyi zbirnyk 1252–1952* (New York: Chervona Kalyna 1953); and Vasyl Mudry, ed., *L'viv: A Symposium on its 700th Anniversary* (New York: Alumni Institutions of Higher Education in L'viv 1962).

See also the shorter collection of essays on all aspects of the city by Gregor Prokoptschuk, *Das ukrainische Lwiw-Lemberg: kulturpolitische Betrachtung* (Munich: Vlg. Ukraine 1953) and the historical memoirs of Stepan Shakh, *L'viv–misto moieï molodosty,* 2 vols (3 pts) (Munich: Khrystyians'kyi holos 1955–56).

107 Ivan Krypiakevych, *Istorychni prokhody po L'vovi,* Vyd. TP, no. 771 (L'viv 1932); Olena Stepaniv, *Suchasnyi L'viv* (Cracow and L'viv: Ukraïns'ke vyd. 1943), 2nd ed. (New York: Hoverlia 1953).

108 Fryderyk Papée, *Historia m. Lwowa w zarysie* (L'viv: Gmina Król. Stoł. Miasta Lwowa 1894), 2nd ed. (L'viv and Warsaw 1924); Józef Rudnicki, *A Page of Polish History: Lwów* (London: Polish Research Centre 1944); Stefan Mękarski, *Lwów: karta z dziejów Polski,* 2nd ed. (London: Koła Lwowian 1962).

See also the comprehensive pre-World War I guidebooks to the city by Józef Wiczkowski, *Lwów: jego rozwój i stan kulturalny oraz przewodnik po mieście* (L'viv: Wydział Gospodarczy X. Zjazdu Lekarzy i Przyrodników Polskich 1907) and to the city and region, n. 86 above; and the more popular collections of essays by Franciszek Jaworski, *Lwów stary i wczorajszy* (L'viv: 'Kurjer Lwowskiego' 1910); idem, *O szarym Lwowie* (L'viv and Warsaw:

geois-nationalist'' Ukrainian and Polish writings and have instead offered their own syntheses, which stress the economic growth and class conflict that had supposedly always existed in the city until the coming of Soviet rule. Their revisionist views appear in two multiauthored histories issued in 1956 in connection with the 700th anniversary of the issuance of L'viv's city charter.[109]

Besides L'viv, there are general histories of other cities and towns in eastern Galicia. Among these, Przemyśl has received the most attention. Recently, Polish scholars produced a comprehensive two-volume history covering events in Przemyśl from earliest times to the present.[110] A memorial book produced by Ukrainian emigrés and an older Polish historical guide and demographic study are also valuable sources of information on Przemyśl.[111]

Each of the other major cities, towns, and even some villages in eastern Galicia have at least one study devoted to them.[112] Already in the second half of the nineteenth century, Venedykt Ploshchans'kyi wrote a series of historical descriptions of thirty-one Galician-Ukrainian towns and villages.[113] Since then, there

---

H. Altenberg, G. Greyfarth, E. Wende 1916); Stanisław Wasylewski, *Historje lwowskie* (L'viv and Poznań: Wyd. Polskiego 1921), 2nd rev. ed. under the title *Bardzo przyjemne miasto* (Poznań: R. Wegner 196?); and Mieczysław Opałek, *Obrazki z przeszłości Lwowa*, Bibljoteka Lwowska, vol. XXX (L'viv 1931).

109 Ivan P. Kryp''iakevych et al., *Narysy istoriï L'vova* (L'viv: Knyzhkovo-zhurnal'ne vyd. 1956); Ie.K. Lazarenko et al., *Istoriia L'vova: korotkyi narys* (L'viv: LU 1956).

110 Franciszek Persowski, Antoni Kunysz, Julian Olszak, eds, *Tysiąc lat Przemyśla: zarys historyczny*, 2 vols (Warsaw and Cracow: PWN 1974). See also the earlier work by Leopold Hauser, *Monografia miasta Przemyśla* (Przemyśl: Braci Jeleniów 1883).

111 B. Zahaikevych, *Peremyshl': zakhidnyi bastion Ukraïny* (New York and Philadelphia: Peremys'kyi vydavnychyi komitet 1961); Mieczysław Orłowicz, *Ilustrowany przewodnik po Przemyślu i okolicy* (L'viv: Zjednoczenie Towarzystw Polskich i Towarzystwo Przyjaciół Nauk w Przemyślu 1917); Walerjan Kramarz, *Ludność Przemyśla w latach 1521–1921* (Przemyśl: Towarzystwo Przyjaciół Nauk w Przemyślu 1930).

For contemporary statistical data, see *Rocznik statystyczny miasta Przemyśla*, Rok I: 1971 (Przemyśl: Powiatowy Inspektorat Statystyczny w Przemyślu 1971).

112 For studies of various towns and cities during specific periods, see below, chapter 3, notes 47–49, 51–55; chapter 4, notes 38–46; and chapter 10, notes 18, 50–74, 88, 96.

113 Venedykt A. Ploshchanskii, ''Korolevskii vol'nŷi horod Drohobŷch–po chasty ystoriy, topografiy y statystyky,'' *Naukovŷi sbornyk Halytsko-russkoi Matytsŷ*, III (L'viv 1867), pp. 162–198; ''Halytsko-russkii horod Stanyslavov po dostovîrnŷm ystochnykam,'' *ibid.*, IV (1868), pp. 15–56; ''Halytsko-russkii torhovel'nŷi horod Brodŷ,'' *ibid.*, IV (1868), pp. 56–69 and pp. 273–288; ''Nîkotorŷy mîstnosty Peremŷshl'skoho okruha (Husakov, Iavorov, Iaroslavl'), *ibid.*, IV, 3–4 (1868), pp. 177–221; ''Halytsko-russkii horod Zholkov,'' *ibid.*, IV, 3–4 (1868), pp. 221–272; ''Nîkotorŷy sela Halytskoi Rusy: Voloshcha, Mainych, Korchyn, Zvynyhorod, Lahodov, Beleluia, Strach, Dobrostanŷ, Rozhorche, Vîtvytsa, Oporets, Labochne, Ternavka, Khytar, Kalne, Tukhol'ka, Plav'e, Oriavchyk, Tysovets', Slavsko,'' *Lyteraturnŷi sbornyk Halytsko-russkoi Matytsŷ* [II] (L'viv 1870), pp. 31–88;

have also appeared histories, encyclopedic surveys, or documentary collections for Belz,[114] Berezhany,[115] Boryslav,[116] Brzozów (Bereziv),[117] Buchach,[118] Chernykhiv,[119] Chortkiv,[120] Drohobych,[121] Horodok,[122] Hrymaliv,[123] Iaslys'ka,[124] Iavoriv,[125] Iezupil',[126] Jarosław,[127] Jasło,[128] Kaminka Strumylova,[129] Kolo-

---

"Zaval'e, selo Halytskoi Rusy," *ibid.*, [III] (L'viv 1871), pp. 65–66; "Busk: horod u b. kniazhestvo na Halytskoi Rusy," *ibid.*, pp. 67–98.

114 Fryderyk Papée, "Zabytki przeszłości miasta Bełza," *Przewodnik Naukowy i Literacki*, XII (L'viv 1884), pp. 97–105 and 209–217.

115 Józef Czernecki, *Brzeżany: pamiątki i wspomnienia* (L'viv: T-wo Nauczycieli Szkół Wyższych 1905); *Brzeżany 1530–1930* (Brzeżany 1930).

116 D.D. Nyzovyi, *Boryslav—misto naftovykiv* (L'viv: Knyzhkovo-zhurnal'ne vyd-vo 1960).

117 Antoni Prochaska, "Z przeszłości Brzozowa," *Przewodnik Naukowy i Literacki*, XVI (L'viv 1888), pp. 43–59, 254–267, 343–355.

118 S. Barącz, *Pamiętniki buczackie* (L'viv 1882).

119 Ia. Kosovs'kyi, *Selo Chernykhiv ternopil's'koho povitu: podiï ta zhyttia sela* (Cherykhiv: Chytal'nia TP 1936).

120 Teofil Kostruba, ed., *Materiialy do istoriï m. Chortkova* (L'viv 1931).

121 Feliks Gatkiewicz, ed., *Z archiwum Drohobycza: zbiór przywilejów, aktów, dekretów granicznych, lustracyi, memoryałów* (Drohobych 1906); Mścisław Mściwujewski, *Królewskie wolne miasto Drohobycz* (L'viv and Drohobych: n.p. 1929).

122 Volodymyr Hrabovets'kyi and Ivan Hopalo, *Horodok: istoryko-kraieznavchyi narys* (L'viv: Kameniar 1968).

123 I.P. Kryp''iakevych, *Korotka istoriia Hrymalova i sil sudovoho Hrymalivs'koho okruha* (Hrymalovo: TP 1931).

124 Antoni Prochaska, "Jaśliska, miasteczko i klucz biskupów przemyskich," *Przewodnik Naukowy i Literacki*, XVII (L'viv 1889), pp. 58–77, 181–188, 263–270, 368–375, 464–473, 563–572, 650–662.

125 Edward Webersfeld, *Jaworów: monografia historyczna, etnograficzna i statystyczna* (L'viv 1909), first published in *Przewodnik Naukowy i Literacki*, XXXVII (L'viv 1909), pp. 369–384, 457–466, 551–564, 649–658, 741–752, 833–848, 903–915.

126 Aleksander Czołowski, "Z przeszłości Jezupola i okolicy," *Przewodnik Naukowy i Literacki*, XVII (L'viv 1889), pp. 821–835, 923–932, 1046–1050, 1184–1245, also separately (L'viv 1890).

127 Franciszek Siarczyński, *Wiadomość historyczna i statystyczna o mieście Jarosławiu* (L'viv: Kuhn i Milikowski 1826); A. Wondaś, *Szkice do dziejów Jarosławia*, 3 vols (Jarosław 1934–36); K. Gottfried, *Illustrowany przewodnik po Jarosławiu* (Jarosław 1937).

128 Ferdynand Bostel, "Przyczynek do dziejów Jaślisk," *Przewodnik Naukowy i Literacki*, XVIII (L'viv 1890).

129 Bronisław Faliński, *Żródła dziejowe starostwa i parafii Kamionka Strumiłowa*, 2 vols (Kaminka Strumylova: Rada Powiatowa i Magistrat Miasta 1928–30).

myia,[130] Lishna,[131] Novovolyns'k,[132] Radymno,[133] Sambir,[134] Sanok,[135] Sokal',[136] Stryi,[137] Stanyslaviv,[138] Ternopil',[139] Tyriava Sil'na,[140] Zboriv,[141] Zhovkva,[142] and Zolochiv.[143]

130 Leopold Waigel, *Rys miasta Kolomyi* (Kolomyia, 1877); Zynovii Knysh, ed., *Nad Prutom u luzi: Kolomyia v spohadakh* (Toronto: Komitet Pokutian 1962).

131 Ivan Fylypchak, ''Z istoriï sela Lishni,'' *Zapysky NTSh*, CXLIX (L'viv 1928), pp. 85–116.

132 B.M. Popov and I.V. Spodarenko, *Novovolyns'k–misto shakhtariv* (L'viv: Knyzhkovo-zhurnal'ne vyd-vo 1962).

133 A. Prochaska, ''Radymno, miasteczko i klucz biskupów przemyskich,'' *Przewodnik Naukowy i Literacki*, XIX (L'viv 1891); K. Gottfried, ''Z przeszłości Radymna,'' *Rocznik Przemyski*, X, 3 (Przemyśl 1965).

134 Aleksander Kuczera, *Samborszczyzna: ilustrowana monografia miasta Sambora i ekonomii samborskiej*, 2 vols (Sambor: Księgarnia Nauczycielska 1935–37).

135 M.K. Ladyzhynskii, ''Sianok i ego okresnosti,'' *Sbornik Galitsko-russkoi Matitsy*, VII (L'viv 1930), pp. 81–84; Stefan Stefański, *Sanok i okolice* (Sanok: Polskie Towarzystwo Turystyczno-krajoznawcze 1974).

136 Fryderyk Papée, ''Skole i Tucholszczyzna,'' *Przewodnik Naukowy i Literacki*, XVIII (L'viv 1890), pp. 448–456, 633–642, 741–747, 820–838, 923–937, 1016–1026, 1140–1164, also separately as *Skole i Tucholszczyzna: monografia historyczna* (L'viv: Gubrynowicz i Schmidt 1891); Mykola Holubets', *Z istoriï mista Sokalia* (L'viv: Nedilia 1929); M.P. Iaremchuk, and A.I. Bil'chenko, *Sokal'* (L'viv: Knyzhkovo-zhurnal'ne vyd-vo 1961).

137 Ferdynand Bostel, ''Z przeszłości Stryja i starostwa stryjskiego,'' *Przewodnik Naukowy i Literacki*, XIV (L'viv 1886), pp. 600–615, 691–720; Antoni Prochaska, *Historia miasta Stryja* (L'viv: Nakł. Miasta Stryja 1926); M.M. Levyts'kyi and V.Ie. Batos'kyi, *Stryi* (L'viv: Knyzhkovo-zhurnal'ne vyd-vo 1962).

138 S. Barącz, *Pamiątki miasta Stanisławowa* (L'viv 1858).

139 P. Bîlenskii, *Ternopôl' y ieho okolytsia*, 2 pts (Ternopil' 1895–96).

140 Ivan Fylypchak, ''Narys istoriï Tyriavy Sil'noï,'' *Zapysky NTSh*, CLIV (L'viv 1937), pp. 115–139.

141 Ivan P. Kryp''iakevych, *Korotka istoriia Zborova*, Nash ridnyi krai, no. 5 (L'viv 1929).

142 Sadok Barącz, *Pamiątki miasta Żółkwi* (L'viv 1852), 2nd rev. ed. (L'viv 1877); Marjan Osiński, *Zamek w Żółkwi* (L'viv: Towarzystwo Opieki nad Zabytkami Sztuki i Kultury we Lwowie 1933).

143 Łucja Charewiczowa, *Dzieje miasta Złoczowa* (Zolochiv 1929).

Chapter 3

Early history to 1340

Archeological studies

Although the history of Galicia traditionally begins with the first documentary references to the territory that reveal its association with Kievan Rus' in the late tenth century, there are also several archeological studies of the region, the results of which have often been used by historians to confirm or deny hypotheses about ''prehistoric'' and later historical developments. Among the more prolific archeologists in the first half of the twentieth century were Bohdan Janusz, Iaroslav Pasternak, and Leon Kozłowski, each of whom wrote one or more general surveys of archeological findings in all or part of Galicia from the Paleolithic Age (300,000 BC) to the tenth century AD.[1] Before World War II, the number of archeological finds was already sufficient enough that monographs could be

1 Bohdan Janusz, *Z pradziejów ziemi lwowskiej,* Biblioteka Lwowska, vol. XXII–XXIII (L'viv 1913); idem, *Kultura przedhistoryczna Podola galicyjskiego* (L'viv: Wyd. Polskie 1919); Aleksander Czołowski and Bohdan Janusz, *Przeszłość i zabytki województwa Tarnopolskiego* (Ternopil': Panstwowa Organizacja Narodowa 1926); Jaroslav Pasternak, *Ruské Karpaty v archeologii,* Filosofická fakulta University Karlovy, Práce z vedĕckých ústavů, vol. XVIII (Prague 1928); Iaroslav Pasternak, *Korotka arkheolohiia zakhidno-ukraïns'kykh zemel',* Vydannia Bohosloviï, no. 11–12 (L'viv 1932), first published in *Bohosloviia,* X, 1, 2, and 3 (L'viv 1932), pp. 38–79, 147–164, and 229–248; the appropriate sections in idem, *Arkheolohiia Ukraïny* (Toronto: NTSh 1961); Leon Kozłowski, *Zarys pradziejów Polski Południowo-Wschodniej,* in *Polska Południowo-Wschodnia,* vol. I, ed. Zygmunt Czerny (L'viv: Związek Polskich Towarzystw Naukowych 1939), pp. 62–164.

See also the earlier survey by Vladimir Demetrykiewicz, ''Vorgeschichte [Galiziens],'' in *Die österreichisch-ungarische Monarchie in Wort und Bild,* vol. XII: *Galizien* (Vienna K.K. Hof- und Staatsdruckerei 1898), pp. 111–136; and the popular history by Omelian Partytskyi, *Starynna istoryia Halychyny,* vol. I: *vid VII-oho viku pered Khrystom do roky 110 po Khrysti* (L'viv 1894).

devoted to specific periods of archeological development in Galicia, in particular to what was called Scythian culture and the Roman Age.[2] Medieval cities, especially Halych and L'viv, have also been a traditional focus of attention for archeological studies.[3]

Archeological research in Galicia actually began in a serious manner in the second half of the nineteenth century, and a description of this early work was published by the local cultural activist Iakiv Holovats'kyi.[4] Since that time, the ever increasing number of archeological finds has been successively cataloged, beginning with the years before World War I,[5] continuing during the interwar years,[6] and culminating with the Soviet period after 1945, when archeological research in the region became particularly active. The results of the extensive Soviet work in Galicia and neighboring regions can be found in a journal devoted specifically to the subject, *Materialy i doslidzhennia z arkheolohiï Prykarpattia i Volyni* (Kiev 1958–present), as well as in numerous monographs and articles.[7]

2 Volodymyr Hrebeniak, ''Slidy skyts'koï kul'tury v Halychyni,'' *Zapysky NTSh,* CXVII–CXVIII (L'viv 1914), pp. 9–25; Tadeusz Sulimirski, *Scytowie na zachodniem Podolu,* Prace Lwowskiego Towarzystwa Prehistorycznego, vol. II (L'viv 1936); Karol Hadaczek, ''Kultura dorzecza Dniestru w epoce cesarstwa rzymskiego,'' in *Materyałów archeologiczno-antropologicznych,* XII (Cracow 1912), pp. 22–32; Marcyan Śmiszko, *Kultury wczesnego okresu epoki cesarstwa rzymskiego w Małopolsce Wschodniej* (L'viv: Towarzystwo Naukowe 1932); M. Śmiszko, T. Sulimirski, and K. Myczkowski, *Przyczynki do poznania epoki cesarstwa rzymskiego południowo-wschodniej Polski,* Prace Lwowskiego Towarzystwa Prehistorycznego, vol. I (L'viv 1934).

3 See notes 47–55 below.

4 Iakov Golovatskii, ''Ob izsliedovanii pamiatnikov russkoi stariny v Galichinie,'' *Trudy I. arkheologicheskago s''iezda v Moskvie,* I (Moscow 1869), pp. 219–241.

5 Władysław Przybysławski, *Repertoryum zabytków przedhistorycznych Galicyi wschodniej* (L'viv 1906); Volodymyr Hrebeniak, ''Novi arkheol'ogichni nakhidky na terytoriï Skhidnoï Halychyny,'' *Zapysky NTSh,* CXXII (L'viv 1915), pp. 5–28; Bohdan Janusz, *Zabytki przedhistoryczne Galicyi wschodniej,* Prace Naukowe Wydawnictwa Tow. dla Popierania Nauki Polskiej, sect. 1, vol. V (L'viv 1918).

6 Iurii Polians'kyi, ''Novi arkheol'ogichni znakhidky z Halychyny,'' *Zapysky NTSh,* CXLIX (L'viv 1928), pp. 9–30; Iaroslav Pasternak, ''Novovidkryti ryms'ki pam''iatky z Halychyny i Volyni,'' *Zapysky NTSh,* CLI (L'viv 1931), pp. 1–17; idem, ''Persha bronzova doba v Halychyni v svitli novykh rozkopok,'' *Zapysky NTSh,* CLII (L'viv 1933), pp. 63–112; idem, ''Novi arkheolohichni nabutky (1929–1932),'' *Zapysky NTSh,* CLII (L'viv 1933), pp. 113–130; idem, ''Novi arkheolohichni nabutky Muzeiu NTSh u L'vovi za chas vid 1933–1936,'' *Zapysky NTSh,* CLIV (L'viv 1937), pp. 242–268.

7 See the catalog of archeological sites in Galicia in O.O. Ratych, *Drevn'orus'ki arkheolohichni pam''iatky na terytoriï zakhidnykh oblastei URSR* (Kiev: AN URSR 1957); the comprehensive bibliography in *Arkheolohichni pam''iatky Prykarpattia i Volyni u rann'oslov''ians'kyi ta davn'orus'kyi chasy* (Kiev: Naukova dumka 1982); and the monographs on specific periods by O.P. Chernysh et al., eds., *Arkheolohichni pam''iatky Prykarpattia i Volyni kam''ianoho viku* (Kiev:

A problem that links archeological "prehistory" with the historical era of Galician development is that of the Croats or White Croats, who are known to have inhabited the upper Dniester and Buh regions sometime between the fifth and tenth centuries AD. Insufficient written documentary evidence and differing views regarding the available archeological and linguistic data have produced an extensive though controversial literature about the White Croats and Galicia. The controversy centers on several problems: (1) the origins of the group (whether they were autochthonous or an Irano-Alanic tribe or military/merchant elite from the Caucasus who migrated north of the Carpathians and then were absorbed by the sedentary western and eastern Slavs over whom they ruled and to whom they bequeathed their name); (2) the territorial extent of their rule (whether or not they formed a "Croatian Empire" stretching from the Oder valley in the west to the upper Dniester and Buh valleys in the east); (3) their migration southward (whether in the fifth, or sixth, or seventh centuries) and their relationship to the ancestors of the modern-day Croats; (4) their relationship to Moravia (whether or not they were annexed in the ninth century by the Greater Moravian state, which then established centers like Przemyśl and introduced Christianity); and finally (5) their "ethnicity" (whether they were eastern Slavs, western Slavs, or a confederation of tribes of which only one was the White Croatian in Galicia).

The best introductory survey on the White Croats is the concise encyclopedic article by Gerard Labuda, that outlines the various problems and reviews the existing literature on the subject.[8] In 1863, the Galician-Ukrainian writer Omelian

---

Naukova dumka 1981); Ivan K. Svieshnikov, *Pidsumky doslidzhennia kul'tur bronzovoï doby Prykarpattia i Zakhidnoho Podillia* (L'viv 1958); Larysa I. Krushel'nyts'ka, *Pivnichne Prykarpattia i Zakhidna Volyn' za doby rann'oho zaliza* (Kiev: Naukova dumka 1976); O.P. Chernysh et al., eds, *Naselennia Prykarpattia i Volyni za doby rozkladu pervisnoobshynnoho ladu ta v davn'orus'kyi chas* (Kiev: Naukova dumka 1976); Volodymyr D. Baran, *Ranni slov''iany mizh Dnistrom i Pryp''iattiu* (Kiev: Naukova dumka 1972); and the appropriate sections in *Arkheolohiia Ukraïns'koï RSR*, 3 vols (Kiev: Naukova dumka 1971–75).

For the results of post-World War II archeological research in Poland, especially in the region of the Cherven cities, see n. 27 below.

8 Gerard Labuda, "Chorwacja Biała," in *Słownik starożytności słowiańskich*, vol. I, pt 2 (Wrocław, Warsaw, and Cracow: ZNIO–PAN 1961), pp. 255–256.

Much of the controversy stems from differing interpretations of the tenth-century description of the White Croats by the Byzantine author Constantine Porphyrogenitus, in his *De administrando imperio*, Greek text ed. Gyula Moravcsik, English trans. R.J. H. Jenkins (Budapest 1949), especially pp. 147–161, and vol. II: *Commentary*, ed. R.J.H. Jenkins (London: Athline Press of the University of London 1962), especially pp. 97–132 *passim*. See also the extensive historiographical discussion of the Croat problem in Václav Polák, "Etnogenese slovanů s hlediska jazykového," in *Vznik a počátky slovanů*, vol. I (Prague: Československá akademie věd 1956), pp. 34–47.

Partyts'kyi put forth what has come to be the traditional view of the White Croats: that they were an autochthonous East Slavic population that had created a strong state in Galicia by the seventh century and had then united with Kievan Rus' in the early tenth century.[9] With some adjustments, this view has been maintained by most Ukrainian writers, as well as in more recent times by Soviet archeologists and historians anxious to reveal the existence of state structures among the eastern Slavs before the coming of the Varangians in the ninth century.[10] The Soviets are particularly opposed to Polish scholars (some of whom place the center of the White Croats along the upper Vistula, others along the upper Dniester), because they do not stress the supposedly exclusive eastern Slavic aspect of the Croats, and in at least one instance (Paszkiewicz) argue that they are all western Slavs.[11] The Czech specialists on early Slavic and medieval history, Lubor Niederle and Francis Dvornik, argue that the White Croats, centered along the upper Vistula River, were originally neither East Slavic nor West Slavic (having originated as an Irano-Alanic group from the Caucasus region), and that it was only after the majority of the group migrated southward (during the sixth century) that the remnants left behind were absorbed by local Slavs to whom they gave their name, so that only by the ninth and tenth centuries can one speak of "Polish," "Czech,"

9 Omelian Partytskyi, "Chervonnaia Rus' v chasakh pred-historychnŷkh," *Halychanyn: lyteraturnŷi sbornyk*, I, 3–4 (L'viv 1863), pp. 208–226.

10 For the non-Soviet Ukrainian view, see Yaroslav Pasternak, "Peremyshl of the Chronicles and the Territory of White Croats," *Proceedings of the Shevchenko Scientific Society, Historical-Philosophical Section*, II (Paris, New York, and Toronto 1957), pp. 36–40, expanded in a Ukrainian version as "Kniazhyi horod Peremyshl'," in V. Zahaikevych, ed., *Peremyshl': zakhidnii bastion Ukraïny* (New York and Philadelphia: Peremys'kyi vydavnychyi komitet 1961), pp. 7–24. On the other hand, Mykhailo Hrushevs'kyi expressed skepticism about the existence of an East Slavic (Ukrainian) branch of Croats. Cf. his *Istoriia Ukraïny-Rusy*, vol. I, 3rd rev. ed. (Kiev 1913; reprinted New York: Knyho-spilka 1954), pp. 210–213.

For the Soviet view, see M.Iu. Smishko, "Rann'oslov''ians'ka kul'tura karpats'koho pidhir''ia," *Naukovi zapysky Instytutu suspil'nykh nauk AN URSR*, I (Kiev 1953); and V. Koroliuk, "K voprosu ob otnosheniiakh Rusi i Pol'shi v X veke," *Kratkie soobshcheniia Instituta slavianovedeniia*, IX (Moscow 1952), pp. 43–50.

11 Józef Widajewicz, *Państwo Wiślan*, Biblioteka Studium Słowiańskiego Uniwersytetu Jagiellońskiego, seria A, nr. 2 (Cracow 1947), especially pp. 13–30; Gerard Labuda, *Pierwsze państwo słowiańskie: państwo Samona*, Biblioteka Historyczna Poznańskiego Towarzystwa Przyjaciół Nauk, vol. IV (Poznań 1949), especially pp. 194–262; Tadeusz Lehr-Spławiński, "Zagadnienie Chorwatów nadwiślańskich," *Pamiętnik Słowiański*, II (Cracow 1951), pp. 17–32; Józef Widajewicz, "Pierwotne dzieje Polski," *Przegląd Zachodni*, VIII, 11–12 (Poznań 1952), especially pp. 374–380; Henryk Łowmiański, *Początki Polski*, 5 vols (Warsaw: PWN 1963–73), especially vol. II, pp. 114–200; Henryk Paszkiewicz, *The Origins of Russia* (London: George Allen and Unwin 1954), especially pp. 359–361.

or "Rus' " Croats.[12] The presence of Moravian-Czech influence in Galicia during the tenth century, to which the founding of Przemyśl (c. 970s) and the introduction of a hybrid Latin/Byzantine form of Christianity are attributed, forms the subject of studies by Iaroslav Pasternak and Václav Chaloupecký.[13]

Background

The traditional starting point of Galician history is the year 981, when, according to the Rus' Primary Chronicle, the grand prince of Kiev, Volodymyr (reigned 980–1015), went to the Liakhs and took Przemyśl, Cherven, and other cities. The same source mentions that in 993 Volodymyr attacked the Croats who allegedly inhabited Galicia at the time. These terse statements in the Primary Chronicle have generated numerous and yet unresolved questions about the status of Galicia before Volodymyr's appearance–for example, was the region retaken by the Rus' prince, or did he take it for the first time from Poland or Great Moravia? Whatever answers subsequent writers have provided to such questions, it is certain that after the late tenth century Galicia and its White Croatian inhabitants became part of the political, socioeconomic, and cultural sphere of Kievan Rus'.

Kievan Rus' was itself no more than a loosely knit federation of principalities, each with its own ruler or rulers representing various branches of the founding Rurykovych dynasty and nominally subordinate, though more often than not independent of the senior, or grand prince residing in Kiev. More important as a unifying factor was culture and religion. Galicia received Christianity in its eastern Orthodox form from Kiev in the late tenth century and later a cultural language, Old Slavonic, from the same source.

It was also arrangements reached within the Kievan political order that provided Galicia, in the second half of the eleventh century, with its own branch of the Rurykovych dynasty, the Rostyslavyches from Prince Rostyslav (d. 1065), grandson of the powerful prince of Kiev, Iaroslav the Wise (reigned 1019–1054). Rostyslav's three sons, the real founders of the Galician dynasty, divided the

12 Lubor Niederle, *Slovanské starožitnosti,* vol. II: *Původ a počátky slovanů jižních,* pt 1 (Prague: Bursík a Kohout 1906), pp. 244–280 and vol. IV: *Původ a počátky Slovanů východních* (Prague: Bursík a Kohout 1924), pp. 154–156; Francis Dvornik, *The Making of Central and Eastern Europe* (London 1949), 2nd rev. ed. (Gulf Breeze, Florida: Academic International Press 1974), especially pp. 268–304. See also Václav Hrubý, "Původní hranice biskupství pražského a hranice říše české v 10. století," *Časopis Matice Moravské,* I (Brno 1926), pp. 85–154.

13 See n. 10 above; and Václav Chaloupecký, "Česká hranice východní koncem XI st.," *Český časopis historický,* XXXII (Prague 1926), pp. 334–342.

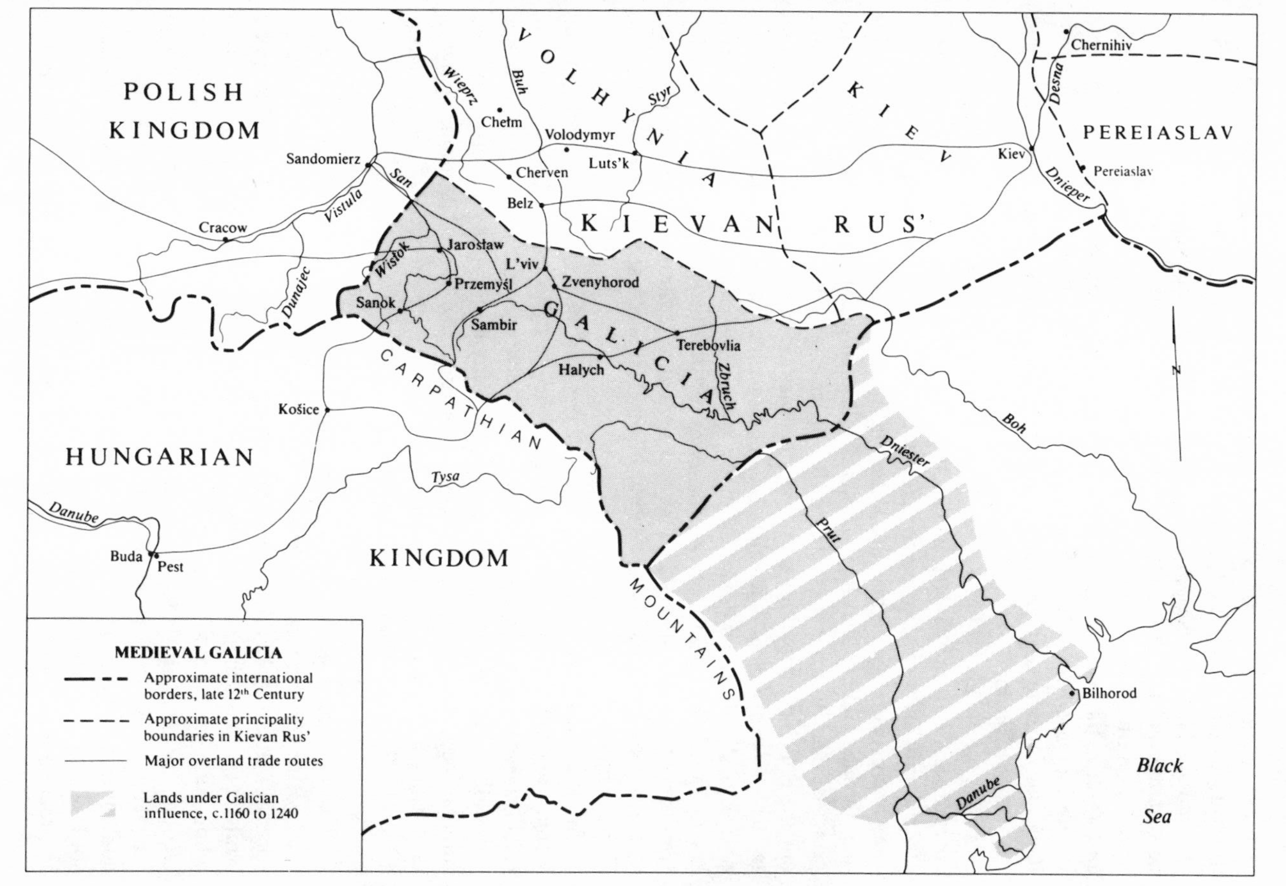
MEDIEVAL GALICIA
Approximate international borders, late 12th Century
Approximate principality boundaries in Kievan Rus'
Major overland trade routes
Lands under Galician influence, c.1160 to 1240
POLISH KINGDOM
HUNGARIAN KINGDOM
VOLHYNIA
KIEV
PEREIASLAV
KIEVAN RUS'
GALICIA
CARPATHIAN MOUNTAINS
Black Sea
N
Chernihiv
Pereiaslav
Kiev
Desna
Dnieper
Chełm
Volodymyr
Luts'k
Cherven
Belz
Buh
Wieprz
Styr
Sandomierz
San
Vistula
Cracow
Dunajec
Wisłok
Jarosław
L'viv
Przemyśl
Zvenyhorod
Sanok
Sambir
Terebovlia
Halych
Zbruch
Košice
Tysa
Danube
Buda
Pest
Boh
Dniester
Prut
Bilhorod
Danube

realm and ruled from the fortresses of Zvenyhorod, Przemyśl, and Terebovlia, but their successors during the twelfth century–Volodymyrko (reigned 1124–1153) and Iaroslav Osmomysl' (reigned 1153–1187)–united these cities, founded a new capital at Halych (1141), and extended the principality's territorial extent from its original base along the upper Buh and Dniester rivers toward the southeast as far as the Black Sea. It was also during this period that Galicia's economic wealth increased, mainly because of its exports of salt (mined near Halych) to Kiev and revenue derived from international trade with Byzantium, Kiev, and east-central Europe.

Like other lands within Kievan Rus', Galicia experienced several periods of chronic wars caused by interprincely rivalry over the throne of Kiev and over each other's principalities. During the eleventh and twelfth centuries, the princes of Kiev and especially neighboring Volhynia frequently attempted to take the Galician throne. Galicia also had problems that distinguished it from other Kievan principalities. Both the neighboring Hungarian Kingdom south of the Carpathians and the Polish principalities to the west claimed Galicia as their patrimony and on numerous occasions invaded the region (sometimes at the invitation of Galician princes or discontented boyars). Finally, the boyars (a class of wealthy landowners) grew to be a politically and economically influential group, and after the twelfth century often served as a potent restraint on centralized princely authority; at times they contributed to internal chaos that was exploited by the Poles or Hungarians.

In 1199, the Rostyslavych dynasty died out, and the local boyars invited Prince Roman of Volhynia (reigned 1199–1205) to be their ruler. This heralded the establishment of a new branch of the Rurykovych dynasty–the Romanovyches–as well as the unification of Galicia and Volhynia through the person of their ruling prince. After a period of civil war, foreign invasion, and declining economic fortunes, Galicia-Volhynia reached its apogee under Danylo (reigned 1238–1262) and his son Lev (reigned 1264–1301). And since Kiev had already lost its preeminent political and economic role by the early thirteenth century, Galicia-Volhynia replaced it as the dominant force within the southern Rus' lands. This position was maintained even after the Mongol invasion, which devastated parts of Galicia in 1240. Danylo reached an accommodation with the Mongols, while at the same time negotiating with western states, including the Pope, from whom he received a crown in 1253. As king of Rus' (*Rex Rusiae*), Danylo was recognized as a full-fledged monarch in the context of the western European feudal order. The Kingdom of Galicia-Volhynia (*regnum Galiciae et Lodomeriae*) continued to flourish, especially in the economic sphere, under Danylo's successor Lev. It was also at this time (1260s) that L'viv was made the capital of Galicia. In order to enhance further the prestige of the Galician-Volhynian Kingdom, a new Galician Orthodox metropolitanate was established in 1303 with its seat in Halych.

However, at the moment of its seeming height, a period of decline set in, which ultimately was to prove fatal. The first decades of the fourteenth century witnessed the death of the last male in the Romanovych dynasty (1323), an increase in antiprincely activity on the part of the boyars, new friction with the Mongols, and frequent incursions on the part of the Poles, Hungarians, and a new power from the north, the Lithuanians. In 1340, the last Romanovych ruler (on the female side) was poisoned by the boyars. This act immediately plunged the kingdom into a period of internal civil war and anarchy as well as foreign invasion and diplomatic maneuvering that was to last for almost half a century, at the end of which Galicia was annexed by the Polish Kingdom.

Sources

The most important sources for the study of Galicia during the medieval period are the Old Rus' chronicles. Of these, the Kievan Chronicle (covering the years 1113–1200) and especially the Galician-Volhynian Chronicle (covering the years 1201–1292) are of greatest value for Galician events. The Galician-Volhynian Chronicle has, like the other chronicles, survived only in later-day copies, the oldest of which is found in the second part of the so-called Hypatian text (from the early fourteenth century). The Hypatian text has been published four times.[14] There are also annotated translations in English and Ukrainian.[15] The Hypatian text and its second component part, the Galician-Volhynian Chronicle, have been the subject of numberous studies, mostly of a linguistic nature. These studies, as well as the various existing texts and translations, are listed in a comprehensive bibliography on the chronicles by Rufina P. Dmitrieva and in a historiographical survey by George A. Perfecky.[16] From the historical point of view, the analysis of

14 *Polnoe sobranie russkikh lietopisei*, vol. II: *Ipatievskaia lietopis'* (St Petersburg: Arkheograficheskaia kommissia 1843), 2nd rev. ed. (St Petersburg: Arkheograficheskaia kommissia 1908; reprinted Moscow: Izd. vostochnoi literatury Instituta istorii AN SSSR, 1962); A.S. Petrushevych, ed., *Volŷnsko-Halytskaia lîtopys' sostavlennaia s kontsem XIII vîka 1205–1292* (L'viv 1871), supplement to *Lyteraturnyi sbornyk Halytsko-russkoi Matytsy*, [III–IV] (L'viv 1870–71); *Lietopis' po Ipat'evskomu spisku* (St Petersburg: Arkheograficheskaia kommissia 1871).

15 George Perfecky, *The Galician-Volynian Chronicle: The Hypatian Codex*, pt 2, Harvard Series in Ukrainian Studies, vol. XVI, pt 2 (Munich: Fink Vlg. 1973); L. Makhovets', "Halyts'ko-volyns'kyi litopys," *Zhovten'*, XXXIII, 7 (L'viv 1982), pp. 14–87.

16 R.P. Dmitrieva, comp., *Bibliografiia russkago letopisaniia* (Moscow and Leningrad: Akademii Nauk SSSR 1962); George Perfecky, "Studies on the Galician-Volynian (Volhynian) Chronicle," *Annals of the Ukrainian Academy of Arts and Sciences in the United States*, XII, 1–2 (New York 1969–72), pp. 62–112.

Izydor Sharanevych and the establishment of the chronicle's chronology (the Hypatian text had no dates) by Mykhailo Hrushevs'kyi are invaluable.[17] The Galician-Volhynian Chronicle as well as other Rus' chronicles and western European, Byzantine, and Arabic sources for the history of medieval Galicia are discussed in works by Ivan Lynnychenko, Mykhailo Hrushevs'kyi, Vladimir Ikonnikov, Dmytro Bahalii, and Vladimir Pashuto.[18]

General histories of Galicia-Volhynia

The medieval Galician-Volhynian principality and later kingdom marked the only time when the area was more or less independent. It is not surprising, then, that some of the earliest histories written by natives of the region concentrated on what they considered to be their homeland's heroic period. As early as 1837, Denys Zubryts'kyi published a Polish-language history of Galicia covering the years 988 to 1340.[19] This was followed by a three-volume history providing much greater detail, though the narrative ended with 1337.[20]

Besides glorifying the era of Galician princely rule, Zubryts'kyi also put forth two propositions that were to become standard in writings on the subject: that the Rus' population of Galicia was autochthonous, and that it originally was settled much farther west than the nineteenth-century Polish-Ukrainian ethnographic boundary. Other surveys of medieval Galician Rus' history were published by the

17 Isidor Szaraniewicz, *Die Hypatios-Chronik als Quellen-Beitrag zur österreichischen Geschichte* (L'viv: Karl Wild 1872); Mykhailo Hrushevs'kyi, ''Khronol'ogiia podiï halyts'ko-volyns'koï litopysy,'' *Zapysky NTSh,* XLI (L'viv 1901), 72 pp.

18 Ivan Linnichenko, *Vzaimnyia otnosheniia Rusi i Pol'shi do poloviny XIV stolietiia,* pt 1: *Rus' i Pol'sha do kontsa XII vieka* (Kiev 1884), especially pp. 1–24; Mykhailo Hrushevs'kyi, *Istoriia Ukraïny-Rusy,* vol. II, 2nd rev. ed. (L'viv 1905; reprinted New York: Knyho-spilka 1954), pp. 569–580 and vol. III, 2nd rev. ed. (L'viv 1905; reprinted New York: Knyho-spilka 1954), pp. 504–534; V.S. Ikonnikov, *Opyt russkoi istoriografii,* vol. II, pt 1 (Kiev 1908), pp. 539–600; Dmytro Bahalii, *Narys ukraïns'koï istoriohrafiï,* vol. I: *Litopysy,* Zbirnyk Istorychno-filolohichnoho viddilu UAN, vol. I (Kiev 1923), especially pp. 89–98; V.T. Pashuto, *Ocherki po istorii Galitsko-Volynskoi Rusi* (Moscow: AN SSSR 1950), especially pp. 17–133.

19 D. Zubrzycki, *Rys do historyi Narodu Ruskiego w Galicyi i hierarchii cerkiewnej w temże królestwie,* pt 1: *Zaprowadzenie chrześciańswa na Rusi aż do opanowania Rusi Czerwonej przez Kazimierza W. od r. 988 do 1340* (L'viv 1837). This was revised and brought down to 1583 in two works by the author that were translated into Russian by Osyp Bodians'kyi and A. Maikov: Denis Zubritskii, *Kritiko-istoricheskaia poviest' vremennykh liet Chervonoi ili Galitskoi Rusi* (Moscow: Imperatorskoe Obshchestvo istorii i drevnostei rossiiskikh 1845); idem, ''Galitskaia Rus' v XVI st.,'' *Chteniia obshchestva istorii i drevnostei rossiiskikh pri Moskovskom universitetie,* pt 3 (Moscow 1862), 84 pp.

20 Denis Zubritskii, *Istoriia drevniago galichsko-russkago kniazhestva,* 3 vols (L'viv 1852–55).

local scholar, Izydor Sharanevych, who brought his coverage down to the mid-fifteenth century,[21] and in briefer works by the Galician philologist Iakiv Holovats'kyi and the Russian and Polish historians Mikhail Smirnov and Anatol Lewicki.[22]

Since medieval Galicia was part of the Kievan federation, and since both Russian and Ukrainian writers consider Kievan Rus' the starting point for the development of their respective nations, it is not surprising that Galician Rus' often figures to a greater or lesser degree in Russian and Ukrainian national histories. Russian historians generally give Galicia only scant attention, because they consider it a peripheral area, i.e. the farthest western land of Kievan ''Russian'' influence, but one which had little impact on developments that eventually led to the growth of Muscovy. The best representative of the Russian national school is Sergei Solov'ev, who in the second and third volume of his monumental *History of Russia from Oldest Times* discusses at some length events in the Galician principality and Galician-Volhynian Kingdom.[23]

Medieval Galicia plays a more important role in Ukrainian national histories, since the area is viewed as one where the ''true'' culture of Kiev was preserved (something much different from what later arose in Muscovy)–at first independently, then within the Polish-Lithuanian Commonwealth, until it was carried on later in Ukrainian history during the Cossack era. The idea of Galicia as a crucial link in the Ukrainian historical continuum from Kievan Rus' to the present was developed by the greatest Ukrainian historian, Mykhailo Hrushevs'kyi. As a

21 Yzydor Sharanevych, *Ystoriia halytsko-volodymyrskoy Rusy ôt naidavnîishykh vremen do roku 1453* (L'viv: p.a. 1863). See also Isidor Szaraniewicz, *Kritische Blicke in die Geschichte der Karpaten-Völker im Alterthum und im Mittelalter* (L'viv: p.a. 1871).

22 [Iakiv Holovats'kyi], ''Velikaia Khorvatiia ili Galitsko-Karpatskaia Rus','' *Moskvitianin,* I, 11 and 12 (Moscow 1841), pp. 213–232 and 457–467, reprinted under the pseudonym ''Ia.'' in *Vînok Rusynam,* pt 2, ed. Ivan B. Holovatskii (Vienna 1847), pp. 133–206; M. Smirnov, *Sud'by Chervonoi ili Galitskoi Rusi do soedineniia ee s Pol'shei* (St Petersburg 1860), translated into Ukrainian in M. Smyrnov et al., *Monohrafiy do ystoriy Halytskoy Rusy,* Ruska ystorychna biblioteka, vol. V (Ternopil' 1886), pp. 1–57; Anatol Lewicki, ''Ruthenische Theilfürstenthümer bis Vereinigung mit Polen 1387,'' in *Die österreichisch-ungarische Monarchie in Wort und Bild* [vol. XI]: *Galizien* (Vienna: K.K. Hof- und Staatsdruckerei 1898), pp. 158–180.

23 Sergei Solov'ev, *Istoriia Rossii s drevnieishikh vremen,* vol. II, 3rd ed. (Moscow 1862), especially chapters 4, 5, and 6, and vol. III, 3rd ed. (Moscow 1862), especially chapter 2. This history has been republished in 15 volumes (Moscow 1960).

For a recent survey of medieval Galicia within the context of ''Russian'' history, see the excellent chapter by Günther Stökl, ''Das Fürstentum Galizien-Wolhynien,'' in *Handbuch der Geschichte Russlands,* Vol. I, ed. Manfred Hellman (Stuttgart: Anton Hiersemann 1976), pp. 485–533.

result, the Galician-Volhynian principality is given much attention in two volumes of his *History of Ukraine-Rus'*.[24]

Specific periods and problems

There are numerous studies devoted to specific periods or problems in the history of the medieval Galician-Volhynian principality and kingdom. The very first mention of Galician territory in the Primary Chronicle's entry for 981 has itself been the subject of a large and controversial literature. The traditional view that Volodymyr attacked the Cherven cities and Liakhs in order to unite or reunite them with his realm has been challenged by Polish historians like Stefan Mária Kuczyński and Henryk Paszkiewicz, who argue that the attack was really directed against the so-called Lendians, a West Slav or Polish tribe, and that therefore the whole Galician-Volhynian borderland as far east as the Styr River was originally Polish, not East Slavic.[25] This view is forcefully challenged by the Soviet specialist Vladimir Koroliuk, who supports the traditional view that the Cherven cities in question were White Croatian, and therefore East Slavic, and that the Liakhs mentioned in the chronicle simply referred to temporary political control of the region by Poles.[26] The Cherven cities, mentioned in the 981 chronicle entry and

24 Mykhailo Hrushevs'kyi, *Istoriia Ukraïny-Rusy,* vol. II, 2nd rev. ed. (L'viv 1905; reprinted New York: Knyho-spilka 1954), pp. 407–485 and vol. III, 2nd rev. ed. (L'viv 1905; reprinted New York: Knyho-spilka 1954), pp. 1–142.

The Ukrainian view of the Galician-Volhynian principality (often referred to as kingdom) is presented in more recent surveys by Pavlo Hrytsak, *Halyts'ko-volyns'ka derzhava*, NTSh, Biblioteka ukraïnoznavstva, vol. V (New York: NTSh i Vyd–vo Obnova 1958), Ivan P. Kryp''iakevych, *Halyts'ko-volyns'ke kniazivstvo* (Kiev: Naukova dumka 1984); and in several chapters of more general histories of the medieval Ukraine by Stepan Tomashivs'kyi, *Ukraïns'ka istoriia*, vol. I (L'viv 1919), reprinted as *Istoriia Ukraïny starynni i seredni viky* (Munich: Ukraïns'kyi vil'nyi universytet 1949); Omelian Terlets'kyi, *Istoriia ukraïnskoï derzhavy*, vol. I: *Kniazha doba* (L'viv 1923; reprinted New York: Vyd-vo Chartoriis'kykh 1972); V. Budzynovs'kyi, *Istoriia Ukraïny* [vol. I]: *Kniazhyi vik* (L'viv: p.a. 1924), especially pp. 91–160; for Bahalii's work, see n. 18 above.

25 Stefan M. Kuczyński, ''Wschodnia granica państwa polskiego w X wieku (przed 980 r.),'' in *Początki państwa polskiego: księga tysiąclecia,* vol. I: *Organizacja polityczna* (Poznań: Poznańskie Towarzystwo Przyjaciół Nauk 1962), pp. 233–252; Stefan Mária Kuczyński, ''O wyprawie Włodzimierza I ku Lachom na podstawie wziamki z r. 981 w opowiéci lat doczesnych,'' 2nd rev. ed. in his *Studia z dziejów Europy Wschodniej X–XVII w.* (Warsaw PWN 1965), pp. 33–118; Henryk Paszkiewicz, ''The Earliest Rus'ian-Polish Borderlands,'' in his *The Making of the Russian Nation* (London: Darton, Longman, and Todd 1963), especially pp. 336–397.

26 Vladimir D. Koroliuk, *Zapadnye slaviane i Kievskaia Rus' v X–XI vv.* (Moscow: Nauka 1964), especially pp. 73–108.

located between the San-Vistula and Buh valleys along the western border of both Galicia and Volhynia, have also been the subject of much writing. The discussion centers on how many there actually were (Brest, Belz, Cherven/Czerwień, and Przemyśl being the best known), and whether they were originally "Polish," "Czech," "East Slavic," or, in the opinion of A.V. Longinov (one of the first writers to analyze the problem in depth), part of a principality that was independent of both Poland and Kievan Rus'.[27]

Closely related to the problem of Volodymyr's 981 and 993 expeditions against the Liakhs, the Croats, and the Cherven cities is the question of the ethnographic boundary between the Polish and Rus' populations. The subsequent rise of national consciousness in nineteenth-century Galicia provoked friction between Poles and Ukrainians, both of whom tried to buttress their views by pointing to supposed ethnographic boundaries in the early medieval period. The controversy began after studies by the Galician and Subcarpathian Russophile authors Denys Zubryts'kyi and Adol'f Dobrians'kyi argued that in the medieval period the Rus' population was settled as far west as the Dunajec River, thus making the Cherven cities and regions farther west all East Slavic.[28] Subsequent studies by the Russian

27 A.V. Longinov, *Chervenskie goroda: istoricheskii ocherk v sviazi s étnografiei i topografiei Chervonoi Rusi* (Warsaw 1885). For a historiographical survey of the Cherven problem, see Ia.D. Isaievych, "Dzherela pro zakhidni mezhi ukraïns'koï etnichnoï terytoriï v period feodalizmu," *Ukraïns'kyi istorychnyi zhurnal,* XII, 12 (Kiev 1968), pp. 78–84.

Polish writers have argued both for and against the original east Slavic character of the region: Henryk Łowiański, "Problematyka historyczna Grodów Czerwieńskich," *Kwartalnik Historyczny,* LX (Warsaw 1953), pp. 58–85; Andrzej Poppe, "Grod Wołyń," in *Studia Wczesnośredniowieczne,* vol. IV (Warsaw and Wrocław: ZNIO–PAN, 1958); and Konrad Jażdżewski, "Stosunki polsko-ruskie we wczesnym średniowieczu w świetle archeologii," *Pamiętnik Słowiański,* IV (Wrocław and Poznań 1954), pp. 340–360. See also n. 30 below.

The Ukrainian view has recently been presented in Ia.D. Isaievych, "Terytoriia i naseleniia 'chervens'kykh hradiv'," in *Ukraïns'kyi istoryko-heohrafichnyi zbirnyk,* vol. I (Kiev: Naukova dumka 1971), pp. 71–83. See also n. 29 below.

The results of Polish archeological work during the early 1950s in the area of the Cherven cities is discussed in A. Gieysztor, "Prace badawcze na obszarze Grodów Czerwieńskich," *Kwartalnik Historyczny,* LX, 1 (Warsaw 1953), pp. 302–316; A. Gieysztor, "Polskie badania na Grodach Czerwieńskich w latach 1952 i 1953," *Kwartalnik Instytutu Polsko-Radzieckiego,* I, 6 (Warsaw 1954), pp. 144–153; and Henryk Łowmiański, "Problematyka historyczna Grodów Czerwieńskich w związku z planem zespołowych badań polsko-radzieckich," *Kwartalnik Historyczny,* LXVII, 1 (Warsaw 1959), pp. 68–74.

28 Dionysius Zubrzycki, *Gränzen zwisçhen der russinischen und polnischen Nation in Galizien* (L'viv 1849), published in Polish as *Granice między ruskim i polskim narodem w Galicyi* (L'viv 1849); A.I. D [obrianskii], "O zapadnych granitsakh Podkarpatskoi Rusi so vremen sv. Vladimira," *Zhurnal Ministerstva narodnago prosvieshcheniia,* CCVIII (St Petersburg 1880), 134–159.

and Ukrainian authors Evgenii Kryzhanovskii, Ivan Filevych, Myron Korduba (the best on the subject), and most recently Iaroslav Isaievych confirmed the idea of a more westward extension of the Rus' population,[29] while the Poles Adam Szelągowski, Józef Widajewicz, Franciszek Persowski, and Józef Skrzypek strongly oppose such views and consider the region, at least as far east as the Buh River, to have originally been Polish.[30] The whole question of Polish-Rus' relations during the medieval period, which were marked by frequent conflict over the Cherven cities and Polish interference in Galician political life, has been surveyed by the West German specialist Gotthold Rhode, who is skeptical of any Polish presence as far east as the Cherven cities before the eleventh century, as well as by Bronisław Włodarski, who presents the Polish view, and Vladimir D. Koroliuk, who represents the current Soviet view.[31]

The reigns of a few Galician rulers have also been the subject of special studies. As might be expected, the thirteenth-century apogee of Galician history under Prince and later King Danylo has received the most attention in solid monographs by Mykola Dashkevych and Vladimir Pashuto, and in a more recent semipopular biography by Mykola Kotliar.[32] The other reign to be singled out for

29 E.M. Kryzhanovskii, ''Zabuzhnaia Rus','' in his *Sobranie sochinenii*, vol. II (Kiev 1880), pp. 304–404; Ivan Filevich, ''Ocherk karpatskoi territorii i naseleniia,'' *Zhurnal Ministerstva narodnago prosvieshcheniia*, CCXCVIII, 4 (St Petersburg 1895), pp. 361–385, and CCXCIX, 5, pp. 156–218; Myron Korduba, ''Zakhidne pohranyche Halyts'koï Derzhavy mizh Karpatamy ta dolishnym Sianom,'' *Zapysky NTSh*, CXXXVIII–CXL (L'viv 1925), pp. 159–245; idem, ''Stosunki polsko-ukraińskie w wieku X–XIII,'' *Sprawy Narodowościowe*, VII, 6 (Warsaw 1933), pp. 755–759; Ia.D. Isaievych, ''Do pytannia pro zakhidnyi kordon Kyïvs'koï Rusi,'' in *Istorychni dzherela ta ïkh vykorystannia*, vol. VI (Kiev: Naukova dumka 1971), pp. 83–100.

30 Adam Szelągowski, *Kwestya ruska w świetle historyi* (Warsaw: Przegląd Narodowy 1911); Józef Widajewicz, *Południowo-wschodnie kresy Polski w X i XI wieku*, Poznańskie Towarzystwo Przyjaciół Nauk, Prace Komisiji Historycznej, vol. XI, pt 2 (Poznań 1937); Franciszek Persowski, *Studia nad pograniczem polsko-ruskim w X–XI wieku* (Wrocław, Warsaw, and Cracow: ZNIO–PAN 1962); Józef Skrzypek, *Studia nad pierwotnym pograniczem polsko-ruskim w rejonie Wołynia a Grodów Czerwieńskich* (Warsaw: PWN 1962).

31 Gotthold Rhode, *Die Ostgrenze Polens: politische Entwicklung, kulturelle Bedeutung und geistige Auswirkung*, vol. I: *Im Mittelalter bis zum Jahre 1401* (Köln and Graz: Böhlau-Vlg. 1955); Bronisław Włodarski, *Polska i Ruś 1194–1340* (Warsaw: PWN 1966); see the Koroliuk study in n. 26 above, especially pp. 207–232 and 297–330.

See also the more specialized studies by M. Buxbaum, ''Stosunki polsko-ruskie w latach 1288–1328,'' in *Sprawozdanie Dyrekcji Państwego Gimnazjum w Końskich za r. 1931–1932* (Końskie 1932); and Kazimierz Górski, ''Stosunki Kazimierza Sprawiedliwego z Rusią,'' *Przewodnik Naukowy i Literacki*, III (L'viv 1875), pp. 572–584, 649–656, 750–757.

32 Nikolai Dashkevich, *Kniazhenie Daniila Galitskago po russkim i inostrannym izviestiiam* (Kiev 1873), first published in *Universitetskaia izviestiia*, no. 6 (Kiev 1873), 24 p., translated into

special attention is that of Iurii II (reigned 1323–1340), the last ruler of an independent Galicia-Volhynia.[33]

Galicia's importance during the medieval period was due in large measure to its strategic location at the crossroads of major trading routes connecting Kiev and Constantinople in the east and southeast, and with Poland and Hungary in the west and southwest. Izydor Sharanevych has provided an extremely detailed description of the geography of these routes.[34] As for the region's internal socioeconomic structure, Mykhailo Hrushevs'kyi and Myron Korduba have provided descriptions of the various social strata that comprised the region–the prince, burghers, peasants, and powerful boyars.[35] Several Soviet writers have also provided descriptions of the Galician social structure, although they seem especially anxious to stress instances of rebellious discontent among the lower classes.[36] The impact of the Mongol invasion after 1240 upon Galicia has been a focus of specific attention. A controversy has arisen over the degree to which the Galician-Volhy-

---

Ukrainian and published in M. Smyrnov et al., *Monohrafiy do ystoriy Halytskoy Rusy,* Ruska ystorychna biblioteka, vol. V (Ternopil' 1886); V. Pashuto, "Galitsko-Volynskoe kniazhestvo vremen Daniila Romanovicha," *Uchenye zapiski Leningradskago gosudarstvennago universiteta,* no. 67 (Leningrad 1941), pp. 25–82; see also his *Ocherki po istorii Galitsko-Volynskoi Rusi* (Moscow: AN SSSR 1950); Mykola F. Kotliar, *Danylo Halyts'kyi* (Kiev: Naukova dumka 1979). On Danylo's relations with the Vatican, see below, notes 43–44.

33 Jan Řežábek, "Jiří II, poslední kníže veškeré Malé Rusi," *Časopis musea království českého,* LVII (Prague 1883), pp. 120–141 and 194–218; Ernst Kunik, ed., *Boleslav Iurii II: kniaz' vsei Maloi Rusi* (St Petersburg 1907); Mykola Andrusiak, "Ostanni Romanovychi (nashchadky Mstyslava i Romana Danylovychiv)," *Naukovyi zbirnyk Ukraïns'koho Vil'noho Universytetu,* V (Munich 1948), pp. 1–12; and A.V. Longinov, *Gramoty malorusskago kniazia Iuriia II i vkladnaia zapis'kniazia Iuriia Danilovicha Kholmskago XIV vieka* (Moscow 1887). Longinov's study can be supplemented by an extensive critical review: I.A. Linnichenko, "Kriticheskii obzor novieishei literatury po istorii Galitskoi Rusi," *Zhurnal Ministerstva narodnago prosvieshcheniia,* CCLXXV (St Petersburg 1891), especially pp. 147–170.

See also the several documents on the relations between Iurii II and other Galician princes with Muscovy in L.V. Cherepnin, ed., *Dukhovnye i dogovornye gramoty velikikh i udel'nykh kniazei XIV–XVI vv.* (Moscow and Leningrad: Akademiia Nauk SSSR 1950), reprinted as Slavic Reprint Nr. 40 (Düsseldorf and Vaduz, Leichtenstein: Brücken Vlg. and Europe Printing 1970), especially docs 14, 24, 29–38.

34 Ysydor Sharanevych, "Yzslîdovanie na poly otechestvennoi heohrafiy y ystoriy," *Lyteraturnŷi sbornyk Halytsko-russkoi Matytsŷ,* [I], 1–4 (L'viv 1869), pp. 46–139.

35 Mykhailo Hrushevs'kyi, "Halyts'ke boiarstvo XII–XIII v.," *Zapysky NTSh,* XX [6] (L'viv 1897), 20 pp.; Myron Korduba, "Suspil'ni verstvy ta polïtychni partyï v Halyts'kim kniazïvstvi do polovyny XIII stolïtia," *Zapysky NTSh,* XXXI–XXXII (L'viv 1899), 42 pp.

36 Kseniia A. Sofronenko, *Obshchestvenno-politicheskii stroi galitsko-volynskoi Rusi XI–XIII vv.* (Moscow: Gos. izd. iuridicheskoi literatury 1955); V.V. Mavrodin, "O narodnykh dvizheniiakh v Galitsko-Volynskom kniazhestve v XII–XIII vv.," *Uchenye zapiski Leningradskogo gosudarstvennogo universiteta,* no. 48 (Leningrad 1939).

nian Kingdom was obliged to submit to the Golden Horde–some scholars (George Vernadsky and Vladimir Pashuto) seeing total subordination, others (Mykhailo Zhdan) considering the region to have been basically independent, even if its rulers had to pay personal obeisance as well as tribute to the Mongol khans.[37]

Galician-Hungarian relations

Medieval Galicia's relationships with Hungary are an important aspect of the region's history and a considerable literature has grown up on this subject. After reaching the crest of the Carpathian Mountains, Hungary's kings considered expanding into Galicia. Their intervention began in the late eleventh century. Then in 1205 Hungary's ruler András II (reigned 1205–1235), taking advantage of the disarray in Galicia after the death of Prince Roman, added to his royal title–King of Galicia and Lodomeria–a designation that remained part of Hungarian title until the fall of the Habsburgs in 1918. On the basis of this claim, András II, in cooperation with the Polish grand duke, Leszek the White (reigned 1202–1227), had his son Kálmán placed on the Galician throne where the son ruled briefly in 1215–1216 and again in 1220–1221. Hungarian efforts to dominate Galician princes or to annex the region outright were to continue, often with the cooperation of local Galician boyars and Polish rulers, for the next century and a half.

The first period of extensive Hungarian intervention in Galicia during the late twelfth and early thirteenth centuries has received the most attention. There are a few documents from this era published in two multivolume collections on Hungarian diplomacy compiled by György Fejér and Gusztáv Wenzel.[38] Also, all sec-

37 See Pashuto's studies in n. 32; George Vernadsky, "The Royal Serfs (*servi Regales*) of the 'Ruthenian Law' and their Origin," *Speculum,* XXIV, 2 (Cambridge, Mass. 1951), pp. 255–264; Michael B. Zdan, "The Dependence of Halych-Volyn' Rus' on the Golden Horde," *Slavonic and East European Review,* XXXV [85] (London 1957), pp. 505–522; Mykhailo B. Zhdan, "Do pytannia pro zalezhnist' halyts'ko-volyns'koï Rusy vid Zolotoï Ordy," *Ukraïns'kyi istoryk,* IV, 1–2 (New York and Munich 1967), pp. 23–37, IV, 3–4 (1967), pp. 95–102, and V, 1–4 (1968), pp. 69–81.

38 Georgii Fejér, ed., *Codex diplomaticus Hungariae ecclesiasticus ac civilis,* 11 vols in 40 (Buda 1829–1844), see vols, 3, 9, 10, and especially vol. 4, parts 1 and 2. An index to the Fejér collection, with several references to Galicia, is found in Mór Czinár, *Fejér György magyarországi okmánytárának betürendű tárgymutatója* (Pest 1866). Gusztáv Wenzel, ed., *Codex diplomaticus Arpadianus continuatus Árpádkori új okmánytár,* 12 vols [1001–1301], in *Monumenta Hungariae historica / Magyar történelmi emlékek,* vols. VI–XIII, XVII, XVIII, XX, XXII (Pest 1860–74).

tions pertaining to Hungary that appear in the Kievan and Galician-Volhynian chronicles have been collected into one volume, which includes the original Slavonic texts as well as Hungarian translations.[39]

As for secondary works, Hungarian-Galician relations during the late twelfth and early thirteenth centuries have been surveyed by the Subcarpathian scholar Ivan Haraida, while the interaction between Polish and Hungarian interests in Galicia during this same period are discussed in works by Bronisław Włodarski and Ludwik Droba.[40] There are also specific studies devoted to Prince Danylo's mid-century accord with Hungarians and to the familial ties between the Galician and Hungarian royal houses.[41]

Church history

The history of the church has always been of central concern for Galician historians and Antin Petrushevych has written an extensive chronological survey covering the twelfth and thirteenth centuries.[42] As the farthest western Orthodox Rus' land, Galicia was in constant contact with Roman Catholic Poland and Hungary and it was inevitably exposed to the efforts of Rome to unite the Christian world. Indeed, attempts at church union were tried several times throughout the thirteenth century, and these have been investigated with sympathy and in great detail by Mykola Chubatyi.[43] One of the high points in these efforts came in 1253 when

39 Antal Hodinka, comp., *Az orosz évkönyvek magyar vonatkozásai* (Budapest: Magyar tudományi akadémia kiadása 1916), especially pt 3, pp. 275–486, which includes excerpts from the Kievan and Galician-Volhynian chronicles (Hypatian manuscript) as well as the Hustyn Chronicle, covering the years 1188 to 1292.

40 Yvan Haraida, "Halyts'ka polytyka uhorskykh korolëv Beilŷ III-ho y Andriia II-ho," *Zoria/Hajnal*, III, 1–4 (Uzhhorod 1943), pp. 119–176; Bronisław Włodarski, *Polityka ruska Leszka Białego* (L'viv 1925); Ludwik Droba, "Stosunki Leszka Białego z Rusią i Węgrami," *Rozprawy .., Wydziału Historyczno-filozoficznego Akademii Umiejętnośći*, XIII (Cracow 1881), pp. 361–429.

41 Bohdan Barvins'kyi, *Zizd kniazia Danyla z uhors'kym korolem Beloiu IV v Preshburzi 1250 r.* (L'viv 1901); A.V. Longinov, "Rodstvennye otnosheniia russkikh kniazei s vengerskim korolevskim domom," *Trudy Vilenskago predvaritel'nago komiteta po ustroistve v Vil'ne IX arkheologicheskago s''ezda* (Vilnius 1893).

42 Anton Petrushevych, "O sobornoi bohorodychnoi tserkvî v Halychî" and "O halytskykh epyskopakh so vremen uchrezhdeniia Halytskoi eparkhii dazhe do kontsa XIII vîka," *Halytskii ystorycheskii sbornyk ... Halytsko-russkoi Matytsŷ*, vols I-III (L'viv 1853–60), pp. 49–150, 3–195, 3–59 and clxxix pp. See also A.S. Petrushevych, *Kratkoe ystorycheskoe yzvîstie o vvedeniy khrystianstva v Predkarpatskykh stranakh vo vremena sv. Kyrylla y Mefodiia* (L'viv: Halytsko-russkaia Matytsŷ 1882).

43 Mykola Chubatyi, "Zakhidna Ukraïna i Rym u XIII vitsï u svoïkh zmahaniakh do tserkovnoï uniï," *Zapysky NTSh*, CXXIII–CXXIV (L'viv 1917), 108 pp.

Prince Danylo, seeking western allies in his struggle against the Tatars, agreed to receive a royal crown from the Pope. Danylo's short-lived relations with Rome are the subject of extensive studies by Mykola Dashkevych, who treats them in the diplomatic context of medieval *Realpolitik,* and the Soviet scholar Vladimir Pashuto, who considers the episode as but another in a series of Vatican-inspired acts of aggression against the people of Rus'.[44]

With the transfer in 1299 of the metropolitan seat of the Rus' church from Kiev northward to Vladimir-Suzdal and then in 1328 to Moscow, Galician rulers became convinced of the need for their own metropolitan. At the same time, the Byzantine Orthodox patriarch feared the movements toward union with Rome that continued to exist in Galicia. Thus, in 1303 he authorized the creation of a Galician metropolitanate, with its seat in Halych. The Muscovite metropolitans feared this new rival, however, and eventually succeeded in having the Galician metropolitanate abolished in 1347. The complex negotiations of secular and religious leaders that led to the creation of the Galician metropolitanate, as well as its short-lived history and the efforts to revive it throughout the rest of the fourteenth century, are treated in detail by I. Tikhomirov and A. Pavlov.[45]

Cultural and urban history

Medieval Galicia-Volhynia also made important cultural advances, especially in literature, art, and architecture. Iaroslav Isaievych has provided general surveys of these achievements.[46] Further details are available in the several studies that

---

On the mission of two papal emissaries to gain peace with the Mongols and at the same time their activity on behalf of church union in Galicia, see Boleslaw Szczęśniak, ''Benoît le Polonais, dit le Vrtislavien et son rôle dans l'union de la Ruthénie de Halicz avec Rome en 1246,'' *Antemurale,* I (Rome 1954), pp. 39–50; and idem, ''The Mission of Giovanni di Plano Carpini and Benedict the Pole of Vratislavia to Halicz,'' *Journal of Ecclesiastical History,* VII, 1 (London 1956), pp. 12–20.

44 Nikolai Dashkevich, *Pervaia uniia iugozapadnoi Rusi s katolichestvom* (Kiev 1884), first published in *Universitetskiia izviestiia,* no. 8 (Kiev 1884); V.T. Pashuto, ''O politike papskoi kurii na Rusi (XIII v.),'' *Voprosy istorii,* V, 5 (Moscow 1949), pp. 52–76.

See also the chapter, ''Secret Talks of Danylo Romanovych with the Roman Curia,'' in A.S. Petrushevych, *Ystorycheskoe yzvîstie o tserkvy sv. Panteleimona blyz horoda Halycha, teper' kostelî sv. Stanyslava oo. Frantsyskanov, iako drevnîishem pamiatnykî romanskoho zodchestva na Halytskoi Rusy s pervoi polovynŷ XIII stolîtiia* (L'viv 1881).

45 A. Pavlov, *O nachalie Galitskoi i Litovskoi mitropolii i o pervykh tamoshnykh mitropolitakh po vizantiiskim dokumental'nym istochnikam XIV vieka* (St Petersburg 1894), first published in *Russkoe obozrienie,* V, 5 (St Petersburg 1894), pp. 214–251; I.D. Tikhomirov, *Galitskaia mitropoliia: tserkovno-istoricheskoe izsliedovanie* (St Petersburg 1895).

46 Ia.D. Isaevich, ''Kul'tura Galitsko-Volynskoi Rusi,'' *Voprosy istorii,* XXIX, 1 (Moscow

deal with individual medieval Galician cities. Many of these works focus on archeological remains, which serve as primary sources for historical descriptions. The most extensive literature is on Halych, which was founded at the turn of the tenth century, served as capital of the Galician-Volhynian principality (1141–1241), and then was the seat of Galicia's short-lived metropolitanate (1301–1347). After some debate, it was established that medieval Halych was located at the village of Krylos, about six kilometers south of the present-day town of Halych. The earliest histories and archeological descriptions of Halych were done in the nineteenth century by Izydor Sharanevych, Antin Petrushevych, and Aleksander Czołowski.[47] The results of later archeological discoveries prompted new studies by Iaroslav Pasternak[48] and by several Soviet authors.[49] There are also historico-archeological studies of L'viv, capital of the Galician-Volhynian princi-

---

1973), pp. 92–107; idem, "Iz istorii kul'turnykh sviazei Galitsko-volynskoi Rusi s zapadnymi slavianami v XII–XIV vv.," in B.A. Rybakov, ed., *Pol'sha i Rus': cherty obshchnosti i svoeobraziia v istoricheskom razvitii Rusi i Pol'shi XII–XIV vv.* (Moscow: Nauka 1974), pp. 261–275.

47 Ysydor Sharanevych, *Staroruskii kniazhii horod Halych: krytychne studium* (L'viv: Zoria 1880), first appeared as "Na kotrôm mîsttsy nŷnîshnoho Halycha y ieho okrestnosty stoiav staroruskii kniazhii horod Halych?" *Zoria*, I, 10–13 (L'viv 1880), pp. 127–129, 140–143, 155–158, and 172–175: Izydor Szaraniewicz, *Trzy opisy historyczne staroksiążęcego grodu Halicza w roku 1860, 1880 i 1882* (L'viv: Gubrynowicz i Schmidt 1883); idem, "O rezultatach poszukiwań archeologicznych w okolicy Halicza w r. 1883," *Przegląd Archeologiczny*, III (L'viv 1883), pp. 3–9 and "O rezultatach poszukiwań archeologicznych w okolicy Halicza w roku 1884 i 1885," *ibid.*, IV (1886), also separately (L'viv 1886); A. Petrushevych, *Krytyko-ystorycheskiia razsuzhdeniia o naddnîstrianskom horodî Halychî y eho dostopamiatnostiakh* (L'viv 1888); Aleksander Czołowski, *O położeniu starego Halicza*, in *Pamiętnik II. Zjazdu historyków polskich* (L'viv 1899).

48 Iaroslav Pasternak, *Staryi Halych: arkheolohichno-istorychni doslidy u 1850–1943 rr.* (Cracow and L'viv: Ukraïns'ke vyd-vo 1944). See also the earlier: idem, "Halyts'ka katedra u Krylosi (tymchasove zvidomlennia z rozkopiv u 1936 i 1937 r.)," *Zapysky NTSh*, CLIV (L'viv 1937), pp. i–xxi; and Lev Chachkovs'kyi and Iaroslav Khmilevs'kyi, *Kniazhyi Halych* (Stanyslaviv 1938), 2nd rev. ed. (Chicago: Ukraïns'kyi Arkhiv-Muzei 1959).

49 V.K. Honcharov, *Arkheolohichni doslidzhennia drevn'oho Halycha u 1951 r.* (Kiev 1955); idem, "Drevnyi Halych," *Visnyk AN URSR*, XXVII, 1 (Kiev 1956), pp. 61–67; V. Hrabovets'kyi and P. Arsenych, *Halych* (L'viv 1964).

principality after 1241;[50] of Zvenyhorod,[51] Przemyśl,[52] and Terebovlia,[53] ancient centers that served as the seats of Galician princes before the territory was united with Volhynia; and of Belz[54] and Sambir.[55]

50 Isydor Sharanevych, *Starodavnŷi L'vôv,* Starodavnŷy halytskïi horodŷ, pt 2 (L'viv 1861); A.S. Petrushevych, *Lynhvystychesko-ystorycheskiia yzslîdovaniia o nachatkakh horoda L'vova y okresnostei eho s vozzrîniem na predystorycheskiia vremena pereseleniia slovenskykh y rumŷnskykh plemen yz prydunaiskykh stran v predkarpatskiia oblasty* (L'viv 1893); Aleksander Czołowski, ''Lwów za ruskich czasów,'' *Kwartalnik Historyczny,* V, 4 (L'viv 1891), pp. 779–812.

51 Vasylii Yl'nytskïi, *Starodavnŷi Zvenyhorod,* Starodavnŷy halytskïy horody, vol. I (L'viv 1861); Mykhailo Hrushevs'kyi, ''Zvenyhorod halyts'kyi: istorychno-arkheol'ogichna rozvidka,'' *Zapysky NTSh,* XXXI–XXXII (L'viv 1899), 28 p.; V.V. Hrabovets'kyi, *Zvenyhorod* (L'viv: Knyzhkovo-zhurnal'ne vyd-vo 1959).

52 Anatol Lewicki, *Obrazki z najdawniejszych dziejów Przemyśla* (Przemyśl 1881); Franciszek Sikora, *Dokumenty i kancelaria Przemysła i oraz Bolesława Pobożnego 1239–1279 na tle współczesnej dyplomatyki Wielkopolskiej,* PAN-Oddział w Krakowie, Prace Komisiji Nauk Historycznego, vol. XXII (Wrocław, Warsaw, and Cracow: ZNIO–PAN 1969).

53 Vasylii Yl'nytskïi, *Starodavna Tieriebovlia,* Starodavnŷy halytskïy horodŷ, vol. III (L'viv 1862).

54 Lev Chachkovs'kyi, ''Kniazhyi Belz,'' *Zapysky NTSh,* CLIV (L'viv 1937), pp. 15–30.

55 I.P. Kryp''iakevych, ''Kniazhyi Sambir i Sambirs'ka volost','' *Litopys Boikivshchyny,* no. 10 (Sambir 1938), pp. 26–33.

Chapter 4

1340–1772

Background

The years 1340 to 1772 comprise the Polish era of Galician history. This era actually began with a transition period following the assassination in 1340 of Iurii II, the last Romanovych ruler of the Galician-Volhynian Kingdom, and the entry of Polish forces dispatched by Casimir the Great (reigned 1333–1370), who laid dynastic claims to Galicia as part of his expansive drive toward the east. For close to half a century, from 1340 to 1387, Galicia was to experience almost continuous instability because of foreign invasion by Tatars and by various claimants to rule Galicia and Volhynia, as well as revolts led by local boyars. Among the claimants to the Galician-Volhynian patrimony were its neighbors, Poland, Lithuania, and Hungary, each of which ruled the territory for varying periods of time. Finally, by 1387, Poland reached agreements with Lithuania and Hungary, so that from that time Galicia remained under the jurisdiction of the kings of Poland. As for the principality of Belz (which since 1234 had been part of Galicia), it too came under Polish sovereignty, but first as part of Mazovia and then as a distinct palatinate; neighboring Volhynia was incorporated into the Grand Duchy of Lithuania.

Within Poland, Galicia was initially known as the Rus' land (*Ziemia Ruska* or *Ruś Czerwona*). Its boundaries more or less coincided with those of the medieval principality of Galicia (before the 1234 acquisition of Belz), and it was ruled by deputies (*starosta*) appointed by the king to handle administrative, legal, and military affairs. During the first decades of the fifteenth century, Galicia was administratively integrated with other lands in the Polish Kingdom, and it became the Rus' palatinate (*Województwo Ruskie*) with its administrative center in L'viv. The Rus' palatinate was further divided into four administrative-territorial units known as lands (*ziemie*): L'viv, Halych, Przemyśl, and Sanok. During the sixteenth century, a fifth land, Chełm, was added to the Rus' palatinate. By 1434, the

GALICIA IN THE POLISH-LITHUANIAN COMMONWEALTH
International borders, c.1600
Polish palatinates
Lands (Ziemie) of the Galician Rus' palatinate
Sanok Administrative centers of the Galician Rus' lands
0 50 MILES
0 50 KILOMETERS
N
SANDOMIERZ
LUBLIN
GALICIA (RUS')
Chełm
Zamość
Wieprz
Buh
Volodymyr
Luts'k
VOLHYNIA
BELZ
Belz
CRACOW
Vistula
San
Wisłok
Przeworsk
Jarosław
Przemyśl
Sudova Vyshnia
Zhovkva
L'viv
Brody
Pochaiv
Zbarazh
Ternopil'
Krosno
GALICIA
Univ
Sanok
Lesko
Sambir
Berezhany
Rohatyn
Dunajec
Mshanets'
Drohobych
Dniester
Zbruch
Seret
Halych
PODOLIA
CARPATHIAN
MOUNTAINS
(RUS')
Košice
Uzhhorod
Kam''ianets' Podil's'kyi
HUNGARY
Kolomyia
Tysa
Cheremosh
Chernivtsi
Prut
MOLDAVIA
OTTOMAN EMPIRE

Polish court system was introduced and the Galician nobility was given more clearly defined privileges by the king.

Even before consolidating its control in 1387, Poland's rulers tried to make Galicia politically, socially, and culturally a part of Poland. With regard to Galicia's traditional ruling class, the landowning boyars, those who had fought against Polish expansion were forced to give up their holdings and emigrate to Orthodox Rus' lands held by Lithuania in the east or to Orthodox Moldavia and Wallachia in the south. On the other hand, many boyars received charters from Polish kings confirming their property rights and even awarding them new lands. A portion of the Galician ruling elite was thereby co-opted into the new political system, and although they retained their Rus' faith, as members of Poland's heraldic nobility (*szlachta*) they later came to consider themselves Poles in terms of political loyalty. Noble status was particularly important in Poland, because by the sixteenth century that country had, in essence, become a ''republic of nobles,'' in which at the national and in particular the local level, political, legal, socioeconomic, and to a large extent cultural life was controlled or directed by the nobility. To be sure, there were great discrepancies between wealth and therefore power in the different strata of the nobility–magnates, gentry, petty gentry–but in theory all were politically equal and held hereditary rank. The desire among Galicians to enjoy all the privileges and social prestige of noble status in Poland led many to abandon their Rus'-Ukrainian faith and language for Roman Catholicism and Polish culture. This assimilatory trend among the upper strata of Galician-Ukrainian society was particularly marked beginning with the second half of the sixteenth century.

Polish rule also brought into the Galician countryside an influx of Polish and central European nobles as well as Roman Catholic peasants. In towns and cities, the numbers of Germans, Poles, and Armenians increased, and these were later joined by Jews. Since the noble's wealth depended on landholding and the exploitation of agriculture, and since Poland's economy was restructured to respond to the demand for grain exports during the sixteenth century, the need for a fixed labor supply became paramount, resulting in the legal enserfment of the peasantry. Although there were variations throughout Galicia, by the end of the sixteenth century, serfdom was the norm and some peasants were obliged to provide an ever increasing number of work days for the domains of their lords.

The Polish presence in Galicia also affected culture. As in the rest of Poland, Latin became the official language of administration. The Roman Catholic church expanded its activity, establishing a Latin rite archdiocese in Halych as early as 1365; it was later transferred to L'viv in 1414. The L'viv archdiocese also became the metropolitan see for Roman Catholic dioceses serving not only the Rus' palatinate (L'viv-Halych, Przemyśl, Chełm), but all the Ukrainian lands as well.

Concomitantly, there was a decline in the status of the Orthodox church (comprising the dioceses of Halych-L'viv, Chełm, and Przemyśl in Galicia). The distinct Galician Orthodox metropolitanate formed at the outset of the fourteenth century to unite these dioceses fell victim to the complexities of eastern church politics, especially the opposition from the metropolitan of Kiev and all Rus' residing in Moscow. In 1401, the Galician metropolitanate was abolished and its dioceses made subordinate once again to the metropolitan see of Kiev. Even more serious was the fact that the Orthodox bishop of Halych was not replaced after 1406, and for the next 130 years the diocese was administered by lay persons, many of whom were appointed by the Roman Catholic archbishop of L'viv-Halych. Although the Orthodox bishopric of Halych was restored in 1539, the fate of the Orthodox church in Galicia–which was the symbol of Rus'-Ukrainian culture in the region–continued to decline.

The Ukrainian reaction to these developments took different forms. Whereas the increase in serfdom prompted sporadic peasant uprisings, the most famous being one in southeastern Galicia in 1490–1492, led by a Moldavian named Mukha, a more typical pattern was flight eastward. In fact, much of the virgin Ukrainian steppe in the Dnieper valley was settled during the sixteenth and seventeenth century by peasants fleeing Galicia.

On the cultural front, there occurred a revival during the sixteenth century aimed at restoring the legal and moral status of the Orthodox church and in improving its intellectual standards. First led in the 1570s by Orthodox nobles from Galicia and most especially Volhynian magnates led by Prince Konstantyn of Ostrih (1527–1608), the cultural and religious revival was before long centered in the cities, especially L'viv. There, in the 1580s, a group of townsmen and petty nobles founded a brotherhood in association with the Orthodox Church of the Assumption. Although established at lay initiative, the L'viv Assumption Brotherhood strove to enhance the status of the Orthodox church and community through the establishment of schools, printing houses, hospitals, and orphanages. Most important, the L'viv brotherhood received, in 1589, the status of stauropegia, that is, it was responsible only to the patriarch, or head of the Orthodox church in Constantinople, and not to the local Orthodox bishop. The L'viv Assumption, or Stauropegial Brotherhood, also became the leader and provided the model for other brotherhoods that were established not only in Galicia (Przemyśl, Rohatyn, Horodok) but also in Kiev and other cities of Volhynia and Belorussia.

In a sense, by the late sixteenth century, Galicia, and especially L'viv, became the most important center of religious and intellectual life for all Orthodox Rus' lands within Poland. It is, therefore, not surprising that the controversial question of church unity was related in large measure to developments in Galicia. Actually, since the split between Rome and Constantinople in 1054, there had been several attempts to unite the Catholic and Orthodox worlds. Even the magnates who led the Orthodox Rus' cultural revival in Poland during the 1570s discussed the feasibility of church union.

It was actually the Orthodox bishop of L'viv, Gedeon Balaban (1530–1607, consecrated 1569), who initiated a new attempt at union. Jealous of the prerogatives and what he perceived as interference in church affairs by the Stauropegial Brotherhood, Balaban turned to the Roman Catholic archbishop of L'viv and began to discuss the possibility of union. Balaban was joined by several other Orthodox bishops and the metropolitan of Kiev; encouraged by the Polish king, two Orthodox hierarchs journeyed to Rome and declared for union. Upon their return they called a synod at Brest in 1596 and proclaimed the union. In the meantime, however, Bishop Balaban had changed his mind, and backed by several Orthodox magnates and the brotherhood, he opposed the Union of Brest that had brought into being the so-called Uniate church, that is, one whose liturgy and practices (including married clergy) remained Eastern Orthodox but which recognized the Pope as supreme authority. For his part, the Polish king not only recognized the new Uniate church as legal, he at the same time outlawed the Orthodox church and its supporters.

The precarious position of the Orthodox church in Galicia and other Rus' lands within Poland was somewhat improved by the issuance of several decrees legalizing its existence and culminating in a royal charter of 1632. However, after the Zaporozhian Cossack revolution of 1648, the position of the Orthodox church worsened considerably and Orthodox hierarchs in Galicia at first secretly and then openly passed over to the Uniate church. Finally, in 1708, the Stauropegial Brotherhood, which from its establishment had been the primary defender of Orthodoxy, became Uniate. While the more than century-long struggle since the Union of Brest resulted in the abolition of Orthodoxy in Galicia, it also prompted a spirited Uniate-Orthodox polemic enhanced by numerous publications produced on local printing presses and written by talented authors like Ivan Vyshens'kyi (c. 1550–1620) and Lavrentii Zyzanii (d.c. 1634), who were either natives of or worked in Galicia. The territory also produced a number of Orthodox leaders who emigrated eastward where they played an important role in Ukrainian developments, such as the Zaporozhian Cossack hetman, Petro Konashevych Sahaidachnyi (d. 1622); archimandrite of the Monastery of the Caves in Kiev, Ielysei Pletenets'kyi (1550–1624); and metropolitan of Kiev, Iov Borets'kyi (d. 1631, consecrated 1620). Finally, while the Uniate church was subordinate to Rome, it did maintain the liturgy and traditions of the Orthodox world, so that by the eighteenth century this hybrid ecclesiastical structure was well on its way to becoming the symbol of Galician-Ukrainian culture and identity.

In reality, Galician society during the Polish era became divided into several different classes that coincided largely with different ethnic groups. The Ukrainians comprised the vast majority of the enserfed peasant masses and a small strata of Orthodox and later Uniate clergy. The Ukrainian elite, that is, the few magnates and larger number of gentry who had at least retained their ancestral Orthodox faith before the Union of Brest, rapidly converted to Latin Rite Catholicism and assimilated totally to Polish culture during the seventeenth century. This process was to a lesser degree true among the petty gentry (especially in the villages), many of whom remained adherents of the eastern church and continued to use Ukrainian in their everyday lives. As for burghers, these were primarily Jews and smaller numbers of Armenians and Germans who dominated urban and small-town commercial and artisan activity. The Poles, including some rural peasants and urban dwellers, dominated the administrative/noble class, which was made up either of individuals who had immigrated from western Polish lands or local polonized Ukrainians.

Polish domination over Galicia–both political and cultural–seemed complete during the late seventeenth and most of the eighteenth centuries. The only brief threat came during the great Cossack revolution of 1648 led by Hetman Bohdan Khmel'nyts'kyi (c. 1595–1657). Khmel'nyts'kyi invaded Galicia twice and laid siege to L'viv in 1648 and 1655, but his presence did not alter the existing sociopolitical system, although discontented peasants revolted and then fled eastward when the Cossacks retreated.

Another form of protest against Polish rule–peasant uprisings and the brigand movement (*opryshky*)–occurred during the late seventeenth and early eighteenth centuries. However, the peasant movement was sporadic, while the brigands restricted their activity to the Carpathian Mountains and the Pokuttia region as far as the Dniester River. Thus, Polish rule remained firmly entrenched in Galicia and was basically undisturbed by internal developments. It was only the international situation of the 1770s, leading to the first partition of Poland by her neighbors, that was to have a decisive impact on Galicia's future.

General surveys and sources

There are no general surveys that concentrate exclusively on the history of Galicia during the era of Polish rule. The closest to such a survey is the chronicle of events undertaken as part of a lifetime project by Antin Petrushevych. Four of his volumes and the beginnings of a fifth cover the years 1500 to 1549 and 1600 to 1772.[1]

1 Petrushevych's incomplete chronicle for the sixteenth century was published posthumously by

While there may be no general surveys of the era of Polish rule, in contrast, the amount and quality of published sources is better than for any other period of Galician history. The Soviet Ukrainian scholars Ivan Kryp''iakevych, Mykola Koval's'kyi, and Iaroslav Isaievych have prepared comprehensive guides to the wide variety of published sources about Galicia before 1772.[2] Numerous collections of documents exist on the history of the church, the brotherhood movement, the Khmel'nyts'kyi era, and the city of L'viv.[3] Of a more general nature are four collections, which deal with manorial administration, urban life, legal questions, and the socioeconomic conditions of the peasantry from the mid-fourteenth through the seventeenth centuries.[4]

The most ambitious undertaking of documentary sources is found in the twenty-five volumes from local castle (*grodzkie*) and regional (*ziemskie*) court registers found in the Bernardine Archive in L'viv and compiled by Polish scholars beginning in the second half of the nineteenth century. The first nine volumes contain documents from the years 1244 to 1768 that deal with problems

---

Pylyp Svystun: A.S. Petrushevych, ''Svodnaia lietopis' 16-ago vieka,'' *Viestnik 'Narodnago Doma'*, XXXII (X), 1–7? (L'viv 1914), pp. 3–17, 35–46, 60–70, 92–104. Later years are covered in idem, *Svodnaia halytsko-russkaia lîtopys' s 1600 po 1700 hod* (L'viv 1874), first appearing in *Lyteraturnŷi sbornyk Halytsko-russkoi Matytsŷ, 1872 y 1873* [IV–V] (L'viv 1874), pp. 1–700; idem, *Dopolneniia ko Svodnoi halytsko-russkoi lîtopysy s 1600 po 1700 hod yzdannoi vo L'vovî 1874 h.* (L'viv 1891); idem, *Svodnaia halychsko-russkaia lîtopys' s 1700 do kontsa avhusta 1772 h.* (L'viv 1887); idem, *Dopolneniia 'Svodnoi halytsko-russkoi lîtopysy s 1700–1772 hh.'*, pt 1 (L'viv 1896) and pt 2 in *Lyteraturnŷi sbornyk Halytsko-russkoi Matytsŷ, za 1897 hod* (L'viv 1897), pp. 1–519.

2 See the works of Kryp''iakevych and Koval's'kyi, chapter 1, n. 3, and of Isaievych and Koval's'kyi in notes 65 and 73 below.

3 See notes 29, 50–53, 66–68, 88–89 below.

4 Iakov F. Holovatskii and A.S. Petrushevych, eds, ''Pamiatnyky dyplomatycheskoho y sudebno-dîlovoho iazŷka russkoho v drevnem Halytsko-Volodymyrskom kniazhestvî y v sumezhnŷkh russkykh oblastiakh, s vtoroi polovynŷ XIV stolîtiia,'' *Naukovŷi sbornyk Halytsko-russkoi Matytsŷ,* I (L'viv 1865), pp. 180–200; II (1866), pp. 36–56; III (1867), pp. 135–161; Mykhailo Hrushevs'kyi, ''Materialy do istoriï suspil'no-politychnykh i ekonomichnykh vidnosyn Zakhidn'oï Ukraïny,'' *Zapysky NTSh,* LXIII–LXIV (L'viv 1905), v and 94 pp. and LXIX (1906), pp. 84–166; idem, ed., *Opysy korolïvshchyny v zemliakh rus'kykh XVI viku: Liustratsiï zemel' Halyts'koï, Peremys'koï, Sianots'koï, Kholms'koï, Belz'koï i L'vivs'koï,* 4 vols, Zherela do istoryï Ukraïny-Rusy, vols. I–III, VII (L'viv: Arkheografichna komisyia NTSh 1895–1903); Kazimierz Arłamowski, Wanda Kaput, and Emilia Arłamonowska, eds, *Lustracja Województwa Ruskiego 1661–1665,* vol. I: *Ziemia przemyska i sanocka,* vol. II: *Ziemia Lwowska,* vol. III: *Ziemie halicka i chełmska,* Lustracje dóbr królewskich XVI–XVIII wieku (Wrocław, Warsaw, Cracow, and Gdańsk: ZNIO–PAN 1970–76). See also ''Lustracya starostwa Halickiego 1566 roku,'' in *Biblioteka Ordynacyi Krasińskich, Muzeum Konstantego Swidzińskiego,* vol. II (Warsaw 1876), pp. 354–402.

of manorial land administration and city life. Volumes eleven through nineteen contain the results of court proceedings from tribunals at Sanok, 1423–1552 (volumes 11 and 16); Halych, 1435–1475 (volume 12); Przemyśl and Przeworsk, 1436–1506 (volumes 13 and 18); L'viv, 1440–1500 (volumes 14–15); Przemyśl and L'viv, 1469–1506 (volume 17); and Przeworsk, 1458–1506 (volume 19). The last six volumes contain the proceedings of the dietines (*sejmiki*) at Sudova Vyshnia, 1572–1732 (volumes 20–22); Sudova Vyshnia, L'viv, Przemyśl, Sanok, 1731–1772 (volume 23); and Halych, 1575–1772 (volumes 24–25).[5]

Period of transition, 1340–1387

The first problem to receive attention in the literature is the transition period between 1340 and 1387, when Poland, Lithuania, and Hungary put forth claims for the Galician-Volhynian inheritance, while at the same time local boyars, led for a time by Dmytro Ded'ko (d. 1349), allied with one or more of the surrounding rival states, as well as with the Tatars in an attempt to maintain authority over their homeland. Control over all or part of Galicia-Volhynia changed numerous times during these years, and the actions of all the powers concerned have been outlined by Ivan Filevych, Mykhailo Hrushevs'kyi, and more recently Gotthold Rhode.[6] The Polish viewpoint regarding these complicated years was put forth by Kazimierz Gorżycki and in a comprehensive monograph by Henryk Paszkiewicz, both of whom emphasize Poland's supposed historical right to Galicia, whose eventual unity with Poland they consider to have been advantageous to the otherwise unfortunate province.[7] The problem of succession to the Galician-Volhynian

5 Oktaw Pietruski, Xawery Liske, Antoni Prochazka, and Wojciech Hejnosz, eds, *Akta grodzkie i ziemskie z czasów Rzeczypospolitej Polskiej z archiwum tak zwanego Bernardyńskiego we Lwowie,* 25 vols (L'viv 1868–1935).

6 Ivan P. Filevich, *Bor'ba Pol'shi i Litvy-Rusi za galitsko-vladimirskoe nasliedie* (St Petersburg 1890), first published in *Zhurnal Ministerstva narodnago prosvieshcheniia,* CCLXVI–CCLXVII (St Petersburg 1889), pp. 135–187, 280–304 and CCLXVIII (1890), pp. 95–135, 253–302, and 119–168; Mykhailo Hrushevs'kyi, *Istoriia Ukraïny-Rusy,* vol. IV (L'viv 1903), 2nd rev. ed. (Kiev 1907; reprinted New York: Knyho-spilka 1955), especially pp. 20–62 and 101–124; Gotthold Rhode, *Die Ostgrenze Polens,* vol. I: *im Mittelalter bis zum Jahre 1401* (Köln and Graz: Böhlau-Vlg. 1955), especially pp. 172–206, 228–241, and 260–316. See also Volodymyr Myl'kovych, *Studiï krytychni nad istoriieu rus'ko-pol's'koiu (1340–1387)* (L'viv: Stavropihiia 1893).

7 Kazimierz Gorżycki, *Połączenie Rusi Czerwonej z Polską za Kazimierza Wielkiego* (L'viv 1889); Henryk Paszkiewicz, *Polityka ruska Kazimierza Wielkiego,* Rozprawy Historyczne Towarzystwa Naukowego Warszawskiego, vol. IV (Warsaw 1925).

See also Stanisław Zakrzewski, "Wpływ sprawy ruskiej na państwo Polskie w XIV w.," *Przegląd Historyczny,* XXIII, 1 (Warsaw and L'viv 1921), pp. 66–121; and the extensive critique of Gorżycki by Ivan Linnichenko, "Kriticheskii obzor novieishii literatury po istorii

inheritance and whether the Polish king, Casimir the Great, ever established any real control over the area during the 1340s are the subjects of solid studies by Antoni Prochaska and Omelian Terlets'kyi.[8] Finally, a recent work by Paul Knoll surveys Polish policies toward Galicia and the east throughout the reign of Casimir, while earlier works by Ivan Matiïv, Ernest Breiter, and Aleksy Gilewicz focus on the Polish-Hungarian struggle for Galicia and on Władysław Opolski, the Polish duke who ruled Galicia from 1372 to 1378.[9]

The establishment and impact of Polish rule

The changes that occurred in the administrative and social structure of Galicia as a result of Polish rule have been the subject of numerous studies. During the late nineteenth century, Polish scholars had already compiled a multivolume encyclopedia-like work describing the geography, demography, economy, growth of cities, and administration of pre-partition Poland; it includes extensive sections dealing specifically with Galicia (*Województwo Ruskie*).[10] Similar works describing all aspects of Galicia appeared at the outset of the twentieth century by the Polish historians Aleksander Jabłonowski, who covered the sixteenth century, and Władysław Łoziński, who concentrated on the first half of the seventeenth century, the apogee of Polish power and influence in eastern Europe.[11] More recently,

---

Galitskoi Rusi,'' *Zhurnal Ministerstva narodnago prosvieshcheniia*, CCLXXVI (St Petersburg, 1891), pp. 454–492.

8 Antoni Prochaska, ''W sprawie zajęcia Rusi przez Kazimierza Wielkiego,'' *Kwartalnik Historyczny*, VI, 1 (L'viv 1892), pp. 1–33; Antoni Prochaska, ''Pryczynek do sprawy zajęcia Rusi przez Kazimierza W.,'' in his ''Urywki z dziejów XIV wieku,'' *Kwartalnik Historyczny*, XVIII, 2 (L'viv 1904), pp. 210–213; Omelian Terletskyi, ''Politychni podiï na halytskii Rusy v r. 1340 po smerti Boleslava Iuriia II,'' *Zapysky NTSh*, XII, 4 (L'viv 1896), 24 pp.

9 Paul W. Knoll, *The Rise of the Polish Monarchy: Piast Poland in East Central Europe, 1320–1370* (Chicago and London: University of Chicago Press 1971), especially pp. 121–177; Johann Matijów, ''Der polnisch-ungarische Streit um Galizien und Lodomerien,'' in *Jahresbericht des k.k. zweiten Obergymnasiums im Lemberg für 1886* (L'viv 1886); Ernest T. Breiter, *Władysław książe Opolski, pan na Wieluniu, Dobrzyniu i Kujawach, palatyn węgierski i wielkorządca Polski i Rusi: zarys biograficzny* (L'viv: p.a. 1889); Aleksy Gilewicz, ''Stanowisko i działalność gospodarcza Władysława Opolczyka na Rusi w latach 1372–1378,'' in *Prace Historyczne . . . ku uczczeniu . . . Akademickiego Koła Historyków Uniwersytetu Jana Kazimierza we Lwowie 1878–1928* (L'viv: Akademicke Kolo Historyków 1929), pp. 3–52.

10 Michał Baliński and Tymoteusz Lipiński, *Starożytna Polska pod względem historycznym, jeograficznym i statystycznym opisana*, 3 vols in 4 pts (Warsaw: S. Orgelbrand 1843–50), 2nd rev. ed. by F.K. Martynowski, 4 vols (Warsaw: S. Orgelbrand 1885–86); vol. II, pp. 650–985, covers the *Województwo Ruskie*.

11 Aleksander Jabłonowski, *Polska XVI wieku pod względem geograficzno-statystycznym*, vol. VII, 2 pts, *Ziemie Ruskie–Ruś Czerwona* (Warsaw 1902–03), pt 2: ''Ruś Czerwona'' reprinted

Soviet and Czechoslovak researchers have analyzed the political, administrative, and socioeconomic life in the Carpathian foothills of southern Galicia.[12]

By the early fifteenth century, after Poland had consolidated its rule in Galicia, it was able to institute an administrative, judicial, and legal system on the Polish model. Several local dietines (*sejmiki*) composed of deputies from the nobility were established; this process is described in a monograph on the administrative structure of Galicia in the fifteenth century by Przemysław Dąbkowski.[13] The early and subsequent activity of the dietines, which for all practical purposes determined how Galicia was ruled and chose its deputies to the Polish national diet (*sejm*), is also the subject of several studies,[14] as is the structure of office holding in the Galician administration.[15] Finally, Polish legal historians have analyzed the impact of old Rus' law on the new Polish judicial system introduced after 1435.[16]

---

in *Pisma Aleksandra Jabłonowskiego,* vol. IV (Warsaw: E. Wende 1911), pp. 408–519; Władysław Łoziński, *Prawem i lewem: obyczaje na Czerwonej Rusi za panowania Zygmunta III* (L'viv 1903). The second revised edition appeared as *Prawem i lewem: obyczaje na Czerwonej Rusi w pierwszej połowie XVII wieku,* 2 vols (L'viv 1904), reprinted in 3rd ed. (L'viv 1911), 4th ed. (L'viv 1931), and 5th ed. (Cracow: Wydawnictwo Literackie 1957).

12 Iurii H. Hoshko, *Naselennia ukraïns'kykh Karpat XV–XVIII st.: zaselennia, mihratsiï, pobut* (Kiev: Naukova dumka 1976). The following work compares conditions in southern Galicia to those in the neighboring mountainous regions of the northeastern Hungarian Kingdom (Slovakia and the Transcarpathian oblast): Omelian Stavrovs'kyi, *Slovats'ko-pol's'ko-ukraïns'ke prykordonnia do 18 stolittia* (Bratislava and Prešov: Slovats'ke pedahohichne vydavnytstvo, viddil ukraïns'koï literatury 1967).

13 P. Dąbkowski, *Podzial administracyjny województwa Ruskiego i Belzkiego w XV wieku,* Zabytki Dziejowe, Towarzystwo Naukowe we Lwowie, vol. V (L'viv 1939).

14 Henryk Chodynicki, *Sejmiki ziem ruskich we wieku XV,* Studya nad Historyą Prawa Polskiego, vol. III, pt 1 (L'viv 1906); Stanisław Śreniowski, *Organizacja sejmiku halickego,* Studja nad Historją Prawa Polskiego imienia Oswalda Balzera, vol. XVI, no. 3 (L'viv 1938); Tadeusz Kostkiewicz, *Dzialalność kulturalna sejmiku ruskiego,* Pamiętnik Historyczno-Prawny, vol. XIII, no. 2 (L'viv 1939); Stanisław Piotrkowski, *Uchwały podatkowe sejmiku generalnego wiszeńskiego 1572–1772,* Studja nad Historją Prawa Polskiego imienia Oswalda Balzera, vol. XIII, no. 4 (L'viv 1932); Antoni Prochaska, ''Sejmiki wiszeńskie w czasach trzech elekcyi pojagiellońskich,'' *Kwartalnik Historyczny,* XVII (L'viv 1903), pp. 363–404 and 544–595.

15 Karol Maleczynski, *Urzędnicy grodzcy i ziemscy lwowscy w latach 1352–1783,* Zabytki Dziejowe, Towarzystwo Naukowe we Lwowie, vol. VI, no. 1 (L'viv 1938); Maurycy Dzieduszycki, ''Starostowie ruscy i lwowscy,'' *Przewodnik Naukowy i Literacki,* III (L'viv 1875), pp. 428–445; Ludwik Ehrlich, *Starostwa w Halickiem w stosunku do starostwa lwowskiego w wiekach średnich (1390–1501),* Studya nad Historyą Prawa Polskiego, vol. VI, pt 1 (L'viv 1914); Stefan Sochaniewicz, *Wojtowstwa i sołtystwa pod względem prawnym i ekonomicznym w ziemi lwowskiej.* Studya nad Historyą Prawa Polskiego, vol. VII (L'viv 1921).

16 Wojciech Hejnosz, *Ius Ruthenicale: przeżytki dawnego ustroju społecznego na Rusi Halickiej w XV wieku,* Studja nad Historją Prawa Polskiego imienia Oswalda Balzera, vol. XII, no. 1

As for the impact of Polish rule on Galicia's social structure, there are numerous works by Ukrainian and Polish scholars who have focused in particular on the changes brought about during the late fourteenth to sixteenth centuries.[17] The role of the nobility in Galicia, made up especially of middle and petty gentry who were either immigrants from Polish lands or from the polonized local Ukrainian elite, has traditionally been the object of attention in specialized Polish genealogical studies.[18] An indication of the wide variety of literature on this topic is available in a bibliography of a recent study on the petty nobility.[19] Individual family histories are particularly well represented in two heraldic journals published in L'viv during the twentieth century: *Rocznik Towarzystwa Heraldycznego we Lwowie* (L'viv 1908–32) and *Miesięcznik Heraldyczny* (L'viv 1908–39). The problem of the petty nobility in the Carpathian region has received particular attention,[20] and there are more general studies on nobles' attitudes toward military levies,[21] their role in the manorial agricultural economy over which they had complete control,[22]

(L'viv 1928); Przemysław Dąbkowski, *Zemsta, okup i pokora na Rusi halickiej w wieku XV i pierwszej połowie wieku XVI* (L'viv: Gubrynowicz i Schmidt 1898).

17 I.A. Linnichenko, *Cherty iz istorii soslovii v iugo-zapadnoi (Galitskoi) Rusi XIV–XV vv.* (Moscow 1894), translated into Ukrainian as *Suspil'ni verstvy Halyts'koï Rusy XIV–XV v.*, Rus'ka Istorychna Biblioteka, vol. VII (L'viv: NTSh 1904); Isydor Szaraniewicz, *Rys wewnętrznych stosunków w Galicyi wschodniej w drugiej połowie piętnastego wieku na podstawie źródeł* (L'viv: p.a. 1869), translated into Ukrainian in M. Smyrnov et al., *Monohrafiy do istoriy Halytskoy Rusy*, Rus'ka istorychna biblioteka, vol. V (Ternopil' 1886), pp. 107–196; Mykhailo Hrushevs'kyi, *Istoriia Ukraïny-Rusy*, vols V and VI (L'viv and Kiev 1905–07; reprinted New York: Knyho-spilka 1955); Andrzej Janeczek, ''Polska ekspansja osadnicza w ziemi lwowskiej w XIV–XVI w.,'' *Przegląd Historyczny*, LXIX, 4 (Warsaw 1978), pp. 597–622.

18 A useful introduction with extensive bibliographical references to the problem of the nobility in all Ukrainian lands including Galicia is found in Frank E. Sysyn, ''The Problem of Nobilities in the Ukrainian Past: the Polish Period, 1569–1648,'' in Ivan L. Rudnytsky, ed., *Rethinking Ukrainian History* (Edmonton: Canadian Institute of Ukrainian Studies, University of Alberta 1981), pp. 29–102.

19 Maria Biernacka, *Wsie drobnoszlacheckie na Mazowszu i Podlasiu: tradycje historyczne a współczesne przemiany* (Wrocław, Warsaw, and Cracow: ZNIO–PAN 1966).

20 Przemysław Dąbkowski, *Szlachta zaściankowa w Korczynie i Kruszelnicy nad Stryjem*, Wschód, vol. XIII (L'viv 1936); Władysław Pulnarowicz, *Rycerstwo polskie Podkarpacia: dawne dzieje i obecne obowiązki szlachty zagrodowej na Podkarpaciu* (Przemyśl 1937); Bohdan Barvins'kyi, ''Konashevychi v peremyskii zemli v XV i XVI st.: henealochichno-istorychna monohrafiia,'' *Zapysky NTSh*, C (L'viv 1930), pp. 9–175.

21 Kazimierz Hahn, *Pospolite ruszenie wedle uchwał sejmikowych ruskich od XVI do XVIII wieku*, Pamiętnik Historyczno–Prawny, vol. IX, no. 4 (L'viv 1928).

22 I.A. Linnichenko, ''Iuridicheskie formy shliakhetskago zemlevladeniia i sud'ba drevnerusskago boiarstva v Iugo-Zapadnoi Rusi XIV–XV vv.,'' *Iuridicheskii viestnik*, XI, 3–4 (St Petersburg 1892); Kazimierz Arłamowski, *Zapatrywania i dążenia gospodarcze szlachty*

and their attempts to direct the administration and economies of the Galician cities.[23]

The other social component of the manorial system that prevailed in Galicia was made up of peasants; their status, affected by the increasing demands of serfdom, is described in the general studies on the Galician social structure discussed above, as well as in the monographs on the rural population during the fifteenth century.[24] Soviet and Polish Marxist authors have given particular attention to the Galician peasantry in works that stress the exploitative aspects of the ''feudal'' pre-partition Polish economy and that trace all documented instances of the seemingly continual peasant ''revolutionary'' activity from the late fifteenth century revolt led by the Moldavian leader Mukha through numerous uprisings until the eighteenth century.[25] Finally, the Orthodox and Uniate clergy, especially the question of their social origins and the impact of the Union of Brest on their social status, is the subject of older analyses by Izydor Sharanevych and Mykhailo Hrushevs'kyi.[26]

---

czerwonoruskiej XVII wieku (L'viv 1927); V.F. Inkin, ''K voprosu ob evoliutsii feodalnoi renty v Galichine v XVI–XVIII vv.,'' *Ezhegodnik po agrarnoi istorii vostochnoi Evropy 1963* (Vilnius 1964), pp. 224–245; Iu.M. Grossman, ''Folvarki gosudarstvennykh imenii Russkogo i Belzkogo voevodstva vo vtoroi polovine XVI v.,'' *Ezhegodnik po agrarnoi istorii vostochnoi Evropy 1961* (Riga 1963), pp. 135–146; Iu.M. Hrossman, ''Orendy maietkiv ta ïkh vplyv na stanovyshche zakhidno-ukraïns'kykh selian v pershii polovyni XVII st.,'' *Pytannia z istoriï SRSR* (Kiev 1958), pp. 107–119.

23 Antoni Prochaska, *Lwów i szlachta*, Biblioteka Lwowska, vol. XXIV, no. 5 (L'viv 1919); S.T. Bilets'kyi, ''Borot'ba mischchan L'vova proty zasyllia shliakhty v pershii polovyni XVII st.,'' in *Z istoriï zakhidnoukraïns'kykh zemel'*, vol. I (Kiev: AN URSR 1957), pp. 15–24.

24 See notes 11–12, 17, 22 above; and S. Rundstein, *Ludność wieśniacza ziemi halickiej w wieku XV*, Studya nad Historyą Prawa Polskiego, vol. II, pt 2 (L'viv 1903); Ludwik Ehrlich, ''Obciążenie stanu wieśniacznego na Rusi Czerwonej (w dawnem Województwie Ruskiem) w odrębie XV stulecia,'' *Przewodnik Naukowy i Literacki*, XLIII, 11 (L'viv 1917).

25 N.A. Mokhov, ''Vosstanie ukrainskikh i moldavskikh krest'ian pod rukovodstvom Mukhi v 1490–1492 gg.,'' *Izvestiia Moldavskogo filiala AN SSSR*, no. 3–4 (Kishenev 1953), pp. 17–40; Volodymyr V. Hrabovets'kyi, *Selians'ke povstannia na Prykarpatti pid provodom Mukhy 1490–1492 rokiv* (L'viv: LU–Vyshcha shkola 1979); Maurycy Horn, *Walka chłopów czerwonoruskich z wyzyskiem feudalnym w latach 1600–1648*, pt 1: *Zbiegostwo i zbójnictwo karpackie*, and pt 2: *Chłopi dóbr koronnych w walce przeciw zwiększaniu robocizny i danin*, Zeszyty Naukowe Wyższej Szkoły Pedagogicznej, Seria B, no. 40 (Opole 1974); idem, ''Epidemie chorób zakaźnych na Rusi Czerwonej w latach 1600–1647,'' *Studia Historyczne*, XI, 1 (Cracow 1968), pp. 13–31; M.V. Gorn, ''Klassovaia bor'ba krest'ian zapadno-ukrainskikh zemel' v 1638–1648 godakh,'' *Voprosy istorii*, X, 2 (Moscow 1954), pp. 58–70; V.V. Hrabovets'kyi, *Selians'kyi rukh na Prykarpatti v druhii polovyni XVII–pershii polovyni XVIII st.* (Kiev: AN URSR 1962); V.V. Hrabovets'kyi, ''Selians'kyi rukh na halyts'komu Pidkarpatti v druhii polovyni XVII st.,'' in *Z istoriï zakhidnouraïns'kykh zemel'*, vol. II (Kiev: AN URSR 1957), pp. 32–57.

26 See notes 53 and 59 below.

Urban and economic history

The early centuries of the Polish era, at least until the mid-seventeenth century, brought economic prosperity to Galicia. International trade routes continued to flourish connecting Galicia with the Ukrainian steppe in the east, with Cracow and central Europe in the west, with the lower Vistula and Baltic Sea to the north, and with the Hungarian kingdom to the south. Protected by Polish military might and enriched by the growing wealth of the country's grain exports, Galicia's cities maintained prosperous commercial and artisan activity until the mid-seventeenth century. Most of the extensive literature dealing with this period focuses on specific cities and towns in Galicia. Two contemporary Polish social historians, Elżbieta Hornowa and Maurycy Horn, have, however, provided descriptions of demographic and socioeconomic developments in all Galicia's cities and towns during the height of the Polish economy–the sixteenth and first half of the seventeenth century.[27]

By far, the most important urban center in Galicia was L'viv, which in fact was the largest city throughout all Ukrainian territory during the era of Polish rule. As early as 1356, L'viv received from the Polish king the right of self-rule as outlined in the privileges of Magdeburg Law, and about 1435 it became the administrative center of the Rus' palatinate. To enhance its importance, the city was heavily fortified. Accompanying the changes under Polish rule was an influx of German and to a lesser degree Armenian settlers, who dominated the city's merchant and artisan classes until the late fifteenth century. Urban life was organized according to guilds whose number increased to thirty by the mid-seventeenth century. Among the city's chief manufactures were iron works and weapons.

---

27 Elżbieta Hornowa, *Stosunki ekonomiczno-społeczne w miastach ziemi Halickiej w latach 1590–1648*, Zeszyty Naukowe Wyższej Szkoły Pedagogicznej w Opolu, Seria B: Studia i Rozprawy, nr. 4 (Opole 1963); Maurycy Horn, *Osadnictwo miejskie na Rusi Czerwonej w latach 1501–1648*, Zeszyty Naukowe Wyższej Szkoły Pedagogicznej: Historia, vol. XIII (Opole 1977); idem, *Walka klasowa i konflikty społeczne w miastach Rusi Czerwonej w latach 1600–1647 na tle stosunków gospodarczych* (Wrocław, Warsaw, Cracow, and Gdansk: ZNIO 1972).

On earlier periods, see the numismatic study that provides much information on the economic life of Galicia: M.F. Kotliar, *Halyts'ka Rus' u druhii polovyni XIV–pershii chverti XV st.: istoryko-numizmatychne doslidzhennia* (Kiev: Naukova dumka 1968); and Maurycy Horn, "Miejski ruch osadniczy na Rusi Czerwonej do końca XV wieku," *Roczniki Dziejów Społecznych i Gospodarczych*, XXXIV (Poznań 1974), pp. 49–74.

Despite Polish military superiority in eastern Europe until the mid-seventeenth century, it was still not possible to eliminate Tatar raids from the east. For their impact on the Galician economy as late as the first half of the seventeenth century, see idem, *Skutki ekonomiczne najazdów tatarskich z lat 1605–1633 na Ruś Czerwoną* (Wrocław: ZNIO 1964).

By the seventeenth century, most of the Germans and Armenians became polonized and the city took on a distinctly Polish character. Only Roman Catholics (Poles and polonized Germans) enjoyed the urban privileges of Magdeburg Law, while the growing Jewish population was restricted to living in its ghettos and to engaging only in those economic activities (especially money lending and certain trades) permitted them by royal decrees. The Orthodox Ukrainians had no particular privileges, and they were limited to one section of the city (*Rus'ka ulytsia*) and especially to its suburbs. It was this generally unfavorable situation among the Ukrainians in L'viv that provided the stimulus to the brotherhood movement and Orthodox cultural revival of the sixteenth century.

L'viv's prosperity began to decline precipitiously with the second half of the seventeenth century. Although L'viv was besieged briefly by the Cossacks under Hetman Bohdan Khmel'nyts'kyi in 1648 and again in 1655, the city was not substantially affected by these campaigns.[28] The overall changes within Poland after the Khmel'nyts'kyi revolution, however, did have a deep effect on L'viv, and its economy declined, beginning with the second half of the seventeenth century, because of three factors: constant wars throughout Poland during its "period of ruin"; a change in trade patterns; and the unfavorable influence of the landowning nobility on Poland's economic policies.

There are several volumes of documents dealing with L'viv during the era of Polish rule. The Polish scholar Aleksander Czołowski has published the earliest extant municipal register books from 1382 to 1448, while the Soviet historian Iaroslav Kis' has published documents from the years 1507 to 1771.[29] Besides the several general histories of L'viv that contain much data on the Polish era,[30] Aleksander Czołowski has written a general survey covering the period before 1772, while Franciszek Jaworski, Władysław Łoziński, and Łucja Charewiczowa have focused on specific periods.[31] Other subjects that have received attention are

28 For literature on these sieges, see notes 91 and 93 below.

29 Aleksander Czołowski and Franciszek Jaworski, eds, *Pomniki dziejowe Lwowa z archiwum miasta*, vol. I: *Najstarsza księga miejska 1382–89* (L'viv 1892); vol. II: *Księga przychodów i rozchodów miasta 1404–1414* (L'viv 1896); vol. III: *Księga przychodów i rozchodów miasta 1414–1426* (L'viv 1905); vol. IV: *Księga Ławnicza miejska 1441–1448* (L'viv 1921); Ia.P. Kis', ed., *Sotsial'na borot'ba v misti L'vovi v XVI–XVIII st.: zbirnyk dokumentiv* (L'viv: LU 1961).

30 See chapter 2, notes 106–109.

31 A. Czołowski, *Historia Lwowa od zalożenia do 1600 r.* (L'viv 1925); idem, *Historia Lwowa od 1600/1772 r.* (L'viv 1927); Fr. Jaworski, *Lwów za Jagiełły*, Biblioteka Lwowska, vol. XI–XII (L'viv 1910); Władysław Łoziński, *Patrycyat i mieszczaństwo lwowskie w XVI i XVII wieku* (L'viv 1890), 2nd ed. (L'viv: Gubrynowicz i Schmidt 1892); Łucja Charewiczowa, "Lwów na przelomie XVII i XVIII wieku," in *Studja z historji społecznej i gospodarczej poświęcone prof. dr. Franciszkowi Bujakowi* (L'viv 1931), pp. 347–374.

the legal system in L'viv,[32] the attempts of the nobility to influence city life,[33] the social structure of the population,[34] and the respective fates of the Germans, Armenians, Jews, and Ukrainians.[35] L'viv's economy in particular has been the subject of much attention. Soviet historians have prepared general surveys of economic development during the era of Polish "feudalism,"[36] but the most valuable data come from several interwar Polish monographs on trade, financing, the price structure, artisans, and guilds during the seventeenth and eighteenth centuries.[37] Although L'viv has by far the most well-developed literature, several other regions, towns, even villages in Galicia have documentary collections, general surveys, or detailed monographs about developments during the Polish

32 Aleksy Gilewicz, "Przyjęcia do prawa miejskiego we Lwowie w latach 1405/1604," in *Studja z historji społecznej i gospodarczej poświęczone prof. dr. Franciszkowi Bujakowi* (L'viv 1931), pp. 375–414.

33 See n. 23 above.

34 S.T. Bilets'kyi, "Sotsial'na struktura naselennia L'vova v seredyni XVII st.," in *Z istoriï zakhidnoukraïns'kykh zemel'*, vol. IV, ed. I.P. Kryp"iakevych (Kiev: AN URSR 1960), pp. 3–14; Maurycy Horn, *Lwowska ludność rzemieślnicza i jej walka w pierwszej połowie XVII wieku (w latach 1600–1648)*, Zeszyty Naukowe Wyższej Szkoły Pedagogicznej: Historia, vol. I (Opole 1960).

35 On Germans, Armenians, and Jews during this period, see chapter 10, notes 15–18, 86, 88, and 90. On the Ukrainians, see Ivan Krypiakevych, "L'vivs'ka Rus' v pershii polovyni XVI viku," *Zapysky NTSh*, LXXVII (L'viv 1907), pp. 77–106; LXXVIII (1907), pp. 26–50; LXXIX (1907), pp. 5–51; Ivan Kryp"iakevych, "Rusyny vlastyteli u L'vovi v pershii pol. XVI st.," *Naukovyi zbirnyk prysviachenyi profesorovy Mykhailovy Hrushevs'komu* (L'viv: Vydannie Komitetu 1906), pp. 219–236; and the more popular Mykola Holubets', *Za ukraïns'kyi L'viv: epizody borot'by XIII–XVIII v.* (L'viv: Novyi chas 1927).

36 Iaroslav P. Kis', *Promyslovist' L'vova u period feodalizmu (XIII–XIX st.)* (L'viv: LU 1968); V. Inkin, *Narys ekonomichnoho rozvytku L'vova u XVIII st.* (L'viv 1959).

37 Łucja Charewiczowa, *Handel średniowiecznego Lwowa* (L'viv: ZNIO 1925); R. Zubyk, *Gospodarka financowa m. Lwowa w l. 1624–1635*, Badania z Dziejów Społecznych i Gospodarczych, vol. VII (L'viv 1930); Michał Wąsowicz, *Kontrakty lwowskie w latach 1676–1686* and Stanisław Siegel, *Kontrakty lwowskie w latach 1717–1724*, Badania z Dziejów Społecznych i Gospodarczych, vol. XIX (L'viv 1935); Stanisław Hoszowski, *Ceny we Lwowie w XVI i XVII wieku*, Badania z Dziejów Społecznych i Gospodarczych, vol. IV (L'viv 1934), translated into French as *Les prix à Lwow (XVIe–XVIIe siècles)*, Oeuvres étrangères de l'École pratique des Hautes Études– VIe section, vol. I (Paris 1954); Łucja Charewiczowa, *Lwowskie organizacje zawodowe za czasów Polski przedrozbiorowej* (L'viv: ZNIO 1929); Władysław Łoziński, "Kupiectwo lwowskie w XVI w.," *Biblioteka Warszawska*, XLVIII, 3 (Warsaw 1981); M. Kowalczuk, *Cech budowniczych we Lwowie za czasów polskich (do roku 1772)* (L'viv 1927); Tadeusz Mańkowski, *Lwowski cech malarzy w XVI–XVII wieku*, Biblioteka Lwowska, vol. XXXVI (L'viv 1936).

See also Ivan Krypiakevych, "Materialy do istoriï torhovli L'vova," *Zapysky NTSh*, LXV (L'viv 1905), 45 pp.

era. These include Berezhany,[38] Brody,[39] Drohobych,[40] Jarosław,[41] Krosno,[42] Lesko,[43] Mshanets',[44] Przemyśl,[45] Sambir,[46] and Sanok.[47]

38 M. Maciszewski, *Brzeżany w czasach Rzeczypospolitej Polskiej: monografia historyczna* (Brody: F. West 1911).

39 Ivan Sozans'kyi, ''Z mynuvshyny m. Brodiv (prychynky do istoriï mista v XVII v.),'' *Zapysky NTSh*, XCVII (L'viv 1910), pp. 5–25, XCVIII (1910), pp. 10–30, CII (1911), pp. 88–115, also separately (L'viv: NTSh 1911).

40 Helena Polaczkówna, ed., *Księga radziecka miasta Drohobycza 1542–1563*, Zabytki Dziejowe, vol. IV, pt 1 (L'viv 1936); Ia.D. Isaievych, ''Do kharakterystyky remesla i torhivli v Drohobychi v 30–60–kh rokakh XVIII st.,'' in his *Z istoriï zakhidnoukraïns'kykh zemel'*, vol. IV, ed. I.P. Kryp''iakevych (Kiev: AN URSR 1960), pp. 30–39; Ia.D. Isaievych, ''Administratyvno-pravovyi ustrii Drohobycha v dobu feodalizmu (do kintsia XVIII st.),'' in *Z istoriï Ukraïns'koï RSR*, vol. VI–VII (Kiev: AN URSR 1962), pp. 3–20; idem, ''Gorod Drogobych v XVI–XVIII vv.,'' *Goroda feodal'noi Rossii: sbornik statei pamiati N.V. Ustiugova* (Moscow: Nauka 1966), pp. 160–167. See also chapter 2, n. 121.

41 W.A. Wagner, *Handel dawnego Jarosława do połowy XVII w.*, Prace Historyczne ... Uniwersytetu Jana Kazimierza we Lwowie (L'viv 1929).

42 Anatol Lewicki, *Krosno w wiekach średnich* (Krosno 1933); Antoni Prochaska, ''Starostwo krośnieńskie w XVII–XVIII wiekach,'' *Przewodnik Naukowy i Literacki*, XLVII (L'viv 1921).

43 Adam Fastnacht, ''Ludność miasta Leska w XV i XVI wieku'' *Rocznik ZNIO*, IV (Wrocław 1953), pp. 77–116.

44 Mykhailo Zubryts'kyi, ''Selo Mshanets' Starosambirs'koho povita: materiialy do istoriï halyts'koho sela,'' *Zapysky NTSh*, LXX (L'viv 1906), pp. 114–167; LXXI (1906), pp. 96–133; LXXIV (1906), pp. 93–128; LXXVII (1907), pp. 114–170.

45 Jan Smołka, ed., *Księga ławnicza, 1402–1445* (Przemyśl: Gmina Miasta Przemyśla 1936); M. Horn, ''Zaludnienie miast ziemi przemyskiej i sanockiej w drugiej połowie XVI i pierwszej połowie XVII wieku,'' *Roczniki Dziejów Społecznych i Gospodarczych*, XXXI (Poznań 1970); Maurycy Horn, *Ruch budowlany w miastach ziemi przemyskiej i sanockiej w latach 1550–1650 na tle przesłanek urbanizacyjnych*, Zeszyty Naukowe Wyższej Szkoły Pedagogicznej, Seria B: Studia i Monografie, vol. XXIII (Opole 1968); M. Horn, ''Lokalizacja cechów i specjalności rzemieślniczych w miastach ziemi przemyskiej i sanockiej w latach 1550–1650,'' *Przegląd Historyczny*, XLI, 3 (Warsaw 1970), pp. 403–427; idem, ''Rzemiosła skórzane w miastach ziemi przemyskiej i sanockiej w latach 1550–1650,'' *Kwartalnik Historii Kultury Materialnej*, XX, 1 (Warsaw 1972), pp. 71–101; idem, ''Rzemiosła metalowe w miastach ziemi przemyskiej i sanockiej w latach 1550–1650,'' in *Wyroby rzemieślnicze w Polsce w XIV–XVIII wieku*, Studia i Materiały z Historii Kultury, vol. XLV (Wrocław: ZNIO 1971), pp. 23–68; Marjan Ungeheuer, *Stosunki kredytowe w ziemi przemyskiej w połowie XV wieku*, Badania z Dziejów Społecznych i Gospodarczych, vol. VI (L'viv 1929). See also the general histories of Przemyśl, chapter 2, notes 110–111.

46 Anna Dörflerówna, ed., *Materiały do historii miasta Sambora 1390–1795, Zabytki Dziejowe*, vol. IV, pt 2 (L'viv 1936); R. Rybarski, *Kredyt i lichwa w ekonomiji samborskiej w XVIII w.*, Badania z Dziejów Społecznych i Gospodarczych, vol. XXX (L'viv 1936); V.F. Inkin, ''Rozvytok feodal'noï renty v sambirs'kii ekonomiï u druhii polovyni XVI–na pochatku XVII stolittia,'' *Visnyk LDU–Seriia istorychna*, 4 (L'viv 1967), pp. 79–91. See also n. 44 above.

47 Władysław Kucharski, ed., *Dokumenty z ziemi Sanockej* (Sanok 1908); idem, *Sanok i sanocka ziemia w dobie Piastów i Jagiellonów* (L'viv 1905); Przemysław Dąbkowski, *Ziemia sanocka w XV stuleciu*, 2 vols (L'viv: Wschód 1931); Alojzy Winiarz, ''Ziemia sanocka w latach

Church history

There is much literature on the religious history of each of the groups–Ukrainians, Poles, Jews, Armenians–who inhabited Galicia during the period of Polish rule. As the official and representative church of Polish culture, Roman Catholicism first made its organizational appearance with the establishment of an archdiocese in Halych (1365) that was later transferred to L'viv (1414). Władysław Abraham has written two monographs on the early years of the Roman Catholic church in Galicia as well as a biography of its first archbishop, Jakob Strepa (consecrated 1391, died 1409).[48] There are also several studies of Jewish communities in Galicia, which at least before 1772 were governed by their own laws as formulated and enforced by religious leaders, as well as of the Armenians whose Apostolic church accepted union with Rome during the first decades of the seventeenth century.[49]

But by far the most extensive literature dealing with church history from this period concerns Ukrainians. In a sense, because they lived in a Polish state, had lost their traditional elite social strata during the process of polonization, and were deprived of a middle class owing to their exclusion from legal privileges enjoyed by other urban groups, the Ukrainians of Galicia maintained a distinct cultural and national identity primarily because of their membership in the Orthodox Rus' and later Uniate church. Thus, in many ways, the history of Ukrainians in Galicia between 1387 and 1772 is the history of their Orthodox and Uniate churches.

Documents originating from Galicia and dealing with religious history during the era of Polish rule appeared in three of the volumes on ''South-West Russia''

1463–1553,'' *Kwartalnik Historyczny,* X (L'viv 1896), pp. 286–306; Adam Fastnacht, *Osadnictwo ziemi sanockiej w latach 1340–1650,* Prace Wrocławskiego Towarzystwa Naukowego: Seria A, no. 84 (Wrocław 1962); Władysław Kucharski, *Ludność ziemi Sanockiej na schyłku XVIII w. w świetle protokołu magistratu Sanockiego* (Sanok 1907).

48 Władysław Abraham, *Powstanie organizacji kościoła łacińskiego na Rusi* (L'viv 1904); idem, *Początki arcybiskupstwa łacińskiego we Lwowie,* Biblioteka Lwowska, vol. VII (L'viv 1909); idem, *Jakob Strepa, arcybiskup halicki (1391–1409)* (Cracow 1908).

See also the earlier survey by Kazimierz Stadnicki, *O początkach arcybiskupstwa i biskupstw katolickich łac. obrz. na Rusi halickiej i Wołyniu* (L'viv: Zelman Iglo 1882); the history of the Roman Catholic Cathedral in L'viv (dedicated in 1434), Maurycy Dzieduszycki, *Kościół katedralny lwowski obrządku łacińskiego* (L'viv: X.O. Hołyński 1872); and the biographies of two hierarchs: Antoni Prochaska, ''Z życia biskupa przemyskiego (Aleksandra Trzebieńskiego),'' *Przegląd Historyczny,* VII (Warsaw 1908), pp. 75–83 and 204–311, and Stefan Szydelski, *Konstanty Zieliński, arcybiskup lwowski* (Cracow: Akademija Umiejętności 1910).

49 On Jewish and Armenian religious history during this period, see chapter 10, notes 15–18, 82–83.

published by the Commission for the Study of Ancient Documents in Kiev.[50] All nine series of documents from the Vatican archives on Ukrainian church history also include much material on Galicia before 1772.[51] As for the efforts at church unity that began in the late sixteenth century and continued during the seventeenth century, there are many documents not only in the Vatican series but also in three volumes published earlier by the Archeographic Commission in St Petersburg.[52] Finally, two works contain numerous documents pertaining especially to the tithes due the clergy by the Ukrainian peasantry.[53]

As for secondary literature, the years of Polish rule are covered in great detail in the first histories of the Galician church by Mykhailo Harasevych and Antin Dobrians'kyi,[54] as well as in a more recent history of the church in Poland, in which Ludomir Bieńkowski surveys the organization of the eastern church on Polish territory from the sixteenth to eighteenth centuries.[55] To be sure, the most important event in Galician-Ukrainian religious history during these centuries was the Union of Brest (1595), and therefore a large portion of the secondary literature deals with the union and its aftermath, although most analyses pertain to the Ukrainian population in the Polish-Lithuanian Commonwealth as a whole, not just to Galicia. Because of the controversial circumstances in which the Union of Brest came about, the act and its implications for Ukrainians under Polish rule have been either adamantly defended or attacked by latter-day apologists or critics. Defenders of the Union of Brest see it either as a positive step toward ''reuniting'' the Orthodox ''schismatics'' into the one Catholic church and/or a symbol of Poland's ''civilizing mission'' in the east whereby the level of culture,

50 The 285 documents relating to the ''Galician-Russian Orthodox Church'' were compiled by A. Krilovskii in *Arkhiv Iugo-zapadnoi Rossii,* Chast' pervaia: vols X–XII (Kiev: Kommissiia dlia razbora drevnykh aktov 1904).

51 See chapter 2, notes 47–55.

52 *Akty otnosiashchiesia k istorii Zapadnoi Rossii,* 5 vols. [1340–1699] (St Petersburg: Arkheograficheskaia kommissiia 1846–53), especially vols 2–4.

See also A.S. Petrushevych, *Aktŷ otnosiashchiesia k ystorii iuzhnozapadnoi Rusy* (L'viv 1868), first published in *Naukovŷi sbornyk ... Halytsko-russkoi Matytsŷ,* III, 1–4 (L'viv 1868), pp. 365–378 and IV, 1–4 (1868), pp. 70–159 and 289–352; Onufrii Lepkii, ed., ''Aktŷ otnosiashchiysia k ystoriy Iuzhno-zapadnoi Rusy,'' *Lyteraturnŷi sbornyk Halytsko-russkoi Matytsŷ* [II] (L'viv 1870), pp. 89–104; and several documents that appear in the collection of S. Golubev, ''Materialy dlia istorii zapadno-russkoi pravoslavnoi tserkvi (XVI i XVII stol.),'' *Trudy Kievskoi dukhovnoi akademii,* XIX, 1 and 3 (Kiev 1878), pp. 197–219 and 17–416.

53 Jan X. Pociej, *Zbiór wiadomości historycznych i akt dotyczących dziesięcin kościelnych na Rusi* (Warsaw 1845); M. Hrushevs'kyi, ''Storinka z istoryï ukraïns'ko-rus'koho sil's'koho dukhovenstva (po sambirs'kym aktam XVI v.),'' *Zapysky NTSh,* XXXIV (L'viv 1900), 82 pp.

54 See chapter 2, notes 57 and 60.

55 Ludomir Bieńkowski, ''Organizacja Kościoła Wschodniego w Polsce,'' in *Kościół w Polsce,* vol. II: *wieki XVI–XVIII* (Cracow: ZNAK 1970), pp. 781–1049.

especially among the former Orthodox clergy, was substantially raised.[56] Opponents of the Union of Brest consider it a forcible act supported by the Polish government and Roman Catholic church to enhance further their control over the Ukraine and Belorussia and to create a more favorable basis for the eventual conversion of the Rus' populace to Roman Catholicism.[57] Whereas Soviet writers are not concerned with the religious aspect of the Union of Brest, their view is a corollary to the Orthodox position in that they consider the union as a symbol of foreign aggression and domination over the Rus' people and therefore an "act of shame and treachery."[58] In a less impassioned approach to religious develop-

56 On the Union of Brest as an act of Christian reunification, see the general studies by Galician Greek Catholic (Uniate) prelates, chapter 2, notes 57, 58, 60; *Nacherk ystoriy uniy ruskoy tserkvy z Rymom* (L'iviv: Komitet iuvileinyi 1896); Ivan Rudovych, *Uniia v l'vovskoi eparkhii* (L'viv 1900); and by the former Roman Catholic archbishop of L'viv, Edward Likowski, *Historya Unii kościoła ruskiego z kościołem Rzymskim* (Poznań: M. Leitgeber, 1875) and his *Unja Brzeska r. 1596* (Poznań: p. a. 1896).

For the stress on Polish cultural expansion as well as religious unity, see Antoni Prochaska, "Unia brzeska," *Przegląd Polski*, XII (L'viv 1896), pp. 441–462; Antoni Prochaska, "Z dziejów unii brzeskiej," *Kwartalnik Historyczny*, XII (L'viv 1896), pp. 522–577; Oscar Halecki, *From Florence to Brest (1439–1596)*, Sacrum Poloniae Millenium, vol. V (New York: Fordham University Press 1958), and rev. ed. (New York: Archon Books 1968).

57 Makarii [Sergei Golubev], *Istoriia russkoi tserkvi*, vol. IX: *Istoriia zapadno-russkoi ili litovskoi mitropolii* (St Petersburg 1879; reprinted Vaduz, Liechtenstein: Europe Printing Establishment 1969); Vladimir Antonovich, "Ocherk sostoianiia pravoslavnoi tserkvi v iugo-zapadnoi Rossii," introduction to *Arkhiv Iugo-Zapadnoi Rossii*, pt 1, vol. IV: *Akty ob unii i sostoianii pravoslavnoi tserkvi s poloviny XVII v. (1648–1798)* (Kiev: Vremennaia kommissiia dlia razbora drevnikh aktov 1871), also separately (Kiev 1871) and reprinted in his *Monografii* (Kiev 1885) and *Tvory* (Kiev 1932), translated in Ukrainian for the series Rus'ka istorychna biblioteka, vol. VIII (L'viv: NTSh 1900), and reprinted as Volodymyr Antonovych, *Shcho prynesla Ukraïni Uniia: stan Ukraïns'kii Pravoslavnoï Tserkvy vid polovyny XVII do kintsia XVIII st.* (Winnipeg 1952); Ivan Vlasovs'kyi, *Narys istoriï Ukraïns'koï Pravoslavnoï tserkvy*, 4 vols in 5 (New York and Bound Brook, NJ: Ukraïns'ka Pravoslavna Tserkva v Z.D.A. 1955–56), especially vol. I–II, the only two of which have been translated into English: *Outline History of the Ukrainian Orthodox Church*, 2 vols (New York: Ukrainian Orthodox Church of the USA 1974–79). See also Kazimierz Chodynicki, *Kościół prawosławny a Rzeczpospolita Polska 1370–1632* (Warsaw 1934).

58 See the works by V. Dobrychev and S. Danilenko in chapter 2, n. 59. The Soviet view is also expressed in analyses of the anti-Uniate polemic literature that arose at the time, the most famous tract being the *Perestoroha (Warning)*, which had its origins in L'viv. Porfyrii K. Iaremenko, *'Perestoroha' – ukraïns'kyi antyuniats'kyi pamflet pochatku XVII st.* (Kiev: AN URSR, 1963).

For other anti-Uniate polemical texts, many of which were authored by natives of Galicia who served as Orthodox hierarchs in the Ukraine, see Peter Gil'tebrandt, ed., *Pamiatniki polemicheskoi literatury v Zapadnoi Rusi*, in *Russkaia istoricheskaia biblioteka*, vol. IV (St Petersburg: Arkheograficheskaia Kommissiia 1878); and *Arkhiv Iugo-Zapadnoi Rossii*, pt 1, vol. VII: *Pamiatniki literaturnoi polemiki pravoslavnykh iuzhno-russtsev s latino-uniatami*, intro. by S. Golubev (Kiev: Vremennaia kommissiia dlia razbora drevnikh aktov 1887).

ments during this period, the nineteenth-century Galician historian Izydor Sharanevych has in three studies traced the reaction of the Orthodox Patriarch in Constantinople toward the Uniate movement and how the socioeconomic status of the lower clergy changed as a result of its entry into the Uniate church.[59]

Besides the problem of church union, there are also several studies dealing with other aspects of Ukrainian religious history during the era of Polish rule. These include works on the continuing efforts to revive the Galician metropolitanate,[60] histories of individual dioceses and parishes,[61] descriptions of the important role played by monasteries before their abolition in 1785,[62] and biographies of individual Orthodox and Uniate bishops.[63]

59 Izydor Szaraniewicz, *Patryarchat wschodni wobec kościoła ruskiego i Rzeczpospolitej Polskiej* (Cracow 1879), first published in *Rozprawy Wydziału Historyczno-Filozoficznego Akademii Umiejętności,* vols VIII and X (Cracow 1878–79), pp. 255–344 and 1–80; Isydor Sharanevych, *Tserkovnaia unyia na Rusy y vliianie ey na zmienu obshchestvennogo polozheniia myrskogo ruskogo dukhoven'stva* (L'viv 1897), translated into Polish as *Kościelna unia na Rusi i wpływ jej na zmianę społecznego stanowiska świeckiego duchowieństwa ruskiego* (L'viv 1899); Izydor Sharanevych, *Rzut oka na beneficya kościoła ruskiego za czasów Rzeczpospolitej polskiej* (L'viv 1875), 2nd rev. ed. entitled *Cherty iz istorii tserkovnykh benefitsii i mirskogo dukhovenstva v Galitskoi Rusi* (L'viv 1902).

See also the descriptions of the clergy based on the visitation of M. Shadurs'kyi between 1759 and 1763 in Melaniia Bordun, ''Z zhyttia ukraïns'koho dukhovenstva l'vivs'koï eparkhiï v druhii pol. XVIII v. (na osnovi vizytatsiï M. Shadurs'koho 1759–1763),'' *Zapysky NTSh,* CXXXIV–CXXXV (L'viv 1924), pp. 137–160.

60 Myron Stasiw, *Metropolia Haliciensis (eius historia et iuridica forma),* Analecta OSBM, series II, sectio I: opera, vol. XII (Rome 1954), 2nd ed. (Rome 1960).

61 Leonid Sonevyts'kyi, ''Ukraïns'kyi iepyskopat peremys'koï i kholms'koï ieparkhiï v XV–XVI st.,'' *Analecta OSBM,* series II, sectio II, vol. II, 1–2 (Rome 1954), pp. 23–64 and vol. II, 3–4 (1956), pp. 348–394, also separately in Analecta OSBM, series II, sectio I: Opera, vol. VI (Rome 1955); Stepan Tomashivs'kyi, ''Do istoriï Peremyshlia i ioho iepyskops'koï katedry,'' *Zapysky ChSVV,* III, 1–2 (Zhovkva 1928), pp. 179–190.

62 Ivan P. Kryp''iakevych, ''Serednovichni monastyri v Halychyni: sproba katalohu,'' *Zapysky ChSVV,* II, 1–2 (Zhovkva 1926), pp. 70–104; Anton Petrushevych, ''Kratkaia rospys' russkym tserkvam y Monastŷriam v horodî L'vovî,'' *Halytskii ystorycheskii sbornyk . . . Halytsko-russkoi Matytsŷ,* I (L'viv 1853), pp. iii–iv, 1–48; M. Holubets', ''Materialy do katalohu vasyliians'kykh monastyriv v Halychyni (dodatky do kataloha I.P. Kryp''iakevych),'' *Zapysky ChSVV,* III (Zhovkva 1930), pp. 165–170; Borys Balyk, ''Manastyri peremys'koï ieparkhiï za vladytstva Innokentiia Vynnyts'koho (1679–1700),'' *Analecta OSBM,* series II, sectio II, vol. III, 1–2 (Rome 1958), pp. 69–97; Iuliian Tselevych, ''Ystoriia Skytu Maniavskoho vôd ieho osnovania azh do prystuplenia l'vôvskoy eparkhiî do uniî (1611–1700),'' in *Spravozdanie dyrektora ts. k. hymnaziî akademychnoy u L'vovî za rôk shkôl'nŷi 1885/6* (L'viv 1886), pp. 1–72; idem, *Ystoriia Skytu Maniavskoho vraz z zbôrnykom hramot, lystôv y deiakykh sudovŷh dokumentôv, dotŷchnŷkh toho monastŷria* (L'viv: p.a. 1887); Venedykt A. Ploshchanskii, ''Lavrov: selo y monastŷr' v samborskom okruzî,'' *Naukovŷi sbornyk Halytsko-russkoi Matytsŷ,* II (L'viv 1866), pp. 318–339; idem,

Cultural history: the brotherhoods

Closely connected with the history of the church were the brotherhoods (*bratstvos*), which by the late sixteenth century had taken the lead in the Orthodox cultural revival. The oldest and most influential of these associations, the L'viv Assumption, later Stauropegial, Brotherhood (L'vivs'ke Uspens'ke [Stavropihiis'ke] Bratstvo), has received the most attention in both documentary collections and secondary literature.[64] The Soviet Ukrainian specialist on this period, Iaroslav Isaievych, has prepared a comprehensive handbook outlining the existing source material on the brotherhoods, on education, and on publishing.[65] Five volumes of documents cover the activity of the Stauropegial Brotherhood between the years 1519 and 1881,[66] while two studies by Izydor Sharanevych have extensive appendices that include minutes of the brotherhood's meetings between 1605 and 1725.[67] Factual information is found in Denys Zubryts'kyi's chronicle of the L'viv Brotherhood (1453–1793),[68] in the more general chronicles of Antin

''Dobromyl': monastŷr' Chyna Sv. Vasyliia Velykoho y nîskol'ko slov ob otnosheniiakh horoda,'' *Naukovŷi sbornyk Halytsko-russkoi Matytsŷ,* III (L'viv 1867), pp. 210–259.

63 Mykola Andrusiak, ''Ivan Khlopets'kyi, peremys'kyi pravoslavnyi epyskop-nominat v 1632–1633 rr.,'' *Zapysky NTSh,* CXLVII (L'viv 1927), pp. 131–140; Mikołaj Andrusiak, *Józef Szumlański: pierwszy biskup unicki lwowski 1667–1708,* Archiwum Towarzystwa Naukowego we Lwowie, Series B, vol. XVI, no. 1 (L'viv 1934); Borys I. Balyk, *Inokentii Ivan Vynnyts'kyi: iepyskop peremys'kyi, sambirs'kyi, sianits'kyi (1680–1700),* Analecta OSBM, series II, sectio I: Opera, vol. XXXVIII (Rome 1978).

64 Much information on the L'viv Brotherhood during its early years is found in the general collections of documents on the period by Petrushevych and Lepkii, note 52 above, as well as in general histories of the organization, chapter 2, n. 67.

65 Iaroslav D. Isaievych, *Dzherela z istorii ukraïns'koï kul'tury doby feodalizmu XVI–XVIII st.* (Kiev: Naukova dumka 1972).

66 *Monumenta confraternitatis Stauropigianae Leopoliensis sumptibus Instituti Stauropigiani,* ed. Wladimirus Milkowicz, vol. I, 2 pts (L'viv 1895–98); *Diplomata statutaria a Patriarchis Orientalibus confraternitati Stauropigianae Leopoliensi, 1586–1592 data,* vol. II, ed. Ivan Krystyniats'kyi (L'viv 1895); *Arkhiv Iugo-zapadnoi Rossii,* chast'pervaia: vols XI–XII, comp. with an intro. by A. Krilovskii (Kiev: Kommissiia dlia razbora drevnykh aktov 1904). See also fourteen documents in *Pamiatniki, izdannye Vremennoiu Kommissieiu dlia razbora drevnikh aktov,* 4 vols (Kiev 1845–59), 2nd rev. ed. (Kiev 1898–1900), vol. III, pt 1.

67 Izydor Sharanevych, *Nikolai Krassovskii (Mikolai Krasuvskii) ot goda 1686 do g. 1692 pisar' upravleniia, a ot g. 1692 do g. 1697 starieishina Stavropigiiskogo Bratstva vo L'vovie* (L'viv 1895); Izydor Sharanevych, *Iurii Eliiashevich (Georgii Il'iashevich) ot 1720 g. chlen i v 1722–1735 gg. odin iz seniorov Stavr. Bratstva v L'vovie* (L'viv 1895).

68 Dionisii Zubrytskii, ''Lietopis' L'vovskago Stavropigial'nago Bratstva,'' *Zhurnal Ministerstva narodnago prosvieshcheniia,* LXII (St Petersburg 1849), pp. 1–22, 59–99, 131–163; LXVI, 2–3 (1850), pp. 61–96 and 121–146; LXVII (1850), pp. 1–43.

Petrushevych,[69] and in a collection of articles on the brotherhood's activity during the eighteenth century.[70] The brotherhood movement throughout the Ukraine is surveyed in two larger works by Mykhailo Hrushevs'kyi[71] and in specialized monographs by Iaroslav Isaievych and Fedir Sribnyi,[72] each of whom concentrates largely on activity in L'viv.

Cultural history: book culture, art, and architecture

A large literature has developed about book printing in Galicia during Polish rule. Despite indications of the existence of earlier printing establishments, it is generally assumed that the beginnings of book printing in Galicia, as well as in the Ukraine as a whole, should be dated with the arrival in L'viv of an emigré from Moscow, Ivan Fedorov / Fedorovych (d. 1583). In 1574, Fedorovych issued from his press the first books printed on Ukrainian territory. He left for Volhynia the following year and then returned to L'viv in 1581. After Fedorovych's death, printing in L'viv was continued at the printshop of the Assumption Brotherhood (est. 1586), which for the next 350 years was to remain one of the most important in Galicia. In the seventeenth century a few other presses were established in Galicia as well.

Iaroslav Isaievych and Mykola Koval's'kyi have written works describing the source materials available for the early history of Ukrainian printing, in which L'viv and other Galician centers are discussed at length.[73] The enormous secondary literature on Fedorovych and printing developments in Galicia is found in a

69 See n. 1 above.

70 Adrian Kopystianskii, ed., *Iubileinii sbornik v pamiat' 350-liettia l'vovskago stavropigiona: materialy otnosiashchisia k istorii l'vovskago stavropigiona v 1700–1767 gg.* (L'viv: Institut Stavropigionu 1936).

71 Mykhailo Hrushevs'kyi, *Istoriia Ukraïny-Rusy,* vol. VI (Kiev 1907; reprinted New York: Knyho-spilka 1955), pp. 498 ff.; Mykhailo Hrushevs'kyi, *Kul'turno-natsional'nyi rukh na Ukraïni v XVI–XVII vitsï* (Kiev and L'viv 1912), 2nd ed. (Vienna: Dniprosoiuz 1919).

72 Iaroslav D. Isaievych, *Bratstva ta ïkh rol' v rozvytku ukraïns'koï kul'tury XVI–XVIII st.* (Kiev: Naukova dumka 1966); Fedir Sribnyi, "Studiï nad organïzatsiieiu l'vivs'koï Stavropigiï vid kintsia XVI do polovyny XVII st.," *Zapysky NTSh,* CVI (L'viv 1911), pp. 25–40; CVIII (1912), pp. 5–38; CXI (1912), pp. 5–24; CXII (1912), pp. 59–73; CXIV (1913), pp. 25–56; CXV (1913), pp. 29–76.

See also F. Labenskii, "Russkiia tserkvi i bratstva na predgradiiakh l'vovskikh v XVI–XVII stolietiiakh," *Viestnik 'Narodnogo Doma',* XXIX (VII), 2–3 (L'viv 1911), pp. 18–31, 35–55.

73 See especially pages 110–143 of Isaievych's work mentioned in note 65 above, and M.P. Koval's'kyi, *Dzherela pro pochatkovyi etap drukarstva na Ukraïni (diial'nist' pershodrukaria Ivana Fedorova v 70-kh–na pochatku 80-kh rr. XVI st.)* (Dnipropetrovs'k: Dnipropetrovs'kyi derzhavnyi universytet 1972).

comprehensive bibliography by Evgenii Nemirovskii.[74] A recent collection of 137 documents on printing activity between 1573 and 1648 also includes much material on Fedorovych and Galicia.[75]

Several general histories of Ukrainian printing by Ilarion Svientsits'kyi, Ivan Ohiienko, Serhii Maslov, Isaak Kahanov, and Iakym Zapasko all contain one or more chapters on early printing activity in Galicia.[76] There are also several studies devoted primarily to Galicia, whether to the earliest pre-Fedorovych enterprises[77] or to the flowering of Galician printing in the seventeenth and eighteenth centuries.[78] As might be expected, Fedorovych has been the subject of much writing by Ukrainian, Russian, and Polish scholars, the most important being recent works

74 E.L. Nemirovskii, *Nachalo knigopechataniia v Moskve i na Ukraine: zhizn' i deiatel'nost' pervopechatnika Ivana Fedorova, ukazatel' literatury 1574–1974* (Moscow: Gosudarstvennaia biblioteka SSSR im. V.I. Lenina 1975).

See also Edward Kasinec, "Soviet Ukrainian Works on the Old Ukrainian Book" *Recenzija*, V, 1 (Cambridge, Mass. 1974), pp. 47–68.

75 Ia.D. Isaievych et al., *Pershodrukar Ivan Fedorov ta ioho poslidovnyky na Ukraïni (XVI–persha polovyna XVII st.: zbirnyk dokumentiv)* (Kiev: Naukova dumka 1975).

76 Ilarion Svientsyts'kyi, *Pochatky knyhopechatania na zemliakh Ukraïny* (Zhovkva: O.O. Vasyliiany 1924); Ivan Ohiienko, *Istoriia ukraïns'koho drukarstva*, vol. I: *istorychno-bibliohrafychnyi ohliad ukraïns'koho drukarstva XV–XVIII vv.* (L'viv 1925; reprinted Winnipeg: Tovarystvo 'Volyn', 1983), especially pp. 33–156; S.I. Maslov, *Ukraïns'ka drukovana knyha XVI–XVIII vv.* (Kiev 1925); I.Ia. Kahanov, *Ukraïns'ka knyha kintsia XVI–XVII stolit' : narysy z istoriï knyhy* (Kharkiv: Knyzhkova palata URSR 1959); Ia.P. Zapasko, *Mystetstvo knyhy na Ukraïni v XVI–XVIII st.* (L'viv: LU 1971).

See also the short survey by Lubomyr R. Wynar, *History of Early Ukrainian Printing, 1491–1600*, Studies in Librarianship, vol. I, no. 2 (Denver: University of Denver Graduate School of Librarianship 1962).

77 O.Ia. Matsiuk, "Chy bulo knyhodrukovannia na Ukraïni do Ivana Fedorova?" *Arkhiv Ukraïny*, XXII, 2 (Kiev 1968), pp. 2–14; O. Hubko, "Do pochatkiv ukraïns'koho drukarstva," *Arkhiv Ukraïny*, XXIII, 3 (Kiev 1969), pp. 12–28.

78 D. Zubrzycki, *Historyczne badania o drukarniach rusko-słowiańskich w Galicyi* (L'viv 1836), translated into Russian: "O slavianorusskikh tipografiiakh v Galitsii i Lodomirii," *Zhurnal Ministerstva narodnago prosvieshcheniia*, XIX, 2 (St Petersburg 1838), pp. 560–585; Ilarion Svientsits'kyi, "Deshcho pro pechatniu Uspens'koho Bratstva u L'vovi ta ïï vydannia," in *Zbirnyk L'vivs'koï Stavropyhiï: mynule i suchasne*, vol. I (L'viv 1921), pp. 325–339; A. Kawecka-Gryczowa, K. Korotajowa, and W. Krajewski, *Drukarze dawnej Polski od XV do XVIII wieku*, vol. VI: *Małopolski–Ziemie Ruskie* (Wrocław: ZNIO 1959); H.I. Koliada and Ia.D. Isaievych, "Drukars'ka sprava na zakhidnoukraïns'kykh zemliakh (XVI–XVIII st.)," in *Knyhy i drukarstvo na Ukraïni* (Kiev: Naukova dumka 1964), pp. 42–69; Ia.D. Isaevich, "Izdatel'skaia deiatel'nost' L'vovskogo bratstva v XVI–XVIII vekakh," *Kniga*, vol. VII (Moscow 1962), pp. 199–238; Iakym Zapasko, *Kolyska ukraïns'koho drukarstva* (L'viv: AN URSR–LNBS 1970). See also the listings compiled by Ia. Holovats'kyi, A. Petrushevych, and F. Maksymenko, chapter 1, notes 28, 78, and 83.

by Evgenii Nemirovskii and Iaroslav Isaievych.[79] The monastery printshops at Pochaïv (est. c. 1630), just over the border in Volhynia, which competed with the jealously guarded prerogatives of the L'viv Assumption Brotherhood, and the one at Univ (est. 1647), are also the subject of individual studies.[80]

The era of Polish rule resulted in significant artistic creativity in the realm of architecture and painting. Familiarity with the achievements in these art forms provides a fuller understanding of the life-style of the secular and religious cultural elite in Galicia. Beginning with the late nineteenth century and continuing down to the present, an extensive literature has developed on architecture and painting produced in Galicia during the seventeenth and eighteenth centuries.[81] There are several general introductions to architectural monuments in Galicia,[82] and L'viv in particular has been the focus of attention in comprehensive monographs by the prewar Polish art historians Władysław Łoziński and Tadeusz Mańkowski and more recently by the Soviet scholar Grigorii Ostrovskii.[83] The

79 E.L. Nemirovskii, *Nachalo knigopechataniia na Ukraine: Ivan Fedorov* (Moscow: Kniga 1974); Ia.D. Isaievych, *Pershodrukar Ivan Fedorov i vynyknennia drukarstva na Ukraïni* (L'viv: Vyshcha shkola 1975).

See also the older studies of Stanisław L. Ptaszycki, *Iwan Fedorowicz, drukarz ruski we Lwowie z końca XVI wieku* (Cracow: G. Gebethner 1884), originally published in *Rozprawy Wydziału Filologicznego Akademii Umiejętnósci,* XI (Cracow 1884); Ivan Krevets'kyi, Ivan Ohiienko, Volodymyr Doroshenko et al., ''Ivan Khvedorovych,'' *Stara Ukraïna,* II–V (L'viv 1924), pp. 19–74; V. Romanovs'kyi, ''Druka Ivan Fedorovych, ioho zhyttia ta diial'nist',''' in *Ukraïns'ka knyha XVI–XVII–XVIII st.*, Trudy Ukraïns'koho naukovoho instytutu knyhoznavstva, vol. I (Kiev 1926), pp. 1–55; Semeon Iu. Bendasiuk, ''Obshcherusskii pervopechatnik Ivan Fedorov,'' *Vremennik Stavropigiiskogo Instituta na 1935 god,* LXXI (L'viv 1934), also separately (L'viv, 1934); P. Berezov, *Pervopechatnik Ivan Fedorov* (Moscow 1952); Ia. Zapasko, *Pershodrukar Ivan Fedorov* (L'viv 1964).

80 ''Pochaevskaia tipografiia i bratstvo l'vovskoe v XVIII viekie,'' *Volynskiia eparkhial'nyia viedomosti,* XVIII, 35–38 (Zhytomir 1909), pp. 726–732, 757–758, 781–785, and 807–810; A. Shchurovs'kyi, ''Do pytannia pro pochatok Pochaïvs'koï drukarni,'' *Zapysky NTSh,* VII (L'viv 1895), misc., pp. 1–3; Ivan Ohiienko, ''Pochatok drukarstva v Unevi,'' *Zapysky NTSh,* CXLI–CXLII (L'viv 1925).

81 References to the extensive literature on art and architecture in L'viv are found in the monographs of Loziński, Mańkowski, Zholtovs'kyi, and Gębarowicz, notes 83, 85, and 86 below. See also the historiographical survey of art scholarship on Galicia during the early decades of this century in Tadeusz Mańkowski, ''Dzieje sztuki na Ziemi Czerwieńskiej (przegląd badań 1918–1934),'' *Ziemia Czerwieńska,* I (L'viv 1935), pp. 290–302.

82 Ladislaus Luszczkiewicz, ''Die Architektur,'' in *Die österreichisch-ungarische Monarchie in Wort und Bild: Galizien* (Vienna: Vlg. der K. K. Hof- und Staatsdruckerei 1898), pp. 665–720; Aleksander Czołowski, ''Dawne zamki i twierdzy na Rusi halickiej,'' *Teka Konserwatorska,* I (L'viv 1892), and separately (L'viv: p.a. 1892); G. K. Lukomskii, *Galitsiia v eia starine: ocherki po istorii arkhitektury XII–XVIII vv.* (Petrograd: R. Golike i A. Vil'borg 1915).

83 Władysław Łoziński, *Sztuka lwowska w XVI i XVII wieku: architektura i rzeżba* (L'viv: H.

wooden church architecture in the Carpathian foothills of southern Galicia has in particular been singled out in numerous studies.[84]

Introductions to secular and religious painting in Galicia from the era of Polish rule are found in the interwar studies of Mykola Holubets' as well as in the extensive sections on Galicia in the more recent and beautifully illustrated works by the Soviet art historians Platon Bilets'kyi and Pavlo M. Zholtkovs'kyi.[85] Special attention has also been given to secular portraiture in L'viv,[86] and to the extensive religious art (especially icons) found in churches and monasteries throughout Galicia.[87]

Altenberg 1898), 2nd ed. (L'viv 1901); Tadeusz Mańkowski, *Dawny Lwów: jego sztuka i kultura artystyczna* (London: Fundacja Lanckorońska i Polska Fundacja Kulturalna 1974); Grigorii S. Ostrovskii, *L'vov: khudozhestvennye pamiatniki* (Leningrad and Moscow: Iskusstvo 1965), 2nd rev. ed. (1975).

See also Bohdan Janusz, *Zabytki monumentalnej architektury Lwowa* (L'viv: 'Wiadomośći Konserwatorskie' 1928). On the artistic heritage of the older medieval capital, Halych, see the comprehensive monograph of Józef Pełeński, *Halicz w dziejach sztuki średniowiecznej* (Cracow: Akademia Umiejętności 1914).

84 Among the more important works are W. Zaloziecky [Volodymyr Zalozets'kyi], *Gotische und barocke Holzkirchen in den Karpatenländern* (Vienna 1926); Mykhailo Dragan, *Ukraïns'ki derev''iani tserkvy,* 2 vols (L'viv 1937); and Vladimír Sičynśkyj [Sichyns'kyi], *Dřevěné stavby v karpatské oblasti,* Carpatica, series III, no. 3 (Prague 1940). See also the beautifully illustrated chapter on Galicia and Carpathian architecture in David Buxton, *The Wooden Churches of Eastern Europe: An Introductory Survey* (Cambridge, London, New York, New Rochelle, Melbourne, and Sydney 1981), pp. 87–147; and the studies of wooden architecture in southern Galicia in Ivan Hvozda, *Derev''iana arkhitektura ukraïns'kykh Karpat/Wooden Architecture of the Ukrainian Carpathians* (New York: Lemko Research Foundation 1978).

85 Mykola Holubets', ''Ukraïns'ke maliarstvo XVI–XVII st. pid pokrovom Stavropyhiï,'' in *Zbirnyk l'vivs'koï Stavropyhiï: mynule i suchasne,* ed. Kyrylo Studyns'kyi (L'viv 1921), pp. 247–324; idem., *Halyts'ke maliarstvo* (L'viv: Dobra knyzhka 1926); Platon Bilets'kyi, *Ukraïns'kyi portretnyi zhyvopys' XVII–XVIII st.: problemy stanovlennia i rozvytku* (Kiev 1969) and Pavlo M. Zholtovs'kyi, *Ukraïns'kyi zhyvopys XVII–XVIII st.* (Kiev: Naukova dumka 1978).

86 Mieczysław Gębarowicz, *Portret XVI–XVIII wieku we Lwowie* (Wrocław, Warsaw, and Cracow: ZNIO–PAN, 1960); see also a monograph about the leading Ukrainian painter of the seventeenth century, Vira Svientsits'ka, *Ivan Rutkovych i stanovlennia realizmu v ukraïns'komu maliarstvi XVII st.* (Kiev: Naukova dumka 1966).

87 The best introductions to eastern church art (especially icon painting) in Galicia are found in Władysław Łoziński, ''Malarstwo cerkievne na Rusi,'' *Kwartalnik Historyczny,* I (L'viv 1887); Ilarion Svientsits'kyi, *Ikonopys Halyts'koï Ukraïny XV–XVI st.* (L'viv 1928); idem., *Ikony Halyts'koï Ukraïny XV–XVI st.* (L'viv 1929); and in analyses of the artistic heritage of two monasteries: *Skyt Maniavs'kyi i Bohorodchans'kyi ikonostas* (L'viv 1926); and Mykola Holubets', ''Lavriv,'' *Zapysky ChSVV,* II, 1–2 (Zhovkva 1926), pp. 30–69 and 3–4 (1927), pp. 317–335.

Cossacks in Galicia and the brigand movement

Historians have also devoted attention to two other aspects of the Ukrainian reaction to Polish rule in Galicia: the military campaigns led by the Zaporozhian Cossack Hetman Bohdan Khmel'nyts'kyi, and the uprisings and protest movements of peasants and mountain brigands. Although Khmel'nyts'kyi's appearance in Galicia was brief (he laid siege to L'viv in 1648 and again in 1655), the central importance of the Cossack leader for Ukrainian history has prompted Galician historians to analyze in detail the activity of this national leader in their native province.

Stepan Tomashivs'kyi has devoted the most attention to the Khmel'nyts'kyi era in Galicia. He prepared three volumes of documents containing the acts of the Galician dietines, materials on the peasant movement (1648–1651), and chronicles describing the Cossack wars around L'viv (1648–1657).[88] Numerous documents dealing with the Cossacks in Galicia are also found in a mid-nineteenth-century collection published by the Kiev Commission for the Study of Ancient Documents and in the three-volume set put out by the Soviets in 1953 on the eve of the three-hundredth anniversary of the "reunification" of the Ukraine with Russia.[89] Soviet writers are, of course, quite interested in stressing Muscovy's interest in the fate of the "western Rus'" lands not only during the Khmel'nyts'kyi era, but throughout the seventeenth century.[90]

Several monographs focus on specific aspects of Khmel'nyts'kyi's activity in Galicia. The best of these are by Stepan Tomashivs'kyi, in which he analyzes both the military and diplomatic aspects of Khmel'nyts'kyi's first campaign (1648) in the L'viv region and the revolutionary response of the local peasantry.[91] The uprisings of Galician-Ukrainian peasants against Polish landlords between 1648

88 Stefan Tomashivs'kyi, ed., *Materyialy do istoryi Halychyny,* 3 vols, in *Zherela do istoryï Ukraïny-Rusy,* vols IV–VI (L'viv: Arkheografichna komisyia NTSh 1898–1913). See also his analysis of the diary of a mid-seventeenth century L'viv official: Stepan Tomashivs'kyi, "Samuil Kazymyr Kushevych, raitsia l'vivs'kyi i ioho zapysna knyzhka," *Zapysky NTSh,* XV, 1 (L'viv 1897), 24 pp.

89 *Pamiatniki, izdannye Vremennoiu kommissieiu dlia razbora drevnikh aktov,* 4 vols (Kiev, 1845–59), 2nd rev. ed. (Kiev 1898–1900); *Vossoedinenie Ukrainy s Rossiei: dokumenty i materialy* [1620–1654], 3 vols (Moscow AN SSSR 1953).

90 Ivan P. Kryp''iakevych, *Zv''iazky Zakhidnoï Ukraïny z Rosiieiu do seredyny XVII st.* (Kiev: AN URSR 1953); M.P. Koval's'kyi, "Politychni zv''iazky zakhidnoukraïns'kykh zemel' z rosiis'koiu derzhavoiu v druhii polovyni XVII st.," *Naukovi zapysky LDU,* XLIII: *Seriia istorychna,* 6 (L'viv 1957), pp. 120–144.

91 Stefan Tomashivs'kyi, *Pershyi pokhid Bohdana Khmel'nyts'koho na Halychynu: dva misiatsi ukraïns'koï polityky 1648 r.* (L'viv 1914). This work is actually a reprint of a chapter that originally appeared in the third volume of his documentary collection (see n. 88 above); Stepan Tomashivs'kyi, "Narodni rukhy v halyts'kii Rusy 1648 r.," *Zapysky NTSh,* XXIII–XXIV (L'viv 1898), 138 pp.

and 1654 are the focus of attention in a monograph by the Soviet scholar Volodymyr Hrabovets'kyi,[92] while the siege of L'viv in 1655 has been the subject of three older Polish studies, each of which considers the eventual departure of Khmel'nyts'kyi as a victory for Polish civilization over the ''unruly eastern hordes.''[93]

The most recent literature on Polish rule in Galicia is from Poland and the Soviet Ukraine, and it reflects the interests of Marxist scholarship in the interminable class conflicts that are considered the dominant feature of all history before the Soviets came to power. The most prolific writers in this regard are the Pole Maurycy Horn and the Ukrainian Volodymyr Hrabovets'kyi. In separate studies, they have described the economic situation and resultant peasant disturbances in Galicia throughout the seventeenth and early eighteenth centuries.[94] Both have also written about one particular aspect of primitive revolt, the brigand movement, based largely in the Carpathian Mountains and led by many local ''Robin Hoods,'' the most famous of whom was Oleksa Dovbush (1700–1745).[95]

See also the brief survey by Ivan P. Kryp''iakevych, ''Bohdan Khmel'nyts'kyi v Halychyni,'' in *Iz velykykh dniv: zbirka v 250-littia smerti Bohdana Khmel'nyts'koho* (L'viv: Narodnyi Komitet 1907), pp. 13–29; and Ludwik Kubala, *Oblężenie Lwowa w roku 1648*, Bibljoteczka Universytetów Ludowych i Młodzieży Szkolnej, no. 120 (Warsaw 1930).

92 V.V. Hrabovets'kyi, *Zakhidnoukraïns'ki zemli v period narodno-vyzvol'noï viiny 1648–1654 rr.* (Kiev: Naukova dumka 1972).

93 Fr. Rawita Gawroński, *Krwawy gość we Lwowie: kartka ze smutnych dziejów Polski i Rusi* (L'viv: H. Altenberg 1905); Franciszek Jaworski, *Obrona Lwowa* (L'viv 1905); Ludwik Kubala, ''Oblężenie Lwowa z r. 1655,'' *Lamus*, II (Warsaw 1908–09), pp. 185–216.

The Ukrainian view of the 1655 siege of L'viv is best described by Mykhailo Hrushevs'kyi, *Istoriia Ukraïny-Rusy*, vol. IX, pt 2 (Kiev 1931; reprinted New York: Knyho-spilka 1957), pp. 1091–1126.

94 See n. 25 above.

95 V.V. Hrabovets'kyi, *Antyfeodal'na borot'ba karpats'koho opryshkivstva XVI–XIX st.* (L'viv: LU 1966); idem, ''Rukh zakarpats'kykh opryshkiv naperedodni i v roky vyzvol'noï viiny 1648–1654 rr.,'' in *Z istoriï zakhidnoukraïns'kykh zemel'*, vol. I (Kiev: AN URSR 1957); idem, ''Opryshkivs'kyi rukh u halyts'kii zemli v pershii polovyni XVIII st. (1700–1738 roky),'' in *Z istoriï zakhidnoukraïns'kykh zemel'*, vol. IV, ed. I.P. Kryp''iakevych (Kiev: AN URSR 1960), pp. 15–29; V.V. Hrabovets'kyi, ''Rukh halyts'kykh opryshkiv u druhii polovyni XVIII st.,'' *Z istoriï Ukraïns'koï RSR*, vol. VI–VII (Kiev: AN URSR 1962); V. Grabovetskii, *Oleksa Dovbush: legendarnyi geroi ukrainskogo naroda* (Moscow: Izd. sotsial'no-ékonomicheskoi literatury 1959); and pt 1 of Maurycy Horn's *Walka chłopów czerwonoruskich*, n. 25 above.

See also E. Drakokhrust, ''Galitskoe Prikarpat'e XVI veka i dvizhenie oprishkov,'' *Voprosy istorii*, IV, 1 (Moscow 1948), pp. 35–58; the historical and sociodemographic studies on the Carpathian region during this period by Stavrovs'kyi and Hoshko, n. 12 above; and the earlier works by Iuliian Tselevych, *Opryshky*, Rus'ka istorychna biblioteka, vol. XIX (L'viv: NTSh 1897), and his Polish work–Julian Celewicz, *O Oleksie Dowbuszczuku, jego poprzednikach i następcach* (n.p., n.d.); and Antoni Prochaska, ''Samorząd województwa ruskiego w walce z opryszkami,'' *Rozprawy Akademii Umiejętności, Wydział Historyczno-Filozoficzny: Serya II*, XXIV (Cracow 1907), pp. 269–336.

Chapter 5

1772–1848

Background

The internal decline of the Polish-Lithuanian Commonwealth, which had already begun in the second half of the seventeenth century, and the simultaneous increase in the strength of neighboring Prussia, Austria, and Russia were factors that were to have a direct effect on the future of Galicia. In 1772, Prussia, Austria, and Russia carried out the first of three partitions of Polish territory that less than a quarter of a century later, in 1795, were to result in the removal of Poland from the map of Europe. In 1772, the Austrian empress Maria Theresa (reigned 1740–1780) had laid claim, as sovereign of Hungary, to the lands of the medieval Galicia-Volhynian Kingdom, which the Hungarian royal house had, in its turn, claimed since the thirteenth century as part of its own patrimony. On the basis of this claim, Austria received territory known as the Kingdom of Galicia and Lodomeria (the Latin form of Volhynia), which became one of the crown lands or provinces of the empire.

Despite its official name, Austria's new territorial acquisition included hardly any of Volhynia (except for a small region around Zbarazh). On the other hand, the province of Galicia did include all the former Polish palatinates of Rus' (minus the northern half of the Chełm land), Belz, and Podolia west of the Zbruch River–that is, territory that coincided with the medieval, pre-Polish, Galician principality. Added to these core lands inhabited primarily by Ukrainians were Polish-inhabited lands father west (the Sandomierz and Cracow palatinates south of the Vistula River), which Austria also received in 1772.

The new province of Galicia comprised 83,000 sq. km and an estimated 2,797,000 inhabitants (1786). In 1787, Austria added to Galicia the province of Bukovina (75,000 inhabitants), which it had recently (1774) acquired from the Ottoman Empire; then as a result of the third partition of Poland in 1795, Austria

RUSSIAN EMPIRE
GERMAN EMPIRE
SILESIA
GALICIA
VOLHYNIA
PODOLIA
BUKOVINA
HUNGARIAN KINGDOM
CARPATHIAN MOUNTAINS
N
Częstochowa
Kielce
Lublin
Chełm
Zamość
Volodymyr Volyns'kyi
Luts'k
Rivne
Vistula
San
Wieprz
Buh
Styr
Horyn
Tarnobrzeg
Nisko
Mielec
Kolbuszowa
Sokal'
Chrzanów
Oświęcim
Cracow
Podgórze
Wieliczka
Dąbrowa
Tarnów
Ropczyce
Łańcut
Cieszanów
Rava Rus'ka
Kaminka Strumylova
Brody
Biała
Wadowice
Brzesko
Bochnia
Dunajec
Pilzno
Rzeszów
Przeworsk
Jarosław
Iavoriv
Zhovkva
Żywiec
Myślenice
Limanowa
Strzyżów
Wisłok
Mostys'ka
L'viv
Zolochiv
Nowy Sącz
Gorlice
Jasło
Brzozów
Przemyśl
Horodok
Peremyshliany
Zboriv
Grybów
Krosno
Dobromyl'
Rudky
Bibrka
Zbarazh
Nowy Targ
Sanok
Lesko
Staryi Sambir
Sambir
Berezhany
Ternopil'
Skalat
Zbruch
Poprad
Drohobych
Zhydachiv
Rohatyn
Seret
Terebovlia
Stryi
Dniester
Pidhaitsi
Husiatyn
Turka
Skole
Kalush
Buchach
Chortkiv
Dolyna
Stanyslaviv
Borshchiv
Košice
Tovmach
Zalishchyky
Bohorodchany
Horodenka
Uzhhorod
Nadvirna
Kolomyia
Sniatyn
Pechenizhyn
Tysa
Kosiv
Cheremosh
Chernivtsi
Prut
0 50 MILES
0 50 KILOMETERS
GALICIA IN THE AUSTRO-HUNGARIAN EMPIRE
International borders, 1850
Boundary between Hungarian Kingdom and Austrian crownlands
Austrian crownland boundaries
Boundaries between west and east Galician judicial districts
Approximate Polish-Ukrainian ethnolinguistic boundary
County seats in Galicia

once again expanded northward, almost doubling Galicia's size. This last acquisition was lost in 1809 to the Duchy of Warsaw, which soon after became the Congress Kingdom of Poland within the Russian Empire. The only other territorial change came in 1847, when the Austrian administered city/state of Cracow (including the city and some territory north of the Vistula River) was made an integral part of Galicia. With the exception of this last minor acquisition, the boundaries of Austrian Galicia were more or less fixed in 1809. Thus, from the outset of the nineteenth century, Austrian Galicia included historical Galicia inhabited primarily by Ukrainians (71 percent in 1849) as well as some Polish-inhabited territory west of the San and Wisłok rivers. In keeping with the principles outlined in the introduction to this study, the following two chapters on the Austrian period will deal with developments in historic, or "eastern" Galicia.

Galicia entered the Austrian Empire at a time when that state was ruled by "enlightened" rulers, Maria Theresa and her son Joseph II (reigned 1780–1790), both of whom were anxious to strengthen their realm through a program of national planning and governmental centralization. By 1786, Austrian laws replaced Polish ones; the old dietines *(sejmiki)* were abolished; and after a while, the elected urban councils (whose privileges had been guaranteed under Magdeburg Law) were replaced by bureaucrats appointed by the imperial administration in Vienna. As in other Austrian provinces, an Assembly of Estates was set up. Located in L'viv, which under the name of Lemberg remained the administrative capital, the assembly comprised magnates, gentry, and clergy. However, it could only send petitions to the emperor; real power rested in the hands of the emperor's appointee, the governor *(gubernator/naczelnik)*, who ruled with his administration from L'viv. To administer the province more effectively, it was divided into nineteen regions *(Kreise)*. The era of the enlightened, or reforming, Austrian rulers, which Galicia first experienced, had a profound effect on the province's life. The formerly all-powerful position of the Polish nobility *(szlachta)* was broken: the theoretical equality of all nobles was replaced by the creation of two separate estates–magnates and gentry; tax-exempt status for nobles was abolished; their domination of the legal system ended; and their control over the serfs was strictly defined. Emperor Joseph II even went so far as to abolish serfdom in 1781, although his social experiment ended after his death and serfdom was restored. Nontheless, despite these and other reforms from above, life for the masses of the population was unchanged. Galicia still remained an overwhelmingly agrarian society in which the vast majority of the populace was composed of enserfed peasants whose lives, especially in the economic sphere, were dependent on a small class of magnates and gentry.

In one area, Austrian rule brought longer lasting change. Equality for all religions was proclaimed and backed up by concrete governmental support, especially in the realm of education. The established church for Ukrainians, now known as Greek Catholic (Uniate was dropped because the hierarchy felt the term was derogatory), received government funding to create Greek Catholic seminaries both in Galicia and in the imperial capital. Elementary education was also encouraged and the first university in Galicia was established at L'viv (1784), where before long an institute (Studium Ruthenum) to train Greek Greek Catholic Ukrainians was set up. The prestige of Ukrainian Greek Catholics was raised even further by the revival of the Galician metropolitanate in 1808.

One result of these developments was the growth of a Galician-Ukrainian intelligentsia. Though small in number and almost exclusively composed of Greek Catholic clergy, this group had become exposed to the ideas of romantic nationalism that dominated contemporary thought in Germany and east-central Europe and that placed an almost mystical faith in the supposed virtues of the *Volk*–unique ethnolinguistic groups. One of these groups comprised the Ukrainians of Galicia, and from educational centers in Vienna, Przemyśl, and L'viv, the beginnings of a Ukrainian cultural revival took place in the first half of the nineteenth century. Of course, this was only the very embryonic stage of national development; the vast majority of the population was still composed of serfs, and the small intelligentsia was confined to struggling over issues of education and the question of formulating an acceptable literary language. Any participation by the masses in this process or any demands for political change had to await the revolution of 1848.

Historical surveys and descriptive works

The vast majority of writings on the period between 1772 and 1848 consists of secondary literature dealing with three topics: the establishment of the Austrian administration, socioeconomic developments, and most especially cultural history. There are only a few general histories that cover the period as a whole. One of the earliest was written in 1846 by Iakiv Holovats'kyi, whose work provides the perspective not only of a contemporary but of a participant in the historical process as well.[1] The period is treated at greater length in the first volume of Pylyp Svystun's history of Ukrainians under Austrian rule. Svystun, who was a Galician Russophile, is generally critical of the Austrian government which, because of its fear of the Russian Empire he argues, cooperated with Galician-Polish magnates and the Greek Catholic hierarchy to restrict contacts between Galician ''Rus-

1 Havryło Rusyn [Iakiv Holovats'kyi], ''Zustände der Russinen in Galizien,'' *Jahrbücher für slawische Literatur, Kunst und Wissenschaft*, IV (Leipzig 1846; reprinted Leipzig: Zentralantiquariat der DDR, 1974), pp. 361–379.

sians'' and their brethren in the east.[2] The Ukrainian viewpoint, which is much more favorably disposed toward the efforts of Austria during its initial years of rule in Galicia, is presented by Tyt Voinarovs'kyi as part of a larger work on Ukrainians under Polish rule before 1851.[3] The Polish view of Galicia's history, which focuses primarily on the western Polish-inhabited areas, is presented by Kazimierz Bartoszewicz.[4] Useful for factual data is the last volume of Antin Petrushevych's chronicle of Galician history, covering the years 1772 to 1800.[5]

Several important descriptions of Galicia as a whole during the years 1772 to 1848 are available. Among the first of these is a statistical analysis of the province at the outset of the nineteenth century by Michał Wiesiołowski.[6] This has been followed by a solid monograph by A. Brawer on Galician society as it was when the Austrians first acquired it, and by detailed accounts by Walerian Kalinka and Stanisław Grodziski on the historical, social, religious, political, legal, economic, and military aspects of the province throughout the first seventy-five years of Austrian rule.[7] These same years are also described in contemporary accounts by native and foreign visitors; the more important of these are by the first Austrian governor of Galicia, Count Anton Pergen, the director of police in L'viv, Leopold von Sacher-Masoch, the Moravian leader, Karel Zap, and the local Galician leader, Iakiv Holovats'kyi.[8] The impressions of several other writers have been

2 Filipp I. Svistun, *Prikarpatskaia Rus' pod vladieniem Avstrii*, pt 1: *1772–1850* (L'viv: Izd. O.A. Markova 1896; reprinted Trumbull, Conn.: Peter S. Hardy 1970).
See also *Galitskaia Rus' v evropeiskoi polititsie* (L'viv: Novyi prolom 1886).

3 Titus von Wojnarowskyj, *Das Schicksal des ukrainischen Volkes unter polnischer Herrschaft*, vol. I (Vienna: p.a. 1921), especially pp. 57–256.

4 Kazimierz Bartoszewicz, *Dzieje Galicyi: jej stan przed wojną i 'wyodrębnienie'* (Warsaw, Lublin, Łodź, and Cracow: Gebethner i Wolff 1917).
See also the earlier critique of Austrian rule in Galicia from a Polish patriotic and democratic point of view in Michel Kubrakiewicz, *Essai sur le gouvernement paternel et les mystères d'Autriche* (Paris 1846).

5 A.S. Petrushevych, *Svodnaia halychsko-russkaia lîtopys' s 1772 do kontsa 1800 h.* (L'viv 1889), published first in *Lyteraturnŷi sbornyk Halytsko-russkoi matytsŷ za 1888 hod* (L'viv 1889).

6 Michał Wiesiołowski, *Rys statystyczno-jeograficzny Galicyi austryjackiej skreślony r. 1811* (Poznań: W. Stefański 1842).

7 A. Brawer, *Galizien wie es an Österreich kam: eine historisch-statistische Studie über die inneren Verhältnisse des Landes im Jahre 1772* (Leipzig and Vienna 1910); Waleryan Kalinka, *Galicya i Kraków pod panowaniem austryackiem* (Paris: K. Królikowski 1853), reprinted under the same title in *Dziela Ks. Waleryana Kalinki*, vol. X (Cracow: Społka Wydawnicza Polska 1898); Stanisław Grodziski, *Historia ustroju społeczno-politycznego Galicji 1772–1848*, PAN, Oddział w Krakowie, Praci Komisji Nauk. Historycznych, vol. XXVIII (Wrocław, Warsaw, Cracow, and Gdańsk 1971).

8 Ludwik Finkel, ''Memoryał Antoniego hr. Pergena pierwszego gubernatora Galicyi, o stanie

preserved in anthologies compiled by Stanisław Schnür-Pepłowski and Marian Tyrowicz.[9]

Establishment of Austrian and foreign affairs

The establishment of an Austrian administration for Galicia is described in several works. Beginning in 1778, the imperial government issued handbooks *(schematisma)* almost every year, outlining the administrative structure of the entire Habsburg empire. Several pages in each volume were devoted to Galicia.[10] Another series was issued between 1789 and 1914, covering solely the Kingdom of Galicia and Lodomeria.[11] Besides these official handbooks, the administrative system set up by Maria Theresa and most especially by Joseph II is analyzed in great detail by Wacław Tokarz and Horst Glassl.[12] The colonization program of the Austrian rulers that brought several thousand new settlers, especially Germans, to Galicia has received detailed statistical analysis in several works.[13] The

---

kraju,'' *Kwartalnik Historyczny,* XIV, 1 (L'viv 1900), pp. 24–43; Hofrath von Sacher-Masoch, ''Memoiren eines österreichischen Polizeidirektors,'' *Auf der Höhe,* no. 2 (Leipzig 1882), pp. 104–123 and 431–449; Karel V. Zap, *Cesty a procházky po haličské zemi* (Prague 1843), 2nd ed. (Prague 1863); J.F.H. [Iakiv Holovats'kyi], ''Cesta po halické a uherské Rusi,'' *Časopis českého musea,* XV, 2, 3, 4 (Prague 1841), pp. 183–223, 302–317, 423–437; XVI, 1 (1842), pp. 42–62; idem, ''O halické a uherské Rusi,'' *Časopis českého musea,* XVII, 1 (Prague 1843), pp. 12–52.

9 Stanisław Schnür-Pepłowski, *Galiciana, 1778–1812* (L'viv 1896) and *Cudzoziemcy w Galicyi (1787–1841)* (Cracow: Społka Wyd. Polska 1898); Marian Tyrowicz, ed., *Galicja od pierwszego rozbioru do wiosny ludów 1772–1849* (Cracow and Wrocław: ZNIO, 1956).
See also the historical gudebook by Stanisław Schnür-Pepłowski, *Obrazy z przeszłości Galicyi i Krakowa (1772–1858)* (L'viv: Gubrynowicz i Schmidt 1896).

10 *Schematismus des kaiserlichen auch kaiserlich-königlichen Hofes und Staates;* later *Hof- und Staats-Schematismus des österreichischen Kaiserthumes;* and from 1844 to 1868 *Hof- und Staats-Handbuch des österreichischen Kaiserthumes* (Vienna: K.K. Hof- und Staats-Druckerei 1778–1868); *Hof- und Staats-Handbuch der oesterreichisch-ungarischen Monarchie,* vols I–XLIV (Vienna: K.K. Hof- und Staatsdruckerei 1874–1914).

11 *Schematismus der Königreiche Galizien und Lodomerien* [1789–1843] / *Provinzial-Handbuch der Königreiche Galizien und Lodomerien* [1844–1884] / *Handbuch der Lemberger Stathalterei-Gebietes in Galizien* [1855–1869] / *Szematyzm Królewstwa Galicyi i Lodomeryi z Wielkim Ks. Krakowskim* [1870–1914] (L'viv 1789–1914).

12 Wacław Tokarz, *Galicya w początkach ery józefińskiej w świetle ankiety urzędowej z roku 1783* (Cracow: Akademia Umiejętności 1909); Horst Glassl, *Das österreichische Einrichtungswerk in Galizien (1772–1790),* Veröffentlichungen des Osteuropa-Institutes München, vol. XLI (Wiesbaden: Otto Harrassowitz 1975).
See also Bronisław Łoziński, ''Początki ery jósefińskiej w Galicyi,'' *Kwartalnik Historyczny,* XXIV (L'viv 1910), pp. 163–206.

13 See chapter 10, n. 93.

Austrian police administration and the creation of an albeit ineffectual Assembly of Estates, or Diet (1817–1845), to replace old local Polish dietines are also the subject of two studies.[14]

In comparison to preceding and subsequent periods, Galicia between 1772 and 1848 was not a focus of interest for international concern and Austria's control of the area was never seriously challenged. Nevertheless, there are some studies that treat Galicia's relations with the outside world, such as the diplomatic and military aspects of Austria's takeover of L'viv in 1772;[15] the occupation of the Ternopil' area by the Russian army between 1809 and 1815;[16] the reaction of Poles and Ukrainians in the province to the Polish revolution of 1831 and their cooperation in later conspiracy movements;[17] and the periodic attempts (1790, 1825–27, 1830) of Hungary to lay claim to Galician territory during its negotiations with Vienna for more self-rule.[18]

14 Antoni Kurka, *Dzieje i tajemnice lwowskiej policji z czasów zaboru austrjackiego 1772–1918* (L'viv: Gubrynowicz i syn 1930): Bronisław Łoziński, *Galicyjski sejm stanowy (1817–1845)* (L'viv: H. Altenberg 1905).

See also the text (in French) of the abortive Austrian plan for a constitution for Galicia in Stanisław Grodziski and Artur St. Gerhardt, eds, *Projekt konstytucji dla Galicji z 1790 r. (''Charta Leopoldina'')*, Zeszyty Naukowe Uniwersytetu Jagiellońskiego, vol. DLXXXXVIII: Prace Prawnicze, no. 94 (Warsaw and Cracow 1981).

15 Bronisław Pawłowski, *Zajęcie Lwowa 1772*, Biblioteka Lwowska, vol. XIV (L'viv 1911).

16 Jan Leszczyński, *Rządy rosyjskie w kraju Tarnopolskim 1809–1814*, Monografie w Zakresie Dziejów Nowożytnych, vol. III (Cracow and Warsaw 1903); idem, ''Cesya wschodnio-galicyjska na rzecz Rosyi (Rokowania cesyjne: październik 1809-czerwiec 1810),'' *Kwartalnik Historyczny*, XVI, 1 (L'viv 1902), pp. 23–53. See also the description of L'viv, which in 1809 was occupied by Polish, then Russian, troops before being retaken by the Austrians: Bronisław Pawłowski, *Lwów w 1809 r.*, Biblioteka Lwówska, vol. III (L'viv 1909).

17 Józef Białynia Chołodecki, *Lwów w czasie powstania listopadowego*, Biblioteka Lwowska, vol. XXIX (L'viv 1930); Ivan Krevets'kyi, ''Fal'shovannie metryk dlia pol's'kykh povstantsiv z 1830–31 rr. (prychynok do kharakterystyky halyts'ko-rus'koho dukhovenstva pershoï polovyny XIX st),'' *Zapysky NTSh*, LXXVII (L'viv 1907), pp. 107–113; Kyrylo Studyns'kyi, ''Pol'ski konspiratsiï sered rus'kykh pytomtsïv i duchovens'tva v Halychynï v rokakh 1831–46,'' *Zapysky NTSh*, LXXX (L'viv 1907), pp. 53–108 and LXXXII (1908), 87–177; Hryhorii Iu. Herbil's'kyi, ''Do pytannia pro z''viazky ukraïns'kykh i pol's'kykh prohresyvnykh diiachïv u Halychyni v pershii polovyni XIX st.,'' *Visnyk LDU: Seriia istorychnna*, no. 1 (L'viv 1962), pp. 87–99; Włodzimierz Borys, ''Do historii ruchu społeczno-politycznego studentów Universytetu i mlodzieży rzemieślniczej Lwowa w latach 1832–46,'' *Przegląd Historyczny*, XIV, 3 (Warsaw 1963), pp. 418–431; Bolesław Łopuszański, *Stowarzyszenie Ludu Polskiego (1836–1841): geneza i dzieje* (Cracow: Wydawnictwo Literackie 1975).

18 Szymon Askenazy, ''Galicya a Węgry,'' *Nowe Wczasy* (Warsaw 1910), pp. 264–274.

Socioeconomic developments

Historians have devoted considerable attention to socioeconomic developments in Austrian Galicia before 1848. Separated from the trade routes and markets of the Polish economic sphere of which it had been a part, the economic life of Galicia stagnated. The Austrian government initially made some investments in the area, but soon decided that the province should remain an agricultural region that would supply food products to the rest of the empire while at the same time becoming a market for products from the more industrialized western provinces. Investments were not encouraged; industry was limited to a few ineffectual textile mills, iron works, glass works, and breweries; and the urban areas were neglected. As a result, Galicia became a kind of internal colony and the most economically depressed and backward area within the Austrian half of the empire.

Agriculture declined as well. The Josephine reforms aimed at improving the status of the enserfed peasantry were short-lived or their intention distorted. Most of the land remained in the hands of Polish magnates and gentry, and peasant obligations remained in force. The situation was further aggravated by a rapid growth in population that could not be absorbed by a nonexistent industrial sector or by an agricultural sector that offered no credit and a decreasing amount of available land.

Agrarian conditions in eastern Galicia have been the special focus of attention in a collection of documents[19] and in general surveys of the period by Mykhailo Herasymenko and Evdokiia Kosachevskaia.[20] The effect on the peasantry of the Josephine reforms has been discussed in great detail in two monographs and a collection of documents by Roman Rozdol's'kyi, while the domanial (demesne) and rustical (peasant) division of all land put into effect by the Austrians has been analyzed on the basis of lord/serf agreements from the period by Bronisław Łoziński.[21]

19 *Klasova borot'ba selianstva skhidnoï Halychyny (1772–1849): dokumenty i materialy* (Kiev: Naukova dumka 1974). Actually, more than half of the 301 documents in this collection pertain to the peasant uprisings of 1846 and to the revolutionary years 1848–1849.

20 M.P. Herasymenko, *Ahrarni vidnosyny v Halychyni v period kryzy panshchynnoho hospodarstva* (Kiev: AN URSR 1959); Evdokiia M. Kosachevskaia, *Vostochnaia Galitsiia nakanune i v period revoliutsii 1848 g.* (L'viv: LU 1965).

21 Roman Rozdolski, *Wspólnota gminna w b. Galiciji Wschodniej i jej zanik*, Badania z Dziejów Społecznych i Gospodarczych, vol. XXVII (L'viv 1936); idem, *Stosunki poddańcze w dawnej Galicji*, 2 vols (Warsaw: PWN 1962); Bronisław Łoziński, "Z czasów i aktów dominikalnych (przyczynek do historyi administracyi w Galicyi)," *Kwartalnik Historyczny*, XX, 1–2 (L'viv and Warsaw 1906), pp. 252–285; idem, "Z czasów nowicyatu administracyjnego Galicyi," *Kwartalnik Historyczny*, XXI, 1 and 2–3 (L'viv and Warsaw 1907), pp. 105–116 and 411–440.

The phenomenon of serfdom and the manner in which it changed between 1772 and 1848 are analyzed by Ludwig von Mises and Ivan Franko.[22] Soviet historians are particularly concerned with the reactions of the peasants to their plight: Fedir Steblii has traced peasant ''rebellions'' and the brigand movement in eastern Galicia during the first half of the nineteenth century, as well as the peasant uprising of 1846. This event, although based in Polish-inhabited areas of western Galicia during the early spring of that year, nonetheless had repercussions in Ukrainian eastern Galicia as well, especially during the late spring and summer months.[23] The problem of serfdom in Galicia became an important issue in Polish revolutionary circles, especially after 1830, and this development as well as its impact on Ukrainians in eastern Galicia is the basis of extensive studies by Ostap Terlets'kyi and Ivan S. Miller.[24]

Developments in industry and the status of the working class throughout Galicia as a whole are treated in a general survey of the period by the Polish

---

See also E. Barwiński and M. Wasowicz, ''Reformy Józefa II i jego następców i ich pozostałości archiwalne,'' *Ziemia Czerwieńska,* I, 2 (L'viv 1935), pp. 251–289; P. Pyrozhenko and K. Sivers'ka, *Iosyfins'ka (1785–1788) i frantsyskans'ka (1819–1820) metryky, pershi pozemel'ni kadastry Halychyny: pokazhchyk naselenykh punktiv* (Kiev: Naukova dumka 1965); Ivan Krevets'kyi, ''Pomichni dnï: prychynky do istoriï panshchyny v Halychynï v XIX v.,'' *Zapysky NTSh,* LXXVI (L'viv 1907), pp. 142–155.

22 Ludwig von Mises, *Die Entwicklung des gutsherrlich-bäuerlichen Verhältnisses in Galizien (1772–1848),* Wiener Staatswissenschaftliche Studien, vol. IV, pt 2 (Vienna and Leipzig 1902); Ivan Franko, *Panshchyna i ïï skasovanie v 1848 roku* (L'viv: Prosvita 1898).

See also the more general work by V. Budzynovskyi, *Panshchyna, ieï pochatok i skasovanie* (Chernivtsi 1898).

23 Fedir I. Steblii, *Borot'ba selian Skhidnoï Halychyny proty feodal'noho hnitu v pershii polovyni XIX st.* (Kiev: AN URSR 1961); F.I. Steblii, ''Pro selians'ki zavorushennia v Halychyni u 1805 rotsi,'' *Pytannia istoriï narodiv SRSR,* vol. III (Kharkiv 1966), pp. 81–86; Volodymyr Borys, ''Antyfeodal'na ahitatsiia v Skhidnii Halychyni v polovyni 30-kh na pochatku 40-kh rr. XIX st.,'' *Arkhivy Ukraïny,* XXII, 3 (Kiev 1968), pp. 76–84; F.I. Steblii, ''Selians'kyi rukh u Skhidnii Halychyni v 1846 rotsi,'' *Z istoriï zakhidnoukraïns'kykh zemel',* vol. V, ed. I.P. Kryp''iakevych (L'viv: AN URSR 1960), pp. 37–56; F.I. Steblii, ''Skhidna Halychyna i selians'ke povstannia 1846 r.,'' *Ukraïns'kyi istorychnyi zhurnal,* XIV, 5 (Kiev 1971), pp. 21–29.

See also the memoirs of the events of 1846 by a Greek Catholic priest, Iurii Hladylovych, ''Spomyny rus'koho s'viashchenyka pro rizniu 1846 roku,'' *Zapysky NTSh,* XII, 4 (L'viv 1896), 20 pp.

24 Ivan Zanevych [Ostap Terlets'kyi], *Znesenie panshchyny v Halychyni: prychynok do istoriï suspil'noho zhytia i suspil'nykh pohliadiv 1830–1848 rr.,* pt 1 (L'viv 1896); I.S. Miller, ''Nakanune otmeny barshchiny v Galitsii,'' *Uchenye zapiski Instituta slavianovedeniia,* I (Moscow and Leningrad 1949), pp. 119–240.

scholar Walentyna Najdus.[25] The city of L'viv has been given special attention, especially in the solid work of the Polish economic historian Stanisław Hoszowski.[26] There are also studies on the discrepancies between the legally defined social groups and the actual class structure of society, on metalwork artisans, on the role of granaries in the countryside, and on trade in the city of Brody.[27]

Cultural history: background

The establishment of Austrian rule in Galicia initially brought several advantages in the cultural sphere to the Ukrainian population, although many of these lost their effectiveness in the early decades of the nineteenth century. In their efforts to strengthen the internal structure of the Habsburg realm, Maria Theresa and Joseph II established a network of schools, and while the activity of the monasteries was curtailed, the status of the Uniate church (renamed the Greek Catholic church in 1774) was raised; it was made the legal and social equal of the predominant Roman Catholic church. Although supported by the state, educational advances for Ukrainians in Galicia were closely linked to the Greek Catholic church. To ensure that the Greek Catholic church would be able to fulfill its new role, cadres of priests had to be educated, and for that purpose theological seminaries were established in Vienna (the Barbareum, 1775–1784) and L'viv (1783). Also, at the University of L'viv (est. 1784), a special collegium, the Studium Ruthenum (1787–1809), was set up to instruct Ukrainians who were still unable to understand Latin. Finally, the prestige of the Greek Catholic church was raised substantially when the Galician metropolitanate was restored in 1808, with its seat in

25 Walentyna Najdus, ''Galicja,'' in *Polska klasa robotnicza: zarys dziejów,* vol. I, pt 1, ed. Stanisław Kalabiński (Warsaw: PWN 1974), pp. 507–659.

26 Stanisław Hoszowski, *Ekonomiczny rozwój Lwowa w latach 1772–1914* (L'viv 1935) and his *Ceny w Lwowie w latach 1701–1914,* Badania z Dziejów Społecznych i Gospodarczych, vol. XIII (L'viv 1934).

See also the more specialized works on the city during the first decades of Austrian rule: Janina Bielecka, *Kontrakty Lwowskie w latach 1768–1775: wpływ pierwszego rozbioru Polski, 1772 r., na kontrakty lwowskie,* Badania z Dziejów Społecznych i Gospodarczych, vol. XXXVI (Poznań 1948); and F.I. Svistun, ''Russkie domovladiel'tsy v L'vovie v XVIII vieku,'' *Viestnik Narodnago Doma,* XXVII (V) (L'viv 1909), pp. 171–181.

27 M.P. Herasymenko, ''Klasy i sotsial'ni hrupy v Halychyni v kintsi XVIII st.,'' in *Z istoriï zakhidnoukraïns'kykh zemel',* vol. II, ed. I.P. Kryp''iakevych (L'viv 1957), pp. 78–107; Ivan Karpynets', ''Halyts'ki zalizni huty ta ïkh produktsiia v rr. 1772–1848,'' *Zapysky NTSh,* CLIV (L'viv 1937), pp. 141–182; Ivan Franko, ed., *Hromads'ki shpikhlïri v Halychynï 1784–1840 r.,* in *Ukraïns'ko-rus'kyi arkhyv,* vol. II (L'viv 1907); Tadeusz Lutman, *Studja nad dziejami handlu Brodów w latach 1773–1880,* Badania z Dziejów Społecznych i Gospodarczych, vol. XXVI (L'viv 1937).

L'viv and dioceses in L'viv and Przemyśl. The result of these developments was the creation of a Galician-Ukrainian intelligentsia, albeit mostly clergymen, trained in a western-oriented educational tradition.

By the early nineteenth century, however, the Barbareum and Studium Ruthenum had ceased functioning, the University of L'viv (from 1817) offered instruction only in German, and the network of elementary schools offered instruction for the most part only in Polish. As a result, the younger generations were becoming rapidly polonized, while the older leaders were left to argue among themselves as to how best to maintain their recently obtained social status, even if that meant assimilation to Polish culture. On the other hand, if some kind of local patriotism was being espoused, it usually got no further than discussions concerning the problem of which literary language should be used for Galician-Ukrainian cultural affairs. The few attempts at establishing cultural societies had failed, there were no newspapers or journals in the native tongue, and very few books were published. This situation changed only slightly when a group of three seminary students, known later as the Rusyn Triad *(Rus'ka triitsa),* published the first book in the vernacular–*Rusalka dnîstrovaia* (1837). This stimulated the appearance of a few more literary works and grammars in the 1840s. A Galician-Ukrainian cultural revival had begun.

Because this revival is looked to as the source for more intense cultural developments in the second half of the nineteenth century, the pre-1848 years, especially the 1830s and 1940s when the Rusyn Triad was active, have received extensive treatment in secondary literature. These writings may be divided into general cultural histories of the whole period and studies focusing on education, the church, literature, individual writers, and contacts with intellectual currents abroad.

Cultural history: sources and surveys

Three collections of documents covering all or part of the period 1772 to 1848 have been edited by Ivan Franko, Mykhailo Tershakovets', and Stepan Tomashivs'kyi. The varied materials deal with the local clergy, establishment of elementary schools, the Studium Ruthenum, textbooks, and censorship.[28]

28 Ivan Franko, ed., *Materiialy do kul'turnoï istoriï Halyts'koï Rusy XVIII i XIX viku,* Zbirnyk istorychno-fil'osofichnoï sektsiï NTSh, vol. V (L'viv: NTSh 1902). Each of the several sections in the collection has an introduction written by its compiler: Mykhailo Zubryts'kyi, Iurii Kmit, Ivan Kobylets'kyi, Ivan E. Levyts'kyi, and Ivan Franko. Mykhailo Tershakovets', ed., *Materialy i zamitky do istoriï natsional'noho vidrodzhenia Halyts'koï Rusy v 1830–40 rr. (Dodatok: Do istoriï moskvofil'stva v Uhors'kii Rusy),* in *Ukraïns'ko-rus'kyi arkhyv,* vol. III

As for general surveys, only a few older ones cover all aspects of cultural development during the whole period in question. These include works by Mykhailo Vozniak and Volodymyr Hnatiuk who, as representatives of a Ukrainophile view, paint with sympathy the late eighteenth-century achievements of the Austrian government and the early efforts to create a vernacular-based cultural movement in the 1830s and 1840s.[29] In contrast, a monograph on this same period by Ivan Filevych expounds the Russophile view, which is generally critical of the Viennese government for its efforts to ''de-Russianize'' the local population and for its acquiescence, with the help of the Greek Catholic hierarchy, in allowing further polonization.[30] Variations of the above interpretations are found in studies by Iakiv Holovats'kyi, Ivan E. Levyts'kyi, Ivan Franko, and Serhii Iefremov, all of whom focus on cultural developments before 1820.[31] The Soviet Marxist view of the early nineteenth century is best outlined in two monographs by Hryhorii Herbil's'kyi.[32] Fulfilling Marxist criteria, Herbil's'kyi seeks out and distinguishes progressive from reactionary cultural leaders. Progressive figures are somewhat difficult to find during this period, however, since almost all are clergy

---

(L'viv: Fil'osofichna sektsiia NTSh 1907); Stefan Tomashivs'kyi, ed., *Materiialy do istoriï halyts'ko-rus'koho shkil'nytstva XVIII i XIX vv.*, in *Ukraïns'ko-rus'kyi arkhyv,* vol. IV (L'viv: Istorychno-fil'osofichna sektsiia NTSh 1909). Each section of the Tomashivs'kyi collection has an introduction written by its compiler: Ilarion Svientsits'kyi, Iurii Kmit, Stepan Tomashivs'kyi, and Ivan Krevets'kyi.

29 Mykhailo Vozniak, *Iak probudylosia ukraïns'ke narodnie zhyttia v Halychyni za Avstriï,* Biblioteka 'Novoho chasu', no. 1 (L'viv 1924); Volodymyr Hnatiuk, *Natsional'ne vidrodzhennie avstro-uhors'kykh ukraïntsiv (1772–1880 rr.)* (Vienna: Soiuz Vyzvolennia Ukraïny 1916).

See also the extensive discussion of general cultural developments in Omelian Ohonovskii, *Ystoriia lyteraturŷ ruskoy,* 4 vols (L'viv: NTSh, 1887–94), vol. II, pp. 48–155.

30 Ivan P. Filevich, *Iz istorii Karpatskoi Rusi: ocherki galitsko-russkoi zhizni s 1772 g.* (Warsaw 1907).

31 Ia.F. Holovatskii, ''O pervom lyteraturno-umstvennom dvyzhenii Rusynov v Halytsii so vremen Avstriiskoho vladîniia v toi zemlî,'' *Naukovŷi sbornyk ... Halytsko-russkoi Matytsŷ,* I (L'viv 1865), pp. 65–103; Jan Lewicki, *Ruch Rusinów w Galicji w pierwszej połowie wieku panowania Austriji (1772–1820)* (L'viv: p.a. 1879); I. Franko, ''Szkice z dziejów literatury rusińskiej w Galicji,'' *Głos,* III, 2, 4, 5, 12 (Warsaw 1888), pp. 14, 42, 52, and 137, translated into Ukrainian as ''Narysy z istoriï ukraïns'koï literatury v Halychyni,'' in Ivan Franko, *Tvory,* vol. XVI (Kiev: Derzhavne vyd. khudozhn'oï literatury 1955), pp. 141–156; Sergei A. Iefremov, ''Iz istorii vozrozhdeniia Galichiny,'' *Golos minuvshogo,* III, 2 (Moscow 1915), p. 5–33.

32 Hryhorii Iu. Herbil's'kyi, *Rozvytok prohresyvnykh idei v Halychyni u pershii polovyni XIX st. (do 1848 r.)* (L'viv: LU 1964); idem, *Peredova suspil'na dumka v Halychyni* (L'viv: LU 1959).

See also Włodzimierz Mokry, ''Życie kulturalno-literackie Ukraińców w Galicji w pierwszym 30-leciu XIX wieku,'' *Slavia Orientalis,* XXX, 1 (Warsaw 1981), pp. 45–60.

in the "reactionary" Greek Catholic church. Herbil's'kyi does, nonetheless, discuss the secular writings and ideas of the most important figures before the 1830s; he then dwells at great length on the activity of the Rusyn Triad, the first really acceptable "progressive" cultural movement. But the best works on the era of the Rusyn Triad are by the Ukrainian academician Kyrylo Studyns'kyi, who elucidates in great detail the reaction of the Viennese government to the Triad's activity, and more recently by the Polish historian Jan Kozik, who stresses the influences of Polish intellectuals upon the Triad, as well as their subsequent contacts with other Slavic leaders.[33]

Cultural history: education, church, theater, press

Several studies have been devoted to the Ukrainian educational system. Pylyp Svystun has traced the history of elementary schools throughout the period, Ambrosii Androkhovych secondary schools, and Kyrylo Studyns'kyi the L'viv Theological Seminary during the years when the Rusyn Triad was active.[34] Special attention has been devoted to the Barbareum (1774–1784) and imperial boarding school (*konvikt,* 1803–1893) attached to the St Barbara Church in Vienna, which served as a meeting place not only for young seminarians from Galicia but also for influential leaders from throughout Austria's Slavic lands.[35] Similarly, the Studium Ruthenum, the first, if short-lived, experiment in Ukrainian education at the modern university level, is analyzed by Ivan Krevets'kyi and in a major monograph by Ambrosii Androkhovych.[36]

33 Kyrylo Studyns'kyi, "Prychynky do istoriï kul'turnoho zhytia Halyts'koï Rusy v lïtakh 1833–47," in *Korespondentsiia Iakova Holovats'koho v lïtakh 1835–49,* in *Zbirnyk fil'ol'ogichnoï sektsiï NTSh,* XI–XII (L'viv 1909), pp. i–cxxxviii; Jan Kozik, *Ukraiński ruch narodowy w Galicji w latach 1830–1848* (Cracow: Wyd. Literackie 1973).

34 [F.I. Svistun], "Zachatki russkikh narodnykh shkol v Galichinie," *Viestnik 'Narodnogo Doma',* XXVIII (VI), 6–12 (L'viv 1910), pp. 98–100, 113–121, 135–140, 149–156, 168–192; F.I. Svistun, "Galitsko-russkiia shkoly v pervoi polovinie XIX st.," *Zhivoe slovo,* I, 6 (L'viv 1899), pp. 328–340; Ambrozii Androkhovych, "Obrazky z istoriï seredn'oho shkil'nytstva v Halychyni v XVIII i XIX st.," *Zapysky NTSh,* C (L'viv 1930), pp. 289–310; Kyrylo Studyns'kyi, *L'vivs'ka dukhovna seminariia v chasakh Markiiana Shashkevycha 1829–1843* (L'viv 1916).

35 M. Hornykewitsch, *Griechisch-Katholische Zentralpfarrei zu St. Barbara in Wien* (Vienna 1934); Willibald M. Plöchl, *St. Barbara zu Wien: die Geschichte der griechisch-katholischen Kirche und Zentralpfarre St. Barbara,* 2 vols (Vienna: Vlg. Herder 1975). In the 1830s, the Barbareum's influence spread as far south as Italy: Iaroslav Hordyns'kyi, "Osnovanie hr.-kat. tserkvy v kniazïvstvi Liukka v Italiï," *Zapysky NTSh,* CXXV (L'viv 1918), pp. 55–89.

36 Ivan Krevets'kyi, "Neopravdani dokory: do istoriï t. zv. 'Rus'koho Instytutu' (Studium Ruthenum) na l'vivs'kim unïversytetï," *Zapysky NTSh,* CII (L'viv 1911), pp. 117–126; Ambrozii Androkhovych, "L'vivs'ke 'Studium Ruthenum'," *Zapysky NTSh,* CXXXI (L'viv

The history of the church has also been the focus of attention. The several series of documents from Vatican archives each contain material on Galicia during this period, especially pertaining to the efforts of Maria Theresa and Joseph II to raise the status of Greek Catholicism and to the negotiations over the restoration of the Galician metropolitanate.[37] The correspondence of Metropolitan Mykhailo Levyts'kyi (1774–1858, consecrated 1816), Bishop of Przemyśl Ivan Snihurs'kyi (1784–1848, consecrated 1817), and Bishop of Przemyśl Hryhorii Iakhymovych (1792–1863, consecrated 1849) has been published,[38] as well as smaller collections of documents on the rural priesthood in the Przemyśl diocese and on the episcopal effort to control "revolutionary" activity in the L'viv Theological Seminary.[39] The history of the Greek Catholic church throughout the years 1772 to 1848 is covered in one survey,[40] while certain specific problems, such as the sociocultural status of the L'viv diocesan clergy in the late eighteenth century, the development of monasteries before 1848, the establishment of Basilian churches, and the career of Bishop Ivan Snihurs'kyi, are treated in separate studies.[41] None is as comprehensive, however, as the two-volume analysis by Władysław Chotkowski of church politics during the last years (1772–1780) of Maria Theresa's reign. Chotkowski discusses in great detail the Basilian monasteries, the question of a metropolitanate for Galicia, and the role of Bishop of L'viv Lev Sheptyts'kyi (1717–1779, consecrated 1749).[42]

1921), pp. 123–195; CXXXII (1922), pp. 185–217; CXXXVI–CXXXVII (1925), pp. 43–105; CXLVI (1927), pp. 33–118; CL (1929), pp. 1–80.

37 See chapter 2, notes 47–55.

38 Vasyl' Shchurat, ed., *Lysty mytropolyta M. Levyts'koho do epyskopa Iv. Snïhurs'koho i ofitsiial'ni dokumenty ïkh spil'noï diial'nosty (1813–1847)*, in *Ukraïns'kyi arkhyv*, vol. XII (L'viv 1924); Kyrylo Studyns'kyi, ed., *Materiialy do istoriï kul'turnoho zhytia v Halychynï v 1795–1857 rr.: zamitky i teksty*, in *Ukraïns'ko-rus'kyi arkhyv*, vol. XIII–XIV (L'viv 1920).

39 Mykhailo Zubryts'kyi, "Prychynky do istoriï rus'koho dukhovenstva v Halychynï vid 1820–1853 r.," *Zapysky NTSh*, LXXXVIII (L'viv 1909), pp. 118–150; Iurii Kmit, "Prychynky do istoriï rus'koho dukhovnoho seminaria u L'vovi vid 1837–1851 r.," *Zapysky NTSh*, XCI (L'viv 1909), pp. 151–158.

40 Anton Korczok, *Die griechisch-katolische Kirche in Galizien*, Osteuropa Institut in Breslau (Leipzig and Berlin: Teubner 1921).

41 Melianïia Bordun, "Z zhytia ukraïns'koho dukhovenstva L'vivs'koï eparkhiï v druhii polovynï XVIII v.," *Zapysky NTSh*, CIX (L'viv 1912), pp. 39–90; CX (1912), pp. 55–100; Władysław Chotkowski, *Historya polityczna dawnych klasztorów panieńskich w Galicyi 1773–1848 na podstawie akt cesarskiej Kancelaryi Nadwornej* (Cracow: Gebethner 1905); Mykhailo Vavryk, "Do istoriï vasyliians'kykh kapitul u Halychyni v XVIII–XIX stolitti," *Analecta OSBM*, series II, sectio II, vol. III, 1–2 (Rome 1958), pp. 46–68; Iustin Zhelekhovskii, *Ioann Sniegurskii: ego zhizn' i dieiatel'nost' v Galitskoi Rusi* (L'viv: Stavropigiiskii Institut 1894).

42 X. Władysław Chotkowski, *Historya polityczna kościoła w Galicyi za rządów Maryi Teresy*, 2 vols (Cracow: Akademia Umiejętności 1909), especially vol. II, pp. 379–500.

A few other topics in the cultural history of Ukrainian Galicia after 1772 have received attention. These include the beginnings of Ukrainian amateur theatrical performances sponsored mainly by the rural clergy;[43] a history of the press in eastern Galicia, which begins with the *Gazette de Léopol* (1776–although neither this nor subsequent organs were intended for Ukrainians;[44] the role of the Kurzbeck printshop (1770–1792) in Vienna in diffusing Cyrillic books;[45] the rivalry between the printshops of the Stauropegial Institute and Pochaïv Monastery;[46] the impact of the history of Galicia-Volhynia (1792–1793) on the Galician-Ukrainian intelligentsia by the Austrian scholar Johann Christian Engel (1770–1814);[47] and the abortive attempts (1842 and 1848) of the Austrian government to provide Ukrainians with their own literary journal.[48]

Cultural history: literature (Rusyn Triad)

Of all the aspects of cultural history during the period 1772 to 1848, it is the history of literature that has received the most attention. Not surprisingly, most concern has been devoted to the activity of the Rusyn Triad during the 1830s and 1840s. This is evident in early essays by Iosyf Levyts'kyi, a contemporary who may be considered the first literary historian of the era,[49] in the writings of Ostap

43 Mykhailo Vozniak, "Ukraïns'ki dramatychni vystavy v Halychynï v pershii polovyni XIX stolïtia (zamitky i materialy)," *Zapysky NTSh*, LXXXVII (L'viv 1909), pp. 79–91; LXXXVIII (1909), pp. 51–93.

44 Ivan Krevets'kyi, "Pochatky presy na Ukraïni, 1776–1850," *Zapysky NTSh*, CXLIV (L'viv 1926), pp. 185–208.

45 Ambrozii Androkhovych, " 'Illiriis'ka' drukarnia i knyharnia Osypa Kurtsbeka 1770–1792 r. ta ïï zviazky z uhors'koiu i halyts'koiu zemleiu," *Zapysky NTSh*, CL (L'viv 1929), pp. 109–120.

46 Mykhailo Vozniak, "Do istoriï pochaïvs'kykh vydan' XVIII v.," *Zapysky NTSh*, CXXX (L'viv 1930), pp. 107–119.

47 F.I. Svistun, "Sbornik o. Mikhaila Petrushevicha," *Viestnik 'Narodnogo Doma'*, XXIX (VII), 1 (L'viv 1911), pp. 2–16.

48 F.I. Svistun, "Proekt pervoi avstro-russkoi literaturnoi vremenopisi v 1842 g.," *Viestnik 'Narodnogo Doma'*, XXIII (I), 4–7 (L'viv 1905), pp. 60–62, 65–70, 82–87, 111–119; idem, "Vtoroi proekt avstro-russkoi literaturnoi vremenopisi v 1848 g." *ibid.*, pp. 180–183.

49 Józef Lewicki, *Listy tyczące się piśmiennictwa ruskiego w Galicyi* (Przemyśl, 1843). An unsigned article by this same author that originally appeared the same year (1843) stressed primarily the writings of Bishop Mykhailo Levyts'kyi and Ivan Mohyl'nyts'kyi: "Das Schicksal der gallizisch-russischen Sprache und Literatur," *Jahrbücher für slawische Literatur, Kunst und Wissenschaft*, II (Leipzig 1844; reprinted Leipzig: Zentralantiquariat der DDR 1974), pp. 183–185 and 206–210.

Terlets'kyi who has produced the most comprehensive cultural history of this period,[50] and in later Soviet scholarship on the subject as well.[51]

The most famous literary work of the period was the Rusyn Triad's *Rusalka dnîstrovaia* (1837), in a sense a revolutionary cultural phenomenon because it was the first book for Galician Ukrainians written in the vernacular and in the modern, civil alphabet *(hrazhdanka)*. Banned by the local censor, *Rusalka dnîstrovaia* had to be published in Buda[pest]. The history of this work's encounters with official censors, its eventual appearance, and its very limited distribution (though nonetheless enormous influence) have been the subject of several critical studies.[52]

Most of the studies devoted to individual writers from this period focus on members of the Rusyn Triad: Iakiv Holovats'kyi (1814–1888), Ivan Vahylevych (1811–1866), and most especially Markiian Shashkevych (1811–1843). The Soviet scholars Mykhailo Humeniuk and Ivan Kravchenko have prepared a comprehensive bibliography of the writings of the Triad,[53] while the group as a whole is given much attention in several of the general histories and general literary histories mentioned above,[54] as well as in popular accounts by the interwar Galician Russophile Vasilii Vavrik and the Soviet writer Osyp Petrash.[55]

50 Ivan Zanevych [Ostap Terlets'kyi], "Literaturni stremlinnia halyts'kykh Rusyniv vid 1772 do 1872," *Zhytie i slovo*, I, 2 and 3 (L'viv 1894), pp. 207–215 and 354–370; II, 4, 5, and 6 (1894), pp. 69–80, 198–204, and 428–451; III, 1, 2, and 3 (1895), pp. 99–110, 274–285, and 430–461; IV, 4, 5, and 6 (1895), pp. 112–160, 272–302, and 385–454.

51 Ostap Makarushka, "Pochatky novoho ukraïns'koho pys'menstva v Halychyni," *Ukraïna*, 2 [27] (Kiev 1928), pp. 41–46; P.K. Volyns'kyi, "Literaturno-teoretychni vystupy v zakhidnykh zemliakh Ukraïny v 1830-kh rokakh," *Radians'ke literaturoznavstvo*, I, 1 (Kiev 1957), pp. 103–123; Petro K. Volyns'kyi, *Teoretychna borot'ba v ukraïns'kii literaturi (persha polovyna XIX st.)* (Kiev: Derzhavne vyd-vo khudozhn'oï literatury 1959); M. Pyvovarov, *Literaturnyi rukh v Halychyni v 30-40-kh rokakh XIX st.* (Kiev 1960). See also the anthology of works by western Ukrainian writers, *Pys'mennyky Zakhidnoï Ukraïny 30-50-kh rokiv XIX st.* (Kiev: Dnipro 1965), with an introductory essay by I.I. Pil'huk, "Literaturne vidrodzhennia na Zakhidnii Ukraïni (30-50-i roky XIX st.)," pp. 5–33.

52 See the study by Kyrylo Studyns'kyi in n. 33 above, and Mykhailo Tershakovets', "Pro naklad 'Rusalky Dnïstrovoï,'" *Zapysky NTSh*, CVIII (L'viv 1912), pp. 117–139; O.O. Markov, "K istorii 'Russalki Dniestrovoi'," *Viestnik 'Narodnogo Doma'*, XXIX (VII), 4 (L'viv 1911), pp. 57–69; O.I. Bilets'kyi, "Rusalka Dnîstrovaia," in M. Shashkevych, *Rusalka Dnistrova*, reprint of the 1837 edition (Kiev: Derzhlitvydav 1950), 2nd ed. (Kiev: Dnipro 1972), pp. 3–31, reprinted in *Materialy do vyvchennia istoriï ukraïns'koï literatury*, vol. II, comp. I.P. Skrypnyk and P.M. Sirenko (Kiev: Radians'ka shkola 1961), pp. 347–359.

53 M.P. Humeniuk, and I.I. Kravchenko, eds, *M. Shashkevych, I. Vahylevych, I. Holovats'kyi: bibliohrafichnyi pokazhchyk* (L'viv 1962).

54 See notes 2, 29, 30, 32, 33, 50, 51 above.

55 Vasilii R. Vavrik, *Rus'ka Troitsia* (L'viv 1933); Osyp Petrash, *Rus'ka Triitsia* (Kiev: Dnipro 1972).

Of the three, it is Markiian Shashkevych who has received the most attention. This is probably because he died young and did not have to go through the complicated and consequently controversial intellectual development after 1848 that his colleagues Vahylevych and Holovats'kyi experienced. As a result, Shashkevych remained "pure" and has become a prime subject for glorification in the local national pantheon, whether he is being described by a traditionalist Old Ruthenian, Ukrainophile, Russophile, or Soviet Marxist author. The cult of Shashkevych itself has become an object of study.[56] The most reliable edition of Shashkevych's writings is by Mykhailo Vozniak.[57] Vozniak and, later, the Ukrainian emigré Stepan Shakh and the Soviet author Mykhailo Shalata have written the best analyses of the life and work of the poet.[58] Several other shorter biographies of Shashkevych have been written, including more popular essays by Omelian Ohonovs'kyi, Ivan Franko, and Bohdan Lepkyi.[59]

56 O. Kul'chyts'kyi, "Kult Markiiana Shashkevycha, iak psykhosotsiial'na problema," *Naukovi zapysky Ukraïns'koho Vil'noho Universytetu,* VII (Munich 1963), pp. 208–222. Examples of the cult of Shashkevych in the Americans are the memorial book, *Propamiatna knyha amerykans'kykh ukraïntsiv vydana u stolitniu richnytsiu smerty o. Markiiana Shashkevycha pershoho probudytelia Halyts'koï Ukraïny* (Philadelphia, Pa.: O.O. Vasyliian 1943); and the annual journal *Shashkevychiiana* (Winnipeg 1963–present).

57 Mykhailo Vozniak, ed., *Pysannia Markiiana Shashkevycha,* Zbirnyk Fil'ol'ogichnoï sektsiï NTSh, vol. XIV (L'viv 1912).

See also the biographical data, unpublished works, and other documents in Mykhailo Tershakovets', "Prychynky do zhytiepysu Markiiana Shashkevycha ta deshcho iz ioho pys'mens'koï spadshchyny," *Zapysky NTSh,* LVIII (L'viv 1904), 48 pp.; idem, "Do zhytiepysy Markiiana Shashkevycha," *Zapysky NTSh,* CIV (L'viv 1911), pp. 92–115; CVI (1911), pp. 77–134.

58 Mykhailo Vozniak, *U stolittia 'Zori' Markiiana Shashkevycha (1834–1934): novi rozshuky pro diial'nist' ioho hurtka,* Pratsi Ukraïns'koho Bohoslovs'koho Naukovoho Tovarystvo, vols IX–X (L'viv 1936), pp. 147–324; Mykhailo S. Vozniak, "Istorychne znachennia diial'nosti Markiiana Shashkevycha," *Naukovi zapysky Instytutu suspil'nykh nauk AN URSR (L'vivs'kyi filial),* I (L'viv 1953), reprinted in *Materialy do vyvchennia istoriï ukraïns'koï literatury,* vol. II (Kiev: Radians'ka shkola 1961), pp. 347–359; Stepan Shakh, *O. Markiian Shashkevych ta halyts'ke vidrodzhenia,* Vydannia Ukraïns'koho khrystyians'koho rukhu, no. 2 (Paris and Munich 1961); Mykhailo I. Shalata, *Markiian Shashkevych: zhyttia, tvorchist' i hromads'ko-kul'turna diial'nist'* (Kiev: Naukova dumka 1969).

See also the extensive sections on Shashkevych in Omelian Ohonovskii, *Ystoriia lyteraturŷ ruskoy,* vol. II (L'viv 1889), pp. 354–393, and in Osyp Petrash, *Rus'ka triitsia* (Kiev: Dnipro 1972), pp. 18–81.

59 Omelian Ohonovskii, *Markiian Shashkevych: pro ioho zhytie i pys'ma,* Biblioteka TP, no. 95 (L'viv 1886); Ivan Franko, "M. Shashkevych i halyts'ko-rus'ka literatura," *Zhytie i slovo,* II (L'viv 1894), pp. 147–53, reprinted in his *Tvory,* vol. XVII (Kiev: Derzhavne vyd-vo khudozhnoï literatury 1955), pp. 226–233; Bohdan Lepkyi, *Markiian Shashkevych,* Zahal'na biblioteka, no. 106–107 (Kolomyia: Iakiv Orenshtain 1911).

More controversial and less well studied is Ivan Vahylevych. Estranged from the Greek Catholic church and eventually a convert to Protestantism, in 1848 Vahylevych considered cooperation with the Poles as the best way to guarantee the future of Ukrainians in Galicia. Though he never advocated national assimilation, he nonetheless is often unjustly viewed as a polonizer by some Ukrainophile and Russophile writers. The best introductory biography on Vahylevych is by the Canadian historian Peter Brock.[60] Ivan Franko has published much of Vahylevych's correspondence and large parts of his autobiography;[61] Iakiv Holovats'kyi and Vasilii Vavrik have written biographies.[62]

Even more controversial is Iakiv Holovats'kyi, the prolific ethnographer, historian, linguist, poet, and beginning in 1848 holder of the first chair in Ruthenian language and literature at the University of L'viv. Subsequently disillusioned with Austria's policy toward Galicia's Ukrainians, Holovats'kyi emigrated to the Russian Empire (Vilnius) in 1867. Partly because of this, he is praised during the earlier part of his career for participating in the Rusyn Triad, but criticized, at least by Soviet and non-Soviet Ukrainian authors, for his "reactionary" Russophile tendencies in later life. The best sources on Holovats'kyi's complex career are his memoirs covering the period before 1848 and the two volumes of his correspondence (1835–1862), which have been meticulously

---

See also Vladymir Kotsovskii, *Zhytie y znachenie Markiiana Shashkevycha y v dodatku materiialŷ y zamîtŷ do henezy rusko narodnoho ôdrodzhenia v Halychynî* (L'viv 1886); I. Jeluka, *Odrodzenie ruskiej literatury w Galicyi i Markijan Szaszkiewicz* (Berezhany 1911); Damaskyn Popovych, *Markiian Shashkevych na tli vidrodzhennia Halyts'koï Ukraïny* (Mundare, Alberta: O.O. Vasyliiany 1944); Luka Lutsiv, *Markiian Shashkevych: biohrafiia i kharakterystyka tvorchosty* (New York: Svoboda 1963).

60 Peter Brock, "Ivan Vahylevych (1811–1866) and the Ukrainian National Identity," *Canadian Slavonic Papers,* XIV, 2 (Ottawa 1972), pp. 153–190, reprinted with minor revisions in Andrei S. Markovits and Frank E. Sysyn, eds, *Nationbuilding and the Politics of Nationalism* (Cambridge, Mass.: Harvard Ukrainian Research Institute 1982), pp. 111–148.

61 Ivan Franko, "Do biografiï Ivana Vahylevycha," *Zapysky NTSh,* LXXIX (L'viv 1907), pp. 97–141. For further published correspondence of Vahylevych, see notes 76, 84, and 88 below.

62 Iakov Golovatskii, "Sud'ba odnogo galitsko-russkago uchenago–k biografii Ivana Nikolaevicha Vagilevicha," *Kievskaia starina,* II, 7 (Kiev 1883), pp. 453–472; Vasilii R. Vavrik, *Zhizn' i deiatel'nost' Ivana Nikolaevicha Dalibora Vagilevicha* (L'viv 1934), originally published in *Sbornik Galitsko-russkoi matitsy,* VIII (L'viv 1934), pp. 65–92.

See also the sections on Vahylevych in Omelian Ohonovskii, *Ystoriia lyteratury ruskoy,* vol. IV (L'viv: NTSh 1894), pp. 119–150; Ivan Zanevych [Ostap Terlets'kyi], "Literaturni stremlinnia halyts'kykh Rusyniv vid 1772 do 1872," *Zhytie i slovo,* II, 6 (L'viv 1894), pp. 434–451; Osyp Petrash, *Rus'ka triitsia* (Kiev: Dnipro 1972), pp. 82–105. On his grammatical works, see the study of Mykhailo Vozniak, n. 73 below.

compiled by Kyrylo Studyns'kyi.[63] The Ukrainian view of Holovats'kyi's career is expressed in works by Omelian Ohonovs'kyi, Ostap Terlets'kyi, and Osyp Petrash; the Russophile view is found in works by Fedor Aristov and Vasilii Vavrik, both of whom are favorably disposed toward Holovats'kyi's ''Russophile'' inclinations.[64]

Besides the works and activity of the Rusyn Triad, a critical edition of the philological works of Ivan Mohyl'nyts'kyi (1777–1831) and the autobiographical notes of the linguist and ethnographer Iosyf Lozyns'kyi (1807–1889) have appeared.[65] Finally, biographies of a few other early nineteenth century Galician-Ukrainian national and cultural leaders exist: the influential member of the Stauropegial Brotherhood Ivan Horbachevs'kyi (1743–1806);[66] the writer and educator Stefan Petrushevych (1772–1859);[67] the churchman and educator Ivan Lavrivs'-

63 Ia.F. Holovatskii, ''Perezhytoe y perestradannoe: zapysky,'' *Lyteraturnŷi sbornyk ... Halytsko-russkoi Matytsŷ* (L'viv 1885), pp. 10–41, 127–140, and (1886), pp. 198–207; Kyrylo Studyns'kyi, ed., *Korespondentsyia Iakova Holovats'koho v lïtakh 1835–49 [and] 1850–62,* 2 vols, in Zbirnyk fil'ol'ogichnoï sektsyi NTSh, VIII–IX and XI–XII (L'viv 1905–09). For Holovats'kyi's correspondence with Osyp Bodians'kyi, see chapter 6, n. 196; for his correspondence with Czech leaders, see notes 76 and 78 below.

64 Omelian Ohonovskii, *Ystoriia lyteraturŷ ruskoy,* vol. IV (L'viv: NTSh 1894), pp. 60–119; Ivan Zanevych [Ostap Terlets'kyi], ''Literaturni stremlinnia halyts'kykh Rusyniv vid 1772 do 1872,'' *Zhytie i slovo,* II, 6 (L'viv 1894), pp. 428–451; Osyp Petrash, *Rus'ka triitsia* (Kiev: Dnipro 1972), pp. 106–141; F.F. Aristov, *Karpato-russkie pisateli,* vol. I (Moscow 1916), 2nd rev. ed. (Bridgeport, Conn.: Carpatho-Russian Literary Association 1977), pp. 76–128; Vasilii P. Vavrik, *Iakov Fedorovich Golovatskii: iego dieiatel'nost' i znacheniie v galitsko-russkoi slovesnosti* (L'viv 1925).

On Holovats'kyi's activity after 1848, see also chapter 6, n. 133; on his travels throughout eastern Galicia and northeastern Hungary, see Olena Rudlovchak, ''Na podorozhakh z Ia. Holovats'kym,'' *Duklia,* XII, 4 (Prešov 1964), pp. 79–83, as well as his own description of those travels, n. 8 above; on his scholarly activity and contacts with other Slavic peoples, see chapter 1, n. 27, and I.P. Vishnevskii, ''Nekotorye problemy slavianskogo edinstva v trudakh galitskikh prosvetitelei XIX v.,'' in *Ocherki po istorii slavianskikh literaturnykh sviazei* (L'viv: Vishcha shkola 1978), pp. 9–47; on his linguistic work, see the study of Mykhailo Vozniak, n. 73 below.

65 Mykhailo Vozniak, ed., *Fil'ol'ogichni pratsï Ivana Mohyl'nyts'koho,* in *Ukraïns'ko-rus'kyi arkhyv,* vol. V (L'viv 1910); Iosyf Lozynskii, ''Avtobiohrafycheskii zapysky,'' *Lyteraturnŷi sbornyk ... Halytsko-russkoi Matytsŷ,* 1–4 (L'viv 1885), pp. 114–126. On the grammatical work of Mohyl'nyts'kyi and Lozyns'kyi, see n. 73 below.

66 Ambrozii Androkhovych, ''O. Ivan Horbachevs'kyi, prymirnyi parokh Stavropyhiis'koho Bratstva,'' in *Zbirnyk L'vivs'koï Stavropyhiï: mynule i suchasne,* ed. Kyrylo Studyns'kyi (L'viv 1921), pp. 54–98.

67 F.I. Svistun, ''O. Stefan Petrushevich'' [1772–1859], *Viestnik 'Narodnago Doma',* XXVI (IV), 8–11 (L'viv 1908), pp. 166–170, 176–181, 191–198.

kyi (1773–1846);[68] the historian Denys Zubryts'kyi (1777–1862);[69] the ethnographer Hryhorii Il'kevych (1803–1841);[70] and the national benefactor Mykhailo Kachkovs'kyi (1802–1872), whose name was later used for one of the more influential Galician popular cultural societies.[71]

Cultural history: the language question

One aspect of literary and cultural history has received special attention–the language question. Like other groups in the earliest stages of their national development, the Galician-Ukrainian intelligentsia argued among itself about which linguistic form would have sufficient prestige to represent their culture. The debate arose in the 1830s, and in the years before 1848 it revolved primarily around two problems: external form, i.e. which alphabet should be used–the traditional Cyrillic *(kyrylytsia),* modern civil *(hrazhdanka),* or Latin-based Polish *(latynyka)* alphabet; and content, i.e. whether the language should reflect the local vernacular or be traditional Church Slavonic.

General surveys of the language question in Galicia by Vasyl' Lev and Paul R. Magocsi include a discussion of developments before 1848.[72] The most extensive

68 Ambrozii Androkhovych, "Ivan Lavrivs'kyi: odyn iz pioniriv ukraïns'koho vidrodzhenia v Halychyni," *Zapysky NTSh,* CXXVIII (L'viv 1919), pp. 51–120.

69 Ia. Golovatskii, "Denis Zubritskii," *Viestnik iugo-zapadnoi i zapadnoi Rossii,* I (Kiev 1862), pp. 56–61 and 219–229; F.F. Aristov, *Karpato-russkie pisateli,* vol. I (Moscow 1916), 2nd rev. ed. (Bridgeport, Conn.: Carpatho-Russian Literary Association 1977), pp. 33–48. Zubryts'kyi's letters to Iakiv Holovats'kyi are found in the correspondence edited by Studyns'kyi, vol. I, n. 63 above. Some of Zubryts'kyi's correspondence with leaders in other Slavic lands appears in: Kyrylo Studyns'kyi, "Z korespondentsyï Denysa Zubryts'koho rr. 1840–1853," *Zapysky NTSh,* XLIII (L'viv 1901), 66 pp.; and in works by Studyns'kyi and Svistun, n. 79, and Popov, n. 84 below. On Zubryts'kyi as a historian, see chapter 1, n. 13. For his linguistic views, see n. 74 below.

70 Andrii Franko, "Hryhorii Il'kevych iak etnograf," *Zapysky NTSh,* CIX (L'viv 1912), pp. 91–122; CX (1912), pp. 123–156; CXI (1912), pp. 117–139.

71 Bohdan A. Dîdytskii, *Mykhayl Kachkovskii y sovremennaia halytsko-russkaia lyteratura: ocherk biohrafycheskii y ystoryko-lyteraturnŷi,* pt 1 (L'viv: Halytsko-ruska Matytsa 1876).

72 Vasyl' Lev, "Borot'ba za ukraïns'ku literaturnu movu v Halychyni ta kharakter ïï," *Zbirnyk na poshanu Ivana Mirchuka,* in *Ukraïns'kyi Vil'nyi Universytet, Naukovyi zbirnyk,* vol. VIII (Munich, New York, Paris, and Winnipeg 1974), pp. 67–86; Paul R. Magocsi, "The Language Question as a Factor in the National Movement in Eastern Galicia," in Andrei S. Markovits and Frank E. Sysyn, eds, *Nationbuilding and the Politics of Nationalism: Essays on Austrian Galicia* (Cambridge, Mass.: Harvard Ukrainian Research Institute 1982), pp. 220–238. A shorter version of this work appeared earlier: Paul R. Magocsi, *The Language Question in Galicia,* Ukrainian Heritage Notes, no. 2 (Cambridge, Mass.: Ukrainian Studies Fund 1978).

research has been done by Osyp Makovei and Mykhailo Vozniak on the earliest published and unpublished grammars from the period,[73] and by Ivan Franko, Mykhailo Vozniak, and Vasyl' Shchurat on the controversies during the 1830s over proposals to introduce a Polish-based Latin alphabet.[74]

Relations with other Slavs

The first half of the nineteenth century was a period when the budding intelligentsias among each of the Slavic peoples became conscious not only of their own national cultures but also of the fact that they were related to other Slavs living within the Russian, Austrian, and Ottoman empires. This resulted in a movement known as Pan-Slavism, which stressed ideas of cultural and sometimes political interdependence among the Slavs, and which prompted eager efforts among members of each group to discover and study the life of all the others. Ukrainian Galicia was the object of attention among Slavs abroad; at the same time local leaders closely followed developments in other Slavic lands. An extensive literature on Galician-Ukrainian and Slavic interrelations has developed.

Relations with the Czechs were especially well advanced, since Galician-Ukrainian leaders saw in this westernmost Slavic group that had achieved so much in the national/cultural sphere a model to be followed. Václav Židlický and Vladimír Hostička have surveyed the interest in Galicia displayed by Czech leaders before 1848.[75] Ivan Bryk has traced the important influence of the Czech linguist and patron saint of Pan-Slavism, Josef Dobrovský (1753–1829), on Galician-Ukrainian grammarians, and he has published the correspondence between Ivan Vahylevych, Iakiv Holovats'kyi, and several Czech leaders.[76] The

73 Osyp Makovei, "Try halyts'ki hramatyky: Ivan Mohyl'nyts'kyi, Iosyf Levyts'kyi i Iosyf Lozyns'kyi," *Zapysky NTSh,* LI and LIV (L'viv 1903), 96 pp.; Mykhailo Vozniak, "Studiï nad halyts'ko-ukraïns'kymy hramatykamy XIX v.," *Zapysky NTSh,* LXXXIX (L'viv 1909), pp. 111–143; XC (1909), pp. 33–118; XCI (1909), pp. 126–150; XCIII (1910), pp. 90–131; XCIV (1910), pp. 107–161; XCV (1910), p. 83–106; XCVIII (1910), pp. 77–146.

74 Ivan Franko, "Azbuchna viina v Halychynï 1859 r.," *Zapysky NTSh,* LXXXI, 1 (L'viv 1908), pp. 134–144; Mykhailo Vozniak, "Avtorstvo azbuchnoï statti z 1834 r.," *Zapysky NTSh,* CXXXVI–CXXXVII (L'viv 1925), pp. 107–118; idem, "Apologiia kyrylytsi Denysa Zubryts'koho," *Zapysky NTSh,* CL (L'viv 1929), pp. 122–142; Vasyl' Shchurat, "Azbuchnia statia Mykoly Kmytsykevycha z 1834 r.," *Zapysky NTSh.* LXXXI (L'viv 1908), pp. 134–144.

75 Václav Židlický, "Naše styky s haličskými ukrajinci v době národního obrození," in *Věčná družba: sborník prací k třístému výročí opětného sjednocení Ukrajiny s Ruskem* (Prague: Svět Sovětů 1957), pp. 283–300; Vladimír Hostička, "Ukrajina v názorech české obrozenecké společnosti do roku 1848," *Slavia,* XXXIII, 4 (Prague 1964), pp. 558–578.

76 Ivan Bryk, "Iosyf Dobrovs'kyi i ukraïnoznavstvo," *Zapysky NTSh,* CXLI–CXLIII (L'viv 1925), 35 pp.; idem, *Materiialy do istoriï ukraïns'ko-ches'kykh vzaiemyn v pershii polovyni XIX st.,* in Ukraïns'ko-rus'kyi arkhyv, vol. XV (L'viv 1921).

trips of several Czechs to Galicia, especially Karel Zap (1812–1871), as well as the influence of the Slovaks Ján Kollár (1793–1852) and Pavel Šafárik (1814–1876) on Galician Ukrainians have been studied,[77] while the letters of Karel Zap to Iakiv Holovats'kyi and of Iakiv Holovats'kyi and Denys Zubryts'kyi to Václav Hanka (1791–1861) have been published.[78]

One of the single most important influences on Galician-Ukrainian leaders was provided by the Slovenian philologist Jernej Kopitar (1780–1844). From his post as imperial censor of Slavic books and director of the Austrian National Library, Kopitar urged through his writings the promotion of each of the various Slavic cultures and vernacular languages. His impact on all the major Galician-Ukrainian leaders before 1848 is traced in detail by Mykhailo Tershakovets', while his ties with Denys Zubryts'kyi and Bishop Ivan Snihurs'kyi are discussed at length by Kyrylo Studyns'kyi and Vasyl' Shchurat.[79] The cultural relations of the Rusyn

77 Vladimír Hostička, ''Karel Vladislav Zap a haličští Ukrajinci,'' in *Kapitoly z dějin vzájemných vztahů národů ČSR a SSSR* (Prague: Československá akademie věd 1958), pp. 69–115; Jiří Horák, ''Tři čeští spisovatelé v Haliči,'' *Národopisný věstník českoslovanský,* X (Prague 1915), pp. 101–156, reprinted in a shorter version in Jiří Horák, *Z dějin literatur slovanských: stati a rozpravy* (Prague: Jos. R. Vilímek 1948), pp. 209–273; I. Paňkevyč, ''Západoukrajinské literárne obrodenie a Ján Kollár,'' in *Z dejín československo-ukrajinských vzt'ahov: Slovanské štúdie,* I (Bratislava: Slovenská akadémia vied 1957), pp. 269–294, translated into Ukrainian as ''Zakhidnoukraïns'ke literaturne vidrodzhennia i Ian Kollar,'' in *Z istoriï chekhoslovats'ko-ukraïns'kykh zv''iazkiv* (Bratislava: Slovats'ke vyd-vo khudozhn'oï literatury 1959), pp. 253–280; Kyrylo Studyns'kyi, ''Pavlo Iosyp Shafaryk i ukraïntsi,'' *Nasha kul'tura,* I, 7 (L'viv 1935), pp. 401–412; Vl. Hostička, ''Pavel Josef Šafařík a ukrajinci,'' in *Z dejín československo-ukrajinských vzt'ahov: Slovanské štúdie,* I (Bratislava: Slovenská akadémia vied 1957), pp. 295–318, translated into Ukrainian as ''Pavel Iozef Shafaryk i ukraïntsi,'' in *Z istoriï chekhoslovats'ko-ukraïns'kykh zv''iazkiv* (Bratislava: Slovats'ke vyd-vo khudozhn'oï literatury 1959), pp. 281–306.

On relations with other Czechs, see Zdeněk Hájek, ''Styky Jakiva a Ivana Holovackých z Josefem Podlipským a Františkem Cyrilem Kampelíkem,'' in *Franku Wollmanovi k sedmdesátinám: sborník prací* (Prague: Státní pedagogické nakladatelství 1958), pp. 213–227; Hryhorii Omel'chenko, *Ian Pravoslav Koubek i ioho ukraïns'ki sympatiï* (Prague: Ches'ko-ukraïns'ka knyha 1933).

78 Kyrylo Studyns'kyi, ed., *Korespondentsyia Iakova Holovats'koho v lïtakh 1835–49,* in Zbirnyk fil'ol'ogichnoï sektsyi NTSh, VIII–IX (L'viv 1905); V.A. Frantsev, ed., *Pis'ma k Viacheslavu Gankie iz slavianskikh zemel'* (Warsaw 1905), pp. 222–238 and 378–392.

79 Mykhailo Tershakovets', ''Vidnosyny Vartolomeia Kopitara do halyts'ko-ukraïns'koho pys'menstva,'' *Zapysky NTSh,* XCIV (L'viv 1910), pp. 84–106; XCV (1910), pp. 107–154; Kyrylo Studyns'kyi, ''Kopitar i Zubryts'kyi,'' *Zapysky NTSh,* CXXV (L'viv 1918), pp. 115–164; Vasyl' Shchurat, ''V. Kopitar i ep. Iv. Snihurs'kyi,'' *Zapysky NTSh,* CXXV (L'viv 1918), pp. 165–200.

The correspondence between Zubryts'kyi and Kopitar is found in the study by Studyns'kyi, n. 69 above, and in F.I. Svistun, ''Korrespondentsiia Denisa Zubritskogo s Kopitarom,''

Triad with other southern Slavs, especially the Serbs, are also the subject of two studies.[80]

With regard to the Polish influences on Galician Ukrainians, especially the Rusyn Triad, the best work is by Jan Kozik.[81] There are also several studies on the cooperation between Ukrainians and Poles, especially students in L'viv, in the conspiratorial Polish revolutionary movement during the 1830s and the 1840s.[82] The growth of interest in Ukrainian Galicia on the part of Polish ethnographers like Wacław Zaleski (Wacław z Oleksa, 1799–1849) and Żegota Pauli (1814–1895) and the writer Tomasz Padurra (1801–1871) is outlined in Aleksander Pypin's monumental history of Russian ethnography and in Zdzisław Niedziela's survey of L'viv writers before 1848.[83]

Unlike the mutual interest between Galician Ukrainians and western and southern Slavic peoples that before 1848 were basically cultural in nature, the relationship with Russia took on political overtones from the very beginning. The ideas of Pan-Slavism, which had originated in the writings of Ján Kollár and Pavel Josef Šafárik, were understood by some Russian publicists, most notable among them Mikhail P. Pogodin (1800–1875), as the first stage in a development that would eventually lead to the unity of all the Slavic peoples under the hegemony of Russia. Pogodin and other writers in the tsarist empire were hopeful that the inheritance of Kievan Rus' (and this included eastern Galicia) would some day be ''reunited'' with Russia. Pogodin traveled to many Slavic lands and undertook extensive correspondence with local leaders in Galicia, the most notable being Denys Zubryts'kyi and Ivan Vahylevych.[84]

Viestnik 'Narodnogo Doma', XXIV (II), 3–6 (L'viv 1906), pp. 47–52, 63–67, 105–109, 121–122.

80 M.Ia. Holberg, ''Pivdennoslov''ians'ki zv''iazky 'Rus'koï triitsi' (Z istoriï pershykh ukraïns'kykh perekladiv serbs'kykh narodnykh pisen'),'' in *Mizhslov''ians'ki literaturni vzaiemyny*, vol. II (Kiev: AN URSR 1961), pp. 225–237; Jan Kozik, ''Czeskie i południowosłowiańskie powiązania 'Ruskiej trójcy','' *Studia Historyczne*, XI, 3 (Cracow 1968), pp. 323–341.

81 See his monograph, n. 33 above, pp. 205–217; and also Jan Kozik, ''Wpływy polskie na kształtowanie się świadomości narodowej Ukraińców w Galicji,'' *Studia Historyczne*, X, 1–2 (Cracow 1967), pp. 87–112.

82 See n. 17 above.

83 Aleksander N. Pypin, *Istoriia russkoi étnografii*, 4 vols (St Petersburg 1890–91), especially vol. III (1891), pp. 114–138; Zdzisław Niedziela, *Słowiańskie zainteresowania pisarzy lwowskich w latach 1830–1848*, Zeszyty Naukowe Universytetu Jagiellońskiego, vol. CXLIV: Prace Historyczno-literackie, no. 12 (Cracow 1966), especially pp. 75–89.

84 The letters of Zubryts'kyi and Vahylevych to Pogodin are found in Nil A. Popov, ed., *Pis'ma k M.P. Pogodinu iz slavianskikh zemel'*, vol. III (Moscow 1880), pp. 537–621 and 622–651. See also the comments on the Vahylevych-Pogodin correspondence in Iakov Golovatskii, ''K istorii galitsko-russkoi pis'mennosti (neskol'ko zamiechanii na pis'mo I. Vagilevicha k M.P. Pogodinu),'' *Kievskaia starina*, II [VI], 8 (Kiev 1883), pp. 645–663.

A volume of previously unpublished articles, diaries, correspondence, and other documents compiled by Ilarion Svientsits'kyi reveals the extent of mutual interest between writers in the Russian Empire and "Carpatho Russians" (i.e. Galicians and Subcarpathians) during the first half of the nineteenth century.[85] A discussion of all aspects of these relations is provided in studies by Svientsits'kyi and Evstakhiia Tyshyns'ka.[86]

Ukrainians from the southern part of the Russian Empire were also discovering their brethren in Galicia at this time. Several essays on these relations, especially the activity of Izmaïl Sreznevs'kyi (1812–1880),[87] as well as the correspondence of Ivan Vahylevych to Sreznevs'kyi, Mykhailo Maksymovych (1804–1873), and Osyp Bodians'kyi (1808–1879), have been published.[88]

85 I.S. Svientsitskii, *Materialy po istorii vozrozhdeniia Karpatskoi Rusi*, vol. I: *Snosheniia Karpatskoi Rusi s Rossiei v 1-oi polovinie XIX-ago vieka* (L'viv 1905).

86 I.S. Svientsitskii, "Obzor snoshenii Karpatskoi Rusi s Rossiei v l-uiu polovinu XIX v.," *Izviestiia otdieleniia russkago iazyka i slovesnosti Imp. Akad. Nauk*, XI, 3 (St Petersburg 1906), pp. 259–367; Evstakhiia Tyshyns'ka, "Pogodin i Zubryts'kyi," *Zapysky NTSh*, CX (L'viv 1912), pp. 101–122.

87 Mykhailo Vozniak, "Epizody kul'turnykh znosyn halyts'koï i rosiis'koï Ukraïny v pershii polovyni XIX viku," in *Fil'ol'ogichnyi zbirnyk pamiaty Mykhal'chuka* (Kiev 1915), pt 1 in *Zapysky Ukraïns'koho Naukovoho Tovarystva*, XIII (Kiev 1914), pp. 54–142; Ivan Pil'huk, "Literaturni zv''iazki skhidnoï i zakhidnoï Ukraïnu v pershi polovyni XIX st.," *Radians'ka literatura*, no. 11 (Kiev 1939), pp. 157–162; A. V. Kriukov, "Naukova podorozh I.I. Sreznevs'koho v Zakhidnu Ukraïny," in *Ukraïns'ke literaturoznavstvo*, vol. XVI (L'viv: LU 1972), pp. 23–27; T.V. Polianina, "Iz istorii vzaimootnoshenii I.I. Sreznevskogo i Ia.F. Golovatskogo," in *Voprosy russkoi literatury*, vol. III (15) (L'viv: LU 1970), pp. 90–97. See also the impact of Kotliarevs'kyi's *Aneida* on Galicia in Ivan Franko, "Pysania I.P. Kotliarevs'koho v Halychyni," *Zapysky NTSh*, XXVI (L'viv 1898), 14 pp.

88 "Listy I. Vagilevicha do I. Sreznevskago," *Nauchno-literaturnyi sbornik*, V, 1 (L'viv 1906), pp. 37–48; V. Danilov, ed., "Pis'ma Ivana Vagilevicha k M.A. Maksimovichu," *Russkii filologichnii viestnik*, LXVIII, 4 (Warsaw 1912), pp. 407–416; Fedir Savchenko, ed., "Lysty halychan do Bodians'koho," *Ukraïna*, VI, 5 (Kiev 1929), pp. 85–89.

Chapter 6

1848–1918

Background

The year 1848 witnessed the outbreak of revolutionary activity throughout large parts of the European continent. Galicia was to remain under Austrian rule, but during the next six decades the Ukrainian population underwent a profound social, political, and cultural transformation.

The revolutionary activity that began in March 1848 and threatened to overthrow Habsburg rule spread quickly to eastern Galicia. One month later, an imperial decree repealed serfdom. As a result of this act, a whole class of people (comprising more than ninety percent of the Ukrainian populace) had in effect come into being and had for the first time to be reckoned with as a factor in organized political and cultural life. In May, the freed serfs participated in elections to Austria's first Parliament (the Reichstag). At the same time a small group of Ukrainian leaders, mostly Greek Catholic clergy, set up political and cultural organizations. Although Habsburg authority was reinstated throughout the empire by 1850 and a period of neoabsolutism began, this did not erase the fact that Ukrainians had come into existence as a group; from now on their political and cultural needs had to be and were taken into account by the imperial government in Vienna as well as by the provincial administration in Galicia.

The abolition of serfdom, an increase in the number of Ukrainian elementary and secondary schools, and the resultant advances in literacy contributed, after the 1870s, to the growth of civic consciousness and organizational strength of the peasant masses as well as the evolution of a new, more secular-oriented Ukrainian intelligentsia. This resulted in the establishment of numerous Ukrainian newspapers and journals, publishing houses, cultural societies, theaters, credit associations, economic cooperatives–and in the 1890s, political parties. Thus by the end of the century, Ukrainians in Galicia had created a comprehensive infrastructure for national life that in turn prompted demands for more and more political autonomy.

During this rapid advancement of Galician-Ukrainian society, it is not surprising that the group's political and cultural leaders often suffered from the inability of society to fulfill their ever-rising expectations. Whereas the imperial government permitted and even at times promoted Ukrainian national life, political realities dictated that Vienna reach an accommodation with the most powerful force in Galicia–the Poles. The failure of Austria's neoabsolutist approach to internal administration and its military defeats at the hands of France and Sardinia (1859) and Prussia (1866) forced Vienna to embark on a period of experiment in reorganizing the empire. The result was the establishment of a new parliament (1861), ushering in Austria's constitutional period, and the creation of the Dual Monarchy (1867), permitting self-rule for Hungary. The Galician Poles, who had just witnessed the failure of another Polish revolt (1863) against Russia, were ready to cast their lot fully with the Habsburgs, although they wanted autonomy like the Hungarians had received. Vienna was not prepared to go so far, although in return for their support of the Habsburg monarchy, the Poles were allowed to control the internal affairs of Galicia as they saw fit. As a result, the provincial administration remained basically in Polish hands until the dissolution of the Austro-Hungarian Empire in 1918.

The Ukrainians were left to struggle as best they could to obtain a greater control over the life of the province. It was an uphill battle, fought primarily for more schools, more seats in the Austrian Parliament (Vienna) and Galician Diet (L'viv), and more provincial funds for cultural and economic activity. Like all national groups living within a multinational state and struggling for political autonomy and even independence, the Ukrainians in Austrian Galicia were never satisfied that they had gained enough concessions. Nevertheless, despite continued Polish dominance in the affairs of the province and the generally underdeveloped agrarian-based economy that left the region one of the poorest in the whole Habsburg Empire, the Ukrainians of Galicia made remarkable progress in the political and especially cultural spheres. Their region, small by comparison with the Dnieper Ukraine within the Russian Empire, became the leading center for the Ukrainian national revival in the second half of the nineteenth century.

Such relatively favorable conditions were dependent, however, on the existence of the Austro-Hungarian Empire, which, in 1914, entered a military conflict that four years later was to result in its demise. From the outset of the world conflict, eastern Galicia had become a war zone and it was occupied by tsarist Russia during the winter of 1914 and 1915. Although Ukrainian political leaders and the vast majority of the population remained to the end loyal to the Habsburgs (who fondly referred to them as the Tyrolians of the east), the passing of the

Austro-Hungarian Empire in late October 1918 put an end to the Austrian period in Galician history and opened up a new era in the national life of Galician Ukrainians.

Historical surveys, memoirs, reference works

The general literature on the period 1848–1918 can be divided into several categories: histories of the whole period, memoirs by participants in contemporary political and cultural life, and descriptive works of an encyclopedic and statistical nature. For the period as a whole and in particular for the legal and administrative aspects of Austrian nationality policy throughout the empire, there are excellent studies by Hugo Hantsch, Robert A. Kann, and in several multiauthored works, all of which have specific sections on Galicia and/or its nationalities.[1] With regard to Galicia itself, the leading postwar Polish authority on Galicia, Stefan Kieniewicz, has compiled a volume of documents with a historical essay for the years 1850 to 1914, although the vast majority of his material concerns Polish-inhabited western Galicia.[2] The best introductory surveys about Ukrainians in Galicia during this period are found in articles by Ivan L. Rudnytsky and Wolfdieter Bihl; for Poles, there are similar studies by Piotr Wandycz and Henryk Batowski.[3] There are also several surveys about Jews in Galicia during the last seventy years of Habsburg rule.[4]

1 Hugo Hantsch, *Die Nationalitätenfrage im alten Österreich: Das Problem der konstruktiven Reichsgestaltung*, Wiener Studien, vol. I (Vienna: Herold 1953); Robert A. Kann, *The Multinational Empire: Nationalism and National Reform in the Habsburg Monarchy, 1848–1918*, 2 vols (New York: Columbia University Press 1950; reprinted New York: Octagon Press 1964 and 1970), revised edition in German: *Das Nationalitätenproblem der Habsburgermonarchie*, 2 vols (Graz: H. Bohlaus Nachf. 1964); Karl Gottfried Hugelmann, ed., *Das Nationalitätenrecht des alten Österreichs* (Vienna and Leipzig: W. Braumüller 1934); R. John Rath, ed., *The Nationality Problem in the Habsburg Monarchy in the Nineteenth Century: A Critical Appraisal*, in *Austrian History Yearbook*, III, 3 pts (Houston 1967); Adam Wandruszka and Peter Urbanitsch, eds, *Die Habsburgermonarchie 1848–1918*, vol. III: *Die Völker des Reiches*, 2 pts (Vienna: Österreichische Akademie der Wissenschaften 1980).

2 Stefan Kieniewicz, *Galicja w dobie autonomicznej (1850–1914)* (Wrocław: ZNIO 1952).

3 Ivan L. Rudnytsky, ''The Ukrainians in Galicia Under Austrian Rule'' and Piotr S. Wandycz, ''The Poles in the Habsburg Monarchy,'' in *Austrian History Yearbook*, III, pt 2 (Houston 1967), pp. 261–286 and 394–429, reprinted with revisions in Andrei S. Markovits and Frank E. Sysyn, eds, *Nationbuilding and the Politics of Nationalism: Essays on Austrian Galicia* (Cambridge, Mass.: Harvard Ukrainian Research Institute 1982), pp. 23–93; Wolfdieter Bihl, ''Die Ruthenen'' and Henryk Batowski ''Die Polen,'' in Adam Wandruszka and Peter Urbanitsch, eds, *Die Habsburgermonarchie 1848–1918*, vol. III: *Die Völker des Reiches*, pt 1 (Vienna: Österreichische Akademie der Wissenschaften, 1980), pp. 522–584.

4 See chapter 10, n. 9.

It is from the last decades of the nineteenth century that deep splits occurred within the Ukrainian intelligentsia, especially between the Ukrainophiles and Russophiles, and as a result much of the historiography about Ukrainian life during this era is influenced by these national/ideological divisions. The Ukrainophile view is represented in brief essays by Mykhailo Lozyns'kyi and Volodymyr Levyts'kyi, national activists from the period, who depict Austrian rule in a relatively favorable light, and in two semipopular volumes by Matvii Stakhiv, a political leader from the interwar period, who emphasizes the negative aspects of Austrian cooperation with local Poles that hindered Galician-Ukrainian development.[5] The Russophile view is presented in the second volume of Pylyp Svystun's history of Galician Rus' under Austrian domination. His narrative stops in 1895, and he is extremely critical of both the Vienna government and the Polish provincial administration. Each of them, he argues, promoted in its own way "Ukrainian separatism," thus perpetuating the Austrian policy of *divide et impera* at the expense of the "Russian" population of eastern Galicia, which was forced to remain separated from its brethren in tsarist Russia.[6] Reflecting the continued efforts of Soviet Marxist scholarship to deny anything positive in all the regimes that preceded the Soviet "liberation" of Galicia in 1939, Volodymyr Osechyns'kyi paints in the darkest colors the cooperation between the Habsburg government and the Polish upper classes in Galicia to oppress politically and culturally and to exploit economically the Ukrainian peasant masses.[7] The continual changes in Polish-Ukrainian relations in Galicia during the nineteenth century have been traced by Mykhailo Demkovych-Dobrians'kyi.[8]

Several memoirs date from this period, some of which were conceived as histories of Galicia. The most ambitious of these is the six-volume work by the parliamentarian Kost' Levyts'kyi, whose systematic coverage of political and cultural events during the years 1848 to 1918 (from the Ukrainophile point of

5 Mykhailo Lozyns'kyi, "Obopil'ni stosunky mizh Velykoiu Ukraïnoiu i Halychynoiu v istoriï rozvytku ukraïns'koï politychnoï dumky XIX i XX vv.," *Ukraïna,* V, 2 (Kiev 1928), pp. 83–90; Volodymyr Levyts'kyi, *Iak zhyvet' sia ukraïns'komu narodovy v Avstriï* (Vienna: Vyd–vo Soiuza Vyzvolennia Ukraïny 1915); Matvii Stakhiv, *Zakhidna Ukraïna ta polityka Pol'shchi, Rosiï i zakhodu, 1772–1918,* 2 vols (Scranton, Pa.: Ukraïns'kyi Robitnychyi Soiuz 1958).

6 Filipp I. Svistun, *Prikarpatskaia Rus' pod vladieniem Avstrii,* pt 2: 1850–1895 (L'viv: Izd. O.A. Markova 1897; reprinted Trumbull, Conn.: Peter S. Hardy 1970).

7 V.K. Osechyns'kyi, *Halychyna pid hnitom Avstro-Uhorshchyny v epokhu imperializmu* (L'viv: Knyzhkovo-zhurnal'ne vyd-vo, 1954).

8 Mykhailo Demkovych-Dobrians'kyi, *Ukraïns'ko-pol's'ki stosunky u XIX storichchi,* Ukraïns'kyi Vil'nyi Universytet, Monohrafiï, no. 13 (Munich 1969).

view) is still one of the best chronicle-type histories of the subject.[9] Other memoirs by local leaders focus on shorter periods: Iustyn Zhelekhovs'kyi (1840s–1870s), Anatol Vakhnianyn (1847–1874), Oleksii Zaklyns'kyi (1850s–1870s), Bohdan Didyts'kyi (1860s–1870s), Oleksander Barvins'kyi (1860–1888), Kornylo Ustiianovych (1870s), Tyt Voinarovs'kyi (1880s–1920s), Ievhen Olesnyts'kyi (1870s–1890s), Vasyl' Nahirnyi (1890–1914).[10] Also of importance are several memoirs by Galician Polish leaders, including Prince Leon Sapieha, marshal of the Galician Diet (1861–1875); Kazimierz Chłędowski, writer and government official in Galicia (1868–1880); Józef Doboszyński, state prosecutor and jurist in eastern Galicia (1859–1889); Leon Biliński, imperial minister for Galicia (1895–1897); and Michał Bobrzyński, viceroy of Galicia (1908–1913);[11] as well as memoirs by Mykhailo Drahomanov, the political

9 Kost' Levyts'kyi, *Istoriia politychnoï dumky halyts'kykh ukraïntsiv 1848–1914*, 2 vols (L'viv: p.a. 1926); idem, *Istoriia vyzvol'nykh zmahan' halyts'kykh ukraïntsiv z chasu svitovoï viiny*, 3 vols (L'viv: p.a. 1929–30); idem, *Velykyi zryv: do istoriï ukraïns'koï derzhavnosty vid bereznia do lystopada 1918 r. na pidstavi spomyniv ta dokumentiv* (L'viv: Chervona kalyna 1931), 2nd ed. (New York: Vyd-vo Chartoryis'kykh 1968).

10 ''Avtobiografiia o. Iustina Zhelekhovskago,'' *Viestnik 'Narodnago Doma'*, XXVII (V), 1–4 and 6–12 (L'viv 1909), pp. 9–17, 23–31, 44–51, 65–97 and 97–104, 128–144, 158–164, 166–171, 193–200, 205–210; XXVIII (VI), 1–12 (L'viv 1910), pp. 8–16, 25–28, 40–46, 54–59, 68–72, 82–88, 107–113, 127–134, 142–148, 160–168; Anatol' Vakhnianyn, *Spomyny z zhytia (posmertne vydannie)* (L'viv 1908); Oleksei Zaklyns'kyi, *Zapysky parokha starykh Bohorodchan* (L'viv: Chervonaia Rus' 1890), 2nd ed. (Toronto: Dobra knyzhka 1960); Bohdan Dîdytskii, *Svoezhyt'evŷy zapysky*, pt 1: *Hde-shcho do ystoriy samorozvytiia iazŷka y azbuky Halytskoi Rusy* (L'viv 1907), first published in *Vîstnyk 'Narodnoho Doma'*, nos 2–4, 6–12 (L'viv 1906) and pt 2: *Vzhliad na shkol'noe obrazovanie Halytskoi Rusy v XIX st.* (L'viv 1908); Oleksander Barvins'kyi, *Spomyny z moho zhytia*, 2 vols, Zahal'na biblioteka, no. 115–120 (L'viv: Iakiv Orenshtain v Kolomyï 1912–13); Kornylo N. Ustiianovych, *M.F. Raievskii i rossiiskii panslavyzm* (L'viv: K. Bednarskyi 1884); memoirs of Tyt Voinarovs'kyi are in *Istorychni postati Halychyny XIX–XX st.*, NTSh, Biblioteka ukraïnoznavstva, vol. VIII (New York, Paris, Sydney, and Toronto 1961), pp. 15–75; Ievhen Olesnyts'kyi, *Storinky z moho zhyttia*, 2 vols (L'viv: Dilo 1935); Vasyl' Nahirnyi, *Z moïkh spomyniv* (L'viv: Reviziinyi Soiuz Ukraïns'kykh Kooperatyv 1935).

11 Leon Sapieha, *Wspomnienia (z lat 1803 do 1863 r.)* (L'viv, Warsaw, and Poznań: H. Altenberg, G. Seyfarth, E. Wende, Rzepecki 1912); Kazimierz Chłędowski, *Pamiętniki*, 2 vols, ed. with an introduction by Antoni Knot (Wrocław: ZNIO 1951), especially vol. I: *Galicja (1843–1880);* Józef Doboszyński, ''Pamiętnik,'' in *Pamiętniki urzędników galicyjskich*, ed. with an introduction by Irene Homola and Bolesław Łopuszański (Cracow: Wyd. Literackie 1978), pp. 357–416; Leon Biliński, *Wspomnienia i dokumenty*, 2 vols (Warsaw: F. Hosick, 1924–25); Michał Bobrzyński, *Z moich pamiętników*, ed. with an introduction by Adam Galos (Wrocław and Cracow: ZNIO 1957). The introductions by Knot, Homolka, and Lopuszański referred to above include surveys of Galician-Polish memoir literature.

theorist from the Russian Ukraine who spread ideas of Ukrainianism in Galicia during the late 1860s and 1870s, and Vasilii Kel'siev, the Russian Slavophile who toured Galicia in 1866–1867.[12]

Finally, there are several handbooks, statistical compilations, and descriptive works dealing with the years 1848–1918. The best source material on the administrative structure of Galicia is found in the handbooks for the whole empire published almost every year by the imperial government. Beginning in 1856, each volume contains 100 or more pages devoted to Galicia, listing everyone in the Diet, provincial administration (executive, judicial, fiscal, trade, and rural branches), educational system, the military, and the churches.[13] Comprehensive statistical data are available in 104 volumes of the series entitled *Oesterreichische Statistik*. This series contains data from each of the decennial censuses between 1880 and 1910, dealing with population (place of habitation, age, marriage status, demographic growth and movement, occupation, religion, mother tongue), sanitation, foreign trade, judicial proceedings (civil and criminal), education, banking, parliamentary election results, internal commerce and trade, and communications. Each of these volumes, with the exception of those on foreign trade, contains a section on Galicia.[14]

Statistical data on the size and composition of Galicia's population have received special attention. The Austrian government published the results of four of its decennial censuses between 1857 and 1900. One volume for each census was devoted to Galicia, listing all villages with the total number of houses and persons, the latter figures broken down by sex and sometimes national and religious categories.[15] Yearbooks and other statistical guides for Galicia and the city of L'viv were also published in the late nineteenth century.[16]

12 M. Drahomanov, *Avstro-rus'ki spomyny* [1867–1877], 3 pts (L'viv: Ivan Franko 1889–92), reprinted in his *Literaturno-publitsystychni pratsi*, vol. 2 (Kiev: Naukova dumka 1970), pp. 151–288; Vasilii Kel'siev, *Galichina i Moldaviia: putevyia pis'ma* (St Petersburg 1868; reprinted Bridgeport, Conn.: Carpatho-Russian Literary Association 1976).

See also the shorter A [polinarii] Martyns'kyi, "Poïzdka v Halychynu v 1889 r. (zi spomyniv)," in *'Dnipro': kaliendar na 1924 r.* (Zolochiv 1924), pp. 82–101.

13 See chapter 5, notes 10 and 11.

14 *Oesterreichische Statistik*, 93 vols (Vienna: K. K. Hof- und Staatsdruckerei, 1882–1914) and Neue Folge, 11 vols (1912–14).

15 See chapter 2, n. 18.

16 Władysław Rapacki, *Ludność Galicyi* (L'viv: p. a. 1874); *Rocznik statystyki Galicyi*, 5 vols [1886–1897], ed. T. Rutkowski (L'viv: Krajowe Biuro Statystyczne 1887–98), and *Podręcznik statystyki Galicyi*, 4 vols [1898–1913], ed. by T. Pilat (L'viv: Krajowe Biuro Statystyczne 1900–13); *Wiadomości statystyczne o mieście Lwowie*, 3 vols, ed. Tadeusz Romanowicz (L'viv: Gmina miasta Lwowa 1874–86).

A useful survey of pre-1914 statistical sources on Galicia is provided by Walentyna Najdus,

In an era when the peasant masses were being asked for the first time to identify themselves with some national label (usually they would still identify themselves by religious affiliation), it is not surprising that difficulties developed with respect to the accuracy of the statistical data. Accuracy would have been a problem even in the most objective environment, which Galicia was not, and the census results caused continual controversy (complete with political repercussions) over the exact number of Ukrainians vs Poles or Greek Catholics vs Roman Catholics. Stanislav Dnistrians'kyi has provided an excellent history of census collecting in Austria-Hungary with reference to specific problems in late nineteenth-century Galicia.[17] The problem of national and religious identity among Ukrainians and Poles in eastern Galicia as reflected in contemporary statistical data is analyzed in great detail by Volodymyr Okhrymovych, and an effort to determine correlations between religious background and professional status based on data from the 1900 census was made by Józef Buzek.[18]

Also of use are the encyclopedia-like guides on all aspects of the province during the last years of Habsburg rule: several were prepared in Russia on the eve of the war and reflect the tsarist government's growing interest in Galicia:[19] two others were written by Poles during the war and emphasized the positive aspects of the Polish-dominated administration in the province.[20] Less partisan in approach

''Źródła statystyczne do dziejów klasy robotniczej w Galicji,'' in *Polska klasa robotnicza: studia historyczne,* vol. III (Warsaw: PWN 1972), pp. 367–385.

17 Stanislav Dnïstrians'kyi, ''Natsional'na statystyka,'' in *Studiï z polia suspil'nykh nauk i statystyky,* vol. I–II, ed. M. Hrushevs'kyi (L'viv: Statystychna komisiia NTSh 1909–10), pp. 17–64 and 27–67.

18 Volodymyr Okhrymovych, ''Z polia natsional'noï statystyky Halychyny (pomichenia nad rizhnytsiamy i pereminamy v natsional'nim skladi halyts'koï liudnosty),'' in *Studiï z polia suspil'nykh nauk i statystyky,* vol. I, ed. M. Hrushevs'kyi (L'viv: Statystychna komisiia NTSh 1909), pp. 65–160; Józef Buzek, *Stosunki zawodowe i socyalne ludności w Galicyi według wyznania i narodowości na podstawie spisu ludności z dnia 31 grudnia 1900 r.* (L'viv 1905); J. Buzek, ''Rozsiedlenie ludności Galicji według wyznania i języka,'' *Wiadomości Statystyczne,* XXI, 2 (L'viv 1909).

19 L. Vasilevskii, *Sovremennaia Galitsiia* (St Petersburg 1900); V. Zubkovskii, *Galitsiia: kratkii obzor geografii, étnografii, istorii i ékonomicheskoi zhizni strany* (Kharkiv 1914); Iu.A. Kheifits, *Galitsiia: politicheskoe, administrativnoe i sudebnoe ustroistvo* (Petrograd 1915); N.V. Iastrebov, *Galitsiia nakanunie Velikoi voiny 1914 goda* (Petrograd 1915); N.M. Lagov, *Galichina, eia istoriia, priroda, naselenie, bogatstva i dostoprimiechatel'nosti* (Petrograd: N.P. Karbasnikov 1915); E.S. Vul'fson, *Galitsiia do velikoi evropeiskoi voiny* (Moscow 1915). See also chapter 2, note 38.

20 Bohdan Winiarski, *Ustrój prawno-polityczny Galicyi* (Warsaw: Gebethner i Wolff 1915); Kazimierz Bartoszewicz, *Dzieje Galicyi: jej stan przed wojną i 'wyodrębnienie'* (Warsaw: Gebethner i Wolff 1917).

is a recent work by the Polish scholar Konstanty Grzybowski.[21] An encyclopedic survey on the city of L'viv is also available, and although the chronological coverage is only 1870 to 1895, this work, with long historical sections by Aleksander Czołowski and Kazimierz Ostaszewski-Barański, is perhaps the most comprehensive study on any period of the city's history.[22]

Revolutionary years, 1848–1849

Of the many works devoted to political history during the last seventy years of Austrian rule, the revolutionary period, 1848–1849, has received the most attention. During this period Ukrainians in Galicia entered the modern political sphere for the first time and their activity was played out in three places: in Galicia itself, at the Slav Congress in Prague, and at the newly elected Reichstag, which carried on its short-lived parliamentary career in Vienna and then in the Moravian town of Kroměříž (Kremsier).

In Galicia itself, the enterprising governor Count Franz Stadion (1806–1853) tried to stay on top of the revolutionary situation. He pushed through an important decree on April 22, 1848, liberating the serfs (actually months ahead of lands in the rest of the empire), and in early May encouraged a group of Ukrainian Greek Catholic clergy centered around the St George Cathedral (from which the term *sviatoiurtsi*–St George Circle–derives) to form a political organization, the Central Ruthenian Council (Holovna Rus'ka Rada). The latter development gave rise immediately to Polish accusations that Stadion had created the Ruthenian problem, and consequently the Poles set up a rival Ruthenian Council (Rus'kyi Sobor) composed of "Ruthenians of the Polish nation" *(gente Rutheni natione Poloni).* During 1848, the Ukrainians also established their first newspapers –*Zoria Halytska* and *Dnewnyk ruski;* their first cultural societies–the Congress of Rusyn Scholars (Sobor Rus'kykh Uchenykh) and the Galician-Rus' Matytsia (Halytsko-russka Matytsia); and their first military units–a peasant frontier defense organization, a national guard, and a sharpshooter division.

Outside Galicia, two rival delegations of Ukrainians–one representing the Central Ruthenian Council, the other the pro-Polish Ruthenian Council–journeyed to Prague in June, where they and other national leaders put forth cultural

21 Konstanty Grzybowski, *Galicia 1848–1914: historia ustroju politycznego na tle historii ustroju Austrii* (Cracow, Wrocław, and Warsaw: PAN 1959).

22 *Miasto Lwów w okresie samorządu 1870–1895* (L'viv 1896). See also the demographic analysis by Stanisław Pazyra, "Ludność Lwowa w pierwszej ćwierci XX wieku," in *Studja z historji społecznej i gospodarczej poświęcone prof. dr. Franciszkowi Bujakowi* (L'viv 1931), pp. 415–446; and the history of prices that covers the period down to 1914 by Stanisław Hoszowski, chapter 5, n. 26.

and political demands at the first international Slavic Congress. Between July 10, 1848, and March 6, 1849, thirty-nine Ukrainian deputies (elected in May 1848) called for greater social reform and the division of the province into Ukrainian and Polish halves during debates in the Austrian Parliament (Reichstag).

The many-sided activity of Galician Ukrainians in 1848–1849 is described in a few documentary collections and general histories of the period. The documentary collections concern the peasantry and political movements throughout eastern Galicia;[23] the creation of local affiliates of the L'viv-based Supreme Ruthenian Council;[24] the debates in the Ruthenian-Polish section at the Slav Congress in Prague;[25] and relations with Czech leaders, who did much to defend Ukrainian interests against Polish encroachments.[26] Also, the problem of the constitutional status of Galicia, its possible partition, and the views of Ukrainian and Polish deputies to the Austrian Reichstag are revealed in the published verbatim debates and protocols.[27] Finally, there are several political pamphlets from the era–both those that defend the idea of a distinct Ukrainian nationality with the right to political and cultural independence from the Poles,[28] and those that argue that

23 See the more than 100 documents from 1848–1849 in *Klasova borot'ba selianstva skhidnoï Halychyny (1772–1849): dokumenty i materialy* (Kiev: Naukova dumka 1974), pp. 376–529. See also the description of the March days in L'viv from the diary of Ivan Fedorovych in Ivan Franko, ''Prychynky do istoriï 1848 r.,'' *Zapysky NTSh,* LXXXVIII (L'viv 1909), pp. 94–117, and documents on the varied reactions of L'viv Greek Catholic seminarians to the 1848 events in Iurii Kmit, ''1848 rik i L'vivs'ka rus'ka dukhovna seminaryia,'' *Zapysky NTSh,* (L'viv 1901), 10 pp.

24 On the Brody affiliate, see Ivan Sozans'kyi, ''Kil'ka dokumentiv do istoriï 1848–1849 rr.,'' *Zapysky NTSh,* XC (L'viv 1909), pp. 158–165; on the Berezhany affiliate, see F.I. Svistun, ''Akty berezhanskoi Rady russkoi 1848–1849 gg.,'' *Viestnik 'Narodnogo Doma',* nos 2–9 (L'viv 1909).

25 W.T. Wisłocki, ''Kongres słowiański w roku 1848 i sprawa polska,'' *Rocznik Zakładu Narodowego imienia Ossolińskich,* I–II (L'viv 1927–28), pp. 517–731.

26 Ivan Bryk, *Materiialy do istoriï ukraïns'ko-ches'kykh vzaiemyn v pershii polovyni XIX st.,* in *Ukraïns'ko-rus'kyi arkhiv,* vol. XV (L'viv 1921).

27 *Verhandlungen des österreichischen Reichstages nach der stenographischen Aufnahme,* 5 vols (Vienna: K.K. Hof- und Staatsdruckerei 18?–?); *Protokolle über die Sitzungen des österreichischen Reichstages* (Vienna: K.K. Hof- und Staatsdruckerei 1852); Anton Springer, ed., *Protokolle des Verfassungs-Ausschusses im österreichischen Reichstage 1848–1849* (Leipzig 1885).

28 [Teodor Rozheiovs'kyi], *An die Russinen: mit kurzen historisch-politischen und statistischen Notizen* (L'viv 1848); *Denkschrift der ruthenischen Nation in Galizien zur Aufklärung ihrer Verhältnisse* (L'viv 1848); Antoni Pietruszewicz [Antin Petrushevych], *Słów kilka napisanych w obronie ruskiej narodowości* (L'viv 1848); I. Kołosowicz [Evstakhii Prokopchyts'], *Die ruthenische Frage in Galizien von Anton Dąbczański, Landrath zu Lemberg* (L'viv 1849), second edition published under the cryptonym Eine Russinen, *Die ruthenische Frage in Galizien von Anton Dąbczański* (L'viv 1850); W. Podoliński, *Slowo przestrogi* (Sanok: Karol

Ukrainianism (that is, Ruthenianism) is a dangerously divisive creation of Austrian political circles who are trying to counterbalance Polish influence in the province.[29]

With regard to general histories of the period, the best is by the Polish scholar Jan Kozik, who, on the basis of a wide variety of archival data, describes in great detail all aspects of Ukrainian activity, even though he is critical of what he considers the anti-Polish and pro-Austrian conservative tendencies of the Supreme Ruthenian Council.[30] Such views are also expressed in surveys of the period by the Soviet writer Evdokiia Kosachevskaia and the Slovak Michal Danílak, whose book is the only work to compare developments during these years in northern Bukovina and northeastern Hungary (Subcarpathian Rus') as well as in eastern Galicia.[31] More favorably inclined to the Supreme Ruthenian Council and to Ukrainian achievements in general is the shorter survey by Marta Bohachevsky-Chomiak.[32]

There are also several solid studies devoted to specific aspects of the Galician-Ukrainian experience during 1848–1849. With regard to developments within the province itself, studies by the Ukrainian historian Ivan Krevets'kyi cover a variety of topics during the revolutionary years: the government-organized elections in May 1848,[33] the last days of serfdom followed by agrarian strikes and boycotts

---

Pollak 1848). This last work has been analyzed by Vasyl' Shchurat, ''Rechnyk nezalezhnosty Ukraïny v 1848r. o. Vasyl' Podolyns'kyi,'' in his *Na dosvitku novoï doby: statti i zamitky do istoriï vidrodzhennia halyts'koï Ukraïny* (L'viv: NTSh 1919), pp. 134–178; and by F.I. Steblii, '' 'Slovo perestorohy' V. Podolyns'koho,'' *Ukraïns'kyi istorychnyi zhurnal,* X, 12 (Kiev 1966), pp. 44–51.

29 Anton Dąbczański, *Die ruthenische Frage in Galizien* (L'viv 1848); Anton Dąbczański, *Wyjaśnienie sprawy ruskiej* (L'viv 1848; reprinted L'viv: L. Piller 1885); Kaspar Cięglewicz, *Rzecz czerwono-ruska 1848 roku* (L'viv 1848); Kaspar Cięglewicz, *Die roth-reussischen Angelegenheiten im Jahre 1848: eine Berichtigung der Denkschrift der Ruthenen in Galizien zur Aufklärung ihrer Verhältnisse* (Vienna 1848).

30 Jan Kozik, *Między reakcją a rewolucją: studia z dziejów ukraińskiego ruchu narodowego w Galicji w latach 1848–1849,* Zeszyty Naukowe Uniwersytetu Jagiellońskiego, CCCLXXXI: Prace Historyczne, pt 52 (Warsaw and Cracow 1975).

31 Evdokiia M. Kosachevskaia, *Vostochnaia Galitsiia nakanune i v period revoliutsii 1848 g.* (L'viv: LU 1965); Mikhal Danylak, *Halyts'ki, bukovyns'ki, zakarpats'ki ukraïntsi v revoliutsiï 1848–1849 rokiv* (Bratislava and Prešov: Slovens'ke pedahohichne vyd-vo, viddil ukraïns'koï literatury 1972).

32 Martha Bohachevsky-Chomiak, *The Spring of a Nation: The Ukrainians in Eastern Galicia in 1848* (Philadelphia: Shevchenko Scientific Society 1967).

33 Ivan Krevets'kyi, ''Z vyborchoho rukhu u skhidniï Halychyni v 1848 r. (vybir Ivana Kapushchaka),'' *Zapysky NTSh,* LXX (L'viv 1906), pp. 73–85.

calling for greater economic freedom,[34] the psychological atmosphere in 1848,[35] the political struggle led by the Supreme Ruthenian Council for the division of Galicia,[36] and the establishment of a Rusyn national guard, a Rusyn peasant frontier defense organization, and a Rusyn sharpshooter's battalion, all supported by the imperial government in its effort to contain the Hungarian revolution from spreading to Galicia and involving Polish revolutionaries.[37] Other studies dealing with military and revolutionary activity focus on the Hutsul uprising and the imperial army's bombardment of L'viv in November 1848, which resulted in the return of strict Austrian control over the provincial capital.[38] More recently, Marxist historians in both the Soviet Ukraine and Poland have focused on the activity of the peasantry in Galicia during the rapidly changing events of 1848–1849.[39] As for cultural work, the importance of the first Ukrainian cultural organization, the Galician Rus' Matytsia, is seen in a collection of speeches and other documents by participants dating from the initial years of the Matytsia's

34 Ivan Krevets'kyi, ''Tsutsylivs'ka trivoha v 1848 r.: prychynky do istoriï ostannikh dnïv panshchyny v Halychynï,'' in *Naukovyi zbirnyk prys'viachenyi prof. Mykhailovy Hrushevs'komu . . .* (L'viv 1906), pp. 446–482; Ivan Krevets'kyi, *Agrarni straiky i boikoty u skhidnii Halychyni v 1848–1849 rr.: do istoriï borot'by za suspil'no-ekonomichne vyzvolenie ukraïns'kykh mas u skhidnii Halychyni* (L'viv: 'Dilo' 1906).

35 Ivan Krevets'kyi, ''Do psykhol'ogiï 1848 roku (sprava St. Hoshovs'koho),'' *Zapysky NTSh,* XC (L'viv 1909), pp. 137–157.

36 Ivan Krevets'kyi, ''Sprava podïlu Halychyny v rr. 1846–1850,'' *Zapysky NTSh,* XCIII (L'viv 1910), pp. 54–69; XCIV (1910), pp. 58–83; XCV (1910), pp. 54–82; XCVI (1910), pp. 94–115; XCVII (1910), pp. 105–154.

37 Ivan Krevets'kyi, ''Oboronna organïzatsiia rus'kykh selian na halyts'ko-uhors'kim pohranychu v 1848–1849 rr.,'' *Zapysky NTSh,* LXIII–LXIV (L'viv 1905), 58 pp.; idem, ''Do istoriï organïzovannia natsional'nykh gvardiï v 1848 r.,'' *Zapysky NTSh,* LXXIII (L'viv 1906), pp. 125–142; idem, ''Batalïon rus'kykh hïrskykh stril'tsïv 1849–1850,'' *Zapysky NTSh,* CVII (L'viv 1912), pp. 52–72; idem, ''Proby organïzovania rus'kykh natsional'nykh gvardii u Halychynï 1848–1849,'' *Zapysky NTSh,* CXIII (L'viv 1913), pp. 77–146. See also the shorter essay by F.I. Svistun, ''Galitsko-russkoe voisko v 1848–1849 godakh,'' *Zhivoe slovo* I (L'viv 1899), pp. 30–39.

38 Ivan Franko, ''Lukian Kobylytsia: epizod iz istoriï Hutsul'shchyny v pershii polovynï XIX v.,'' *Zapysky NTSh,* XLIX (L'viv 1902), 40 pp., reprinted in his *Tvory,* vol. XIX (Kiev: Derzhavne vyd-vo khudozhn'oï literatury 1956), pp. 716–752; Ia. Levyts'kyi, ''l y 2 padolysta 1848 r. v L'vovi,'' *Zapysky NTSh,* XXV (L'viv 1898), pp. 1–43.

39 F.I. Steblii, ''Selians'kyi rukh u Skhidnii Halychyni pid chas revoliutsiï 1848–1849 rr.,'' *Ukraïns'kyi istorychnyi zhurnal,* XVI, 6 (Kiev 1973), pp. 28–38; Jan Kozik, ''Kwestia włościańska w Galicji Wschodniej w polityce Hołownej Rady Ruskiej 1848–1849,'' in *Prace Historyczne,* no. 50, *Zeszyty Naukowe Uniwersytetu Jagiellońskiego,* CCCLXIV (Warsaw and Cracow 1974), pp. 63–93; and Stefan Kieniewicz, *Pomiędzy Stadionem a Goslarem: sprawa włościańska w Galicji w 1848 r.* (Wrocław: ZNIO 1980).

existence (1848–1850) as well as in a study of its establishment by Mykhailo Vozniak.[40]

Relations between Galicia's two major nationalities, especially the reaction by Poles to the efforts of Ukrainians to become a distinct national and political force, are discussed in a general survey by Jan Kozik.[41] More specifically, the activity of the pro-Polish Ruthenian Council (Rus'kyi Sobor) is analyzed by Nina Pashaeva in a factually accurate though critical account, while Marceli Handelsman has dealt with the Ukrainian question in a monograph on Prince Adam Czartoryski (1770–1861), the influential Polish exile in Paris who urged that Galician Poles cooperate with local Ukrainians as part of his larger effort to undermine Russia and restore an independent Polish state.[42] An insight into Polish-Ukrainian relations is also provided in biographies of Galicia's governors during the revolutionary years: the Austrian Franz Stadion, who ostensibly "invented the Ruthenians," and Wacław Zaleski, the student of Ukrainian folklore and the first Pole to hold the governor's post.[43]

Ukrainian activity outside Galicia during 1848–1849 has also been studied extensively. Recent articles by historians in Poland have given particular attention to Ukrainian participation in the parliamentary debates at Vienna and Kroměříž,[44]

40 Yvan Holovatskii, ed., *Ystorychieskii ocherk osnovaniia Halytsko-ruskoy Matytsî y spravozdan'e pervoho soboru uchenŷkh ruskykh y liubytelei narodnoho prosvîshcheniia* (L'viv: Yzd. Halytsko-russkoi Matytsŷ 1850); Mykhailo Vozniak, "Do istoriï ukraïns'koï naukovoï i prosvitnoï organïzatsiï v Halychynï 1848 r.," *Zapysky NTSh,* CX (L'viv 1912), pp. 163–182.

41 Jan Kozik, "Stosunki ukraińsko-polskie w Galicji w okresie rewolucji 1848–1849: proba charakterystyki," in *Z dziejów współpracy Polaków, Ukraińców i Rosjan,* in *Zeszyty Naukowe Uniwersytetu Jagiellońskiego,* CCCCXVI: *Prace Historyczne,* no. 54 (Warsaw and Cracow 1975), pp. 29–54.

42 N.M. Pashaeva, "Otrazhenie natsional'nykh i sotsial'nykh protivorechii v Vostochnoi Galichine v 1848 g. v listovkakh Russkogo Sobora," in *Slavianskoe vozrozhdenie,* ed. S.A. Nikitin et al. (Moscow: Nauka 1966), pp. 48–62; Marceli Handelsman, *Ukraińska polityka ks. Adama Czartoryskiego przed wojną krymską,* in Pratsi Ukraïns'koho Naukovoho Instytutu, vol. XXXV (Warsaw 1937), especially the chapter on Galicia (pp. 60–97) and the decrees of the L'viv Polish National Council regarding Galician Ukrainians in 1848 (pp. 151–162).

43 On Stadion, see the reminiscences about him by a contemporary, R. Hirsch, *Franz Graf Stadion* (Vienna, 1861); and the biography by Rudolf Mattausch, "Franz Graf Stadion (1806–1853)," in *Neue österreichische Biographie ab 1815: grosse Österreicher,* vol. XIV (Zurich, Leipzig, and Vienna: Amalthea Vlg. 1960), pp. 62–73. On Zaleski, see the biography by K. Ostaszewski-Barański, *Wacław Michał Zaleski, 1799–1849: zarys biograficzny* (L'viv 1912). On Zaleski's earlier cultural activities, see also chapter 5, n. 83.

44 Włodimierz Borys, "Wybory w Galicĵi i debaty nad zniesieniem pańszczyzny w parlamencie wiedeńskim w 1848 r.," *Przegląd Historyczny,* LVIII (Warsaw 1967), pp. 28–45; Jan Kozik, "Galizische Ukrainer im konstituierenden Reichstag von Wien und Kremsier (1848–1849)," in *Studia austro-polonica,* vol. I, in *Zeszyty Naukowe Uniwersytetu Jagiellońskiego,*

while the prewar Ukrainian scholar Ivan Bryk has provided the most detailed account of Galician-Ukrainian participation at the Slav Congress in Prague.[45] The Czech historians Vladimír Hostička and Václav Žaček have described Czech-Ukrainian relations at the Slav Congress and in the Reichstag, where Czech leaders opposed the Ukrainian demand to divide Galicia but supported all their efforts for cultural and political autonomy in the face of Polish opposition.[46]

Political developments, 1850–1914

After the Austrian defeat (with Russian help) of the Hungarian revolutionaries in August 1849, the Viennese government under the new emperor, Franz Joseph (reigned 1848–1916), embarked on a policy of centralized neoabsolutist control of the empire. In Galicia, martial law remained in effect until 1854, and the province was ruled by the Polish governor Count Agenor Gołuchowski (1812–1875)–renamed viceroy *(Statthalter/namiestnik)* about 1865–whose policy of full cooperation with Austria was not yet appreciated by Polish political circles, whether conservative or liberal. As for the Ukrainians, the Supreme Ruthenian Council dissolved itself in 1852, and following that, most of the group's concerns revolved around cultural issues, such as the maintenance of Ukrainian cultural institutions, use of the Ukrainian language in public life, and preference for German instead of Polish as the official language in the school system. There are

---

CCCCLXXXII: *Prace Historyczne,* no. 57 (Warsaw and Cracow 1978), pp. 129–155; and the more general work by Roman Rosdolsky, *Die Bauernabgeordneten im konstituierenden österreichischen Reichstag 1848–1849,* Ludwig Boltsmann Institut für Geschichte der Arbeiterbewegung, vol. V (Vienna: Europaverlag 1976).

45 Ivan Bryk, *Slavians'kyi zïzd u Prazï 1848 r. i ukraïns'ka sprava* (L'viv: NTSh 1920), 81 pp., first published in *Zapysky NTSh,* CXXIX (L'viv 1920), pp. 141–217; idem, "Shafaryk u roli suddi v terminolohichnomu ukraïns'ko-pol's'komu spori 1849 r.," *Zapysky NTSh,* CL (L'viv 1929), pp. 253–269.

See also the documents from Prague in the collections edited by Bryk and Wisłocki, notes 25 and 26 above, and in Ivan Sozans'kyi, "Do istoriï uchasty halyts'kykh Rusyniv u slovians'kim kongresï v Prazï 1848 r.," *Zapysky NTSh,* LXXII (L'viv 1906), pp. 112–121.

46 Vladimír Hostička, *Spolupráce Čechů a haličských Ukrajinců v letech 1848–1849,* Rozpravy Československé akademie věd: Řada společenských věd, vol. LXXV, no. 12 (Prague 1965); V. Žáček, "Ze styků Čechů a západních Ukrajinců v revolučních letech 1848 a 1849," in *Z dejín československo-ukrajinských vzt'ahov: Slovanské štúdie,* I (Bratislava: Slovenská akadémia vied 1957), pp. 351–374, translated into Ukrainian as "Pro zv"iazky chekhiv i zakhidnykh ukraïntsiv u revoliutsiinykh 1848 ta 1849 rokakh," in *Z istoriï chekhoslovats'ko-ukraïns'kykh zv"iazkiv* (Bratislava: Slovats'ke vyd-vo khudozhn'oï literatury 1959), pp. 343–369.

See also the older essay by Florian Zapletal, *Rusíni a naši buditelé* (Prague: Kolokol 1921); and the more recent Michal Danilák, "Ukrajinci a Slovanský zjazd v Prahe roku 1848," *Slovanské štúdie,* X: *História,* 4 (Bratislava 1968), pp. 5–28.

several studies on Ukrainian life during the 1850s' decade of absolutism as well as the 1860s, which witnessed the first stirrings of a populist Ukrainian cultural movement.[47] The Polish struggle to gain political superiority in Galicia during these years has also been given much attention in a biography of governor Gołuchowski by Bronisław Łoziński and in several monographs on specific aspects of Polish political activity.[48] Ukrainian reaction to Polish strivings was expressed in cultural terms, and in particular the language question, a problem that took on elements of a Ukrainian *cause célèbre* when Gołuchowski's administration proposed in 1859 that the Latin alphabet (in its Czech, not Polish form) be introduced for all Ukrainian publications.[49] The provincial government's unsuccessful intervention in the Ukrainian language question has been treated in two collections of documents[50] and in studies on the cultural aspects ("the language war") and political aspects (the role of Gołuchowski) of the problem.[51]

47 M. T-ov [M. Drahomanov], "Russkie v Galitsii: literaturnyia i politicheskiia zamietki," *Viestnik Evropy,* VIII, 1 and 2 (St Petersburg 1873), pp. 114–152 and 769–798; Natal' Vakhnianyn, *Prychynky do istoriï ruskoï spravy v Halychyni v lïtakh 1848–1870* (L'viv: Lev Lopatyns'kyi 1901); Ivan P. Filevich, *Iz istorii Karpatskoi Rusi: ocherki galitsko-russkoi zhizni s 1772 g. (1848–1866)* (Warsaw 1907); Sergei Efremov, "Galichina v nachalie konstitutsionnoi éry," *Golos minuvshago,* V, 9–10 (Moscow 1917), pp. 154–180; Iaroslav Hordyns'kyi, *Do istoriï kul'turnoho i politychnoho zhytia v Halychyni v 60-tykh rr. XIX v.,* in *Zbirnyk Fil'ol'ogichnoï sektsiï NTSh,* vol. XVI (L'viv 1917); S.M. Trusevych, *Suspil'no-politychnyi rukh u Skhidnii Halychyni v 50-70-kh rokakh XIX st.* (Kiev: Naukova dumka 1978).

48 Bronisław Łoziński, *Agenor Hrabia Gołuchowski w pierwszym kresie rządów swoich (1846–1859)* (L'viv: H. Altenberg 1901); Kazimierz Wyka, *Teka Stańczyka na tle historii Galicji w latach 1849–1869,* Instytut Badań Literackich, Studia Historyczno-Literackie, vol. IV (Wrocław: ZNIO 1951); Michał Bobrzyński, Władysław Leopold Jaworski, and Józef Milewski, *Z dziejów odrodzenia politycznego Galicyi, 1859–1873* (Warsaw: G. Gebethner i Wolff 1905); Irena Pannenkowa, *Walka Galicji z centralizmem wiedeńskim: dzieje rezolucyi Sejmu Galicyjskiego z 24. września 1868* (L'viv 1918); Jakub Forst-Battaglia, "Die polnisch-ukrainischen Beziehungen in Galizien zwischen 1866 und 1873," in *Studia austro-polonica,* vol. I, in *Zeszyty Naukowe Uniwersytetu Jagiellońskiego,* CCCCLXXXII: *Prace Historyczne,* LVII (Warsaw and Cracow 1978), pp. 47–62.

See also the memoirs of Leon Sapieha, marshal of the Galician Diet, covering the period up to 1863, n. 11 above.

49 The proposal was drawn up by the Czech scholar and official in the Ministry of Religion and Education in Vienna, Joseph Jireček, *Ueber den Vorschlag das Ruthenische mit lateinischen Schriftzeichen zu schreiben* (Vienna: K.K. Hof- und Staatsdruckerei 1859).

50 *Die ruthenische Sprach- und Schriftfrage in Galizien* (L'viv 1861); Ivan Franko, "Azbuchna viina v Halychynï 1859 r.," *Zapysky NTSh,* CXIV (L'viv 1913), pp. 81–116; CXV (1913), pp. 131–153; CXVI (1913), pp. 87–125.

51 Ivan Franko, ed., *Azbuchna viina v Halychynï 1859 r.: novi materiialy,* in *Ukraïns'ko-rus'kyi arkhyv,* vol. VIII (L'viv 1912); Kazimierz Ostaszewski-Barański, *Agenor Gołuchowski i Rusini w roku 1859* (L'viv: M. Schmitt 1910); F.I. S[vistun], *Gr. Agenor Golukhovskii i Galitskaia Rus' v 1848–1859 gg.* (L'viv 1901).

The 1860s inaugurated the constitutional period in Austrian history. In February 1861, a two-chamber parliament *(Reichsrat)* consisting of a House of Lords *(Herrenhaus)* and House of Deputies *(Abgeordnetenhaus)* was established by imperial patent in Vienna, while during the same year the Galician Diet *(Landtag/Sejm)* in L'viv was transformed into a representative assembly. The Diet consisted of representatives elected by four *curiae* (great landowners, chambers of commerce, towns, and rural communes), and a few Ukrainians were chosen from the last three *curiae*. Initially, representatives to the House of Deputies in Vienna were designated by the Galician Diet, then after 1873 a four-*curiae* system was initiated for elections to the parliament as well. In 1895, a fifth *curia* was established opened to all male voters, and finally in 1907 the *curia* system was abolished and replaced by universal male suffrage. In the upper house of parliament, Ukrainian Greek Catholic bishops were members ex-officio from the very beginning.[52]

To be sure, the Ukrainians, despite their rough equivalency in numbers to the Poles, were always underrepresented in both the Austrian Parliament and Galician Diet. Between 1861 and 1914, the number of Ukrainians in any one session ranged from 38 (1861) to 3 (1867) in Parliament and from 46 (1861) to 13 (1883 and 1901) in the Diet, which meant at best never more than 30 percent of the total allotment in either of the representative bodies. Nonetheless, Galician Ukrainians did participate in the political process and, as a result, a whole new generation of leaders and a politically aware populace had come into being by the outbreak of World War I.

The secondary literature on Ukrainian political developments during the Austrian constitutional period is not very good; it consists for the most part of polemical essays, sometimes with documents appended, on specific issues, or of memoir-like histories, the best of which is by Kost' Levyts'kyi.[53] On the other

---

See also the several memoirs by Galician-Ukrainian activists during these years, especially Didyts'kyi, n. 10 above. On Euzebiusz Czerkowski, the Ukrainian-born Polonophile school inspector who favored the introduction of the Latin alphabet in its Polish form, see n. 119 below.

52 A useful survey of the activity of Ukrainian deputies in the Vienna Parliament is Theodore Bohdan Ciuciura, ''Ukrainian Deputies in the Old Austrian Parliament, 1861–1918,'' *Mitteilungen: Arbeits- und Föderungsgemeinschaft der ukrainischen Wissenschaften,* XIV (Munich 1977), pp. 38–56. For emphasis on the first decade of the twentieth century after the introduction of universal male suffrage, see Ignacy Winiarski, *Rusini w Radzie państwa 1907–1908,* Nasze sprawy na Rusi, vol. III (L'viv 1909); and Teodor Bohdan Tsiutsiura, ''Borot'ba ukraïntsiv u videns'komu parliamenti za zahal'ne vyborche pravo i natsional'nu avtonomiiu (zokrema v rokakh 1905–1907),'' *Ukraïns'kyi istoryk,* XVII, 1–4 (New York, Toronto, and Munich 1980), pp. 23–44.

53 See n. 9 above.

hand, Polish historiography contains several important studies on Polish politics and the results achieved in Galicia during the period of de facto autonomy between 1871 and 1914.[54]

Important source materials exist, however, in the form of the debates and other materials from the Parliament in Vienna and the Diet in L'viv. The complete stenographic record of the twenty-two sessions of the Austrian Parliament between 1861 and 1918 is available for both the House of Deputies (374 volumes) and the House of Lords (74 volumes). Each session begins with a set of chronologically numbered volumes that contain the verbatim debates *(Sitzungen)* followed by several volumes of law proposals and other documents *(Beilagen)*.[55] Extremely valuable are the 50 volumes of indices for both houses, each of which contains a subject index and lists of laws debated, members and their presentations, committees, delegates according to province, and *Beilagen*.[56] The vast majority of the texts in the stenographic record are in German, although toward the end of the empire some other languages were used (including Ukrainian during the very last session). Certain speeches of Ukrainian deputies have been published separately.[57]

54 William Feldman, *Stronnictwa i programy polityczne w Galicyi, 1846–1906,* 2 vols (Cracow, 1907); Konstanty Grzybowski, *Galicja 1848–1914: historia ustroju politycznego na tle historii ustróju Austrii* (Warsaw and Wrocław: ZNIO, 1959); and the chapters on Galicia in Bohdan Winiarski, *Ustrój polityczny ziem polskich w XIX w.* (Poznań: Fiszer a Majewski 1923), translated into French as *Les institutions politiques en Pologne au XIXe siècle* (Paris: Picat 1924).

See also n. 48 above; n. 72 below; the memoir literature, note 11 above; and the biography of the marshal of the Galicia Diet from 1880 to 1886, who was of Ukrainian descent *(gente Ruthenus, natione Polonus):* Irena Homola Dzikowska, *Mikołaj Zyblikiewicz (1823–1887)* (Wrocław, Warsaw, and Cracow: ZNIO 1964).

55 *Stenographische Protokolle des Hauses der Abgeordneten des Reichsrathes* [1861–1868]/ *Stenographische Protokolle über die Sitzungen des Hauses der Abgeordneten des österreichischen Reichsrathes* [1869–1918], [374 vols] (Wien: K.K. Hof- und Staatsdruckerei 1862–1918); *Stenographische Protokolle des Herrenhauses des Reichrathes* [1861–1872]/ *Stenographische Protokolle über die Sitzungen des Herrenhauses des österreichischen Reichsrathes* [1873–1918], [74 vols] (Vienna: K.K. Hof- und Staatsdruckerei 1862–1918).

56 *Index zu den stenographischen Protokollen des Abgeordnetenhauses des österreichischen Reichsrathes,* 28 vols (Vienna: K.K. Hof- und Staatsdruckerei 1862–1920); *Index zu den stenographischen Protokollen des Herrenhauses des österreichischen Reichsrathes 1867–1918,* 22 vols (Vienna: K.K. Hof- u. Staatsdruckerei 1869–1920).

57 *Besïda posla Hryhoryia Tsehlyns'koho vyholoshena na zasïdaniu palaty posliv pry budzhetovii debatï dnia 19. hrudnia 1907* (Przemyśl: Selian'ska Rada 1908); *Ukraïns'ko-pol's'ka sprava v avstriis'kim parliamentï: promovy posliv tt. Iatska Ostapchuka, Hnata Dashyns'koho i Semena Vityka pry halyts'kii debatï v avstriis'kim parliamenti (20–26 maia 1908 r.)* (L'viv: Vyd-vo 'Chervonyi prapor' 1908).

The complete stenographic record of the Galician Diet between 1861 and 1914 is also available. It consists of three series: debates *(posiedzenia,* 54 volumes), addenda (*alegaty,* 90 volumes), and minutes (*protokóły,* 34 volumes).[58] Each volume is preceded by a subject and speaker index, and separate indices have been prepared for the years 1861 to 1895.[59] The Diet proceedings are printed in Polish and Ukrainian (using a Latin-based Polish alphabet), although there is a German translation for the years 1863 and 1865–1867[60] and some individual speeches by Ukrainian deputies have been published in German or Ukrainian.[61]

Biographical data on Ukrainian members in the Austrian Parliament are available in guides by Sigmund Hahn covering the five sessions between 1867 and 1892 and in a handbook by Fritz Freund on the House of Deputies during two sessions beginning in 1907 and 1911.[62] Longer biographies of several Ukrainian deputies in both the Vienna Parliament and the Galician Diet are found in works by Kost' Levyts'kyi, Izydor Sokhots'kyi, and Stepan Volynets'.[63]

58 *Stenograficzne Sprawozdania Sejmu Krajowego Królestwa Galicyi i Lodomeryi wraz z Wielkiem Księstwem Krakowskiem: Posiedzenia,* 1861–1914, 50 vols; *Alegaty,* 1865–1914, 90 vols; *Protokóły,* 1876–1914, 34 vols ([L'viv] 1861–1914).

59 Władysław Koziebrodzki, *Repertorjum czynności Galicyjskiego Sejmu krajowego,* 2 vols [vol. I: 1861–1883; vol. II: 1883–1889] (L'viv: Wydział Krajowy 1885–89); Stanisław Miziewicz, *Repertoryum czynności Galicyjskiego Sejmu krajowego,* vol. III: 1889–1895 (L'viv: Wydział Krajowy 1896).

60 *Stenographische Berichte über die Sitzungen des galiz. Landtages* [1863, 1865–67].

61 *Die gegenwärtige Lage der Ruthenen in Galizien in nationaler, politischer und ökonomischer Beziehung, auf Grund parlamentarischer Enunciationen der ruthenischen Landtags-abgeordneten in den Jahren 1889–1892* (L'viv: Russkaja Rada 1892); Ievhen Olesnytskyi, *Besïda vyholoshena v halytskim soimi dnia 14. zhovtnia 1903 pry zahal'nii rozpravi nad zvitom shkil'noï komisyï o stanï serednykh shkil v rr. 1900/1 i 1901/2* (L'viv: 'Dilo' 1903).

62 Sigmund Hahn, *Reichsraths-Almanach: für die Session 1867* (Prague: Carl J. Satow 1867); *für die Session 1873–1874* (Vienna: L. Rosner 1874); *für die Session 1879–1880* (Vienna: Alfred Hölder 1879); *für die Session 1885–1886* (Vienna: Alfred Hölder 1885); *für die Session 1891–1892* (Vienna: Alfred Hölder 1891); Fritz Freund, *Das österreichische Abgeordnetenhaus: ein biographisch-statistisches Handbuch,* 2 vols: *1907–1913 Legislaturperiode* and *1911–1917 Legislaturperiode* (Vienna 1907–11).

63 Kost' Levyts'kyi, *Ukraïns'ki polityky: syl'vety nashykh davnikh posliv i politychnykh diiachiv,* 2 vols (L'viv: 'Dilo' 1936–37); Sokhots'kyi's biographies of seven politicans are in *Istorychni postati Halychyny XIX–XX st.,* NTSh, Biblioteka ukraïnoznavstva, vol. VIII (New York, Paris, Sydney, and Toronto 1961), pp. 77–125; Stephen Volynets', *Peredvisnyky i tvortsi lystopadovoho zryvu: zakhidn'o-ukraïns'ki hromads'ki i politychni diiachi* (Winnipeg: Tryzub 1965).

See also the biography of Ievhen Petrushevych in Ivan O. Maksymchuk, *Narys istoriï rodu Petrushevychiv* (Chicago 1967), pp. 155–170.

The remaining literature on political problems reflects some of the challenges faced by Galician-Ukrainian politicians. In the situation after 1868 when the imperial government in Vienna and eventually local Galician-Polish leaders realized that it was in the interest of both parties to cooperate, the resulting *modus vivendi* meant that Ukrainian political interests would always be secondary to Polish ones. The Ukrainians tried to improve on this situation by demanding (sometimes in cooperation with the Poles) more parliamentary and dietary representation, by renewing their long-standing demand for the division of Galicia into Polish and Ukrainian provinces, by creating political parties, by supporting student strikes, and in at least one instance by engaging in political assassination.

Polish-Ukrainian relations were being commented on in essays by contemporaries and/or participants in the political process. On the Polish side, some writers like the pro-Austrian Cracow conservative intellectuals Józef Szujski, Stanisław Smolka, and Stanisław Tarnowski stressed the need for compromise with Ukrainians and urged recognition of their demands;[64] others like Józef Łokietek took the view that Ukrainians had already gained too much, and considering their eastward "Russophile" tendencies, they posed a serious threat to the well-being of "Polish" Galicia.[65] On the Ukrainian side, leaders like Stefan Kachala and Oleksander Barvins'kyi favored the idea of compromise with the Poles;[66] others criticized the failure of any lasting cooperation with the Poles, the halfhearted

64 For the more general works on Polish-Ukrainian relations in Galicia by Szujski, Smolka, and Tarnawski, see chapter 2 notes 33 and 34. Other Polish views favoring compromise and based on specific political developments include: [Jan L.] Czerwiński, *O Rusinach i do Rusinów* (Cracow 1891); Stanislaus Smolka, *Die Ruthenen und ihre "Gönner" in Berlin* (Vienna and Leipzig: Vlg. 'Austria' Franz Doll 1902); I. Daszyński [I. Żegota], *Mowa o sprawie polsko-ruskiej* (Cracow 1908); Ludwik Kulczycki, *Ugoda polsko-ruska* (L'viv 1912); E. Dubanowicz, "Sejmowa reforma wyborcza a ugoda polsko-ruska," in *Reforma wyborcza sejmowa,* vol. II (L'viv 1912).

On the relations of a leading Polish defender of Galician autonomy, Prince Adam Sapieha, with Ukrainian leaders in the 1860s and 1870s, see the excellent biography by Stefan Kieniewicz, *Adam Sapieha (1828–1903)* (L'viv: ZNIO 1939), especially pp. 347–398.

65 Jił [Józef Łokietek], *Uwagi na czasie,* 5 pts, especially pt 1: *Sprawa ruska: wspomnienia, spostrzeżenia, uwagi, wnioski* (Cracow 1891) and pt 5: *Stosunki narodowósciowe w Galicyi wschodniej: Archidyecezja lwowska obrz. rzym. katolickego* (Cracow: Tow. Szkoły Ludowej 1894).

See also Zygmunt Miłkowski, "Ukrainizm galicyjski," *Przegląd Narodowy,* II, 2 (Warsaw, 1908), pp. 141–156; Alexandre Raciborski and Stanisław Glombiński, *La question ruthène en Galicie* (Paris: Agence polonaise de presse 1911); and the later Franciszek Podleski, *Zagadnienie 'ukraińskie' na tle stosunków austrjackich* (L'viv: B. Połoniecki [1935]).

66 Stefan Kaczała, *Polityka Polaków względem Rusi* (L'viv: p.a. 1879). For Barvins'kyi's views, see his memoirs, n. 10 above.

attempts of the government at electoral reform, the continual electoral abuses, and the support given by Poles to local Russophiles during the first decade of the twentieth century in an attempt to weaken the growing Ukrainian movement.[67]

The Ukrainian efforts to divide the province from 1847 until the outbreak of World War I are surveyed in several pamphlets written by supporters of the idea,[68] while the actual legal status of Ukrainians in Galicia is outlined in a solid description by Mykhailo Lozyns'kyi.[69] The abortive Polish uprising of 1863 against Russia and its specific impact on Ukrainians in Galicia have also been the subject of study.[70] More significant for Ukrainians was their increasing participation in Galician politics toward the end of the century, and the establishment during the 1890s of the Ukrainian Radical, the Ukrainian Social Democratic, the Ukrainian National Democratic, and the Russian National parties is described in several short essays.[71] By the outset of the twentieth century, the Ukrainian

67 Julian Romanczuk, *Die Ruthenen und ihre Gegner in Galizien* (Vienna 1902); Michel Lozynsky, *Notes sur les relations en Galicie pendant les 25 dernières années (1895–1919)* (Paris: Bureau ukrainien 1919); *Hromadna deputatsiia ruska (spravozdanie ruskoho komitetu deputatsiinoho)* (L'viv: Vasyl' Nahôrnyi 1896); L'onhyn Tsehel'skii, *Shcho chuvaty z vyborchoiu reformoiu: proekt bar. Gavcha, shcho z nym dïie sia ta shcho ruskym khlopam chynyty?* (L'viv: Narodnyi Komitet 1906); Roman Sembratowycz, *Polonia irredenta* (Frankfurt-am-Main: Neuer Frankfurter Vlg. 1903); A. von Redlitz, *Unter uns–ohne Maske: eine Antwort auf die Ruthenenfrage von den Ruthenen selbst gegeben*, 2 vols (Vienna 1912). On Polish support for local Russophiles, see n. 193 below.

68 Mykhailo Lozyns'kyi, *Utvorennie ukraïns'koho koronnoho kraiu v Avstriï* (n.p. 1915), in German translation as *Die Schaffung einer ukrainischen Provinz in Oesterreich* (Berlin: C. Kroll 1915), an abridged version of this work is *Ukraïns'ka Halychyna–okremyi koronnyi krai* (n.p.: Partiia Ukr. Sotsiialïstiv-Revoliutsioneriv 1915); Wladimir Singalewytsch von Schilling, *Zur Frage der Sonderstellung Galiziens: ein Streifzug in das galizische Problem* (Vienna: G. Röttig u. Sohn 1917). See also the 1864 petition of Ukrainian leaders to the imperial government: *Denkschrift in Betreff der Theilung Galiziens* (L'viv 1865).

69 Mykhailo Lozyns'kyi, ''Avtonomiia kraïv v avstriisk'kii konstytutsiï,'' in *Studiï z polia suspil'nykh nauk i statystyky*, vol. III, ed. V. Okhrymovych (L'viv: Statystychna komisiia NTSh 1912), 62 pp.

70 Fr. Rawita-Gawroński, *Rok 1863 na Rusi*, 2 vols (L'viv: H. Altenberg 1902–03), especially vol. I: *Ruś Czerwona i Wschód;* and Cyryl Studziński [Studyns'kyi], ''Powstańcy polscy z r. 1863 w redakcji ukraińskiej *Mety*,'' *Ziemia Czerwieńska*, III, 1 (L'viv 1937), pp. 1–43. See also n. 194 below.

71 The Ukrainian Radical party has received the most attention in both Soviet and non-Soviet writings: M.M. Kravets', ''Do pytannia pro rus'ko-ukraïns'ku radykal'nu partiiu u skhidnii Halychyny v 90-kh rokakh XIX st.,'' in *Z istoriï zakhidnoukraïns'kykh zemel'*, vol. II (L'viv: AN URSR 1957), pp. 124–140 and his ''Robitnychyi rukh u Skhidnii Halychni naprykintsi XIX st. (1892–1900 roky),'' in *Z istoriï zakhidnoukraïns'kykh zemel'*, vol. IV, ed. I.P. Kryp''iakevych (Kiev: AN URSR 1960), pp. 40–65; Ivan Makukh, *Na narodnii sluzhbi* (Detroit: Ukraïns'ka vil'na hromada Ameryky 1958), especially pp. 56–192 and the introductory article by Matvii Stakhiv, ''Ukraïns'ka Radykal'na Partiia pered pochatkom

struggle against Polish domination had focused on the Galician Diet, and there are solid studies by Józef Buszko on the electoral reform movement and by Mykhailo Lozyns'kyi and Volodymyr Okhrymovych on the results in Ukrainian territory of the first election (1907) based on universal suffrage.[72]

Not surprisingly, political violence attracted the attention of contemporary writers who discussed at length the assassination of the viceroy of Galicia, Count Andrzej Potocki (1861–1908), by a young Ukrainian student, Myroslav Sichyns'kyi (1887–1980), in 1908. Contemporary Poles regarded this act as nothing less than murder;[73] the Ukrainians saw Sichyns'kyi as a national hero who was forced by circumstances to defend the interests of his downtrodden people.[74] Finally, this period witnessed important Galician contributions to modern Ukrainian political thought: Iuliian Bachyns'kyi's pioneering call for an independent

---

politychnoï diial'nosty d-ra Ivana Makukha,'' pp. 1–55; and John-Paul Himka, ''Ukraïns'kyi sotsiializm u Halychyni (do rozkolu v Radykal'nii partii 1899 r.),'' *Journal of Ukrainian Graduate Studies*, no. 7 (Toronto 1979), pp. 33–51. On the background to the Ukrainian Socialist movement, see John-Paul Himka, *Socialism in Galicia: The Emergence of Polish Social Democracy and Ukrainian Radicalism (1860–1890)* (Cambridge, Mass.: Harvard Ukrainian Research Institute 1983).

On the Ukrainian Social Democratic party, see Matvii Stakhiv, *Proty khvyl': istorychnyi rozvytok ukraïns'koho sotsiialistychnoho rukhu na zakhidnykh ukraïns'kykh zemliakh* (L'viv: Soimovyi kliub USRP 1934); and n. 93 below.

On the Ukrainian National Democratic party, see Stepan Baran, *Nasha prohrama i organizatsiia: prohrama i organizatsiia ukraïns'koï natsional'no-demokratychnoï (narodnoï) partiï* (L'viv: p.a. 1913); and the comparative analysis of its program with the Radical party in Zakhar Skvarko, *Prohramy narodno-demokratychnoï i radykal'noï partiï* (Kolomyia 1913).

On the Russian National party, see *S''iezd muzhei dovieriia russko-narodnoi partii i eia organizatsiia* (L'viv: Obshchestvo 'Russkaia Rada' 1900).

72 Józef Buszko, *Sejmowa reforma wyborcza w Galicji, 1905–1914* (Warsaw: PWN 1956); M. Lozyns'kyi and V. Okhrymovych, ''Z vyborchoï statystyky Halychyny,'' in *Studii z polia suspil'nykh nauk i statystyky*, vol. II, ed. M. Hrushevs'kyi (L'viv: Statystychna komisiia NTSh 1910), pp. 75–104.

For a description of the parliamentary elections of 1885 and the controversy between Old Ruthenian and populist candidates, see Bohdan A. Dîdytskii, *Iak y koho vŷbrala Halytskaia Rus' do Dumŷ derzhavnoi dnia 2 chervnia 1885 h.* (L'viv: Yzd. Obshchestva ym. M. Kachkovskoho 1885); on the Galician Diet before World War I, see Georges Bienaimé, *La Diète de Galicie: ses tendences autonomiques* (Paris 1910).

73 Stanislaus Zieliński, *Die Ermordung des Statthalters Grafen Andreas Potocki: Materialien zur Beurteilung des ukrainischen Terrorismus in Galizien* (Vienna and Leipzig: C.W. Stern 1908). A more recent and well-documented account of Sichyns'kyi's escape from prison and flight to the United States is in Aleksander Janta, ''Ucieczka z więzienia,'' *Kultura*, XX [231] (Paris 1967), pp. 173–205.

74 Mykhailo Lozyns'kyi, *Akt 12 ts'vitnia 1908 roku* (L'viv: p.a. 1908), 2nd rev. ed. (L'viv: p.a. 1909); Iaroslav Vesolovs'kyi and Mykhailo Lozyns'kyi, *Iak sudyly Myroslava Sichyns'koho* (L'viv: Volodymyr Bachyns'kyi 1910).

Ukrainian state and Mykhailo Hrushevs'kyi's suggestion that, despite all its shortcomings, Ukrainian Galicia could serve as a piedmont for such a state.[75]

Socioeconomic developments

The large body of pre-World War I Austrian statistical data with specific sections by province on demography, banking, commerce, trade, and communications is still the most important source for analyzing socioeconomic developments in late nineteenth- and early twentieth-century Galicia.[76] As for secondary literature, there are a few general works and several specific studies dealing with the peasantry, the cooperative movement, emigration, the growth of industry, and the socialist movement.

Among the best general works on all aspects of the Galician economy after 1848 are a brief economic history and a monumental two-volume description of the province's economy published by the Galician-Polish scholar Franciszek Bujak during the first decades of the twentieth century.[77] More recently, the Polish social historian Józef Buszko has described the change in Galicia's socioeconomic structure during the second half of the nineteenth century, while Volodymyr Osechyns'kyi has provided the Soviet view of these decades by stressing the negative aspects of Polish domination over all aspects of the economy in eastern Galicia.[78]

The peasantry has been the focus of particular attention, and rightly so, since as late as 1900, ninety percent of the population in eastern Galicia lived in the countryside. Although the serfs were legally freed from bondage in 1848, they remained economically bound to their landlords. This situation is largely due to the fact that the right of the peasants to use the gentry-owned woods and pastures (the traditional ''servitudes'') was revoked. Now they had to pay for the use of woods or pastures and were forced to rely only on their limited amount of land

75 Iuliian Bachyns'kyi, *Ukraina irredenta* (L'viv 1896), 3rd ed. (Berlin: Ukrains'ka molod' 1924); Mykhailo Hrushevs'kyi, *Nasha polityka* (L'viv: NTSh 1911); idem, ''Ukrainskii P'emont,'' in his *Ukrainskii vopros: stat'i* (Moscow: Tov. 'Rodnaia Riech' 1917), pp. 61–66.

76 See n. 14 above; and *Skorowidz przemysłowo-handlowy Królestwa Galicyi* (L'viv 1912).

77 Franciszek Bujak, *Rozwój gospodarczy Galicyi (1772–1914)* (L'viv: Bernard Połoniecki 1917), reprinted in idem, *Wybór pism*, vol. II (Warsaw 1976), pp. 342–397; idem, *Galicya*, 2 vols (L'viv: H. Altenberg 1908).

78 Józef Buszko, *Zum Wandel der Gesellschaftsstruktur in Galizien und in der Bukowina*, Österreichische Akademie der Wissenschaften, Philosophisch-Historische Klasse, Sitzungsberichte, vol. CCCXLIII (Vienna 1978); V.K. Osechyns'kyi, ''Kolonial'ne stanovyshche Halychyny v skladi Avstro-Uhorshchyny,'' *Naukovi zapysky LDU*, XXXVI: *Seriia istorychna*, 6 (L'viv 1955), pp. 35–65. See also n. 7 above.

(constantly being subdivided), so that they became chronically in debt and were in effect transformed into "economic serfs." Despite continual demands by Ukrainian leaders for a favorable resolution of the "servitude" issue and for more equitable distribution of the land, the Polish gentry, most especially in eastern Galicia, successfully opposed (at least until the end of the century) any real reform; thus by 1900 as much as forty percent of the farmland remained in the hands of large landlords (each owning at least 100 hectares). The plight of the peasantry in eastern Galicia during the last half of the nineteenth century is discussed in three extensive studies by the Soviet Ukrainian scholar Mykola M. Kravets'.[79] The problem of the government's policy toward land division throughout Galicia was first surveyed in 1898 in a book dedicated to the fiftieth anniversary of the repeal of serfdom; it was a kind of apologia for the Austrian regime.[80] A more balanced discussion of the problem is found in a monograph by the Polish scholar Katarzyna Sójka-Zielińska.[81]

The vicious cycle of indebtedness, the subdivision of land into smaller holdings (in 1905 the vast majority of landowners–52,000–held only two to five hectares of land), and rapid demographic growth (the population rose 45 percent between 1869 and 1910)–factors only partially alleviated by emigration to America–led at the turn of the century to a series of agricultural strikes, the largest of which took place in 1902, involving an estimated 200,000 peasants. The history of peasant protest in eastern Galicia during the two decades before the outbreak of World War I and especially the revolt of 1902, which finally prompted some land distribution on the part of the gentry, are discussed in several studies.[82] The

79 Mykola M. Kravets', *Selianstvo Skhidnoï Halychyny i pivnichnoï Bukovyny u druhii polovyni XIX st.* (L'viv: LU 1964); M.M. Kravets', "Selians'kyi rukh u Skhidnii Halychyni v 50-80-kh rokakh XIX st.," *Z istoriï Ukraïns'koï RSR*, vol. VI–VII (Kiev: AN URSR 1962), pp. 57–81; idem, "Masovi selians'ki vystupy u Skhidnii Halychyni v 90-kh rokakh XIX st.," in *Z istoriï Ukraïns'koï RSR*, vol VIII (Kiev: AN URSR 1963), pp. 3–27.

80 Liubomyr Selians'kyi, *U piatdesiatu richnytsiu znesenia panshchyny i vidrodzhenia halytskoï Rusy*, Knyzhochky 'Pros'vity', no. 215–216 (L'viv 1898).

81 Katarzyna Sójka-Zielińska, *Prawne problemy podziału gruntów chłopskich w Galicji na tle austriackiego ustawodawstwa agrarnego*, Dissertationes Universitatis Varsoviensis, no. 14 (Warsaw: PWN 1966).

82 P.V. Sviezhyns'kyi, *Ahrarni vidnosyny na Zakhidnii Ukraïni v kintsi XIX–na pochatku XX st.* (L'viv: LU 1966); Walentyna Najdus, *Szkice z historii Galicji*, vol. I: *Galicja w latach 1900–1904* (Warsaw: Książka i Wiedza 1958); Zbigniew Pazdro, "Strejki rolne w Galicyi wschodniej w r. 1902 i 1903 na podstawie materyałów urzędowych," *Wiadomości Statystyczne o Stosunkach Krajowych Wydane Przez Krajowe Biuro Statystyczne*, XX, 1 (L'viv 1903), pp. 1–68; Jan Rozwadowski, *Ruskie bezrobocie w r. 1902: uwagi o jego terenie* (L'viv 1904).

widespread practice of usury is also carefully analyzed in a contemporary study by Leopold Caro.[83]

In an attempt to alleviate the conditions of the peasantry, the new secular-oriented Ukrainophile populist intelligentsia created a strong cooperative movement which, beginning in the 1880s, led to the formation of numerous agricultural and dairy cooperatives, trade and credit associations, and insurance companies. Such developments in Galicia are described in comprehensive histories of the Ukrainian cooperative movement by Illia Vytanovych and Lev Olesnevych.[84]

When all else failed, another outlet for peasant frustration was emigration to America. Encouraged by steamship agents who visited the Galician countryside, the first emigrants began to depart in the 1880s. Having heard about the success of their brethren through avidly read letters, others established a pattern of chain migration that reached large-scale proportions during the first decade of the twentieth century. By 1914, an estimated 420,000 Galician Ukrainians emigrated to the New World, mainly to the United States and Canada. Several studies by Austrian and Polish scholars provide important statistical analyses of the greatest years of emigration (1904–1914),[85] while the Galician-Ukrainian political think-

83 Leopold Caro, *Studya społeczne*, 2nd ed. (Cracow 1908).

84 Illia Vytanovych, *Istoriia ukraïns'koho kooperatyvnoho rukhu* (New York: Tovarystvo ukraïns'koï kooperatsiï 1964); L.O. Olesnevych, *Kooperatyvni mify i kapitalistychna diisnist': zakhidnoukraïns'ka burzhuazna kooperatsiia (1883–1939)* (Kiev: Naukova dumka 1974).

See also Ivan Bryk and Mykhailo Kotsiuba, eds, *Pershyi ukraïns'kyi pros'vitno-ekonomichnyi kongres uladzhenyi Tovarystvom ''Pros'vita'' ... u L'vovi ... 1909 roku: protokoly i referaty* (L'viv: Pros'vita 1910); and *The Ukrainian (Ruthenian) Co-operative Movement in Galicia (Austria)* (L'viv: Ruthenian Provincial Co-operative Union 1913). On individual cooperative organizations, see chapter 7, n. 68.

85 Richard von Pflügl, ''Die überseeische österreichische Wanderung in den Jahren 1904 und 1905 und die Einwanderungsverhältnisse in den wichtigsten überseeischen Staaten in diesen Jahren,'' *Statistische Monatschrift*, XXXII, N.F. XI (Brno 1906), pp. 495–509, 573–629; idem, ''Die überseeische österreichische Wanderung in den Jahren 1906 und 1907 sowie die Einwanderungs- und sonstigen Verhältnisse in den wichtigsten Einwanderungsstaaten,'' *Statistische Monatschrift*, XIV (Brno 1909), pp. 239–256, 308–324, 355–384, 408–440. See also the comprehensive critique of Pflügl's work with emendations regarding Galician-Ukrainian emigrants: Zenon Kuzelia, ''Prychynky do studiï nad nashoiu emigratsiieiu,'' *Zapysky NTSh*, CI (L'viv 1901), pp. 145–158; CV (1911), pp. 175–204; CVII (1912), pp. 129–163. Johann Chmelar, ''The Austrian Emigration, 1900–1914,'' *Perspectives in American History*, vol. VII (Cambridge, Mass. 1973), pp. 275–378; Hans Chmelar, *Höhepunkte der österreichischen Auswanderung: Die Auswanderung aus den im Reichsrat vertretenen Königreichen und Ländern in den Jahren 1905–1914*, Studien zur Geschichte der Österreichisch-Ungarischen Monarchie, vol. XIV (Vienna: Österreichische Akademie der Wissenschaften 1974).

The views on emigration by a contemporary Galician lawyer are found in several works by

er Iuliian Bachyns'kyi published, in 1914, what has become the classic book on the Ukrainian immigration, with valuable descriptions of the causes of emigration as well as the life of the early immigrants in America.[86] Subsequently, a considerable literature on the Ukrainian immigration (most of which concerns Galicia, the source of three-quarters of all Ukrainian emigrants) developed. It describes life in the New World as well as the conditions in the homeland that prompted the emigration.[87]

The reluctance of the large landowners in eastern Galicia to change the economic status quo (which assured them an unlimited supply of cheap labor) and the general Austrian policy that considered Galicia to be an agricultural zone and marketplace (a kind of "internal colony") for products from the industrially advanced western provinces (Bohemia, Silesia, Lower Austria) are factors that caused the province to remain an economically underdeveloped territory.[88]

Leopold Caro, including *Auswanderung und Auswanderungspolitik in Österreich,* Schriften des Vereins für Sozialpolitik, vol. CXXXI (Leipzig: Dunker und Humbolt 1909); *Statystyka emigracyi polskiej i Austro-węgierskiej do Stanów Zjednoczonych Ameryki Północnej* (Cracow 1907); and "Die Statistik der österreichisch-ungarischen und polnischen Auswanderung nach den Vereinigten Staaten von Nordamerika," *Zeitschrift für Volkswirtschaft, Sozialpolitik und Verwaltung,* XVI (Berlin 1907), pp. 68–113; *Emigracya i polityka emigracyjna ze szczególnem uwzględnieniem stosunków polskich* (Poznań 1914). See also the discussion of the attitude of the Galician Diet toward emigration in Benjamin P. Murdzek, *Emigration in Polish Social-Political Thought, 1870–1914,* East European Monographs, vol. XXXIII (Boulder, Colo.: East European Quarterly 1977), especially pp. 79–131.

86 Iulïian Bachyns'kyi, *Ukraïns'ka immigratsiia v Z''iedynenykh Derzhavakh Ameryky* (L'viv: p.a. 1914). For an interesting history of how this book finally came to be published, see Liubomyr Vynar, "Iuliian Bachyns'kyi–vydatnyi doslidnyk ukraïns'koï emigratsiï," *Ukraïns'kyi istoryk,* VII, 4 (New York and Munich 1970), pp. 30–43.

87 The best general introductions to the Ukrainian immigration in the New World are by Paul R. Magocsi, "Ukrainians," *Harvard Encyclopedia of American Ethnic Groups* (Cambridge, Mass.: The Belknap Press of Harvard University Press 1980), pp. 997–1009; Vasyl Markus, "Ukrainians Abroad: In the United States," in *Ukraine: A Concise Encyclopedia,* vol. II, ed. V. Kubijovyč (Toronto: University of Toronto Press 1971), pp. 110–1151; Ivan Tesla et al., "Ukrainians Abroad: In Canada," in *ibid.,* pp. 1151–1193; O. Boruszenko, "Ukrainians Abroad: In Brazil," in *ibid.,* pp. 1194–1204; E. Onatsky "Ukrainians Abroad: In Argentina," in *ibid.,* pp. 1204–1212; and Walter Dushnyk, "Ukrainians Abroad: In Other Countries of Latin America," in *ibid.,* pp. 1212–1215.

Among other monographs on Ukrainian immigration that include much data on Galicians are Charles H. Young, *The Ukrainian Canadians: A Study in Assimilation* (Toronto: Thomas Nelson and Sons 1931); M. Nastasivs'kyi, *Ukraïns'ka imigratsiia v Spoluchenykh Derzhavakh Ameryky* (New York, 1934); Luka Myshuha, ed., *Propamiatna knyha* (Jersey City, NJ: Ukraïns'kyi Narodnyi Soiuz 1936); Wasyl' Halich, *Ukrainians in the United States* (Chicago: University of Chicago Press 1937); A.M. Shlepakov, *Ukraïns'ka trudova emihratsiia v SShA i Kanadi (kinets' XIX–pochatok XX st)* (Kiev: AN URSR 1960); Vladimir J. Kaye, *Early*

Hence, while Galicia accounted for 25 percent of the land area in the Austrian half of the monarchy, it had in contrast only 9.3 percent of the industrial enterprises—and most of these were in western Galicia. A few sawmills, tanneries, and brick factories existed in eastern Galicia, and in the 1890s oil fields near Drohobych were developed, but the small enterprises were in the hands of Jews, who made up as high as 75 percent of the population in the towns, while the oil industry (which by 1905 accounted for 5 percent of world production) was in the hands of foreign investors (English and Austrian).[89]

The industrial aspect, however small, of the economy in eastern Galicia, and the concomitant rise of an industrial proletariat (which numbered 12,900 in 1890) are traced in great detail in several studies by Soviet scholars like Hryhorii Koval'chak and Mykola Kravets'.[90] Marxist writers are particularly anxious to

---

Ukrainian Settlements in Canada 1895–1900: Dr. Josef Oleskow's Role in the Settlement of the Canadian Northwest (Toronto: University of Toronto Press for the Ukrainian Canadian Research Foundation 1964); Michael H. Marunchak, *The Ukrainian Canadians: A History* (Winnipeg: Ukrainian Free Academy of Sciences 1970).

88 On the large landowners and peasants, see Maurice Lair, ''La noblesse polonaise et les paysans ruthènes,'' *Annales des sciences politiques,* XVIII (Paris 1903), pp. 553–572, 707–717 and XIX (1904). pp. 185–205. On the economic policies of the Galician Diet, see Eljasz Wojtanowicz, ''Polityka agrarna sejmu galicyjskiego w cyfrach budżetów krajowych,'' in *Studja z historiji społecznej i gospodarczej poświęcone prof. dr. Franciszkowi Bujakowi* (L'viv 1931).

89 For an early survey of industry in Galicia, see Wacław Saryusz-Zaleski, *Dzieje przemysłu w b. Galicji 1804-1929* (Cracow: S. Zieleniewski 1930). On the budding oil industry, see Stanisław Bartoszewicz, *Historia i stan przemysłu naftowego w Galicji* (L'viv 1905); and several Soviet studies by S.D. Garkavenko, ''Neft Vostochnoi Galitsii na neftianom rynke Zapadnoi Evropy (1900–1918 gg.)'' and ''Kontsentratsiia proizvodstva i voznikonovenie monopolii v neftianoi promyshlennosti Vostochnoi Galitsii pri Avstro-Vengrii (1892–1918),'' *Nauchnye zapiski L'vovskogo sel'skokhoziastvennogo instituta,* IX (L'vov 1959), pp. 285–351; I.S. Khonihsman, *Pronyknennia inozemnoho kapitalu v ekonomiky Zakhidnoï Ukraïny v epokhu imperializmu* (L'viv: LU 1971).

For a discussion of Galician industry in the context of the Austro-Hungarian Empire, see Helena Madurowicz-Urbańska, ''Die Industrie im Rahmen der wirtschaftlichen Struktur der Donaumonarchie,'' in *Studia austro-polonica,* vol. I, in *Zeszyty Naukowe Uniwersytetu Jagiellońskiego,* CCCCLXXXII, *Prace Historyczne,* LVII (Warsaw and Cracow 1978), pp. 157–173.

90 H.I. Koval'chak, ''Rozvytok kapitalistychnoï promyslovosti skhidnoï Halychyny v pershi desiatyrichchia pislia skasuvannia kriposnoho prava (1848–1870 rr.),'' in *Z istoriï zakhidnoukraïns'kykh zemel',* vol. II (L'viv: AN URSR 1957), pp. 108–123; idem, ''Rozvytok kapitalistychnoï promyslovosti v Skhidnii Halychyni u 70-80-kh rokakh XIX st.,'' *Z istoriï zakhidnoukraïns'kykh zemel',* vol. III, ed. I.P. Kryp''iakevych (Kiev: AN URSR 1958), pp. 3–22; H.I. Koval'chak, ''Rozvytok fabrychno-zavods'koï promyslovosti v Skhidnii Halychyni v kintsi XIX-na pochatku XX st.,'' *Z istoriï zakhidnoukraïns'kykh zemel',* vol. V

uncover any indication of worker protests and strikes[91]–some ostensibly under the influence of the 1905 Russian Revolution and Leninist ideas[92]–in order to point out the insuperable weakness of eastern Galician society as well as Austria-Hungary as a whole, during what is considered the era of world imperialist crisis.

Although Ukrainians comprised only 18 percent of the small industrial proletariat in eastern Galicia, some of their leaders, like Ivan Franko, Mykhailo

---

(Kiev: AN URSR 1960), pp. 57–74; idem, ''Ekonomichne stanovyshche robitnychoho klasu Skhidnoï Halychyny v period imperializmu,'' *ibid.*, pp. 75–112; M.M. Kravets', ''Pochatok robitnychoho rukhu v Skhidnii Halychyni,'' *Z istoriï zakhidnoukraïns'kykh zemel'*, vol. III, ed. I.P. Kryp''iakevych (Kiev: AN URSR 1958), pp. 23–59; M.M. Kravets', ''Robitnychyi rukh u Skidnii Halychyni naprykintsi XIX st. (1892–1900 roky),'' in *Z istoriï zakhidnoukraïns'kykh zemel'*, vol. IV, ed. I.P. Kryp''iakevych (Kiev: AN URSR 1960), pp. 40–65; M.M. Kravets', ''Masovi robitnychni vystupy u Skhidnii Halychyni na pochatku XX st. (1901–1914 roky),'' in *Z istoriï Ukraïns'koï RSR*, vol. VI–VII (Kiev: AN URSR 1962), pp. 113–135.

See also the solid survey of industry and the working class in Galicia before 1870 by Walentyna Najdus, chapter 5, n. 25; and the study by John-Paul Himka, ''Voluntary Artisan Associations and the Ukrainian National Movement in Galicia (the 1870's),'' *Harvard Ukrainian Studies*, II, 2 (Cambridge, Mass. 1978), pp. 235–250, reprinted in Andrei S. Markovits and Frank E. Sysyn, eds. *Nationbuilding and the Politics of Nationalism* (Cambridge, Mass.: Harvard Ukrainian Research Institute 1982), pp. 178–195.

91 V. Makaiev, *Robitnychyi klas Halychyny v ostanii tretyni XIX st.* (L'viv: LU 1968); Ivan I. Kompaniiets', *Stanovyshche i borot'ba trudiashchykh mas Halychyny, Bukovyny ta Zakarpattia na pochatku XX st.* (Kiev: AN URSR 1960); Ievhenii A. Iatskevych, *Stanovyshche robitnychoho klasu Halychyny v period kapitalizmu (1848–1900): narys* (Kiev: AN URSR 1958); K.H. Kakovs'kyi, *Na shliakhu do velykoho zhovtnia: straikovyi ruch v Halychyni kintsia XIX–pochatku XX st.* (L'viv: LU 1970); Ie.A. Iatskevych, ''Z istoriï revoliutsiinoï borot'by trudiashchykh Skhidnoï Halychyny naperedodni velykoï zhovtnevoï sotsialistychnoï revoliutsiï (1908–1917 roky),'' in *Z istoriï zakhidnoukraïns'kykh zemel'*, vol. IV, ed. I.P. Kryp''iakevych (Kiev: AN URSR 1960), pp. 66–76; V.I. Bohaichuk, *Borot'ba trudiashchykh Ternopil'shchyny proty sotsial'noho i natsional'noho hnitu za vozz''iednannia z URSR (1900–1920 rr.)* (Stanislav: Oblasne knyzhkovo-zhurnal'ne vyd-vo 1961).

92 I.V. Dovhal', *Vplyv rosiis'koï revoliutsiï 1905 roku na rozvytok revoliutsiinoho rukhu v Halychyni* (Kiev: Derzhpolitvydav 1952); V.K. Osechyns'kyi, ''Vplyv revoliutsiinoho rukhu v Rosiï na revoliutsiino-vyzvol'nu borot'bu trudiashchykh Halychyny v kintsi i na pochatku XX st.,'' *Naukovi zapysky LDU*, XXV: *Seriia istorychna*, 5 (L'viv 1953); S. Ovnanian ''Vliianie russkoi revolutsii 1905–1907 gg. na pod''em revoliutsionnogo dvizheniia v Galitsii i Bukovine,'' *Sbornik nauchnykh trudov Armenskogo zaochnogo pedagogicheskogo instituta*, I, 1 (Erevan 1954), pp. 165–198; V.K. Osechyns'kyi, ''Vplyv pershoï rosiis'koï revoliutsiï na pidnesennia revoliutsiinoho rukhu v Halychyni 1905–1907 rr.,'' in *50 rokiv Pershoï rosiis'koï revoliutsiï* (L'viv 1955), pp. 118–136; I.S. Pavliuk, ''Revoliutsiine pidnesennia v Halychyni pid vplyvom rosiis'koï revoliutsiï 1905–1907 rr.,'' in *Z istoriï zakhidnoukraïns'kykh zemel'*, vol. I (Kiev: AN URSR 1957), pp. 43–58; M.M. Volianiuk and V.Iu. Malanchuk, *Poshyrennia marksysts'ko-lenins'kykh idei na Zakhidnii Ukraïni* (L'viv: Knyzhkovo-zhurnal'ne vyd-vo 1960); A.D. Iaroshenko, *V.I. Lenin i revoliutsiinyi rukh na zakhidnoukraïns'kykh zemliakh* (L'viv: Kameniar 1968).

Pavlyk, and Ostap Terlets'kyi, took an active part in the Galician socialist movement from the very beginning. Besides the discussions found in many of the Soviet works mentioned above, Volodymyr Levyns'kyi has written two works on the history of Ukrainian socialism in Galicia, in particular its evolution into the Ukrainian Social Democratic party (est. 1900).[93] The relations between Ukrainian socialist leaders and their Polish counterparts as well as their repeated arrests and trials between 1877 and 1892 are also the subject of separate studies.[94]

Cultural history: national identity and national organizations

After the beginnings of a revival in the late 1830s and 1840s, followed by a national "take-off stage" during the revolution of 1848, Ukrainian culture entered a period of fertile development between the 1860s and 1914 that in Galicia was unmatched before and has been unmatched since. This half century witnessed a phenomenal growth in popular and scholarly cultural organizations, the press and other publications, schools, and literary activity. Moreover, all this was taking place at a time when, in the Russian-controlled Dnieper Ukrainian lands, Ukrainian cultural activity was severely curtailed (1863–1905). To be sure, Galician cultural life was not without difficulties, such as the internal controversies over national identity and an acceptable literary language, and the continued reluctance on the part of the provincial administration to allow more Ukrainian schools. Yet these factors may have stimulated as much as hampered the vibrant cultural activity that was the mark of the last half century of Austrian rule in Ukrainian Galicia. The literature on cultural developments between 1848 and 1918 consists of many works dealing with specific topics: the problem of national identity, cultural organizations, the press and publishing, the language question, education, literature, and the church.

National identity became a factor in Galician life only after 1848, when political and social changes forced the leadership (and after the institution of

93 V. Levyns'kyi, *Narys rozvytku ukraïns'koho robitnychoho rukhu v Halychyni* (Kiev 1914), 2nd rev. ed. (Kiev 1930); and his *Pochatky ukraïns'koho sotsiializmu v Halychyni* (Toronto 1918). See also his programmatic statement on land reform: *Selianstvo i sotsialdemokratiia* (L'viv: Zemlia i volia 1910).

The early history of Galician socialism is also covered in S. Podolinskii, *Sotsialisty ukraïntsy v Avstrii* (Geneva [1881]); M. Hrushevs'kyi, *Z pochyniv ukraïns'koho sotsiialistychnoho rukhu: Mykhailo Drahomaniv i zhenevs'kyi sotsiialistychnyi hurtok* (Vienna: Institut sociologique ukrainien 1922); M. Iavors'kyi, *Narysy z istoriï revoliutsiinoï borot'by na Ukraïni*, vol. II, pt 1 (Kharkiv 1928).

94 Jan Kozłowski, "I. Franko a polski ruch robotniczy w Galicji w latach 1870-tych i 1880-tych," *Kwartalnik Instytutu Polsko-Radzieckiego*, I (Warsaw 1954), pp. 93–108; Volodymyr I. Kalynovych, *Politychni protsesy Ivana Franka ta ioho tovaryshiv* (L'viv: LU 1967); Ivan Karpynets', "Do spravy areshtovan' u L'vovi v chervni 1877 r.," *Zapysky NTSh*, CLI (L'viv 1931), pp. 205–216.

decennial censuses, the masses as well) to think in terms of self-identification. Basically, the intelligentsia became divided into three groups: the Old Ruthenians *(starorusyny),* who had a vague sense of belonging to East Slavdom, but whose national horizons did not really transcend the boundaries of Galicia; the populist Ukrainophiles *(narodovtsi),* who considered themselves part of a distinct nationality stretching from the Carpathians to the Caucasus Mountains; and the Russophiles, who rejected both the vagueness of the Old Ruthenians and the ''separatism'' of the Ukrainophiles and who considered the population of eastern Galicia (as well as the Dnieper Ukraine) to be part of one Russian nationality. Most writing on this subject is by partisans of the last two orientations and is usually polemical in nature.[95] More balanced descriptions of the national controversy up until the 1870s are found in contemporary essays by Ostap Terlets'kyi and Mykhailo Drahomanov.[96] The best works on the subject as a whole, however, are by Mykola Andrusiak, who is careful not to lump the Old Ruthenians and Russophiles together or to describe them with the pejorative term *moskvofily,* or to tarnish them as national renegades.[97]

Each of the national orientations had its own cultural organization. The Old Ruthenians controlled the Galician-Rus' Matytsia (est. 1848), the Stauropegial Institute, the National Home (est. 1864), and the Kachkovs'kyi Society (est. 1874), all of which came into the hands of the Russophiles by the outset of the

95 Good examples of the Ukrainian viewpoint are found in M. Pavlyk, *Moskvofil'stvo ta ukraïnofil'stvo sered avstro-rus'koho narodu* [1884–1887] (L'viv 1906); Ivan Franko, ''Iz istoriï 'moskvofil's'koho' pys'menstva v Halychyni'' [1899], in *Ivan Franko: zibrannia tvoriv,* vol. XXXI (Kiev 1981), pp. 458–480; idem, ''Stara Rus','' *Literaturno-naukovyi vistnyk,* XXXIV, 6 (L'viv 1906), pp. 456–473; XXXV, 7 and 9 (1906), pp. 32–51 and 382–392; XXXVI, 10–12 (1906), pp. 66–79, 236–243, and 359–374; Vladimir Kuschnir, *Der Neopanslawismus* (Vienna 1908); and M. Mykolaievych [Matvii Stakhiv], *Moskvofil'stvo: ioho bat'ky i dity* (L'viv: Hromads'kyi holos 1936).

The Russophile view is forcefully expressed in O.A. Monchalovskii, *Literaturnoe i politicheskoe ukrainofil'stvo* (L'viv: 'Galichanin' 1898). For the Old Ruthenian view, see the extensive memoirs of Bohdan Didyts'kyi, n. 10 above.

96 Ostap Terlets'kyi, *Moskvofily i narodovtsi v 70-ykh rr.,* Literaturno-naukova Biblioteka, no. 37 (L'viv 1902); Mykhailo Drahomanov, *Halyts'ko-rus'ke pys'menstvo* (L'viv: NTSh 1876); Mykhailo Drahomanov, ''Halyts'ke-rus'ke pys'menstvo (Perednie slovo do 'Povistei' Osypa Fed'kovycha [1876]),'' reprinted in his *Literaturno-publitsystychni pratsi,* vol. I (Kiev: Naukova dumka 1970), pp. 309–348.

97 Mykola Andrusiak, *Narysy z istoriï halyts'koho moskvofil'stva*, Biblioteka Zhyttia i znannia, no. 15/Vyd. TP, no. 310 (L'viv 1935); there is also a shorter version: *Geneza i kharakter halyts'koho rusofil'stva v XIX–XX st.* (Prague: Ukraïns'ke výd-vo 'Proboiem' 1941). See also Paul R. Magocsi, ''Old Ruthenianism and Russophilism: A New Conceptual Framework for Analyzing National Ideologies in Late 19th Century Eastern Galicia,'' in Paul Debreczeny, ed., *American Contributions to the Ninth International Congress of Slavists* (Columbus, Ohio 1983), pp. 305–324.

twentieth century. The Ukrainophiles founded the Rus'ka Besida (est. 1861), the Prosvita Society (est. 1868), and the prestigious Shevchenko Scientific Society (est. 1873). Oleksander Barvins'kyi has written a useful, if brief, history of these and other cultural, economic, and student societies;[98] in addition, each organization has at least one, if not several, histories of its activity.[99]

Cultural history: the press and the language question

There is no general history of the Ukrainian press during the last era of Austrian rule. There are several solid studies, however, on individual periods or publications. Ivan Krevets'kyi treats the Ukrainian press during the revolutionary years,[100] while the most important publication to arise from that period, *Zoria Halytska* (L'viv 1848–57), is treated in detail by Ivan Bryk.[101] Other studies focus on stillborn publications, censorship,[102] or in Soviet Marxist terms, on "progressive" L'viv newspapers like *Druh* (1874–77), *Hromads'kyi druh* (1878), *Dzvin* (1878), *Molot* (1879), *S'vit* (1881–82) and *Tovarysh* (1888), whose history is traced in a long monograph by Oleksa Dei.[103]

98 Oleksander Barvîn'skii, *Lîtopys' suspôl'noy robotŷ y sylŷ rusynôv avstriiskykh* (L'viv: TP 1885).

99 See chapter 2, notes 67–74. On the libraries of these institutions, see chapter 1, notes 90–91..
On the Rus'ka Besida, see Ia. Dmytriv, *Istoriia prosvitnoho tovarystva Rus'ka Besida* (Chernivtsi 1909). On the activity of the Prosvita Society, especially at the turn of the century, , see Ivan Bryk and Mykhailo Kotsiuba, *Pershyi ukraïns'kyi pros'vitno-ekonomichnyi kongres uladzhenyi Tovarystvom 'Pros'vita' ... u L'vovi ... 1909 roku: protokoly i referaty* (L'viv: Pros'vita 1910). On the Stauropegial Institute printshop, see Ivan Krypiakevych, "Stavropyhiis'ka litografiia v rr. 1847–1854," in *Zbirnyk L'vivs'koï Stavropyhiï: mynule i suchasne,* vol. I (L'viv 1921), pp. 143–159.

100 See chapter 5, n. 44.

101 Ivan Bryk, "Pochatky ukraïns'koï presy v Halychyni i L'vivs'ka Stavropyhiia," in *Zbirnyk L'vivs'koï Stavrophiï: mynule i suchasne,* vol. I, ed. K. Studyns'kyi (L'viv 1921), pp. 99–142.
See also twelve documents concerning *Zoria Halytska* as well as another important newspaper from the period, *Vîstnyk, chasopys' ... dlia Rusynov Avstriïskoi dierzhavŷ* (Vienna 1850–66), in Myhailo Vozniak, "Z-za redaktsiinykh kulïs videns'koho Vistnyka ta Zori Halyts'koï," *Zapysky NTSh,* CVII (L'viv 1912), pp. 73–109.

102 Volodymyr Hnatiuk, "Rukopysni humorystychni chasopysy," *Zapysky NTSh,* CXXX (L'viv 1930), pp. 133–167; M. Vozniak, "Z zarannia ukraïns'koï presy v Halychyni," *Zapysky NTSh,* CXI (L'viv 1911), pp. 140–159; F. Svistun, "Kril. o. Nikita Izhak iako tsenzor galitsko-russkikh izdanii v 1852-1857 gg.," *Viestnik 'Narodnago Doma',* XXV (III), 5–6 (L'viv 1907), pp. 70–76, 90–94. On censorship during the 1850s, see also the works of Studyns'kyi, n. 105 below.

103 Oleksa I. Dei, *Ukraïns'ka revoliutsiino-demokratychna zhurnalistyka* (Kiev: AN URSR 1959).

Closely related to the growth of the Ukrainian press in Galicia was the language question. The need for publications, prompted by the increase in the size of the secular intelligentsia and educated general public, forced editors to face a practical question, albeit with large cultural and national implications: what literary language should be used? By the beginning of the twentieth century, the Galician recension of Church Slavonic (described as the *iazychie* by its detractors), which was used by the Old Ruthenians, and literary Russian, used by the Russophiles, were both rejected by the majority of the populace (and by the Austrian government) in favor of the Ukrainophile solution of a vernacular-based language. After protracted debate with Ukrainians in the Russian Empire, this eventually became standard Ukrainian based on the Poltava dialects in the Dnieper Ukraine. The history and resolution of the language question during this period is traced in works by Vasyl' Lev and Paul R. Magocsi.[104] The most seriously researched period is the 1850s, as in the excellent monograph by Kyrylo Studyns'kyi on the whole decade[105] and in several works on the government-inspired ''alphabet war'' of 1859.[106]

Cultural history: education

For nationalities that have no decisive control over their own political fate and that lack a sufficient number of nationally conscious leaders willing to defend and promote the interests of the group, much emphasis is placed on creating new

---

On *Svit,* see also I.I. Doroshenko, ''Do istoriï vydannia zhurnalu 'Svit' (1881–1882),'' *Naukovi zapysky LDU,* XLII: *Pytannia zhurnalistyky,* 1 (L'viv 1958), pp. 39–46; on *Tovarysh,* see also O.I. Dei, ''Zhurnal 'Tovarysh' (epizod iz zhurnalistychnoï diial'nosti I. Franka),'' *Doslidzhennia tvorchosti Ivana Franka,* vol. II (Kiev 1959), pp. 103–132. Two of the newspapers have been indexed: P.H. Bab''iak, *Svit, 1881–1882: systematychnyi pokazhchyk zmistu zhurnalu* (L'viv: LNBS–AN URSR 1970); P.H. Bab''iak and V.I. Khoma, *Khliborob, 1891–1895; systematychnyi pokazhchyk zmistu* (L'viv: LNBS–AN URSR 1971).

104 See chapter 5, n. 72; and the chapters on Galicia in George Y. Shevelov, *Die ukrainische Schriftsprache 1798–1865: ihre Entwicklung unter dem Einfluss der Dialekte* (Wiesbaden: Otto Harrassowitz 1966); as well as studies on the problem of orthography until the 1890s in Kost' Kysilevs'kyi, ''Istoriia ukraïns'koho pravopysnoho pytannia: sproba syntezy,'' *Zapysky NTSh,* CLXV (New York and Paris 1956), pp. 74–114; and specifically during 1848 in Mykhailo Vozniak, ''Proiekt pravopysy Ivana Zhukivs'koho na z''ïzdï 'rus'kykh uchenykh','' *Zapysky NTSh,* LXXXII, 2 (L'viv 1908), pp. 53–86.

On Austrian language laws in Galicia, see n. 107 below.

105 The comprehensive work by Studyns'kyi actually appears as an extensive (untitled) introduction to the second volume of *Korespondentsyia Iakova Holovats'koho v lïtakh 1850-62,* in *Zbirnyk fil'ol'ogichnoï sektsyi NTSh,* VIII–IX (L'viv 1905), pp. i–clxi.

106 See above, notes 49 to 51.

cadres for future leadership roles. As a result, education becomes a crucial factor, and Galician-Ukrainian political and cultural leaders put great emphasis on expanding the group's educational facilities during the last decades of the twentieth century. A closely related problem was the legal status of language. After 1867, Polish replaced German as the language of instruction in secondary schools, while at the elementary level the decision was left up to local community councils.[107] As a result of these provisions, Ukrainian leaders were forced to begin a long campaign of constant pressure on the provincial and imperial governments in an attempt to increase the number of Ukrainian schools at all levels.

By the outbreak of World War I, they had obtained certain achievements in eastern Galicia. These included 2510 elementary schools (71 percent of the total number in the region) and six *gymnasia* (Przemyśl, Kolomyia, Ternopil', Stanyslaviv, two in L'viv) with Ukrainian as the language of instruction, as well as two *gymnasia* (Berezhany and Stryi) with parallel classes in Ukrainian, and ten teacher's colleges (seminaries) where Ukrainian was taught alongside Polish. Ukrainians remained unsatisfied, however (there was, for instance, one Polish *gymnasium* for every 60,400 Poles, but one Ukrainian *gymnasium* for every 546,000 Ukrainians), and founded private schools run by educational societies or by the Greek Catholic church, which by 1914 included sixteen elementary schools, ten *gymnasia,* and three teacher's colleges.

The best source material on education during this period is found in the statistical data issued by the Austrian government[108] and in a series of annual yearbooks *(zvity)* published by most of the Ukrainian *gymnasia,* which include

107 For an introductory historical survey of Austrian language laws to 1870 (with praise for the final acceptance of Polish in the school system), see F. Kasparek, ''Du droit en vigueur en Galicie en ce qui concerne l'usage officiel des différentes langues,'' *Revue de droit international et de législation comparée,* VI (Gand 1874), pp. 667–686. On the legal status of Ruthenian (Ukrainian), see Kost' Levytskii, *Pro prava ruskoy movŷ* (L'viv: TP 1896).

108 *Österreichische Statistik: Statistik der Unterrichtsanstalten,* vol. IX, pt 1: 1882/83; vol. XII, pt 3: 1883/84; vol. XVI, pt 2: 1884/85; vol. XVIII, pt 2: 1885/86; vol. XXI, pt 1: 1886/87; vol. XXII, pt 4: 1887/88; vol. XXV, pt 3: 1888/89; vol. XXVIII, pt 4: 1889/90; vol. XXXV, pt 4: 1890/91; vol. XXXVIII, pt 4: 1891/92; vol XLIV, pt 4: 1892/93; vol XLVIII, pt 4: 1893/94; vol. LI, pt 1: 1894/95; vol. LII, pt 3: 1895/96; vol. LIV, pt 2: 1896/97; vol. LV, pt 4: 1897/98; vol. LXII, pt 1: 1898/99; vol. LXVIII, pt 3: 1899/1900; vol LXX, pt 3: 1900/01; vol. LXXIII, pt 1: 1901/02; vol. LXXVI, pt 1: 1902/03; vol. LXXVII, pt 2: 1903/04; vol. LXXIX, pt 3: 1904/05; vol. LXXXVI, pt 2: 1905/06; vol. LXXXVIII, pt 2: 1906/07; vol. XCI, pt 2: 1907/08; vol. XCIII, pt 1: 1908/09; *Neue Folge,* vol. VII, pt 3: 1909/10; vol. VIII, pt 2: 1910/11 (Vienna: K.K. Hof- und Staatsdruckerei 1885–1913).

See also *Statistik der öffentlichen und Privatvolksschulen 1870–1871* [and] *1875–1876* (Vienna: K.K. Hof- und Staatsdruckerei 1872–76); and *Schematismus der allgemeinen Volksschulen und Bürgerschulen 1890* [and] *1900* (Vienna: A. Hölder 1892–1901).

protocols of academic activity, retrospective histories, and the names of all students and faculty.[109] A recent study by Ann Sirka surveys the history of Ukrainian education in Galicia between 1867 and 1914.[110] There are also several histories of Galician schools that cover all or part of the period between 1848 and 1918: Mieczysław Baranowski on elementary schools throughout Galicia and Lev Iasinchuk on Ukrainian schools;[111] Józef Buzek, Stefan Możdżeń, and Stepan Baran on Galician *gymnasia;*[112] Iaroslav Bilen'kyi on Ukrainian private schools;[113] and Zygmunt Dulczewski on the struggle over schools as reflected in debates in the Galician Diet.[114] The question of a Ukrainian university, with its political/cultural symbolism as well as its purely educational function, was the

109 *Spravozdanie* (later *Zvit) dyrektsiî ts. k. hymnaziî Akademychnoy vo L'vovî*, 40 vols (L'viv 1877–1917); *Zvit dyrektsiî ts. k. hymnaziî v Kolomyî*, 14 vols (Kolomyia 1900–13); *Zvît dyrektsiî ts. k. hymnaziî Frants-Iosyfa I. v Ternopoly*, 9 vols (Ternopil' 1905–13); *Zvït dyrektsiî ts. k. hymnaziî z rus'koiu movoiu vykladovoiu u Stanyslavovî*, 6 vols (Stanyslaviv 1908–13); *Zvît dyrektsiî ts. k. hymnaziî z rus' kym vykladovym iazŷkom v Peremyshly*, 8 vols (Przemyśl 1910–17); *Zvît dyrektsiî lytseia rus'koho instytuta dlia divchat v Peremyshly*, 14 vols (Przemyśl 1903–17); *Zvît dyrektsiï pryv[atnoî] hymnaziï z pravom pryliudnosty ... v Turtsi* (Turka 1913); *Zvit dyrektsiï pryvatnoï hymnaziï z rus'koiu vyklad. movoiu v Iavorovi*, 2 vols (Iavoriv 1912–13); *Zvit dyrektsiï pryvatnoï gimnaziï z ukraïns'koiu vykladovoiu movoiu Kruzhka Ukraïns'koho Tovarystva Pedagogichnoho v Rohatyni*, 4 vols (L'viv 1909–12); *Zvit dyrektsiï pryvatnoï zhens'koï gimnazyi ss. Vasyliianok u L'vovi*, 8 vols (L'viv 1906–13); *Zvit dyrektsiï pryvatnoï zhinochoï real'noï gimnaziï S.S. Vasyliianok v Stanislavovi* (Stanyslaviv 1912); *Zvit upravy i komitetu pryvatnoï gimnaziï z rus'koiu movoiu vykladovoiu u Zbarazhi*, 3 vols (Zbarazh, 1910–12).

110 Ann Sirka, *The Nationality Question in Austrian Education: The Case of Ukrainians in Galicia 1867–1914*, European University Studies, CXXIV (Frankfurt-am-Main: Peter D. Lang 1979).

111 See chapter 2, notes 77 and 79.

112 Józef Buzek, *Rozwój stanu szkół średnich w Galicyi w ciągu ostatnich lat 50* (L'viv 1909); Stefan I. Możdżeń, *Ustrój szkoły średniej w Galicji i próby jego modernizacji w latach 1848–1884*, Acta Universitatis Wratislaviensis, vol. CCXXX (Wrocław 1974); Stepan Baran, "Z polia natsional'noï statystyky halyts'kykh serednïkh shkil," in *Studiï z polia suspil'nykh nauk i statystyky*, vol. II, ed. V. Okhrymovych (L'viv: Statystychna komisiia NTSh 1910), pp. 107–178 and "Konfesiini i natsional'ni pereminy v halyts'kykh serednikh shkolakh v rr. 1896–1908," in *ibid.*, vol. III (1912), 66 p.

113 Ia. Bilen'kyi, *Ukraïns'ki pryvatni shkoly v Halychyni* (L'viv 1922).

114 Zygmunt Dulczewski, *Walka o szkołę na wsi galicyjskiej w świetle stenogramów Sejmu Krajowego 1861–1914* (Warsaw: Ludowa Społdzielnia Wyd. 1953).

See also the more polemical accounts of education in Galicia: the anti-Polish Ukrainian view is by Bohdan Dîdytskii, *Svoezhyt'evŷy zapysky*, pt 2: *Vzhliad na shkol'noe obrazovanie Halytskoi Rusy v XIX st.* (L'viv 1908), first published in *Vîstnyk 'Narodnoho Doma'*, XXV (III), 6–12 (L'viv 1907) and XXVI (IV), 1–9 (L'viv 1908); the anti-Austrian Polish view by Swiatłomir [H. Zaleski], *Ciemnota Galicyi w świetle cyfr i faktów 1772–1902: czarna księga szkolnictwa galicyjskiego* (L'viv: Polskie Towarzystwo Nakładowe 1904).

subject of several contemporary publications.[115] The Austrian authorities belatedly acquiesced to the Ukrainian demands for a university only in 1912; thus, before World War I, Ukrainian education at the highest level in Galicia was limited to ten chairs in Ukrainian subjects or using the Ukrainian language at the University of L'viv. Ukrainian educational activity and personnel at that institution are discussed in several general histories of the University of L'viv.[116] There are also histories of individual *gymnasia* and teacher's colleges, the L'viv Theological Seminary, and the short-lived Greek Catholic Seminary in Vienna (1852–55);[117] an analysis of teaching Galician history in *gymnasia;*[118] a biography of the

115 Observator, *Sprava ukraïns'ko-rus'koho universytetu u L'vovi* (L'viv 1899); Stanislav Dnistrians'kyi, *Prava rus'koï movy u l'vivs'koho universytetu* (L'viv 1902); *Za ukraïns'kyi universytet u L'vovi: zbirka statei v universytets'kii spravi* (L'viv: Ukraïns'kyi Students'kyi Soiuz 1910).

A good survey of the Ukrainian struggle is found in a later work: Vasyl' Mudryi, *Borot'ba za ohnyshche ukraïns'koï kul'tury v zakhidnykh zemliakh Ukraïny* (L'viv: Ukraïns'ka Kraieva Students'ka Rada 1923).

116 See chapter 2, notes 82 and 83. On the establishment of the influential chair of Ukrainian History in 1894, see Aleksander Barvins'kyi, ''Zasnovannie Katedry istoriï Ukraïny v L'vivs'komu universyteti,'' *Zapysky NTSh,* CXLI–CXLIII (L'viv 1925), 18 pp. On the activity of the first holder of the history chair, Mykhailo Hrushevs'kyi, see n. 212 below. For a brief survey of the Ukrainian rectors at L'viv, see Makarii Karovets', *Ukraïntsi-rektory L'vivs'koho universytetu* (Zhovkva 1936), first published in *Dobryi pastyr,* no. 2–3 (L'viv 1936).

117 Besides the individual *gymnasia* yearbooks (n. 109 above), see also *Zur polnisch-ruthenischen Frage in Galizien: die Verhandlung im galizischen Landtage über den Antrag auf Errichtung eines ruthenischen Gymnasiums in Stanislau* (L'viv: I. Vereinsbuchdruckerei 1903), 2nd ed. (L'viv: Mychajło Petryckyj 1904); I. Fylypchak and R. Lukan', ''Ts. K. okruzhna holovna shkola v Lavrovi, 1788/89–1910/11,'' *Zapysky ChSVV,* V, 1–4 (Zhovkva 1942), pp. 1–192, reprinted in *Analecta OSBM,* series II, sectio II (Rome 1967); Vasyl' Veryha, *Tam de Dnister kruto v'iet'sia: istorychnyi narys vykhovno-osvitn'oï polityky v Halychyni na prykladi Uchytel's'koï Seminariï ta gimnaziï v Zalishchykakh, 1899–1939,* Kanads'ke NTSh, vol. XIV (Toronto: Sribna Surma 1974); Bohdan Romanenchuk and Oleksander Dombrovs'kyi, eds, *Iuvileina knyha Ukraïns'koï Akademichnoï Gimnaziï u L'vovi,* 2 vols (Philadelphia and Munich: Ukraïns'kyi Vil'nyi Universytet 1978–81); Roman Kukhar, *Do blakytnykh vershyn: persha Ukraïns'ka Akademichna Himnaziia u L'vovi v istorychnii perspektyvi* (London: Ob''iednannia absol'ventiv Ukraïns'koï Akademichnoï Himnaziï 1981); Vasyl' Lev, ed., *Propam''iatna knyha Himnaziï sester Vasyliianok u L'vovi,* NTSh Ukraïns'kyi arkhiv, vol. XXII (New York, Paris, Sydney, and Toronto 1980); Iaroslav Levyts'kyi, *L'vivska dukhovna seminaryia v lïtakh 1897–1901* (L'viv: A. Khoinats'kyi 1901); Iaroslav Hordyns'kyi, ''Viden's'ka hr. k. dukhovna seminariia v. rr. 1852–1855,'' *Zapysky NTSh,* CXV (L'viv 1913), pp. 77–130.

118 Wanda Zwolska, ''Sprawa nauczania historii kraju rodzinnego w gimnazjach galicyjskich w latach 1867–1914,'' *Małopolskie Studia Historyczne,* IX, 1–2 (Cracow 1966), pp. 25–45.

Ukrainian-born school inspector Euzebiusz Czerkawski (1822–1896), who was instrumental in polonizing the educational system in the 1850s and 1860s;[119] and finally descriptions of the influential student societies–Druzhnyi Lykhviar (est. 1871) and Akademichne Bratstvo (est. 1882) in L'viv, and the St Cyril and Methodius Society (est. 1864) and Sich (est. 1868) in Vienna.[120]

Cultural history: literary history surveys

The last half century before the outbreak of World War I witnessed a vibrant growth of Ukrainian literary activity in Galicia, dominated largely by the prolific and talented Ivan Franko (1856–1916). Despite the richness of Galician-Ukrainian literature at this time, there is no general history devoted specifically to the years 1848–1918. Instead, it is necessary to consult the general Ukrainian literary (and cultural) histories by the Galicians Omelian Ohonovs'kyi and Ivan Franko, which include special sections on Galician developments to the 1890s, and the more recent Soviet Ukrainian multivolume literary history that brings the story down to 1918.[121] Ivan Franko also wrote a stimulating and critical essay of Galician-Ukrainian literary and cultural developments in general during the last decades of the nineteenth century.[122] The postrevolutionary decade beginning in 1848 and the early development of a popular, vernacular-based literature in the early 1860s are analyzed in some detail by Ivan Verkhrats'kyi and Ostap Terlets'kyi.[123]

The growth of the populist Ukrainian literary movement in Galicia derives

119 Aleksander Skorski, *Euzebiusz Czerkawski, jego życie i działalność pedagogiczna: przyczynek do historyi rozwoju szkolnictwa,* pt 1 (L'viv 1898).

120 Ivan Franko, ed., "Z istoriï ukraïns'koï molodïzhy v Halychynï, 1871–1884," *Zapysky NTSh,* LV (L'viv 1903), misc., pp. 1–26; Vasyl' Shchurat, "Videns'ke 'Obshchestvo sv. Kyryla i Metodiia'," *Zapysky NTSh,* CXXVIII (L'viv 1919), pp. 177–202; *'Sïch', 1868–1898: al'manakh v pamiat' 30-ykh rokovyn osnovania tovarystva 'Sïch' u Vidny* (L'viv 1898); Zenon Kuzielia and Mykola Chaikivs'kyi, *Sïch: al'manakh v pamiat' 40-ykh rokovyn osnovania tovarystva 'Sïch' u Vidnï* (L'viv, 1908).

There is also a study of the Ukrainian student organization, Hromada, in Cracow: Władysław A. Serczyk, " 'Akademiczna Hromada' w Krakowie (1887–1895)," in *Studia z dziejów młodzieży Universytetu Krakowskiego od oświecenia do połowy XX wieku,* vol. I, ed. Celina Bobińska (Cracow 1964), pp. 219–240.

121 See chapter 2, notes 63 and 64.

122 Ivan Franko, *Moloda Ukraïna,* pt 1: *Providni ideï i epizody* (L'viv: Ukraïns'ko-rus'ka vydavnycha spilka 1910).

123 Ivan Verkhrats'kyi, "Z pervykh lït narodovtsïv (1861–1866)," *Zapysky NTSh,* CXXII (L'viv 1914), pp. 79–101; Ostap Terlets'kyi, *Halyts'ko-rus'ke pys'menstvo 1848–1865 rr. na tlï tohochasnykh suspil'no-politychnykh zmahan' halyts'ko-rus'koï intelïgentsiï* (L'viv 1903).

largely from the inspiration of Taras Shevchenko (1814–1861), the great nineteenth-century writer from the Dnieper Ukraine who, although known by some before, was really discovered by Galician society only during the 1860s. By the end of the century, he had become an object of national reverence, and the resultant cult of Shevchenko among Galician Ukrainians (expressed in festivals, memorials, and publications) has itself become the subject of study.[124] Less well known is the ''cult'' of Nikolai Gogol (Hohol', 1809–1852), Shevchenko's contemporary and countryman, who chose to write in Russian. Osyp Markov has shown how, for Galician Old Ruthenians and Russophiles, Gogol became a symbol of the pan-Russian *(obshcherusskii)* national and cultural ideals they espoused.[125] With regard to Russian literature in general in Galicia, Viktor Malkin has written an informative history of its impact on those local writers who tried, with varying success, to write in that language.[126] Finally, the Ukrainian modernist literary group in Galicia known as Moloda Muza (1906–1909) is the subject of memoirs by one of its members, Petro Karmans'kyi.[127]

Theater and ethnography are also related to literary activity. Several essays or parts of larger works trace the history of the Ukrainian theater in Galicia, especially after its rise to significance in national life after the creation in 1864 of the Rus'ka Besida Theater.[128] The history of ethnographic research in Galicia (which actually began seriously in the 1830s) was first surveyed by Aleksander Pypin in

124 Viktor Petrykevych, *Istoryia kul'tu Shevchenka sered gimnazyial'noï molodizhy* (Przemyśl 1914), first published in *Zvit Dyrektsyï ts. k. gimnazyi z ruskoiu vykladovoiu movoiu v Peremyshly za shkil'nyi rik 1913/1914* (Przemyśl: Naukovyi Fond 1914), pp. iii–lxviii; Bohdan Zahaikevych, ''Kul't Shevchenka v Halychyni do pershoï svitovoï viiny,'' in *Taras Shevchenko,* in *Zapysky NTSh,* CLXXVI (New York, Paris, and Toronto 1962), pp. 253–262. See also Mykhailo Vasyl'ev, ''Perve pomynal'ne bohosluzhenie za upokoi Tarasa Shevchenka 1862 roku u L'vovi,'' *Zapysky NTSh,* CVIII (L'viv 1912), pp. 145–157; and M. Dubyna, *Shevchenko i Zakhidna Ukraïna* (Kiev: Kyïvs'kyi universytet 1969).

125 O.O. Markov, ''N.V. Gogol' v galitsko-russkoi literaturie,'' *Izviestiia otdieleniia russkago iazyka i slovesnosti Imp. Akademii nauk,* XVIII, 2 (St Petersburg 1913), pp. 37–78.

126 Viktor A. Malkin, *Russkaia literatura v Galitsii* (L'viv: LU 1957). See also the critical response by Andrii Brahinets' et al., ''Domysly i perekruchennia pid vyhliadom nauky,'' *Zhovten',* IX, 2 (L'viv 1959), pp. 132–145.

127 Petro Karmans'kyi, *Ukraïns'ka bohema, storinky vchorashn'oho: z nahody 30-littia 'Molodoï Muzy'* (L'viv: 'Krasa i syla' 1936).

128 Stanisław Schnür-Pepłowski, *Teatr ruski w Galicyi* (L'viv: 'Dziennik Polski' 1887); H. Tsehlyns'kyi, *Rus'kyi teatr,* I (L'viv 1892); Ivan Franko, ''Rus'ko-ukraïns'kyi teatr: istorychni obrysy'' (1894), in his *Tvory,* vol. XVI (Kiev: Derzhavne vyd-vo khudozhn'oï literatury 1955), pp. 209–245; S. Charnets'kyi, *Narys istoriï ukraïns'koho teatru v Halychyni* (L'viv: Prosvita 1934).

the section on the Ukraine in his multivolume history of Russian ethnography.[129] More recently, the Soviet scholars Vyktoriia Malanchuk and Roman Kyrchiv have written monographs on the history of ethnography in Galicia.[130]

Cultural history: individual writers and national leaders

More developed than general literary and cultural histories is the literature on individual writers and national leaders from this period, both the publication of their writings and biographies of their activity. After the 1848 revolution, Galician-Ukrainian cultural life was dominated by the Old Ruthenians, whose national horizons were based for the most part on local patriotism and loyalty to Austria, although a few looked toward tsarist Russia for national salvation and eventually emigrated to that country. Some of the writings of these figures are contained in the second volume of Ilarion Svientsits'kyi's compilation of material on Old Ruthenians and Russophiles in the Austro-Hungarian Rus' lands.[131] The best-researched figure among the older generation of leaders is Iakiv Holovats'kyi, the former member of the Rusyn Triad who held the first chair in Ruthenian language and literature at the University of L'viv from 1849 until 1867, when he emigrated to Russia. Kyrylo Studyns'kyi has published Holovats'kyi's correspondence from this period,[132] while Mykhailo Vozniak has studied his national views in 1848 and Fedir Savchenko his subsequent clash with the Austrian authorities.[133] There are

129 Aleksander N. Pypin, *Istoriia russkoi étnografii*, 4 vols (St Petersburg 1890–91), especially vol. III (1891), pp. 223–258 ff. and 413–418.

130 Vyktoriia A. Malanchuk, *Rozvytok etnohrafichnoï dumky v Halychyni kintsia XIX–pochatku XX st.* (Kiev: Naukova dumka 1977); Roman F. Kyrchiv, *Etnohrafichne doslidzhennia Boikivshchyny* (Kiev: Naukova dumka 1978).

131 I.S. Svientsitskii, *Materialy po istorii vozrozhdeniia Karpatskoi Rusi*, vol. II: *Karpatorusskoe slavianofil'stvo i ugrorusskoe dvizhenie perioda vozrozhdeniia* (L'viv 1909), first published in *Nauchno-literaturnyi sbornik za 1908 god*, VI, 3–4 (L'viv 1908).

See also Ivan Franko, ''Shist' lystiv halyts'kykh 'starorusiv' z rr. 1853–1863,'' *Zapysky NTSh*, XLVIII (L'viv 1902), misc., pp. 3–12.

132 For Studyns'kyi's edited collection of Holovats'kyi's correspondence, which covers the period through 1862, see chapter 5, n. 63. For other correspondance of Holovats'kyi, see notes 195 and 215 below.

133 Mykhailo Vozniak, ''Do vyiasnennia natsional'nykh pohliadiv Iakova Holovats'koho v 1848 r. (persha redaktsiia 'Rozpravy o iazytsï iuzhno-ruskim i ieho narichiiakh'),'' *Zapysky NTSh*, CXXI (L'viv 1914), pp. 133–172; Fedir Savchenko, ''Protest Iakova Holovats'koho do avstriis'koho ministerstva z pryvodu trusu v ioho meshkanni,'' *Zapysky NTSh*, C (L'viv 1930), pp. 379–388.

For general biographies of Holovats'kyi as well as works on his pre-1848 career, see chapter 5, n. 64. On Holovats'kyi as a bibliographer, see the several works of Mykhailo Humeniuk, chapter 1, n. 27.

also biographies and some unpublished writings of other old Ruthenian leaders: Mykhailo Kachkovs'kyi (1802–1872),[134] Rev. Antin Dobrians'kyi (1810–1877),[135] Rev. Mykola Ustiianovych (1811–1885),[136] Rev. Antin Mohyl'nyts'kyi (1811–1873),[137] Rev. Antin Petrushevych (1821–1913),[138] Rev. Ivan Hushalevych (1823–1903),[139] Rev. Ivan Naumovych (1826–1891),[140] Rev.

134 F.I. Svistun, ''Pis'ma Mikhaila Kachkovskago,'' *Viestnik 'Narodnago Doma'*, XXVII (V), 11–12 (L'viv 1909); XXVIII (VI), 1–4, 6 (1910), pp. 3–8, 18–24, 35–40, 59–64. On Kachkovs'kyi's career before 1848, see chapter 5, n. 71.

135 Bohdan A. Didytskii, *Antonii Dobrianskii: eho zhyzn' y dîiatel'nôst' v Halytskoi Rusy* (L'viv: Izd. Ob-va ym. M. Kachkovskoho 1881).

136 Iaroslav Hordyns'kyi, ''Do biografiï i kharakterystyky Mykoly Ustiianovycha,'' *Zapysky NTSh*, CIV (L'viv 1911), pp. 83–122. See also the extensive sections on Ustiianovych in Omelian Ohonovskii, *Ystoriia lyteraturŷ ruskoy*, vol. II, pt 1 (L'viv 1889), pp. 393–426; F.F. Aristov, *Karpato-russkie pisateli*, vol. I (Moscow 1916), 2nd rev. ed. (Bridgeport, Conn.: Carpatho-Russian Literary Association 1977), pp. 62–75. For some of Ustiianovych's writings, see the collection, *Rus'ka pys'mennist'*, n. 137 below.

137 K. Luchakovskii, ''Antôn Liubych Mohyl'nytskii, ieho zhytie y ieho znachînie,'' in *Spravozdanie Dykretsiî ts. k. hymnaziî akademychnoy u L'vovi za rôk shkôl'nŷi 1886/7* (L'viv 1887), pp. 5–73.

Some works of Mohyl'nyts'kyi and a brief biography of him appear in Omel'ian Partyskii, *Pys'ma Antoniia Liubycha Mohyl'nyts'koho* (L'viv: Zoria 1885) and in *Rus'ka pys'mennist'*, vol. III: *Tvory Markiiana Shashkevycha, Iakova Holovats'koho, Nykoly Ustiianovycha, Antona Mohyl'nyts'koho* (L'viv: TP 1906), pp. 495–623 and 2nd ed. (L'viv: TP 1913), pp. 339–512.

138 Biobibliographic data on Petrushevych is found in F.F. Aristov, *Karpato-russkie pisateli*, vol. I (Moscow 1916), 2nd rev. ed. (Bridgeport, Conn.: Carpatho-Russian Literary Association 1977), pp. 234–291; and in Ivan O. Maksymchuk, *Narys istoriï rodu Petrushevychiv* (Chicago 1967), especially pp. 97–138 and 242–263. See also Ahatanhel Kryms'kyi, ''Epihony davn'oï halyts'koï nauky (1894),'' in his *Rozvidky, statti ta zamitky*, in *Zbirnyk istorychno-filolohichnoho viddilu UAN*, vol. LVII (Kiev 1928), pp. 285–286. For works on Petrushevych as an historian, see chapter 1, n. 14.

139 Ivan Franko, ''Ivan Hushalevych,'' *Literaturno-naukovyi vistnyk*, XXIII, 8 and 9 (L'viv 1903), pp. 111–128 and 163–187; XXIV, 11 (1903), pp. 92–120, reprinted in his *Tvory*, XVII (Kiev: Derzhavne vyd-vo khudozhn'oï literatury 1955), pp. 346–406; F.F. Aristov, *Karpato-russkie pisateli*, vol. I (Moscow 1916), 2nd rev. ed. (Bridgeport, Conn.: Carpatho-Russian Literary Association 1977), pp. 292–304.

Some of Hushalevych's correpondence was published by Iaroslav Hordyns'kyi, ''Do dïial'nosty Ivana Hushalevycha v rr. 1867–1881,'' *Zapysky NTSh*, XCIII (L'viv 1910), pp. 144–157. See also n. 215 below.

140 I.G. Naumovich, *Sobranie sochinenii*, ed. A. Gensiorskii (L'viv: Obshchestvo M. Kachkovskago 1929–27).

On Naumovich's career, see O.A. Monchalovskii, *Zhit'e i dieiatel'nost' Ivana Naumovicha* (L'viv: Russkaia Rada 1899); and Vasilii R. Vavrik, *Prosvietitel' Galitskoi Rusi Ivan G. Naumovich* (L'viv and Prague 1926).

Iustyn Zhelekhovs'kyi (1821–1910),[141] Bohdan Didyts'kyi (1827–1908),[142] and Izydor Sharanevych (1829–1901).[143]

The next generation of Galician-Ukrainian leaders, who began to be active in the 1860s, were known first as populists *(narodovtsi)* and later as Ukrainophiles. The bulk of existing literature focuses on their most outstanding and prolific representative, Ivan Franko (1856–1916). The dynamic Franko was active in the student movement in the 1870s, was one of the first Ukrainian socialists in the 1880s,[144] and was a leading figure in the propagation of Ukrainian identity and cultural activity from the 1890s until his death. He is best remembered for his enormous output of poetry, prose, literary criticism, journalistic essays, and bibliographical and historical works.[145]

Franko's literary works and some of his correspondence have been published many times. The most extensive multivolume editions appeared in the Soviet Ukraine between 1924 and 1929 (thirty volumes)[146] and again between 1950 and 1956 (twenty volumes).[147] These collections contained basically Franko's belletristic works, although the 1950–56 edition included four volumes with some of his literary criticism, historical studies, and letters.[148] Recently, a fifty-volume

141 F.I. Svistun, ed., ''Iz rukopisnago nasliediia po bl. p. Iustinie Zhelekhovskom,'' *Viestnik 'Narodnago Doma'*, XXX (VIII), 4–9/10 (L'viv 1912), pp. 53–66, 70–75, 86–93, 109–114, 121–122. For his memoirs, see n. 10 above.

142 On Didyts'kyi as a literary figure, see Omelian Ohonovskii, *Ystoriia lyteraturŷ ruskoy,* vol. II, pt 1 (L'viv 1889), pp. 302–315. For some of his correspondence, see n. 215 below. For his memoir-like history of Galicia after 1848, see n. 10 above.

143 Ivan Franko, ''Shist' lystiv pok. Izydora Sharanevycha z rr. 1862–1864,'' *Zapysky NTSh,* XLV (L'viv 1902), misc., pp. 6–9. On Sharanevych as an historian, see chapter 1, n. 15.

144 The student activist and socialist aspect of Franko's career is treated at length in many recent Soviet studies on Galicia. Cf. n. 94 above.

145 Of the many attempts to list Franko's works (Mykhailo Pavlyk, 1898; Volodymyr Doroshenko, 1918; Ivan Boiko, 1954 and 1956; M. Humeniuk et al., 1956; *Ukraïns'ki pys'mennyky,* vol. III, 1963), the most comprehensive bibliography is by M.O. Moroz, *Ivan Franko: bibliohrafiia tvoriv 1874–1964* (Kiev: L'vivs'ka derzhavna biblioteka, Instytut literatury im. Shevchenka AN URSR 1966).

146 Ivan Franko, *Tvory,* 30 vols, ed. S. Pylypenko (Kiev and Kharkiv: Rukh, 1924–29), several volumes appeared in a second edition (Kiev and Kharkiv: Rukh 1927–31 and Knyhospilka 1924–29). Large parts of the first edition together with works from other editions were reprinted in 20 vols (New York: Knyho-Spilka 1956–62).

147 Ivan Franko, *Tvory,* 20 vols (Kiev: Derzhavne-literaturne vyd-vo 1950–56).

148 Several journalistic works that did not appear in the multivolume editions are contained in Ivan Franko, *V naimakh u susidiv: zbirnyk prats' pysanykh pol's'koiu ta nimets'koiu movamy v perekladi z poiasneniamy ta dodatkamy avtora,* vol. I: *Stati na suspil'no-politychni temy. pysani v rr. 1886–1890,* Pysania Ivana Franka, vol. VII (L'viv 1914), and in Mykhailo Vozniak, ed., ''Do publitsystychnoï diial'nosty Iv. Franka v rr. 1879–1883,'' in *Za sto lit,* vol. IV, in *Zapysky Istorychnoï sektsiï* VUAN (Kiev 1929), pp. 225–268. For Franko's

edition has begun to appear in Kiev, and this promises to include more of Franko's writings than have previously been republished.[149] Franko's German-language studies on social developments as well as cultural and literary history in Galicia have been republished in an anthology of his writings in East Germany.[150]

The repeated publication of Franko's works reflects the degree to which he is glorified within present-day official Soviet Ukrainian historico-cultural iconography. Reflective of Franko's stature is the amount that has been written about him, including a yearbook, later succeeded by a journal, devoted to recent research,[151] a collection of documents on his life and subsequent influence,[152] collections of contemporary memoirs about him,[153] and a huge corpus of books and articles about virtually every aspect of his career.[154] Several biographies have also appeared, beginning in 1926 with one by Serhii Iefremov and an anthology of studies edited by Mykhailo Hrushevs'kyi,[155] and continuing after World War II

---

correspondence with Dnieper Ukrainian and other Slavic leaders, see notes 191, 199, and 214 below.

149 Ivan Franko, *Zibrannia tvoriv,* 50 vols (Kiev: Naukova dumka 1976–). As of 1981, thirty-one volumes have appeared.

150 Ivan Franko, *Beiträge zur Geschichte und Kultur der Ukraine: ausgewählte deutsche Schriften des revolutionären Demokraten, 1882–1915,* eds E. Winter and P. Kirchner, Quellen und Studien zur Geschichte Osteuropas, vol. XIV (Berlin 1963).

151 *Ivan Franko: statti i materialy,* 12 vols (L'viv: LU 1948?–65); *Ukraïns'ke literaturoznavstvo* (L'viv 1966–present). Despite the general title of the latter, it is devoted primarily to Franko.

152 *Ivan Franko: dokumenty i materialy 1856–1965* (Kiev: Naukova dumka 1966).

153 O.I. Dei and N.P. Korniienko, eds, *Ivan Franko u spohadakh suchasnykiv* (L'viv 1956); O.I. Dei, ed., *Ivan Franko u spohadakh suchasnykiv,* pt 2 (L'viv 1972).

154 O. Moroz and M. Moroz, ''Radians'ke frankoznavstvo za dvadtsiat' rokiv (1939–1959): materialy do bibliohrafiï,'' in *Ivan Franko: statti i materialy,* vol. VIII (L'viv: LU 1960), pp. 179–388. See also the lists of works about Franko in I.Z. Boiko, *Ivan Franko: bibliohrafichnyi pokazhchyk,* 2nd ed. (Kiev: AN URSR 1956), pp. 129–226 and 272–278; M.P. Humeniuk et al., *Ivan Iakovych Franko: kataloh tvoriv pys'mennyka ta literatury pro n'oho* (L'viv: L'vivs'ka Biblioteka AN URSR 1956), pp. 134–155: *Ukraïns'ki pys'mennyky: biobibliohrafichnyi slovnyk,* vol. III (Kiev: Derzhavne vyd-vo khudozhn'oï literatury 1963), pp. 504–563; O.N. Moroz, *Ivan Franko: seminarii* (Kiev 1966), 2nd ed. (Kiev: Vyshcha shkola 1977).

155 S. Iefremov, *Ivan Franko: krytychno-biohrafychnyi narys,* 2nd ed. (Kiev: Slovo 1926); *Ukraïna,* III, 6, ed. Mykhailo Hrushevs'kyi (Kiev 1926).

See also the earlier works by Omelian Ohonovskii, *Ystoriia lyteratury̑ ruskoy,* vol. III, pt 1 (L'viv 1891), pp. 915–1072; Mykhailo Vozniak, *Zhyttia i znachennia Ivana Franka* (L'viv 1913) and his *Pam'iati Ivana Franka: opys zhyttia, diial'nosti i pokhoronu* (Vienna 1916); and Mykhailo Lozyns'kyi, *Ivan Franko* (Vienna: Soiuz Vyzvolennia Ukraïny 1917).

with two works by Mykhailo Vozniak and works by many other Soviet authors.[156]

Writings on other later nineteenth-century Galician-Ukrainian cultural and literary figures are much fewer. These include works on the writer Sofron Vytvyts'kyi (1819–1879);[157] the writer and pedagogue Rev. Vasyl' Il'nyts'kyi (1823–1895);[158] the writer Rev. Pavlo Leontovych (1825–1880);[159] the literary historian and linguist Rev. Omelian Ohonovs'kyi (1833–1894);[160] the writer and painter Kornylo Ustiianovych (1839–1903);[161] the writer, actor, and teacher, born in the Dnieper Ukraine but after 1863 active in Galicia, Pavlyn Svientsits'kyi (1841–1876);[162] the writer and economist Volodymyr Navrots'kyi (1847–

156 M.S. Vozniak, *Z zhyttia i tvorchosti Ivana Franka* (Kiev: AN URSR 1955) and his *Narysy pro svitohliad Ivana Franka* (L'viv: LU 1955); O.I. Bilets'kyi, I.I. Bass and O.I. Kysel'ov, *Ivan Franko: zhyttia i tvorchist'* (Kiev: AN URSR 1956); Iurii Kobylets'kyi, *Tvorchist' Ivana Franka: do storichchia z dnia narodzhennia (1856–1956)* (Kiev: Derzhlitvydav Ukraïny 1956), translated into Russian as *Ivan Franko: ocherk zhizni i tvorchestva* (Moscow: Sovetskii pisatel' 1960); Leonid Khinkulov, *Franko* (Moscow: Molodaia gvardiia 1961); Ievhen Kyryliuk, *Vichnyi revoliutsioner: zhyttia i tvorchist' Ivana Franka* (Kiev: Dnipro 1966); I.I. Bass, *Ivan Franko: biohrafiia* (Kiev: Naukova dumka 1966).

Among non-Soviet studies on Franko in the post-World War II era is an interesting analysis of his student days in Vienna, which includes his extensive curriculum vitae written in 1893: Günther Wytrzens, "Ivan Franko als Student und Doktor der Wiener Universität," *Wiener Slawistisches Jahrbuch,* VIII (Vienna 1960), pp. 228–241. On Franko as a historian, see chapter 1, n. 10.

157 Roman Smal'-Stots'kyi, "Sofron Vas'kevych-Vytvyts'kyi," *Naukovyi zbirnyk Ukraïns'koho Vil'noho Universytetu,* VI (Munich 1956), pp. 235–243.

158 For biographical data on Il'nyts'kyi, see Omelian Ohonovskii, *Ystoriia lyteraturŷ ruskoy,* vol. III, pt 1 (L'viv 1891), pp. 554–567. For his writings on Galician society, see Ivan Sozans'kyi, "Z lïteraturnoï spadshchyny Vasylia Il'nyts'koho," *Zapysky NTSh,* LXVI (L'viv 1905), 59 pp.

159 Kyrylo Studyns'kyi, "Pavlo Leontovych," *Zapysky NTSh,* CXXXI (L'viv 1921), pp. 197–229; CXXXII (1922), pp. 135–184, CXXXVI–CXXXVII (1925), pp. 159–196.

160 Ivan Franko, "Profesor Omelian Ohonovs'kyi," *Narod,* nos 20, 21, 23–24 (L'viv 1894), pp. 316–318, 334–336 and 382–385; "Dr. Omelian Ohonovs'kyi," *Pravda,* XXIII (L'viv 1894), pp. 767–778; Ahatanhel Kryms'kyi, "Omel'ian Ogonovskii," *Étnograficheskoe obozrienie,* VI (23) (St Petersburg 1894), pp. 176–177, revised version in his *Rozvidky, statti ta zamitky,* in *Zbirnyk istorychno-filolohichnoho viddilu UAN,* vol. LVII (Kiev 1928), pp. 286–291; Leonid Bilets'kyi, *Omelian Ohonovs'kyi,* Ukraïns'ki vcheni, no. 2 (Winnipeg: Ukraïns'ka Vil'na Akademiia Nauk 1950).

For some of Ohonovs'kyi's published correspondence, see n. 201 below.

161 Ostap Hrytsai, "Kornylo Ustyianovych iak dramaturg," in *Zvit Dykretsyï ts. k. Akademichnoï gimnazyï u L'vovi za shkil'nyi rik 1911/12* (L'viv, 1912).

162 Volodymyr Radzykevych, "Pavlyn Svientsitskyi: publïtsystychna, naukova ta literaturna ioho diial'nist'," *Zapysky NTSh,* CI (L'viv 1911), pp. 109–129; CII (1911), pp. 127–147; CIII (1911), pp. 113–190.

1882);[163] the political activist and scholar Ostap Terlets'kyi (1850–1902);[164] the bibliographer Ivan E. Levyts'kyi (1850–1913);[165] the radical political activist Mykhailo Pavlyk (1853–1915);[166] the editor and economist Kost' Pan'kivs'kyi (1855–1915);[167] the writer and social activist Nataliia Kobryns'ka-Ozarkevych (1855–1920);[168] the writer Uliana Kravchenko (Iuliia Shneider, 1860–1947);[169]

163 Some of Navrots'kyi's writings have appeared in his *Tvory,* with an essay on the author by Ostap Telets'kyi (L'viv: Akademychne bratstvo 1884). On the author, see also Illia Vytanovych, *Volodymyr Navrots'kyi (1847–1882): pershyi ukraïns'kyi statystyk-ekonomist v Halychyni na tli svoieï doby* (L'viv 1934).

164 Ivan Franko, "Dr. Ostap Terlets'kyi: spomyny i materiialy," *Zapysky NTSh,* L (L'viv 1902), 64 pp.; Oleksandr Lysenko, "Ostap Terlets'kyi," *Zhovten',* IX, 5 (L'viv 1959), pp. 107–117. On Terlets'kyi as a historian see chapter 1, n. 18. On Terlets'kyi as a social activist, see n. 94 above.

165 Ivan Krevets'kyi, "Ivan Em. Levyts'kyi: posmertna hadka," *Zapysky NTSh,* CXIII (L'viv 1913), pp. 155–159. On Levyts'kyi as a bibliographer, see the several studies listed in chapter 1, n. 27.

166 Pavlyk's extensive correspondence with Drahomanov has been published, see n. 200 below. For some of his other writings, see Mykhailo Pavlyk, *Vybrani tvory* (L'viv: Knyzhkovo-zhurnal'ne vyd-vo 1955) and his *Tvory* (Kiev: Derzhlitvydav Ukraïny 1959).

For works about Pavlyk, see Ivan Franko, "Mykhailo Pavlyk (zamist' iuvileinoï syl'vetky)," *Literaturno-naukovyi vistnyk,* XXIX, 3 (L'viv 1905), pp. 160–186; Mykhailo Lozyns'kyi, *Mykhailo Pavlyk: ioho zhyttie i diïal'nist'* (Vienna: Soiuz vyzvolennia Ukraïny 1917; reprinted Irvington, NJ: SMB 1974); Pavlo Iashchuk, *Mykhailo Pavlyk: literaturno-krytychnyi narys* (L'viv: Knyzhkovo-zhurnal'ne vyd-vo 1959); I.O. Denysiuk, *Mykhailo Pavlyk* (Kiev: Derzhlitvydav Ukraïny 1960); and O.Ia. Lysenko, "Mykhailo Pavlyk i ioho mistse v suspil'no-politychnomu zhytti Halychchyny ostann'oï chverti XIX st.," *Ukraïns'kyi istorychnyi zhurnal,* IV, 1 (Kiev 1960), pp. 36–45.

167 Illia Vytanovych, *Kost' Pan'kivs'kyi: idealist hromads'koï pratsi i viry u vlasni syly narodu* (New York: Tov. Ukraïns'kykh Kooperatoriv 1954). For Pan'kivs'kyi's correspondence with Drahomanov, see n. 208 below.

168 Some of Kobryns'ka's writings have appeared in two collections: Nataliia Kobryns'ka, *Vybrani opovidannia* (L'viv: Knyzhkovo-zhurnal'ne vyd-vo 1954) and *Vybrani tvory* (Kiev: Derzhlitvydav Ukraïny 1958). For her correspondence with Drahomanov, see n. 206 below.

On Kobryns'ka, see Omelian Ohonovskii, *Istoriia lyteraturŷ ruskoy,* vol. III, pt 2 (L'viv 1893), pp. 1263–1305; Irena Knysh, *Smoloskyp v temriavi: Nataliia Kobryns'ka i ukraïns'kyi zhinochyi rukh* (Winnipeg 1957); Pavlo Iashchuk, "Natalia Kobryns'ka," *Zhovten',* VI, 4 (L'viv 1956), pp. 93–103; Martha Bohachevsky-Chomiak, "Natalia Kobryns'ka: A Formulator of Feminism," in Andrei S. Markovits and Frank E. Sysyn, eds, *Nationbuilding and the Politics of Nationalism* (Cambridge, Mass.: Harvard Ukrainian Research Institute 1982), pp. 196–219.

169 Some of Kravchenko's writings have appeared in four collected works: *Vybrani poeziï* (Kiev: Radians'kyi pys'mennyk 1941); *Vybrane,* with an essay on the author by P. Iashchuk (L'viv: Knyzhkovo- zhurnal'ne vyd-vo 1956); *Vybrani tvory,* with an essay on the author by A.A. Kaspruk (Kiev: Derzhlitvydav Ukraïny 1958); and *Tvory* (Toronto: M. Kozak 1975). Her correspondence with Ivan Franko appeared in D. Lukiianovych, ed., "Neopublikovani lysty

the writer and pedagogue Osyp Makovei (1867–1925);[170] the ethnographer and politician Volodymyr Okhrymovych (1870–1931);[171] the ethnographer and linguist Volodymyr Hnatiuk (1871–1931);[172] the writer and parliamentarian Vasyl' Stefanyk (1871–1936);[173] the writer and social activist Konstantyna Malyts'ka

---

Ivana Franka (do Uliany Kravchenko),'' *Zhovten'*, IV, 10 (L'viv 1954), pp. 112–115 and ''Lysty I. Franka do Uliany Kravchenko,'' in *Ivan Franko: statti i materialy*, vol. V (L'viv 1956), pp. 132–178.

On the author, see Omelian Ohonovskii, *Ystoriia lyteraturŷ ruskoy*, vol. II, pt 1 (L'viv 1889), pp. 697–701; and Pavlo Iashchuk, ''Uchenytsia velykoho vchytelia,'' *Zhovten'*, VI, 1 (L'viv 1956), pp. 105–116.

170 For a comprehensive bibliography of Makovei's writing, see O.P. Kushch, *Osyp Makovei: bibliohrafichnyi pokazhchyk* (L'viv: L'vivs'ka biblioteka AN URSR 1958). Some of his writings appear in three collected volumes (each with a brief biography of Makovei): *Vybrani tvory* (Kharkiv and Kiev: Knyhospilka 1930); *Vybrani tvory* (Kiev: Derzhlitvydav Ukraïny 1954); *Vybrane* (L'viv: Knyzhkovo-zhurnal'ne vyd-vo 1956). Also D. Lukiianovych, ed., ''Avtobiohrafiia O. Makoveia,'' *Literaturno-naukovyi vistnyk*, LXXXVIII, 11 (L'viv 1925), pp. 230–240.

The most comprehensive biography is F. Pohrebennyk, *Osyp Makovei: krytyko-biohrafichnyi narys* (Kiev: Derzhlitvydav Ukraïny 1960).

171 Viktoriia A. Malanchuk, *Etnohrafichna diial'nist' V. Iu. Okhrymovycha* (Kiev: Naukova dumka 1972).

172 Some of Hnatiuk's writings are reprinted in Volodymyr Hnatiuk, *Vybrani statti pro narodnu tvorchist' na 110-richchia narodzhennia*, ed. Bohdan Romanenchuk, in *Zapysky NTSh*, CCI (New York, Paris, Sydney, and Toronto 1981); and (together with a comprehensive bibliography and essays on his life) in Mykola Mushynka, ed., *Naukovyi zbirnyk Muzeiu ukraïns'koï kul'tury v Svydnyku*, vol. III: *prysviachenyi pam''iati Volodymyra Hnatiuka* (Bratislava and Prešov 1967), especially pp. 17–220. On Hnatiuk's scholarly career, see chapter 1, n. 20.

173 The most comprehensive bibliography of Stefanyk's writings and studies about him is O.P. Kushch, *Vasyl' Stefanyk: bibliohrafichnyi pokazhchyk* (Kiev: AN URSR 1961). Among the several anthologies of Stefanyk's writings, the oldest is Vasyl' Stefanyk, *Vybrani tvory* (Kharkiv: Derzhavne vyd-vo Ukraïny 1927), 2nd ed. (1928), 3rd ed. (1929); the most complete collection is idem, *Povne zibrannia tvoriv*, 3 vols (Kiev: AN URSR 1949–54).

Studies on Stefanyk's life and work include: S. Kryzhanivs'kyi, *Vasyl' Stefanyk: krytyko-biohrafichnyi narys* (Kiev: Derzhlitvydav Ukraïny 1946); Oleksandra Bandura, *Vasyl' Stefanyk* (L'viv: Knyzhkovo- zhurnal'ne vyd-vo 1956); N. Zhuk, *Vasyl' Stafanyk: literaturnyi portret* (Kiev: Derzhavne vyd-vo khudozhn'oï literatury 1960); V.M. Lesyn, *Tvorchist' Vasylia Stefanyka* (L'viv: LU 1965), 2nd rev. ed. under the title *Vasyl' Stefanyk–maister novely* (Kiev: Dnipro 1970); Vasyl' Kostashchuk, *Volodar dum selians'kykh*, 2nd rev. ed. (Uzhhorod: Karpaty 1968); *Vasyl' Stefanyk u krytytsi ta spohadakh: statti, vyslovliuvannia, memuary* (Kiev: Dnipro 1970); Luka Lutsiv, *Vasyl' Stefanyk: spivets' ukraïns'koï zemli* (New York and Jersey City, NJ: Svoboda 1971); D.S. Struk, *A Study of Vasyl' Stefanyk: The Pain at the Heart of Existence* (Littleton, Colo.: Ukrainian Academic Press 1973); V.L. Mykytas', *Pravda pro Vasylia Stefanyka: proty burzhuazno-natsionalistychnykh fal'syfikatsiï tvorchosti pys'mennyka* (Kiev: Naukova dumka 1975).

(1872–1947);[174] the literary scholar and writer Bohdan Lepkyi (1872–1941);[175] and the writers Les' Martovych (1871–1916),[176] Mykhailo Iatskiv (1873–1961),[177] Marko Cheremshyna (1874–1927),[178] Oleksander Kozlovs'kyi (1876–1898),[179] and Ostap Luts'kyi (1883–1941).[180]

174 On Malyts'ka's life, see *Vykhovnytsia pokolin' Konstantyna Malyts'ka: hromads'ka diiachka, pedahoh i pys' mennytsia* (Toronto: Svitova federatsiia ukraïns'kykh zhinochykh orhanizatsiï 1965).

175 Comprehensive bibliographies of Lepkyi's writings together with essays on his life and work are found in Ievhen Iu. Pelens'kyi, ed., *Bohdan Lepkyi, 1872–1941: zbirnyk u poshanu pam''iati poeta* (Cracow and L'viv: Ukraïns'ke vydavnytstvo 1943); Ievhen Iulii Pelens'kyi, *Bohdan Lepkyi, 1872–1941: tvorchyi shliakh–bibliografiia tvoriv* (Cracow and L'viv: Ukraïns'ke vydavnytstvo 1943); and in the comprehensive biography by Vasyl' Lev, *Bohdan Lepkyi, 1872–1941: zhyttia i tvorchist'*, in *Zapysky NTSh*, CXCIII (New York, Paris, Sydney, and Toronto 1976).

For some of his literary works, see Bohdan Lepkyi, *Pysannia*, 2 vols (Kiev, Leipzig, Kolomyia, and Winnipeg: Ukraïns'ka nakladnia [1920]).

176 For a bibliography of Martovych's writings, see Mykhailo Humeniuk, *Les' Martovych, 1871–1916: korotkyi pokazhchyk literatury* (L'viv: LNBS–AN URSR 1955). Of the many collections of Martovych's works, the most comprehensive is *Tvory*, 3 vols, ed. Iu. Hamorak (Cracow and L'viv: Ukraïns'ke vydavnytstvo 1943). For a more recent edition of some of his writings, see Les' Martovych, *Tvory* (Kiev: Derzhavne vyd-vo khudozhn'oï literatury 1963).

On the author, see Vasyl' Lesyn, *Les' Martovych: literaturnyi portret* (Kiev: Derzhavne vyd-vo khudozhn'oï literatury 1963); and Fedir Pohrebennyk, *Les' Martovych: zhyttia i tvorchist'* (Kiev: Dnipro 1971).

177 Some of Iatskiv's writings have appeared in *Vybrane*, introduction by Iurii Mel'nychuk (L'viv: Knyzhkovo-zhurnal'ne vyd-vo 1957); and *Vybrani tvory*, introduction by Mykola Il'nyts'kyi (Kiev: Dnipro 1973).

On the author, see Iurii Mel'nychuk, ''Mykhailo Iatskiv,'' *Zhovten'*, VI, 7 (L'viv 1956), pp. 68–86; O.K. Babyshkin, ''Mykhailo Iatskiv (sproba kharakterystyky tvorchosti 1909–1917 rr.),'' *Radians'ke literaturoznavstvo*, I, 2 (Kiev 1957), pp. 83–103; Iu. Mel'nychuk, *Slovo pro pys'mennykiv* (L'viv: Knyzhkovo-zhurnal'ne vyd-vo 1958), especially pp. 170–234.

178 For comprehensive bibliographies of Cheremshyna's writings, see Ie.Ie. Kravchenko and N.V. Semaniuk, *Marko Cheremshyna: bibliohrafichnyi pokazhchyk* (Kiev: AN URSR 1962). Of the numerous collections of Cheremshyna's works, the most complete is his *Tvory: povne vydannia*, 3 vols (L'viv: Izmahard 1937); and the most recent *Tvory*, 2 vols (Kiev: Naukova dumka 1974).

Of the many works about the author, see especially A. Krushel'nyts'kyi, ''Pro zhyttia i tvorchist' Ivana Semaniuka-Marka Cheremshyna: krytychnyi narys,'' in M. Cheremshyna, *Vybrani tvory* (L'viv 1929), pp. 3–23; Mykola Zerov, ''Marko Cheremshyna, ioho zhyttia i tvorchist',''' in M. Cheremshyna, *Vybrani tvory* (Kharkiv and Kiev: Knyhospilka 1930), pp. v–xxxiv; Nataliia Semaniuk, *Spivets' Hutsul'shchyny : spohady pro Marka Cheremshynu* (Uzhhorod: Karpaty 1970); and Oleksa Zasenko, *Marko Cheremshyna: zhyttia i tvorchist'* (Kiev: Dnipro 1974).

179 Mykhailo Mochul's'kyi, ''Oleksander Kozlovs'kyi: biografichno-lïteraturnyi narys,'' in

Church history

As a result of the enormous political and social changes that took place in Galician society after 1848, the church no longer played the undisputed dominant role that it once had. Nevertheless, several Greek Catholic priests as well as the hierarchy (from the inner sanctum of the St George Circle at the L'viv Cathedral chapter) did hold a commanding influence over Galician-Ukrainian developments, especially before the 1870s. The continuing role of Greek Catholic priests in transmitting national ideas from the intelligentsia to the peasantry is the subject of a brief study by John-Paul Himka, whose work is one of the few general studies on the Galician church between 1848 and 1918.[181]

Most of the literature dealing with the church during these decades focuses on the activity of individual hierarchs. Luigi Glinka has provided a comprehensive biography of the life and times of Rev. Hryhorii Iakhymovych (1792–1863), the bishop of Przemyśl (1849–1859) and metropolitan of L'viv (1860–1863), who played a decisive role in Ukrainian political and cultural developments in the 1848 revolution and during the decade that followed.[182] Iakhymovych's successor, Metropolitan Spyrydon Lytvynovych (1810–1869, consecrated 1863), has been the subject of study, and some of Przemyśl Bishop Ivan Stupnyts'kyi's (1816–1890, consecrated 1871) correspondence has been published as well.[183] Most of

---

Naukovyi zbirnyk prys'viachenyi profesorovy Mykhailovy Hrushevs'komu (L'viv 1906), pp. 524–537.

180 For some of Luts'kyi's writings and an essay on his literary career and the activity of the Moloda Muza by Bohdan Rubchak, see Iurii Luts'kyi, ed., *Ostap Luts'kyi–molodomuzets'* (New York: Slovo 1968). On Luts'kyi's life, especially his work in the cooperative movment during the interwar period, see the biography by Andrii Kachor, chapter 7, n. 68.

181 John-Paul Himka, ''Priests and Peasants: The Greek Catholic Pastor and the Ukrainian National Movement in Austria, 1867–1900,'' *Canadian Slavonic Papers*, XXI, 1 (Ottawa 1979), pp. 1–14.

See also the compilation of legal matters related to the church in Michael Malinowski, *Die Kirchen- und Staatssatzungen bezüglich des griechisch-katolischen Ritus der Ruthenen in Galizien* (L'viv 1861); and the description of the priesthood in a travel account by the Russian T. Tytov, *Russkoe dukhovenstvo v Galichinie: iz nabliudenii puteshestvennyka, tserkovno-istoricheskii ocherk* (Kiev 1903).

182 Luigi Glinka, *Gregorio Jachymovyč–Metropolita di Halyč ed il suo tempo (1840–1865)*, 2nd ed., Analecta OSBM, series II, sectio I, vol. XXX (Rome 1974).

See also the earlier description of Iakhymovych as defender of ''Russian'' culture in eastern Galicia by Dmitrii Vientskovskii, *Grigorii Iakhimovich i vremennoe russkoe dvizhenie* (L'viv 1892). For correspondence of Bishop Iakhymovych, see chapter 5, n. 38.

183 F. Svistun, ''Mitropolit Spiridon Litvinovich i o. Iv. Naumovich v 1864 g.,'' *Nauchno-literaturnyi sbornik 'Galitsko-russkoi Matitsy'*, IV, 1 (L'viv 1905); Kyrylo Studyns'kyi, ed.,

the existing literature, however, is devoted to Rev. Andrei Sheptyts'kyi (1865–1944) who, after serving less than a year as bishop of Stanyslaviv, became Greek Catholic Metropolitan of L'viv in 1900. Born into a polonized aristocratic family, Sheptyts'kyi soon embraced the Ukrainian cause and became its staunchest defender under Austrian and later Polish rule.[184] Sheptyts'kyi's pastoral letters from 1899 to 1901 and some of his ascetic and ethical works have been published.[185] Among the best works that contain much information on Sheptyts'kyi's career before 1914 are biographies by Stepan Baran, Hryhorii Prokopchuk, and Kyrylo Korolevs'kyi.[186] Because of his overwhelming stature in Galician-Ukrainian life, Sheptyts'kyi has not been ignored by Soviet writers, although everything the Greek Catholic hierarch accomplished is depicted in a negative way.[187]

''Lysty min. Fl'oriiana Ziemialkovs'koho do ep. Ivana Stupnyts'koho,'' *Zapysky NTSh,* LXXXV, 5 (L'viv 1908), pp. 106–133.

184 Sheptyts'kyi was also forced to take sides between the competing Ukrainophile and Russophile intelligentsias. He chose the Ukrainian cause. Cf. the documents in *Mitropolit galitskii Andrei Sheptitskii i 'Galitsko-russkaia Matitsa'* (L'viv: Galitsko-russkaia Matitsa 1905).

185 Andrei Sheptyts'kyi, *Tvory,* vol. I: *pastyrs'ki lysty: 2. VIII.1899–7.IX.1901,* Pratsi Ukraïns'koho Bohoslovs'koho Naukovoho Tovarystva, vol. XV (Toronto 1965); idem, *Tvory (asketychno-moral'ni),* Pratsi Hreko-Katolyts'koï Bohoslovs'koï Akademiï, vol. XLV–XLVII (Rome 1978). For his later writings, see chapter 8, n. 12.

186 Stepan Baran, *Mytropolyt Andrei Sheptyts'kyi: zhyttia i diial'nist'* (Munich: Vernyhora 1947); Gregor Prokoptschuk, *Der Metropolit: Leben und Wirken des grossen Förderers der Kirchenunion Graf Andreas Scheptytzkyj* (Munich: Vlg. Ukraine 1955); Cyrille Korolevskij, *Metropolite André Szeptyckyj 1865–1944,* Pratsi Ukraïns'koho Bohoslovs'koho Naukovoho Tovarystva, vol. XVI–XVII (Rome 1964).

See also the shorter biographies by Lonhyn Tsehel's'kyi, *Mytropolyt Andrii Sheptyts'kyi: korotkyi zhyttiepys i ohliad ioho tserkovno-narodnoï diial'nosty* (Philadelphia, Pa.: 'Ameryka' 1937); Feuillen Mercenier, ''Le Métropolite André Szeptyckyj,'' *Irénikon,* XIX, 1 (Brussels 1946), pp. 49–69; Theodosius Halusczynskyj, ''Andreas Szeptyckyj, O.S.B.M., Metropolita Haliciensis,'' *Analecta OSBM,* series II, sectio II, vol. I, 2–3 (Rome 1950), pp. 268–284; Volodymyr Doroshenko, *Velykyi Mytropolyt* (Yorkton, Saskatoon: Logos 1958); and two volumes of memoirs by Sheptyts'kyi's mother: Zofia z Fredrów Szeptycka, *Wspomnienia z lat ubiegłych* (Wrocław, Warsaw, and Cracow: ZNIO 1967) and Sofiia z Fredriv Sheptyts'ka *Molodist' i poklykannia o. Romana Sheptyts'koho* (Winnipeg and Toronto: D. Mykytiuk 1965).

187 V.K. Osechyns'kyi, ''Hreko-katolyts'ka tserkva na sluzhbi u avstro-nimets'koho imperializmu i fashysts'kykh zaharbnykiv,'' *Naukovi zapysky LDU, X: Seriia istorychna,* 3 (L'viv 1948), pp. 5–21; Serhii T. Danylenko, *Dorohoiu han'by i zrady (istorychna khronika)* (Kiev: Naukova dumka, 1970), 2nd rev. ed. (Kiev: Naukova dumka 1972).

Relations with other Slavs

The contacts that first developed between Galician Ukrainians and other Slavic peoples before 1848 were expanded to include political as well as cultural interaction during the second half of the nineteenth century. The revolutionary years 1848–1849 brought Galician Ukrainians especially close to the Czechs, who at the time were respected by their fellow Slavs as one of the most advanced groups among the subject peoples in the Habsburg Empire. The literature on Czech-Galician-Ukrainian relations in 1848–1849 is well developed,[188] and although relations continued in subsequent years, they were less intense and limited primarily to the cultural realm. There are no general surveys of Czech-Galician-Ukrainian relations after 1848; the existing literature deals only with ties among individual leaders. Kyrylo Studyns'kyi has described the relations between Iakiv Holovats'kyi and the Czech writer Karel Jaromír Erben (1811–1870), while the interest of the Czech ethnographer František Řehoř (1857–1890) in Galicia has been discussed and his correspondence with Ukrainian leaders there published.[189] The most attention, however, has been devoted to Ivan Franko. There exist studies of his relations with Czechs and Slovaks,[190] as well as a volume including Franko's articles on and correspondence with leaders of those groups as well as the commentary on the Galician-Ukrainian writer in the contemporary Czech and Slovak press.[191]

Besides the more general political histories and polemical works mentioned above that include material on Polish-Galician-Ukrainian relations, the literature devoted specifically to this topic is limited to two recent monographs by the Polish scholar Elżbieta Hornowa on Mykhailo Drahomanov and his impact upon Polish

188 See notes 45 and 46 above.

189 Kyrylo Studyns'kyi, "Karel Iaromir Erben i Iakiv Holovats'kyi," *Zapysky NTSh,* CLV (L'viv 1937), pp. 6–28; M.M. Mundiak, "Frantishek Rzhehorzh i Ukraïna," *ibid.*, pp. 279–287; Petro Bogatyrev, "Z lystuvannia Frantishka Rzhegorzha," in *Za sto lit,* vol. IV, *Zapysky Istorychnoï sektsiï VUAN,* XXX (Kiev 1929), pp. 269–299.

190 Jozef Hrozienčik, ed., *Z dejín československo-ukrajinských vzt'ahov: Slovanské štúdie,* I (Bratislava: Slovenská akadémia vied 1957), translated into Ukrainian as *Z istoriï chekhoslovats'ko-ukraïns'kykh zv''iazkiv* (Bratislava: Slovats'ke vyd-vo khudozhn'oï literatury 1959). This work (especially pp. 41–186 of the Slovak version and pp. 39–202 of the Ukrainian version) contains eight essays on Franko's relations with Czechs. See also Mikuláš Nevrlý, "Ivan Franko a česká kultura," in *Věčná družba: sborník prací k třístému výročí opětného sjednocení Ukrajiny s Ruskem* (Prague: Svět Sovětů 1957), pp. 317–354; I.Iu. Zhuravs'ka, "Franko i rozvytok ches'ko-ukraïns'kykh literaturnykh zv''iazkiv," *Mizhslov''ians'ki literaturni vzaiemyny,* vol. I (Kiev: AN URSR 1958), pp. 262–278.

191 Mykhailo Mol'nar and Mariia Mundiak, eds, *Zv''iazky Ivana Franka z chekhamy ta slovakamy* (Bratislava: Slovats'ke vyd-vo khudozhn'oï literatury 1957).

left-wing intellectuals, including Poles and Ukrainians in Galicia,[192] and to works by Mykhailo Lozyns'kyi that are critical of the pro-Russian elements within the Polish movement on the eve of World War I, including "Polish Russophiles" in Galicia.[193] There is also a recent collection of documents, including many from L'viv and other cities in eastern Galicia, which reveal the Galician reaction to the anti-Russian Polish uprising of 1863.[194]

Ultimately the most influential relations for Galician Ukrainians were those that they had with their brethren in the Dnieper Ukraine. The writings of Shevchenko and the visits and correspondence of several leading Dnieper Ukrainian writers prompted the beginnings of the populist literary movement in Galicia in the 1860s and the blossoming of Ukrainian literary and cultural activity in the decades that followed. The only general studies of these developments focus on Galician-Dnieper Ukrainian interrelations during the 1860s and the activity of Galician students in Kiev during the 1870s.[195]

Most of the existing literature deals with relations between certain individuals. From the immediate post-1848 revolutionary years dates the correspondence of

192 Elżbieta Hornowa, *Ukraiński obóz postępowy i jego współpraca z polską lewicą społeczną w Galicji 1876-1895* (Wrocław, Warsaw, and Cracow, 1968); Elżbieta Hornowa, *Problemy polskie w twórczości Michała Drahomanowa* (Wrocław, Warsaw, Cracow, and Gdańsk: PAN 1978).

193 Michael Lozynskyj, *Die russische Propaganda und ihre polnischen Gönner in Galizien* (Vienna: Allgemeiner Ukrainischer Nationalrat in Österreich 1914); idem, *Dokumente des polnischen Russophilismus* (Berlin: Allgemeiner Ukrainischer Nationalrat in Österreich 1915).

194 S. Kieniewicz and I. Miller, eds, *Galicia w powstaniu styczniowym / Galitsiia v vosstanii 1863 goda* (Wrocław, Warsaw, Cracow, and Gdańsk: ZNIO–PAN 1980). See also the earlier studies on the specific impact of the 1863 revolt on Ukrainians and eastern Galicia, n. 70 above.

195 Kyrylo Studyns'kyi, "Do istoriï vzaiemyn Halychyny z Ukraïnoiu v rr. 1860–1873," *Ukraïna*, 2 [27] (Kiev 1928), pp. 6–40; Andronyk Stepovych, "Do kyïvo-halyts'kykh zv"iazkiv pochatku 1870-kh rokiv," in *Za sto lit*, vol. V, in *Zapysky Istorychnoï sektsiï VUAN*, XXXI (Kharkiv and Kiev 1930), pp. 183–191. See also the correspondence in Kyrylo Studyns'kyi, ed., *Halychyna i Ukraïna v lystuvanni 1862–1884 rr.: materialy do istoriï ukraïns'koï kul'tury v Halychyni ta ïï zv"iazkiv z Ukraïnoiu* (Kharkiv and Kiev: VUAN–Komissiia Zakhidnoï Ukraïny 1931).

Galician-Dnieper Ukrainian relations during the late nineteenth and early twentieth centuries are also covered in a polemical essay by Andrii Kamins'kyi, *Zahadka Ukraïny i Halychyny* (L'viv 1927), although the author is more concerned with trying to prove Galicia's alleged cultural backwardness.

Iakiv Holovats'kyi and Osyp Bodians'kyi.[196] The best-documented coverage is on the Dnieper Ukrainian Mykhailo Drahomanov (1841–1895), the historian and political theorist who travelled to Galicia and subsequently corresponded with and influenced many of the most important Galician-Ukrainian activists. It was Drahomanov who convinced several Old Ruthenians (including Ohonovs'kyi, Franko, and Pavlyk) of their national affiliation with Dnieper Ukrainians and of the fact that the success of nationalism in the region was dependent upon the socioeconomic transformation of Galician society. There are a few general descriptions of Drahomanov's contacts with Galicia and in particular his meetings with students in the early 1870s.[197] More important are Drahomanov's "Austro-Hungarian memoirs," which dwell in great detail on his visit to the area in 1873,[198] and in particular several volumes of his correspondence with Galician Ukrainian leaders, including Ivan Franko,[199] Mykhailo Pavlyk,[200] Omelian Ohonovs'kyi,[201] Iuliian Bachyns'kyi (1870–193?),[202] Teofil Okunevs'kyi (1858–1937),[203] Volodymyr Navrots'kyi,[204] Meliton Buchyns'kyi (1847–

196 Fedir Savchenko, "Lystuvannia Ia. Holovats'koho z O. Bodians'kym (1843–1876 rr.)," in *Za sto lit*, vol. V, in *Zapysky Istorychnoï sekstsiï UVAN*, XXXI (Kharkiv and Kiev 1930), pp. 121–169.

197 Yaroslav Bilinsky, "Mykhaylo Drahomanov, Ivan Franko, and the Relations between the Dnieper Ukraine and Galicia in the Last Quarter of the 19th Century," *Annals of the Ukrainian Academy of Arts and Sciences in the U.S.*, VII, 1–2 (New York 1959), pp. 1542–1566; Kyrylo Studyns'kyi, "Persha zustrich Mykhaila Drahomanova z halyts'kymy studentamy," *Ukraïna*, III, 2–3 (Kiev 1926), pp. 70–75. See also Iliarion Svientsits'kyi, *Drahomanov i Halychane* (L'viv: Natsional'nyi Muzei 1922; reprinted Saskatoon, Sask. 1975); Mykhailo Pavlyk, *Mykhailo Drahomanov i ioho rolia v rozvoiu Ukraïny* (L'viv 1907).

198 See n. 12 above, and the supplement, Mykhailo Vozniak, "Dopovnennia M.P. Drahomanova do ioho 'Avstro-rus'kykh spomyniv' u vidpovid' retsenzentovi 'Dila'," *Ukraïna*, III, 2–3 (Kiev 1926), pp. 78–89.

199 *Lysty M. Drahomanova do Ivana Franka i ynshykh*, vol. I: 1881–1886, vol. II: 1887–1895 (L'viv: Ivan Franko 1906–08); Mykhailo Vozniak, ed., *Lystuvannia I. Franka i M. Drahomanova*, Materiialy dlia kul'turnoï i hromads'koï istoriï Zakhidn'oï Ukraïny, vol. I, in *Zbirnyk Istorychno-filolohichnoho viddilu VUAN*, vol. III (Kiev: Komisiia Zakhidn'oï Ukraïny VUAN 1928).

200 Mykhailo Pavlyk, ed., *Perepyska M. Drahomanova z M. Pavlykom*, 7 vols [numbered II–VIII] (L'viv and Chernivtsi: Ukraïns'ko-rus'ka vydavnycha spilka i Lev Kohut 1901–12).

201 M. Pavlyk, ed., "Perepyska M.P. Drahomanova z d-rom Omelianom Ohonovs'kym," *Zhytie i slovo*, VI, 5–6 (L'viv 1897), pp. 363–400.

202 Iuliian Bachyns'kyi, *Moia perepyska s Mykhailom Drahomanovym* [1894] (L'viv: p.a. 1900).

203 M. Pavlyk, ed., *Perepyska Mykhaila Drahomanova z d-rom Teofilem Okunevs'kym (1883, 1885–1891, 1893–1895)* (L'viv: 'Dilo' 1905).

204 Kyrylo Studyns'kyi, "Perepyska M. Drahomanova z V. Navrots'kym (z pochatkiv sotsiialistychnoho rukhu v Halychyni)," in *Za sto lit*, vol. I, in *Zapysky Istorychnoï sektsiï UAN*, XXIV (Kiev 1927), pp. 83–153.

1903),[205] Nataliia Kobryns'ka-Ozarkevych,[206] Oleksander Borkovs'kyi (1841–1921),[207] Kost' Pan'kivs'kyi,[208] and Iuliian Iavors'kyi (1873–1937).[209] Second to Drahomanov in influence over Galician Ukrainians was the historian and belletrist Panteleimon Kulish (1819–1897), who lived for a while in Warsaw (1868–1871) and in Austria, from where he corresponded with leaders in Galicia whom he finally visited in 1881. While Kulish was successful in promoting the populist-Ukrainian movement in Galicia, he failed to achieve his other goal–Polish-Ukrainian cooperation. Osyp Makovei, Oleksander Hrushevs'kyi, Mykhailo Vozniak, and Kyrylo Studyns'kyi have written solid studies of Kulish's impact on Galicia;[210] some of his correspondence with local leaders has been published as well.[211]

The third Dnieper Ukrainian to have had a lasting influence on Galicia was Mykhailo Hrushevs'kyi (1866–1934). Unlike his predecessors, Hrushevs'kyi actually lived in Galicia, where he held the chair of Ukrainian history at the University of L'viv (1894–1914) and was president of the Shevchenko Scientific Society (1897–1914). He was largely responsible for making the Shevchenko Scientific Society an "unofficial" Ukrainian Academy of Sciences, transforming the previously provincial Ukrainian scholarly atmosphere of L'viv into an environment that matched the standards of other European intellectual centers at the

205 Mykhailo Pavlyk, ed., *Perepyska Mykhaila Drahomanova z Melitonom Buchyns'kym 1871–1877*, in *Zbirnyk Fil'ol'ogichnoï sektsiï NTSh*, vol. XIII (L'viv 1910).

206 M. Pavlyk, ed., *Perepyska Drahomanova z Nataliieiu Kobryns'koiu (1893–1895)* (L'viv: M. Pavlyk 1905).

207 M. Drahomanov, "Lysty do O. Borkovs'koho (1888–1889)," *Zhytie i slovo*, VI, 1 and 2 (L'viv 1897), pp. 62–69, 74–76 and 141–145.

208 M. Drahomanov, "Lysty do K. P[ankiv]s'koho, 1886, 1893–1894," *Zhytie i slovo*, VI, 2 (L'viv 1897), pp. 151–158.

209 M. Drahomanov, "Lysty do Iuliiana Iavors'koho (1891–1894)," *Zhytie i slovo*, V, 5 (L'viv 1896), pp. 378–391.

210 Osyp Makovei, "Pan'ko Olel'kovych Kulish: ohliad ioho diialnosti," *Literaturno-naukovyi vistnyk*, IX, 3 (L'viv 1900), pp. 161–183; X, 4, 5, 6 (1900), pp. 1–28, 77–107 and 169–188; XI, 9 (1900), pp. 145–161; XII, 10, 11, 12 (1900), pp. 30–43, 92–114, 150–169, also separately (L'viv 1900); Oleksander Hrushevs'kyi, "Halyts'ka molod' ta Kulish v 1860-kh rr.," *Zapysky Istorychno-filolohichnoho viddilu UAN*, XX (Kiev 1928), pp. 325–342; Mykhailo Vozniak, "Ostanni znosyny P. Kulisha z Halychanamy (z dodatkom ioho lystuvannia z M. Pavlykom)," *Zapysky NTSh*, CXLVIII (L'viv 1928), pp. 165–240; Kyrylo Studyns'kyi, "Slidamy Kulisha," *Zapysky NTSh*, CXLVIII (L'viv 1928), pp. 241–306.

211 O. Monchalovskii, "Pis'ma P.A. Kulisha otnosiashchiiasia k vremeni i tsieli ego prebyvaniia vo L'vovie," *Nauchno-literaturnyi sbornik Galitsko-russkoi Matitsy*, III, 1 and 2 (L'viv 1904), pp. 59–72 and 1–44; Ivan Franko, ed., "Iz perepysky P. Kulisha z Halychanamy 1870–71 r.," *Zapysky NTSh*, XXVI (L'viv 1898), misc., pp. 7–16.

time. Lubomyr Wynar has surveyed Hrushevs'kyi's career in Galicia in several studies.[212]

Studies also exist on the relations and influence of five other Dnieper Ukrainians upon Galicia: the writers Stepan Karpenko (1816–1886), Oleksandr Konys'kyi (1836–1900), Pavlo Hrabovs'kyi (1864–1902), and Mykhailo Kotsiubyns'kyi (1864–1913), and the historian Volodymyr Antonovych (1834–1908).[213] Finally, some of the correspondence between the writer Ivan Nechui-Levyts'kyi (1838–1918) and the Galician intelligentsia he so harshly criticized has been published.[214]

The relations between Galician Ukrainians and Russians had from the very beginning political overtones, reflecting the foreign-policy interests of the Russian Empire. As the nineteenth century progressed, and as Russia saw itself as more than ever a protector for all the Slavs, it could not help but take a special interest in its ''Russian'' brethren living within the Habsburg Empire. As a result, by the beginning of the twentieth century, the territorial acquisition of eastern Galicia had become a foreign-policy goal of the tsarist empire. Russia's actual activity in Galicia between 1848 and 1914 took the form of moral and sometimes financial support for Old Ruthenian and later Russophile leaders and their publications as well as encouragement of the Orthodox movement either directly or via immigrants who returned from the United States.

212 Liubomyr Vynar, ''Halyts'ka doba zhyttia Mykhaila Hrushevs'koho 1894–1914,'' *Ukraïns'kyi istoryk*, IV, 1–2 (New York and Munich 1967), pp. 5–22; idem, ''Mykhailo Hrushevs'kyi iak holova Naukovoho tov. im. Shevchenka,'' *Ukraïns'kyi istoryk*, VI, 1–3 (New York and Munich 1973), pp. 5–46; idem, *Mykhailo Hrushevs'kyi i Naukove Tovarystvo im. Tarasa Shevchenka 1892–1930* (Munich: Dniprova khvylia 1970). See also the more general idem, ''Zhyttia i naukova diial'nist' Mykhaila Hrushevs'koho,'' *Ukraïns'kyi istoryk*, III, 1–2 (New York and Munich 1966), pp. 15–31.

213 Kyrylo Studyns'kyi, ''Zv''iazky Stepana Karpenka z halychanamy (1865–8 rr.),'' in *Naukovyi zbirnyk profesorovi doktorovi Ivanovi Ohiienkovi* (Warsaw: Iuvileinyi komitet 1937), pp. 154–168; idem, ''Zv''iazky Oleksandra Konys'koho z Halychynoiu v rr. 1862–1866,'' *Zapysky NTSh*, CL (L'viv 1929), pp. 271–338; M. Vozniak, ''Zv''iazky Pavla Arsenovycha Hrabovs'koho z zakhidnoiu Ukraïnoiu,'' *Naukovi zapysky LDU*, III: *Seriia filolohichna*, 3 (L'viv 1946), pp. 3–71; idem, ''Do zv''iazkiv M.M. Kotsiubyns'koho z Halychynoiu,'' *Zapysky istor. ta filol. fakultetiv L'vivs'koho universytetu*, I (L'viv 1940), pp. 149–202; Myron Korduba, ''Zv''iazky V. Antonovycha z Halychynoiu,'' *Ukraïna*, V, 5 [30] (Kiev 1928), pp. 33–78; Leonid Sonevyts'kyi, ''Volodymyr Antonovych i ukraïns'ka istorychna nauka v Halychyni,'' *Ukraïns'kyi istoryk*, XVIII, 1–4 (New York, Toronto, and Munich 1981), pp. 98–104.

214 Mykhailo Vozniak, ''Z lystuvannia Ivana Nechuia-Levyts'koho z Halychanamy,'' *Zapysky Istorychnoï sektsiï VUAN*, XXVI, (Kiev 1927), pp. 97–133. Included is correspondence with the Galicians Ivan Belei, Volodymyr Lukych-Levyts'kyi, Ivan Franko, Nataliia Kobryns'ka, and Volodymyr Barvins'kyi.

There are several general studies on the early stages of Russian Pan-Slavism and its relations with Slavs living in the Austro-Hungarian Empire, as well as a volume containing letters from local leaders, including several Galician Old Ruthenians, to Mikhail F. Raevskii (1811–1884), an Orthodox priest at the Russian embassy in Vienna who served as tsarist liaison to Slavs in Austria-Hungary.[215] As for Galicia in particular, Fedir Savchenko has described Russian support for the newspaper *Slovo* (L'viv 1861–88).[216] There is also much important data in biographies of Adol'f Dobrians'kyi (1817–1901), the Russophile leader from Subcarpathian Rus' who, together with his daughter Olga Grabar (the mother of the famous art historian and painter Igor Grabar), was a defendant at a treason trial held in L'viv in 1882 at which the defendants were acquitted, but which embarrassed the Old Ruthenian movement sufficiently to end not only its "Russian connection," but its general effectiveness in Galician cultural life as well.[217]

The second stage of Russian relations with Galician Russophiles occurred during the two decades preceding the outbreak of World War I. The views of tsarist diplomats regarding the Russophile as well as Ukrainophile movements in Galicia are found in scattered documents from the uncompleted multivolume collection published by the Soviets on Russian foreign policy covering part of the years 1911 and 1912.[218] Secondary literature on this period consists only of brief

215 Mieczysław Tanty, "Kontakty rosyjskich komitetów Słowiańskich ze Słowianami z Austro-Węgier (1868–1875)," *Kwartalnik Historyczny,* LXXI, 1 (Warsaw 1964), pp. 59–77; V. Matula and I.V. Churkina, eds, *Zarubezhyne slaviane i Rossiia: dokumenty arkhiva M.F. Raevskogo 40-80 gody XIX veka* (Moscow: Nauka 1975). Included is correspondence from Bohdan Didyts'kyi, Iakiv Holovats'kyi, and Ivan Hushalevych.

216 Fedir Savchenko, "Sprava pro shchorichnu, taiemnu subsydiiu l'vivs'komu 'Slovu'," *Zapysky NTSh,* CL (L'viv 1929), pp. 391–404.

217 F.F. Aristov, *Karpato-russkie pisateli,* vol. I (Moscow 1916), 2nd rev. ed. (Bridgeport, Conn.: Carpatho-Russian Literary Association 1977), pp. 145–233; Stepan Dobosh, *Adol'f Ivanovich Dobrianskii: ocherk zhizni i dieiatel'nosti* (Bratislava: Slovenské vydavatel'stvo krásnej literatúry 1956).

For correspondence from this period among Dobrians'kyi, Ivan Naumovych, and Russian leaders, see I.S. Svientsitskii, *Materialy po istorii vozrozhdeniia Karpatskoi Rusi,* vol. II (L'viv 1909), pp. 94–104. On the 1882 trial, see the report of the editor of *Slovo* and one of the defendants, Venedikt Ploshchanskii, *Iz istorii galitskoi Rusi s 1882 goda: politicheskii protsiess russkikh galichan voobshche, riedaktora Slova v osobiennosti* (Vilnius: I. Syrkin 1892).

218 SSSR–Kommissiia po izdaniiu dokumentov épokhi imperializma, *Mezhdunarodnye otnosheniia v épokhu imperializma: dokumenty iz arkhivov tsarskogo i Vremennogo pravitel'stv 1878–1917 gg.,* series II: 1900–1913, vols XVIII–XX, pt 1 [14.V.1911–13.VIII.1912] (Moscow: Gosudarstvennoe izd. politicheskoi literatury 1938–39).

studies on the Orthodox movement,[219] contemporary polemics in defense of Russian Orthodoxy,[220] reports of the activity of the Galician-Russian Benevolent Society (Galitsko-russkoe Blagotvoritel'noe Obshchestvo) in St Petersburg,[221] and a study of Galicians at the Kiev *gymnasium* who were later to play leading roles in the Russophile movement in Galicia.[222]

World War I

The last phase of Austrian rule in Galicia began in August 1914, with the outbreak of World War I. It ended four years later with the dissolution of the Habsburg Empire in October 1918. From the outset of hostilities, Galicia, especially its eastern, Ukrainian-inhabited half, was a theater for military operations. After a brief advance onto Russian territory, the Austro-Hungarian army led by Field Marshal Conrad von Hötzendorf (1852–1925) was turned back by a series of swift Russian victories that began on August 5; one month later the tsarist armies reached the San River and the well-defended walls of Przemyśl. During their rapid retreat, Habsburg troops, especially the Hungarian *Honvéds,* took revenge upon many inhabitants whom they considered to be Russian spies. Several hundred people–both local Russophiles and Ukrainophiles, Orthodox and Greek Catholics–were summarily shot, hanged, or herded off to concentration camps, the most infamous being Talerhof in Styria.

Militarily in control of eastern Galicia, the Russian government installed a civilian administration headed by Count Georgii Bobrinskii, who immediately cooperated with local Russophiles, including Semeon Bendasiuk (1877–1965) and Volodymyr Dudykevych (1861–1922), and pro-Russian Poles, including Professor Stanisław Grabski (1871–1949) and Count Leon Piniński (1857–1938). Ukrainian cultural and educational institutions were closed, plans were

219 Alexander Pelipenko, ''Die politische Propaganda der russischen Heiligen Synode in Galizien vor dem Kriege,'' *Berliner Monatshefte für internationale Aufklärung,* XII, 2 (Berlin 1934), pp. 825–838; Rudolf Kiszling, ''Die russische Orthodoxie und der Nordosten des ehemaligen Habsburgerreiches 1908–1914,'' *Ostdeutsche Wissenschaft,* IX (Munich 1962), pp. 287–300. See also the contemporary description of Russophilism by a Ukrainophile editor in Vienna: Vladimir Kuschnir, *Der Neopanslawismus* (Vienna 1908).

220 Mykhail Sharych, *Bratskii priviet brat'iam i sestram karpatorussam, zhivushchim v predielakh karpatskikh gor i v Amerikie* (St Petersburg 1893); V.A. Bobrinskii, *Prazhskii s''iezd: Chekhiia i Prikarpatskaia Rus'* (St Petersburg 1909).

221 *Otchet o dieiatel'nosti Galitsko-russkago Blagotvoritel'nago Obshchestva v S.-Peterburgie za 1912 god* (St Petersburg 1913); ... *za 1913–1914 god* (St Petersburg 1914).

222 F.I. Svistun, ''Galitskie urozhentsi–uchiteli pervoi kievskoi gimnazii,'' *Viestnik 'Narodnago Doma',* XXIX (VII), 7–8 (L'viv 1911), pp. 132–140.

made to dismantle the Greek Catholic church, and several leaders, including Metropolitan Andrei Sheptyts'kyi, were arrested and deported to Russia. Those Ukrainians who managed to flee westward before the Russian advance settled in refugee camps, the largest of which was at Gmünd in Upper Austria. The tsarist army captured Przemyśl in March 1915 and advanced even farther westward into Galicia as far as Gorlice and Tarnów on the Dunajec River. Finally, an Austrian counteroffensive (with German help) began in May 1915. Within a month the Russian government was driven out of L'viv and the tsarist army was pushed back, so that it managed to retain only the far eastern section of Galicia, south of Ternopil' between the Seret and Zbruch rivers. The rest of Galicia remained under the control of an Austrian military and civilian administration until November 1,1918. The Russians held most of eastern Galicia again briefly during the offensive led by General Aleksei Brusilov (1853–1926) in the summer of 1916, but by the fall of that year they were driven back to the region around Ternopil', which they were finally forced to abandon in July 1917.

During the war years, Galician-Ukrainian leaders set up new interparty political organizations in Vienna. The first of these, the Supreme Ukrainian Council (Holovna Ukraïns'ka Rada), within a week of its establishment on August 1, 1914, united the Ukrainian units in the Austrian army into a military formation known as the Ukrainian Sich Riflemen (Ukraïns'ki Sichovi Stril'tsi). This unit fought within the Austrian ranks against the tsarist army on the eastern front. The Supreme Ukrainian Council cooperated with the Union for the Liberation of the Ukraine (Soiuz Vyzvolennia Ukraïny), also founded in Vienna in August by Ukrainians from the Russian Empire.

Eventually, two factions arose among the Galician Ukrainians, which were in basic agreement about ultimate goals but not about tactics. The General Ukrainian Council (Zahal'na Ukraïns'ka Rada, est. May 5, 1915) led by parliamentarian Kost' Levyts'kyi (1859–1941) supported the idea of an independent state for Dnieper Ukrainians in the Russian Empire but called only for national autonomy for Galicia within Austria. The other faction, the Ukrainian Parliamentary Representation, led by Ievhen Petrushevych (1863–1940) and supported by the Ukrainian Sich Riflemen was after 1916 less conciliatory toward the Austrians and demanded the separation of Galicia and a guarantee of Ukrainian autonomy even before hostilities ceased. The imperial Habsburg government made some token concessions but never fulfilled the basic demands of either Ukrainian faction. By 1918, when the end of the war was in sight and it was clear that Austria was to be on the losing side, Ukrainian leaders met in L'viv on October 19, stated their intention to declare an independent western Ukrainian state (comprising northern Bukovina and northeastern Hungary as well as eastern Galicia), and carried out that intention after the breakup of the Habsburg Empire less than two weeks later.

Documents from Austrian archives on the Ukrainian problem in Galicia have been published in a multivolume collection about Ukrainian developments during World War I. Austrian attitudes toward the Ukrainian problem within and beyond its borders, the formation of the Sich Riflemen, the activity of Metropolitan Sheptyts'kyi in exile, the implications of the Treaty of Brest-Litovs'k (February 1918) for Galicia, and the role of Habsburg Archduke Wilhelm in Galician-Ukrainian affairs are among the subjects for which there are numerous documents in this collection.[223]

With regard to general histories of the war years, there are none that deal competently with all aspects of eastern Galicia (political, socioeconomic, cultural, military) during the years of World War I. Of the general surveys that do exist, Józef Skrzypek presents the view of a supporter of Polish rule in Galicia;[224] Volodymyr Osechyns'kyi reflects the highly critical Soviet attitude toward all actors in the drama, whether local Poles, Ukrainophiles, Russophiles, the Austrian government, the Greek Catholic church, or the ''reactionary'' tsarist military machine and civil administration;[225] and Helga Grebing and Wolfdieter Bihl provide dispassionate accounts of Austro-Hungarian policy toward Ukrainians during the war.[226]

223 Theophil Hornykiewicz, ed., *Ereignisse in der Ukraine 1914–1922, deren Bedeutung und historische Hintergründe*, 4 vols (Horn, Austria and Philadelphia: Ferdinand Berger Vlg. for the W.K. Lypynsky East European Institute 1966–69).

See also the small collection of documents from the Russian occupation (1914–1915) in Bohdan Janusz, *Dokumenty urzędowe okupacyi rosyjskiej Lwowa* (L'viv: Księgarnia Akademicka 1916).

224 Józef Skrzypek, ''Ukraińcy w Austrii podczas wielkiej wojny i geneza zamachu na Lwów,'' *Niepodległość*, XIX, 1 (Warsaw 1939), pp. 28–82.

See also the analysis of Polish policies and Polish-Ukrainian relations in Galicia in Konstanty Skrokowski, *N.K.N.: zarys historji Naczelnego Komitetu Narodowego* (Cracow: Krakowska Spółka Wydawnicza 1923).

225 V.K. Osechyns'kyi, ''Avstriis'kyi viis'kovo-politseis'kyi teror v Halychyni pid chas pershoï svitovoï viiny,'' *Naukovi zapysky LDU*, XLIII: *Seriia istorychna*, 6 (L'viv 1957), pp. 65–91. See also Jurij Křížek, ''Ukrajinská a polská otázka v Haliči na začátku první světové války,'' *Historie a vojenství*, XIX, 3 (Prague 1970), pp. 319–345.

226 Helga Grebing, ''Österreich-Ungarn und die 'Ukrainische Aktion' 1914–1918,'' *Jahrbücher für Geschichte Osteuropas*, N.F., VII, 3 (Munich 1959), pp. 270–296; Wolfdieter Bihl, ''Einige Aspekte der österreichisch-ungarischen Ruthenenpolitik 1914–1918,'' *Jahrbücher für Geschichte Osteuropas*, N.F., XIV (Wiesbaden 1966), pp. 537–550.

See also the discussion of the Austrian government's eventually aborted plans to divide Galicia along nationality lines: Heinz Lemke, ''Die Regierung Stürgkh und die Pläne zur Theilung Galiziens,'' in *Österreich–Ungarn in der Weltpolitik 1900 bis 1918* (Berlin: Akademie Vlg. 1965), pp. 267–283.

The initial months of the war and in particular the Russian occupation during the fall and winter of 1914–1915 have received much attention. Since it is precisely from this period that the real animosity and deep-seated hatred between Galician Ukrainophiles and Russophiles derives, it is not surprising that several accounts of the Russian occupation, most of which were written during the war years, are highly polemical in nature. The Ukrainophile viewpoint, best represented by Ivan Kryp''iakevych, stresses the degree to which Ukrainians suffered under Russian occupation.[227] The Russophile view considers the tsarist army to be liberators who, however briefly, restored the ''true Russian'' character of the land. They have given particular attention to the ''Talerhof martyrs,'' loyal patriots who suffered for their nation.[228] As might be expected, both the Ukrainophiles and Russophiles, in an effort to discredit their opponents, accuse each other of duplicity and cooperation with the Austrians, Russians, or local Poles.

The Polish view of 1914–1915, best expressed in contemporary accounts by Feliks Przysiecki and Józef Białynia Chołodecki, tries to explain in a larger Polish context the reason why some local Poles, influenced by their countrymen in the Congress Kingdom (Roman Dmowski among others), found it necessary to cooperate with the Russian administration.[229] On the other hand, Soviet writers

227 Ivan Petrovych [Ivan Kryp''iakevych], *Halychyna pidchas rosiis'koï okupatsiï: serpen' 1914-cherven' 1915* (L'viv: Politychna biblioteka 1915).

See also Austriacus, *Polnische Russophilen und Massenverhaftungen staatstreuer Ukrainer in Galizien* (Berlin: Carl Kroll 1915); Bedwin Sands [George Raffalovich], *The Russians in Galicia* (New York: Ukrainian National Council 1916); M.H. Tsehlyns'kyi, *Halyts'ki pohromy: trahichna storinka z zhyttia halyts'kykh ukraïntsiv v chasy evropeis'koï viiny 1914–1915 rr.* (Cleveland: Robitnyk 1917); and the memoirs of the Dnieper Ukrainian Dmytro Doroshenko, who served with the Russian government in Galicia, *Moï spomyny pro nedavnie mynule (1914–1918)*, vol. I: *Halyts'ka ruïna*, 1914–1917 (L'viv: Chervona Kalyna 1923; reprinted in Munich: Ukraïns'ke vydavnytstvo 1969).

228 A. Cholovskii, *L'vov vo vremena russkago vladychestva* (Petrograd? 1915); *Talergofskii al'manakh: propamiatnaia kniga avstriiskikh zhestokostei, izuvierstv i nasilii nad karpato-russkim narodom vo vremia vsemirnoi voiny 1914–1917 gg.*, 4 vols (L'viv: Talergofskii Komitet 1924–32), reprinted with additions as *Voennye prestupleniia Gabsburgskoi monarkhii 1914–1917 gg.: Galitskaia golgofa* (Trumbull, Conn.: Peter S. Hardy 1964). The supplemented reprint also includes an essay by Bohdan Svitlynskii, ''Avstro-Uhorshchyna i Talerhof,'' 39 pp.

On Galician Ukrainophiles in Talerhof and another camp at Gmünd in Upper Austria, see Vasyl' Makovs'kyi, *Talerhof: spohady i dokumenty* (L'viv: p.a. 1934); and Vasyl' Makovs'kyi, *Gmind: tabir ukraïns'kykh zbihtsiv i vyhnantsiv u chasy svitovoï viiny 1914–1918 rr.* (L'viv 1935).

229 Feliks Przysiecki, *Rządy rosyjskie w Galicyi wschodniej* (Piotrków: Wyd. 'Wiadomości Polskich' 1915); Józef Białynia Chołodecki, *Lwów w czasie okupacji rosyjskiej (3 września 1914–22 czerwca 1915)*, Wschód, vol. IV (L'viv 1930).

are highly critical of a policy that they believe strove to preserve the interest of local Polish aristocratic and bourgeois "exploiters."[230] Some documents and studies on Russian policy toward the Greek Catholic church and descriptions of Metropolitan Sheptyts'kyi as "prisoner of the tsar" between 1914 and 1917 are also available.[231]

Because of the Russian invasion during the first weeks of hostilities, most Ukrainian political leaders fled from Galicia and remained in Vienna for the duration of the war. Their activity on behalf of the homeland is chronicled in the four-volume historical memoir of Kost' Levyts'kyi: three volumes deal with events up to March 1918, and the fourth concerns the crucial changes in the attitudes of Galician national leaders between March and October of that year.[232] There are also available decrees and other documents issued by the General Ukrainian Council and the Ukrainian Parliamentary Representation,[233] as well as studies on Galician interaction with the Vienna-based Union for the Liberation of the Ukraine founded by Ukrainians from the Russian Empire living in Austria.[234] The generally loyal stance of Galicia's leaders toward the Austrian Empire until

---

See also Stanisław Rossowski, *Lwów podczas inwazyi* (L'viv: H. Altenberg 1917); and Bohdan Janusz, *293 dni rządów rosyjskich w Lwowie (3. IX. 1914–22. VI. 1915)* (L'viv and Warsaw: Bernard Połoniecki–Gebethner i Wolff 1915).

230 I.I. Bieliakevych, "Polityka pol's'kykh burzhuazno-pomishchyts'kykh diiachiv Skhidnoï Halychyny (VIII.1914–VII.1915)," *Visnyk LDU: Seriia istorychna*, IV (L'viv 1967), pp. 44–53. See also n. 225 above.

231 See the top secret report by the head of the Russian gendarmerie in L'viv (dated 17. I.1915) in S. Iefremov, "Do istoriï 'halyts'koï ruïny' 1914–1915 rr.," *Ukraïna*, I, 4 (Kiev 1924), pp. 127–144; a Russian report on the goals to destroy the Greek Catholic church (dated 24.III.1915) in Mykhailo Kornylovych, "Plany 'vozsoiedyneniia halyts'kykh uniiativ' v 1914–1915 rr.," *Ukraïna*, I, 4 (Kiev 1924), pp. 144–152; and the memoirs of a Russian ecclesiastic who was instrumental in working for the conversion of Galician Greek Catholics to Orthodoxy: Mitropolit Evlogii [Vasilii Georgievskii], *Put' moiei zhizni: vospominaniia Mitropolita Evlogiia* (Paris: YMCA Press 1947), especially pp. 242–283. See also the documents in the Hornykiewicz collection, n. 223 above.

232 See Levyts'kyi's *Istoriia vyzvol'nykh zmahan'* and *Velykyi zryv*, n. 9 above.

233 *Zvidomlenie zahal'no-ukraïns'koï kul'turnoï rady (vid liutoho 1915 do zhovtnia 1917 r.)* (L'viv: Zahal'no-ukraïns'ka kul'turna rada 1917); *Die österreichische Politik gegen die Ruthenen: ein Appell an die öffentliche Meinung Österreichs* (Vienna 1914).

234 Wolfdieter Bihl, "Österreich-Ungarn und der 'Bund zur Befreiung der Ukraina'," in *Österreich und Europa: Festgabe für Hugo Hantsch zum 70. Geburtstag* (Graz, Vienna, and Köln: Vlg. Styria 1965), pp. 505–526; idem, "Die Tätigkeit des ukrainischen Revolutionärs Mykola Zaliznjak in Österreich-Ungarn," *Jahrbücher für Geschichte Osteuropas*, N.F., XIII (Wiesbaden 1965), pp. 226–230.

On the activity of the Union in prisoners-of-war camps, especially at Freistadt, see *Soiuz Vyzvolennia Ukraïny, 1914–1918 Viden'* (New York: Chervona kalyna 1979).

the very last months of the war is revealed in much pamphlet literature demanding the division of the province and the ''restoration'' of the medieval Galician-Volhynian Kingdom under a Habsburg scepter.[235] The hoped-for ruler of the restored kingdom, the Habsburg Archduke Wilhelm Franz (Vasyl' Vyshyvanyi, 1895–c. 1950), is the subject of separate studies.[236]

As for military developments, there exists an extensive literature on campaigns in the region during World War I, including the Battle of Galicia (August 5–September 11, 1914), the Austro-German counteroffensive against the Russians (May–June 1915), and the short-lived offensive of General Brusilov (June 5–September 1, 1916). These events are covered in great detail in general Austrian and Russian military histories of World War I;[237] in the memoirs of the leading protagonists–the Austrian Field Marshall Conrad von Hötzendorf and the Russian general Aleksei Brusilov;[238] and in studies of individual battles–L'viv (August

235 See n. 68 above; and Michael Lozynskyj, *Wiederherstellung des Königreiches Halytsch-Wolodymyr: Galizien und das ukrainische Problem in Österreich* (L'viv 1918).

236 Wolfdieter Bihl, ''Erzherzog Wilhelms 'austroukrainische' Tätigkeit 1918,'' *Jahrbücher für Geschichte Osteuropas,* N.F., XIV (Wiesbaden 1966), pp. 51–57; and the biography by Nykyfor Hirniak, *Polkovnyk Vasyl' Vyshyvanyi* (Winnipeg: D. Mykytiuk 1956).

237 *Österreich-Ungarns letzter Krieg 1914–1918,* 7 vols in 15 (Vienna: Vlg. der militärwissenschaftlichen Mitteilungen 1930–38), especially vols I, II, IV; A.M. Zaionchkovskii, *Mirovaia voina 1914–1918 gg.,* 3 vols, 3rd ed. (Moscow: Voenizdat 1938–39), especially vol. I.

See also the chapters on Galicia (1914) and the Brusilov offensive (1916) in Norman Stone, *The Eastern Front 1914–1917* (New York: Charles Scribner's Sons 1975) and in the memoir-like account of the journalist Stanley Washburn, *Field Notes from the Russian Front* (London: Andrew Melrose 1915) and his *The Russian Offensive* (London: Constable and Co. 1917); studies of the 1914 campaign in N. Auffenberg-Komarow, *Aus Österreich-Ungarns Teilnahme am Weltkriege* (Berlin and Vienna: Vlg. Ullstein 1920) and in N.N. Golovin, *Iz istorii kampanii 1914 goda na russkom frontie,* vol. III: *Galitsiiskaia bitva* (Paris: Rodnik 1930); and of the 1915 Russian retreat in Mikhail D. Bonch-Bruevich, *Poteria nami Galitsii v 1915 godu,* 2 vols, Trudy Voenno-istoricheskoi komissii, vol. I (Moscow 1920–26) and Hans Niemann, *Die Befreiung Galiziens,* 2nd ed. (Berlin: Ernst Siegfried 1916).

238 Feldmarschall Conrad, *Aus meiner Dienstzeit, 1906–1918,* 5 vols in 8 (Vienna, Leipzig, and Munich 1922–25), especially vols IV and V; A.A. Brusilov, *Moi vospominaniia* (Riga: Mir 1929), French translation: A.A. Brousilov, *Mémoires* (Paris: Hachette 1929), English translation: *A Soldier's Notebook 1914–1918* (London: Macmillan 1930).

See also the memoirs of an Austro-Hungarian officer on the 1914 Galician battle: Octavian C. Tăslăuanu, *Trois mois de campagne en Galicie* (Paris and Neuchatel: Attinger frères 192?).

21–September 11, 1914),[239] San (September 1914),[240] Gorlice (May 1915),[241] and Horodok-L'viv (June 1915).[242]

The history of the Ukrainian Sich Riflemen within the Habsburg army has also been traced from its beginnings as a paramilitary organization in March 1913 to its participation in Carpathian Mountain battles (September 1914) and against the Brusilov offensive (summer 1916) until its incorporation into the Ukrainian Galician Army (November 1918). The best works on the Ukrainian Sich Riflemen are by Osyp Dumin and Stepan Ripets'kyi, who have written histories of the unit and edited collections of articles, documents, and biographies of its leading participants.[243]

239 Max Freiherr von Pitreich, *Lemberg 1914* (Vienna: Adolf Holzhausens Nachfolger 1929).

240 *Kämpfe am San*, Der grosse Krieg in Einzeldarstellungen, vol. XXII (Oldenburg: Gerhard Stalling 1918).

241 V. François, *Gorlice 1915: Der Karpathendurchbruch und die Befreiung von Galizien* (Leipzig: K.F. Koehler 1922); Leonhard von Rothkirch, *Gorlice-Tarnow*, Der grosse Krieg in Einzeldarstellungen, vol. XXI (Oldenburg: Gerhard Stelling 1918); *Gorlitskaia operatsiia: sbornik dokumentov* (Moscow: Voenizdat 1941).

242 Müller-Brandenburg, *Die Schlacht bei Grodek-Lemberg (Juni 1915)*, Der grosse Krieg in Einzeldarstellungen, vol. XXIV (Oldenburg: Gerhard Stalling 1918).

243 Osyp Dumin, *Istoriia Liegionu Ukraïns'kykh Sichovykh Stril'tsiv 1914–1918* (L'viv: Chervona Kalyna 1936); Stepan Ripets'kyi, *Za voliu Ukraïny: istorychnyi zbirnyk USS: v 50-littia zbroinoho vystupu Ukraïns'kykh Sichovykh Stril'tsiv proty Moskvy 1914–1964* (New York: Holovna Uprava Bratstva USS 1967).

See also the earlier general history: Bohdan Hnatkevych, ''Ukraïns'ki Sichovi Stril'tsi,'' in Ivan Kryp''iakevych and Bohdan Hnatkevych, eds, *Istoriia ukraïns'koho viis'ka* (L'viv: Ivan Tyktor 1936; reprinted Winnipeg 1953), pp. 293–356; a collection of essays, *Ukraïns'ki Sichovi Stril'tsi 1914–1920* (L'viv: Ihor Fediv 1935), 2nd ed. (L'viv 1936), 3rd rev. ed. (Montreal 1955); and the memoirs by the first commander of the unit, Mykhailo Halushchyns'kyi, *Z Ukraïns'kymy Sichovymy Stril'tsiamy: spomyny z rr. 1914–1915* (L'viv: 'Dilo' 1934), and by a prominent contemporary journalist, Osyp Nazaruk, *Slïdamy Ukraïns'kykh Sïchovykh Stril'tsïv* (L'viv: Soiuz Vyzvolennia Ukraïny 1916; reprinted New York: Howerla 1975).

Chapter 7

1919–1939

Background

With the dissolution of the Habsburg Empire in late October, 1918, Galician Ukrainians, like most other nationalities (and branches of nationalities) in Austria-Hungary, created national councils, declared their independence, and then set out to achieve in fact what they had declared in word. Ukrainian military and political preparations for the imminent collapse of the Habsburg state had already begun with the establishment in L'viv of a Central Military Committee at the end of September and a Ukrainian National Council (Rada) headed by parliamentarian Ievhen Petrushevych on October 18. Prepared militarily and politically, the Galician Ukrainians took the initiative on November 1 by seizing the Austrian government buildings in L'viv and by establishing a Western Ukrainian People's Republic (Zakhidno-Ukraïns'ka Narodna Respublika).

The next two decades in the history of Ukrainian Galicia–1919 to 1939–can be divided into three phases. The first lasted from November 1918 to July 1919, when the Ukrainians struggled to establish an operative government and to fight off a Polish invasion. The second lasted from July 1919 to March 1923, a period when Poland's control of the area was made secure and was eventually recognized by the Western Powers. The third lasted from 1923 to 1939, when Poland tried to integrate the region and its inhabitants into the administrative and social structure of the Polish state.

The first period was marked primarily by military campaigns between Polish and Ukrainian forces. By November 21–22, 1918, the Poles had driven the Ukrainians out of L'viv. The Ukrainian government moved first to Ternopil' and then at the end of December to Stanyslaviv. Despite a rapidly changing military situation, the Ukrainians managed to establish a government administration and to set up diplomatic representation abroad. The Galicians made known their intention to unite with the Ukrainian National Republic in the Dnieper Ukraine, and did so by a solemn act in Kiev on January 22, 1919. Despite this act of union, the Western Ukrainian People's Republic maintained its own administration and a well-equipped Ukrainian Galician Army. They were no match, however, for the Polish army of General Józef Haller (1873–1960). Sent from France in April 1919 (ostensibly to fight the Russian Bolsheviks), Haller entered Galicia and by July 1919 drove the Ukrainian army and government across the Zbruch River and into lands of the former Russian Empire.

The second historical phase, lasting until 1923, was marked by the establishment of Polish control over all Galicia. The Poles considered all of former Austrian Galicia to be part of their age-long Polish patrimony and were intolerant of any views to the contrary. Thus, despite Poland's acceptance of the provision on minorities in the treaty signed at Versailles on June 28, 1919, the new Polish administration in Galicia instituted a policy of retaliation against Ukrainians who had fought against them. This resulted in the arrest and deportation of several thousand Ukrainians and in restrictions placed on Ukrainian political, cultural, and educational activity. The Ukrainian reaction took the form of strikes, election boycotts, patriotic demonstrations, and acts of sabotage carried out by the newly founded Ukrainian Military Organization (UVO) headed by Colonel Ievhen Konovalets' (1891–1938). Also, some Ukrainians in the eastern extreme of Galicia (around Ternopil') lent their support to the short-lived Galician Soviet Republic set up under the protection of Bolshevik armies between July and September 1920.

Forced out of its homeland, the Ukrainian Galician Army first fought alongside the forces of the Ukrainian National Republic and thereby became embroiled in the Ukrainian struggle for independence and the civil war that was raging on lands of the former Russian Empire. Acting without the consent of the Western Ukrainian government, the Ukrainian Galician Army joined in November 1919 the anti-Bolshevik White Russian Army of General Anton Denikin (1872–1947), only later to switch sides and become the Red Ukrainian Galician Army (January 1920), a unit that operated with Bolshevik forces until its final dissolution in April 1920.

For its part, the Western Ukrainian government set up an administration in exile, first in Kamianets'-Podil's'kyi (July–November 1919), then in Vienna (to March 1923), where under the leadership of Ievhen Petrushevych it tried to convince the Entente Powers of the need to guarantee the existence of an independent and neutral Galician-Ukrainian state in the face of Polish aggression. In the end, the Council of Ambassadors of the Associated and Allied Powers accepted (on March 14, 1923) the incorporation of eastern Galicia into Poland.

With no practical access to outside aid, Galician Ukrainians were faced with the prospect of being ruled directly by the Poles; moreover, they had no recourse to higher authority, such as was possible with the central government in Vienna during the prewar Habsburg days. Basically, the Ukrainian leadership and the vast majority of the population considered the Poles as representing a regime of occupation. None of the plans for autonomy that were proposed in either Polish or Entente diplomatic circles between 1919 and 1923 were ever put into effect, and the new regime in Warsaw attempted to make all of Galicia an integral part of Poland. By 1920, the former Austrian crownland of Galicia (with its local diet and educational administration) was abolished and divided into four Polish provinces *(województwa):* Cracow, L'viv, Stanyslaviv, and Ternopil'. The last three of these provinces, comprising the core area of pre-1772 historic Galicia and inhabited predominantly by Ukrainians, were renamed Eastern Little Poland *(Małopolska Wschodnia)*. Not only were Ukrainians denied autonomous status in Eastern Little Poland, they were also deprived of the achievements in political, cultural, and educational affairs made previously under the Austrians, even to the degree of replacing the name Ukrainian with the Polish term Ruthenian *(Rusini, rusiński, ruski)* in official matters.

The Ukrainian reaction ranged from participation in the political process (although election or economic boycotts were frequent), to an outright rejection of Polish rule resulting in sabotage, so that by the 1930s a virtual state of war existed between the Polish authorities and large segments of the Ukrainian population. After the Entente decision of 1923, when it became clear that Poland was to rule eastern Galicia, these two basic approaches to the new situation prevailed. Beginning in 1925, the largest political parties united into the Ukrainian National Democratic Union (Ukraïns'ke Natsional'ne Demokratychne Ob''iednannia–UNDO), which, carrying on the tradition of the prewar Ukrainian National Democratic party, followed the model of organic work adopted under Austrian rule and attempted to improve the status of the Ukrainian population through rational political, social, and economic action. This group included both older politicians (Kost' Levyts'kyi, Dmytro Levyts'kyi, Stepan Baran) and younger leaders (Vasyl' Mudryi, Liubomyr Makarushka, Ostap Luts'kyi). There were also several other Galician parties that participated in interwar Polish political life. Among them were the old prewar Ukrainian radical, later Ukrainian Socialist-Radical party and the Ukrainian Social Democratic party, as well the Ukrainian Catholic National party, several Russophile parties, and finally the Communist party of the Western Ukraine.

The second approach, that of revolutionary activity and military action, was represented by the Ukrainian Military Organization (UVO), which by 1929 provided the initiative for the formation of the Organization of Ukrainian Nationalists (OUN). Led by Colonel Konovalets' and sharing many of the ideological tenets of

INTERWAR GALICIA
International borders, 1920-1939
Territory claimed by Western Ukrainian National Republic, 1918-1919
Polish palatinates (Województwa), 1920-1939
0 50 MILES
0 50 KILOMETERS
N
KIELCE
LUBLIN
Chełm
Zamość
Vistula
Buh
San
POLISSIA
Luts'k
VOLHYNIA
VOLHYNIA
POLAND
Brody
UKRAINIAN
S.S.R.
Dunajec
CRACOW
Nowy Sącz
Wisłok
L'VIV
Przemyśl
L'viv
Seret
Sanok
Ternopil'
LEMKIAN REGION
Berezhany
Zbruch
Drohobych
CARPATHIAN
Dniester
TERNOPIL'
Prešov
Chortkiv
CZECHOSLOVAKIA
Stanyslaviv
SLOVAKIA
STANYSLAVIV
Kam"ianets' Podil's'kyí
Zalishchyky
MOUNTAINS
Uzhhorod
Kolomyia
Khotin
SUBCARPATHIAN RUS'
Tysa
Cheremosh
Chernivtsi
Prut
BUKOVINA
HUNGARY
Sighet
ROMANIA

the integral nationalism developed by Dmytro Dontsov (1883–1973), the OUN demanded strict discipline from its members and advocated a Ukrainian national ideal that would embrace all aspects of Galician society. The isolated acts of terror, assassinations, bombings, and sabotage directed by the UVO during the 1920s against Polish authority prompted acts of government retaliation that reached their most intense pitch during the so-called pacification campaign, carried out by the Polish army and gendarmerie between September 16 and November 30, 1930. Pacification took the form of beatings and arrests leveled against Ukrainians especially in villages, and the sacking and closing of Ukrainian reading rooms, cultural centers, newspaper offices, and cooperatives.

As a result of the pacification campaign, Polish and Ukrainian societies became totally polarized, so that the more moderate tactics of the UNDO were rapidly superseded by an increase in the number of violent acts carried out by the OUN. There still were attempts at Polish-Ukrainian political compromise during the mid-1930s (the so-called period of ''normalization''), but this resulted in no real change in the situation. By 1938, both Ukrainian and Polish societies were wracked by anxiety over the imminent outbreak of armed conflict in Europe. On Steptember 1, 1939, that conflict did come and within a few weeks Polish control of Ukrainian Galicia came to an end.

General surveys

For the most part, the literature on interwar Ukrainian Galicia is marked by a decided lack of serious scholarly writings. What is available consists primarily of a few general accounts and many more works that deal with specific topics or time periods. These are primarily: (1) accounts by participants in the historical process (usually of factual value but often lacking in perspective); (2) polemics defending Polish or Ukrainian viewpoints; (3) documents of a diplomatic nature; and (4) writings by Soviet authors who are intent upon emphasizing the plight of the Ukrainian workers and the activity of the Communist party in the region.

Only a few works focus specifically on the two decades of interwar Ukrainian Galicia. These consist of an extended essay by three Polish writers who in 1938 already reflected on the failure of Warsaw's efforts to carry out a policy of national assimilation in eastern Galicia,[1] and of monographs by Mykola Kravets', Mykhailo Herasymenko, and Bohdan Dudykevych, the leading Soviet writers on the period, who are very critical of both ''imperialist'' Polish rule and the activity of

1 Aleksander Bocheński, Stanisław Łoś, and Włodzimierz Bączkowski, *Problem polsko-ukraiński w Ziemi Czerwieńskiej,* 2nd ed. (Warsaw: Polityka 1938).

"bourgeois-nationalist" Ukrainian leaders.[2] More representative of the existing literature are numerous polemical pamphlets. From Polish writers, these works reflect views expressed in 1919, trying to justify Polish control over all of Galicia because of the "absolute inferiority of the Ruthenian element,"[3] and later essays that may express sympathy for some Ukrainian demands, although they still argue for the advantages of Polish rule in Galicia.[4] Ukrainian essays on the same period stress the absolute need for self-determination, whether it be brought about by political or military means.[5] A collection of twelve polemical pamphlets from

2 Mykola M. Kravets', *Narysy robitnychoho rukhu v Zakhidnii Ukraïni v 1921–1939 rr.* (Kiev: AN URSR 1959); M.P. Herasymenko and B.K. Dudykevych, *Borot'ba trudiashchykh Zakhidnoï Ukraïny za vozz''iednannia z Radians'koiu Ukraïnoiu (1921–1939 rr.)* (Kiev: Derzhpolitvydav URSR 1955); M. Herasymenko and B. Dudykevych, *Borot'ba trudiashchykh Zakhidnoï Ukraïny za vozz''iednannia z Radians'koiu Ukraïnoiu* (Kiev 1960).

See also V.Iu. Tverdokhlib, *Solidarnist' u borot'bi za vyzvolennia: dopomoha hromads'kosti Kraïny Rad zakhidno-ukraïns'kym trudiashchym u borot'bi za vozz''iednannia v iedynii ukraïns'kii radians'kii derzhavi, 1917–1939* (L'viv: Vyshcha shkola 1978).

3 The quote comes from Henri Grappin, *Polonais et ruthènes: la question de Galicie* (Paris 1919). See also W. Lutosławski and E. Romer, *The Ruthenian Question in Galicia* (Paris 1919); I. Panenko, *La Galicie: pays polonais* (Paris: Bureau polonais de publications politiques 1919); I. Pannenkowa, *Punkty Wilsona a Galicja wschodnia* (Warsaw and L'viv: Polskie Towarzystwo Nauczycieli Szkół Wyższych 1919); and Eugeniusz Romer, *W obronie Galicyi* (L'viv: Książnica polska, 1919).

4 The Polish pamphlet literature from the interwar period is very extensive: see the national minority bibliography listed in chapter 1, n. 34. The most prolific authors were M. Feliński, *Ukraińcy w Polsce odrodzonej* (Warsaw 1931), in Ukrainian as *Ukraïntsi u vidrodzhenii Pol'shchi* (L'viv 1931), in English as *The Ukrainians in Poland* (London: p.a. 1931), and in French as *Les ukrainiens dans la Pologne restaurée* (Warsaw: Institut polonais de collaboration avec l'étranger 1931), the latter reprinted in *Seeds of Conflict* (see n. 6 below); Stanisław Łoś, "The Ukrainian Question in Poland," *Slavonic and East European Review*, IX [27] (London 1931), pp. 116–125; idem, "O konstruktywną politykę ukraińska w Polsce," *Nasza Przyszłość*, XXI (Warsaw 1932), pp. 82–113, reprinted as *O konstruktywną politykę na Rusi Czerwonej* (Warsaw 1932) and in Ukrainian as *Za konstruktyvnu polityku na Chervonii Rusy* (L'viv: UNO 1933); idem, *Mizhnarodnie polozhennia Pol'shchi ta halyts'ki ukraïntsi* (L'viv 1932); and idem, "Sytuacja międzynarodowa a Ukraińcy haliccy," *Nasza Przyszłość*, XXX (Warsaw 1933), reprinted separately (Warsaw 1933); and Leon Wasilewski, *Polska dla Polaków czy dla wszystkich obywateli polskich* (Warsaw 1924); idem, *Sprawa kresów i mniejszości narodowych w Polsce* (Warsaw, 1925).

There is also some Polish irredentist literature on eastern Galicia from the post-1945 period: Stanisław Skrzypek, *The Problem of Eastern Galicia* (London: Polish Association for the South-Eastern Provinces 1948); S. Skrzypek, *Sprawa ukraińska* (London 1953); and Stanisław J. Paprocki, *Kwestia ukraińska* (London 1953).

5 *The Ukrainian Question: A Peace Problem* (Geneva: Executive of Ukrainian Nationalists 1928); Stepan Tomashivs'kyi, *Desiat' lit ukraïns'koho pytannia v Pol'shchi* (L'viv: p.a. 1929); Basil Paneyko, "Galicia and the Polish-Ukrainian Problem," *The Slavonic and East European Review*, IX [27] (London 1931), pp. 567–587; Gregory Chomyszyn, *Problem ukraiński*

these years representing both Polish and Ukrainian viewpoints on Galicia was recently reprinted.[6]

As for statistical data, these are available in the published results of the Polish censuses of 1921 and 1931. Three volumes from each census are devoted to Galicia, indicating the size, location, and occupation of the inhabitants.[7] Because of the sensitivity about national identity and the resultant accusations of national assimilation, the official statistics became themselves the subject of both praise and criticism.[8] The controversial problem of the ethnographic boundary between Poles and Ukrainians and the interrelationship between religious and national identity has also engendered a large literature, especially by the Ukrainian Volodymyr Kubiiovych and the Pole Alfons Krysiński.[9]

(Warsaw 1933), originally in *Nasza Przyszłość,* XXIX and XXX (Warsaw 1933); Semen Shevchuk, *Pora skazaty pravdu pro nashi vyzvol'ni zmahannia dobytysia voli dlia halyts'koï zemli 1918–1939* (Toronto: p.a. 1965).

6 *Seeds of Conflict Series I: Irredentist and National Questions in Central Europe, 1913–1939,* vol. 8: *Poland,* 2 pts (Nendeln, Liechtenstein: Kraus Reprint 1973).

7 *Statystyka Polski: pierwszy powszechny spis Rzeczypospolitej Polskiej z dnia 30 września 1921–mieszkania, ludność, stosunki zawodowe,* vol. XXIII: *Województwo Stanisławowskie;* vol. XXVII: *Województwo Lwowskie;* and vol. XXIX: *Województwo Tarnopolskie* (Warsaw: Główny Urząd Statystyczny Rzeczypospolitej Polskiej 1927).

8 M. Prószyński, *Spis ludności i jego wielka ważność dla Wschodniej Małopolski* (Warsaw 1921); M. Sadovs'kyi, *Liudnist' zakhidnoukraïns'kykh zemel' po pol's'komu perepysu 30 veresnia 1921* (L'viv 1927); J. Suski, *Statystyka narodowościowa Rzeczypospolitej opracowana na podstawie wyników spisu ludności z dnia 30 września 1921* (Warsaw 1925).

9 Volodymyr Kubijovyč, *Etnichni hrupy pivdennozakhidn'oï Ukraïny (Halychyny) na 1.1. 1939 r.,* in *Zapysky NTSh,* CLX (London, Munich, New York, and Paris 1953); Volodymyr Kubiiovych, *Zakhidni ukraïns'ki zemli v mezhakh Pol'shchi 1920–1939* (Chicago and New York: Ukraïns'kyi publitsystychno-naukovyi instytut 1963), in English: *Western Ukraine Within Poland, 1920–39: Ethnic Relationships* (Chicago: Ukrainian Research and Information Institute 1963); Alfons Krysiński, ''Liczba i rozmieszczenie Ukraińców w Polsce,'' *Sprawy Narodowościowe,* II, 6 (Warsaw 1928), 651–707, also separately in Bibljoteka 'Spraw Narodowościowych', no. 6 (Warsaw 1929); idem, ''Rozwój stosunków etnicznych w Ziemi Czerwieńskiej w Polsce Odrodzonej,'' *Sprawy Narodowościowe,* IX, 5 and 6 (Warsaw 1935), pp. 387–412 and 555–584, also separately (Warsaw 1936); idem, ''Ludność ukraińska (ruska) w Polsce w świetle spisu 1931 r.,'' *Sprawy Narodowościowe,* XI, 6 (Warsaw 1937), pp. 567–591, also separately (Warsaw 1938).

See also Kazimierz Piątkowski, *Rozwój stosunków wyznaniowych i narodowościowych Małopolski Wschodniej: Materiały dła celów pracy społecznej* (L'viv 1936); Aleksander Aland, ''Układ stosunków wyznaniowo-zawodowych wśród ludności z województw południowo-wschodnich,'' *Sprawy Narodowościowe,* XIII, 1–2 (Warsaw 1939), pp. 14–42; and chapter 10, n. 4.

Establishment of Polish rule 1918–1923

The historical literature on certain aspects of the interwar years is more abundant. The most detailed coverage deals with the period from the outbreak of the Polish-Ukrainian war in November 1918 to the international recognition of Polish control of the area in March 1923. Recently published collections of documents on Polish-Ukrainian and Polish-Soviet relations include much material on the military, diplomatic, and social status of Galicia.[10] The most detailed histories of these early years are by the former Sich Riflemen officer Vasyl' Kuchabs'kyi, and the socialist leader Matvii Stakhiv, both of whom describe with sympathy the political, diplomatic, and military efforts to establish a viable western Ukrainian state.[11] On the other hand, in his history of attempts throughout the Ukraine to gain independence between 1917 and 1923, Izydor Nahaievs'kyi includes an extensive chapter on Galicia in which he is very critical of local leaders for their supposed lack of sufficient concern for the larger Ukrainian problem.[12] The Soviet view, which is negative toward both the Polish state (acting in collusion with western imperialists) and "Ukrainian bourgeois nationalists" (struggling for independence in order to preserve their own control over the downtrodden masses), is best outlined in a monogrpah by Iurii Slyvka.[13]

10 *Ukraine and Poland in Documents, 1918–1922*, 2 vols., ed. Taras Hunczak, Shevchenko Scientific Society, Sources for the History of Rus'-Ukraine, Vol. XII (New York, Paris, Sydney, and Toronto 1983); *Dokumenty i materiały do historii stosunków polsko-radzieckich*, ed. Natalia Gąsiorowska-Grabowska, I.A. Chrienow, et al., 9 vols [1917–1949] (Warsaw: Książka i Wiedza 1962–74), see especially vols I–IV (March 1917–May 1926) and the references in the indexes to "Galicja Wschodnia" and "Ukraina Zachodnia."

11 W. Kutschabsky, *Die Westukraine im Kampfe mit Polen und dem Bolschewismus in den Jahren 1918–1925*, Schriften der kriegsgeschichtlichen Abteilung im historischen Seminar der Friedrich-Wilhelms-Universität Berlin, vol. VIII (Berlin: Junker und Dunnhaupt Vlg. 1934); Matvii Stakhiv, *Zakhidna Ukraïna: narys istoriï derzhavnoho budivnytstva ta zbroinoï i dyplomatychnoï oborony v 1918–1923*, 5 vols [given as vol. III, IV, V, VI, pts 1–2] (Scranton, Pa.: Ukraïns'kyi Robitnychyi Soiuz 1959–61), this work combined with two other volumes covering the years 1772 to 1918 has been issued in an abridged English edition: Matthew Stachiw and Jaroslaw Sztendera, *Western Ukraine at the Turning Point of Europe's History, 1918–1923*, 2 vols, Shevchenko Scientific Society Ukrainian Studies (English section), vols. 5–6 (New York 1969–71).

See also Sydir Iaroslavyn, *Vyzvol'na borot'ba na zakhidn'o-ukraïns'kykh zemliakh u 1918–1923 rokakh* (Philadelphia 1956); and Stepan Ripets'kyi, *Ukraïns'ko-pol's'kyi protses 1918–1923 pered svitovym trybunalom* (Chicago and New York: Ukr. publitsystychno-naukovyi instytut 1963), in English translation: *Ukrainian-Polish Diplomatic Struggle 1918–1923* (Chicago: Ukrainian Research and Information Institute 1963).

12 Isidore Nahayewsky, *History of the Modern Ukrainian State 1917–1923* (Munich: Ukrainian Free University and Academy of Arts and Sciences 1966), especially chapter 4.

13 Iurii Iu. Slyvka, *Borot'ba trudiashchykh Skhidnoï Halychyny proty inozemnoho ponevolennia* (Kiev: Naukova dumka 1973).

Polish-Ukrainian war and the Ukrainian Galician Army, 1918–1919

The Polish-Ukrainian war of November 1918 to July 1919 and the campaigns of the Ukrainian Galician Army have been the subject of much writing. The history of the army after 1918 is treated in general histories of the Ukrainian Sich Riflemen, from which it in part evolved after World War I,[14] and in five volumes of memoirs, documents, eyewitness reports, and other studies of the army's activity between 1918 and 1920.[15]

The "November days," which lasted from November 1 to 22, when Ukrainian military forces led by Captain Dmytro Vitovs'kyi (1887–1919) took over L'viv and then fought to maintain eastern Galicia, are treated in detail by both Ukrainian and Polish authors. The Ukrainian view, best represented in detailed works by Oleksa Kuz'ma and Mykhailo Hutsuliak, considers these few weeks as a glorious epoch when Galician Ukrainians were, despite great odds, on the verge of achieving independence for the first time in the modern era.[16] Polish writings on the November days are even more prolific. As evident in several works, the most comprehensive of which are by Czesław Mączyński, Eugeniusz Wawrzkowicz, Józef Klink, and Rosa Bailley, the Poles consider the retaking of L'viv, begun on November 1 with an underground movement led by Captain Czesław Mączyński, as the first step toward what eventually resulted in a successful effort to bring all of Galicia together with other historic Polish lands under the scepter of a restored independent Poland.[17]

14 See chapter 6, n. 243.

15 *Ukraïns'ka Halyts'ka Armiia u 40-richchia ïï uchasty u vyzvol'nykh zmahanniakh*, 5 vols (Winnipeg: Dmytro Mykytiuk 1958–77).

See also the general history by Bohdan Hnatkovych and Osyp Dumin, "Ukraïns'ka Halyts'ka Armiia," in Ivan Kryp''iakevych and Bohdan Hnatkevych, eds, *Istoriia ukraïns'koho viis'ka* (L'viv: Ivan Tyktor 1936; reprinted Winnipeg 1953), pp. 462–535; and the biographical dictionary of chaplains who served in the army: Ivan Lebedovych, *Polevi dukhovnyky Ukraïns'koï Halyts'koï Armiï* (Winnipeg: p.a. 1963).

16 Oleksa Kuz'ma, *Lystopadovi dni 1918 r.* (L'viv: p.a. 1931; reprinted New York: Chervona kalyna 1960); Mykhailo Hutsuliak, *Pershyi Lystopad 1918 roku na zakhidnikh zemliakh Ukraïny zi spohadamy i zhyttiepysamy chleniv komitetu vykonavtsiv lystopadovoho chynu* (New York: Komitet vykonavtsiv lystopadovoho chynu 1973).

See also the shorter essay by Petro Oliinyk, *Lystopadovyi zryv: povstannia ukraïns'koï derzhavy na zakhidnikh zemliakh v Lystopadi 1918 r.*, Narodnia Biblioteka 'Nastup', no. 11 (Prague: Proboiem 1941); and the biography by Myron Zaklyns'kyi, *Dmytro Vitovs'kyi* (New York: Chervona kalyna 1967).

17 Czesław Mączyński, *Boje lwowskie*, pt. 1: *Oswobodzenie Lwowa (1–24 listopada 1918 r.)*, 2 vols (Warsaw: Nakł. Spółki Wyd. Rzeczpospolita 1921); Eugeniusz Wawrzkowicz and Józef Klink, eds, *Obrona Lwowa 1–22 listopada 1918: organizacja listopadowej obrony Lwowa: ewidencja uczestników walk* (L'viv: Nakł. Towarzystwa Badania Historii Obrony Lwowa i

Besides the November days, several other works are devoted to the changing fortunes of the Polish-Ukrainian war to July 1919;[18] the last major (Chortkiv) offensive of the Ukrainian Galician Army in early June 1919;[19] the alliance in November 1919 with the White Russian General Denikin and, because of this, the resultant trial of the unit's commander, General Myron Tarnavs'kyi (who was acquitted);[20] and the last stage of the Ukrainian Galician Army's existence as part of the Bolshevik Red Army (March–April 1920).[21] There are also several memoirs by participants in various Galician-Ukrainian diplomatic efforts and military campaigns from the era,[22] and a few studies on the fate of Galician-Ukrainian

---

Województw Południowo-Wschodnich 1939); Rosa Bailly, *A City Fights for Freedom: The Rising of Lwów in 1918–1919* (London: Publishing Committee Leopolis 1956).

See also the shorter works by Władysław Stesłowicz, *Relacja z czasu walk listopadowych o Lwów* (n.p., n.d.); Stanisław Łapiński-Nilski and Alexander Kron, *Listopad we Lwowie (1918 r.)* (Warsaw: Ogniwo 1920); Witold Hupert, *Walki o Lwów* (Warsaw 1933); Stanisław Rutkowski, *Odsiecz Lwowa w listopadzie 1918* (L'viv 1928); and Jan Rogowski, *W obronie Lwowa* (L'viv: Nakł. Księgarni A. Krawczyński 1939). On the international aspects of the Polish-Ukrainian war in Galicia, see Aleksy Deruga, *Polityka wschodnia Polski wobec ziem Litwy, Białorusi i Ukrainy (1918–1919)* (Warsaw: Książka i Wiedza 1969), especially pp. 223–253.

18 The Ukrainian viewpoint is best represented in three comprehensive works: *'Zoloti vorota': istoriia Sichovykh Stril'tsiv 1917–1919* (L'viv: Chervona kalyna 1937); Vasyl' Kuchabs'kyi et al., *Korpus Sichovykh Stril'tsiv: voienno-istorychnyi narys* (Chicago: Iuvileinyi komitet dlia vidznachennia 50-richchia stvorennia formatsiï Sichovykh Stril'tsiv 1969); Lev Shankovs'kyi, *Ukraïns'ka Halyts'ka Armiia: voienno-istorychna studiia* (Winnipeg: D. Mykytiuk 1974); and in shorter studies by V.K., *Sichovi Stril'tsi: ïkh istoriia i kharakter* (L'viv: Ivan Kvasnytsia 1920); Mykhailo Omelianovych-Pavlenko, *Ukraïns'ko-pol's'ka viina 1918–1919* (Prague 1929); Marko Bezruchko, *Sichovi Stril'tsi v borot'bi za derzhavnist'* (Kalisz 1932); and Antin Krezyb [Osyp Dumin], *Narys istoriï ukraïns'ko-pol's'koï viiny 1918–1919* (L'viv: Chervona kalyna 1933; reprinted New York: Oko 1966).

The Polish viewpoint appears in Józef Sopotnicki, *Kampania polsko-ukraińska: doświadzenia operacyjne i bojowe* (L'viv: Spółka Nakł. 'Odrodzenie' 1921); *W obronie Lwowa i kresów wschodnich polegli od 1go listopada 1918 do 30go czerwca 1919 r.* (L'viv: Nakł. Straży Mogił Polskich Bohaterów 1926).

19 *Chortkivs'ka ofenzyva* (Munich: Bratstvo Kol. Voiakiv 1-oï Ukraïns'koï Dyviziï UNA 1953).

20 Ievhen Konovalets', *Prychynky do istoriï ukraïns'koï revoliutsiï* (L'viv 1928), 2nd ed. (n.p.: Provid ukraïns'kykh natsionalistiv 1948); Myron Tarnavs'kyi, *Protses henerala Myrona Tarnavs'koho* (Winnipeg: Dmytro Mykytiuk 1976). On the Tarnavs'kyi trial, see also the diary of the supreme commander of the Ukrainian Galician Army, in n. 22, *Dennyk,* below.

21 Nykyfor Hirniak, *Ostannii akt trahediï Ukraïns'koï Halyts'koï Armiï* (Perth Amboy, NJ: Ukraïns'kyi Viis'kovo-Istorychnyi Instytut n.d.).

22 Osyp Nazaruk, *Rik na Velykii Ukraïni: konspekt spomyniv z ukraïns'koï revolutsiï* (Vienna: Ukraïns'kyi prapor 1920; reprinted New York: Hoverlia 1978); Osyp Levyts'kyi, *Halyts'ka armiia na Velykii Ukraïni (spomyny z chasu vid lypnia do hrudnia 1919)* (Vienna 1921); Evhen Borodyievych, *V chotyrokutnyku smerty: prychynky do trahediï UHA na Velykii Ukraïni*

World War I prisoners of war in Russia. After the Bolshevik Revolution, many were released and in November 1917 formed the Voluntary Battalion of Sich Riflemen, a unit led by Colonel Ievhen Konovalets' that served in the army of the Ukrainian National Republic in the Dnieper Ukraine. However, a few other Galicians, mostly Russophiles, joined the Czechoslovak Legion, which had its own Carpatho-Russian unit that lasted from August 1918 until the following spring when it merged with White Russian armies.[23] Others joined the White Russian Volunteer Army of General Lavr Kornilov (1870–1918) in the hope of creating a democratic Russia that would include Galicia within its borders.[24] Finally, as the Soviet Ukrainian historian Iaroslav Dashkevych has pointed out, several leftist and socialist-oriented Galician prisoners of war took part in the Ukrainian section of the Tashkent Bolshevik party and later played leading roles in the new Turkestan Soviet Republic.[25]

Galicia and the international scene, 1918–1923

Writings that deal with the period 1919 to 1923, when the legal status of eastern Galicia was not yet decided upon in the international forum, consist primarily of studies and documents on four subjects: the initial years of the Polish administration; the diplomatic efforts launched first at home and then abroad by Ukrainian and Polish leaders; the reaction of the Entente to the problem of eastern Galicia; and the establishment of a short-lived Soviet Galician Republic.

Mykhailo Lozyns'kyi and Petro Karmans'kyi have provided the most detailed account of Polish rule between 1918 and 1920. Their account, interspersed with numerous quotations from the contemporary press and lists of arrested Ukrainians, stresses the various kinds of repression that accompanied the Polish ad-

---

(L'viv: 'Nove zhyttia' 1921; reprinted New York: Hoverlia 1975); Iurko Tiutiunnyk, *Zymovyi pokhid 1919–20 rr.* (Kolomyia: Trembita 1923) 2nd ed. (New York: Vyd-vo Chartoryis'kykh 1966); Stepan Shukhevych, *Spomyny z Ukraïns'koï halyts'koï armiï (1918–1920),* 5 vols (L'viv: Chervona kalyna 1928–29); Roman Dashkevych, *Artyleriia Sichovykh Stril'tsiv u borot'bi za zoloti kyïvs'ki vorota* (New York: Chervona kalyna 1965); Osyp Stanymir, *Moia uchast' u vyzvol'nykh zmahanniakh 1917–1920* (Toronto 1966); *Dennyk Nachal'noï Komandy Ukraïns'koï Halyts'koï Armiï* (New York: Chervona kalyna 1974); Volodymyr Galan, *Bateriia smerty* (Jersey City, NJ: Chervona kalyna, 1968).

23 František Šíp, ''Naše finanční pomoc při vzniku karpatoruských vojsk na Sibiři,'' *Naše revoluce,* III (Prague 1925–26), pp. 386–391.

24 V.R. Vavrik, *Karpatorossy v Kornilovskom pokhodie i dobrovol'cheskoi armii* (L'viv 1923).

25 Ia.R. Dashkevych, ''Halychany-internatsionalisty u radians'komu Turkestani v svitli novoznaidenykh dzherel 1917–1920 rr.,'' in *Istorychni dzherel ta ïkh vykorystannia,* vol. III (Kiev: Naukova dumka 1968), pp. 91–116.

vance.[26] There are several other documentary reports compiled by Ukrainians,[27] as well as similar documents and polemics by Polish authors who describe the same events in terms of the alleged ''Ruthenian terror'' in Galicia.[28]

With regard to diplomatic efforts, several memoranda are available indicating that, while leaders from the Western Ukrainian People's Republic were calling for independence or union with Ukrainians in the former Russian Empire, local Russophile leaders were proposing unification of Galicia with a democratic Russia,[29] and when that option proved impractical, they hoped for union at least of the Lemkian region with other ''Carpatho-Russians'' in the new state of Czechoslovakia.[30]

26 Mykhailo Lozyns'kyi and P. Karmans'kyi, *Krivava knyha*, pt 1: *Materialy do pol's'koï invaziï na ukraïns'ki zemli Skhidnoï Halychyny 1918–1919* (Vienna 1919) and pt 2: *Ukraïns'ka Halychyna pid okupatsiieiu Pol'shchi v rr. 1919–1920* (Vienna: Vydannia Uriadu Zakhidno-Ukraïns'koï Narodn'oï Republyky 1921).

27 *Das Buch der blutigen Greueltaten: Beiträge zur Martyrologie der ukrainischen Bevölkerung Ostgaliziens während der polnischen Invasion, 1918/19* ([Vienna]: Regierung der Westukrainischen Volksrepublik 1919), translated into English as *The Bloody Book: Returns Concerning the Invasion of the Poles in Ukrainian Territory of East-Galicia in 1918/19* ([Vienna]: Government of the West Ukrainian Republic 1919) and reprinted in *Seeds of Conflict Series I,* vol. VIII: *Poland,* pt 1 (Nendeln, Liechtenstein: Kraus Reprint 1973); Voldemar Temnytsky and Joseph Bouratchinski, *Les atrocités polonaises en Galicie ukrainienne* (Paris: Bureau ukrainien 1919), reprinted also in *Seeds of Conflict Series I;* Osyp Megas, *Tragediia halyts'koï Ukraïny: materiialy pro pol's'ku invaziiu, pol's'ki varvarstva i pol's'ku okupatsiiu Skhidnoï Halychyny za krovavi roky: 1918, 1919 i 1920* (Winnipeg 1920); *A Plea for the Right to Live in Behalf of the People of East Galicia* (New York: Ukrainian Information Bureau 1922).

28 Henri Grappin, *La terreur ruthène en Galicie* (Paris 1919); *Documents rutheno-ukrainiens* (Paris: Bureau polonais de publications politiques 1919).

29 *Supplique: les Russes des Karpathes délaissés et dignes de protection* (Marburg 1917?); Dmitrij Markoff, *Mémoire sur les aspirations nationales des petits-russiens de l'ancien empire austro-hongrois* (n.p. 1918); *La Russie Carpathique: les raisons de sa réunion à la Russie* (Paris 1919).

30 Anthony Beskid and Dimitry Sobin, *The Origin of the Lems, Slavs of Danubian Provenance: Memorandum to the Peace Conference Concerning their National Claims* (Prešov 1919); Dimitrij Sobin, *Protêt contre le partage de la contrée russe des Carpathes: appel à la justice du Congrès de la Paix à Paris* (Prague: Ed. Grégr et fils 1919).

See also the Soviet explanation of these developments in R.H. Symonenko, ''Do pytannia pro Skhidnu Halychynu naperedodni Paryz'koï myrnoï konferentsiï 1919 r.,'' in *Naukovi zapysky Instytutu istoriï,* vol. IX (Kiev: AN URSR 1957). For Czechoslovak policy toward the Ukrainian problem during this period, including eastern Galicia, see Krzysztof Lewandowski, *Sprawa ukraińska w polityce zagranicznej Czechosłowacji w latach 1918–1932* (Wrocław: ZNIO–PAN 1974).

The more important, although ultimately unsuccessful, diplomatic efforts were carried out by the Western Ukrainian People's Republic headed by Ievhen Petrushevych. By late 1919 this government had its headquarters in exile in Vienna and its representatives in several European capitals, most especially at the Paris Peace Conference. A member of the government, Mykhailo Lozyns'kyi, has provided the best account of its activity in Vienna, Paris, and its relations with Dnieper Ukrainians; in another work, he has focused on the role of president-designate Petrushevych.[31] The memoirs of the Western Ukrainian government's minister of foreign affairs, L'ongin Tsehel's'kyi, are also useful.[32] After most of the Dnieper Ukraine was overrun by the Bolsheviks, White Russians, and peasant anarchists, and the government of the Ukrainian National Republic had concluded an alliance with Poland, Galician-Ukrainian leaders pressed their case for a separate independent western Ukrainian state. The government's laws and policy statements,[33] its petitions to the Entente and other powers,[34] and its calls justifying independence in economic as well as political terms have been published.[35] There

31 Mykhailo Lozyns'kyi, *Halychyna v rr. 1918–1920* (Vienna: Institut sociologique ukrainien 1922), reprinted with intro. by Ivan Kedryn (New York: Chervona kalyna 1970); idem, *Moie spivrobitnytstvo z Prezydentom Petrushevychom* (L'viv 1925).

32 L'ongin Tsehel's'kyi, *Vid legend do pravdy: spomyny pro podiï v Ukraïni zviazani z pershym lystopadom 1918 r.* (New York and Philadelphia: Bulava 1960).

33 *Les documents les plus importants de la république ukrainienne de l'ouest* (Vienna 1918); Ivan Khrapko, *Zbirnyk zakoniv i postanov ukraïns'koho pravytel'stva vidnosno zakordonnykh instytutsiï* (Vienna 1919).

34 Michael Lozynsky, *Décisions du conseil suprême sur la Galicie orientale* (Paris: Bureau ukrainien 1919); Mykhailo Lozyns'kyi, *Pol's'ka kol'onizatsiia Skhidnoï Halychyny* (Vienna: 'Ukraïns'kyi Prapor' 1921); *Politychne pytannia Skhidnoï Halychyny (Memorial Z.U.T. Ligy Natsiï na VII. Konferentsiiu Tov. Ligy Natsiï u Vidni)* (Vienna 1923); *For Galicia! Appeal to world democracy* (Geneva: Ukrainian Socialistic Revolutionary Party 1920); Julian Batchinsky, *Protest of the Ukrainian Republic to the United States against the delivery of Eastern Galicia to the Polish domination* (Washington, DC 1919); *To the civilised nations of the world* (Geneva: Committee of the Independent Ukraine 1920); E. Petrusevic [Petrushevych], *Mémoire concernant les territories ukrainiens sous la domination polonaise présenté par la président du Conseil National Ukrainien à la 5me Assemblée de la Société des Nations* (Geneva 1924). See also the several documents in the collection edited by Hunzak, above, note 10.

35 The arguments that eastern Galicia was potentially an economically self-sufficient unit were put forth most forcefully in *La situation économique de la Galicie Orientale et son importance pour la reconstruction de l'Europe* (Geneva: Conseil national ukrainien 1922); and *Eastern Galicia an Independent Commonwealth* (n.p.: National Council of Eastern Galicia n.d.). See also S.R. [Stepan Rudnyts'kyi], *Ekonomichni osnovy halyts'koï derzhavnosti* (L'viv and Vienna: 'Ukraïns'kyi prapor' 1921); and S.R. [Stepan Rudnyts'kyi], *Halychyna i novi derzhavy Ievropy* (Vienna: Ukraïns'kyi prapor 1921).

The political argument that a Ukrainian-Galician state could become the Switzerland of the east is found in Mykhailo Lozyns'kyi, *Za derzhavnu nezalezhnist' Halychyny: chomu*

are also studies of the Western Ukrainian government's presence during the negotiations and its protests over the treaty signed at Riga on March 18, 1921, when Soviet Russia and Soviet Ukraine recognized Polish control over all of Galicia.[36] The diplomatic activity of the Polish government at the Paris Peace Conference regarding eastern Galicia is revealed in a collection of over 100 documents from late 1918 and 1919,[37] as well as in two solid studies by the Polish scholars Zofia Zaks and Andrzej Partyka, who also discuss the aborted Polish proposals for autonomy in the region.[38]

With regard to the Entente and its participation in redrawing the map of eastern Europe after World War I, there are still no general studies of western policy toward Galicia during this period. Certain aspects have been treated, however, such as the views of western experts and Peace Conference advisers regarding eastern Galicia,[39] the interest of certain countries, especially France and England,

---

ukraïns'ka Halychyna ne mozhe pryity pid Pol'shchu (Vienna: Vydannia Prezydiï Ukraïns'koï Natsional'noï Rady 1921); *Nekhai zhyve Nezalezhna Halyts'ka Derzhava!: zbirka statei* (Vienna: 'Ukraïns'kyi prapor' 1922); *Pour l'indépendence de la Galicie: pourquoi la Galicie ne doit pas faire partie de la Pologne* (Vienna: Présidence du Conseil national ukrainien 1921), reprinted in *Seeds of Conflict Series I,* vol. 8, pt 2 (Nendeln, Liechtenstein 1973); *The Case for the Independence of Galicia* (London: President of the Ukrainian National Council 1922), in French translation as *Preuves pour l'Indépendence de la Galicie Orientale* (Vienna: Présidence du Conseil national ukrainien 1922).

36 *Ukraïns'ka delegatsiia Skhidnoï Halychyny v Ryzi* (Vienna 1920); O.Iu. Karpenko, "Pytannia pro skhidnu Halychynu na radians'ko-pol's'kykh perehovorakh u Ryzi v 1920 r.," in *Pytannia istoriï narodiv SRSR,* vol II (Kharkiv 1966), pp. 54–63. See also the memoirs of a Galician participant at Riga: Osyp Nazaruk, *Halyts'ka delegatsiia v Ryzi 1920 r.: spomyny uchasnyka* (L'viv 1930).

37 *Sprawy polskie na Konferencji Pokojowej w Paryżu w 1919 r.: dokumenty i materiały,* vol. II (Warsaw PWN 1967), especially pt 4, "Galicja Wschodnia," pp. 213–376. See also the *Mémoire sur la Galicie* (Paris: Commission polonaise des travaux préparatiores au Congrès de la Paix 1919), reprinted in *Seeds of Conflict,* see n. 6 above.

38 Zofia Zaks, "Galicja Wschodnia w polskiej polityce zagranicznej (1921–1923)," in *Z dziejów stosunków polsko-radzieckich,* vol. VIII (Warsaw: Książka i Wiedza 1971), pp. 3–36; Andrzej Partyka, "Polskie koncepcje autonomii Galicji Wschodniej w latach 1919–1922," *Studia Historyczne,* XIX, 4 (Cracow 1976), pp. 563–576.

39 Leonid C. Sonevytsky, "The Ukrainian Question in R.H. Lord's Writings on the Paris Peace Conference," *Annals of the Ukrainian Academy of Arts and Sciences in the U.S.,* X, 1–2 (New York 1962–63), pp. 65–84; Henryk Batowski, "Linia Curzona a była Galicja Wschodnia," in *Z dziejów stosunków polsko-radzieckich,* vol. III (Warsaw: Książka i Wiedza 1968), pp. 170–177; Taras Hunczak, "Sir Lewis Namier and the Struggle for Eastern Galicia," *Harvard Ukrainian Studies,* I, 2 (Cambridge, Mass. 1977), pp. 198–210. See also Laurence Orzell, "A 'Hotly Disputed' Issue: Eastern Galicia at the Paris Peace Conference," *The Polish Review,* XXV, 1 (New York 1980), pp. 49–68.

in the oil fields of eastern Galicia,[40] the problem of eastern Galicia as a factor during the Polish-Soviet war of 1920,[41] and the role–as viewed by Soviet writers–of ''American imperialists'' in making eastern Galicia part of the mid-European buffer zone against Bolshevik Russia.[42]

Soviet interest in Galicia immediately after World War I took several concrete forms. Soviet writers are in particular concerned with stressing the importance of the Communist-led ''Drohobych armed revolt'' in the fall of 1919[43] and of the Galician Socialist Soviet Republic, which in the wake of Red Army victories against Poland was established in the region around Ternopil' between July 15 and September 23, 1920.[44] These and other revolutionary developments are considered by Soviet writers to have been of greater significance than the ''bourgeois and counterrevolutionary'' Western Ukrainian People's Republic.[45] Less emo-

40 Zofia Zaks, ''Walka dyplomatyczna o naftę wschodniogalicyjską 1918–1923,'' in *Z dziejów stosunków polsko-radzieckich*, vol. IV (Warsaw: Książka i Wiedza 1969), pp. 37–60; Barbara Ratyńska, *Rola nafty w kształtowaniu stosunku państw zachodnich do sprawy Galicji Wschodniej 1918–1919* (Warsaw: Polski Instytut Spraw Międzynarodnych 1957).

41 Zofia Zaks, ''Problem Galicji Wschodniej w czasie wojny polsko-radzieckiej,'' in *Studia z dziejów ZSRR i Europy Środkowej*, vol. VIII (Wrocław, Warsaw, Cracow, and Gdańsk: ZNIO–PAN 1972), pp. 79–109.

42 O.H. Tsybko, ''Amerykans'ki imperialisty–orhanizatory i natkhnennyky zakhvatu zakhidnoukraïns'kykh zemel' pol's'kymy panamy,'' *Naukovi zapysky LDU*, XXV: *Seriia istorychna*, 5 (L'viv 1953), pp. 47–54.

43 H. Barbara, *Drohobyts'ke povstannia* (L'viv: Tsentral'nyi komitet KPZU 1929); I. Bohodyst, *Borot'ba trudiashchykh Halychyny za Radians'ku vladu v 1918–1920 rr.* (L'viv: Knyzhkovo-zhurnal'ne vyd-vo 1952); O.Iu.Karpenko, ''Borot'ba robitnychoho klasu Skhidnoï Halychyny proty vlady ukraïns'koï burzhuaziï pid chas isnuvannia ZUNR,'' *Z istoriï zakhidnoukraïns'kykh zemel'*, vol. III, ed. I.P. Kryp''iakevych (Kiev: AN URSR 1958), pp. 69–96; O.Iu. Karpenko, ''Z istoriï revoliutsiinoï borot'by zakhidnoukraïns'kykh trudiashchykh za vladu Rad, za vozz''iednannia z Radians'koiu Ukraïnoiu (1918–1919 rr.),'' *Visnyk LDU: Seriia istorychna* [I] (L'viv 1965), pp. 64–71.

44 B.I. Tyshchyk, *Halyts'ka sotsialistychna Radians'ka respublika (1920)* (L'viv: LU 1970).
See also the memoirs of Galicians who were in Russia during the Bolshevik Revolution and then returned home to propagate revolution: *Za vladu Rad: spohady uchasnykiv Velykoï Zhovtnevoï sotsialistychnoï revoliutsiï ta borot'by za Radians'ku vladu na zakhidnoukraïns'kykh zemliakh* (L'viv: Knyzhkovo-zhurnal'ne vyd-vo 1957).

45 A.D. Iaroshenko, ''Vplyv Zhovtnevoï revoliutsiï na rozvytok revoliutsiinoho rukhu trudiashchykh zakhidnoukraïns'kykh zemel' (1917–1919 rr.),'' in *Bil'shovyky Ukraïny v borot'bi za peremohu Zhovtnevoï revoliutsiï* (Kiev 1957), pp. 377–410; V. Osechyns'kyi and P. Chelak, ''Vplyv velykoï zhovtnevoï sotsialistychnoï revoliutsiï na revoliutsiino-vyzvol'nu borot'bu trudiashchykh Zakhidnoï Ukraïny 1918–1923,'' in *40 rokiv Velykoho Zhovtnia* (L'viv 1957), pp. 153–186.
See also the Polish writer on this period: Janusz Radziejowski, ''Ideologiczne i organizacyjne kształtowanie się ruchu komunistycznego na terenie Ukrainy Zachodniej w latach 1918–1923,'' *Z Pola Walki*, XIV, 2 (Warsaw 1971), pp. 27–48.

tional is Zofia Zaks' analysis of Soviet Russia's continued interest (1920–1923) in eastern Galicia, first as a stepping stone to a potentially revived Soviet Hungary, then as terrain for revolutionary activity against Polish rule.[46]

Political developments, 1923–1939

A comprehensive and balanced history of Ukrainian Galicia between 1923 and 1939 remains to be written. For the most part, the published material that does exist consists of descriptions of a memoiristic and documentary nature, dealing with the negative aspects of Polish-Ukrainian relations and the reaction of both sides to an increasingly tense situation.

The best documentary source materials for this period are the stenographic records containing the debates and publications of the Polish Parliament. While Ukrainians from parts of Volhynia, Podlachia, Polisia, and the Chełm area participated in elections to the Polish Parliament in 1922, it was not until 1928 that the first Ukrainians from Galicia entered both the house of deputies (*Sejm*) and Senate (*Senat*). The interpellations of Ukrainian parliamentarians and the responses of their Polish counterparts provide a good picture of the kinds of problems that wracked eastern Galicia.[47] Some of the parliamentary debates from this period have been published separately,[48] and there are several studies of Galician Ukrainians in the Polish Parliament and of individual Ukrainian political parties.[49] Much valuable factual data from this period are also available in the

46 Zofia Zaks, "Radziecka Rosja i Ukraina wobec sprawy państwowej przynależności Galicji Wschodniej 1920–1923," in *Z dziejów stosunków polsko-radzieckich*, vol. VI (Warsaw: Książka i Wiedza 1970), pp. 69–95.

47 *Sprawozdanie stenograficzne Sejmu Ustawodawczego* [1919–1921] and *Sprawozdanie stenograficzne Sejmu Rzeczypospolitej* [1922–1937], 44 vols; *Sprawozdanie stenograficzne Senatu Rzeczypospolitej* [1922–1937], 8 vols. These volumes are unfortunately not indexed.

48 *Z trybuny: promovy ukraïns'kykh posliv i senatoriv u pol's'komu Soimi i Senati* (L'viv, Luts'k, Chełm, and Brest: Ukraïns'kyi posol's'kyi kliub 1925); *Sabotaż ukraiński i akcja pacyfikacyjna* (Warsaw: Polski Institut Współpracy z Zagranicą 1931).

49 Pavlo Lysiak, "Ukraïns'ke parliamentarne predstavnytstvo," *Kaliendar Tovarystva 'Prosvity' na rik 1929* (L'viv 1928), pp. 141–170; M. Feliński, "Ukraińcy w Izbach Ustawodawczych Polski Odrodzonej," *Sprawy Narodowościowe*, V, 6 (Warsaw 1931), pp. 566–600; idem, "Program polityczny Ukraińskiego Narodowo-Demokratycznego Objednanja (UNDO)," *ibid.*, I, 4 (Warsaw 1927), pp. 381–388; idem, "Program ukraińskiej Socjalistyczno-Radykalnej Partji," *ibid.*, II, 1 (Warsaw 1928), pp. 32–40.

See also the chapters on Ukrainian parties in the context of interwar Polish political life in Jerzy Holzer, *Mozaika polityczna Drugiej Rzeczpospolitej* (Warsaw: Książka i Wiedza 1974), especially pp. 241–253 and 531–551. On the Communist and other related parties, see also notes 72–80 below.

systematic chronicle of events on Ukrainians and Old Ruthenians that appeared six times a year between 1927 and 1939 in a Warsaw journal on minority affairs,[50] as well as in the memoirs of the Ukrainian Radical leader Ivan Makukh, Social Democrat Antin Chernets'kyi, and the journalist and UNDO supporter Ivan Kedryn-Rudnyts'kyi.[51]

Perhaps the most informative surveys on the interwar years are found in a balanced account by the Canadian-Ukrainian historian Bohdan Budurowycz and in several chapters dealing with eastern Galicia in monographs by the Polish scholars Mirosława Papierzyńska-Turek (on Ukrainians in Poland between 1922 and 1926) and Ryszard Torzecki (on the Ukrainian question and the Third Reich after 1933).[52] The Polish view of eastern Galicia during the interwar period is also found in chapters on Ukrainians in three works dealing with all minorities in Poland. Two of these works were published in the 1930s, and they argue that indeed the Polish government was trying to live in peace with Ukrainians and to protect their rights; the third is a recent monograph by Andrzej Chojnowski, who is much more critical of Poland's interwar minority policy.[53] The inevitable failure of Polish efforts at compromise was hastened by the formation of the fascist-oriented uniparty Bloc of National Unity (Obóz Zjednoczenia Narodowego), whose establishment in 1937 is described by E. Wynot.[54]

The largest amount of literature on political developments after 1923 deals on the one hand with the revolutionary and military approach to the Galician-Ukrainian problem adopted by the Ukrainian Military Organization (UVO) and its successor, the Organization of Ukrainian Nationalists (OUN), and on the other hand with the Polish reaction to such activity that took the form of periodic arrests and trials followed in the early 1930s by half hearted attempts at repression–a

50 See the sections ''Kronika ukraińska'' and ''Kronika: Starorusini'' in *Sprawy Narodowościowe*, I–XIII (Warsaw 1927–39); also the monthly *Biuletyn Polsko-Ukraiński*, I–VIII (Warsaw 1932–39).

51 Ivan Makukh, *Na narodnii sluzhbi* (Detroit: Ukraïns'ka vil'na hromada Ameryky 1958); Antin Chernets'kyi, *Spomyny z moho zhyttia* (London: Nashe slovo 1964); Ivan Kedryn, *Zhyttia-podiï-liudy: spomyny i komentari* (New York: Chervona kalyna 1976), especially pp. 102–337.

52 Bohdan Budurowycz, ''Poland and the Ukrainian Problem, 1921–1939,'' *Canadian Slavonic Papers*, XXV, 4 (Toronto, 1983), pp. 473–500; Mirosława Papierzyńska-Turek, *Sprawa ukraińska w Drugiej Rzeczypospolitej 1922–1926* (Cracow: Wydawnictwo Literackie 1979); Ryszard Torzecki, *Kwestia ukraińska w polityce III Rzeszy (1933–1945)* (Warsaw: Książka i Wiedza 1972), especially pp. 41–74, 79–91, 154–192.

53 Kazimierz Kierski, *Ochrona praw mniejszości w Polsce* (Poznań: p.a. 1933); S.J. Paprocki, ed., *Minority Affairs and Poland* (Warsaw: Nationality Research Institute 1935); Andrzej Chojnowski, *Koncepcje polityki narodowościowej rządów polskich w latach 1921–1939* (Wrocław, Warsaw, Cracow, and Gdańsk: ZNIO–PAN 1979).

54 E. Wynot, Jr., ''The Ukrainians and the Polish Regime, 1937–1939,'' *Ukraïns'kyi istoryk*, VII, 4 (New York and Munich 1970), pp. 44–60.

policy known as pacification. As for Ukrainian nationalism, the best work on its ideological background and subsequent practice as carried out by Galician leaders both at home and in the emigration (Vienna, Prague, Berlin) is a recent monograph by Alexander J. Motyl.[55] For greater details on the UVO and other revolutionary activity during the 1920s, one has to rely on the historical memoirs of two of its members, Volodymyr Martynets' and in particular Zynovii Knysh.[56] The more radically nationalist and revolutionary OUN, which came into being in 1929, is covered in a collection of documents and in several sympathetic histories of the movement, the most comprehensive by Petro Mirchuk.[57] There are also several memoirs by former OUN members on the organization's activity during the 1930s,[58] and a study by a postwar Polish emigré on the OUN's most publicized act–the assassination of Minister of Interior Bronisław Pieracki (1895–1934) in 1934.[59] The OUN leader, Ievhen Konovalets', has been the object of praise in a

55 Alexander J. Motyl, *The Turn to the Right: The Ideological Origins and Development of Ukrainian Nationalism, 1919–1929,* East European Monograph Series, vol. LXV (Boulder, Colo. and New York: Columbia University Press for East European Monographs 1980).

56 V. Martynets', *Ukraïns'ke pidpillia vid U.V.O. do O.U.N.* (n.p. 1949); Zynovii Knysh, ed., *Spohady i materiialy do diiannia UVO* (Toronto: Sribna Surma 1963); idem, ed., *Sribna Surma: pochatky UVO v Halychyni* (Toronto: Sribna Surma 1963); idem, *Pry dzherelakh ukraïns'koho orhanizovanoho natsionalizmu* (Tornoto: Sribna Surma 1970); idem, *Dva protsesy iak naslidok diial'nosty UVO v 1924 rotsi* (Toronto: Sribna Surma, 1968); idem, *Na povni vitryla: Ukraïns'ka Viis'kova Orhanizatsiia v 1924–1926 rokakh* (Toronto: Sribna Surma 1970); idem, *Dalekyi prytsil: UVO v 1927–1929 rokakh* (Toronto: Sribna Surma 1970).

See also the detailed account of the 1926 trial held in L'viv in *12 ukraïntsiv pered l'vivs'kym sudom (protses Paslavs'koho i tov.),* Biblioteka 'Novoho Chasu', no. 11 (L'viv 1926); and the report found in the German Foreign Ministry Archives on UVO activity between 1921 and 1926 by a former officer in the Sich Riflemen, Osip Dumin, "Die Wahrheit über die ukrainische Organisation," report dated Berlin, May 1926, translated into Polish as "Prawda o Ukraińskiej Organizacji Wojskowej," *Zeszyty Historyczne,* XXX (Paris 1974), pp. 103–137.

57 *OUN v svitli postanov velykykh zboriv, konferentsii ta inshykh dokumentiv z borot'by 1929–1955 r.: zbirka dokumentiv* (n.p.: Zakordonni chastyny OUN 1955); Petro Mirchuk, *Narys istoriï Orhanizatsiï Ukraïns'kykh Natsionalistiv,* vol. I: *1920–1939* (Munich, London, and New York: Ukraïns'ke vyd-vo 1968).

See also *Orhanizatsiia Ukraïns'kykh Natsionalistiv 1929–1954* (Paris: OUN 1955) and R. Lisovyi, *Rozlam v OUN* (n.p. 1949).

58 Zynovii Knysh, *Dryzhyt' pidzemnyi huk: spohady z 1930 i 1931 rokiv u Halychyni* (Winnipeg 1953); Iurii Mozil', *Zapysky polityv''iaznia: spomyny z pol's'koï tiurmy* (Toronto: Dobra knyzhka 1958); Lev Rebet, *Svitla i tini ǑUN* (Munich: 'Ukraïns'kyi samostiinyk' 1961); Mykola Klymyshyn, *V pokhodi do voli: spomyny,* vol. I (Toronto: Liga Vyzvolennia Ukraïny and Doslidnyi Instytut Studiï 1975).

59 Władysław Żeleński, *Zabójstwo ministra Pierackiego* (Paris: Instytut Literacki 1973).

recently published large collection of essays about his life and times,[60] although he had been criticized by some in his lifetime for not being able to fulfill the role of a strong and charismatic leader that national idealists hoped to have during the 1930s.[61]

The ideological framework for interwar Galician-Ukrainian nationalism was provided by Dmytro Dontsov, a native of the Dnieper Ukraine, who emigrated to L'viv before World War I. Between 1922 and 1939 he worked in L'viv as editor of the leading literary and publicist journal *Literaturno-naukovyi vistnyk* (L'viv 1922–32), later *Vistnyk* (1933–39), and was the author of several works that had a great impact on the disillusioned interwar Galician-Ukrainian youth. Dontsov espoused the ideal of integral nationalism and the necessity to act, which was translated into illegal or terrorist activity by the Galician OUN in its efforts to achieve the goals of Ukrainian independence from Poles and later from the Russians. Dontsov's works and several biographies about him are available.[62]

The brief pacification campaign carried out against Ukrainians in 1930 became a *cause célèbre* not only for aggrieved Ukrainian writers but for liberals in the West as well. Almost immediately, Ukrainians compiled several documentary "black books" that outlined in graphic detail and with photographs the wounds, physical and psychological, inflicted on the Ukrainian population.[63] Similar publications sponsored by Ukrainians in the United States appeared at the same

60 *Ievhen Konovalets' ta ioho doba* (Munich: Fundatsiia im. Ievhena Konoval'tsia 1974). See also the memorial book issued soon after his death: *Ievhen Konovalets'* ([Paris] 194?).

61 R.K., *Istoriia odnoho kandydata na 'vozhda': politychnyi zhyttiepys providnyka 'natsionalistiv' E. Konoval'tsia* (L'viv: Hromada 1934).

62 Some of Dontsov's writings have appeared in the collection *Khrestom i mechem: tvory* (Toronto: Liga Vyzvolennia Ukraïny 1967). Among his more influential political writings from the L'viv period are *Natsionalizm* (L'viv and Zhovkva: 'Nove zhyttia' 1926); 2nd ed. (Munich 1958); 3rd rev. ed. (London: Ukraïns'ka Vydavnycha Spilka 1966); *Patriotyzm* (L'viv: Knyhozbirnia Vistnyka 1936); and *Masa i provid* (L'viv: Kvartal'nyk Vistnyka 1939), reprinted in *Khrestom i mechem*.

The most comprehensive biography is by Mykhailo Sosnovs'kyi, *Dmytro Dontsov: politychnyi portret* (New York and Toronto: Trident International 1974). See also Rostyslav Iendyk, *Dmytro Dontsov: ideoloh ukraïns'koho natsionalizmu* (Munich: Ukraïns'ke vyd-vo, 1955), and the early critical essay by Volodymyr Levyts'kyi, *Ideol'og fashyzmu: zamitky do ideol'ogiï Dmytra Dontsova* (L'viv: Hromads'kyi holos 1936).

63 *Na vichnu han'bu Pol'shchi, tverdyni varvarstva v Evropi* (Prague: Provid Ukraïns'kykh Natsionalistiv 1931); 2nd ed. (New York: Howerla 1956); Vladimir J. Kushnir, *Polish Atrocities in the West Ukraine* (Vienna: Gerold and Co. 1931); *Kryvavyi pokhid pol's'koho fashyzmu na okupovanykh zemliakh Zakhidnoï Ukraïny* (L'viv and New York: Komunistychna partiia Zakhidnoï Ukraïny 1931).

time,[64] and the issue also became a subject of debate in the British House of Commons.[65] Always anxious about its image in western, and especially British, political circles, the Polish government issued explanations defending the pacification and even found support among some British parliamentarians as well.[66]

Socioeconomic developments and the Galician Communist party

Besides the more publicized activity of the UVO and OUN, there were also efforts made on the part of the Ukrainian leadership to continue the policy of organic work in order to strengthen the social fabric from within–a policy that had met with success under Austrian rule during several decades of the late nineteenth and early twentieth centuries. The history of this less dramatic, though not unimportant, aspect of interwar Galicia remains to be written.

In a still largely underdeveloped agrarian society, such organic work was considered most important in the economic sphere, and despite opposition from the Polish government, several self-help cooperative societies like the Audit Union of Ukrainian Cooperatives (Reviziinyi Soiuz Ukraïns'kykh Kooperatyv), the Central Union (Tsentrosoiuz), the Dairy Union (Maslo-soiuz) and the Agricultural Association (Sil's'kyi Hospodar) continued to prosper. Each of the major cooperatives had its own journal, and these are valuable sources of information about the movement.[67] General histories of cooperatives by Illia Vytanovych and of merchants and industrialists by Volodymyr Nestorovych, as well as histories of individual organizations, provide a good survey of the Ukrainian cooperative movement in Galicia during the interwar period.[68]

64 Emil Revyuk, ed., *Polish Atrocities in Ukraine* (New York: United Ukrainian Organizations of U.S. 1931).

65 James Barr and Rhys J. Davies, *Report on the Polish-Ukrainian Conflict in Eastern Galicia* (Chicago: United Ukrainian Organizations 1931); *Poland and Ukraine: the Danger Spot of Europe* (London: Ukrainian Bureau n.d.).

66 *The Situation in Southeastern Poland (''Eastern Galicia'')*, Polish Library of Facts, no. 2 (New York: American-Polish Chamber of Commerce and Industry 1931); John Berger, *Who is Oppressing the Ukrainians?* (London: Reynolds 1931). See also the extensive apologia of Polish rule by M. Feliński, n. 4 above.

67 The Audit Union of Ukrainian Cooperatives published *Hospodars'ko-kooperatyvna rodyna* (L'viv 1934–39), and the scientific-ideological journal, *Kooperatyvna respublika* (L'viv 1928–39). The Dairy Union published *Kooperatyvne molocharstvo* (L'viv 1926–39), and the Agricultural Association *Sil's'kyi hospodar* (L'viv 1926–39). For more details on the cooperative press during this period, see Andrii Zhuk, *Ukraïns'ka hospodars'ko-kooperatyvna presa* (L'viv 1931).

68 Illia Vytanovych, *Istoriia ukraïns'koho kooperatyvnoho rukhu* (New York: Tovarystvo Ukraïns'koï Kooperatsiï 1964), especially pp. 315–496; Volodymyr T. Nestorovych, *Ukraïns'ki kuptsi i promyslovtsi v Zakhidnii Ukraïni 1920–1945* (Toronto and Chicago: Kliub

In general, however, Ukrainian Galicia was destined to remain, as before, a basically agricultural region that would serve as a source of raw materials and a market for manufactured goods from other parts of Poland. The only difference from prewar Austrian days was that the continually unstable Polish economy exacerbated by the depression could not even maintain the meager standard of living that existed before 1914.

The economic history of Ukrainian Galicia during the interwar period has been left almost entirely to Soviet writers. They have produced an extensive literature, which is often based on archival sources and a wide variety of statistical data. Their basic concern, however, is to highlight every instance, however small, of ''revolutionary'' activity (i.e. strikes and other forms of protests) among the peasantry and the still relatively small industrial proletariat. The revolutionary movement was ostensibly led by the local Communist party whose goals were liberation of the Ukrainian masses from the oppression of the Polish government and landlords, as well as from the local ''Ukrainian bourgeois nationalists'' and Greek Catholic church, and unification with the Ukrainian Soviet Socialist Republic.

To make more plausible the writing of such histories, Soviet authors have prepared eight volumes of documents on revolutionary activity in interwar eastern Galicia.[69] As for the secondary literature, most Soviet histories of the interwar

---

Ukraïns'kykh Profesionalistiv i Pidpryiemtsiv 1977); E. Khraplyvyi, *Sorok lit pratsi Kraievoho Hospodars'koho Tovarystva 'Sil's'kyi Hospodar' (1899–1939)* (L'viv 1939); Andrii Kachor, *Ukraïns'ka molochars'ka kooperatsiia v Zakhidnii Ukraïni* (Munich 1949); Pavlo Dubrivnyi, ed., *Kraiove hospodars'ke tovarystvo 'Sil's'kyi Hospodar' u L'vovi 1899–1944* (New York: Ukraïns'ka Vil'na Akademiia Nauk 1970); Ivan Martiuk, *Tsentrosoiuz, soiuz kooperatyvnykh soiuziv u L'vovi v rokakh 1924–1944: spohady spivuchasnyka pratsi i zmahan' ukraïns'koho kooperatyvnoho rukhu* (Jersey City, NJ: M.P. Kots' 1973).

See also one of the earliest surveys: Andrii Zhuk, *Ukraïns'ka kooperatsiia v Pol'shchi* (L'viv 1934); the negative Marxist view of the movement: L.O. Olesnevych, *Kooperatyvni mify i kapitalistychna diisnist': zakhidnoukraïns'ka burzhuazna kooperatsiia (1883–1939)* (Kiev: Naukova dumka 1974); and the biographies of several activists in the cooperative movement by Andrii Kachor: *Ol'ha Bachyns'ka: narys ïï zhyttia ta hromads'ko-kooperatyvnoï pratsi* (Winnipeg: Bratstvo Maslosoiuznykiv u Kanadi i SShA 1954); *Denys Korenets': nacherk ioho zhyttia ta pratsi na tli ukraïns'koho fakhovoho shkil'nytstva i sil's'ko-hospodars'koï kooperatsiï v Zakhidnii Ukraïni* (Winnipeg: Kooperatyvna hromada 1955); *Ostap Luts'kyi: pam''iati vyznachnoho hromads'koho diiacha* (Winnipeg: Kooperatyvna hromada 1952); *Muzhi ideï i pratsi: Andrii Palii i Andrii Mudryk, tvortsi 'Maslosoiuzu' i modernoï ukraïns'koï kooperatsiï v Zakhidnii Ukraïni* (Winnipeg: Bratstvo Maslosoiuznykiv u Kanadi i SShA 1974).

69 *Pid praporom Zhovtnia: vplyv Velykoï Zhovtnevoï sotsialistychnoï revoliutsiï na pidnesennia*

period adopt a fourfold periodization scheme: 1921–1923–the period of revolutionary crisis; 1923–1928–a period of temporary stabilization of capitalism; 1929–1933–economic crisis; 1933–1939–attempts by workers to create a national front against fascism. Besides the general Soviet histories on the interwar era by Mykhailo Herasymenko, Bohdan Dudykevych, and Mykola Kravets',[70] there are numerous monographs and articles on the history of industry and especially the industrial workers, as well as the peasantry, during one or more of the above outlined periods.[71]

---

revoliutsiinoho rukhu v Zakhidnii Ukraïni: dokumenty i materialy, 3 vols (L'viv: Knyzhkovo-zhurnal'ne vyd-vo and Kameniar 1957–66); D.A. Iaremchuk et al, eds, *Borot'ba za vozz''iednannia Zakhidnoï Ukraïny z Ukraïns'koiu RSR, 1917–1939: zbirnyk dokumentiv ta materialiv* (Kiev: Naukova dumka 1979); *Stanovyshche trudiashchykh L'vova 1917–1939: dokumenty ta materialy* (L'viv: Knyzhkovo-zhurnal'ne vyd-vo 1961); Ivan P. Kryp''iakevych, ed., *Z istoriï revoliutsiinoho rukhu u L'vovi 1917–1933: dokumenty i materialy* (L'viv: Knyzhkovo-zhurnal'ne vyd-vo 1957); *Revoliutsiina borot'ba na Ternopil'shchyni 1917–1939: dokumenty ta materialy* (Ternopil': Oblvydav 1959); P.M. Iatskiv, ed., *Borot'ba trudiashchykh Prykarpattia za svoie vyzvolennia i vozz''iednannia z Radians'koiu Ukraïnoiu: dokumenty i materialy, 1921–1939* (Stanislav: Oblvydav 1957).

70 See n. 2 above.

71 On the working class and industrial development in general, see Iurii H. Hoshko, *Hromads'kyi pobut robitnykiv Zakhidnoï Ukraïny (1920–1939 rr.)* (Kiev: Naukova dumka 1967); I.P. Bohodyst, *Revoliutsiina borot'ba trudiashchykh Zakhidnoï Ukraïny (1917–1939 rr.)* (L'viv 1958); P. Iova, *Borot'ba trudiashchykh Zakhidnoï Ukraïny za vozz''iednannia z Radians'koiu Ukraïnoiu* (L'viv: Knyzhkovo-zhurnal'ne vyd. 1954); H.I. Koval'chak, "Stanovyshche fabrychno-zavods'koï promyslovosti Skhidnoï Halychyny v 20-30-kh rokakh XX st.," *Z istoriï Ukraïns'koï RSR*, vol. VIII (Kiev: AN URSR 1963), pp. 28–41; Ivan I. Kompaniiets', *Revoliutsiinyi rukh v Halychyni, Bukovyni ta Zakarpats'kii Ukraïni pid vplyvom idei Velykoho Zhovtnia (1917–1920 rr.)* (Kiev: AN URSR, Instytut istoriï 1957); P.P. Chelak, "Revoliutsiina borot'ba trudiashchykh mas Zakhidnoï Ukraïny proty okupatsiinoho rezhymu pans'koï Pol'shchi (zhovten' 1920–1923 rr.)," in *300 rokiv vozz''iednannia Ukraïny z Rosiieiu: naukovyi zbirnyk* (L'viv: LU 1954), pp. 134–151; I.K. Vasiuta, "Revoliutsiina borot'ba trudiashchykh Zakhidnoï Ukraïny v 1924-travni 1926 rr.," in *ibid.*, pp. 152–168; T.I. Zhukov, "Borot'ba robitnykiv i selian Zakhidnoï Ukraïny za vozz''iednannia z Radians'koiu Ukraïnoiu u 1928–1933 rr.," in *ibid.*, pp. 169–186; Mark I. Zil'berman, *Revoliutsiina borot'ba trudiashchykh Zakhidnoï Ukraïny (1924–1928 rr.)* (L'viv: LU 1968); O.H. Tsybko, *Revoliutsiino-vyzvol'na borot'ba trudiashchykh Zakhidnoï Ukraïny za vozz''iednannia z URSR (1934–1939 rr.)* (L'viv 1963).

For focus on the peasantry alone, see A.H. Boiko, *Stanovyshche selian Zakhidnoï Ukraïny v pans'kii Pol'shchi (1919–1939)* (L'viv 1951); L.Ia. Korniichuk, *Stanovyshche trudiashchoho selianstva zakhidnykh oblastei Ukraïny pid vladoiu pans'koï Pol'shchi* (Kiev: AN URSR, Institut ekonomiky 1957); I.K. Vasiuta, *Selians'kyi rukh na Zakhidnii Ukraïni v 1919–1939 rr.* (L'viv: LU 1971); P. Chelak, "Revoliutsiinyi selians'kyi rukh u Zakhidnii Ukraïni v 1921–1923 rr.," in *U borot'bi za Radians'ku vladu i sotsializm* (L'viv 1960); and P.P.

According to Soviet Marxist historical iconography, the vanguard of the working classes is the Communist party, which is considered solely responsible for the success of the revolutionary movement. Thus, it is not surprising to find an extensive literature on the history of the party. The Communist party of Eastern Galicia (Komunistychna Partiia Skhidnoï Halychyny–KPSH) was established in February 1919 and was soon made part of the Communist party (Bolshevik) of the Ukraine. On orders from the Comintern in July 1921, the KPSH was to become a regional party organization of the Communist party of Poland, but reluctance on the part of Galician party leaders (O. Vasyl'kiv) delayed unification until 1923, when the organization was renamed the Communist party of Western Ukraine (Komunistychna Partiia Zakhidnoï Ukraïny–KPZU). The KPZU was forbidden to function legally in Poland, and although the Galician Communists attracted some Ukrainian youth during the 1920s (especially since the Ukrainianization policy in the Soviet Ukraine made that area seem potentially more attractive than Polish-dominated Galicia), by the 1930s it was overshadowed by legal Ukrainian political movements and most especially by the appeal of the OUN. Moreover, throughout its brief history, the KPZU was wracked by internal difficulties, such as friction with the Polish party apparatus to which it was subordinate and its support for the Soviet Ukrainianization policies of the 1920s, which were later disavowed by the Communist party (Bolshevik) of the Ukraine. In fact, accusations of ''bourgeois-nationalist deviation'' were given as the justification for the Comintern's dissolution of the KPZU in 1938.

In one of the few non-Soviet works on the KPZU, Roman Solchanyk has written a solid study elucidating the cloudy beginnings of the KPSH between 1919 to 1921.[72] There are several documents on the party included in the eight volumes

---

Mykhailyk, ''Stanovyshche trudiashchykh selian Zakhidnoï Ukraïny v period fashysts'koï dyktatury Pilsuds'koho (1929–1933 rr.),'' *Pratsi kafedr suspil'nykh nauk LDU*, I (L'viv 1954), pp. 39–51.

On the period 1919 to 1923, see also notes 43 and 45 above. On the statistical relationship between varying national/religious groups and industrial employment, see Jerzy Tomaszewski, ''The National Structure of the Working Class in the Southeastern Part of Poland (1918–1939),'' *Acta Poloniae Historica*, XIX (Wrocław, Warsaw, and Cracow 1968), pp. 89–111.

72 Roman Solchanyk, ''The Foundation of the Communist Movement in Eastern Galicia, 1919–1921,'' *Slavic Review*, XXX, 4 (Seattle, Wash. 1971), pp. 774–794.

For the Soviet view of this period, see O.Iu. Karpenko, ''Do pytannia pro vynyknennia i orhanizatsiine oformlennia Komunistychnoï partiï Skhidnoï Halychyny (1919–1923 rr.),'' in *Z istoriï zakhidnoukraïns'kykh zemel'*, vol. II (Kiev: AN URSR 1957), pp. 163–190; N.K. Kucherov, ''K voprosu o vozniknovenii i organizatsionom oformlenii kommunisticheskoi partii Vostochnoi Galitsii (1919–1923),'' *Voprosy istorii KPSS*, IX, 12 (Moscow 1965), pp. 59–68;

on revolutionary activity in interwar Galicia,[73] as well as two anthologies of memoirs by some of its former members.[74] Soviet writers have written several general histories and have also focused on specific periods of the KPZU: the most comprehensive are by Valentyn Malanchuk and Ievhen Halushko.[75] The split of 1928, which resulted from accusations by the Comintern and the Communist party (Bolshevik) of the Ukraine that the KPZU had become dominated by revisionists, pseudo-Ukrainian bourgeois nationalists, and even local Russophiles, has received special attention. Several contemporary criticisms, including one by then Soviet Ukrainian party boss Mykola Skrypnyk, present the view of those who wanted to put the KPZU back on the "correct" ideological path.[76] A

---

idem, "Bor'ba trudiashchikhsia Galitsii za sovetskuiu vlast' v 1918–1923 godakh," *Voprosy istorii*, XXVII, 5 (Moscow 1971), pp. 102–111.

The Ukrainian Communist movement in Poland was actually strongest in Volhynia. Cf. Alexander J. Motyl, "The Rural Origins of the Communist and Nationalist Movements in Wolyn Województwo, 1921–1939," *Slavic Review*, XXXVII, 3 (Columbus, Ohio 1978), pp. 412–420. Most of the works on the KPZU mentioned in the following notes deal with developments in Volhynia as well as Galicia.

73 See n. 69 above.

74 *KPZU-orhanizator revoliutsiinoï borot'by: spohady kolyshnikh chleniv Komunistychnoï partiï Zakhidnoï Ukraïny* (L'viv: Knyzhkovo-zhurnal'ne vyd-vo 1958); *Na choli vyzvol'noï borot'by: spohady kolyshnikh aktyvnykh diiachiv komunistychnoï partiï Zakhidnoï Ukraïny* (Kiev: Vyd-vo politychnoï literatury Ukraïny 1965). See also the memoirs of another KPZU activist, M.M. Tesliuk, *U borot'bi za vozz''iednannia: storinky spohadiv* (L'viv Kameniar 1979).

75 V.Iu. Malanchuk, *Torzhestvo lenins'koï natsional'noï polityky: Komunistychna partiia–orhanizator rozv''iazannia natsional'noho pytannia v zakhidnykh oblastiakh URSR* (L'viv: Knyzhkovo-zhurnal'ne vyd-vo 1963); Ie.M. Halushko, *Narysy istoriï ideolohichnoï ta orhanizatsiinoï diial'nosti KPZU v 1919–1928 rr.* (L'viv: LU 1965).

See also H.I. Koval'chak, Iu.Iu. Slyvka, and V.P. Chuhaiov, *Podiia velykoho istorychnoho znachennia* (Kiev: Vyd-vo politychnoï literatury Ukraïny 1979); M.I. Panchuk, *U polum''ï klasovykh bytv: pro borot'bu KPZU za internatsional'ne zhurtuvannia zakhidnoukraïns'kykh trudiashchykh proty burzhuaznoho natsionalizmu* (Kiev: Politvydav Ukraïny 1979); and M.M. Kravets' and Iu.Iu. Slyvka, "Z istoriï komunistychnoï partiï Zakhidnoï Ukraïny (1929–persha polovyna 1932 r.)," *Z istoriï Ukraïns'koï RSR*, vol. VIII (Kiev: AN URSR 1963), pp. 42–62. On cooperation with the Polish Communist party and other Galician progressive parties (i.e. Sel-Rob), see Oleh M. Shvydak, *Internatsional'na iednist' trudiashchykh Zakhidnoï Ukraïny i Pol'shchi u revoliutsiino-vyzvol'nii borot'bi (1929–1939 rr.)* (Kiev: Kyïvs'kyi universytet 1972).

76 Mykola Skrypnyk, *Dzherela ta prychyny rozlamu v KPZU* (Kharkiv 1928); *Natsional'ne pytannia na Ukraïni ta rozlam v KPZU: zbirnyk statei i dokumentiv* (Kharkiv: Vyd-vo Proletariï 1928); Andrii Khvylia, "Bliudolyzy hrafiv Bobryns'kykh," *Bil'shovyk Ukraïny*, III, 18 (Kharkiv 1928), pp. 76–90; J. Bratkowski, *Na drogach nacjonalizmu, oportunizmu i zdrady* (L'viv: Komunistyczna Partja Zachodniej Ukrainy 1928).

contemporary Polish Communist view of these developments was provided by Jan Regula, while more recently Janusz Radziejowski has provided a solid history of the KPZU in the 1920s, especially of the problems surrounding the split of 1928.[77] The pro-Communist Ukrainian Peasant and Workers Socialist Union (Sel-Rob) and the Communist youth organization in eastern Galicia, Komsomol, have also been the subject of several studies;[78] and there is a collection of documents and monographs about the Anti-Fascist Congress of Cultural Activists which was held in L'viv (1936) and was dominated by local Polish and Jewish Communists as well as a few leftist Ukrainian writers.[79] Finally, the Communist press and other "progressive" organs that continued to appear throughout the interwar period have been analyzed in great detail in several books and articles by Iosyf Ts'okh and Iaroslav Dashkevych.[80]

77 Jan A. Regula, *Historja Komunistycznej partji Polski w świetle faktów i dokumentów* (Warsaw: Drukprasa 1934); Janusz Radziejowski, *Komunistyczna Partia Zachodniej Ukrainy 1919–1929: węzłowe problemy ideologiczne* (Cracow: Wydawnictwo Literackie 1976), in English: *The Communist Party of Western Ukraine, 1919–1929* (Edmonton, Alta.: Canadian Institute of Ukrainian Studies 1983).

78 On the Sel-Rob, see M. Feliński, "Ukraińskie Selansko-Robitnycze Socjalistyczne Objednanie (Sel-Rob)," *Sprawy Narodowościowe*, I, 5 (Warsaw 1927), pp. 495–502; and Janusz Radziejowski, "Geneza partiï 'Sel-Rob'," *Z Pola Walki*, IX, 2 (Warsaw 1966), pp. 47–70. On the Komsomol, see V.Iu. Malanchuk, *Boiovyi shliakh Komsomolu Zakhidnoï Ukraïny* (L'viv: Knyzhkovo-zhurnal'ne vyd-vo 1957); and his "Borot'ba trudiashchoï molodi Zakhidnoï Ukraïny pid kerivnytstvom KPZU proty nastupu fashyzmu za stvorennia iedynoho narodnoho frontu (1934–1935 rr.)," *Naukovi zapysky L'vivs'koho filialu Tsentral'noho muzeiu V.I. Lenina*, I (L'viv 1959), pp. 115–139.

79 T.E. Kozachuk, ed., *Antifashistskii kongress rabotnikov kul'tury vo L'vove v 1936 g.: dokumenty i materialy* (L'viv 1956); B.K. Dudykevych, *Pid praporom Narodnoho frontu: do istoriï kvitnevych podii 1936 roku u L'vovi* (L'viv: Knyzhkovo-zhurnal'ne vyd-vo 1956).

80 I.T. Ts'okh, *Komunistychna presa v Zakhidnii Ukraïni (1919–1932 rr.)* (L'viv: LU 1958); idem, *Komunistychna presa Zakhidnoï Ukraïny: rol' drukovanoï propahandy v ideolohichnii diial'nosti KPZU, 1919–1939 rr.* (L'viv: LU 1966); idem, *Slovo buremnykh rokiv* (L'viv: Knyzhkovo-zhurnal'ne vyd-vo 1961); idem, *Hazeta 'Sel-Rob'* (L'viv: LU 1958); Ia.R. Dashkevych, "Z istoriï vydavnychoï diial'nosti komunistychnoï partiï Zakhidnoï Ukraïny," in *Z istoriï Ukraïns'koï RSR*, vol. VI–VII (Kiev: AN URSR 1962), pp. 95–125; idem, "Pidpil'na presa Komunistychnoï Partiï Zakhidnoï Ukraïny v 1921–1938 rokakh," *Z istoriï zakhidnoukraïns'kykh zemel'*, vol. IV, ed. I.P. Kryp''iakevych (Kiev: AN URSR 1960), pp. 108–120; Ia.R. Dashkevych, "Pidpil'na presa komunistychnoï spilky molodi Zakhidnoï Ukraïny (1922–1938 roky)," in *Z istoriï zakhidnoukraïns'kykh zemel'*, vol. V, ed. I.P. Kryp''iakevych (Kiev: AN URSR 1960), pp. 136–152; Ia. R. Dashkevych, "Komunistychna ta radians'ka presa v Zakhidnii Ukraïni u 1919–1920 rr.," *Ukraïns'kyi istorychnyi zhurnal*, II, 1 (Kiev 1958), pp. 117–124.

See also M.M. Oleksiuk, *Prohresyvna presa Zakhidnoï Ukraïny v borot'bi na zakhyst SRSR (20-30-ti roky)* (Kiev: Naukova dumka 1973).

Cultural history: education

In comparison with the prewar Austrian period, Ukrainian cultural activity in Galicia declined in intensity and influence after 1918. There were several reasons for this: (1) by 1907, the focus of all Ukrainian cultural life had begun to shift from L'viv to Kiev where it blossomed anew during the 1920s; (2) as a result of the Polish-Ukrainian war, many Galician-Ukrainian intellectuals fled to the West or to the Soviet Ukraine; and (3) the relatively permissive cultural atmosphere that prevailed under Austria was replaced by a restrictive and sometimes repressive Polish regime. This does not mean that Ukrainian cultural activity ceased altogether in interwar Galicia, but the region did once again return to the position of a regional area of secondary importance in the larger Ukrainian cultural sphere. These reasons perhaps explain in part the paucity of studies dealing with Ukrainian cultural developments in Galicia between 1919 and 1939. All that exists are a few studies on the educational system, the Greek Catholic church, and Communist and left-wing cultural activists.

The growth of a Ukrainian educational system at all levels that had made such steady progress under Austrian rule was to be curtailed in interwar Poland. In 1921, the provincial school administration based in L'viv was abolished and the local county school boards had to give up whatever effective power they once had to the centralized Ministry of Education and Religion in Warsaw. Although the total number of schools increased in eastern Galicia between 1919 and 1939, their character changed. Initially, the Ukrainian system, especially at the elementary level, was left largely intact, while new Polish schools were founded. Then, as a result of a 1924 law sponsored by the government of Prime Minister Władysław Grabski (1874–1938), Ukrainian and Polish schools were unified and made bilingual. By the 1930s, many of these officially bilingual schools became Polish. At the university level, all the chairs in Ukrainian studies and other appointments were abolished at the University of L'viv in 1919.

The Ukrainian reaction to these developments was to expand, at the community's own expense, the number of private schools. By the 1937/38 school year, 59 percent of all Ukrainian gymnasia, teachers' colleges, and professional schools with approximately 40 percent of Ukrainian students at those levels were privately operated. The growth of private schools was due largely to the Ukrainian Pedagogical Society, founded in 1881 and renamed Ridna Shkola in 1926. At the university level, courses sponsored by several Ukrainian cultural institutes began in 1919, and an underground Ukrainian University was founded in L'viv in 1921. The university operated with as many as 1500 students until 1925 when, after constant pressure by Polish authorities, it was closed, forcing Galician Ukrainians to attend universities abroad, especially in Prague.

The only comprehensive history of Ukrainian education in interwar Galicia is a recent monograph by the Polish scholar Mieczysław Iwanicki.[81] Besides this, there are a few short studies by Soviet writers covering the whole period,[82] several works focusing on the years 1919 to 1924,[83] and a history of Ukrainian elementary schools to 1931.[84] Somewhat better developed is the literature on individual institutions; there are good histories of the Greek Catholic Theological Academy in L'viv,[85] the Ukrainian Academic Gymnasium, the Basilian Sister's Gymnasi-

81 Mieczysław Iwanicki, *Oświata i szkolnictwo ukraińskie w Polsce w latach 1918–1939*, Rozprawy Wyższej Szkoły Pedagogicznej w Siedlcach, vol. V (Siedlce 1975).

See also the chapter on Ukrainian schools in Stanisław Mauersberg, *Szkolnictwo powszechne dla mniejszości narodowych w Polsce w latach 1918–1939* (Wrocław, Warsaw, and Cracow: ZNIO–PAN 1968), especially pp. 59–103.

82 I.S. Pavliuk, ''Borot'ba za narodnu osvitu v Zakhidnii Ukraïni (1919–1939 rr.),'' in *Z istoriï zakhidnoukraïns'kykh zemel'*, vol. II (Kiev: AN URSR 1957), pp. 191–205; L.A. Ivanenko, ''Do pytannia pro borot'bu trudiashchykh Zakhidnoï Ukraïny proty natsional'noho pryhnichennia, za demokratyzatsiiu shkoly i kul'turno-osvitnykh ustanov,'' *Naukovi zapysky LDU, XLIII: Seriia istorychna* 6 (L'viv 1957), pp. 30–44; V.I. Kalynovych, ''Borot'ba trudiashchykh Zakhidnoï Ukraïny za ukraïns'ku shkolu i kul'turu v period panuvannia pans'koï Pol'shchi, 1918–1939 rr.,'' in *40 lit Velykoho Zhovtnia* (L'viv 1957); L.A. Ivanenko and T.H. Sokolovs'ka, ''Borot'ba trudiashchykh Zakhidnoï Ukraïny za proletars'ku i demokratychnu kul'turu (1919–1939),'' in *U borot'bi za svitli idealy komunizmu* (L'viv 1970).

83 The Ukrainian view of this period is presented by K. Fedorovych, *Ukraïns'ki shkoly v Halychyni u svitli zakoniv i praktyky* (L'viv: Sekretariaty ukraïns'kykh partiï: Trudovoï, Radykal'noï i Natsional'noï roboty 1924); Ivan Harasymovych, *Ukraïns'ki shkoly pid pol's'koiu vladoiu* (Stanyslaviv: Bystrytsia 1924); idem, *Zbroina i kul'turna viina* (L'viv: p.a. 1925); Ia. Rudnyts'kyi, *Ukraïns'ka shkola* (L'viv 1926); S. Sivpolko, *Ukraïns'ki shkoly v Halychyni* (Prague 1928).

The Polish view is in Stanislas Sobiński, *L'enseignement public [sic] en Petite Pologne (Galicie) orientale au point de vue national* (L'viv: Office national de l'académie de Léopol, section de manuels scolaires 1923); S. Lehnert, *Szkolnictwo w Małopolsce* (L'viv 1924); and by the minister of education Stanisław Grabski, *Szkoła na kresach wschodnich: w obronie ustawy szkolnej z 31 lipca 1924 r.* (Warsaw 1927).

84 Lev Iasinchuk, *50 lit Ridnoï Shkoly 1881–1931* (L'viv: Tovarystvo 'Ridna shkola' 1931).

85 Pavlo Senytsia, *Svityl'nyk istyny: dzherela do istoriï Ukraïns'koï Katolyts'koï Bohoslovs'koï Akademiï u L'vovi 1928 / 1929–1944*, 3 vols., Vydannia Ukr. Kat. Univ. im. sv. Klymenta Papy, vols. XXXIV, XLIV, LX (Toronto and Chicago 1973–83). See also Vasyl' Lentsyk, ''Mytropolyt Iosyf Slipyi iak rektor Dukhovnoï Seminariï i Bohoslovs'koï Akademiï u L'vov,'' *Naukovi zapysky Ukraïns'koho Vil'noho Universytetu*, X (Munich, Paris, and New York 1968), pp. 226–248; and the early reports: *Hreko-katolysts'ka Bohoslovs'ka Akademiia u L'vovi v pershim / druhomu / tret'omu tr'okhlittiu svoioho istnuvannia (1928–1937)*, 3 vols (L'viv: Akademiia 1932–41), reprinted in *Tvory Kyr Iosyfa Verkhovnoho Arkhiepyskopa i Kardynala*, vol. III–IV (Rome: Ukraïns'kyi Katolyts'kyi Universytet 1970), pp. 257–727.

um, and Student Home in L'viv,[86] the Teacher's College and Gymnasium in Zalishchyky,[87] the Ukrainian underground university,[88] and the Ridna Shkola organization.[89]

Cultural history: the church, national identity, literature

The history of the church during the interwar period is limited to a detailed history of the Ukrainian Theological Scholarly Society (Ukraïns'ke Bohoslovs'ke Naukove Tovarystvo, 1922–39)[90] and to biographies of the bishop of Przemyśl, Iosafat Kotsylovs'kyi (1876–1947, consecrated 1916),[91] the bishop of Stanyslaviv, Hryhorii Khomyshyn (1867–1947, consecrated 1904),[92] and most especially Metropolitan Andrei Sheptyts'kyi, the Greek Catholic hierarch whose stature and reputation made him one of the few leaders respected by most factions of the Ukrainian community, as well as in Polish government circles.[93] Interwar Polish authors wrote tracts that were often critical of the role played by Ukrainian churches,[94] while later Soviet writers have also traced the history of the Greek Catholic church during this period and have criticized all aspects of its work, especially the activity of Metropolitan Sheptyts'kyi, who is invariably depicted as one of the greatest enemies of the Galician-Ukrainian people.[95]

86 See the works by B. Romanenchuk, O. Dombrovs'kyi, R. Kukhar, and V. Lev, chapter 6, n. 117; and Iuliian Beskyd [Iuliian Tarnovych], *Ukraïns'kyi Akademichnyi Dim u L'vovi* (Toronto: 'Na Storozhi' 1962).

87 See the history by V. Veryha, chapter 6, n. 117, especially pp. 95–197.

88 Vasyl' Mudryi, *Borot'ba za ohnyshche ukraïns'koï kul'tury v zakhidnykh zemliakh Ukraïny* (L'viv: Ukraïns'ka kraieva students'ka rada 1923); idem, *Ukraïns'kyi Universytet u L'vovi 1921–1925* (Nürnberg: Chas 1948).

89 *Ridna Shkola / Ukraïns'ke Pedahohichne Tovarystvo: diial'nist' za administratsiinyi rik 1925–1926* (L'viv 1926).

90 Volodymyr Ianiv, ''Narys istoriï Ukraïns'koho Bohoslovs'koho Naukovoho Tovarystva,'' *Naukovi zapysky Ukraïns'koho Vil'noho Universytetu*, X (Munich, Paris, and New York 1968), pp. 139–225, reprinted in idem, *Studiï ta materiialy do noviishoï ukraïns'koï istoriï*, Ukraïns'kyi Vil'nyi Universytet, Seriia monohrafiï, no. 16 (Munich 1970), pp. 3–94.

91 Irynei Nazarko, *Iosafat Kotsylovs'kyi, ChSVV: iepyskop peremys'kyi 1916–1946* (Toronto: O.O. Vasyliian 1954).

92 Petro Mel'nychuk, *Vladyka Hryhorii Khomyshyn: patriot-misionar-muchenyk* (Rome and Philadelphia: n.p. 1979).

93 See the sections covering the interwar period of Sheptyts'kyi's long career in the biographies of Baran, Prokoptschuk, and Korolevs'kyi, chapter 6, n. 186.

94 H. Łubieński, *Kóściół Grecko-Katolicki ŵ województwach południowo-wschodnich*, Bibljoteka 'Spraw Narodowościowych', no. 21 (Warsaw 1935); W. Piotrowicz, *Unia czy demonstracja: o obrządku wschodnio-słowiańskim w Polsce* (Vilnius 1933).

95 Petro A. Petliakov, *Uniats'ka tserkva–ideinyi voroh trudiashchykh: krytyka ideolohiï i*

Some Dnieper Ukrainians fleeing Soviet rule settled in Galicia where they played a role in cultural affairs. Their activity as well as the cultural work of Galician-Ukrainian intellectuals who left their homeland for other countries, most especially Czechoslovakia, is surveyed in detail by Symon Narizhyni.[96] The controversy between local Ukrainophiles and Russophiles over national identity, which had been a dominant feature of Galician life under Austrian rule, was after 1919 resolved for the most part in favor of the Ukrainophiles. The Russophiles and their organizations did continue to exist, although in ever dwindling numbers. They seemed strongest only in the westernmost Lemkian region in the Carpathian Mountains where, with cooperation from the Polish government (which for its own reasons favored the idea of a separate Lemkian people), Russophilism continued to persist.[97] There are a few essays available that on the one hand rephrase Russophile ideals under Polish rule or on the other criticize the Ukrainophiles for their supposed lack of total commitment to the Ukrainian cause.[98]

There are no histories that attempt to cover all aspects of Ukrainian literary development during the whole interwar period in Galicia. Ievhen Pelens'kyi prepared a survey of literary production during the first half of the 1930s, and there are works on several authors who began their literary careers before World War I and who were still active during the interwar years.[99] But it is the Commu-

---

polityky klerykal'noho antykomunizmu (L'viv: Vyshcha shkola 1976); Violla V. Dobretsova, *Natsionalizm i relihiia na sluzhbi antykomunizmu: pro kontrrevoliutsiinu diial'nist' burzhuazno-natsionalistychnykh i klerykal'nykh orhanizatsiï na zakhidnoukraïns'kykh zemliakh u 20-30-kh rokakh ta borot'bu proty nykh prohresyvnykh syl* (L'viv: Vyshcha shkola 1976).

96 Symon Narizhnyi, *Ukraïns'ka emigratsiia: kul'turna pratsia ukraïns'koï emigratsiï mizh dvoma svitovymy viinamy,* Studiï Muzeiu vyzvol'noï borot'by Ukraïny, vol. I (Prague 1942). For a contemporary Soviet view of Ukrainian emigrés in Galicia, see M. Motuzka, *Ukraïns'ka kontrrevoliutsiina emigratsiia* (Kharkiv: Derzhpolitvydav Ukraïny 1928).

97 On Polish governmental policy toward the Lemkians, see the studies listed in chapter 2, n. 97. As part of the government's support of Lemkian separatism, Warsaw succeeded in convincing the Vatican to create in 1934 a separate Greek Catholic apostolic administration for the Lemkian region. See S. Iadlovs'kyi, comp., *Shematyzm hreko-katolytskoho dukhoven'stva apostol'skoï administratsiï Lemkovshchyny 1936* (L'viv: Apostol'ska administratsiia Lemkovshchyny 1936), reprinted with preface by Wasyl Lencyk (Stamford, Conn.: Ukraïns'kyi muzei i biblioteka 1970).

98 H.S. Malets, *Potuhy roz''edyneniia y oslableniia russkoho naroda* (L'viv: p.a. 1924); F. Podleski, *Rusofilizm a ukrainizm* (L'viv 1931); Andrei Kaminskii, *Narodniki i obshcherussy: ich istoricheskaia stoimost'* (L'viv 1930); Andrei Kamins'kyi, *Zahadka Ukraïny i Halychyny* (L'viv: p.a. 1927).

99 Ievhen Iu. Pelens'kyi, *Suchasne zakhidn'o-ukraïns'ke pys'menstvo: ohliad za 1930–1935 rr.* (L'viv: Literaturna biblioteka 1935). For works by and about V. Stefanyk, B. Lepkyi, M. Iatskiv, M. Cheremshyna, and O. Luts'kyi, see chapter 6, notes 173, 175, 177, 178, 180.

nist and other leftist cultural activists who have received the most attention. Guides to revolutionary writers active in Galicia were prepared already in the 1920s,[100] and especially after 1945 they have been idolized in literary histories of the period[101] and in bibliographies, biographies, and re-publications of the works of several authors, including Stepan Tudor (1892–1941),[102] Myroslav Irchan (1897–1937),[103] Petro Kozlaniuk (1904–1965),[104] Oleksandr Havryliuk (1911–1941),[105] and most especially Iaroslav Galan (1902–1949).[106]

100 D. Zahul, V. Atamaniuk, and S. Semko, eds, *Zakhidna Ukraïna* (Kiev 1927). See also the later biobibliographical dictionary: M.P. Humeniuk, comp., *Pys'mennyky radians'koho L'vova* (L'viv: Knyzhkovo-zhurnal'ne vyd-vo 1960).

101 Stepan Trofymuk, *Rozvytok revoliutsiinoï literatury v Zakhidnii Ukraïni 1921–1929* (Kiev 1957); Stepan Trofymuk, *Revoliutsiina poeziia zakhidnoï Ukraïny 1917–1939* (L'viv LU 1970); Mykola Dubyna, *Surmachi vozz''iednannia: literaturno-krytychni narysy* (Kiev: Radians'kyi pys'mennyk 1976); B. Buriak, *Sluzhinnia narodovi: narysy pro zhyttia i tvorchist' Stepana Tudora, Oleksandra Havryliuka, Iaroslava Halana, Petra Kozlaniuka* (Kiev 1954).

See also the extensive sections on literature in eastern Galicia during the interwar period by B.S. Buriak, in *Istoriia ukraïns'koï literatury,* vol. VI (Kiev: Naukova dumka 1970), pp. 435–486 and vol. VII (1971), pp. 318–370.

102 Some of Tudor's writings, including journalist essays, have been published in his *Tvory,* ed. Ia. Tsehel'nyk (Kiev: Derzhlitvydav Ukraïny 1959) and *Tvory,* 2 vols, ed. P.M. Dovhaliuk (Kiev: AN URSR 1962). Among the works about him are: A.S. Elkin, *Stepan Tudor: kritiko-biograficheskii ocherk* (Moscow: Sovetskii pisatel' 1956); M.M. Oleksiuk, *Filosofs'ko-ateistychni pohliady S. Tudora* (L'viv LU 1962); Ia.Kh. Tsehel'nyk, *Stepan Tudor (1892–1941): literaturnyi portret* (Kiev: Derzhlitvydav Ukraïny 1962); 2nd ed. (Kiev: Dnipro 1968); and Stepan M. Trofymuk, *Tvorchist' Stepana Tudora* (Kiev: AN URSR 1963).

103 For a bibliography of Irchan's works, see V.V. Mashotas, *Myroslav Irchan: bibliohrafichnyi pokazhchyk* (Kiev: AN URSR 1961). Some of his writings, including publicist works, have appeared in Myroslav Irchan, *Vybrani tvory,* 2 vols, ed. L.M. Novychenko (Kiev: Derzhlitvydav Ukraïny 1958).

For works about him, see L.M. Novychenko, *Myroslav Irchan: literaturnyi portret* (Kiev: Derzhlitvydav Ukraïny 1958); Vladlen P. Vlasenko and Petro I. Kravchuk, *Myroslav Irchan: zhyttia i tvorchist'* (Kiev: Radians'kyi pys'mennyk 1960); Ie.M. Antoniuk, ''Diial'nist' Myroslava Irchana iak holovy Spilky revoliutsiinykh pys'mennykiv 'Zakhidna Ukraïna','' *Ukraïns'ke literaturoznavstvo,* vol. XVIII (L'viv: Vyshcha shkola pry LU 1973), pp. 64–70.

104 For a bibliography of Kozlaniuk's works, see M.P. Humeniuk, *Petro Kozlaniuk: bibliohrafichnyi pokazhchyk literatury* (L'viv: L'vivs'ka biblioteka AN URSR 1954); 2nd rev. ed. (L'viv 1957). For some of his works, including publicist essays, see his *Tvory,* 2 vols (Kiev: Derzhlitvydav Ukraïny 1954); *Tvory,* 3 vols (Kiev: Derzhlitvydav Ukraïny 1960); and *Tvory,* 4 vols (Kiev: Dnipro 1974).

On his life and work, see B. Buriak, ''Petro Kozlaniuk,'' in *Ukraïns'ki radians'ki pys'mennyky: krytychni narysy* (Kiev 1957), pp. 240–283; Iu.S. Mel'nychuk, ''Petro Kozlaniuk,'' in his *Slovo pro pys'mennykiv* (L'viv 1958), pp. 312–377; and Iu. Baida, *Petro Kozlaniuk: zhyttia i tvorchist'* (Kiev: Radians'kyi pys'mennyk 1959).

105 For a bibliography of Havryliuk's writings, see O.P. Kushch, *Oleksandr Havryliuk (1911–*

1941): bibliohrafichnyi pokazhchyk (Kiev: AN URSR, 1957). For some of his works, including publicist essays, see his *Vybrani tvory,* ed. Iu. Mel'nychuk (Kiev: Radians'kyi pys'mennyk 1949); *Izbrannoe* (Moscow: Sovetskii pisatel' 1950); 2nd rev. ed. (1952); and *Vybrane,* ed. Iu. Mel'nychuk (Kiev: Derzhlitvydav Ukraïny 1955).

For studies on him, see Iurii Mel'nychuk, *Oleksandr Havryliuk: zhyttia, revoliutsiina i literaturna diial'nist'* (L'viv: Knyzhkovo-zhurnal'ne vyd-vo 1955); Volodymyr Radchenko, *Bezsmertia bortsia: zhyttia, revoliutsiina diial'nist' i tvorchist' O. Havryliuka* (Kiev: Radians'kyi pys'mennyk 1956); and Stepan M. Trofymuk, *Oleksandr Havryliuk* (Kiev: Dnipro 1968).

106 For a bibliography of Galan's writings, see M.P. Humeniuk, O.P. Kushch, and I.I. Shapovalov, *Iaroslav Halan: bibliohrafichnyi pokazhchyk* (L'viv: L'vivs'ka biblioteka AN URSR 1956). The most complete collections of his works, including his numerous feuilletons, is the recent: Iaroslav Halan, *Tvory,* 4 vols (Kiev: Naukova dumka 1977–).

The most comprehensive studies of his career are by Iurii Mel'nychuk, *Iaroslav Halan: zhyttia, revoliutsiina i literaturna diial'nist'* (L'viv: Knyzhkovo-zhurnal'ne vyd-vo 1953); Anatolii Elkin, *Iaroslav Galan: ocherk zhizni i tvorchestva* (Moscow: Sovetskii pisatel' 1955); Kuz'ma N. Mlynchenko, *Zbroieiu polum''ianoho slova: publitsystychna diial'nist' Ia. Halana v radians'kii presi* (Kiev: AN URSR 1963). See also the popular biographies by Vladimir P. Beliaev and Anatolii S. Elkin, *Iaroslav Galan* (Moscow: Molodaia gvardiia 1971); Hryhorii H. Kulinych, *Iaroslav Halan: zhyttia i tvorchist'* (Kiev: Dnipro 1977); and the emigré study that focuses on Galan's later years and tries to justify his assassination by a Ukrainian patriot: Petro Tereshchuk, *Istoriia odnoho zradnyka: Iaroslav Halan* (Toronto: Liga Vyzvolennia Ukraïny 1962).

Chapter 8

1939–1944

Background

September 1, 1939, marked the beginning of World War II. It also marked the beginning of a five-year holocaust during which society in Galicia was completely torn apart. The initial invasion of the Red Army resulted in the decimation of segments of the Ukrainian and Polish populations and the establishment of a radically new form of government; warring factions of the Organization of Ukrainian Nationalists (OUN) fought with each other, with the Germans, with the Poles, with Soviet partisans, and with the Red Army; Ukrainians sympathetic to Soviet rule were ousted by those who accepted German rule, who were in turn forced to flee in the face of the returning Red Army in 1944. The local German populace was "voluntarily" relocated to the German fatherland while the large and vibrant Galician Jewish community was physically liquidated.[1] It seemed that during these five years, no matter what side an inhabitant chose, it would sooner or later be the wrong one. And if individuals tried to remain apolitical, they still would be hard pressed to avoid the raids, artillery, or bombing of one of the many competing factions.

Galicia's fate was decided on August 23, 1939, when the Ribbentrop-Molotov nonaggression pact was signed between Germany and the Soviet Union. Both countries agreed not to attack each other while they were engaging in the total destruction of Poland. Germany's attack from the west on September 1 was followed by a Soviet attack from the east on September 17. By mutual agreement, the Red Army occupied L'viv and the rest of Galicia east of the San River. As a

1 On the German and Jewish minorities during World War II, see chapter 10, notes 46–74 and 97–98.

GALICIA SINCE 1939
International borders since 1945
Oblast boundaries
German-Soviet demarcation line Sept. 1939-June 1941
0 50 MILES
0 50 KILOMETERS
N
POLAND
Chełm
Wieprz
Vistula
Dunajec
Nowy Sącz
Wisłok
San
Przemyśl
Sanok
LEMKIAN REGION
Dukla Pass
Prešov
CZECHOSLOVAKIA
Košice
Uzhhorod
Tysa
HUNGARY
CARPATHIAN MOUNTAINS
TRANSCARPATHIA
Sighet
ROMANIA
BUKOVINA
VOLHYNIA
Luts'k
Buh
RIVNE
Brody
UKRAINIAN S. S. R.
L'viv
L'VIV
Drohobych
Stryi
Dniester
Ivano-Frankivs'k (Stanyslaviv)
IVANO-FRANKIVS'K
Kolomyia
Cheremosh
Chernivtsi
CHERNIVTSI
Prut
Ternopil'
TERNOPIL'
Seret
Zbruch
Khmel'nyts'kyi (Proskuriv)
KHMEL'NYTS'KYI
Kam"ianets' Podil's'kyi

result, only Ukrainian-inhabited areas around Przemyśl and the Lemkian region in the Carpathians remained under German control as part of a large area stretching as far as Warsaw and known as the *Generalgouvernement*.

In lands under the control of the Red Army, Soviet-style elections were organized on October 22 for a People's Assembly of the Western Ukraine. Four days later, this body, which in large part was composed of local communists and their sympathizers as well as delegates sent from the Soviet Ukraine, requested to be incorporated into the Ukrainian SSR. The request was granted on November 1, and immediately a Soviet administration was set up throughout eastern Galicia. Soviet rule lasted until June 22, 1941, when the Germans broke their nonaggression pact and invaded the Soviet Union. Within a few days, eastern Galicia was overrun by German troops and on August 1, it was made the fifth province of the *Generalgouvernement*.

For almost three years, the area was ruled by the Germans. Ukrainians were employed only at the lowest levels of the administration and a few organizations were permitted: a branch of the Cracow-based Ukrainian Central Committee, some schools, a publishing house, and a theater. None of the older political parties abolished by the Soviets were permitted to be revived, and both factions of the OUN, which before 1941 had reached an accommodation with the Germans, were banned. A military force was allowed, however; in April 1943, the Galician Division was formed from Ukrainian volunteers and it fought within the ranks of the German Waffen SS. But as the Germans began their retreat from Soviet territory, Galicia again became a theater of military operations. By mid-1943, Ukrainian nationalist and some Soviet partisans were operating in the region, and by March 1944, the Red Army controlled all territory east of Kolomyia and Ternopil'. On July 27, the Soviets took L'viv and by early August controlled all of eastern Galicia. The area was once again a part of the Ukrainian Soviet Socialist Republic and a Soviet administration and government were installed.

Historical surveys and sources

The literature on these war years includes some general studies, some Soviet writings on the period of Communist rule, and several works on the OUN and military operations in the region. As with the interwar period, the historical literature consists primarily of memoirs or personal histories by participants in one of the numerous political factions, or of highly partisan accounts defending a Ukrainian nationalist, Nazi German, Soviet, or Polish viewpoint.

The only attempt at an objective account of this period is found in John Armstrong's history of Ukrainian nationalism between 1939 and 1945. Although he deals with the Ukrainian problem in general, much of his account focuses on

Galicia and the activity of the OUN.[2] Also of value is a two-volume study by Roman Ilnytzkyj, whose analysis of German-Ukrainian relations between 1934 and 1945 contains much information on Galicia.[3]

Besides several works on the initial two years of Galicia's existence as part of the Soviet Ukraine (1939–1941),[4] Soviet writers have also prepared a collection of documents[5] and histories of the peasantry and the underground Communist party during the years 1941 to 1944.[6] Their views are straightforward and unchanging: Galician Ukrainians who sympathized with the two factions of the OUN, with the German administration, or with political, cultural, and religious movements that stemmed from the interwar period, all these are dastardly traitors who for their own "bourgeois-nationalist" ends allied with Hitler's fascists in a barbaric exploitation of the working classes.[7]

Other general works that reflect an understanding of events from various and often conflicting perspectives are contemporary German handbooks on the *Gene-*

2 John Armstrong, *Ukrainian Nationalism, 1939–1945,* Studies of the Russian Institute (New York: Columbia University Press 1955), 2nd rev. ed. (New York: Columbia University Press, 1963; reprinted Littleton, Colorado: Ukrainian Academic Press, 1980).

3 Roman Ilnytzkyj, *Deutschland und die Ukraine 1934–1945: Tatsachen europäischer Ostpolitik,* 2 vols (Munich: Osteuropa-Institut 1955–56), 2nd ed. (1958).

4 See notes 15 to 22 below.

5 *Borot'ba trudiashchykh L'vivshchyny proty nimets'ko-fashysts'kykh zaharbnykiv (1941–1944 rr.): zbirnyk dokumentiv i materialiv* (L'viv: Vil'na Ukraïna 1949).

See also the appropriate documents in note 15 below, and M.K. Ivasiuta et al., eds, *Z istoriï kolektyvizatsiï sil's'koho hospodarstva zakhidnykh oblastei Ukraïns'koï RSR: zbirnyk dokumentiv* (Kiev: Naukova dumka 1976); *Radians'kyi L'viv, 1939–1955: dokumenty i materialy* (L'viv: Knyzhkovo-zhurnal'ne vyd. 1956); and M.P. Hlyns'kyi and M.M. Nesterets', comps, *Radians'ka Ternopil'shchyna 1939–1958: dokumenty i materialy* (L'viv: Kameniar 1971).

6 M.K. Ivasiuta, "Stanovyshche selianstva zakhidnykh oblastei Ukraïns'koï RSR pid chas tymchasovoï nimets'ko-fashysts'koï okupatsiï i ioho borot'ba z zaharbnykamy ta ïkh naimytamy (cherven' 1941–zhovten' 1944 roku)," *Z istoriï zakhidnoukraïns'kykh zemel',* vol. V (Kiev: AN URSR 1960), pp. 168–186; Volodymyr O. Zamlyns'kyi, *Z viroiu u peremohu: komunistychna partiia na choli partyzans'koï borot'by proty nimets'ko-fashysts'kykh zaharbnykiv u zakhidnykh oblastiakh Ukraïny 1941–1944* (Kiev: Vyshcha shkola 1976).

7 V. Rudniev, *Ukraïns'ki burzhuazni natsionalisty–ahentura mizhnarodnoï reaktsiï* (Kiev: Derzhpolitvydav URSR 1955); Volodymyr O. Zamlyns'kyi, *Shliakh chornoho zradnytstva: zlochyny ukraïns'kykh burzhuaznykh natsionalistiv v zakhidnykh oblastiakh Ukraïny naperedodni i v roky Velykoï Vitchyznianoï viiny* (L'viv 1969); Klym Ie. Dmytruk, *Pid shtandartamy reaktsiï i fashyzmu: krakh antynarodnoï diial'nosti uniats'koï ta avtokefal'noï tserkov* (Kiev: Naukova dumka 1976). See also the earlier polemics: B. Dudykevych and Ia. Vitoshyns'kyi, *Ukraïns'ki burzhuazni natsionalisty–naimantsi mizhnarodnykh imperialistiv* (L'viv: Knyzhkovo-zhurnal'ne vyd-vo 1952); O. Poltorats'kyi, *Ukraïns'ki burzhuazni natsionalisty–nailiutishi vorohy ukraïns'koho narodu* (Kiev: Derzhpolitvydav URSR 1953).

ralgouvernement;[8] a comparative view of German policy toward Galicia and Slovenia;[9] detailed descriptions of the period by Kost' Pan'kivs'kyi (1897–1974), who had served as general secretary of the Ukrainian National Council (1941) and head of the Ukrainian Land Committee (1942–1944) in L'viv;[10] studies of the impact of Soviet, German, and again Soviet rule upon Poles especially in L'viv;[11] and letters and decrees of Metropolitan Andrei Sheptyts'kyi, the influential Greek Catholic hierarch who tried with some success to limit the extreme actions of the Germans and various factions of the Ukrainian leadership.[12]

Soviet rule, 1939–1941

The first two years of the war have received much attention. Volodymyr Kubiiovych's detailed history of Ukrainians in the *Generalgouvernement* from 1939 to 1941 includes much information on those parts of Ukrainian Galicia (the area around Przemyśl and the Lemkian Region) that had at the outset of the war come under German rule.[13]

8 *Die ukrainische Volksgruppe im Generalgouvernement,* Bevölkerungswesen und Fürsorge, vol. I, 2nd ed. (Cracow: Volkspolitischer Informationsdienst der Regierung des Generalgouvernements innere Verwaltung 1940); Karl Baedeker, *Das Generalgouvernement: Reisehandbuch* (Leipzig: K. Baedeker's Vlg. 1943).

9 Ihor Kamenetsky, "The National-Socialist Policy in Slovenia and Western Ukraine During World War II," *Annals of the Ukrainian Academy of Arts and Sciences in the United States,* XIV, 37–38 (New York 1978–80), pp. 39–67.

10 Kost' Pan'kivs'kyi, *Vid derzhavy do Komitetu (lito 1941 roku u L'vovi)* (New York and Toronto: Zhyttia i mysli 1957), 2nd ed. (New York and Toronto: Kliuchi 1970); idem, *Roky nimets'koï okupatsiï (1941–1944)* (New York and Toronto: Zhyttia i mysli 1965).

On the Ukrainian National Council, see also the recent study by Stepan M. Horak, "Ukraïntsi i druha svitova viina: dosvid u spivpratsi z Nimechchynoiu, 1941–1942," *Ukraïns'kyi istoryk,* XVI, 1–4 (New York, Toronto, and Munich 1979), p. 23–40.

11 Zygmunt Sobieski, "Reminiscences from Lwow, 1939–1946," *Journal of Central European Affairs,* VI, 4 (Boulder, Colo. 1947), pp. 350–374; Zygmunt Albert, *Lwowski Wydział Lekarski w czasie okupacji hitlerowskiej 1941–1944,* Prace Wrocławskiego Towarzystwa Naukowego, seria B, vol. CLXXXIX (Wrocław 1973).

See also comments on the Polish-Ukrainian problem in Galicia as discussed in Polish underground and emigré circles during World War II: Ryszard Torzecki, "Kontakty polsko-ukraińskie na tle problemu ukraińskego w polityce polskiego rządu emigracyjnego i podziemia (1939–1944)," *Dzieje Najnowsze,* XIII, 1–2 (Warsaw 1981), pp. 319–346.

12 Andrei Sheptyts'kyi, *Pys'ma-Poslannia·z chasiv nimets'koï okupatsiï [Tvory],* pt 2, Biblioteka Lohosu, vol. XXX (Yorkton 1969).

13 Volodymyr Kubiiovych, *Ukraïntsi v Heneral'nii Hubernii 1939–1941: istoriia Ukraïns'koho tsentral'noho komitetu* (Chicago: Vyd-vo Mykola Denysiuka 1975).

The period of Soviet rule that lasted from September 1939 to June 1941 in the part of Galicia that was east of the German-Soviet demarcation line (San River) is the subject of several works by Soviet Ukrainian authors. They view this period as one in which the local population was finally liberated from the centuries-long period of oppression by foreign rulers in cooperation with local Ukrainian bourgeois elements–a ''dark era'' that had lasted since the fall of the Galician-Volhynian principality in the fourteenth century until 1939, when the region was finally ''reincorporated'' into the bosom of the Soviet Ukrainian motherland.[14]

The Soviets have prepared a collection of documents on the unification of the western Ukrainian lands,[15] histories of the administrative, socioeconomic, and cultural changes that resulted,[16] and a praiseworthy account of the Communist party's role in these developments.[17] They have also written individual studies on what are considered the many positive achievements of Soviet rule: nationalization of industry,[18] collectivization of the land,[19] restrictions on the church and reorganization of the educational system,[20] and the ''creation of a new Soviet

14 For contemporary works outlining the general Soviet historical view of Galicia, see chapter 2, n. 45.

On the Red Army's military operations in September 1939, see the recollections of the participants in U.P. Krikun, *Geroizm otvaga, muzhestvo i doblest': rasskazy uchastnikov boev za osvobozhdenie trudiashchikhsia Zapadnoi Ukrainy i Zapadnoi Belorussii* (Kiev: Gospolitizdat 1940).

15 *Vozz''iednannia ukraïns'koho narodu v iedynii Ukraïns'kii Radians'kii derzhavi (1939–1949 rr.): zbirnyk dokumentiv i materialiv* (Kiev: Derzhpolitvydav URSR 1949).

16 Vasyl' L. Varets'kyi, *Sotsialistychni peretvorennia u zakhidnykh oblastiakh URSR (v dovoiennyi period)* (Kiev: AN URSR 1960); B.M. Babii, *Vozz''iednannia Zakhidnoï Ukraïny z Ukraïns'koiu RSR* (Kiev: AN URSR 1954).

17 *Narysy istoriï l'vivs'koï oblasnoï partiinoï orhanizatsiï*, 2nd rev. ed. (L'viv: Kameniar 1969), especially pp. 62–125.

18 V.L. Varets'kyi, ''Sotsialistychne peretvorennia promyslovosti zakhidnykh oblastei Ukraïny v 1939–1941 rr.,'' *Z istoriï borot'by za vstanovlennia radians'koï vlady na Ukraïni, Naukovi zapysky Instytutu istoriï AN URSR*, XI (Kiev 1957), pp. 289–323; H.I. Koval'chak, ''Rozvytok sotsialistychnoï promyslovosti v zakhidnykh oblastiakh URSR u 1939–1941 rokakh,'' in *Z istoriï zakhidnoukraïns'kykh zemel'*, vol. IV, ed. I.P. Kryp''iakevych (Kiev: AN URSR 1960), pp. 121–131; D.D. Nyzovyi, ''Sotsialistychna perebudova naftovoï promyslovosti radians'koho Prykarpattia v 1939–1941 rokakh,'' *Z istoriï zakhidnoukraïns'kykh zemel'*, vol. V (Kiev: AN URSR 1960), pp. 153–167.

19 M.K. Ivasiuta, ''Pershi uspikhy kolektyvizatsiï sil's'koho hospodarstva v zakhidnykh oblastiakh URSR (1939–1941 roky),'' in *Z istoriï zakhidnoukraïns'kykh zemel'*, vol. IV, ed. I.P. Kryp''iakevych (Kiev: AN URSR, 1960), pp. 132–144.

20 F.I. Steblii, ''Perebudova i rozvytok vyshchoï osvity v zakhidnykh oblastiakh URSR v pershi roky radians'koï vlady (veresen' 1939–cherven' 1941 rr.),'' in *Z istoriï Ukraïns'koï RSR*, vol. VI–VII (Kiev: AN URSR 1962), pp. 126–141; T.H. Sokolovs'ka, ''Ideino-vykhovna ta

intelligentsia."[21] Of course, the forcible character of the process that led to such "achievements," even though they were carried out with a Ukrainian national coloring and in the name of the Ukrainian people, is not to be found in Soviet accounts, but rather in a collection of mostly anonymous eyewitness accounts of the period edited by the former parliamentary deputy Milena Rudnyts'ka.[22]

Political developments

In an era of war, rapid political change, and extreme violence, it is not surprising that the activist movement founded in Galicia during the interwar period–the OUN–would come to play a dominant role in Ukrainian affairs. After the generally respected head of the OUN, Ievhen Konovalets', was assassinated in 1938 by a Soviet agent, the directorate (*Provid*) of the organization chose Andrii Mel'nyk (1890–1964) as its new leader. Mel'nyk had fought in the Ukrainian Sich Riflemen during World War I and was arrested in 1924 by the Poles for being the leader of the underground Ukrainian Military Organization (UVO) during the 1920s. But his generally moderate attitude toward political change and reluctance to use violent methods as well as his close relationship with Metropolitan Sheptyts'kyi–all of which made Mel'nyk a leader who could appeal to a broad spectrum of Galician-Ukrainian public opinion–were at the same time characteristics deplored by the younger, more radical, and military-minded members of the OUN. These included Stepan Bandera (1910–1959), Mykola Lebed' (b. 1910), Roman Shukhevych (Taras Chuprynka, 1907–1950), and Iaroslav Stets'ko (b. 1912), who were suspicious of anything that suggested compromise, a policy that had been adopted by older Ukrainian leaders and which they believed had failed totally.

These differences in attitude came to the fore when, as a result of Germany's defeat of Poland, many imprisoned younger members of the OUN were released.

---

kul'turno-osvitnia robota v zakhidnykh oblastiakh URSR (veresen' 1939–cherven' 1941 r.)," *Naukovi zapysky LDU*, XLIII: *Seriia istorychna*, 6 (L'viv 1957), pp. 16–29.

21 L.V. Nazarova, "Pershi uspikhy Radians'koï vlady u stvorenni novoï, radians'koï intelihentsiï v zakhidnykh oblastiakh Ukraïny (1939–1941 rr.)," *Naukovi zapysky L'vivs'koho politekhnichnoho instytutu*, XLVII: *Seriia suspil'nykh nauk*, no. 1 (L'viv 1957), pp. 30–44. For literary activities during these two years, see T.H. Sokolovs'ka, "Rozvytok literatury i mystetstva v zakhidnykh oblastiakh URSR v pershi roky radians'koï vlady (veresen' 1939–cherven' 1941 rr.)," in *Pytannia istoriï SRSR* (L'viv: LU 1958), pp. 5–18; V.V. Lesyk, "Diial'nist' Oleksy Desniaka u L'vovi," *Naukovi zapysky L'vivs'koho derzhavnoho universytetu*, XIX: *Literaturno-krytychnyi zbirnyk*, 1 (L'viv 1951), pp. 110–119.

22 Milena Rudnyts'ka, ed., *Zakhidna Ukraïna pid bol'shevykamy: IX. 1939–VI. 1941* (New York: NTSh v Amerytsi 1958).

They proceeded to denounce Mel'nyk and the OUN directorate and in February 1940 established a rival Revolutionary Directorate of the OUN headed by Stepan Bandera. This was the origin of the struggle between the Melnykites (*Mel'nykivtsi*) and Banderites (*Banderivtsi*), which severely weakened Ukrainian political and military efforts during World War II. The activist Banderites formed military units (*Nachtigall* and *Roland*) that fought with the German Army against the Soviets, and when Germany took over Galicia, Banderite leaders declared the existence of a Ukrainian National Government in L'viv on June 30, 1941. The German government was displeased by such an act and it put Bandera and some of his associates under house arrest in Berlin. The interned Banderite leaders were still able to maintain contact with Galicia, where in the spring of 1943 the Ukrainian Insurgent Army (Ukraïns'ka Povstans'ka Armiia–UPA) was established. The UPA, led by Roman Shukevych (Chuprynka), fought against the Germans and, following the rapid disintegration of the eastern front in 1944, against the Red Army as well. As for Mel'nyk, who like Bandera was confined to Berlin until 1944, some of his supporters also conducted partisan warfare, although most were arrested by the Germans or eliminated by their Banderite rivals.

The literature on the OUN reflects strongly Melnykite and Banderite partisanship. On the Melnykite side, there exists a collection of essays on that faction's activity,[23] histories and memoirs by participants in the movement,[24] and studies on the life and work of Andrii Mel'nyk.[25] On the Banderite side, there is a collection of decrees issued by that OUN faction,[26] an extensive work by Iaroslav Stets'ko on the June 30, 1941 declaration of an independent state for which he was prime minister,[27] and a biography by Petro Mirchuk of Stepan Bandera.[28] Both

23 *Orhanizatsiia Ukraïns'kykh Natsionalistiv 1929–1954* (Paris: OUN 1955).

24 H. Polikarpenko, *Orhanizatsiia Ukraïns'kykh Natsionalistiv pidchas druhoï svitovoï viiny,* 4th rev. ed. (n.p. 1951); Zynovii Knysh, *Pered pokhodom na skhid: spohady i materiialy do diiannia OUN u 1939–1941 rokakh,* 2 vols (Toronto: Sribna Surma n.d.); idem, *Rozbrat: spohady i materiialy do rozkolu OUN u 1940–1941 rokakh* (Toronto: Sribna Surma 1960); idem, *B'ie dvanadtsiata: spohady i materiialy do diiannia OUN naperedodni nimets'ko-moskovs'koï viiny 1941 r.* (Toronto: Sribna Surma n.d.).

25 Zynovii Knysh, ed., *Nepohasnyi ohon' viry: zbirnyk na poshanu polkovnyka Andriia Mel'nyka, holovy Provodu ukraïns'kykh natsionalistiv* (Paris: Natsionalistychne vyd-vo v Europi 1974).

26 *OUN v svitli postanov velykykh zboriv, konferentsii ta inshykh dokumentiv z borot'by 1929–1955 r.: zbirka dokumentiv* (n.p.: Zakordonni chastyny OUN 1955).

27 Iaroslav S. Stets'ko, *30 chervnia 1941: proholoshennia vidnovlennia derzhavnosty Ukraïny* (Toronto: Liga Vyzvolennia Ukraïny, Orhanizatsiia Oborony Chotyr'okh Svobid Ukraïny and Ukraïns'ka Vydavnycha Spilka 1967). See also the memoirs of Lev Rebet and Mykola Klymyshyn, chapter 7, n. 58.

28 Petro Mirchuk, *Stepan Bandera: symvol revoliutsiinoï bezkompromisovosty* (New York and Toronto: OOChSU and Liga Vyzvolennia Ukraïny 1961).

Polish and Soviet writers have provided extensive histories of the OUN, which they view simply as the most treacherous of all bourgeois-fascist elements and which they argue did irreparable harm to the Ukrainian people of Galicia.[29] An exception to such an approach has been put forth by the Polish scholar Ryszard Torzecki, who has provided relatively objective accounts of the split between the Melnykites and the Banderites as well as of German policy toward Ukrainians during the war years.[30]

Military developments

Several works are devoted to Galician-Ukrainian military developments during World War II. A general survey of the battles fought by the various Galician-Ukrainian military formations is found in a large work by the Polish military historians Antoni B. Szczęśniak and Wiesław Z. Szota.[31] Individual aspects of the Galician-Ukrainian war effort have also been analyzed, whether they be OUN-Banderite volunteers in the units *Roland* and *Nachtigall,* which participated in the German invasion of the Soviet Union in June 1941 until they were recalled late in the year and finally disbanded in 1941 because of their opposition to German policy;[32] the so-called marching groups (*pokhidni hrupy*) dispatched by both factions of the OUN to organize the local population and lay the foundations for a new state on Soviet Ukrainian territory occupied by German forces between 1941

29 The Polish view is presented in Antoni Szczęśniak, ''Niektóre problemy stosunków polsko-ukraińskich w latach 1939–1947,'' in *Polska Ludowa,* vol. VII (Warsaw: PWN 1968), pp. 59–106; Tadeusz Cieślak, ''Hitlerowski sojusz z nacjonalizmem ukraińskim w Polsce,'' in *Z dziejów stosunków polsko-radzieckich,* vol. V (Warsaw: Książka i Wiedza 1969), pp. 93–108; and Edward Prus, ''Utworzenie kolaboracyjnego rządu ukraińskich nacjonalistów i ogłoszenie we Lwowie w 1941 r. 'Samostijnej derżawy' pod protektoratem Trzeciej Rzeszy,'' in *Z dziejów stosunków polsko-radzieckich,* vol. IX (Warsaw: Książka i Wiedza 1972), pp. 107–138.

The Soviet view is in V. Bieliaiev and M. Rudnyts'kyi, *Pid chuzhymy praporamy* (Kiev: Radians'kyi pys'mennyk 1958); and Klym Dmytruk, *Bezbatchenky: pravda pro uchast' ukraïns'kykh burzhuaznykh natsionalistiv i tserkovnykh iierarkhiv u pidhotovtsi napadu fashysts'koï Nimechchyny na SRSR* (L'viv: Kameniar 1972).

30 Ryszard Torzecki, ''Geneza rozłamu w Organizacji Ukraińskich Nacjonalistów,'' in *Studia z dziejów ZSRR i Europy Środkowej,* vol. V (Wrocław, Warsaw, and Cracow: ZNIO–PAN 1969), pp. 147–158; idem, ''Niektóre aspekty hitlerowskiej polityki wobec Ukraińców (1940–1944),'' in *Z dziejów stosunków polsko-radzieckich,* vol. V (Warsaw: Książka i Wiedza 1969), pp. 155–160.

31 Antoni B. Szczęśniak and Wiesław Z. Szota, *Droga do nikąd: działalność Organizacji Ukraińskich Nacjonalistów i jej likwidacja w Polsce* (Warsaw: Wojskowy Instytut Historyczny 1973), especially pp. 64–206 on activity to 1944.

32 *Druzhyny ukraïns'kykh natsionalistiv v 1941–42 rokakh* ([Winnipeg] 1953).

and 1943;[33] the Division SS Galicia (SS Division Galizien) formed in 1943 by the Germans from Galician-Ukrainian volunteers who fought against the Soviets on the eastern front until its defeat at Brody in July 1944;[34] the division's successor, the Ukrainian National Army formed in late 1944 to fight alongside the Germans in Austria until the end of the war;[35] or the Ukrainian Insurgent Army (UPA) of Stepan Bandera, which not only fought a guerilla war in Galicia and Volhynia against the retreating Germans and advancing Red Army during the last years of World War II, but continued its military operations against the Communist government of Poland until 1948, and the Soviet Union until as late as the early 1950s.[36]

33 Lev Shankovs'kyi, *Pokhidni hrupy OUN: prychynky do istorii pokhidnykh hrup OUN na tsentral'nykh i skhidnikh zemliakh Ukraïny v 1941–1943 rr.* (Munich: Ukraïns'kyi samostiinyk 1958).

34 See the brief but objective analysis of the German motivation behind the formation of this unit in Basil Dmytryshyn, "The Nazis and the SS Volunteer Division 'Galicia'," *American Slavic and East European Review,* XV, 1 (New York 1956), pp. 1–10; an account of the unit's military activity by a member of the German general staff assigned to the division: Wolf-Dietrich Heike, *Ukraïns'ka dyviziia 'Halychyna': istoriia formuvannia i boiovykh dii u 1943–45 rokakh,* in *Zapysky NTSh* CLXXXIII (Toronto, Paris, and Munich 1970), and German edition: *Sie wollten Freiheit: Die Geschichte der Ukrainischen Division 1943–45* (Dorheim: Podzun Vlg. 1973); the extensive history by Jorge Tys-Krojmaluk [Krokhmaliuk], *Guerra y libertad: historia de la Division 'Halychyna' (DUI) del ejercito nacional ucraino, 1943–1945* (Buenos Aires: Editorial Ucraino 1961); and the memoirs by a member in the unit: Roman Krokhmaliuk, *Zahrava na skhodi: spohady i dokumenty z pratsi u viis'kovii upravi 'Halychyna' v 1943–45 rokakh* (Toronto: Bratstvo kolyshnykh voiakiv 1-oï Ukraïns'koï Dyvizii UNA 1978).

35 Mykola Kapustians'kyi, "Persha ukraïns'ka dyviziia Ukraïns'koï Natsional'noï Armii," in Myron Levyts'kyi, ed., *Istoriia ukraïns'koho viis'ka,* 2nd rev. ed. (Winnipeg: Ivan Tyktor 1953), pp. 604–634. See also the memoirs of the army's commander, Pavlo Shandruk, *Arms of Valor* (New York: Robert Speller 1958).

36 For sympathetic histories of the UPA, see Petro Mirchuk, *Ukraïns'ka Povstans'ka Armiia, 1942–1952* (Munich 1953); Mykola Lebed', *UPA: ii geneza, rist i dii u vyvol'nii borot'bi ukraïns'koho narodu za ukraïns'ku samostiinu sobornu derzhavu,* pt I: *Nimets'ka okupatsiia Ukraïny* (n.p.: Vyd. Presovoho biura UHVR 1946); O. Martovych, *The Ukrainian Insurgent Army* (Munich 1950); Lev Shankovs'kyi, "Ukraïns'ka Povstancha Armiia," in Myron Levyts'kyi, ed., *Istoriia ukraïns'koho viis'ka,* 2nd rev. ed. (Winnipeg: Ivan Tyktor 1953), pp. 635–819; Enrique Martínez Codó, "Guerilla Warfare in the Ukraine," *Military Review,* XL, 8 (Fort Leavenworth, Kan. 1960), pp. 3–14; idem, *Guerrillas tras la Cortina de hierro* (Buenos Aires: Instituto informativo–Editorial ucranio 1966); Yuriy Tys-Krokhmaliuk, *UPA Warfare in Ukraine* (New York: Society of Veterans of the Ukrainian Insurgent Army 1972). On the UPA's postwar activity, see n. 31 above and chapter 9, notes 3–8, 11–12.

Although critical of UPA activity, a useful description of the army's organization during World War II is in Wiesław Szota, "Zarys rozwoju Organizacji Ukraińskich Nacjonalistów i Ukraińskiej Powstańczej Armii," *Wojskowy Przegląd Historyczny,* VIII, 1 (Warsaw 1963), pp. 163–218.

Soviet writers have glorified the underground military activity of various pro-Soviet partisan units that fought against the Germans and Ukrainian nationalists.[37] Special attention has, of course, been given to the heroic efforts of the Red Army, which "liberated" eastern Galicia from the German fascist military machine and made possible the "reunification" of the region with the Soviet Ukraine.[38] The Red Army's advance into Galicia began with its victories after the siege of Ternopil' (March–April 1944) and Battle of Brody (July 7–22, 1944), and ended in the fierce struggle to acquire the Dukla Pass in the Carpathian Mountains (September–November 1944), which opened the way to the Danube Basin.[39] In the wake of these military victories, it was once again possible to install a Soviet regime.

37 Special attention has been given to the Soviet guerilla leader, Sydir Kovpak, who made a daring raid behind the German front line deep into Galicia in July 1943, an act that prompted other pro-Soviet partisan units as well as the UPA into action. Part of Kovpak's memoirs deal with his action in Galicia. The original Russian-language edition was translated into English as S.A. Kovpak, *Our Partisan Course* (London and New York: Hutchinson 1947?) and into Ukrainian as *Vid Putyvlia do Karpat* (Kiev: Dnipro 1968), 2nd ed. (Kiev: Vyd-vo politychnoï literatury Ukraïny 1973).

See also Volodymyr O. Zamlyns'kyi, *Karaiucha zemlia* (L'viv: Kameniar 1965); Vira D. Variahina and Havriil S. Vakulenko, *Narodna hvardiia imeni Iv. Franka: storinky heroichnoï borot'by pidpil'no-partyzans'koï orhanizatsiï zakhidnykh oblastei Ukraïny, 1942–1944 roky* (L'viv: Kameniar 1967); and the extensive Soviet literature on World War II Galician partisan activity in the bibliography (items 414–604), *Zakhidni oblasti,* listed in chapter 1, n. 55.

On cooperation between pro-Polish and Ukrainian partisans, see Mieczysław Juchniewicz and Julian Tobiasz, "Polsko-ukraińskie współdziałanie w ruchu podziemnym i partyzanckim w latach II wojny światowej," in *Z dziejów stosunków polsko-radzieckich,* vol. V (Warsaw: Książka i Wiedza 1969), pp. 109–131; and Ihor Brechak, *Boiovi pobratymy: z istoriï uchasti pol's'kykh antyfashystiv u radians'komu partyzans'komu rusi na Ukraïni v roky Velykoï Vitchyznianoï viiny* (L'viv: Kameniar 1974).

38 I.V. Parot'kin, *Vyzvolennia zakhidnoï Ukraïny* (Kiev: Ukraïns'ke vyd-vo politychnoï literatury 1946); O. Tsybko, "Vyzvol'nyi pokhid Chervenoï Armiï v Zakhidnu Ukraïnu ta vozz''iednannia Zakhidnoï Ukraïny z Radians'koiu Ukraïnoiu," in *300 rokiv vozz''iednannia Ukraïny z Rosiieiu: naukovyi zbirnyk* (L'viv 1954), pp. 187–212; M.A. Polushkin, *Na Sandomirskom napravlenii: l'vovsko-sandomirskaia operatsiia, iul'-avgust 1944 g.* (Moscow: Voenizdat 1969); Viktor B. Ananiichuk, *Vyzolennia zakhidnykh oblastei Ukraïny vid nimets'ko-fashysts'kykh okupantiv* (Kiev: Vyd-vo Kyïvs'koho universytetu 1969); Iu.K. Strizhkov, *Geroi Peremyshlia* (Moscow: Nauka 1969).

See also the collection of articles and memoirs in B.V. Samarin et al., *V boiakh za L'vovshchinu* (L'viv: Kameniar 1965) and *Geroi osvobozhdeniia Prikarpat'ia* (Uzhhorod: Karpaty 1970); B.S. Venkov, ed., *V boiakh za Karpaty* (Uzhhorod: Karpaty 1975), as well as the extensive Soviet literature listed in the bibliography (items 1068–1225), *Zakhidni oblasti URSR* ..., chapter 1, n. 55.

39 For works on the Battle of Brody in which the Galician Division participated, see the emigré

memorial book: Oleh Lysiak, ed., *Brody: zbirnyk stattei i narysiv* (Munich: Bratstvo kolyshnikh voiakiv Pershoï UDUNA 1951), 2nd ed. (New York 1974), and the memoirs of a participant: Volodymyr Molodets'kyi, *U boiu pid Brodamy 28.VI–28.VII.1944* (Toronto: Dobra Knyzhka 1952). For the Soviet interpretation, see the collection of memoirs, documents, and articles in *Brodovskii kotel,* comp. M.V. Verbinskii and B.V. Samarin (L'viv: Kameniar 1974).

On the battle for the Dukla Pass, see D.M. Proiektor, *Cherez duklinskii pereval* (Moscow: Voennoe izd. Ministerstva oborony SSSR 1960). Because of its extreme importance in Communist Czechoslovakia's historical iconography, the Battle of Dukla, especially the operations on the southern slopes of the Carpathian Mountains, has received extensive treatment in Czech and Slovak Marxist writings. See the bibliography, *Dukla: výberový zoznam literatúry* (Prešov: Štátna vedecká knižnica 1959).

Chapter 9

1945 to the present

Background

The Red Army's success in driving the Germans out of eastern Galicia by the autumn of 1944 and the area's reincorporation into the Ukrainian Soviet Socialist Republic did not mean the end of military hostilities. The Ukrainian Insurgent Army (UPA), headed since 1943 by Roman Shukhevych (General Taras Chuprynka), together with the political wing of the movement, the Ukrainian Supreme Liberation Council (Ukraïns'ka Holovna Vyzvol'na Rada–UHVR, est. July 1944), continued to fight against what they considered the Soviet aggressor and its allies, the Communist-controlled governments of Poland and later Czechoslovakia. Against overwhelming odds, the UPA held out in the Carpathian Mountains and continued to make raids into the Galician lowlands until the early 1950s. By then, most of the UPA members had been killed or had escaped to Austria and West Germany via Czechoslovakia.

Despite such continued military resistance to Soviet rule, the new government proceeded with the transformation of Galician society. Ukrainian-inhabited Galicia was divided by the new Polish-Soviet border that ran northward from the Carpathians along the San River, then followed a northeast line, leaving Przemyśl within Poland. This meant that the Lemkian region and other Ukrainian areas around Przemyśl were returned to Polish rule. Under a Communist government, Polish authorities began to deport the Lemkian population from its homeland, at first eastward to the Soviet Ukraine, then in the spring and summer of 1947 westward and northward to lands (Wrocław, Zielona Góra, Szczecin, Olsztyn) acquired by Poland from Germany after the war.

The larger part of Galicia came under Soviet rule. The old administrative divisions were abolished and four new Soviet Ukrainian oblasts were created–

L'viv, Drohobych (made part of L'viv after 1959), Stanislav (renamed Ivano-Frankivs'k in 1962), and Ternopil'–which covered almost all of former eastern Galician territory. The new government proceeded to nationalize industries, banks, and the whole private business sector, as well as to collectivize the land and to reorganize educational and cultural facilities according to the Soviet model. Ukrainianization, again according to the Soviet model, was the official policy in all levels of life, although in practice Russian soon came to be a parallel and in some areas dominant linguistic medium. The Greek Catholic church was abolished in March 1946, when a group of priests "voluntarily" annulled the 1596 union with Rome and joined the Orthodox church. Recalcitrant Greek Catholic priests and hierarchs were jailed, while the legal Orthodox church was restricted in its activity. Besides this, several hundred thousand persons, including most of the prewar Galician-Ukrainian intelligentsia, were uprooted. A large number had fled westward before the advancing Red Army in 1944. Of those remaining behind, many were suspected of being opposed to the government or of having familial ties to known resisters and were deported to other parts of the Soviet Union.

As a result of these administrative, socioeconomic, cultural, religious, and demographic changes, Ukrainian Galicia, which had functioned as a historico-cultural unit since the early medieval era, had in fact ceased to exist after 1945. As part of an unofficial region known as the western Ukraine (which included northern Bukovina and Transcarpathia as well), eastern Galicia was profoundly transformed and very soon it was not significantly different from any other part of the Soviet Ukraine. Considering these factors, the following discussion of the basic literature on post-1945 "Galicia" is but a brief postscript to the periods discussed in the rest of this book.

Ukrainian resistance movement

The literature on post-World War II Galicia consists of works dealing with two subjects: the Ukrainian resistance movement led by the UPA and the transformation of Galician society under Soviet auspices. The views expressed in almost all works on these subjects reflect an absolute polarization. Consequently, members of the UPA either represent the last in a long line of military heroes fighting for the freedom of the Ukraine, or are considered fascist cutthroats trying to reverse the progressive course of Soviet history. Similarly, the transformation to a Soviet society is considered either as the highest stage in the history of Ukrainian Galicia, or as an inhumane imposition of an alien system upon a people that continues to suffer under totalitarian rule imposed by Moscow.

There is perhaps only one study of this period that has risen above the level of polemics. This is Yaroslav Bilinsky's history of the Soviet Ukraine after 1945, which includes two excellent chapters on the Soviet transformations in Galicia and the struggle of the Ukrainian Insurgent Army.[1]

Favorable views of the UPA's postwar military actions are found in general histories of that army by Petro Mirchuk, Iurii Tys-Krokhmaliuk, and Lev Shankovs'kyi.[2] There are also three volumes of documents on the postwar activity of the UPA and its political wing, the UHVR (the Ukrainian Supreme Revolutionary Council),[3] several memoirs,[4] a biography of UPA commander General Taras Chuprynka (Roman Shukhevych),[5] and a bibliography of the UPA underground press.[6] The Organization of Ukrainian Nationalists, from which the UPA and UHVR developed, continues its political activity in the West, as revealed in several collections of documents and other materials.[7]

Immediately after the war, the UPA was particularly well entrenched in the Lemkian region under Polish control, and it tried to stop the deportation of the local populace. The Ukrainian interpretation of these devastations and massacres is found in several articles published by the World Lemkos' Federation.[8] The Polish explanation for these ''population transfers'' is outlined in a monograph on

1 Yaroslav Bilinsky, *The Second Soviet Republic: The Ukraine after World War II* (New Brunswick, NJ: Rutgers University Press 1964).

2 See chapter 8, n. 36.

3 *Ukraïns'ka Povstans'ka Armiia: zbirka dokumentiv za 1942–1950 rr.*, 2 vols (n.p.: Vydannia Zakordonnykh Chastyn OUN 1957–60); *Ukraïns'ka Holovna Vyzvol'na Rada: zbirka dokumentiv za 1944–1950 rr.* (n.p.: Vydannia Zakordonnykh Chastyn OUN 1956).

4 Petro Mirchuk and V. Davydenko, eds, *V riadakh UPA: zbirka spomyniv buv. voiakiv Ukraïns'koï Povstans'koï Armiï* (New York: Tovarystvo b. Voiakiv UPA v ZDA i Kanadi 1957). See also Stepan Khrin, *Zymoiu v bunkri, 1947–48: spohady-khronika* (Augsburg: Do zbroï 1950).

5 Petro Mirchuk, *Roman Shukhevych (Gen. Taras Chuprynka): komandyr armiï bezsmertnykh* (New York, Toronto, and London: Tovarystvo Kolyshnikh Voiakiv UPA v ZSA, Kanadi i Evropi 1970).

6 Lev Shankovs'kyi, *U.P.A. ta ïï pidpil'na literatura* (Philadelphia: Ameryka 1952).

7 *OUN v svitli postanov velykykh zboriv, konferentsii ta inshykh dokumentiv z borot'by 1929–1955 rr.: zbirka dokumentiv* (n.p.: Zakordonni chastyny OUN 1955); *Chetvertyi velykyi zbir Orhanizatsiï Ukraïns'kykh Natsionalistiv*, 2 vols (n.p.: Vydannia OUN 1969); *Ukraïna spil'ne dobro vsikh ïï hromadian: materiialy VII velykoho zboru Ukraïns'kykh Natsionalistiv (VZUN)* (Paris and Baltimore: Smoloskyp 1971); Petro Mirchuk, *Za chystotu ukraïns'koho vyzvol'noho rukhu* (Munich and London 1955); Roman Krychevs'kyi, *Orhanizatsiia Ukraïns'kykh Natsionalistiv v Ukraïni–Orhanizatsiia Ukraïns'kykh Natsionalistiv Zakordonom i ZChOUN* (New York and Toronto 1962); *Orhanizatsiia Ukraïns'kykh Natsionalistiv 1929–1954* (Paris: OUN 1955).

8 See the articles by Walter Dushnyck, Ivan F. Evseev, Andrzej Kwilecki, John Hvosda, Bohdan Czajkowski, and Ievhen Vrets'ona in *Annaly Svitovoï Federatsiï Lemkiv*, II (Camillus, NY 1975), pp. 5–133.

the Lemkians by Andrzej Kwilecki;[9] the changes that have taken place in the Lemkian region since that time are analyzed in a solid sociological study by Maria Biernacka.[10] As for the immediate postwar years, several other works by former Polish officers describe in detail what they consider the heroic efforts of the Polish People's Republic's army to liquidate the "roaming bands" of the UPA, especially after they killed General Karol Świerczewski (1897–1947) in March 1947.[11] Czechoslovak Marxist authors have also compiled polemical studies and a collection of documents in an attempt to reveal the "dastardly" work of the UPA (often in supposed cooperation with the local Greek Catholic church) on Czechoslovak territory, where, nonetheless, some units did meet with sympathy from the Rusyn/Ukrainian population and other anti-Communist elements in Slovakia.[12]

9 Andrzej Kwilecki, *Łemkowie: zagadnienie migracji i asymilacji* (Warsaw: PWN 1974).

10 Maria Biernacka, *Kształtowanie się nowej społeczności wiejskiej w Bieszczadach*, Biblioteka Etnografii Polskiej, no. 29 (Wrocław, Warsaw, Cracow, and Gdańsk: ZNIO–PAN 1974).

11 The most comprehensive Polish history of postwar UPA military activity is in Antoni B. Szczęśniak and Wiesław Z. Szota, *Droga do nikąd: działalność Organizacji Ukraińskich Nacjonalistów i jej likwidacja w Polsce* (Warsaw: Wojskowy Instytut Historyczny 1973), especially pp. 207–468.

See also W. Szota, "Ukraińskie nacjonalistyczne podziemie zbrojne: zarys powstania i działalności," in Władysław Góra, ed., *1944–1947 w walce o utrwalenie władzy ludowej w Polsce* (Warsaw: Książka i Wiedza 1947), pp. 106–134; Ignacy Blum, "Udział Wojska Polskiego w obronie narodowych i społecznych interesów ludu polskiego oraz w umacnianiu władzy ludowej w latach 1945–1948," in *Sesja naukowa poświęcona wojnie wyzwoleńczej narodu polskiego 1939–45: materiały* (Warsaw: Ministerstwo Obrony Narodowej 1959), pp. 241–265; idem, "Udział Wojska Polskiego w walce o utrwalenie władzy ludowej: walki z bandami UPA," *Wojskowy Przegląd Historyczny*, IV, 1 (Warsaw 1959), pp. 3–29, reprinted in chapter 3 of his *Z dziejów wojska polskiego w latach 1945–1948* (Warsaw: Ministerstwo Obrony Narodowej 1960); Jan Gerhard, "Dalsze szczegóły walk z bandami UPA i WIN na południowo-wschodnim obszarze Polski," *Wojskowy Przegląd Historyczny*, IV, 4 (Warsaw 1959), pp. 304–335; Jan Borkowski, "Miejsce Polskiego Stronnictwa Ludowego w obozie reakcji (1945–1947)," *Z Pola Walki*, II, 2 (Warsaw 1959), pp. 56–79; Ryszard Halaba and Bolesław Szwejgiert, "Jeszcze o walkach ludowego Wojska Polskiego z reakcyjnym podziemiem," *Wojskowy Przegląd Historyczny*, V, 3 (Warsaw 1960), pp. 323–333; Tadeusz Pląskowski, "Bój pod Jabłonką 28 marca 1947 r.: śmierć generała Karola Świerczewskiego," *Małopolskie Studia Historyczne*, VII, 1–2 (Cracow 1964), pp. 79–95; Jan Czapla, "Walka z OUN–UPA w latach 1944–1947 (kureń 'Żeleźniaka')," in Maria Turlejska, ed., *Z walk przeciwko zbrojnemu podziemiu, 1944–1947* (Warsaw: Ministerstwo Obrony Narodowej 1966), pp. 359–424; Stanisław Walach, *Był w Polsce czas* (Cracow: Wydawnictwo Literackie 1969); Stanisław Rzepski, "Udział 8. Dywizji Piechoty w walce z bandami UPA w latach 1945–1947," *Wojskowy Przegląd Historyczny*, XIV, 2 (Warsaw 1969), pp. 113–157; and the extensive studies by Mieczysław Redziński, Wiesław Piątkowski, Mikołaj Tyliszczak, and Stanisław Janicki in Maria Turlejska, ed., *W walce ze zbrojnym podziemiem 1945–1947* (Warsaw: Ministerstwo Obrony Narodowej 1972), pp. 34–257.

12 Among the earliest examples of this genre of writing were Václav Slavík, *Pravá tvář*

Establishment of Soviet rule

Soviet writers have prepared much material describing the achievements of the Communist-led government in its transformation of Galician society. The administrative structure of the three oblasts that cover most of former Galicia has been outlined in great detail in a handbook covering the whole Ukrainian SSR,[13] and statistics for some of the oblasts have been published as well.[14] Several collections of documents have also been devoted to all or part of the Soviet period.[15]

The best general Soviet descriptions of the post-1945 period are found in the volumes on the L'viv, Ivano-Frankivs'k, and Ternopil' oblasts that are part of the twenty-six-volume history of cities and oblasts in the Ukrainian SSR. Although these large volumes cover developments from earliest times, most of the discussion focuses on the years after 1945.[16] There are, of course, other studies devoted to individual oblasts[17] and to achievements in the areas of industrialization,[18]

Banderovců: Akce B proti civilní síti (Prague 1948); and A. Svoboda, A. Tučková, and K. Svobodová, *Smlouva Vatíkanu proti ČSR* (Prague: Československá Akademie Věd 1950), translated into Russian as *Zagovor Vatikana protiv ChSR* (Moscow 1950).

Subsequent works have tried to put forward a more scholarly tone, although they are still anti-UPA, as in J. Fiala, "Československá armáda v boji proti Banderovcům v roce 1947," *Historie a vojenství*, IX, 3 (Prague 1960), pp. 237–283; and the collection of documents in František Kaucký and Ladislav Vandůrek, *Ve znamení trojzubce* (Prague: Naše vojsko 1965).

13 D.O. Sheliahin, comp., *Ukraïns'ka RSR: adminstratyvno-terytorial'nyi podil na 1 sichnia 1972 roku* (Kiev: Vyd-vo politychnoï literatury Ukraïny 1973), especially pp. 185–202, 271–301, and 410–429.

14 *Narodne hospodarstvo L'vivs'koï oblasti: statystychnyi zbirnyk* (L'viv: Derzhstatvydav 1958); *Narodnoe hospodarstvo Ternopil's'koï oblasti: statystychnyi zbirnyk* (Ternopil': Ternopil's'ke oblasne vyd-vo 1957).

15 See the appropriate sections in the documentary collections listed in chapter 8, n. 5.

16 See chapter 2, n. 101; and V. Malanchuk, *Sotsialistychni peretvorennia v zakhidnykh oblastiakh Ukraïns'koï RSR* (Kiev 1957).

17 V. Malanchuk and I. Petriv, *Nas iednaie velyka meta* [L'vivs'ka oblast'] (L'viv: Kameniar 1965); I.Ia. Kosharnyi, M.V. Pidpryhorshchuk, I.I. Hapshenko, and K.I. Skrypnyk, *Radians'ka Drohobychchyna* (Drohobych: Drohobyts'ke oblasne vyd-vo 1957); *Pro sotsialistychni peretvorennia na Stanislavshchyni* (Stanislav: Stanislavs'ke oblasne vyd-vo 1957).

18 V. Petrushko, *Rozvytok promyslovosti zakhidnykh oblastei Ukraïny* (Kiev 1958); V. Zasans'kyi, *Stvorennia i utverdzhennia sotsialistychnykh vyrobnychykh vidnosyn v promyslovosti zakhidnykh oblastei URSR* (L'viv 1958); Hryhorii I. Koval'chak, *Rozvytok promyslovosti v zakhidnykh oblastiakh Ukraïny za 20 rokiv radians'koï vlady (1939–1958 rr.): istoryko-ekonomichnyi narys* (Kiev: Naukova dumka 1965); Hryhorii I. Koval'chak, *Industrial'nyi rozvytok zakhidnykh oblastei Ukraïny v period komunistychnoho budivnytstva* (Kiev: Naukova dumka 1973).

collectivized agriculture,[19] education and culture,[20] and finally to the Communist party under whose direction such transformations were carried out.[21] The American specialist Roman Szporluk has provided a brief history of the post-1945 press and discusses linguistic assimilation, especially in western Ukrainian urban areas.[22]

As for the Greek Catholic church, the official proceedings of its liquidation (March 8–10, 1946) have been published,[23] while more recently Serhii Danylenko has written two editions of a historical chronicle, which attempts to show how during the twentieth century, the church, in cooperation with Polish landlords, Ukrainian bourgeois-nationalists, and German fascists, had been a source of intrigue in Galicia, and how after 1945 it supposedly continued from centers in the West its efforts to undermine the achievements of the Soviet Ukrainian homeland.[24] The innumerable arrests, life-long imprisonments, and death of many clergy and faithful, including the last metropolitan of L'viv, Cardinal Iosyf

19 I.P. Bohodyst, ''Sotsialistychna perebudova zakhidno-ukraïns'koho sela,'' *Ukraïns'kyi istorychnyi zhurnal,* I, 2 (Kiev 1957), pp. 69–82; H.I. Koval'chak, ed., *Sotsial'ni peretvorennia u radians'komu seli: na prykladi sil zakhidnykh oblastei Ukraïns'koï RSR* (Kiev: Naukova dumka 1976); M.K. Ivasiuta, *Narys istoriï kolektyvizatsiï sil's'koho hospodarstva Drohobychchyny: zbirnyk* (Drohobych: Obkom KP(b)U 1948).

20 A.I. Hliadkivs'ka and T.H. Sokolovs'ka, ''Kul'turna revoliutsiia v SRSR i kul'turne budivnytstvo v zakhidnykh oblastiakh Ukraïny,'' *300 rokiv vozz''iednannia Ukraïny z Rosiieiu* (L'viv 1954), pp. 260–279; O.K. Zuban', ''Rozvytok narodnoï osvity na L'vivshchyni za roky Radians'koï vlady,'' *Naukovi zapysky L'vivs'koho politekhnichnoho instytutu,* XLVII: *Seriia suspil'nykh nauk,* no. 1 (L'viv 1957); I.Ia. Zabokryts'kyi, ''Rozvytok narodnoï osvity na Ternopil'shchyni za roky radians'koï vlady,'' *Naukovi zapysky Kremenets'koho pedahohichnoho instytutu,* III (Ternopil' 1957); H.S. Davydova and L.A. Ivanenko, ''Braters'ka dopomoha narodiv Radians'koho Soiuzu u vidbudovi i rozvytky vyshchoï shkoly v zakhidnykh oblastiakh URSR (1939–1950 rr.),'' *Visnyk LDU: Seriia istorychna,* no. 10 (L'viv 1974), pp. 28–45.

21 *Narysy istoriï l'vivs'koï oblasnoï partiinoï orhanizatsiï,* 2nd rev. ed. (L'viv: Kameniar 1969); Fedor F. Cherniavskii, *Po puti sotsializma: deiatel'nost' kommunisticheskoi partii po ukrepleniiu rukovodiashchei roli rabochego klassa pri postroenii osnov sotsializma v zapadnykh oblastiakh Ukrainskoi SSR (1939–1950)* (L'viv: Vishcha shkola 1978).

22 Roman Szporluk, ''West Ukraine and West Belorussia,'' *Soviet Studies,* XXXI, 1 (Glasgow 1979), pp. 76–98.

23 *Diiannia soboru hreko-katolyts'koï tserkvy 8–10 bereznia 1946 r. u L'vovi* (L'viv: Presidium of the Synod 1946).

24 S.T. Danylenko, *Dorohoiu han'by i zrady: istorychna khronika* (Kiev: Naukova dumka 1970), 2nd rev. ed. (1972). A particularly negative description of supposed contacts between the Greek Catholic church and the Germans during World War II has been published by the Soviets in English: K. Dmytruk, *In Holy Robes: The Truth About the Contacts Between the Hierarchy of the Uniate Church and the Nazi Aggressors* (Kiev: Ukraina Society 1978).

Slipyi (b. 1892), who served eighteen years in Soviet concentration camps before being released and allowed to go to Rome in 1963–all these developments are outlined in a collection of documents and in other works published in the West.[25]

25 *First Victims of Communism: White Book on the Religious Persecution in Ukraine* (Rome 1953).

Since his release, Cardinal Slipyi has led a persistent though unsuccessful campaign to have the Vatican recognize him as the Patriarch of an ecclesiastically independent and united Ukrainian (Greek) Catholic church. His efforts have become a *cause célèbre* for national pride among certain circles in the Ukrainian immigration; as a result, he has been the subject of many works. See the biography with emphasis on his post-1963 career by Milena Rudnyts'ka, *Nevydymi styhmaty* (Rome, Munich, and Philadelphia: Tovarystvo za patriiarkhal'nyi ustrii Ukraïns'koï Katolyts'koï tserkvy 1971). For Slipyi's autobiography during the war years (1939–1944) and other works about him, see the special volume devoted to his career: *Prychynky do istoriï Ukraïns'koï Katolyts'koï Tserkvy mizh dvoma svitovymy viinamy,* in *Naukovi zapysky Ukraïns'koho Vil'noho Universytetu,* X (Munich, Rome, and Paris 1968). For his work in the ecumenical movement as well as a complete bibliography of his writings, see Wolodymyr Janiw, ''Der ökumenische Gedanke im Leben und Wirken des Märtyrer-Patriarchen,'' *Mitteilungen: Arbeits- und Förderungsgemeinschaft der ukrainischen Wissenschaften,* XIV (Munich 1977), pp. 7–37. For his historical and ecclesiastical writings, see *Tvory Kardynala Iosyfa Verkhovnoho arkhiepyskopa,* ed. Ivan Khoma, Iurii Fedoriv, and Ivan Muzychka, 8 vols (Rome: Ukraïns'kyi Katolyts'kyi Universytet 1968–76).

Chapter 10

Minorities

The vast majority of historical literature discussed in the preceding chapters has dealt with the Ukrainian and to a lesser degree the Polish population of Galicia. Indeed, the Ukrainians always made up the majority of inhabitants, and it is therefore not surprising that most of the writings on the region deal with the experiences of that nationality. Nonetheless, it should be remembered that eastern Galicia was also the homeland of other national groups, in particular Jews, Armenians, Germans, and Karaites, each of whom has a literature dealing with its ''own'' history in Galicia. It would seem most appropriate, therefore, to mention at least some of the major works that treat the history of each of these groups.

POLES

Background

While the Poles were always a numerical minority in eastern, or Ukrainian Galicia, it is difficult to speak of them as a minority, because from at least the mid-fourteenth through mid-twentieth centuries they were the dominant political, social, and cultural force in the area. Polish tradesmen were already living in the cities of eastern Galicia during the medieval period of the Galician principality, and beginning with the second half of the fourteenth century and Poland's general expansion eastward into Ukrainian (Rus') lands, larger numbers of Poles began to arrive. They were, in particular, brought by Polish magnates and gentry who were granted estates by King Casimir the Great (reigned 1339–1370) in the newly acquired territory of Galicia *(Ruś Czerwona)*. The expansion of Polish influence was accompanied by the establishment of a Roman Catholic diocese in Halych (1375), which was later moved to L'viv (1412).

Yet despite the gradual settlement of Poles eastward, most observers of Galicia at the time of its incorporation into Austria (1772) claimed that, with the exception of urban areas, the eastern half of the province was inhabited primarily by Ukrainians. This ethnodemographic situation changed substantially during the second half of the nineteenth century, when the first nationality censuses were taken. Between 1869 and 1910, the number of Poles (i.e. Roman Catholics) in eastern Galicia almost doubled, from 753,700 (21.8 percent of the population) to 1,350,800 (25.3 percent). To be sure, within the category Roman Catholic there were many polonized Ukrainians (including the so-called Latynnyky–Roman Catholics who spoke Ukrainian but who often did not have a clear sense of their national identity). But the main reason for the dramatic rise of Poles was large-scale immigration. In 1890 alone, 288,609 Poles residing in eastern Galicia were registered as having immigrated from western Galicia.

Bearing in mind the tenuous nature of nationality statistics, it seems safe to say that by 1914 there were well over one million Poles living in eastern Galicia. As for the socioeconomic composition of the Roman Catholic population (which reflected largely the Poles), in 1910, 68 percent were peasants, 16 percent were engaged in industry, 8.5 percent in trade and transport, and 7.5 percent in administration, the professions, and service jobs.

After World War I, when all of Galicia became part of the independent Polish Republic, the number of Poles (i.e. Roman Catholics minus *Latynnyky*) continued to grow in eastern Galicia (Ternopil', Stanyslaviv, and L'viv provinces), so that there were over 1,232,000 in 1931. The plight of the Poles in eastern Galicia changed dramatically with the coming of World War II. During the first brief period of Soviet rule (1939–1941), Polish "colonists," that is, those who came during the interwar period, were deported eastward, and most of the Polish cultural institutions in L'viv and elsewhere were either ukrainianized or closed. After 1945, several hundred thousand Poles were sent to postwar Poland as part of the Polish-Soviet population exchange, so that by 1959 only 93,000 Poles remained on former eastern Galician territory.

Studies

As is evident from the preceding chapters, there is an enormous literature in Polish about Galicia. Most of these works, however, deal with the province as a whole (as defined by its borders during the last years of Austrian rule), and more frequently than not they stress developments in western Galicia. This approach is evident in both general works and those that concentrate on specific periods. Thus, the literature specifically on Poles in eastern Galicia is limited in the main to works about the Polish aspect of individual cities and regions or to Polish religious, cultural, and educational institutions in the area, such as the Roman

Catholic archdiocese, the Ossolineum, the University of L'viv, the Polish Historical Society, and the Polish Theater. Located in L'viv, these institutions flourished because of Austria's more liberal policy towards its national minorities (in contrast to the German and Russian empires where Poles also lived), thereby making eastern Galicia a leading center of the Polish national revival. Eastern Galicia (especially L'viv) was also the home of numerous Polish newspapers, literary and scholarly journals, and publishing houses, and the region produced a long line of writers (some of Ukrainian descent) who enriched Polish literature from the Renaissance–Bishop Grzegorz of Sanok (1407–1477), Mikołaj Rej (1505–1569), Sebastian Klonowic (1545–1602), Szymon Szymonowic (1558–1629), Samuel Twardowski (d. 1661)–to the nineteenth century–Aleksander Fredro (1793–1876), Tymon Zaborowski (1799–1828), Kornel Ujejski (1823–1897), Jan Zachariasiewicz (1825–1906), Zygmunt Kaczkowski (1825–1896), Jan Lam (1838–1886).[1]

Nonetheless, with few exceptions, the achievements of eastern Galicia for Polish national life are not treated in isolation, but rather as part of Galician or general Polish political, social, and cultural history. The reason for this approach is simple. From the Polish point of view, all of Galicia has since the Middle Ages been considered an integral part of historic Poland. If one adopts such a premise, then there should be no reason to single out for special analysis the Poles living in any one part of "Polish" territory. Consequently, there are only a few studies

1 For the numerous guidebooks and histories of individual regions, cities, and towns, see chapter 2, notes 85–94, 102–103, 108–111, and 114–143. On the Roman Catholic archdiocese, see chapter 4, n. 48; on the Ossolineum, see chapter 2, notes 68–70; on the University of L'viv, see chapter 2, n. 82.

On the Polish Historical Society (est. 1886), see the introductory article by Tadeusz Manteuffel and Marian Serejski in *Polskie Towarzystwo Historyczne 1886–1956* (Warsaw: PWN 1958), pp. 3–28. On the Polish Theater, see Stanisław Schnür-Pepłowski, *Teatr polski we Lwowie 1780–1881* (L'viv: Gubrynowicz i Schmidt 1889); idem, *Teatr polski we Lwowie 1881–1890* (L'viv: Gubrynowicz i Schmidt 1891); Barbara Lasocka, *Teatr lwowski w latach 1800–1842* (Warsaw: Państwowy Instytut Wydawniczy 1967); and Franciszek Pajączkowski, *Teatr lwowski pod dyrekcją Tadeusza Pawlikowskiego 1900–1906* (Cracow: Wyd. Literackie 1961).

For introductory studies on the Polish press in Galicia, see Irena Homola, "Prasa galicyjska w latach 1831–1866," in Jerzy Łojek, ed., *Prasa polska w latach 1661–1864* (Warsaw: PWN 1976), pp. 199–246; and Jerzy Myśliński, "Prasa polska w Galicji w dobie autonomicznej 1867–1918," in idem, *Prasa polska w latach 1864–1918* (Warsaw: PWN 1976), pp. 114–176.

For bibliographic data on Polish writers mentioned here and others from eastern Galicia, see *Bibliografia literatury polskiej: Nowy Korbut,* 17 vols (Warsaw: Państwowy Instytut Wydawniczy 1953–81).

focusing specifically on Poles living in what was the eastern half of old Austrian Galicia. Both the Polish and Ukrainian encyclopedias published outside the homeland contain general information on Poles in eastern Galicia.[2] Not surprisingly, the problem of the ethnographic boundary between Poles and Ukrainians and the difficulty in assigning a national identity to the *Latynnyky* have prompted the publication of studies both during and after World War I.[3] Yet perhaps the only work dealing specifically with Poles as an element in eastern Galicia is Alfons Krysiński's extended statistical analysis of the group, with emphasis on their status during the 1920s.[4]

JEWS

Background

Of all the minorities in Galicia the Jews (known in Jewish circles by the often derogatory designation *Galizianer*) were the most important not only in numerical terms but with regard to their economic, cultural, and political influence as well. It is not surprising, therefore, that the historical literature on Jews is more voluminous than for any of the other groups.

The early history of Jews in Galicia does not differ significantly from the experience of Jews in other areas under the control of the Polish Kingdom and later the Polish-Lithuanian Commonwealth. Jews began immigrating to Poland from Germany in the eleventh and twelfth centuries, but it was after the Tatar invasion of 1241 that they came in large numbers, welcomed, together with Germans, by Polish kings anxious to rebuild the devastated urban areas of the country. Under Bolesław V the Pious (reigned 1239–1279), the Jews received a

2 See especially the two chapters on ''East Galicia'' by Włodzimierz Wakar, in *The Polish Encyclopedia,* vol. II: *Territory and Population of Poland* (Geneva and Fribourg: Committee for the Polish Encyclopedia Publications 1924), pp. 503–552; and the sections on Galicia (Halychyna) in ''Poliaky na Ukraïni,'' in *Entsyklopediia ukraïnoznavstva: slovnykova chastyna,* Vol. VI (Paris and New York: Molode zhyttia for the NTSh 1970), pp. 2215–2228.

3 A. Petrov, *Ob étnograficheskoi granitsie russkago naroda v Avstro-Ugrii* (Petrograd 1915); Stanisław Pawłowski, *Ludność rzymsko-katolicka w polsko-ruskiej częsci Galicji,* Prace Geograficzne, vol. III (L'viv: Polska Spółka Oszczędności 1919); Franciszek Persowski, *Osadnictwo w dorzeczu średniego Sanu: próba rekonstrukcji krajobrazu z XV w.* (L'viv 1931).
See also the comprehensive studies by Volodymyr Okhrymovych, chapter 6, n. 18; by Volodymyr Kubiiovych and Alfons Krysiński, chapter 7, n. 9; and the extensive literature on the Polish-Rus' ethnographic border during the medieval period, chapter 3, notes 28–30.

4 Alfons Krysiński, ''Liczba i rozmieszczenie ludności polskiej na kresach wschodnich,'' *Sprawy Narodowościowe,* III, 3–4, 5, 6 (Warsaw 1929), pp. 413–450, 618–640, 772–784.

special charter (Statute of Kalisz, 1264), which placed them under the protection of the royal Polish house and defended them as a group whose main business was money lending. As Poland expanded eastward into Galicia and farther into the Ukraine, the Jews were encouraged to follow; they became an integral part of a social structure composed of the royal house, a Polish aristocracy, a Jewish (and to a lesser degree Armenian and German) burgher class, and a Ukrainian or Polish peasantry. The Jews settled primarily, although not exclusively, in the towns and cities of Galicia *(Ruś Czerwona)*. Their numbers grew steadily, and if there were only 3500 Jews in 1538, by 1648 there were as many as 54,000. The main occupations of the Jewish population in Galicia as in other parts of Poland were trade and finance, small handicrafts, the collecting of taxes, and the leasing of magnate-owned lands, mills, and breweries.

The Jews were appreciated for their economic prowess and, in return for loyal service to the state, they were granted a wide degree of self-government. Beginning in the sixteenth century, their judicial, administrative, and religious autonomy was administered through a system known as the Council of Lands, which met twice annually during the fairs in Lublin and Jarosław. Galicia was one of the four lands of the council, which met also from time to time in Jewish centers of Galicia like Przeworsk, Zolochiv, and Brody, as well as in Jarosław. Throughout this period, the Jews played a decisive role in the economic system of Galicia. The province (especially L'viv and the small town of Iwanie near the southeasternmost tip of Galicia) also became the center in the 1750s for the Frankist movement, a Jewish sect that eventually converted to Christianity.

Jewish life was profoundly affected by the incorporation of Galicia into the Austrian Empire in 1772. The system of the Council of Lands had already ceased to function on the eve of Poland's first partition. Moreover, the Austrian government, during its era of enlightened reform under Maria Theresa (reigned 1740–1780) and Joseph II (reigned 1780–1790), was determined to change (from its point of view to improve) the status of the Jews as well as other groups for what was considered the greater good of the state. Initially, the Austrians set up their own form of internal Jewish autonomy with the establishment of a system of congregational districts presided over by a general directorate *(Generaldirektion)* headed by the community's chief rabbi *(Oberlandesrabbiner)*.

Such a system clashed with Joseph II's goals of centralized authority, however, and the *Generaldirektion* as well as rabbinical civil law was abolished in 1785. From Vienna's point of view, Jews should be totally assimilated and be no different from other citizens: they should not be discriminated against, should pay the same taxes as others, serve in the army, and use German, not Yiddish.

As with Joseph's sweeping reforms in other areas of Austrian life, his efforts at benevolent reform of the Jews were undone by his successors. Soon new restrictions were placed on Jews that affected their freedom of movement and their ability to serve in certain offices and professions. As a result, the status of the Jews in Galicia fluctuated with the internal political fortunes of the Habsburg Empire. During the revolutionary period of 1848–1849, they were granted full equality, only to lose certain rights during the era of reaction that began in earnest in 1850. In the era of constitutionalism that began in 1861, the Jews undertook a political struggle for legal equality that finally met with success after 1867. Thus, during the last decades of the nineteenth century, Jewish life flourished in Galicia. While it is true that the masses lived under conditions of severe poverty, forcing as many as 236,504 (172,514 from eastern Galicia) to emigrate between 1881 and 1910, especially to the United States, it is equally true that the same era witnessed the rise of Jewish wealth in Galician banking, trade, oil, industry, and large landowning, as well as the growth of Jewish political influence at the local, urban, and provincial levels.

In the final analysis, the period of Austrian rule (1772–1918) represented the high point of Jewish life in Galicia. The size of the group grew–as a result of a high birth rate, as well as of government-induced immigration and flights from pogroms in Russia–from a low of 144,200 people in 1776 to 448,971 in 1850 and, despite increasing emigration, to 871,895 in 1910. Three-quarters of Galicia's Jews lived in the eastern part of the province, most especially in cities and towns like Brody, Belz, Buchach, Rohatyn, Peremyshliany, Deliatyn, and Sokal', which were almost entirely Jewish, and L'viv, Zhovkva, Drohobych, Stanyslaviv, Ternopil', and Kolomyia, where they made up a significant proportion of the population. Their largely urban residence was reflected in the group's socioeconomic status. In 1910, 53 percent of Galicia's Jews were engaged in commerce, 24.6 percent in industry and crafts, 11.4 percent in civil service and the liberal professions, and only 10.7 percent in agriculture.

Besides the group's demographic, political, and economic growth, the period of Austrian rule also coincided with a vibrant Galician-Jewish cultural experience marked by very creative if competitive and often violently antagonistic trends: traditional rabbinic talmudism, Hasidism, Haskalah, assimilation, Zionism, and socialism. With the disintegration of Poland and the traditional system of Jewish autonomy in the second half of the eighteenth century, the old rabbinic-led way of life was challenged. In such an environment, a popular religious movement known as Hasidism came into being. Although originating in the middle of the eighteenth century in what was still Polish-ruled Podolia, Hasidism rapidly spread northward into Lithuania and westward to nearby Galicia. The followers of Hasidism were noted for their belief in the emotional aspect of religious experience, which favored mass enthusiasm, group cohesion, and charismatic leadership. Because of its mystical and "superstitious" nature, Hasidism was castigated by both traditionalist rabbis (the *mitnaggedim* or opponents) as well as by Austria's enlightened reformers, who found allies among those Jews favoring an end to the group's isolation and instead assimilation with the dominant German culture. Nonetheless, by the 1830s Hasidism had become the dominant way for Jewish life in Galicia.

The reformers, led by Naphtali Herz Homberg (1749–1841), the imperial superintendent for the new 104 German-language Jewish schools set up in Galicia between 1787 and 1806, argued that Jews should abandon their closed communities *(shtetl),* traditional dress, talmudic education, and the "bastardized dialect"–Yiddish. Although the government-sponsored schools were abolished in 1806, the modernizing and secular trend in Jewish life was carried on by the Haskalah (enlightenment) movement and its supporters known as the *maskilim*. The Haskalah first arose among Jews in Germany during the mid-eighteenth century, but it soon spread eastward to Galicia where it was eventually centered in the town of Brody. Great emphasis was placed on creating a modern secular Jewish educational system on the model of the Jewish *gymnasium* in Brody and German school in Ternopil', both founded in 1815 by Josef Perl (1777–1839). The Haskalah also favored the establishment of reformed Jewish temples, the first of which was founded in L'viv in 1846, and it contributed much to modern Hebrew literature and scholarship as in the writings of Nachman Krochmal (1785–1840), Solomon J. Rapoport (1790–1867), Isaac Erter (1792–1851), and Joshua Heschel Schorr (1814–1895).

Late nineteenth-century Jewish cultural life in Galicia was marked by a struggle between assimilationists who favored German culture and assimilationists who favored Polish culture as well as political cooperation with the Poles. After 1870, the Polonophile assimilationists had won out, but while some embraced wholeheartedly the Polish national cause, others allied with Polish and Ukrainian socialists in an attempt to transform the socioeconomic base of Galician life. Still another group initially rejected ideas that real improvement for Jews could ever be achieved in Galicia or anywhere else in Europe. These were the Zionists, who from their first Galician organization in Przemyśl (1874) saw emigration to a Jewish homeland–Palestine–as the only salvation for Jews. The Zionists soon realized, however, that such a solution would take time to realize, and in the interim they favored the idea of self-emancipation as formulated by the Galician-born Nathan Birnbaum (1864–1937), which meant participation in local politics in order to improve the status of Jews while they still remained in Europe.

The twentieth century and the outbreak of World War I marked the beginning of the end of Galicia's Jewish community. As the Russian army advanced into eastern Galicia in August and September 1914, tens of thousands of Jews (many of whom had fled tsarist oppression less than half a century before) fled to

Hungary, Vienna, and other provinces in the western half of the Habsburg Empire. Those who remained behind suffered during the several months of Russian occupation until the return of an Austrian administration in the summer of 1915.

In late 1918, with the breakup of the Habsburg monarchy, the Jews were again caught between the Ukrainians and Poles who were struggling for control of eastern Galicia. Each of the Slavic rivals for power accused the Jews of cooperating with its opponent, and when Polish troops finally took L'viv from the Ukrainians, a Jewish pogrom took place on the night of November 22–23, the first serious incident of its kind on the territory of former Austrian Galicia.

As a result of these developments, the Jewish population declined from a high of 872,975 in 1910 to only 740,323 in 1921 (in eastern Galicia the decline was from 659,706 in 1910 to 534,651 in 1921). During the interwar years under a Polish regime, the Jews suffered discrimination, especially in the professions and universities, where their numbers were increasingly restricted by a government-imposed *numerus clausus*. The Polish government was particularly alarmed that Jews made up such a disproportionately high percentage in certain fields. In eastern Galicia alone, they accounted for 66.6 percent of the total number of lawyers in 1931 and 51.1 percent of the total number of doctors in 1927. As a result, severe restrictions were placed on their further entrance to universities. While 24.4 percent of the student body in Polish universities was Jewish in 1923–24, only 8.2 percent was Jewish in 1938–39.

The outbreak of World War II in September 1939, the German and Soviet occupation of Poland, and finally Germany's complete control of Galicia between the summers of 1941 and 1944 resulted in the complete destruction of the Jewish community in Galicia. As in other parts of Nazi-controlled or Nazi-influenced Europe, Jews were physically uprooted and annihilated in concentration camps. Old Jewish quarters, synagogues, even cemeteries were destroyed. If in 1931 there were 789,886 Jews in Galicia (567,554 in eastern Galicia), by 1945 only a few thousand had managed to survive the holocaust. For all intents and purposes, by the end of World War II, Galicia's once-vibrant Jewish community ceased to exist.

Bibliographies

Writings on the Jews in Galicia are treated primarily within the larger realm of Polish-Jewish historiography. Moreover, with the exception of regional or local studies, most writings that deal with Jews in Galicia are concerned with the province as a whole according to its boundaries during the Austrian era. Nonetheless, since almost three-quarters of the Jews in Galicia inhabited the eastern half of the province (known in some Jewish writings as Red Russia), and since the leading Jewish cultural center was L'viv (Lemberg), much of the general Galician descriptions pertain in fact to the community in the eastern half of the former Austrian province.

Several bibliographical works on Jews in Poland contain many writings that deal specifically with Galicia. These include annotated bibliographies and historiographical studies by Meir Balaban and Philip Friedman, both of whom are outstanding Jewish historians and natives of Galicia.[5] There is also a comprehensive bibliography of late nineteenth-century statistical and sociodemographic writings on Jews in Galicia.[6] Since World War II, numerous memorial books have been compiled by survivors of Galician Jewry living mainly in Israel and the United States. An analysis of the historical value of these memorial books and a list of the 342 published between 1943 and 1972 (twenty-one of which deal with communities in eastern Galicia) have been prepared by Abraham Wein and David Bass.[7]

Historical surveys and documentary collections

There are no general histories of Jews in Galicia, let alone eastern Galicia, which cover the period from their earliest settlement in the Middle Ages to the destruc-

5 Majer Bałaban, *Bibliografia historii Żydów w Polsce i w krajach ościennych za lata 1900–1930,* Pisma Instytutu Nauk Judaistycznych, vol. X (Warsaw 1939). This incomplete work was reprinted with an introduction by Ezra Mendelsohn and supplementary title pages in Hebrew and English: Mayer Balaban, *Bibliography on the History of Jews in Poland and in Neighboring Lands: Works Published During the Years 1900–1930* (Jerusalem: World Federation of Polish Jews 1978); Majer Balaban, ''Przegląd literatury historyi Żydów w Polsce, 1899–1907,'' *Kwartalnik Historyczny,* XXII, 2–3 (L'viv 1908), pp. 494–524; Majer Bałaban, ''Przegląd literatury historyi Żydów w Polsce 1899–1903,'' *ibid.,* XVII, 3 (L'viv 1903), pp. 475–486; idem, ''Notatki bibliograficzne do historyi Żydów,'' *ibid.,* XVIII, 3–4 (L'viv 1904), pp. 635–640; idem, ''Przegląd literatury historyi Żydów w Polsce, 1907–1911,'' *Przegląd Historyczny,* XV, 2 and 3 (Warsaw 1912), pp. 231–248 and 369–385, XVI, 2 (1913), pp. 243–256, and XVII, 1 (1913), pp. 75–91; Philip Friedman, ''Polish Jewish Historiography Between the Two Wars (1918–1939),'' *Jewish Social Studies,* XI, 4 (New York 1949), pp. 373–408, reprinted in his *Roads to Extinction: Essays on the Holocaust* (New York and Philadelphia: Jewish Publication Society of America 1980), pp. 467–499.

6 See the section, ''Galizien,'' in Alfred Nossig, ed., *Jüdische Statistik* (Berlin: Jüdischer Vlg. 1903), pp. 104–114.

7 Abraham Wein, '' 'Memorial Books' as a Source for Research into the History of Jewish Communities in Europe,'' *Yad Vashem Studies,* IX (Jerusalem 1973), pp. 255–272; David Bass, ''Bibliographical List of Memorial Books Published in the Years 1943–1972,'' *ibid.,* pp. 273–321.

tion of the community during World War II. This is because Galicia is considered an integral part of Polish-Jewish history before 1772 and again for the years 1918 to 1945. Thus, the concept of Galician-Jewish history per se is limited for the most part to the years between 1772 and 1918. As a result, in order to trace the full chronological development of Galician-Jewish history, it is necessary to consult general histories of Jews in Poland. There are several such histories, by Simon M. Dubnow, Meir Balaban, Jacob Schall, Raphael Mahler, Bernard Mark, Bernard Weinryb, and Salo W. Baron, although it must be admitted that Galicia more often than not receives scant treatment.[8]

For Jewish developments specifically in Galicia, it is preferable to consult the several multivolume Jewish encyclopedias–American, Russian, German, Yiddish, and Israeli–which have appeared between 1906 and 1972. Each of these includes articles on Galician-Jewish leaders and each has a comprehensive history of Galicia by leading scholars (M. Balaban, I. Cherikover, G. Deutsch, J. Meisl, A. Duker, N.M. Gelber), although the chronological coverage is limited to the years 1772 to 1918.[9] Also useful is the brief biographical dictionary of Galician-

8 S.M. Dubnow, *History of the Jews in Russia and Poland from the Earliest Times Until the Present Day,* 3 vols (Philadelphia: Jewish Publication Society of America, 1916–20), especially vol. I: Majer Bałaban, *Historja i literatura żydowska ze szczególnem uwzględnieniem historji Żydów w Polsce,* 3 vols (L'viv, Warsaw, and Cracow, 1916–25), vol. I: rev. 2nd ed. (1920) and rev. 3rd ed. (1925); vol. II: rev. 2nd ed. (1925); Jacob Schall, *Historia Żydów w Polsce, Litwie i na Rusi* (L'viv 1934), 2nd ed. (L'viv 1936); Raphael Mahler, *Toledot ha-Yehudim be-Polin* (Merḥavyah 1946); Bernard Mark, *Di Geshikhte fun Yidn in Poyln bizn sof fun XV jh.* (Warsaw: 'Idisz Buch' 1957); Bernard D. Weinryb, *The Jews of Poland: A Social and Economic History of the Jewish Community in Poland from 1100 to 1800* (Philadelphia: Jewish Publication Society of America 1972); Salo Wittmayer Baron, *A Social and Religious History of the Jews,* 2nd rev. ed., 17 vols (New York and London: Columbia University Press 1952–78). Baron's monumental study is actually an ongoing world history of the Jews, although volume XVI (1976) deals exclusively with Jews in Poland-Lithuania from 1500 to 1650.

Also of value are two multiauthored works that include studies by the leading Jewish specialists on Poland: Ignacy Schiper et al., eds, *Żydzi w Polsce odrodzonej: działalność społeczna, oświatowa i kulturalna,* 2 vols (Warsaw: 1932–33); and Israel Halpern, ed., *Beit Yisrael be-Polin mi-yamim rishonim ve-'ad li-yemot ha-ḥurban,* 2 vols (Jerusalem: Ha-maḥlaqah le-'inyenei ha-no'ar shel ha-histadrut ha-ṣiyyonit 1948–53).

9 Isidor Singer, ed., *The Jewish Encyclopedia,* 12 vols (New York and London: Funk and Wagnalls 1906–07), with an article on ''Galicia, Austria'' by Gotthard Deutsch, vol. V, pp. 549–553; *Evreiskaia éntsiklopediia: svod znanii o evreistvie i ego kul'ture v proshlom i nastoiashchem,* 16 vols (St Petersburg: Obshchestvo dlia nauchnykh evreiskikh izdanii i Brokhauz-Efron 1906–13), reprinted in Slavistic Printings and Reprintings, vol. CXCIII, 1–16 (The Hague, Paris, and Vaduz: Mouton and Europe Printing 1969–71), with an article on ''Galitsiia'' by M. Balaban and I. Cherikower, vol. VI, pp. 87–103; Georg Herlitz and Bruno Kirschner, eds, *Jüdisches Lexikon,* 4 vols in 5 (Berlin: Jüdischer Vlg. 1927–30), with an

Jewish leaders by Gershom Bader.[10] There are also a few journals published in Galicia before World War I that contain valuable information about all aspects of the Jewish community in the province.[11]

As with general histories, so too are there no documentary collections devoted specifically to Jews in Galicia. There is, however, much material pertaining to Jewish matters between the fifteenth and eighteenth centuries in the multivolume collections of documents on Galicia and on the city of L'viv.[12] Several collections of documents on Jews in Poland from earliest times to World War II also contain material on communities in eastern Galicia (L'viv, Przemyśl, Brody, Drohobych).[13] For an introduction to these and other materials, there are two essays that survey documentary sources for the study of Jews in Poland.[14]

---

article on "Galizien und Lodomerien" by Joseph Meisl, vol. II, pp. 865–879; *Encyclopaedia Judaica: das Judenthum in Geschichte und Gegenwart*, 10 vols [A–L] (Berlin: Eschkol 1928–34), with an article on "Galizien" by Meir Balaban, vol. VII, pp. 22–69; Isaac Landman, ed., *The Universal Jewish Encyclopedia*, 10 vols (New York: Universal Jewish Encyclopedia 1939–43), with an article on "Galicia" by Abraham G. Duker, vol. IV, pp. 493–499; *Encyclopaedia Judaica*, 16 vols (Jerusalem and New York: Keter Publishing House and Macmillan 1971–72), with an article on "Galicia" by Nathan Michael Gelber, vol. XVI: supplement, pp. 1325–1332.

The only encyclopedic article that attempts, however generally, to survey Galician-Jewish history and life from earliest times appeared in the late nineteenth-century encyclopedia of the Austro-Hungarian Empire: Leo Herzberg-Fränkl, "Die Juden [in Galizien]," *Die österreichisch-ungarische Monarchie in Wort und Bild*, vol. XII: *Galizien* (Vienna: K.K. Hof- und Staatsdruckerei 1898), pp. 475–499.

10 Gershom Bader, *Medinah va-Hakhameha / Galician Jewish Celebrities* (New York: Appel 1934).

11 *Nogah ha-Yareaḥ* (L'viv 1872–73, 1880); *Ojczyzna* (L'viv 1881–86); *Wschód* (L'viv, 1900–13); *Rocznik Żydowski* (L'viv, 1901–06).

12 See chapter 4, notes 4, 5, and 29; and T. Wierzbowski, ed., *Matricularum Regni Poloniae Summaria*, vol. I (Warsaw 1919) and *Regesty z Metryki Koronnej do końca panowania Zygmunta Augusta* (Warsaw 1919).

13 Philipp Bloch, *Die General-Privilegien des polonischen Judenschaft* (Poznań: J. Jolowicz 1892); *Russko-evreiskii arkhiv*, vol. III: *dokumenty k istorii polskikh i litovskikh evreev (1364–1569)* (St Petersburg 1903); Mathias Bersohn, ed., *Dyplomatariusz dotyczący Żydów w dawnej Polsce na źródłach archiwalnych osnuty (1388–1781)* (Warsaw 1910); R. Mahler and E. Ringelbaum, *Teksty źródłowe do nauki historii Żydów we Polsce i we wschodniej Europie*, 2 vols (Warsaw 1930); "Iz chernoi knigi rosiiskago evreistva: materialy dlia istorii voiny 1914–1915," *Evreiskaia starina*, X (Petrograd 1918), pp. 195–296; T. Berenstein et al., eds, *Eksterminacja Żydów na ziemiach polskich w okresie okupacji hitlerowskiej: zbiór dokumentów* (Warsaw: Żydowski Instytut Historyczny 1957).

14 S. Huberband, "Źródła do historii Żydów w krajach słowiańskich ze specjalnym uwzględnieniem Polski i Rosiji," *Biuletyn Żydowskiego Instytutu Historycznego*, no. 2 (Warsaw 1951), pp. 16–46; Janina Morgensztern, "Regesty z Metryki Koronnej do historii

Specific periods and problems

The literature is much better developed for specific periods or topics. The Jewish community in Galicia *(Ruś Czerwona)* during the sixteenth and first half of the seventeenth century has recently been analyzed from the standpoint of demography and socioeconomic developments in a detailed monograph and in several shorter works by Maurycy Horn and his associates at the Jewish Historical Institute in Poland (Żydowski Instytut Historyczny w Polsce).[15] The last decades of Polish rule before 1772 have also received attention in a study by Zbigniew Pazdro on the legal status of Galicia's Jews.[16] Finally, the history of individual Jewish communities before 1772 is the subject of several works. L'viv has received the most attention, especially in the writings of Meir Balaban,[17] and there are also studies on Jews in Brody, Drohobych, Jarosław, Przemyśl, the Sanok region, Stanyslaviv, and Zolochiv from earliest times to the late eighteenth century.[18]

Żydów w Polsce 1574–1660,'' *Biuletyn Żydowskiego Instytutu Historycznego*, no. 47–48 (Warsaw 1963), pp. 113–129, no. 51 (1964), pp. 59–78, no. 58 (1966), pp. 107–150, no. 67 (1968).

15 Maurycy Horn, *Żydzi na Rusi Czerwonej w XVI i pierwszej połowe XVII w.* (Warsaw: PWN for the Żydowski Instytut Historyczny w Polsce 1975); Elżbieta Horn, ''Położenie prawno-ekonomiczne Żydów w miastach ziemi halickiej na przełomie XVI i XVII w.,'' *Biuletyn Żydowskiego Instytutu Historycznego*, nos 71–72 (Warsaw 1969), pp. 39–63; Maurycy Horn, ''Żydowski ruch osadniczy w miastach Rusi Czerwonej do 1648 r.,'' *ibid.*, no. 90 (Warsaw 1974), pp. 3–24.

16 Zbigniew Pazdro, *Organizacya i praktyka żydowskich sądów podwojewodzińskich w okresie 1740–1772 r. na podstawie lwowskich materyałów archiwalnych* (L'viv 1903).

See also Majer Bałaban, ''Spis Żydów i Karaitów Ziemi Halickiej i powiatów Trembowelskiego i Kołomyjskiego w roku 1765,'' *Archiwum Komisyi Historycznej Akademji Umiejętności*, XI (Cracow 1909).

17 M. Bałaban, *Żydzi lwowscy na przełomie XVI i XVII wieku* (L'viv 1909); five essays in his *Skizzen und Studien zur Geschichte der Juden in Polen* (Berlin: Louis Lamm 1911), especially pp. 11–19, 54–76, and 97–127; and his more popular *Dzielnica żydowska: jej dzieje i zabytki*, Biblioteka Lwowska, vol. V–VI (L'viv 1909).

See also the first major general history of the community: Jecheskiel Caro, *Geschichte der Juden in Lemberg von den ältesten Zeiten bis zur Theilung Polens im Jahre 1792* (Cracow: p.a. 1894).

18 D. Wurm, *Z dziejów żydostwa brodzkiego za czasów dawnej Rzeczypospolitej Polskiej (do 1772 roku)* (Brody 1935); J. Wikler, ''Z dziejów Żydów w Drohobyczu (od r. 1648 do upadku Rzeczypospolitej),'' *Biuletyn Żydowskiego Instytutu Historycznego*, nos 71–72 (Warsaw 1969), pp. 39–63; Mojżesz Steinberg, *Żydzi w Jarosławiu od czasów najdawniejszych do połowy XIX w.* (Jarosław 1933); Mojżesz Schorr, *Żydzi w Przemyślu do końca XVIII wieku* (L'viv: Konkurs im. H. Wawelberga, Wydział Filozoficzny Uniwersytetu Lwowskiego 1903); Maurycy Horn, ''Żydzi ziemi sanockiej do 1605 r.,'' *Biuletyn Żydowskiego Instytutu*

The vast majority of literature on Galicia's Jews deals with the era of Austrian rule between 1772 and 1918. Several monographs cover in detail some specific periods, such as Meir Balaban's history of the preconstitutional era (1782–1868);[19] Wolfgang Häusler's description of Jews in Galicia before 1848 based on contemporary descriptions;[20] Michael Stöger's older but still useful analysis of the Jews' legal status under Maria Theresa and Joseph II;[21] Raphael Mahler's discussion of their legal status and cultural development between 1772 and 1815;[22] Philip Friedman's description of the Jewish struggle for political and legal rights between 1848 and 1868;[23] and several studies by Wilhelm Feldman and others on Jewish political life and cooperation with Poles and other groups during the constitutional era (1868–1914).[24] There are also a few contemporary accounts of

---

Historycznego, no. 74 (Warsaw 1970), pp. 3–30; Leon Streit, *Ormianie a Żydzi w Stanisławowie w XVII i XVIII: szkic historyczny* (Stanyslaviv: Kolo Naukowe 'Towarzystwo Przyjaciól Universytetu Hebrajskiego w Jerozolimie, oddział w Stanisławowie' 1936); Jakub Perski, ''Materiały do historii Żydów złoczowskich,'' *Biuletyn Żydowskiego Instytutu Historycznego,* no. 81 (Warsaw 1972), pp. 85–90.

19 Majer Bałaban, *Dzieje Żydów w Galicji i w Rzeczypospolitej krakowskiej 1782–1868* (L'viv and New York: B. Połoniecki and E. Wende 1914). See also his study of Galician Jews during the 1848 revolution: M. Balaban, ''Galitsiiskie evrei vo vremia revoliutsii 1848,'' *Evreiskaia starina,* IV (St Petersburg 1919), pp. 423–452.

20 Wolfgang Häusler, *Das galizische Judentum in der Habsburgermonarchie im Lichte der zeitgenössischen Publizistik und Reiseliteratur von 1772–1848* (Vienna: Vlg. für Geschichte und Politik for Österreich Archiv 1979).

21 Michael Stöger, *Darstellung der gesetzlichen Verfassung der galizischen Judenschaft,* 2 vols (L'viv, Przemyśl, Stanyslaviv, and Tarnów: Kuhn and Millikowski 1833). See also the briefer study by M. Balaban, ''Perekhod pol'skikh evreev pod vlast' Avstrii: galitsiiskie evrei pri Marii Terezii i Iosife II,'' *Evreiskaia starina,* V (Petrograd 1913), pp. 289–307; a description of the Austrian policy toward the Jewish rabbinate: N.M. Gelber, ''Oblastnii ravvinat v Galitsii, 1776–1786,'' *Evreiskaia starina,* VI (Petrograd 1914), pp. 305–317, translated into English as ''Aryeh Leib Bernstein: Chief Rabbi of Galicia,'' *Jewish Quarterly Review,* XIV (Philadelphia 1923–24), pp. 303–328; a history of Austrian tax policy toward Jews in Galicia: Viktor Hoffman v. Wellenhof, ''Die Sonderbesteuerung der jüdischen Bevölkerung in Galizien und der Bukowina bis zum Jahre 1848: eine steuergeschichtliche Studie,'' *Vierteljahrschrift für Sozial- und Wirtschaftsgeschichte,* XII, (Leipzig 1914), pp. 404–448.

22 These are actually several sections on Galicia from a more general work: Raphael Mahler, *A History of Modern Jewry 1780–1815* (London: Vallentine, Mitchell 1971), especially 314–341, 495–525, 587–601.

23 Filip Friedman, *Die galizischen Juden im Kampfe um ihre Gleichberechtigung (1848–1868)* (Frankfurt-am-Main: J. Kauffmann Vlg. 1929). See also the shorter excerpt from the foregoing book: idem, ''Die Judenfrage im galizischen Landtag 1861–1868,'' *Monatsschrift für Geschichte und Wissenschaft des Judentums,* LXXII (Frankfurt-am-Main 1928), pp. 379–390 and 457–477.

24 Wilhelm Feldman, *Stronnictwa i programy polityczne w Galicyi 1846 do 1906,* 2 vols (Cracow

Jewish life in Galicia, especially concerning the influx of immigrants into the border town of Brody after the outbreak of pogroms in Russia in 1881.[25] The period of World War I and its immediate aftermath has received special attention in studies devoted to the Russian occupation (September 1914–June 1915),[26] the pogroms of late 1918,[27] and in memoir-like historical accounts of the whole period, which is viewed as the first time in the modern era that the Jews of Galicia were singled out for destruction.[28]

Economic and demographic analyses of the Jewish community during the Austrian period are available as well. Ignaz Schipper and Philip Friedman have written brief reviews of Galician economic developments after 1772.[29] Studies of later periods tend to dwell on the socioeconomic reasons for the massive Jewish emigration to the United States and to a lesser degree other parts of the Austro-

---

1907), especially vol. II, pp. 265–314; Saul R. Landau, *Der Polenklub und seine Hausjuden* (Vienna 1907); E. Dubanowicz, *Stanowisko ludnośći żydowskiej w Galicji wobec wyborów do parlamentu wiedeńskiego w r. 1907* (L'viv 1907); Stanisław Gruziński, *Materiały do kwestji żydowskiej w Galicji* (L'viv 1910); Leila P. Everett, "The Rise of Jewish National Politics in Galicia, 1905–1907," in Andrei S. Markovits and Frank E. Sysyn, eds, *Nationbuilding and the Politics of Nationalism: Essays on Austrian Galicia* (Cambridge, Mass.: Harvard Ukrainian Research Institute 1982), pp. 149–177.

25 Leo Goldenstein, *Brody und die russisch-judische Emigration* (Frankfurt-am-Main: J. Kauffmann 1882); M. Friedländer, *Fünf Wochen in Brody unter jüdisch-russischen Emigration: Ein Beitrag zur Geschichte der russischen Judenverfolgung,* 2nd rev. ed. (Vienna: M. Waizner 1882); I. Horowitz, "Ein Blick auf die Juden in Galizien," *Monatsschrift für Geschichte und Wissenschaft des Judenthums,* XVI (Breslau 1867), pp. 41–53, 81–93, 125–142.

26 Jakób Schall, *Żydowstwo galicyjskie w czasie inwazji rosyjskiej* (n.p.: I. Madfes 1936). See also the works on this period by Ukrainian, Russian, and Polish authors, chapter 6, notes 227–229.

27 Josef Bendow [Josef Tenenbaum], *Der Lemberger Judenpogrom: November 1918-Jänner 1919* (Vienna and Brno: M. Hickl 1919); L. Chasanovitch, ed., *Les pogromes anti-juifs en Pologne et en Galicie en novembre et decembre 1918: faits et documents* (Stockholm: Bokförlaget Judea 1919).

28 S. An-Ski [Solomon Rappoport], *Der yidisher Khurbn in Poyln, Galizie un Bukovine* (Warsaw 1921); idem, *Ḥurban ha-Yehudim be-Polin, Galiẓyah u-Bukovinah,* 4 vols in 2 (Berlin-Charlottenburg 1929); Josef Tenenbaum, *In fayer* (New York 1926); Ruven Fahn, *Geshikhte fun der yidisher natsional avtonomie inem period fun der mayrev-ukrainisher republik* (L'viv 1933).

29 Ignaz Schipper, "Die galizische Judenschaft in den Jahren 1772–1848 in wirtschaftsstatistischer Beleuchtung," *Neue jüdische Monatshefte,* II, 9–10 (Berlin-Charlottenburg 1918), pp. 223–233; Filip Friedman, "Landwirtschaft, kolonizacje un grundbazyc baj di galicjanisze Jidn in 19-tn jorh.," in *Junger Historiker,* vol. II (Warsaw 1929), pp. 131–142.

See also M. Wischnitzer, "Die Stellung der Brodyer Juden im internationalen Handel in der 2-ten Hälfte des XVIII Jahrhundert," in *Dubnow Festschrift* (Berlin 1930), pp. 113–123.

Hungarian Empire, especially its capital Vienna,[30] and on the economic status of the community during the first decades of the twentieth century.[31] With regard to demographic questions, Polish scholars have provided solid analyses of the Galician-Jewish population: Józef Buzek describes Austria's administrative policies, which at first caused a decline then a growth in the number of Jews in Galicia (244,980 in 1772; 144,200 in 1776; 212,002 in 1785), and Bohdan Wasiutyński reveals the fluctuations in the size of Poland's Jewish population during the nineteenth and first three decades of the twentieth century.[32]

Cultural history

Considering the rich cultural life of Jews in Galicia during the Austrian period, it is not surprising that several studies are devoted to various aspects of that experience. The standard works by Simon Dubnow on Hasidism and by Meir Balaban on the earlier Frankist movement provide general histories as well as discussions of the impact of each of those movements upon Galicia.[33] Rafael Mahler has

30 Raphael Mahler, "The Economic Background of Jewish Emigration from Galicia to the United States," *YIVO Annual of Jewish Social Science*, VII (New York 1952), pp. 255–267; Meir Henisch, "Galician Jews in Vienna," in Josef Fraenkel, ed., *The Jews of Austria* (London: Valentine, Mitchell 1967), 2nd ed. (1970), pp. 361–373. See also the more general Arieh Tartakower, "Jewish Migratory Movements in Austria in Recent Generations," in *ibid.*, pp. 285–310.

31 Sigfried Fleischer, "Enquête über die Lage der jüdischen Bevölkerung Galiziens" and Abraham Korkis, "Zur Bewegung der jüdischen Bevölkerung in Galizien," in Alfred Nossig, ed., *Jüdische Statistik* (Berlin: Jüdischer Vlg. 1903), pp. 209–231 and 311–315; Josef Tenenbaum, *Żydowskie problemy gospodarcze w Galicji* (Vienna 1918); Abraham Korkis, "Die wirschaftliche Lage der Juden in Galizien," *Der Jude*, II (Berlin and Vienna 1917–18), pp. 464–471, 532–538, 608–615. See also the excellent sections on Galicia in Max Rosenfeld, *Die polnische Judenfrage: Problem und Lösung* (Vienna and Berlin: R. Lowit 1918), especially pp. 59–81 and 109–123; and the description of Jews in the eastern Galician towns of Kolomyia, Stanyslaviv, and Boryslav: S.R. Landau, *Unter jüdischen Proletarien: Reiseschilderungen aus Ostgalizien und Russland* (Vienna 1898), especially pp. 1–39.

32 Józef Buzek, "Wpływ polityki żydowskiej rządu austryackiego w latach 1772 do 1788 na wzrost zaludnienia żydowskiego Galicyi," *Czasopismo Prawnicze*, IV (Cracow 1903), pp. 91–130; Bohdan Wasiutyński, *Ludność żydowska w Polsce w wiekach XIX i XX: studjum statystyczne* (Warsaw: Wyd. Kasy im. Mianowskiego, Instytutu Popierania Nauki 1930), especially pp. 90–157.

33 Simon Dubnow, *Geschichte des Chassidismus*, 2 vols (Berlin: Jüdischer Vlg. 1931; reprinted Jerusalem: Jewish Publishing House 1969). An English translation of this work has been completed under the editorship of Prof. Ellis Rivkin of the Hebrew Union College (Cincinnati Ohio) as part of a series, Readings in Modern Jewish History, although it has not yet been published.

focused specifically on the Hasidic movement in Galicia, both its struggle with the Jewish Haskalah enlightenment and its efforts to survive in the face of Austrian government pressure during the first half of the nineteenth century.[34] Two of the early leading assimilationists and modernizers, Herz Homberg and Josef Perl, who often cooperated with the Austrian government against the ''superstitious'' Hasidics or ''reactionary'' traditional talmudists, have been the subject of several works. Meir Balaban has devoted two studies to Homberg,[35] while Perl's writings have been published and his educational work described.[36] Since the struggle between Hasidism and the Haskalah was for the souls as well as the minds of the Jewish community, one product of the Haskalah was the growth of reformed synagogues. There are histories of the first and most important of these in L'viv (est. 1846).[37]

On the Frankist movement, see M. Balaban, *Le-Toledot ha-Tenu'ah ha-Frankit,* 2 vols (Tel Aviv 1934–35) and his earlier ''Studien und Quellen zur frankistischen Bewegung in Polen,'' in *Livre d'hommage à la mémoire du dr. Samuel Poznański* (1869–1921) (Warsaw: M.I. Fried 1927), pp. 25–75.

34 Rafael Mahler, *Ha-ḥasidut ve-ha-haskalah* (Merḥavyah 1961). See also his older study: idem, *Haskole un Khsides in Galitsie in der ershter Helft 19tn Jor-Hundert* (New York: YIVO 1942), chapters 2, 3, and 4 of this work were translated into English as Raphael Mahler, ''The Social and Political Aspects of the Haskalah in Galicia,'' *YIVO Annual of Science,* I (New York 1946), pp. 64–85; idem, ''The Austrian Government and the Hasidim During the Period of Reaction (1814–1848),'' *Jewish Social Studies,* I, 1 (New York 1939), pp. 195–240; idem, ''Censorship of Hasidic, Kabbalistic and Yiddish Literature in Galicia During the Period of Reaction (1815–1848),'' *Journal of Jewish Bibliography,* I, 1 and 2 (New York 1939), pp. 35–39 and 71–82.

35 Majer Bałaban, *Herc Homberg i szkoły jozefińskie dla Żydów w Galicyi (1787–1806): studjum historyczne* (L'viv 1906), first published in *Rocznik Żydowski,* VI (L'viv), revised and translated into German as ''Herc Homberg in Galizien: archivalishe Studie,'' *Jahrbuch für jüdische Geschichte und Literatur,* XIX (Berlin 1916), pp. 189–221, reprinted in his *Z historii Żydów w Polsce: szkice i studia* (Vienna 1920), pp. 190–236.

36 Joseph Perl, *Yidishe ksovim,* ed. with biographical introduction by Israel Weinloes (Vilnius: YIVO, Filologishe aktsie 1937); P. Friedman, ''Di galizishe maskilim oyf der shvel fun 19ten yorhundert,'' in *Fun noentn ovar* (Warsaw 1938), pp. 90–102; idem, ''Josef Perl vi a bildungstuer un zayn shul in Tarnopol,'' *YIVO Bleter,* XXXI–XXXII (New York 1948), pp. 131–190. See also S. Katz, ''Naye materialn fun dem Perl-archiv,'' in *Wachstein Bukh* (Vilnius 1939), pp. 557–577.

The problem of the traditional talmudic versus the modern secular approach to education that caused so much controversy in early nineteenth-century Galician society is dealt with in a comprehensive history of pedagogical thought: Hayim Ormian, *Ha-maḥshavah ha-ḥinukhit shel yahudut polanyah le-'or ha-sifrut ha-pedagogit ve-hapsikhologit* (Tel Aviv 1939).

37 Majer Bałaban, *Historia Lwowskiej Synagogi Postępowej* (L'viv: Synagoga Postępowa 1937), in Yiddish as *Geschikhte fun Lemberger Progresivn Templ* (L'viv 1937).

The second half of the nineteenth century, which witnessed the struggle between Jewish Germanophile and Polonophile assimilationists on the one hand and the rise of Zionism and socialism on the other, is best described in studies about the political activists Wilhelm Feldman (1868–1919) and Alfred Nossig (1864–1943), both of whom began as Germanophiles but became respectively a Polonophile socialist and Zionist;[38] in Nathan M. Gelber's two-volume history of Zionism in Galicia;[39] and in works on the Jewish labor movement in the province.[40]

The cultural richness of nineteenth-century Galician Jewry promoted the growth of talmudic and secular scholarship as well as bellettres in Yiddish and Hebrew, languages which in many ways reflected the competing ideals of the Hasidic and Haskalah movements. Jewish intellectual life in Galicia is treated in several general histories of Hebrew and Yiddish literature, most especially the multivolume works of Israel Zinberg and Meyer Waxman.[41] There are also a few

38 Ezra Mendelsohn, ''Jewish Assimilation in Lvov: The Case of Wilhelm Feldman,'' *Slavic Review*, XXVIII, 4 (Seattle, Wash. 1969), pp. 577–590, reprinted in Andrei S. Markovits and Frank E. Sysyn, eds, *Nationbuilding and the Politics of Nationalism* (Cambridge, Mass.: Harvard Ukrainian Research Institute 1982), pp. 94–110; Ezra Mendelsohn, ''Wilhelm Feldman ve-Alfred Nossig: Hitbolelut ve-Ṣiyyonut bi-Lvov,'' *Gal-Ed*, II (Tel Aviv 1975), pp. 89–111. On Feldman, see also the collection of essays: *Pamięci Wilḥelma Feldmana* (Cracow: Drukarna Narodowa 1922).

On the Germanophile organization Shomer Israel (Guardian of Israel, est. 1868) and the problem of assimilation, see Y.L. Landau, *Ha-haskalah ha-ḥadashah 'o ha-'assimilaṣyah* (L'viv 1883); I. Czaczkes [I. Kirton], ''Do dziejów asymilacji i sjonizmu w Galicyi 1880–1892,'' *Moria*, IV (Vienna 1906), pp. 264–279 and 310–321; Ze'ev Brode [Braude], ''Zikhronotav shel ha-rav,'' in *Zikhron Mordechai Ze'ev Broda* (Jerusalem: Ha-sokhnut ha-Yehudit le-'Ereṣ Yisrael 1960), pp. 15–230; and Joseph Margoshes, *Erinerungen fun mayn lebn* (New York: M.N. Meizel 1936). For Feldman's and Nossig's views of these developments, see Wilhelm Feldmann, *Assimilanten, Zionisten und Polen* (L'viv 1892); and Alfred Nossig, *Próba rozwiązania kwestji żydowskiej* (L'viv 1887).

39 N.M. Gelber, *Toledot ha-tenu'ah ha-ṣiyyonit be-Galiṣyah*, 2 vols (Jerusalem: Ha-sifriya ha-ṣiyyonit 1958).

See also the study of Shabbetai Unger, '''Ivri' ve- 'ha-' 'Ivri' (Pereq be-Toledot Tenu'at ha-'Ovedim ha-Ṣiyyonit be-Galiṣyah),'' *Gal-Ed*, III (Tel Aviv 1976), pp. 83–109.

40 Jacob Bross, ''The Beginnings of the Jewish Labor Movement in Galicia,'' *YIVO Annual of Jewish Social Science*, V (New York 1950), pp. 55–84.

41 Israel Zinberg, *Di Geshikhte fun der Literatur bay Yidn*, 8 vols (Vilnius 1929–37), translated into English as *A History of Jewish Literature*, 12 vols (Cincinnati and New York: Western Reserve University Press, Hebrew Union College Press, and KTAV Publishing House 1972–78); Meyer Waxman, *A History of Jewish Literature*, 5 vols in 6 (New York: Bloch Publishing 1930–36), 3rd ed. (New York and London: Thomas Yoseloff 1960).

See also the discussions of the Galician Haskalah in Max Erik [Zalman Merkin], *Etyudn tsu der geshikhte fun der Haskole (1789–1881)* (Minsk: Melukhe Farlag fun Weisrusland 1934);

studies devoted to specific periods or problems in Galician Jewish literature.[42]

Interwar Poland and the holocaust

Writings of Jews in Galicia after 1919 are largely treated as part of descriptions of Polish Jewry as a whole. A detailed analysis of the 1931 Polish census makes it possible to determine the social and demographic structure of Jews in former eastern Galicia (the L'viv, Stanyslaviv, and Ternopil' provinces), and there is also a statistical study of Jewish participation in the Polish land distribution program in the Stanyslaviv province.[43] The problems faced by Galician Jews in professional and academic life can be gauged from more general discussions of those aspects of interwar Poland by Saul Langnas, Samuel Chmielewski, Raphael Mahler, and

---

the dictionary of Yiddish literature, press, and philology: Zalman Reisen, *Leksikon fun der yidisher literatur, prese un filologia*, 4 vols (Vilnius: B. Kleckin 1927–29); and the sections (albeit brief) on Galician writers in Leo Wiener, *The History of Yiddish Literature in the Nineteenth Century* (New York: Charles Scribner's Sons 1899); I.L. Klauzner, *Novo-evreiskaia literatura (1785–1910)* (Odessa? 1899), 2nd rev. ed. (Odessa: Z.D. Rabinovich 1912); A.A. Roback, *The Story of Yiddish Literature* (New York: Yiddish Scientific Institute 1940); and Sol Liptzin, *A History of Yiddish Literature* (Middle Village, NY: Jonathan David Publishers 1972).

42 Max Weissberg, *Die neuhebräische Aufklärungs-Literatur in Galizien: Eine literar-historische Charakteristik* (Leipzig and Vienna: M. Breitenstein 1898), also in *Monatsschrift für Geschichte und Wissenschaft des Judentums*, LVII (Frankfurt-am-Main 1913), pp. 513–526, 735–749; LXXI (1927), pp. 54–62, 100–109, 371–387; LXXII (1928), pp. 71–88, 184–201; M. Weissberg, "Język literatury żydówskiej w Galicji," *Kwartalnik dla Historii Żydów w Polsce*, II (Warsaw 1912), pp. 1–16 and III (1913), pp. 101–132; Sol Liptzin, "Galician Neoromanticism," *YIVO Annual of Jewish Social Science*, XIV (New York 1969), pp. 209–218.

43 I. Bornstein, "Struktura zawodowa i społeczna ludności żydowskiej w Polsce," *Sprawy Narodowościowe*, XIII, 1–2 (Warsaw 1939), pp. 43–98; Jakub Babicki, "Udział Żydów w akciji parcelacyjnej na terenie województwa stanisławskiego," *Sprawy Narodowościowe* X, 6 (Warsaw 1936), pp. 601–607.

On the interwar period, see also volume II of *Żydzi w Polsce odrodzonej*, n. 8 above, and the impressionistic but useful essays by two natives of Galicia: the Jew Josef Tenenbaum, *Galitsye mayn alte Heym*, Das poylishe Yidntum, no. 87 (Buenos Aires 1952); and the Polish ethnographer and specialist on the Hutsul region, Stanisław Vincenz, *Tematy Żydowskie* (London: Oficyna Poetów i Malarzy 1977).

Nathan Eck.[44] Finally, the Jewish community of L'viv during the interwar period is the subject of two works.[45]

On the World War II years, which resulted in the willful annihilation of Galicia's Jewish community, there is an excellent introduction in Philip Friedman's dispassionate account of Ukrainian-Jewish relations under the Nazi occupation.[46] Friedman and T. Berenstein also have written studies on the physical extermination and forced labor programs,[47] while more details on Galicia can be found in a bibliography and in general histories of the holocaust in eastern Europe,[48] as well as in several memorial books devoted to Galicia as a whole and to several of its individual communities. The memorial books include histories of the community in question as well as several memoirs dealing primarily with the interwar years and the holocaust. Some of the better volumes have appeared in two series: *Enṣiqlopedyah shel galuyyot* (Encyclopedia of the Jewish Diaspora) and *'Arim ve-'Immahot be-Yisrael* (Towns and Mother Cities in Israel). Besides

44 Saul Langnas, *Żydzi a studia akademickie w Polsce w latach 1921–31* (L'viv: Centralna Żydowska Akademia Stowarzyszeniowa Samopomoc. 1933); Samuel Chmielewski, ''Stan szkolnictwa wśród Żydów w Polsce,'' *Sprawy Narodowościowe,* XI, 1–2 (Warsaw 1937), pp. 32–74, and separately (Warsaw: Instytut Badań Spraw Narodowościowych 1937); Raphael Mahler, ''Jews in Public Service and the Liberal Professions in Poland, 1918–39,'' *Jewish Social Studies,* VI, 1 (New York 1944); Nathan Eck, ''The Educational Institutions of Polish Jewry (1921–1939),'' *Jewish Social Studies,* IX, 1 (New York 1947), pp. 3–32.

45 *Lwów: żydowska gmina wyznaniowa* (L'viv 1928); J. Schall, *Przewodnik po zabytkach żydowskich Lwowa* (L'viv 1936).

46 Philip Friedman, ''Ukrainian-Jewish Relations During the Nazi Occupation,'' *YIVO Annual of Jewish Social Science,* XII (New York 1958–59), pp. 259–296, reprinted in his *Roads to Extinction: Essays on the Holocaust* (New York and Philadelphia: Jewish Publication Society of America 1980), pp. 176–208.

47 Filip Friedman, *Zagłada Żydów lwowskich,* Wydawnictwo Centralnej Żydowskiej Komisji Historycznej przy Centralnym Komitecie Żydów Polskich, no. 4 (Łódź 1945), 2nd rev. ed. (Munich 1947); in Hebrew as ''Ḥurban yehudei Lvov.'' in *'Enṣiqlopedyah shel galuyyot: Lwów* (Jerusalem 1956), pp. 599–746; in English as ''The Destruction of the Jews of Lwów,'' in his *Roads to Extinction: Essays on the Holocaust* (New York and Philadelphia: Jewish Publication Society of America 1980), pp. 244–321; T. Berenstein, ''Eksterminacja ludności żydowskiej w dystrykcie Galicja (1941–1943),'' *Biuletyn Żydowskiego Instytutu Historycznego,* no. 61 (Warsaw 1967); idem, ''Prace przymusowe ludności żydowskiej w tzw. dystrykcie Galicja,'' *ibid.,* no. 60 (Warsaw 1969).

See also the description of the notorious camp and interrogation center just outside of L'viv in Leon Weliczker-Wells, *Janowska Road* (New York: Macmillan 1963).

48 Jacob Robinson and Philip Friedman, *Guide to Jewish History Under Nazi Impact,* Yad Washem and YIVO Joint Documentary Projects Bibliographical Series, no. 1 (New York 1960). See also the extensive references in Friedman's study, n. 46 above.

general memorial books on Galicia as a whole,[49] there are volumes for twenty-five towns and cities in eastern Galicia: Bolekhiv,[50] Borshchiv,[51] Brody,[52] Buchach,[53] Dobromyl',[54] Drohobych,[55] Horodenka,[56] Husiatyn,[57] Iavoriv,[58] Kolomyia,[59] Kosiv,[60] Kuty,[61] Lesko,[62] L'viv,[63] Przemyśl,[64] Rohatyn,[65] Sanok,[66]

49 N. Zucker, ed., *Pinkas Galicia* (Buenos Aires 1945); N. Zucker, ed., *Gedenkbukh Galitsye* (Buenos Aires: Zychronot 1964).

50 Y. Eshel, ed., *Sefer Hazikkaron le 'Kedoshei Bolechów* (Tel Aviv 1957).

51 N. Blumental, ed., *Sefer Borszczów* (Tel Aviv 1960).

52 N. Gelber, ed., *Brody,* 'Arim ve-'Immahot be-Yisrael, vol. VI (Jerusalem: Rav Kook Institute 1956).

53 I. Kahan, ed., *Sefer Buchacz: Matsevet Zikkaron le'Kehila Kedosha* (Tel Aviv: Am Oved 1956).

54 M. Gelbart, ed., *Sefer Zikkaron le-Zekher Dobromil / Memorial Book Dobromil* (Tel Aviv: Dobromil Society in New York and the Dobromiler Organization in Israel 1964).

55 N.M. Gelber, ed., *Sefer Zikkaron li-Drohobycz, Boryslaw ve-ha-Sevivah* (Tel Aviv 1959).

56 Sh. Meltzer, ed., *Sefer Horodenka* (Tel Aviv 1963).

57 A.Y. Avitov (Birnboym), *Mi-bet Abba: Pirqei Zikhronot mi-yemei Yaldut be-'Ayarat Moladeti Husiatyn* (Tel Aviv: p.a. 1965).

58 Shmuel Druck, *'Yudenshtodt Yavorov': Der Umkum fun Yavorover Yidn / Swastika over Jaworow* (New York: First Jaworower Independent Association 1950).

59 Sh. Bickel, ed., *Pinqas Kolomey* (New York 1957); D. Noy and N. Schutzman, eds, *Sefer Zikkaron li-qehillat Kolomey ve-ha-sevivah* (Tel Aviv 1972). See also documents from the postwar war criminals trial in T. Friedman, ed., *Schupokriegsverbrecher in Kolomea vor dem Wiener Volksgericht* (Haifa 1957).

60 E. Kresel, *Sefer Kosov–Galiṣyah ha-mizraḥit* (Tel Aviv 1964).

61 Isaac Husen, ed., *Kitever Yizkor Bukh* (New York: Kittiver Sick and Benevolent Society in New York 1958).

62 N. Mark and Friedlander, eds, *Sefer Yizkor: Muqdash li-yehudei ha-'Ayarot she-nispu ba-Sho'ah ba-shanim 1939–44: Linsk [Lesko], Istrik ... ve-ha-sevivah* (Tel Aviv: Libai 1965).

63 Y.L. Fishman (Maimon), ed., *Lwów,* 'Arim ve-'Immahot be-Yisrael, vol. I (Jerusalem: Rav Kook Institute 1947); N.M. Gelber, ed., *'Enṣiqlopedyah shel galuyyot: Lwów* (Jerusalem 1956).

64 A. Menczer, ed., *Sefer Przemyśl* (Tel Aviv 1964).

65 M. Amihai, ed., *Qehillat Rohatyn ve-ha-sevivah / Rohatyn: The History of Jewish Community* (Tel Aviv: Former Residents of Rohatyn in Israel 1962).

66 E. Sharvit, ed., *Sefer Zikkaron li-qehillat Sanok ve-ha-sevivah* (Haifa 1968).

Skalat,[67] Sokal',[68] Stanyslaviv,[69] Stryi,[70] Tartakiv,[71] Ternopil',[72] Turka,[73] and Zhovkva.[74]

ARMENIANS

Background

Armenians first settled in Galicia in the thirteenth century. They did not come directly from Armenia, but rather from the Crimea, where thousands had fled after the Turks took control of their homeland in the late eleventh century. In 1356, Armenians were granted the rights and privileges of Magdeburg Law should they settle in cities under the Polish crown. Indeed, it was in cities that Armenians settled, and L'viv as well as several other towns in southeastern Galicia (Stanyslaviv, Horodenka, and especially Kuty) contained some of the greatest concentrations of Armenians in all of the Polish-controlled Ukraine. The Armenians were engaged almost exclusively in trade and they played an important role in medieval Galicia's economy. By 1363, L'viv was the seat of an Armenian Apostolic bishopric (not in union with Rome); then in the seventeenth century, when Poland was actively engaged in trying to convert its non-Roman Catholic subjects, the Armenian Bishop Nikol Torosovič (1627–1681) accepted union with Rome and an Armenian Catholic archdiocese was established in 1635.

This new religious association hastened an assimilatory process that had already been set in motion decades before, and paradoxically this process became most effective during the seventeenth century, when Armenian culture in Galicia

67 H. Bronstein, ed., *Skałat: Qoveṣ Zikkaron li-qehillah she-ḥarevah ba-Sho'ah* (Tel Aviv 1971). See also Avram Weisbrod, *Es shtarbt a shtetl* (Munich 1949).

68 A. Chomel, ed., *Sefer Sokal, Tartaków ... ve-ha-sevivah* (Tel Aviv 1968).

69 D. Sadan and M. Gelerter, eds. *Stanislawów,* 'Arim ve-'Immahot be-Yisrael, vol. V (Jerusalem: Rav Kook Institute 1952). See also documents from the postwar war criminals trial in T. Friedman, ed., *Schupo- und Gestapokriegsverbrecher von Stanislau vor dem Wiener Volksgericht* (Haifa 1957).

70 N. Kudish et al., eds, *Sefer Stryj / Memorial Book of Stryj* (Tel Aviv: Former Residents of Stryj in Israel 1962). See also documents from the postwar war criminals trial in T. Friedman, ed., *Schupokriegsverbrecher von Stryj vor dem Wiener Volksgericht* (Haifa 1957).

71 See n. 68 above.

72 Ph. Korngruen, ed., *'Enṣiqlopedyah shel galuyyot: Tarnopol* (Jerusalem: Encyclopedia of the Jewish Diaspora 1955).

73 J. Sigelman, ed., *Sefer Zikkaron li-qehillat Turka 'al Nehar Stry ve-ha-sevivah* (Haifa? 1966).

74 N.M. Gelber and Y. Ben-Shem, eds, *Sefer Żołkiew (Qiryah Nisgavah)* (Jerusalem: Encylopedia of the Jewish Diaspora 1969). See also Gerszon Taffet, *Zagłada Żydów żółkiewskich* (Łódź 1946).

entered its most vibrant period. The first Armenian printshop on the territory of the Ukraine was established in 1616 in L'viv; that same city contained rich Armenian libraries and a distinct Armenian architecture. This was the high point of the community's development, however; many had already assimilated to Polish culture and by the eighteenth century the special legal and socioeconomic privileges granted to Armenians in the Middle Ages were abolished. By the outset of the nineteenth century, there were only 1500 Armenians recorded in eastern Galicia. The Armenian Rite Catholic church continued to exist until 1944, when it was liquidated, along with other "Uniate" churches, by the Soviet regime.

Historiography, archives, general surveys

The leading Soviet specialist on Armenians in the Ukraine, Iaroslav Dashkevych, has pointed out in several historiographical studies that a rich body of source material and secondary literature on Armenians, especially in L'viv, developed between the fifteenth and nineteenth centuries.[75] Until the second half of the nineteenth century, the leading repositories of documentary material on Armenians in Galicia were the archives of the Armenian Catholic archbishopric and the cathedral chapter in L'viv. After 1866, part of these materials were transferred to the Ossolineum in L'viv and to the Mechitarist Library in Vienna. After World War II, the Ossolineum Armenian collection was further divided between the Central State Historical Archive in L'viv and the Ossolineum in Wrocław, Poland. The Armenian holdings in all these repositories have been described in several studies.[76]

75 Ia.R. Dashkevich, *Armianskie kolonii na Ukraine v istochnikakh i literature XV–XIX vekov: istoriograficheskii ocherk* (Erevan: Izd. AN Armianskoi SSR 1962); idem, "Dzherela i literatura pro virmens'ki koloniï na Ukraïni v XVI st.," *Naukovo-informatsiinyi biuleten' Arkhivnoho upravlinnia URSR*, XV, 6 (Kiev 1961), pp. 70–79; Yar Dachkévytch, "Les historiens arméniens en Ukraine au XVIIIe siècle," *Revue des études arméniennes*, N.S., IX (Paris 1972), pp. 385–424.

For more recent historiography, see Y. Dachkevytch, "Les études armeniénnes en Ukraine aux XIXe et XXe siècles," *Revue des études arméniennes*, N.S., I (Paris 1964), pp. 389–414; I.P. Kripiakevich, "Sadok Baronch– istorik armian byvshei Galitsii," in *Istoricheskie sviazi i druzhba ukrainskogo i armianskogo narodov* (Erevan: AN Armianskoi SSR 1961), pp. 38–47; M.K. Ivasiuta and S.K. Gutianskii, "Nekotorye voprosy istorii Armenii i ukrainsko-armianskikh sviazei v ukrainskoi sovetskoi istoriografii," in *Istoricheskie sviazi i druzhba ukrainskogo i armianskogo narodov*, vol. III (Erevan: AN Armianskoi SSR 1971), pp. 323–336.

76 On the status of Armenian materials before World War II, see Frédéric Macler, "Rapport sur un mission scientifique en Galicie et en Bukovine (juillet-août 1925)," *Revue des études arméniennes*, VIII (Paris 1927), pp. 79–94; Tadeusz Mańkowski, "Archiwum lwowskiej

Austrian, Polish, and Soviet writers have written brief introductory histories of Armenians in Galicia.[77] The first major histories came from a native of the group, Sadok Barącz (1814–1892). He produced a history and biographical dictionary of Armenians in Poland in which developments in, and natives of, Galicia are treated at great length.[78] A contemporary of Barącz, the Austrian scholar Ferdinand Bischoff, published several documents pertaining to the legal status of Armenians under Polish rule, while later the Polish author Ludwik Piotrkowski discussed the phenomenon of Armenian noble families.[79]

---

katedry ormiańskiej,'' *Archeion,* X (Warsaw 1932), pp. 1–11; Tadeusz Mańkowski, ''Sztuka Ormian lwowskich,'' *Prace Komisiji Historii Sztuki,* VI (Cracow 1934), pp. 136–160; and the manuscript catalogs of the Ossolineum, chapter 1, n. 74. On the holdings in Vienna, see H. Dashian, *C'uc'ak hayerēn jeřagrac' matendaranin Mkhit'arianc' i Vienna / Catalog der armenischen Handschriften in der Mechitharisten-Bibliothek zu Wien* (Vienna: Wiener Mechitharisten Congregation 1895).

On Armenian materials in present day archives in L'viv, see G.S. Sizonenko, ''Arkhivnye materialy k istorii armianskoi kolonii vo L'vove,'' in *Istoricheskie sviazi i druzhba ukrainskogo i armianskogo narodov* (Erevan: AN Armianskoi SSR 1961), pp. 204–209; P.Kh. Pirozhenko, ''Materialy TsGIA Ukrainskoi SSR vo L'vove po istorii armianskikh poselenii na Ukraine,'' in *Istoricheskie sviazi i druzhba ukrainskogo i armianskogo narodov* (Ereven: AN Armianskoi SSR 1961), pp. 237–251; N.F. Vradii, ''Aktovye knigi Tsentral'nogo Gosudarstvennogo Istoricheskogo Arkhiva USSR vo L'vove–istochnik po izucheniiu istorii armianskikh poselenii na Ukraine,'' in *Istoricheskie sviazi i druzhba ukrainskogo i armianskogo narodov: sbornik materialov,* vol. II (Kiev: Naukova dumka 1965), pp. 79–82; O.Ia. Matsiuk, ''Kharakteristika bumagi l'vovskikh armianskikh rukopisei XVI–XVII vv.,'' in *Istoricheskie sviazi i druzhba ukrainskogo i armianskogo narodov,* vol. III (Erevan: AN Armianskoi SSR 1971), pp. 369–375); and the catalog of Armenian manuscripts by Nerses Akinian, *C'uc'ak hayerēn jeřagrac' Lvovi hamalsarani matenadarani ark'episkoposarani ew Stanislawovi / Katalog der armenischen Handschriften in den Bibliotheken zu Lwow und Stanislawow* (Vienna: Wiener Mechitharisten Congregation 1961).

On Armenian materials in Polish libraries, see Ya. Dachkévytch, ''Matériaux pour l'histoire des colonies arméniennes en Ukraine, see trouvant dans les bibliotheques de Cracovie et de Wroclaw,'' *Revue des études arméniennes,* N.S., VII (Paris 1970), pp. 451–472; and volume I of the catalog of the Wrocław Ossolineum, chapter 1, n. 98.

77 Bołoz. Antoniewicz, ''Die Armenier [in Galizien],'' in *Die österreichisch-ungarische Monarchie in Wort und Bild,* vol. XII: *Galizien* (Vienna: K.K. Hof- und Staatsdruckerei 1898), pp. 440–462; Józef Haliczer, ''Ormiane w Polsce południowo-wschodniej,'' *Rocznik Ziem Wschodnich,* V (Warsaw 1939), pp. 79–86; V.V. Grabovetskii, ''Armianskie poseleniia na zapadnoukrainskikh zemliakh,'' in *Istoricheskie sviazi i druzhba ukrainskogo i armianskogo narodov* (Erevan: AN Armianskoi SSR 1961), pp. 92–109.

78 S. Barącz, *Rys dziejów ormiańskich* (Ternopil' 1869); Sadok Barącz, *Żywoty sławnych Ormian w Polsce* (L'viv: Wojciech Maniecki 1856).

79 F. Bischoff, *Urkunden zur Geschichte der Armenier in Lemberg* (Vienna, 1865); Ferdinand Bischoff, ''Das alte Recht der Armenier in Lemberg,'' *Sitzungsberichte der philosophisch-historischen Classe der kaiserlichen Akademie der Wissenschaften,* XL (Vienna 1862), pp. 255–302; [Ludwik Piotrkowski], *Armiańskie rody szlacheckie* (Cracow 1934).

Cultural history, the church, other specific problems

Of all the aspects of Armenian history in Galicia, cultural developments in the late sixteenth and especially seventeenth centuries have received the greatest attention. Iaroslav Dashkevych has contributed the most, having compiled a collection of documents on Ukrainian-Armenian relations during this period as well as several articles on Armenian book culture and printing, especially in L'viv.[80] Art, architecture, and other Armenian cultural phenomena during these centuries are also discussed in several works.[81]

The Armenian church has received special attention in a general historical survey by Czesław Lechnicki and a detailed account of the complicated struggle for union with Rome (1626–1686) by Gregory Petrowicz. Both authors present a sympathetic view of the union.[82] In marked contrast, Apostolic Armenian and Soviet writers have castigated the union as having been detrimental to Armenians

80 Ia.R. Dashkevich, *Ukrainsko-armianskie sviazi v XVII veke: sbornik dokumentov* (Kiev: Naukova dumka 1969); idem, ''Armianskaia kniga na Ukraine XVII stoletii,'' *Kniga*, vol. VI (Moscow 1962), pp. 148–168; Ya. Dachkévytch, ''L'imprimerie arménienne à Lvov (Ukraine) au XVII-è siècle,'' *Revue des études arméniennes*, N.S., VI (Paris 1969), pp. 355–371; Ia.R. Dashkevych, ''Virmens'ke drukarstvo na Ukraïni (do 350-richchia vykhodu v svit pershoï virmens'koï drukovanoï knyhy na Ukraïni),'' *Ukraïns'kyi istorychnyi zhurnal*, X, 12 (Kiev 1966), pp. 132–134.

See also N.K. Krivonos, ''K istorii knizhnoi kul'tury armianskoi kolonii vo L'vove v XVI–XVII vekakh,'' *Kniga*, vol. XXII (Moscow 1971), pp. 206–209; N. Krivonos, ''Nekotorye dannye o bibliotekakh armian vo L'vove v XVII veke,'' *Patma-banasirakan handes / Istoriko-filologicheskii zhurnal* [VI], 1 (Erevan 1963), pp. 271–276; and K.A. Korkotian and N.A. Voskanian, ''Armianskaia kniga v XV–XVI vv. i armianskoe knigopechatanie vo L'vove v XVII v.,'' *Istoricheskie sviazi i druzhba ukrainskogo i armianskogo narodov*, vol. III (Erevan: AN Armianskoi SSR 1971), pp. 308–320.

81 M.M. Kazarian, ''Iz istorii deiatel'nosti l'vovskikh khudozhnikov-armian XVI–XVIII vv.,'' *ibid.*, pp. 294–300; N.K. Krivonos, ''Armiane v kul'turnoi zhizni L'vova,'' in *Istoricheskie sviazi i druzhba ukrainskogo i armianskogo narodov* (Erevan: AN Armianskoi SSR 1961), pp. 132–139; E.A. Iatskevich, ''Pamiatniki armianskoi kul'tury vo L'vove,'' in *ibid.*, pp. 121–131; D. Kajetanowicz, *Katedra ormiańska i jej otoczenie* (L'viv 1930).

82 Czesław Lechnicki, *Kościół ormiański w Polsce: zarys historyczny* (L'viv: Gubrynowicz i Syn 1928); Gregorio Petrowicz, *L'unione degli armeni di Polonia con la Santa Sede (1626–1686)*, Orientalia Christiana Analecta, vol. CXXXV (Rome: Pontificum Institutum Orientalium Studiorum 1950).

See also the introductory history by M.D[zieduszucki], ''Lwowska Archidjecezya obrządu ormiańskiego,'' in *Encyklopedya kościelna*, vol. XII (Warsaw: X. Michał Nowodworski 1879), pp. 509–518; and a Polish translation of a Latin and Italian history of the union: Adolf Pawiński, *Dzieje zjednoczenia Ormian polskich z kościołem rzymskim w XVII wieku*, Żródła Dziejowe, vol. II (Warsaw: Gebethner i Wolff 1876).

in Galicia.[83] Of great value on the administration and structure of the church are the several *schematisma* of the Armenian Catholic diocese of L'viv issued between 1843 and 1939.[84]

The Soviet interest in Ukrainian-Armenian historical relations that began in the 1960s has resulted in several conferences and symposia whose results have been published. Among the subjects other than those mentioned above that have been treated are the earliest settlement of Armenians in L'viv,[85] the socioeconomic developments of the group from the fourteenth to seventeenth centuries,[86] its decline in the nineteenth century,[87] and the history of individual communities–L'viv, Stanyslaviv, Sniatyn, Brody, and Kuty.[88]

83 For an Apostolic Armenian view on the "forcible union," see the collection of documents: *Bṙni miufʻiwn hayocʻ Lehastani ěnd ekełecʻwoyn Hṙomay* (St. Petersburg 1884). For the Soviet view, see S.T. Biletskii, "Bor'ba l'vovskikh armian protiv unii i Vatikana," in *Istoricheskie sviazi i druzhba ukrainskogo i armianskogo narodov* [vol. II] (Kiev: Naukova dumka 1965), pp. 89–92.

84 *Schematismus archidioecesis Leopoliensis ritus Armeno-catholici [1843–1939]* (L'viv 1843–1939).

85 Ivan P. Kripiakevich, "K voprosu o nachale armianskoi kolonii v L'vove," *Patma-banasirakan handes / Istoriko-filologicheskii zhurnal* [VI], 1 (Erevan 1963), pp. 163–171; idem, "K voprosu o nachale armianskoi kolonii vo L'vove," in *Istoricheskie sviazi i druzhba ukrainskogo i armianskogo narodov: sbornik materialov,* vol. II (Kiev: Naukova dumka 1965), pp. 122–127.

86 N.F. Kotliar, "Armiane v ékonomike srednevekovogo L'vova (XIV–XV vv.)," in *Istoricheskie sviazi i druzhba ukrainskogo i armianskogo narodov,* vol. III (Erevan: AN Armianskoi SSR 1971), pp. 201–207; Ia. P. Kis', "Uchastie Armian v razvitii remesla g. L'vova v XV–XVII VV.," in *Istoricheskie sviazi i druzhba ukrainskogo i armianskogo narodov* [vol. II] (Kiev: Naukova dumka 1965), pp. 137–139; N.K. Krivonos, "Rol' l'vovskoi armianskoi kolonii v razvitii torgovli na zapadnoukrainskikh zemliakh v pervoi polovine XVII v.," in *ibid.,* pp. 101–104; idem, "K istorii armianskoi kolonii vo L'vove vo vtoroi polovine XVII v.," in *Istoricheskie sviazi i druzhba ukrainskogo i armianskogo narodov,* vol. III (Erevan: AN Armianskoi SSR 1971), pp. 241–249.

See also the older but still useful I.A. Linnichenko, "Obshchestvennaia rol' armian v proshlom Iugo-zapadnoi Rusi," *Chteniia v istoricheskom obshchestvie Nestora-lietopistsa,* IX (Kiev 1895), pp. 140–147; and Bohdan Janusz, *'Mons Pius' Ormian lwowskich,* Bibljoteka Lwowska, vol. XXVI (L'viv 1928).

87 E.A. Iatskevich, "Armiane v Galitsii v XIX v.," *Patma-banasirakan handes / Istoriko-filologicheskii zhurnal* [III], 3 (Erevan 1960), pp. 59–64; G.S. Sizonenko, "Armianskie deiateli nauki i kul'tury vo L'vove XIX–XX vv.," in *Istoricheskie sviazi i druzhba ukrainskogo i armianskogo narodov,* vol. III (Erevan: AN Armianskoi SSR 1971), pp. 170–176.

88 N. Krivonos and V. Grabovetskii, "Armianskaia koloniia vo L'vove v XIV–XVIII vekakh," *Izvestiia Akademii Nauk Armianskoi SSR,* no. 12 (Erevan 1958); V. Grabovetskii, "Armianskaia koloniia v Stanislave v XVII–XVIII vv.," *ibid.,* no. 6 (Erevan 1958), pp. 43–51. V.V. Grabovetskii, "Armianskaia koloniia v Sniatyne," in *Istoricheskie sviazi i*

GERMANS

Background

The German colonization of Galicia occurred basically in two distinct waves. After the Tatar invasion and devastation of large parts of eastern Europe in 1241, the Polish Kingdom was anxious to have its southeastern borders strengthened with new settlers. This led to the first influx of German settlers (priests, soldiers, artisans, traders), who eventually followed Poland's expansion and incorporation of the Galician-Volhynian principality in the fourteenth century. The German colonists were welcomed for their more advanced trading, artisan, and agricultural skills, and, like the Armenians, they were granted special privileges, especially within cities under Magdeburg Law. During the early period, most German colonists settled in western rather than eastern Galicia, and those that did live in the latter area became largely assimilated to Polish culture by the sixteenth century.

The second wave of German colonists arrived after Galicia became part of the Habsburg Empire in 1772. Anxious to improve the economic status of Galicia and to secure Austrian control of the new province, Emperor Joseph II brought (between 1781 and 1785) more than 15,000 colonists and (between 1802 and 1805) Franz II about 4000 more from the Palatinate and other southwest German states. During the first half of the nineteenth century, another 2000 Germans arrived from the Sudetenland. In contrast to the medieval wave of colonists, these Germans settled in small villages in eastern Galicia, most especially in a belt stretching from Kaminka Strumylova and Zhovkva in the north, then past L'viv to Drohobych, Boryslav, and Stryi in the south. Also, in contrast to their medieval predecessors, the new colonists were able to avoid assimilation. This was due in part to their relatively more isolated rural settlement pattern as well as to numerous cultural societies, agricultural cooperatives, schools (some supported by the Protestant church), and publications, all of which contributed to maintenance of a German identity. By 1910, they had numbered about 65,000, but extensive emigration to Germany and to the New World reduced their numbers to less than 50,000 in the 1930s. Finally, with the outbreak of World War II and Poland's destruction at the hands of Germany and the Soviet Union, the Soviet government (which held eastern Galicia) agreed to the return of Germans to their "true

---

druzhba ukrainskogo i armianskogo narodov [vol. II] (Kiev: Naukova dumka 1965), pp. 140–144; Ia.S. Mel'nichuk, "Armianskoe poselenie v Brodakh," in *ibid.*, vol. III (Erevan: AN Armianskoi SSR 1971), pp. 250–254; V.V. Grabovetskii, "Armianskoe poselenie v Kutakh," in *ibid.*, pp. 255–260.

homeland.'' Thus, between 1939 and 1940, Hitler's government resettled *en masse* the Germans from eastern Galicia into the ''purer'' German soil of the so-called Warthegau in West Prussia.

Bibliographies, historical surveys, specific problems

The historical literature on Germans in Galicia is very well developed, as evidenced in a relatively recent bibliography of the subject that includes more than 2000 studies dealing with the history, religion, culture, economic life, legal status, ethnography, and deportation of the group.[89] The first comprehensive works were produced by Raimund Friedrich Kaindl, who wrote a history of Germans in Galicia and Bukovina and also devoted much attention to them in his three-volume history of Germans in the Carpathian lands.[90] More recent scholarly studies that focus on the period 1772 to 1940 include solid histories by Sepp Müller and a collection of essays on all aspects of the group's life edited by Julius Krämer.[91] These works derive from a small group of researchers in West Germany, who have also set up a Galician German archive in a suburb (Weende) near

89 Sepp Müller, *Schrifttum über Galizien und sein Deutschtum,* Wissenschaftliche Beiträge zur Geschichte und Landeskunde Ost-Mitteleuropas, vol. LXIII (Marburg / Lahn: Johann-Gottfried-Herder Institut 1962).

90 Raimund Friedrich Kaindl, *Die Deutschen in Galizien und in der Bukowina* (Frankfurt-am-Main: Heinrich Keller 1916); idem, *Geschichte der Deutschen in den Karpathenländern,* 3 vols (Gotha: Friedrich Andreas Perthes 1907–11), especially vols I and III; and his study of German law in Galicia, which is a kind of addendum to his three-volume history: idem, *Beiträge zur Geschichte des deutschen Rechtes in Galizien,* Archiv für österreichische Geschichte, vol. C, pt 2 (Vienna 1909).

See also the popular works: *Das Deutschtum in Galizien: seine geschichtliche Entwicklung und gegenwärtige Lage* (L'viv: Bund der christlichen Deutschen in Galizien 1914); Fritz Seefeldt, *Der Deutsche in Galizien,* Der Deutsche im Auslande, vol. IX (Berlin–Leipzig: Vlg. Julius Beltz 1937); *Gedenkbuch zur Erinnerung an die Einwanderung der Deutschen in Galizien vor 150 Jahren* (Poznań: Ausschuss der Gedenkfeier 1931); the annual *Zeitweiser der Galiziendeutschen* (Stuttgart and Bad Cannstatt: Hilfskomitee der Galiziendeutschen, 1954–present); and the introductory encyclopedic article: Łudomil German, ''Die deutsche Colonisation [in Galizien],'' *Die österreichisch-ungarische Monarchie in Wort und Bild,* vol. XII: *Galizien* (Vienna: K.K. Hof- und Staatsdruckerei 1898), pp. 463–474.

91 Sepp Müller, *Von der Ansiedlung bis zur Umsiedlung: das Deutschtum Galiziens, insbesondere Lembergs 1772–1940,* Wissenschaftliche Beiträge zur Geschichte und Landeskunde Ost-Mitteleuropas, vol. LIV (Marburg / Lahn: Johann Gottfried Herder Institut 1961); idem, *Das deutsche Genossenschaftswesen in Galizien, Wolhynien und im Cholm-Lubliner Gebiet,* Quellen und Studien des Instituts für Genossenschaftswesen an der Universität Münster, vol. VII (Karlsruhe: C.F. Müller 1954); Julius Krämer, ed., *Heimat Galizien: ein Gedenkbuch* (Stuttgart–Bad Cannstatt: Hilfskomitee der Galiziendeutschen 1965).

Göttingen: the archive's holdings have been described in an essay by Johann Hennig.[92]

Several studies are devoted to specific periods or areas. The best of these include two collections of documents and monographs by Henryk Lepucki and Ludwig Schneider on the colonization organized under Joseph II.[93] There are also solid analyses of settlement patterns,[94] demography during the interwar years,[95] and descriptions of individual communities.[96] Finally, there are several works describing the voluntary deportations in 1939–1940. Most of these are contempo-

92 Johann Hennig, "Das Galiziendeutsche Heimatarchiv," in *Aufbruch und Neubeginn: Heimatbuch der Galiziendeutschen* , vol. II (Stuttgart–Bad Cannstatt: Hilfskomitee der Galiziendeutschen 1977), pp. 613–616.

93 Fritz Seefeldt, *Quellenbuch zur deutschen Ansiedlung in Galizien unter Kaiser Joseph II*, Ostdeutsche Forschungen, vol. III (Plauen im Vogtlande 1935); Franz Wilhelm and Josef Kallbrunner, *Quellen zur deutschen Siedlungsgeschichte in Südosteuropa*, Schriften der Deutschen Akademie, vol. XI (Munich: Ernest Reinhardt 1936), especially pp. 160–215; Henryk Lepucki, *Działalność kolonizacyjna Marii Teresy i Józefa II w Galicji 1772–1790*, Badania z Dziejów Społecznych i Gospodarczych, vol. XXIX (L'viv 1938); Ludwig Schneider, *Das Kolonisationswerk Josefs II. in Galizien: Darstellung und Namenlisten*, Ostdeutsche Forschungen, vol. IX (Poznań and Leipzig: Historische Gesellschaft für Polen 1939).

94 Walter Kuhn, *Die jungen deutschen Sprachinseln in Galizien*, Deutschtum und Ausland, vol. 26–27 (Münster in Westfalen: Aschendorffsche Vlg. 1930).

95 Walter Kuhn, *Bevölkerungsstatistik des Deutschtums in Galizien*, Schriften des Instituts für Statistik der Minderheitsvölker an der Universität Wien, vol. VII (Vienna 1930); Sepp Müller, *Das Deutschtum in Galizien zwischen den beiden Weltkriegen im Lichte der Statistik* (Stuttgart: Hilfskomitee der Galiziendeutschen 1954).

96 Josef Schmidt, "Das Deutschtum in den ost-galizischen Berzirken Dolina und Kałusz," *Kalender des Bundes der christlichen Deutschen in Galizien*, III (L'viv 1911), pp. 129–146; Heinrich Czerwenzel [Siegfried], "Zur Geschichte des Deutschtums in den Bezirken Stanislau, Bohorodczany und Nadwórna," *ibid.*, IV (L'viv 1912), pp. 137–154, also separately (L'viv: Vlg. des Bundes der christlichen Deutschen in Galizien 1912); Walter Kuhn, "Die deutschen Siedlungen bei Kamionka Strumiłowa," *Dornfelder Blätter*, V, 11–12 (Dornfeld 1928), pp. 508–523; Fritz Seefeldt, *Dornfelds Chronik: 150 Jahre Ausland-Deutschen-Schicksal* (Leipzig: S. Hirzel 1936); idem, *Pfälzer wandern, Kolonisation, Umsiedlung, Vertreibung, Heimkehr: 150 Jahre Auslanddeutschen-Schicksal: Dornfelds Chronik II* (Kaiserslautern 1959); idem, *So war es in Galizien*, 2 vols (Eutin: Struve's Buchdruckerei und Vlg. 1965–66).

rary propagandistic tracts put out by the German government[97] or memoirs of those who participated in the exodus.[98]

KARAITES

Background

The Karaites (also known as Karaims) are a Jewish sect that came into being at the beginning of the eighth century. Their doctrinal distinction from other Jews was based primarily on a denial of the talmudic-rabbinical tradition and, instead, recognition of the scriptures as the sole and direct source of religious law. Their name, Karaite, is an abbreviated form for *Kara'im Ba'alei-Mikra,* which means the people of the scriptures.

The Karaites were known to have already inhabited the Crimea in the twelfth century. Popular tradition ascribes their arrival in Poland-Lithuania to the activity of Grand Duke Vytautas (reigned 1392–1430) who, after defeating the Tatars in 1398, brought back many prisoners, among them Karaites, whom he settled in Trakai (Troki), near Vilnius. From Trakai, some Karaites than migrated south to Luts'k in Volhynia and to Halych in Galicia.

Modern scholarship has proved that Karaites came directly to Galicia from the Crimea during the reign of Prince Danylo in 1246. The Karaites were granted commercial privileges like the Jews and Armenians, and they had their own community and places to worship in L'viv and Halych. After 1475, the remaining Karaites in L'viv moved to Halych, which remained the center of the community in Galicia. In 1578, they received from the Polish king the rights and privileges that were accorded "other Jews." Karaite autonomy was recognized by the Austrians as well.

The Karaite community in Galicia at no time numbered more than several hundred. The largest settlement, in Halych, had only 160 persons in 1921 and 100

97 *Die Heimkehr der Galiziendeutschen,* Unsere Heimat, vol. XIV (Leipzig: S. Hirzel for the Historische Gesellschaft Posen 1940); *Marschziel: Bauernreich Grossdeutschland! Erlebnisberichte vom Wintermarsch der Deutschen aus Galizien, Wolhynien und dem Bielsk-Narewgebiet,* Viktor Wagner: Volkstum im Kampf, vol. IV (Berlin: Vlg. Grenze und Ausland 1940); Kurt Kölsch, *Galizien deutsche Heimkehr: ein Tagebuch* (Neustadt: Westmark Vlg. 1940); Heinz Reichenfelser, *Sie folgten dem Ruf des Führers: Erlebnisse eines SS-Mannes* (Graz: Steirische Verlagsanstalt 1941).

98 Julius Krämer et al., eds, *Aufbruch und Neubeginn: Heimatbuch der Galiziendeutschen,* pt 2 (Stuttgart and Bad Cannstatt: Hilfskomitee der Galiziendeutschen 1977). For other works on the deportations, see entries 2056–2130 in the Müller bibliography, n. 89 above.

in 1939. Despite their minuscule size, the Karaites have been able to maintain their own Turkic language–the Galician branch together with those living in Luts'k speak a southern dialect as opposed to those in Troki near Vilnius who speak a northern dialect. They also experienced a cultural revival during the interwar years in Poland, when Karaite journals and other popular works appeared in Vilnius and Luts'k.[99]

The rise of interest in the Karaite past during the interwar period was accompanied by a fierce debate regarding the Jewish or Turkic origins of the group. This proved to have more than purely academic consequences, because the racially oriented Nazi German government became intensely interested in the problem. Finally, in 1939, the German Ministry of Interior ruled that the Karaites were not racially Jewish; as a result, the few remaining residents in Galicia were spared the fate of their Jewish brethren.[100]

General surveys

The best introduction to the problem of the Karaites in Poland is found in general surveys by Bohdan Janusz and the Karaite scholar Ananiasz Zajączkowski. Both have provided a concise discussion of the history, language, folklore, and culture, as well as an extensive bibliography of the group in historic Poland, which includes the settlements in Trakai (near Vilnius), Luts'k (Volhynia), and Halych (Galicia).[101] Another Karaite scholar, Simon Szyszman, has written a solid his-

99 The scholarly journal *Myśl Karaimska* (Vilnius 1924–39) appeared in Polish and beginning in 1932 it was the official organ of the Society for the Friends of Karaite History and Literature. After World War II, *Myśl Karaimska* was revived in Wrocław, but after two volumes appeared (1945–46 and 1946–47), it was merged with *Przegląd Orientalistyczny* (Wrocław and Warsaw 1949–present). The more popular *Karaj awazy* (Luts'k 1931–39) was published in Karaite.

100 When in 1942, German officials asked leading Jewish scholars like Meir Balaban and Jacob Schall to report on the origins of the Karaites, they refuted their well-known views and claimed instead a Turco-Mongolian origin for the group in the hope (which proved real) that the group would be spared. On this incident, see Philip Friedman, "The Karaites under Nazi Rule," in Max Beloff, ed., *On the Track of Tyranny: Essays Presented by the Wiener Library to Leonard G. Montefiore, O.B.E.* (London 1960), pp. 97–123, reprinted in Philip Friedman, *Roads to Extinction: Essays on the Holocaust* (New York and Philadelphia: Jewish Publication Society of America 1980), pp. 153–175. For a fuller discussion of the interwar historiographic debate on Karaite origins, see Jan Czekanowski, "Z zagadnień antropologii Karaimów," *Myśl Karaimska*, Seria nowa, II [XXIV] (Wrocław 1947), pp. 3–23.

101 Bohdan Janusz, *Karaici w Polsce*, Biblioteczka Geograficzna 'Orbis', Serja III, vol. XI (Cracow 1927); Ananiasz Zajączkowski, *Karaims in Poland: History, Language, Folklore, Science* (Warsaw, The Hague, and Paris: PWN and Mouton 1961).

torical account from earliest times to the present that focuses on the various controversies concerning the origins of the group.[102] The Karaite language, including the linguistic peculiarities of the Halych group, is described by Omeljan Pritsak and in several works by the French-born Polish scholar Tadeusz Kowalski and by Ananiasz Zajączkowski.[103]

Scholars began to turn their attention to the Karaites in the seventeenth century.[104] One of the first studies to treat the group in Galicia was published in 1862 by the Austrian scholar J.V. Goehlert.[105] Subsequent writings on Karaites in Galicia before World War I were generally limited to short essays[106] or to more literary descriptions, as in the work of Reuben Fahn.[107] It was not really until the interwar period that more extensive scholarship was undertaken, and several works were published by both Jewish and Karaite scholars. Most of the attention focuses on the origins of the group. Jewish writers like Meir Balaban, J. Brutzkus, and Gedo Hecht argued that the Karaites were of Jewish origin;[108] the Karaites

102 Simon Szyszman, ''Die Karäer in Ost-Mitteleuropa,'' *Zeitschrift für Ostforschung*, VI, 1 (Marburg 1957), pp. 24–54.

103 Omeljan Pritsak, ''Das Karaïmische,'' *Philologiae Turcicae fundamenta*, I (Wiesbaden 1959), pp. 318–340. A complete bibliography of Kowalski's many works on Karaites is found in Włodzimierz Zajączkowski, ''Bibliografia Tadeusza Kowalskiego,'' *Rocznik Orientalistyczny*, XVII (Cracow 1953), pp. xvii–xxxvi. Zajączkowski's works on the Karaite language are listed in the bibliography to his book; see n. 101 above. For a general bibliography on Karaite language, see W. Zajączkowski, ''Die bibliographischen Materiale zur Erforschung der karaimischen Sprache und Volkskunde,'' *Folia Orientalia*, I, 2 (Cracow 1968), pp. 338–346.

104 For a survey of the earliest scholarship on Karaites in general, see Aleksander Dubiński, ''Początki zainteresowań językiem i literaturą karaimską w nauce europejskiej do końca XIX wieku,'' *Przegląd Orientalistyczny*, XII, 2 (Warsaw 1959), pp. 135–144.

105 J.V. Goehlert, ''Die Karaiten und Mennoniten in Galizien,'' *Sitzungsberichte der philosophisch-historischen Klasse der Kaiserlichen Akademie der Wissenschaften*, XXXVIII (Vienna 1862), pp. 596–603.

106 G. Smólski, ''U Karaimów w Haliczu,'' *Naokoło świata*, (Warsaw 1903); W. Schreiber-Łuczyński, ''Zur Anthropologie der Karaimkinder Galiziens,'' *Archiv für Anthropologie*, IX, 1–2 (Braunschweig 1910); M. Bałaban, ''Do dziejów karaickich (okruchy historyczne),'' *Na Ziemi Naszej*, II, 10 (L'viv 1910), pp. 76–77; Bohdan Janusz, ''Gmina karaicka w Haliczu,'' *Na Ziemi Naszej*, III, 5 (L'viv 1911), pp. 5–7.

107 Reuben Fahn, *Mihaje ha-Karaim: Typy i szkice z życia Karaitów* (Drohobych 1908), translated into German as ''Aus dem Leben der Karaiten,'' *Ost und West*, XII, 1 and 2 (Berlin 1912), pp. 66–70 and 135–144; R. Fahn, *Legenden der Karaiten* (Vienna 1921).

108 Majer Bałaban, ''Karaici w Polsce,'' *Nowe Życie*, I (Warsaw 1924), pp. 1–23, 166–176, 323–340 and II (1924), pp. 14–31, 192–206, reprinted in his *Studia historyczne* (Warsaw: M.J. Fried 1927), pp. 1–92; M. Bałaban, ''Skąd i kiedy przybyli Żydzi do Polski,'' *Miesięcznik Żydowski*, I (Warsaw 1924), pp. 1–12, 112–121; J. Brutzkus, ''Di opshtamung fun di Karayimer in Lite un in Poyln,'' *Yivo Bleter*, XIII (Vilna 1938), pp. 109–123, reprinted in *Wachstein Bukh* (Vilna: YIVO 1939), pp. 109–124; Gedo Hecht, *Karaimi 'Synowie Zakonu'* (Warsaw and L'viv: Warszawski Instytut Wydawniczy 1938).

Ananiasz Zajączkowski, Aleksander Mardkowicz, Szymon Firkowicz, Aleksander Szyszman, and H. Seraja Szapszał countered that the group descended from the Khazars and as such was of Turko-Mongolian origin.[109]

With regard to specific developments among the Karaites in Galicia, the greatest controversy has surrounded their initial settlement. A recent study by Iaroslav Dashkevych, which compares historical data from a Karaite manuscript of 1700 with other sources, has proved that the Karaites first settled in Galicia in 1246, not in the late fourteenth century as local tradition and previous scholarly writings had for so long argued.[110]

109 Ananiasz Zajączkowski, "Na marginesie studium Bałabana: Karaici w Polsce," *Myśl Karaimska*, V, 4–5 (Vilnius 1928), pp. 35–69; Ananjasz Zajączkowski, "Elementy tureckie na ziemiach polskich," *Rocznik Tatarski*, II (Zamość 1934), pp. 199–228; Aleksander Mardkowicz-Kokikow, *Ogniska karaimskie* (Luts'k 1934), 3rd ed. (1936); Szymon Firkowicz, *O Karaimach w Polsce* (Troki 1938); A. Szyszman, "Osadnictwo karaimskie i tatarskie na ziemiach Księstwa Litewskiego," *Myśl Karaimska*, X (Vilnius 1934), pp. 29–36.

Also agreeing with the Karaite view of their origins were the contemporary Ukrainian specialist, Bohdan Janusz, see n. 101 above, and the author of a study published in western Europe: Corrado Gino, "I Caraimi di Polonia e Lituania," *Genus*, II (Rome 1936), pp. 1–56.

110 Jaroslav Stepaniv [Iaroslav Dashkevych], "L'époque de Danylo Romanovyč (milieu du XIIIe siècle) d'après une source Karaïte," *Harvard Ukrainian Studies*, II, 3 (Cambridge, Mass. 1978), pp. 335–373.

Major place names

UKRAINIAN	GERMAN	POLISH	RUSSIAN	YIDDISH
Belz	Belz	Bełz	Belz	Belz
Berezhany	Brzezany	Brzeżany	Berezhany	Berezhan
Boryslav	Boryslau	Borysław	Borislav	Borislav
Brody	Brody	Brody	Brody	Brod
Buchach	Buczacz	Buczacz	Buchach	Buchach
Chortkiv	Czortkow	Czortków	Chortkov	Chortkov
Drohobych	Drohobycz	Drohobycz	Drogobych	Drohobich
Halych	Halicz	Halicz	Galich	Halich
Iaroslav	Jaroslau	Jarosław	Iaroslav	Yaroslav
Horodok	Grodek	Gródek (Jagielloński)	Gorodok	Grodok
Iavoriv	Jaworow	Jaworów	Iavorov	Yavorov
Kalush	Kalusz	Kałusz	Kalush	Kalish
Kaminka Strumylova+	Kamionka	Kamionka Strumiłowa	Kamenka Strumilovaia	Kamenke
Kolomyia	Kolomea	Kołomyja	Kolomyia	Kolomay
L'viv	Lemberg	Lwów	L'vov	Lemberg
Peremyshl'	Przemysl	Przemyśl	Peremyshl'	Pshemishl
Rava Rus'ka	Rawaruska	Rawa Ruska	Rava Russkaia	Rava-Ruska
Sambir	Sambor	Sambor	Sambor	Sambor
Sokal'	Sokal	Sokal	Sokal'	Sokal
Stanyslaviv*	Stanislau	Stanisławów	Stanislavov	Stanislav
Stryi	Stryj	Stryj	Stryi	Stri
Sudova Vyshnia	Sondowa Wischnia	Sądowa Wiśnia (Wisznia)	Sudovaia Vishnia	Sondova Vishna
Terebovlia	Trembowla	Trembowla	Terebovlia	Trembovla
Ternopil'	Tarnopol	Tarnopol	Ternopol'	Tarnopol
Zbarazh	Zbaraz	Zbaraż	Zbarazh	Zbarazh
Zboriv	Zborow	Zborów	Zborov	Zborov
Zhovkva†	Zolkiew	Żółkiew	Zholkva	Zolkva
Zolochiv	Zloczow	Złoczów	Zolochev	Zlochov

+ In 1944, Kam''ianka-Strumylivs'ka (the Soviet Ukrainian version of the historic name) was renamed Kam''ianka-Buz'ka.

* In 1962, Stanislav (the Soviet Ukrainian version of the historic name) was renamed Ivano-Frankivs'k.

† In 1951. Zhovkva was renamed Nesterov.

Index

Numbers immediately following an entry refer to text pages. Boldface numbers within parentheses refer to chapter numbers, and italicized numbers refer to note numbers within the chapter.

Abraham, Władysław, 81, (**4**) *48*

Agricultural Association (Sil's'kyi Hospodar), 193, (**7**) *67*, *68*

Agriculture, *see* Socioeconomic structure

Akademichne Bratstvo, 149

Akinian, Nerses, (**10**) *76*

Aland, Aleksander, (**7**) *9*

Albert, Zygmunt, (**8**) *11*

Allied Powers, 174; Council of Ambassadors of the Associated and, 175

Alphabet, *see* Language/alphabet

Amihai, M., (**10**) *65*

Analecta Ordinis S. Basilii Magni, 22

Ananiichuk, Viktor B., (**8**) *38*

András II, 28, 60

Androkhovych, Ambrosii, 104, (**5**) *34*, *36*, *45*, *66*, *68*

Andrusiak, Mykola, xviii, 143, (**2**) *97*, (**3**) *33*, (**4**) *63*, (**6**) *97*

Annaly Svitovoï Federatsiï Lemkiv, 22

An-Ski, S., *see* Rapoport, Solomon J.

Anti-Fascist Congress of Cultural Activists, 198

Antoniewicz, Boloz., (**10**) *77*

Antoniuk, Ie.M., (**7**) *103*

Antonovych, Volodymyr, 165, (**4**) *57*, (**6**) *213*

Apostolic (Armenian) church, *see* Armenian Apostolic church

Arabic historical sources, 54

Archeographic Commission (St Petersburg), 82

Archeological studies, 26, 46–50, 63–64, (**3**) *7*, *27*

Archive(s), 11–20, 23, 33–34, 82, 105, 169, 234, 245, 250–251, (**1**) *64*, *67*, *98*, (**10**) *13*, *76*; Bernardine (Monastery), 12, 13, 70, (**1**) *61*; Central State Historical (L'viv), 12, 13, 14, 15, 27, 245, (**1**) *69*, (**10**) *76*; of the Galician Viceroys, 13; L'viv City Magistracy, 13, (**1**) *65*; Polish State (Provincial), 12, 13, (**1**) *65*, *66*; Vatican and Propaganda Fidei, 33, (**2**) *47–55*. *See also* Armenian Rite Catholic church; Greek Catholic (Uniate) church; L'viv; Poland;

Przemyśl; Roman Catholic church; Vienna; Warsaw
Argentina, (**6**) *87*
'Arim ve-'Immahot be-Yisrael (Town and Mother Cities in Israel), 242
Aristov, Fedor F., 24, 110, (**1**) *15*, *22*, (**2**) *13*, (**5**) *64*, *69*, (**6**) *136*, *138*, *139*, *217*
Arkhivy Ukraïny, 23
Arłamanowska, Emilia, (**4**) *4*
Arłamowski, Kazimierz, (**4**) *4*, *22*
Armenian Apostolic church, 81, 244, 247
Armenian Rite Catholic church, 244–245, 247–248, (**10**) *82–85*; archives of, 12, 14, (**1**) *67*, *69*
Armenians, xiv, 67, 70, 77–81 passim, 224, 228, 244–248, 249, 252, (**10**) *18*, *75–88*
Armstrong, John, 207, (**8**) *2*
Arsenych, P., (**3**) *49*
Art and architecture, *see* Culture
Askenazy, Szymon, (**5**) *18*
Assembly of Estates (Diet), 95, 99
Association for Jewish Studies Review, xvii
Atamaniuk, V., (**7**) *100*
Audit Union of Ukrainian Cooperatives, 193, (**7**) *67*
Auffenberg-Komarow, N., (**6**) *237*
Austria/Austrian Empire, 6, 112, 252; and Austrian writings, 96, 138, 169, 246; Galician loyalty to, 151; Galician occupation and rule by, xiv, xv, 12, 25, 29–32 passim, 92–109 passim, 116–119, 126, 137, 139, 142, 145, 148, 151, 160, 168, 176, 193, 199, 202, 225–231 passim, 239, 249, (**5**) *4*, *14*, *16*, *26*, (**6**) *107*, *226*; national biographical dictionary, 23–24; national encyclopedia (1835), 28; National Library, xvii, 19, 113; Parliament (Reichstag, Reichsrat), 116, 117, 123, 124, 127–132 passim, (**6**) *27*, *52*, *55–57*, *62*; in World War II, 214, 217. *See also* Austro-Hungarian Empire; Vienna
"Austriacus," (**6**) *227*
Austro-Hungarian Empire (Dual Monarchy), 15, 27–30, 122, 140, 141, 151, 166–173, 237–238, (**2**) *38*, (**6**) *89*, (**10**) *9*; creation (and dissolution) of, 117–118, 167, 174. *See also* Austria/Austrian Empire; Hungarian Kingdom/Hungary
Autonomy, national, *see* Galicia
Avitov, A.Y. (Birnboym), (**10**) *57*

Bab''iak, P.H., (**1**) *86*, (**2**) *2*, (**6**) *103*
Babicki, Jakub, (**10**) *43*
Babii, B.M., (**8**) *16*
Babyshkin, O.K., (**6**) *177*
Bachyns'ka, Ol'ha, (**7**) 68
Bachyns'kyi (Batchinsky), Iuliian, 135, 139, 163, (**6**) *75*, *86*, *202*, (**7**) *34*
Bačka, the, (**1**) *20*
Bączkowski, Włodzimierz, (**7**) *1*
Badecki, Karol, (**1**) *64*, *65*
Bader, Gershom, 234, (**10**) *10*
Baedecker, Karl, (**8**) *8*
Bahalii, Dmytro, 54, (**1**) *2*, (**3**) *18*, *25*
Bahrii, R.S., (**1**) *96*
Baida, Iu., (**7**) *104*
Bailley, Rosa, 182, (**7**) *17*
Balaban, Gedeon, 69
Balaban, Meir, 232, 233, 235, 236, 238, 239, 254, (**10**) *5*, *8*, *9*, *16*, *17*, *19*, *21*, *33*, *35*, *37*, *100*, *106*, *108*, *109*
Baliński, Michał, (**4**) *10*
Balyk, Borys I., (**4**) *62*, *63*
Bandera, Stepan, 211, 212, 214, (**8**) *28*; and Banderites (*Banderivtsi*), 212–213
Bandura, Oleksandra, (**6**) *173*

Bandura, V.F., (**1**) *86*
Barącz, Sadok, 246, (**2**) *118*, *138*, *142*, (**10**) *75*, *78*
Baran, Stepan, 32, 147, 160, 176, (**6**) *71*, *112*, *186*, (**7**) *93*
Baran, Volodymyr D., (**3**) *7*
Baranowski, Mieczysław, 37, 147, (**2**) *77*
Barbara, H., (*7*) *43*
Barbareum, 101, 102, 104, (**5**) *35*
Bardakjian, Kevork B., xviii
Baron, Salo Wittmayer, 233, (**10**) *8*
Barr, James, (**7**) *65*
Bartoszewicz, Kazimierz, 96, (**5**) *4*, (**6**) *20*
Bartoszewicz, Stanisław, (**6**) *89*
Barvins'kyi, Bohdan, 31, (**introd**.) *4*, (**1**) *16*, *90*, (**2**) *41*, (**3**) *41*, (**4**) *20*
Barvins'kyi, Oleksander, 31, 120, 133, 144, (**2**) *39*, *71*, (**6**) *10*, *66*, *98*, *116*
Barvins'kyi, Volodymyr, (**6**) *214*
Barwiński, Eugeniusz, 13, (**1**) *61*, *64*, (**5**) *21*
Basarab, John, (**1**) *8*
Basilian Fathers' Library and Museum, 19
Basilian Order (Rome), 17, 33, 105
Basilian Sisters' Gymnasium, 200–201
Bass, David, 232, (**10**) *7*
Bass, I.I., (**6**) *156*
Batos'kyi, V.Ie., (**2**) *137*
Batowski, Henryk, 118, (**6**) *3*, (**7**) *39*
Battle(s): of Brody, 214, 215, (**8**) *39*; of Dukla Pass, 215, (**8**) *39*; of Galicia, 172, (**6**) *238*. *See also* Wars
Baworowski Library, 17
Bayger, J.A., (**2**) *93*
Belei, Ivan, (**2**) *74*, (**6**) *214*
Beleluia, (**2**) 113
Beloff, Max, (**10**) *100*
Belorussia, 33, 68, 83
Belz, 44, 57, 64, 65, 92, 229, (**2**) *114*, (**3**) *54*, (**4**) *4*, *13*, *22*
Bendasiuk, Semeon Iu., 167, (**2**) *1*, *67*, *71*, (**4**) *79*
Bendow, Josef, *see* Tenenbaum, Josef
Bennett, Patricia, xviii
Ben-Shem, Y., (**10**) *74*
Berenstein, T., (**10**) *13*, *47*
Berezhany (Brzeżany), 40, 44, 80, 146, (**2**) *87*, *99*, *115*, (**4**) *38*, (**6**) *24*
Bereziv, *see* Brzozów
Berezov, P., (**4**) *79*
Berger, John, (**7**) *66*
Berlin, 191, 212
Bernardine (Monastery) Archive, *see* Archive(s)
Bersohn, Mathias, (**10**) *13*
Berżyński, Maks, (**1**) *34*, (**2**) *3*
Beskid, Anthony, (**7**) *30*
Beskid, Iuliian, *see* Tarnovych, Iuliian
Bezruchko, Marko, (**7**) *18*
Bibliographies, 3, 5–11, 36, 53, 75, 87, 107, 203, 231–231, 242, 250, 253
Biblioteka Narodowa (Warsaw), 19, (**1**) *99*
Bickel, Shmuel, (**10**) *59*
Bidermann, Hermann, 28, (**2**) *28*
Bielecka, Janina, (**5**) *26*
Bieliaiev, Volodymyr P., (**7**) *106*, (**8**) *29*
Bieliakevych, I.I., (**6**) *230*
Bielousov, Serhii M., 32, (**2**) *45*
Bienaimé, Georges, (**6**) *72*
Bieńkowski, Ludomir, 82, (**4**) *55*
Bieńkowski, Wiesław, (**1**) *47*, (**2**) *10*
Biernacka, Maria, 220, (**4**) *19*, (**9**) *10*
Bigo, J., (**2**) *18*
Bihl, Wolfdieter, 118, 169, (**6**) *3*, *226*, *234*, *236*
Bil'chenko, A.I., (**2**) *136*
Bilen'kyi, Iaroslav, 147, (**6**) *113*
Bilets'kyi, Leonid, (**6**) *160*

Bilets'kyi, O.I., (**5**) *52*, (**6**) *156*
Bilets'kyi, Platon, 89, (**4**) *85*
Bilets'kyi, S.T., (**4**) *23*, *34*, (**10**) *83*
Biliński, Leon, 120, (**6**) *11*
Bilinsky, Yaroslav, 219, (**6**) *197*, (**9**) *1*
Bilins'kyi, Mykola, (1) *37*
Bilins'kyi, Petro, (**2**) *139*
Biographies and biographical data, 23–25, 81, 84, 108–110 passim, 127, 129, 132, 148–160 passim, 166, 203, 233, 246
Birnbaum, Nathan, 230
Birnboym (A.Y. Avitov), (**10**) *57*
Bischoff, Ferdinand, 246, (**10**) *79*
Bittner, Ludwig, 15, (**1**) *71*
Biuletyn Polsko-Ukraiński, (**7**) *50*
Black Sea, 52
Bloch, Philipp, (**10**) *13*
Bloc of National Unity (Obóz Zjednoczenia Narodowego), 190
Blokh, Mykhailo, (**2**) *100*
Blum, Ignacy, (**9**) *11*
Blumental, N., (**10**) *51*
Bobińska, Celina, (**6**) *120*
Bobrinskii, Georgii, 167
Bobrinskii, Vladimir, (**6**) *220*
Bobrzyński, Michał, 120, (**2**) *32*, (**6**) *11*, *48*
Bocheński, Aleksander, (**7**) *1*
Bodians'kyi, Osyp, 115, 163, (**3**) *19*, (**5**) *63*
Bogatyrev, Petr, (**6**) *189*
Bohachevsky-Chomiak, Marta, 125, (**6**) *32*, *168*
Bohaichuk, V.I., (**6**) *91*
Bohats'kyi, Pavlo, (**1**) *48*
Bohemia, 139
Bohodyst, I. P., (**7**) *43*, *71*, (**9**) *19*
Bohorodchany, (**6**) *10*, (**10**) *96*
Boikian region and people, xvi, 39, (**2**) *96*
Boiko, A.H., (**7**) *71*
Boiko, Ivan Z., (**6**) *145*, *154*
Bolekhiv, 243, (**10**) *50*
Bolesław V (the Pious), 227
Bolsheviks, 175, 184, 186, 188, 196; and Bolshevik Red Army, 183 (*see also* Red Army). *See also* Communist party; Revolutions/uprisings
Bonch-Bruevich, Mikhail D., (**6**) *237*
Bordun, Melaniïa, (**4**) *59*, (**5**) *41*
Borets'kyi, Iov, 69
Borkovs'kyi, Oleksander, 164, (**6**) *207*
Borkowski, Jan, (**9**) *11*
Bornstein, I., (**10**) *43*
Borodiievych, Ievhen, (**7**) *22*
Borshchiv, 243, (**2**) *100*, (**10**) *51*
Boruszenko, O., (**6**) *87*
Borys, Włodzimierz, (**5**) *17*, *23*, (**6**) *44*
Boryslav, 44, 249, (**2**) *116*, (**10**) *31*
Bostel, Ferdynand, (**2**) *128*, *137*
Bouratchinski, Joseph, *see* Burachyns'kyi, Osyp
Boyars, 52, 53, 60, 65, 67, 72. *See also* Socioeconomic structure
Bożemski, A., (**2**) *88*
Brahinets', Andrii, (**6**) *126*
Bratkowski, J., (**7**) *76*
Braude (Brode), Ze'ev, (**10**) *38*
Brawer, A., 96, (**5**) *7*
Brazil, (**6**) *87*
Brechak, Ihor, (**8**) *37*
Breiter, Ernest T., 73, (**4**) *9*
Brest, 57
Brest, Union of, 69, 70, 76, 82–83, (**4**) *56*. *See also* Roman Catholic church
Brest-Litovs'k, Treaty of, 169
Brigand movement, 70, 90–91, 100, (**4**) *95*. *See also* Revolutions/uprisings
Britain, *see* England
Brock, Peter, 109, (**5**) *60*
Brode (Braude), Ze'ev, (**10**) *38*

Brody, 80, 101, 228–237 passim, 243, 248, (**2**) *113*, (**4**) *39*, (**6**) *24*, (**10**) *18*, *25*, *29*, *52*, *88*; Battle of, 214, 215, (**8**) *39*
Bronstein, H., (**10**) *67*
Bross, Jacob, (**10**) *40*
Brotherhood movement, 2, 71, 78, 85–86. *See also* Stauropegial Brotherhood (later Institute)
Bruchnalski, W., (**2**) *68*
Brusilov, Aleksei A., 168, 172, 173, (**6**) *237*, *238*
Bruskin, S., (**1**) *51*
Brutzkus, J., 254, (**10**) *108*
Bryk, Ivan, 112, 128, 144, (**5**) *76*, (**6**) *26*, *45*, *84*, *99*, *101*
Brzeżany, *see* Berezhany
Brzozów (Bereziv), 44, (**2**) *117*
Buchach (Buczacz), 40, 44, 229, 243, (**2**) *99*, *118*, (**10**) *53*
Buchyns'kyi, Meliton, 163, (**6**) *205*
Buczacz, *see* Buchach
Buda[pest], 15, 107
Budurowycz, Bohdan, xviii, 190, (**7**) *52*
Budzynovs'kyi, Viacheslav, (**3**) *24*, (**5**) *22*
Buh River and region, 48, 52, 57, 58
Bujak, Franciszek, 26, 136, (**2**) *22*, (**6**) *77*
Bukovina, xvi, 29, 31, 92, 125, 168, 218, 250, (**2**) *18*, *20*, *26*, *38*, *40*, (**10**) *28*, *76*, *90*
Burachyns'kyi (Bouratchinski), Osyp, (**7**), *27*
Burchak, L., (**2**) *38*
Buriak, B.S., (**7**) *101*, *104*
Busk, (**2**) *113*
Buszko, Józef, 135, 136, (**1**) *1*, (**6**) *72*, *78*
Butych, I.L., (**2**) *25*
Buxbaum, M., (**3**) *31*
Buxton, David, (**4**) *84*
Buzek, Józef, 122, 147, 238, (**6**) *18*, *112* (**10**) *32*
Byzantium, 50, 52, 54, 62. *See also* Constantinople

Canada, 19, 109, 138, (**6**) *87*
Caro, Jecheskiel, (**10**) *17*
Caro, Leopold, 138, (**6**) *83*, *85*
Carpathian Mountains, 48, 52, 70; as boundary, xiv, 60, 143, 217; battles in (World Wars I and II), 173, 215, 217, (**6**) *240*, *241*, *243*, (**8**) *38*, *39*; and Carpathian region, 39, 40, 74, 75, 89, 91, 202, 207, 250
"Carpatho-Russians," 115, 184, 185
Carpatho-Ukraine, *see* Subcarpathia/ Subcarpathian Rus'; Transcarpathia
Casimir III (the Great), 65, 72, 224, (**4**) *7*, *8*
Catholic National party, *see* Ukrainian political parties
Caucasus Mountains and region, 48, 49, 149
Celewicz, *see* Tselevych, Iuliian
Censorship, *see* Press, the
Census(es), 121, 122, 143, 180, 225, 241, (**2**) *18*. *See also* Population; Statistical surveys
Central Library of the Basilian Order, 17
Central Military Committee (L'viv), 174
Central Ruthenian Council, *see* Supreme Ruthenian Council (Holovna Rus'ka Rada)
Central State Historical Archive (L'viv), *see* Archive(s)
Central Union (Tsentrosoiuz), 193, (**7**) *68*
Chachkovs'kyi, Lev, (**3**) *48*, *54*
Chaikovs'kyi, Mykola, I., (**6**) *120*, (**1**) *44*
Chaloupecký, Václav, 50, (**3**) *13*
Chanderys, Szymon, (**2**) *18*
Charewiczowa, Łucja, 42, 78, (**1**) *42*, *80*, (**2**) *143*, (**4**) *31*, *37*
Charnets'kyi, S., (**6**) *128*

Chasanovitch, Leon, (**10**) *27*
Chelak, P. P., (**7**) *45*, *71*
Chełm, 65, 67, 68, 92, 189, (**4**) *4*, *61*, (**10**) *91*
Cheremosh River, xiv
Cheremshyna, Marko, 158, (**6**) *178*, (**7**) *99*
Cherepnin, L.V., (**3**) *33*
Cherikover, I., 233, (**10**) *9*
Chernets'kyi, Antin, 190, (**7**) *51*
Cherniavskii, Fedor F., (**9**) *21*
Chernov, O.O., (**2**) *101*
Chernykhiv, 44, (**2**) *119*
Chernysh, O.P., (**3**) *7*
Cherven/Czerwién region, 50, 56–58, (**3**) *7*, *27*
Chłędowski, Kazimierz, 120, (**6**) *11*
Chmelar, Johann, (**6**) *85*
Chmielewski, Samuel, 241, (**10**) *44*
Chodynicki, Henryk, (**4**) *14*
Chodynicki, Ignacy, 41–42, (**2**) *103*
Chodynicki, Kazimierz, (**4**) *57*
Chojnowski, Andrzej, 190, (**7**) *53*
Chołodecki, Józef Białynia, 170, (**5**) *17*, (**6**) *229*
Cholovskii, A., (**6**) *228*
Chomel, A., (**10**) *68*
Chomyszyn, Gregory, *see* Khomyshyn, Hryhorii
Chortkiv (Czortków), 41, 44, 183, (**2**) *100*, *120*, (**7**) *83*
Chotkowski, Władysław, 105, (**5**) *41*, *42*
Chrienow, I.A., (**7**) *10*
Christianity: conversion to (by Jews), 228; and Christian unity, *see* Roman Catholic church; introduction of, 48, 50. *See also* Greek Catholic church, Orthodox church, Roman Catholic church, Religion(s)
Chubatyi, Mykola, 32, 61, (**3**) *43*
Chuhaiov, Volodymyr, P., (**7**) *75*
Chuprynka, Taras (Roman Shukhevych), 211, 212, 217, 219, (**9**) *5*
Church history, 9, 22, 28, 33–34, 61–62, 68–70, 71, 81–84, 105, 159–160, 201, 222–223, 247–248. *See also* Religion(s).
Church Slavonic, *see* Language/alphabet
Churkina, I.V., (**6**) *215*
Chwalewik, Edward, 13, (**1**) *64*
Cięglewicz, Kaspar, (**6**) *29*
Cieślak, Tadeusz, (**8**) *29*
Ciuciura, *see* Tsiutsiura, Teodor Bohdan
Class conflict, *see* Socioeconomic structure
Codó, Enrique Martínez, (**8**) *36*
Colonization, *see* Emigration/immigration
Comintern, 196, 197
Commission for the Study of Ancient Documents (Kiev), 82, 90, (**4**) *66*, *89*
Communist party, 8, 11, 24, 178, 188, 194, 199, 202–203, 207, 208, (**7**) *49*, *75*, (**8**) *17*, *39*, (**9**) *21*; "achievements" of, 210, 221–222; and anti-Communism, 220; of Eastern Galicia (KPSH), 196, (**7**) *72*; in Poland and Czechoslovakia, 198, 214, 217, (**7**) *72*; of Western Ukraine (KPZU), 176, 196–198, (**1**) *56*, (**7**) *74–80*. *See also* Bolsheviks; Ukrainian political parties
Congress of Rusyn Scholars (Sobor Rus'kykh Uchenykh), 123
Constantinople, 59, 69, 84. *See also* Byzantium
Cooperative movements, collectivization, *see* Socioeconomic structure
Cossacks, xiii, 27, 55, 90; Zaporozhian (and 1648 revolution), 69, 70, 78, 90
Council of Lands, 228
Court proceedings, *see* Judicial system

Cracow, xvi, 15, 76, 92, 94, 133, 176, 207, (**2**) *18*; Free City of, xiv
Crimea, the, 244, 252
Croats, *see* White Croats
Cross, Ruth C., xviii
Culture: art and architecture, 62, 88–89, 245, 247, (**4**) *84*, *86*, *87*; "backwardness" of Galician, (**6**) *195*; and cultural history, 35–38, 62–64, 67–70, 81, 85–89, 95, 101–112, 142–158, 199–203, 226; and cultural revival/development, xiii, 68, 69, 78, 85, 88–89, 95, 102, 116–118, 123, 128–129, 142–154, 159, 162, 253, (vs decline) 53, 199, 225; folklore, 127, (**1**) *20*; and Galicia as cultural link, 55; literature and literary production, 102, 106–111, 149–151, 162, 178, 202, 207–208, 225–226, (**7**) *101*, (**8**) *21*; minority, 229–230, 238–241, 244–245, 247–248, (**10**) *76*, *81*, *87*; Polish, *see* Poland; restrictions on, 142, 175, 176, 178; "Russian," (**6**) *182*; Soviet model and studies of, 218, 222; theater, 106, 116, 150, 207, 226, (**10**) *1*. *See also* Education; Language/alphabet; Press, the; Religion(s)
Curia system, 130. *See also* Elections
Cyrillic, *see* Language/alphabet
Czaczkes, I. (I. Kirton), (**10**), *38*
Czajkowski, Bohdan, (**9**) *8*
Czapla, Jan, (**9**) *11*
Czartoryski, Adam, 127
Czech National Museum, (**1**) *48*
Czechoslovakia: Communist party in, 217; and Czech language, 10, 24, 129; and Czech-Ukrainian/Galician relations, 10, 112–113, 124, 128, 161, (**5**) *77*, (**6**) *190*, (**7**) *30*; emigration to, 202; influence of, 50; as new state, 185; researchers and historians of, 49, 74, 220, (**8**) *39*. *See also* Prešov Region; Rusyn(s), in Subcarpathian Rus'; Subcarpathia
Czechoslovak Legion, 184
Czekanowski, Jan, (**2**) *23*, (**10**) *100*
Czerkawski, Euzebiusz, 149, (**6**) *51*, *119*
Czernecki, Józef, (**2**) *115*
Czerny, Zygmunt, (**2**) *23*, (**3**) *1*
Czerwenzel, Heinrich (Siegfried), (**10**) *96*
Czerwień, *see* Cherven/Czerwień region
Czerwiński, Jan L., (**6**) *64*
Czinár, Mór, (**3**) *38*
Czołowski, Aleksander, 12, 63, 78, 123, (**1**) *60*, (**2**) *92*, *126*, (**3**) *1*, *47*, *50*, (**4**) *29*, *31*, *82*
Czortków, *see* Chortkiv
Czyzewski, Julian, (**2**) *23*

Dąbczański, Antoni, 28, (**2**) *31*, (**6**) *29*
Dąbkowski, Przemysław, 74, (**1**) *61*, *65*, (**4**) *13*, *16*, *20*, *47*
Dąbrowski, R., (**2**) *91*
Dachkevytch, *see* Dashkevych, Iaroslav
Dairy Union (Maslo-soiuz), 193, (**7**) *67*, *68*
Daníłak, Michal, 125, (**6**) *31*, *46*
Danilenko, *see* Danylenko, Serhii T.
Danilov, V., (**5**) *88*
Danube Basin, xiv, 215
Danylenko, Serhii T., 221, (**2**) *59*, (**4**) *58*, (**6**) *187*, (**9**) *24*
Danylo, 52, 58, 61, 62, 252, (**3**) *32*, (**10**) *110*
Dashian, H., (**10**) *76*
Dashkevych, Iaroslav R. (Iaroslav Stepaniv; S. Piskovyi), 3, 8, 184, 198, 245, 247, 255, (**1**) *7*, *38*, *86*, (**2**) *6*, *20*, (**7**) *25*, *80*, (**10**) *75*, *76*, *80*, *110*
Dashkevych, Mykola, 58, 62, (**3**) *32*, *44*

Dashkevych, Roman, (**7**) *22*
Daszyński, I. (I. Żegota), (**6**) *64*
Davies, Rhys J., (**7**) *65*
Davydenko, V., (**9**) *4*
Davydova, H.S., (**9**) *20*
Ded'ko, Dmytro, 72
Dei, Oleksa I., 144, (**6**) *103*, *153*
Deliatyn, 229
Demetrykiewicz, Vladimir, (**3**) *1*
Demkovych-Dobrians'kyi, Mykhailo, 119, (**6**) *8*
Denikin, Anton, 175, 183
Denysiuk, I.O., (**6**) *166*
Deportation, *see* Emigration/immigration
Depta, Pawel, xviii
Deruga, Aleksy, (**7**) *17*
Deutsch, Gotthard, 233, (**10**) *9*
de Vitte, E.I., (**2**) *38*
Diakun, Nadia Odette, xviii
Dictionaries, *see* Encyclopedias and dictionaries
Didyts'kyi, Bohdan A., 35, 120, 153, (**2**) *67*, (**5**) *71*, (**6**) *10*, *51*, *72*, *95*, *114*, *135*, *142*, 215
Distrikt Galizien Generalgouvernement, xvi, 207, 208–209, (**8**) *8*, *13*
Dmitrieva, Rufina P., 53, (**3**) *16*
Dmowski, Roman, 170
Dmytriv, Ia., (**6**) *99*
Dmytruk, Klym Ie., (**8**) *7*, *29*, (**9**) *24*
Dmytryshyn, Basil, (**8**) *34*
Dnewnyk ruski, 123
Dnieper Ukraine, xvi, 31, 35, 117, 142, 143, 145, 150, 155, (**6**) *227*; Cossack state established in, xiii; emigration to and from, 68, 192, 202; independence sought, 168; leaders from, 192, (**6**) *148*; relations with/influence of, 162, 163, 164–165, 186, (**6**) *195*; Ukrainian National Republic in, 175, 184, 186
Dniester River and region, xiv, 48, 49, 52, 70
Dnistrians'kyi, Stanislav, 122, (**6**) *17*, *115*
Dobosh, Stepan, (**6**) *217*
Doboszyński, Józef, 120, (**6**) *11*
Dobretsova, Violla V., (**7**) *95*
Dobrians'kyi, Adol'f I., 57, 166, (**3**) *28*, (**6**) *217*
Dobrians'kyi, Antin, 34, 82, 152, (**2**) *60*, (**6**) *135*
Dobromyl', 243, (**4**) *62*, (**10**) *54*
Dobrostany, (**2**) *113*
Dobrovský, Josef, 112
Dobrychev, Vladimir, (**2**) *59*, (**4**) *58*
Dolyna, (**10**) 96
Domashevs'kyi, Mykola, (**2**) *95*
Dombrovs'kyi, Oleksander, (**6**) *117*, (**7**) *86*
Dontsov, Dmytro, 178, 192, (**7**) *62*
Dörflerówna, Anna, (**4**) *46*
Dornfeld, (**10**) *96*
Doroshenko, Dmytro, (**1**) *1*, (**6**) *227*
Doroshenko, I.I., (**6**) *103*
Doroshenko, Volodymyr, 36, 37, (**1**) *91*, (**2**) *2*, *72*, *74*, (**4**) *79*, (**6**) *145*, *186*
Dovbush, Oleksa, 91
Dovhal', I.V., (**6**) *92*
Dovhaliuk, P.M., (**7**) *102*
Dragan, Mykhailo, (**4**) *84*
Drahomanov, Mykhailo P. (T. T-ov), 120, 143, 161, 162–164, (**2**) *71*, (**6**) *12*, *47*, *96*, *166–168*, *197–209*
Drahomanova-Kosach, O.P., (**2**) *71*
Drakokhrust, E., (**4**) *95*
Droba, Ludwik, 61, (**3**) *40*
Drohobych, 41, 44, 80, 140, 218, 229, 234, 235, 243, 249, (**2**) *100*, *121*, (**4**) *40*, (**10**) *18*, *55*; ''armed revolt'' in (1919), 188, (**7**) *43*
Druck, Shmuel, (**10**) *58*

Druh, 144
Druzhnyi Lykhviar, 149
Dual Monarchy, *see* Austro-Hungarian Empire
Dubanowicz, E., (**6**) *64*, (**10**) *24*
Dubilevs'kyi, E.A., (**1**) *68*
Dubiński, Aleksander, (**10**) *104*
Dubnow, Simon M., 233, 238, (**10**) *8*, *33*
Dubrivnyi, Pavlo, (**7**) *68*
Dubyna, Mykola, (**6**) *124*, (**7**) *101*
Dudik, B., 12, (**1**) *59*
Dudykevych, Bohdan K., 178, 195, (**7**) *2*, *79*, (**8**) *7*
Dudykevych, Volodymyr, 167
Duker, Abraham G., 233, (**10**) *9*
Dukla Pass, Battle of, 215, (**8**) *39*
Dulczewski, Zygmunt, 147, (**6**) *114*
Dumin, Osyp (Antin Krezyb), 173, (**6**) *243*, (**7**) *15*, *18*, *56*
Dunajec River, 57, 168
Dushnyk, Walter, (**6**) *87*, (**9**) *8*
Dvornik, Francis, 49, (**3**) *12*
Dzieduszycki, Maurycy D., (**4**) *15*, *48*, (**10**) *82*
Dzikowska, Irena Homola, (**6**) *11*, *54*, (**10**) *1*
Dz'oban, O.O., (**1**) *86*
Dzvin, 144

East(ern) Galicia (*Ost-Galizien/Skhidna Halychna/Galicja Wschodnia*), xv–xvi, 100, (**7**) *27*, *35*, *66*; cultural views regarding, 29–31, 32, 114, 136, 141, 143, (**2**) *38*; guides to and histories of, 38, 41–43, 137, 140, (**2**) *22*; incorporated into Poland (1923), 175; minorities in, 224, 226, 231; Russian policy toward, 165, 188–189, 207, 217–218; schools in, 146. *See also* Galicia
Eastern Little Poland (*Małopolska Wschodnia*), xvi, 176
Eck, Nathan, 242, (**10**) *44*
Economic conditions and economic history, *see* Socioeconomic structure
Education, 37–38, 85, 101, 117, 142, 145–149, (**6**) *114*, *116*, (**7**) *81*; church and, 38, 68, 95, 101–102, 104, 146, 148, 200, 249, (**2**) *80*; and *gymnasia*, 146–148, 167, 199, 200–201, 230, (**2**) *81*, (**6**) *109*, *117*; Jewish, 230, 231, (**10**) *36*; and literacy, 37, 116; restrictions on, 167, 175, 176, 199, 207; Soviet model and studies of, 2, 218, 221. *See also* Language/alphabet; Student societies and activities; Yearbooks
Efremov, Sergei, *see* Iefremov, Serhii
Ehrlich, Ludwik, (**4**) *15*, *24*
Elections, 116, 125, 189, (**6**) *72*; boycotts of, 175, 176; and electoral reform, 134, 135; Soviet-style (1939), 207; and universal male suffrage, 130, 135, (**6**) *52*
Elkin, Anatolii S., (**7**) *102*, *106*
Emigration/immigration, 67, 69, 136, 171, 191, 192, 199, 237–238, (**6**) *85*, (**7**) *96*; and colonization/settlement, 68, 70, 75, 97, 225, 249–250, 251; deportation and, 168, 175, 205, 218, 219, 225, 250, 251–252; and emigré writings, 40, 43, (**8**) *11*, *39*; to and from Russia, 86, 109, 151, 202, 230–231, 237; to U.S. and Canada, 137, 138–139, 229, 237, (**6**) *73*, *87*, (and return) 165
Encyclopedias and dictionaries, 23–26, 28, 29, 31, 41, 227, 233, (**1**) *99*, (**2**) *9*, *22*, *42*; *Encyclopedia Judaica*, xvii; encyclopedic surveys, 32, 35, 38, 39–

40, 44, 48, 73, 118, 122–123, (**10**) *9*; of the Jewish Diaspora (*Enşiqlopedyah shel galuyyot*), 242. *See also* Language/alphabet
Engel, Johann Christian von, 27–28, 106, (**2**) *27*
England, 27, 140, 187, 193
Enlightenment, the, 27
Entente, the, 175, 176, 184, 186, 187
Episcopal General Theological Seminary Library (New York City), 19
Erben, Karel Jaromír, 161, (**6**) *189*
Erik, Max (Zalman Merkin), (**10**) *41*
Erter, Isaac, 230
Eshel, Y., (**10**) *50*
Estreicher, Karol, 6, (**1**) *31*
Estreicher, Karol (grandson of above), (**1**) *31*
Estreicher, Stanisław, (**1**) *31*
Ethnographic boundary (Polish-Ukrainian), 54, 57, 180, 227, (**10**) *3*
Ethnographic research, 39, 150–151, (**2**) *95–97*
Everett, Leila P., (**10**) *24*
Evlogii (Vasilii Georgievskii), (**6**) *231*
Evseev, Ivan F., (**9**) *8*

Fahn, Reuben, 254, (**10**) *28*, *107*
Faliński, Bronisław, (**2**) *85*, *129*
Falkowski, Jan, (**2**) *95*, *97*
Fascism, 190, 195, 208, 213, 215, 218, 222
Fastnacht, Adam, (**1**) *98*, (**4**) *43*, *47*
Fedoriv, Iurii, (**9**) *25*
Fedorov, L., (**1**) *51*
Fedorov/Fedorovych, Ivan, 86–87, (**4**), *73*, *74*, *75*
Fedorovych, Ivan, (**6**) *23*
Fedorovych, K., (**7**) *83*
Fejér, György, 60, (**3**) *38*
Fekula Collection (Episcopal General Theological Seminary Library, New York City), 19
Feldman, Wilhelm, 236, 240, (**6**) *54*, (**10**) *24*, *38*
Feliński, M., (**7**) *4*, *49*, *66*, *78*
Feudalism, *see* Socioeconomic structure
Fiala, J., (**9**) *12*
Filevych, Ivan P., 58, 72, 103, (**3**) *29*, (**4**) *6*, (**5**) *30*, (**6**) *47*
Finkel, Ludwik, 9, 38, (**1**) *45*, *79*, (**2**) *82*, (**5**) *8*
Firkowicz, Szymon, 255, (**10**) *109*
Fischer, Adam, 36, (**2**) *23*, *70*
Fishman, Y.L. (Maimon), (**10**) *63*
Fleischer, Sigfried, (**10**) *31*
Florinskii, Timofei, (**2**) *38*
Folklore, *see* Culture
Foreign relations, *see* Galicia, relations with
Forst-Battaglia, Jakub, (**6**) *48*
Fraenkel, Josef, (**10**) *30*
France, 117, 187
François, V., (**6**) *241*
Frankist movement, 228, 238, (**10**) *33*
Franko, Andrii, (**5**) *70*
Franko, Ivan, 3, 22, 35, 100, 102, 103, 108, 109, 112, 141, 149, 153–154, 161, 163, (**1**) *27*, *29*, (**2**) *63*, (**5**) *22*, *27*, *28*, *31*, *59*, *61*, *74*, *87*, (**6**), *23*, *38*, *50*, *51*, *95*, *120*, *122*, *128*, *131*, *139*, *143–156*, *160*, *164*, *166*, *169*, *190*, *199*, *211*, *214*
Frantsev, Vladimir A., (**5**) *78*
Franz II, 249
Franz Joseph, 128
Fredo, Aleksander, 226
Freidzon, V.I., (**1**) *6*
Freiherr von Pitreich, Max, (**6**) *239*
Freistadt, (**6**) *234*

Freund, Fritz, 132, (**6**) *62*
Friedlander, (**10**) *62*
Friedländer, M., (**10**) *25*
Friedman, Philip, 232, 236, 237, 242, (**10**) *5*, *23*, *29*, *36*, *46*, *47*, *48*, *100*
Friedman, T., (**10**) *59*, *69*, *70*
Fylypchak, Ivan, (**2**) *79*, *131*, *140*, (**6**) *117*

Gajerski, Stanisław Franciszek, (**1**) *73*
Galan, Iaroslav, 203, (**7**) *101*, 106
Galan, Volodymyr, (**7**) *22*
Galicia (*Halychyna*/*Galitsiia*; *Galizien*), xiii–xvii
– administration of, *see* Austria/Austrian Empire, Poland, Soviet Union
– autonomy of, 22, 29, 32, 98, 117, 128, 131, 168, 176, 179, 182, 186
– Battle of (World War I), 172
– concept of, xiv–xv
– economic growth of, 52 (*see also* Socioeconomic structure)
– minorities in, 224–255
– nomenclature referring to, xv–xvi
– relations with: Austria, 92–94, 97–98 (*see also* Austria/Austrian Empire, Galician occupation and rule by); Czechoslovakia (*see* Czechoslovakia, and Czech-Ukrainian/Galicia relations); Hungary, 60–61 (*see also* Hungarian Kingdom/Hungary, claims of/to Galicia); Poland, 29, 53, 56–59, 119, 127, 133–135, 142, 164, 174, 183, 186, 189–193, 217, 219, 220; Russia (*see* Russian Empire, Galician relations with)
– Russian occupation of, *see* Russian Empire
– Soviet interest in (interwar), 188–189
– in Soviet Ukraine, 207, 208, 210, 217–218
– western policy toward, 187–188.
– *See also* East(ern) Galicia; Red Rus'; Ukrainians
Galicia and Lodomeria, Kingdom of, 92, 97, (**2**) *27*, *28*. *See also* Galician-Volhynian principality
Galician Central Archive of Early Castle and Land Court Records, 12
Galician Diet (*Landtag*/*Sejm*), 117, 120, 121, 130, 131, 132, 135, 147, (**6**) *48*, *54*, *58–60*, *72*, *85*, *88*
Galician district of the General-gouvernement, *see Distrikt Galizien Generalgouvernement*
Galician Division (of German army), 207, (**8**) *34*
Galician Rus' (*Halyts'ka Rus'*/*Galitskaia Rus'*), xv
Galician Rus' Matytsia (Halytsko-russka Matytsia), 21, 36, 123, 126, 143, (**2**) *71*, (**6**) *184*
Galician-Russian Benevolent Society, 167, (**6**) *221*
Galician Socialist Soviet Republic, 175, 184, 188, (**7**) *44*
Galician-Volhynian principality, 1, 28, 29, 32, 54–56, 59–60, 62–64, 65, 72, 92, 210, 249, (**3**) *24*; Chronicle, 53–54, 61, (**3**) *14–17*, *39*; importance of, 31, 52–53, 106; "restoration" of, 172
Galos, Adam, (**6**) *11*
Garkavenko, S.D., (**6**) *89*
Gąsiorowska-Grabowska, Natalia, (**7**) *10*
Gatkiewicz, Feliks, (**2**) *121*
Gawroński, Franciszek Rawita, (**4**) *93*, (**6**) *70*
Gazette de Léopol, 106
Gębarowicz, Mieczysław, (**1**) *75*, (**4**) *81*, *86*

Gelbart, M., (**10**) *54*
Gelber, Nathan Michael, 233, 240, (**10**) *9*, *21*, *39*, *52*, *55*, *63*, *74*
Gelerter, M., (**10**) *69*
Genealogical studies, 75
Generalgouvernement, *see Distrikt Galizien Generalgouvernement*
General Ukrainian Council (Zahal'na Ukraïns'ka Rada), 168, 171
Gensiorskii, A., (**6**) *140*
Georgievskii, Vasilii (Mitropolit Evlogii), (**6**) *231*
Gerhard, Jan, (**9**) *11*
German, Łudomil, (**10**) *90*
Germany, 27, 95, 222, 227, 230; East, 154; Foreign Ministry Archives of, (**7**) *56*; German Empire, 226; and Germanophile Jews, 240, (**10**) *39*; and Germans in Galicia/Poland, xiv, 67, 70, 77, 78, 79, 97, 224, 227, 228, 230, 249–252, (**4**) *35*, (**8**) *1*, (**10**) *90*; and Nazis, 207, 231, 242, 253; -Soviet Union relations, 205, 207, 213, 249; Third Reich, 190; West, 217, 250; in World War I, 168, 172; in World War II, 31, 205, 207–214, 217, 231, 242, 249–250, 253, (**8**) *34*, (**9**) *24*, (**10**) *100*
Gieysztor, Aleksander, (**3**) *27*
Gilewicz, Aleksy, 73, (**4**) *9*, *32*
Gil'tebrandt, Peter, (**4**) *58*
Gino, Corrado, (**10**) *109*
Glassl, Horst, 97, (**5**) *12*
Glinka, Luigi, 159, (**6**) *182*
Glombiński, Stanisław, (**6**) *65*
Gmünd, 168, (**6**) *228*
Goehlert, J.V., 254, (**10**) *105*
Gogol (Hohol'), Nikolai, 150, (**6**) *125*
Golden Horde, *see* Mongols, the
Goldenstein, Leo, (**10**) *25*
Golovatskii, *see* Holovats'kyi, Iakiv F.
Golovin, N.N., (**6**) *237*
Golubev, Sergei (Makarii), (**4**) *52*, *57*, *58*
Gołuchowski, Count Agenor, 128, 129
Góra, Władysław, (**9**) *11*
Górkiewicz, M., (**2**) *69*
Gorlice, battle at, 168, 173, (**6**) *241*
Gorn, *see* Horn, Maurycy
Gorżycki, Kazimierz, 72, (**3**) *31*, (**4**) *7*
Gottfried, K., (**2**) *127*, *133*
Göttingen, 251
Grabar, Olga and Igor, 166
Grabovetskii, *see* Hrabovets'kyi, Volodymyr V.
Grabski, Stanisław, 167, (**7**) *83*
Grabski, Władysław, 199
Grappin, Henri, (**7**) *3*, *28*
Grebing, Helga, 169, (**6**) *226*
Greek Catholic (Uniate) church, 28, 109, 167, 199, 201, 209, (**2**) *17*, (**4**) *56*, (**6**) *23*, (**7**) *94*, *97*, (**9**) *23–25*; archives of, 12, (**1**) *69*; and education, 38, 95, 101, 146, 148, 200, (**2**) *80*; history of, 34, 69, 105, 159–160; and politics, 116, 123, 130; *schematisma* of, 25, (**2**) *19*; Soviet/Marxist view of, 34, 103–104, 169, 194, 201, 220, (**4**) *58*, (**7**) 95, (**9**) *24*, (and destruction of) 168, 171, 218, 221–223, (**6**) *231*, (**9**) *23*, *24*. *See also* Uniate movement
Greek Catholic Theological Academy (L'viv), 200, (**7**) *85*
Grimsted, Patricia Kennedy, xviii, 14, 15, 17, (**1**) *58*, *70*, *73*, *84*, *98*
Gródek, *see* Horodok
Grodziski, Stanisław, 96, (**5**) *7*
Grossman, Iurii M., (**1**) *6*, (**4**) *22*
Grushevskii, Aleksander S., *see* Hrushevs'kyi, Aleksander S.
Grushevskii, M., *see* Hrushevs'kyi, Mykhailo S.

Gruziński, Stanisław, (**10**) *24*
Grzegorczyk, Piotr, (**1**) *34*
Grzegorz (of Sanok), 226
Grzybowski, Konstanty, 123, (**6**) *21*, *54*
Gumetskii, I.I., (**2**) *38*
Gutianskii, S.K., (**10**) *75*
Gymnasia, *see* Education

Habsburg Empire, 27, 60, 97, 101, 116–122; passim, 161, 165, 167, 172, 176, 229, 249; dissolution of, 168, 174, 231. *See also* Austria/Austrian Empire
Haczynski, Leo J., (**introd.**) *1*
Hadaczek, Karol, (**3**) *2*
Hahn, Kazimierz, (**4**) *21*
Hahn, Sigmund, 132, (**6**) *62*
Hájek, Zdeněk, (**5**) *77*
Halaba, Ryszard, (**9**) *11*
Halan, Iaroslav, *see* Galan, Iaroslav
Halecki, Oscar, (**4**) *56*
Halich, Wasyl', (**6**) *87*
Haliczer, Józef, (**10**) *77*
Haller, Józef, 175
Halpern, Israel, (**10**) *8*
Halusczynskyj, Theodosius, (**6**) *186*
Halushchyns'kyi, Mykhailo, (**6**) *243*
Halushko, Ievhen M., 197, (**7**) *75*
Halych, xv, 47, 72, 252, 253, (**introd.**) *3*, (**4**) *83*, (**10**) *106*; as capital, 52, 63, (**3**) *47–49*; as religious center, 53, 62, 67–68, 81, 224, (**3**) *42*; as territorial unit, 65, (**4**) *4*
Halychanyn, 21
Halychyna, *see* Galicia
Halyts'kii ystorycheskii sbornyk, 21
Hamorak, Iu., (**6**) *176*
Handelsman, Marceli, 127, (**6**) *42*
Hanka, Václav, 113
Hantsch, Hugo, 118, (**6**) *1*
Hapshenko, I.I., (**9**) *17*
Haraida, Ivan, 61, (**3**) *40*
Harasevych, Mykhailo, 28, 34, 82, (**2**) *57*
Harasymovych, Ivan, (**7**) *83*
Harvard University Library (Cambridge, Massachusetts), xvii, 19, (**1**) *99*
Hasidic and Haskalah movements, *see* Jews
Hauser, Leopold, (**2**) *110*
Haus- Hof- und Staatsarchiv (Vienna), 15, (**1**) *71*. *See also* Archive(s)
Häusler, Wolfgang, 236, (**10**) *20*
Haynes, Helga, xviii
Havryliuk, Oleksandr, 203, (**7**) *101*, *105*
Hebrew, *see* Language, Hebrew
Hecht, Gedo, 254, (**10**) *108*
Heike, Wolf-Dietrich, (**8**) *34*
Hejnosz, Wojciech, (**4**) *5*, *16*
Hejret, J., (**2**) *73*
Hellman, Manfred, (**3**) *23*
Henisch, Meir, (**10**) *30*
Hennig, Johann, 251, (**10**) *92*
Herasymenko, Mykhailo P., 99, 178, 195, (**5**) *20*, *27*, (**7**) *2*
Herasymovych, Ivan, (**2**) *78*
Herbil's'kyi, Hryhorii Iu., 103–104, (**1**) *13*, (**5**) *17*, *32*
Herlitz, Georg, (**10**) *9*
Herzberg-Fränkl, Leo, (**10**) *9*
Herz Homberg, Naphtali, 230, 239, (**10**) *35*
Himka, John-Paul, xviii, 159, (**6**) *71*, *90*, *181*
Hirniak, Nykyfor, (**6**) *236*, (**7**) *21*
Hirsch, R., (**6**) *43*
History: and historical surveys, 27–33; and historiographical studies, 1–5, 22, 32–33, 42, 75–76, 95–97, 118–128, 131, 245–246, 250–251, 255 (*see also* Soviet Union, historiographical writings of). *See also* Church history; Culture;

Regional history; Socioeconomic structure; Urban history
Hitler, Adolf, 208, 250
Hladylovych, Iurii, (**5**) *23*
Hliadkivs'ka, A.I., (**9**) *20*
Hlyns'kyi, M.P., (**8**) *5*
Hnatiuk, Volodymyr, 4, 103, 157, (**1**) *20*, (**2**) *72*, (**5**) *29*, (**6**) *102*, *172*
Hnatkevych, Bohdan, (**6**) *243*, (**7**) *15*
Hodinka, Antal, (**3**) *39*
Hoffman v. Wellenhof, Viktor, (**10**) *21*
Hohol' (Gogol), Nikolai, 150
Holberg, M.Ia., (**5**) *80*
Holovats'kyi, Iakiv F. (Iakov Golovatskii) (''Ia''; Havryło Rusyn; J.F.H.), 5–6, 26, 28, 47, 55, 95, 96, 103, 107–113 passim, 151, 161, 163, (**1**) *27*, *28*, (**2**) *20*, (**3**) *4*, *22*, (**4**) *4*, *78*, (**5**) *1*, *8*, *31*, *53*, *62–64*, *69*, *77*, *84*, *87*, (**6**) *132*, *133*, *215*
Holovats'kyi, Ivan B., (**3**) *22*, (**6**) *40*
Holubets', Mykola, 89, (**2**) *136*, (**4**) *35*, *62*, *85*, *87*
Holzer, Jerzy, (**7**) *49*
Homberg, Nathali Herz, 230, 239, (**10**) *35*
Homola, Irene, *see* Dzikowska, Irena Homola
Honcharov, V. K., (**3**) *49*
Hoover Institution on War, Revolution, and Peace (Stanford, California), 19, (**1**) *99*
Hopalo, Ivan, (**2**) *122*
Horák, Jiří, (**5**) *77*
Horak, Stephen M., (**2**) 72, (**8**) *10*
Horbach, Oleksa, 32
Horbachevs'kyi, Ivan, 110, (**5**) *66*
Hordyns'kyi, Iaroslav, (**1**) *82*, (**5**) *35*, (**6**) *47*, *117*, *136*, *139*
Horn, Maurycy, 77, 91, 235, (**4**) *25*, *27*, *34*, *45*, *95*, (**10**) *15*, *18*
Hornowa, Elżbieta, 77, 161, (**4**) *27*, (**6**) *192*, (**10**) *15*
Hornykewitsch, M., (**5**) *35*
Hornykiewicz, Theophil, (**6**) *223*, *231*
Horodenka and region, 41, 243, 244, (**2**) *100*, (**10**) *56*
Horodok (Gródek), 44, 68, 173, (**2**) *122*, (**6**) *242*
Horowitz, I., (**10**) *25*
Hoshko, Iurii H., (**2**) *96*, (**4**) *12*, *95*, (**7**) *71*
Hostička, Vladimír, 112, 128, (**5**) *75*, *77*, (**6**) *46*
Hoszowski, Stanisław, 101, (**4**) *37*, (**5**) *26*, (**6**) *22*
Hötzendorf, Conrad von, 167, 172, (**6**) *238*
Hrabovets'kyi (Grabovetskii), Volodymyr V., 91, (**2**) *122*, (**3**) *49*, *51*, (**4**) *25*, *92*, *95*, (**10**) *77*, *88*
Hrabovs'kyi, Pavlo, 165, (**6**) *213*
Hraidans, Iu.M., (**1**) *42*
Hrebeniak, Volodymyr, (**3**) *2*, *5*
Hromada, (**6**) *120*
Hromads'kyi druh, 144
Hrossman, *see* Grossman, Iu.M.
Hrozienčik, Jozef, (**6**) *190*
Hrubý, Václav, (**3**) *12*
Hrushevs'kyi, Mykhailo (M. Grushevskii), xv, 31, 54, 55–56, 59, 72, 76, 86, 136, 154, 164–165, (**introd**.) *2*, (**1**), *2*, (**2**) *40*, (**3**) *10*, *17*, *18*, *24*, *35*, *51*, (**4**) *4*, *6*, *17*, *53*, *71*, *93*, (**6**) *17*, *18*, *72*, *75*, *93*, *116*, *155*, *212*
Hrushevs'kyi, Oleksander (A. Grushevskii), 164, (**2**) *72*, (**6**) *210*
Hryhor'iev, A.M., (**2**) *24*
Hrymaliv, 44, (**2**) *123*
Hrytsai, Ostap, (**6**) *161*
Hrytsak, Pavlo, (**3**) *24*
Huberband, S., (**10**) *14*

Hubko, O., (**4**) *77*
Hugelman, Karl Gottfried, (**6**) *1*
Humeniuk, Ie.M., (**1**) *69*, *86*
Humeniuk, Mykhailo P., 5, 107, (**1**) *27*, (**5**) *53*, (**6**) *133*, *176*, (**7**) *100*, *104*, *106*, *145*, *154*
Hunczak, Taras, (**2**) *99*, (**7**) *10*, *34*, *39*
Hungarian Kingdom/Hungary, 125, 168, 231, (**2**) *38*, (**4**) *12*; claims of, to Galicia, 27–28, 52, 53, 60–61, 65, 72, 73, 92, 98; in Dual Monarchy, 117 (*see also* Austro-Hungarian Empire); Galician frontier with, xiv; *Honvéds* (troops) of, 167; revolution in (1848–49), 126, 128; Soviet, 189; trade with, 59, 77
Hupert, Witold, (**7**) *17*
Hurzhii, I., (**1**) *11*
Husakiv, (**2**) *113*
Husen, Isaac, (**10**) *61*
Hushalevych, Ivan, 152, (**6**) *139*, *215*
Husiatyn, 243, (**10**) *57*
Hustyn Chronicle, (**3**) *39*
Hutsuliak, Mykhailo, 182, (**7**) *16*
Hutsul region and people, xvi, 39, (**2**) *95*, (**6**) *38*, (**10**) *43*; and Hutsul uprising, 126 (*see also* Revolutions/uprisings)
Hvozda, Ivan, (**4**) *84*, (**9**) *8*
Hypatian text, *see* Galician-Volhynian principality, Chronicle

Iadlovs'kyi, S., (**7**) *97*
Iakymovych, Hryhorii, 105, 159, (**6**) *182*
Ianiv, Volodymyr, (**7**) *90*
Iaremchuk, D.A., (**7**) *69*
Iaremchuk, M.P., (**2**) *136*
Iaremenko, Porfyrii K., (**4**) *58*
Iarinovich, Anton, (**2**) *38*
Iaroshenko, A.D., (**6**) *92*, (**7**) *45*
Iaroslav, *see* Jarosław
Iaroslav Osmomysl', 52
Iaroslav the Wise, 50
Iaroslavyn, Sydir, (**7**) *11*
Iashchuk, Pavlo, (**6**) *166*, *168*, *169*
Iasinchuk, Lev, 147, (**2**) *79*, (**7**) *84*
Iaslys'ka (Jaśliska), 44, (**2**) *124*
Iastrebov, N.V., (**6**) *19*
Iatskevych, Ievhenii A., (**2**) *101*, (**6**) *91*, (**10**) *81*, *87*
Iatskiv, Mykhailo, 158, (**6**) *177*, (**7**) *99*
Iatskiv, P.M., (**7**) *69*
Iavoriv (Jaworów), 44, 243, (**2**) *113*, *125*, (**6**) *109*, (**10**) *58*
Iavors'kyi, Iuliian, 5, 7, 164, (**1**) *22*, *32*, (**6**) *209*
Iavors'kyi, M., (**6**) *93*
Iedlins'ka, Uliana Ia., (**1**) *24*
Iefremov, Serhii (Sergei Efremor), 103, 154, (**5**) *31*, (**6**) *47*, *155*, *231*
Iendyk, Rostyslav, (**7**) *62*
Iezupil' (Jezupol), 44, (**2**) *126*
Ihnatiienko, Varfolomii, 8, (**1**) *37*
Ikonnikov, Vladimir S., 54, (**1**) *2*, (**3**) *18*
Iliashevych, Iurii, (**4**) *67*
Il'kevych, Hryhorii, 111, (**5**) *70*
Il'nyts'kyi, Mykola, (**6**) *177*
Il'nyts'kyi, Vasyl' (Vasylii Yl'nytskii), 155, (**3**) *51*, *53*, (**6**) *158*
Ilnytzkyj, Roman, 208, (**8**) *3*
Immigration, *see* Emigration/immigration
Industry, *see* Socioeconomic structure
Inglot, S., (**1**) *75*
Inkin, V.F., (**4**) *22*, *36*, *46*
Institutum Pontificum Orientale (Rome), 19
Iova, P., (**7**) *71*
Irchan, Myroslav, 203, (**7**) *103*
Isaievych, Iaroslav D., 2, 5, 58, 62, 71, 85, 86, 88, (**1**) *5*, *12*, *13*, *26*, *86*, *88*, (**3**) *27*, *29*, *46*, (**4**) *2*, *40*, *65*, *72*, *73*, *75*, *78*, *79*
Isaïv, Petro, 34, (**2**) *60*

Iurii II, 59, 65, (**3**) *33*, (**4**) *8*
Ivanenko, L.A., (**7**) *82*, (**9**) *20*
Ivan Franko L'viv State University Library, 15, 18–19
Ivano-Frankivs'k, 8, 12, 23, 41, 218, 221, (**1**) *57*, (**2**) *101*. *See also* Stanyslaviv
Ivasiuta, M.K., (**1**) *12*, (**8**) *5*, *6*, *19*, (**9**) *19*, (**10**) *75*
Iwanicki, Mieczysław, 200, (**7**) *81*
Iwanie, 228

Jabłonowski, Aleksander, 73, (**4**) *11*
Jandaurek, J., (**2**) *20*
Janeczek, Andrzej, (**4**) *17*
Janicki, Stanisław, (**9**) *11*
Janiw, Wolodymyr, (**9**) *25*
Janta, Aleksander, (**6**) *73*
Janusz, Bohdan, 46, 253, (**2**) *92*, (**3**) *1*, *5*, (**4**) *83*, (**6**) *223*, *229*, (10) *86*, *101*, *106*, *100*
Jarosław, xv, 13–14, 44, 80, 228, 235, (**1**) *66*, (**2**) *113*, *127*, (**4**) *41*, (**10**) *18*
Jaśliska, *see* Iaslys'ka
Jasło, 44, (**2**) *128*
Jaworów, *see* Iavoriv
Jaworski, Franciszek, 78, (**2**) *87*, *108*, (**4**) *29*, *31*, *93*
Jaworski, Władysław Leopold, (**6**) *48*
Jażdżewski, Konrad, (**3**) *27*
Jeluka, I., (**5**) *59*
Jenkins, R.J.H., (**3**) *8*
Jewish Historical Institute in Poland (Żydowski Instytut Historyczny w Polsce), 235
Jews: in Galicia/Poland, xiii, xiv, xv, 67, 70, 79, 81, 118, 140, 198, 224, 225, 227–244, 252, 254; Haskalah and Hasidic movements, 229–230, 238–240, (**10**) *33*, *34*, *38*, *41*; pogroms against, 205, 229, 231, 232–233, 237, 242, 253, (**10**) *47*, *100*; restrictions on, 78, 228–229, 231; and Zionism, 229, 230, 240. *See also* Language, Hebrew and Yiddish
Jezupol, *see* Iezupil'
Jił, *see* Łokietek, Józef
Jireček, Joseph, (**6**) *49*
Joseph II, 94, 97, 101, 105, 236, 249, 251, (**10**) *93*; and Josephine reforms, 99, 228
Juchniewicz, Mieczysław, (**8**) *37*
Judicial system, 74, 79, 81, 94; court proceedings and records, 12, 71–72
Jurkowski, Marian (J. Kozłowski), (**1**) *41*

Kachala, Stefan, 133, (**6**) *66*
Kachkovs'kyi, Mykhailo, 111, 152, (**5**) *71*, (**6**) *134*
Kachkovs'kyi Society, 37, 143, (**2**) *73*
Kachor, Andrii, (**2**) *74*, (**6**) *180*, (**7**) *68*
Kaczkowski, Zygmunt, 226
Kahan, I., (**10**) *53*
Kahanov, Isaak Ia., 87, (**4**) *76*
Kaindl, Raimund Friedrich, 250, (**10**) *90*
Kajetanowicz, D., (**10**) *81*
Kakovs'kyi, K.H., (**6**) *91*
Kalabiński, Stanisław, (**5**) *25*
Kalinka, Walerian, 96, (**5**) *7*
Kallbrunner, Josef, (**10**) *93*
Kálmán, 28, 60
Kal'na, (**2**) *113*
Kalush, (**10**) *96*
Kalynovych, Ivan, (**1**) *40*, *44*
Kalynovych, Volodymyr I., (**6**) *94*, (**7**) *82*
Kamenetsky, Ihor, (**8**) *9*
Kam''ianets'-Podil's'kyi, 175
Kaminka Strumylova (Kamionka Strumiłowa, at present Kam''ianka-Buz'ka), 39, 44, 249, (**2**) *85*, *129*

Kamins'kyi, Andrii, (**6**) *195*, (**7**) *98*
Kampelík, Cyril, (**5**) *77*
Kann, Robert A., xviii, 118, (**6**) *1*
Kapustians'kyi, Mykola, (**8**) *35*
Kaput, Wanda, (**4**) *4*
Karaites, xiv, 224, 252–255, (**10**) *16*, *99–110*. *See also* Jews
Karaj awazy, (**10**) *99*
Karamans'kyi, Petro, 150, 184, (**6**) *127*, (**7**) *26*
Karovets', Makarii, (**6**) *116*
Karpenko, O.Iu., (**7**) *36*, *43*, *72*
Karpenko, Stepan, 165, (**6**) *213*
Karpynets', Ivan, (**5**) *27*, (**6**) *94*
Kasinec, Edward, xviii, (**1**) *26*, *99*, (**4**) *74*
Kasparek, F., (**6**) *107*
Kaspruk, A.A., (**6**) *169*
Kats, R., (**1**) *1*
Katz, S., (**10**) *36*
Kaucký, František, (**9**) *12*
Kawecka-Gryczowa, A., (**4**) *78*
Kaye, Vladimir J., (**6**) *87*
Kazanskii, P.E., (**2**) *38*
Kazarian, M.M., (**10**) *81*
Kedryn-Rudnyts'kyi, Ivan, 32, 190, (**7**) *31*, *51*
Kel'siev, Vasilii, 121, (**6**) *12*
Kermisz, Joseph, xviii
Kętrzynski, Wojciech, (**1**) *74*
Khazars, 255
Kheifits, Iu.A., (**6**) *19*
Khinkulov, Leonid, (**6**) *156*
Khitar, (**2**) *113*
Khlopets'kyi, Ivan, (**4**) *63*
Khmel'nyts'kyi, Bohdan, 70, 71, 78, 90–91
Khmilevs'kyi, Iaroslav, (**3**) *48*
Kholm, *see* Chełm
Khoma, Ivan, (**9**) *25*
Khoma, V.I., (**6**) *103*
Khomyshyn, Hryhorii, 201, (**7**) *5*, *92*
Khonihsman, I.S., (**6**) *89*
Khrapko, Ivan, (**7**) *33*
Khraplyvyi, E., (**7**) *68*
Khrin, Stepan, (**9**) *4*
Khvylia, Andrii, (**7**) *76*
Kieniewicz, Stefan, 118, (**6**) *2*, *39*, *64*, *194*
Kierski, Kazimierz, (**7**) *53*
Kiev, xvi, 15, 50, 52, 55, 58, 68, 154, 167, 175, 199; Kievan Chronicle, 53, 61, (**3**) *39*; metropolitanate of, 62, 68, 69
Kievan Rus', xiii, 29, 30, 32, 46, 49, 50, 52, 55, 57, 114
Kirchner, P., (**6**) *150*
Kirschner, Bruno, (**10**) *9*
Kirton, I. (I. Czaczkes), (**10**) *38*
Kis', Iaroslav P., 78, (**4**) *29*, *36*, (**10**) *86*
Kiszling, Rudolf, (**6**) *219*
Kizlyk, O.D., (**1**) *12*, *24*, *53*
Klauzner, I.L., (**10**) *41*
Klimkova, L.N., (**2**) *71*
Klink, Józef, 182, (**7**) *17*
Klonowic, Sebastian, 226
Klymyshyn, Mykola, (**7**) *58*, (**8**) *27*
Kmit, Iurii, (**5**) *28*, *39*, (**6**) *23*
Kmytsykevych, Mykola, (**5**) *74*
Knoll, Paul W., 73, (**4**) *9*
Knot, Antoni, (**6**) *11*
Knysh, Irene, (**6**) *168*
Knysh, Zynovii, 191, (**2**) *130*, (**7**) *56*, *58*, (**8**) *24*, *25*
Kobryns'ka-Ozarkevych, Nataliia, 156, 164, (**6**) *168*, *206*, *214*
Kobylets'kyi, Iurii, (**6**) *156*
Kobylets'kyi, Ivan, (**5**) *28*
Koliada, H.I., (**4**) *78*
Kolisnyk, V., (**2**) *101*
Kollár, Ján, 113, 114

Kołodziejczyk, Edmund, 10, (**1**) *46*
Kolomyia, 44–45, 146, 207, 229, 243, (**2**) *130*, (**6**) *109*, (**10**) *16*, *31*, *59*
Kołosowicz, I. (Evstakhii Prokopchyts'), (**6**) *28*
Kölsch, Kurt, (**10**) *97*
Kompaniiets', Ivan I., (**6**) *91*, (**7**) *71*
Komsomol, 198, (**7**) *78*
Konashevych family, (**4**) *20*
Konieczny, Zdzisław, (**1**) *42*
Konovalets', Ievhen, 175, 176, 184, 191, 211, (**7**) *20*, *60*, *61*
Konstantyn (of Ostrih), 68
Konys'kyi, Oleksandr, 165, (**6**) *213*
Kopchak, Stepan I., 40, (**2**) *98*
Kopchyntsi, (**2**) 100
Kopitar, Jernej, 113, (**5**) *79*
Kopystians'kyi, Adriian V., 30, (**1**) *15*, (**2**) *37*, *38*, (**4**) *70*
Korchyn, (**2**) *113*, (**4**) *120*
Korczok, Anton, (**5**) *40*
Korduba, Myron, 58, 59, (**3**) *29*, *35*, (**6**) *213*
Kordys, Roman, (**2**) *26*
Korenets', Denys, (**7**) *68*
Korkis, Abraham, (**10**) *31*
Korkotian, K.A., (**10**) *80*
Korngruen, Ph., (**10**) *72*
Korniichuk, L.Ia., (**7**) *71*
Korniienko, N.P., (**6**) *153*
Kornilov, Lavr, 184
Kornylovych, Mykhailo, (**6**) *231*
Korolevs'kyi, Kyrylo, 160, (**6**) *186*, (**7**) *93*
Koroliuk, Vladimir D., 56, 58, (**1**) *49*, (**3**) *10*, *26*, *31*
Korotajowa, K., (**4**) *78*
Kosachevskaia, Evdokiia M., 99, 125, (**5**) *20*, (**6**) *31*
Kosharnyi, I.Ia., (**9**) *17*
Kosiv, 243, (**10**) *60*
Kosovs'kyi, Ia., (**2**) *119*
Kossak, M.N., (**2**) *19*
Kostashchuk, Vasyl', (**6**) *173*
Kostiuk, S.P., (**1**) *86*
Kostkiewicz, Tadeusz, (**4**) *14*
Kostruba, Teofil, (**2**) *120*
Kotel'nykova, V.I., (**1**) *68*
Kotliar, Mykola F., 58, (**3**) *32*, (**4**) *27*, (**10**) *86*
Kotliarevs'kyi, Ivan P., (**5**) *87*
Kotsiuba, Mykhailo, (**6**) *84*, *99*
Kotsiubyns'kyi, Mykhailo, 165, (**6**) *213*
Kotsovs'kyi, Volodymyr (Vladymir Kotsovskii), (**5**) *59*
Kotsylovs'kyi, Iosafat, 201, (**7**) *91*
Koval'chak, Hryhorii I., 140, (**6**) *90*, (**7**) *71*, *75*, (**8**) *18*, (**9**) *18*, *19*
Kovalenko, I.A., (**1**) *11*
Kovalevs'ka, T.M., (**2**) *24*
Koval's'kyi, Mykola P., 2, 71, 86, (**1**) *3*, *5*, (**4**) *2*, *73*, *90*
Kovpak, Sydir, (**8**) *37*
Kowalczuk, M., (**4**) *37*
Kowalski, Tadeusz, 254, (**10**) *103*
Kozachuk, T.E., (**7**) *79*
Kozachuk, T.Iu., (**1**) *86*
Koziebrodzki, Władysław, (**6**) *59*
Kozik, Jan, 104, 114, 125, 127, (**5**) *33*, *80*, *81*, (**6**) *30*, *39*, *41*, *44*
Kozlaniuk, Petro, 203, (**7**) *101*, *104*
Kozlovs'kyi, Oleksander, 158, (**6**) *179*
Kozłowski, J., *see* Jurkowski, Marian
Kozłowski, Jan, (**6**) *94*
Kozłowski, Leon, 46, (**2**) *23*, (**3**) *1*
KPSH, KPZU, *see* Communist party
Krafcik, Patricia A., xviii
Krajewski, W., (**4**) *78*
Kramarz, Walerjan, (**2**) *111*
Krämer, Julius, xviii, 250, (**10**) *91*, *98*

Krasovs'kyi (Krasówski), Mykola, (**4**) *67*
Kravchenko, Ie.Ie., (**6**) *178*
Kravchenko, Ivan I., 107, (**5**) *53*
Kravchenko, Uliana (Iuliia Shneider), 156, (**6**) *169*
Kravchuk, Petro I., (**7**) *103*
Kravets', Mykhailo M., 3, 137, 140, 178, 195, (**1**) *11*, *14*, *15*, (**6**) *71*, *79*, *90*, (**7**) *2*, *75*
Kravtsiv, Bohdan, (**2**) *99*
Kremsier, *see* Kroměříž
Kresel, E., (**10**) *60*
Krevets'kyi, Ivan, 104, 125, 144, (**1**) *37*, (**4**) *79*, (**5**) *17*, *21*, *28*, *36*, *44*, (**6**) *33–37*, *165*
Krezyb, Antin, *see* Dumin, Osyp
Krikun, U.P., (**8**) *14*
Krilovskii, A., 35, (**2**) *67*, (**4**) *50*, *66*
Kripchyns'kyi, O.A., (**1**) *69*
Kriukov, A.V., (**5**) *87*
Krivonos, N.K., (**10**) *80*, *81*, *86*, *88*
Křížek, Jurij, (**6**) *225*
Krochmal, Nachman, 230
Krokhmaliuk, Iurii Tys- (Jorge Tys-Krojmaluk), 219, (**8**) *34*, *36*
Krokhmaliuk, Roman, (**8**) *34*
Kroměříž (Kremsier), 123, 127, (**6**) *44*
Kron, Alexander, (**7**) *17*
Krosno, 39, 80, (**2**) *86*, (**4**) *42*
Krushel'nytsia, (**4**) 20
Krushel'nyts'ka, Larysa I., (**3**) *7*
Krushel'nyts'kyi, Antin, (**6**) *178*
Krychevs'kyi, Roman, (**9**) *7*
Krylos, 63
Kryms'kyi, Ahatanhel, (**6**) *138*, *160*
Kryp''iakevych, Ivan P. (Ivan Petrovych), 1, 3, 32, 42, 71, 170, (**1**) *3*, *12*, *23*, *54*, (**2**) *106*, *107*, *109*, *123*, *141*, (**3**) *24*, *55*, (**4**) *2*, *34*, *35*, *37*, *40*, *62*, *90*, *91*, *95*, (**5**) *23*, *27*, (**6**) *71*, *90*, *91*, *99*, *227*, *243*, (**7**) *15*, *43*, *69*, *80*, (**8**) *18*, *19*, (**10**) *75*, *85*
Krysiński, Alfons, 180, 227, (**7**) *9*, (**10**) *3*, *4*
Krystyniats'kyi, Ivan, (**4**) *66*
Kryzhanivs'kyi, S., (**6**) *173*
Kryzhanovskii, Evgenii M., 58, (**3**) *29*
Kubala, Ludwik, (**4**) *91*, *93*
Kubiiovych, Volodymyr, 32, 180, 209, (**2**) *9*, *42*, *78*, (**6**) *87*, (**7**) *9*, (**8**) *13*, (**10**) *3*
Kubrakiewicz, Michel, (**5**) *4*
Kuchabs'kyi, Vasyl', 181, (**7**) *11*, *18*
Kucharski, Władysław, (**4**) *47*
Kucherov, N.K., (**7**) *72*
Kuczera, Aleksander, (**2**) *134*
Kuczyński, Stefan Mária, 56, (**3**) *25*
Kudish, N., (**10**) *70*
Kuhn, Walter, (**10**) *94*, *95*, *96*
Kukhar, Roman, (**6**) *117*, (**7**) *86*
Kul'chyts'kyi, O., (**5**) *56*
Kulczycki, Ludwik, (**6**) *64*
Kulinych, Hryhorii H., (**7**) *106*
Kulish, Panteleimon, 164, (**6**) *210*, *211*
Kunik, Ernst, (**3**) *33*
Kunysz, Anton, (**2**) *102*, *110*
Kunzek, T., (**2**) *92*
Kupchanko, Hryhorii, 30, (**2**) *36*
Kurka, Antoni, (**5**) *14*
Kuryllo, T., (**2**) *16*
Kurzbeck printshop (Vienna), 106, (**5**) *45*
Kuschnir, Vladimir, *see* Kushnir, Volodymyr
Kushch, O.P., (**6**) *170*, *173*, (**7**) *105*, *106*
Kushevych, Samuïl, (**4**) *88*
Kushnir, Volodymyr (Vladimir Kushnir), (**6**) *95*, *219*, (**7**) *63*
Kutrzeba, Stanisław, (**1**) *64*
Kutschabsky, *see* Kuchabs'kyi, Vasyl'
Kuty, 243, 244, 248, (**10**) *61*, *88*

Kuzelia, Zenon, (**6**) *85*, *120*
Kuz'ma, Oleksa, 182, (**7**) *16*
Kwartalnik Historyczny, 22, (**2**) *3*
Kwilecki, Andrzej, 220, (**9**) *8*, *9*
Kyrchiv, Roman F., 39, 151, (**2**) *96*, (**6**) *130*
Kyryliuk, Ievhen, (**6**) *156*
Kyrylov, I.M., (**1**) *95*
Kysel'ov, O.I., (**6**) *156*
Kysilevs'kyi, Kost', (**6**) *104*

Labenskii, F., (**4**) *72*
Labor, *see* Socioeconomic structure
Labuda, Gerard, 48, (**3**) *8*, *11*
Ladyzhynskii, M.K., (**2**) *135*
Lagov, N.M., (**6**) *19*
Lahodiv, (**2**) *113*
Lair, Maurice, (**6**) *88*
Lam, Jan, 226
Landau, Saul R., (**10**) *24*, *31*
Landau, Y.L., (**10**) *38*
Landman, Isaac, (**10**) *9*
Land ownership and reform, *see* Socioeconomic structure
Langnas, Saul, 241, (**10**) *44*
Language/alphabet: assimilation and, 221; Austrian language laws, (**6**) *107*; and bilingualism, 199; Church (Old) Slavonic, 6, 17, 50, 61, 111, 145, (**introd**.) *5*; Cyrillic, xvi, 106, 111, (**introd.**) *5*; Czech, 10, 24, 129; German, 102, 128, 131, 132, 146, 154, 228, 230; Hebrew, 240, (**10**) *42*; Hungarian, 61; of instruction, 128, 146, (**6**) *107*; Karaite, 253, 254, (**10**) *99*, *103*; ''language/alphabet war,'' 111–112, 129, 145; Latin, 67, 101, 129; Latin-Polish alphabet, 111, 112, 132, (**1**) *39*, (**5**) *74*, (**6**) *49–51*; literary, 95, 102, 142, 145; modern, civil alphabet (*hrazhdanka*), 107, 111; Polish, xvi, 54, 102, 128, 132, 146, 199, (**introd**.), *5*, (**6**) *107*, (**10**) *99*; Russian, 31, 145, 150, 218, (**introd**.) *5*; and transliteration, xvi–xvii; Turkic, 253; Ukrainian/Ruthenian vernacular, xvi, 70, 103, 107, 113, 128–129, 131, 132, 145–149 passim, 225, (**introd**.) *5*, (**5**) *72–74*, (**6**) *105–107*; Yiddish, 228, 230, 240, (**10**) *41*. *See also* Culture; Education; Nationalism; Press, the
Łapinski-Nilski, Stanisław, (**7**) *17*
Lasocka, Barbara, (**10**) *1*
Latynnyky, 225, 227
Lavochne, (**2**) *113*
Lavrivs'kyi, Ivan, 110–111, (**5**) *68*
Lavriv, (**4**) *62*, *87*, (**6**) 117
Law, *see* Judicial system
Lawrynenko, Jurij, (**1**) *56*
Lazarenko, Ie.K., (**2**) *83*, *109*
Lazeba, E.M., (**1**) *42*
Lebed', Mykola, 211, (**8**) *36*
Lebedovych, Ivan, (**7**) *15*
Lechnicki, Czesław, 247, (**10**) *82*
Lehnert, S., (**7**) *83*
Lehr-Spławiński, Tadeusz, (**3**) *11*
Lemberg, 94. *See also* L'viv
Lemke, Heinz, (**6**) *226*
Lemkian region and people, xvi, 9, 40, 185, (**1**) *99*, (**2**) *16*, *97*; German control of, 207, 209; Polish rule of, 202, 217, 219–220, (**7**) *97* (**9**) *8–10*
Lemkyn, Y.F., (**2**) *97*
Lencyk, *see* Lentsyk, Vasyl'
Lendians, 56
Leninism, 141
Lentsyk, Vasyl', (**7**) *85*, *97*
Leontovych, Pavlo, 155, (**6**) *159*
Lepkii, Onufrii, (**4**) *52*, *64*

Lepkyi, Bohdan, 108, 158, (**5**) *59*, (**6**) *175*, (**7**) *99*
Lepucki, Henryk, 251, (**10**) *93*
Leshchenko, M.N., (**1**) *6*
Lesko, 80, 243, (**4**) *43*, (**10**) *62*
Lesyk, V.V., (**8**) *21*
Lesyn, Vasyl' M., (**6**) *173*, *176*
Leszczyński, Jan, (**5**) *16*
Leszek the White, 60
Lev, 52
Lev, Vasyl', 111, 145, (**2**) *72*, *100*, (**5**) *72*, (**6**) *117*, *175*, (**7**) *86*
Levitsky, Eugene, (**2**) *44*
Levoče (Leutschau), 27
Levyns'kyi, Volodymyr, 142, (**6**) *93*
Levyts'kyi, Dmytro, 176
Levyts'kyi, Iaroslav, (**6**) *38*, *117*
Levyts'kyi, Iosyf (Józef Lewicki), 106, (**5**) *49*, *73*
Levyts'kyi, Ivan E. (Jan Lewicki), 5, 6–8, 23, 103, 156, (**1**) *27*, *29*, *30*, *86*, (**2**) *6*, (**5**) *28*, *31*, (**6**) *165*
Levyts'kyi, Kost', 32, 119, 130, 132, 168, 171, 176, (**2**) *8*, (**6**) *9*, *63*, *107*, *232*
Levyts'kyi, Mykhailo M., 105, (**2**) *137*, (**5**) *49*
Levyts'kyi, Myron, (**8**) *35*, *36*
Levyts'kyi, Osyp, (**7**) *22*
Levyts'kyi (Lukych), Volodymyr, 119, (**1**) *27*, (**6**) *5*, *214*, (**7**) *62*
Lewandowski, Krzysztof, (**7**) *30*
Lewicki, Anatol, 55, (**3**) *22*, *52*, (**4**) *42*
Lewicki, Jan, *see* Levyts'kyi, Ivan E.
Lewicki, Józef, *see* Levyts'kyi, Iosyf
Lewicki, Kazimierz, (**1**) *4*
Liakhs, the, 50, 56, 57
Libraries and museums, 15–20, 37, 245. *See also* Archive(s)
Library of Congress (Washington), xvi, 19 (**1**) *99*
Likowski, Edward, (**4**) *56*
Limanowski, Bolesław, (**2**) *33*
Linnichenko, *see* Lynnychenko, Ivan A.
Lipiński, Tymoteusz, (**4**) *10*
Liptzin, Sol, (**10**) *41*, *42*
Lishna, 45, (**2**) 131
Liske, Oktaw, (**1**) *61*
Liske, Xawery, (**1**) *61*, (**4**) *5*
Lisovyi, R., (**7**) *57*
Literature/literary production, *see* Culture
Literaturno-naukovyi vistnyk (later *Vistnyk*), 21, 192
Lithuania and the Lithuanians, 28, 53, 65, 67, 72, 229, 252. *See also* Polish-Lithuanian Commonwealth
Litopys Boikivshchyny, 22
Litopys Chervonoï Kalyny, 22
Litopys Natsional'noho muzeiu, 22
Little Russians, xvi
Lodomeria, *see* Volhynia
Łojek, Jerzy, (**10**) *1*
Łokietek, Józef (Jił), 133, (**6**) *65*
Longinov, A.V., 57, (**3**) *27*, *33*, *41*
Łopuszański, Bolesław, (**5**) *17*, (**6**) *11*
Łoś, Stanisław, (**7**) *1*, *4*
Łowmiański, Henryk, (**3**) *11*, *27*
Łoziński, Bronisław, 99, 129, (**5**) *12*, *14*, *21*, (**6**) *48*
Łoziński, Władysław, 73, 78, 88, (**4**) *11*, *31*, *37*, *81*, *83*, *87*
Lozyns'kyi, Iosyf, 110, (**5**) *65*, *73*
Lozyns'kyi, Mykhailo, 32, 37, 119, 134, 135, 162, 184, 186, (**2**) *44*, *74*, (**6**) *5*, *67*, *68*, *69*, *72*, *74*, *155*, *166*, *193*, *235*, (**7**) *26*, *31*, *34*, *35*
Łubieński, H., (**7**) *94*
Lublin, 228, (**10**) *91*
Lubomirski Museum, 16, (**2**) *75*
Luchakovskii, K., (**6**) *137*

Luchkiv, Ivan, (**1**) *25*
Lukan', R., (**6**) *117*
Lukiianovych, D., (**6**) *169*, *170*
Lukomskii, G.K., (**4**) *82*
Lukych-Levyts'kyi, Volodymyr, *see* Levyts'kyi, Volodymyr
Luszczkiewicz, Ladislaus, (**4**) *82*
Lutman, Tadeusz, (**5**) *27*
Lutosławski, W., (**7**) *3*
Lutsiv, Luka, (**2**) *100*, (**5**) *59*, (**6**) *173*
Luts'k, 252, 253
Luts'kyi, Iurii, (**6**) *180*
Luts'kyi, Ostap, 158, 176, (**6**) 180, (**7**) *68*, 99
Lutsyk, R.Ia., (**1**) *24*, *85*
L'viv (L'vov, Lwów), xv, 9, 26, 39, 198 (**1**) *42*, *57*, (**2**) *103–109*, (**3**) *50*, (**4**) *23*, *29–37*, *83*, *86*, (**5**) *15*, 26, (**6**) *16*, *22*, (**8**) *5*; as administrative, religious, and cultural center, 2, 8, 25, 41–43, 47, 52, 63, 65, 67–69, 71, 72, 77–79, 81, 86, 89, 94, 95, 101–102, 104, 105, 146, 148, 160, 164, 200–201, 224, 226, 228, 232, 239, 244–245, 248, (**4**) *48*, (decline of) 77, 199, (underground university in) 199, 201, (*see also* Galician Diet; L'viv, University of); archives in, 12–14, 15–19, 25–27, 245, (**1**) *68*, *98*, (**10**) *76*; battles for, 168, 172, 173, 182, (**7**) *17*, *18*, (**8**) *38*; besieged, 70, 78, 90, 91, (**4**) *93*; minorities in, 226, 229, 234, 235, 242–245 passim, 248, 252, (**10**) *16*, *17*, *38*, *45*, *47*, *63*, *76*, *79–82*, *85–88*, *91*; occupation of, 98, 126, 174, 205, 207, 209, (**5**) *16*; publications in, 75, 144, 192, 247; as territorial unit, 39, 41, 65, 176, 218, 221, 225, 241, (**1**) *42*, (**2**) *24*, *87*, *101* (**4**) *4*, *14*, (**7**) *69*, (**8**) *5*, (**9**) *14*; treason trials at, 166, (**6**) *217*, (**7**) *56*; yearbooks, (**6**) *109*
L'viv, University of, 17, 31, 38, 95, 101, 102, 109, 148, 164, 199, 226, (**1**) *79*, *85*, *95*, (**2**) *82*, *83*, (**6**) *115*, *116*, (**10**), *1*. *See also* Education
L'viv Assumption Brotherhood, *see* Stauropegial Brotherhood (later Institute)
L'viv Historical Museum, 17, 19, (**1**) *96*
L'viv State Museum of Ukrainian Art (Ukrainian National Museum), 15, (**1**) *97*. *See also* Ukrainian organizations and institutions
L'viv Theological Academy Library, 17
L'viv Theological Seminary, 104, 105, 148
Lwów, *see* L'viv
Lynnychenko, Ivan A., 54, (**1**) *2*, (**3**) *18*, *33*, (**4**) *7*, *17*, *22*, (**10**) *86*
Lysenko, Oleksandr Ia., (**6**) *164*, *166*
Lysiak, Oleh, (**8**) *39*
Lysiak, Pavlo, (**7**) *49*
Lytvynovych, Spyrydon, 159, (**6**) *183*

Maciszewski, M., (**4**) *38*
Macler, Frédéric, (**10**) *76*
Mączyński, Czesław, 182, (**7**) *17*
Maday, Johannes, 34, (**2**) *59*
Madurowicz-Urbańska, Helena, (**1**) *47*, (**6**) *89*
Magdeburg Law, 77, 78, 94, 244, 249
Magocsi, Maria, xviii
Magocsi, Paul R., 111, 145, (**1**) *27*, *99*, (**5**) *72*, (**6**) *87*, *97*
Mahler, Raphael, 233, 236, 238, 241, (**10**), *8*, *13*, *22*, *30*, *34*, *44*
Maikov, A., (**3**) *19*
Maikov, V., (**1**) *51*
Maimon (Y.L. Fishman), (**10**) *63*
Mainych, (**2**) *113*
Makaiev, V., (**6**) *91*
Makarii, *see* Golubev, Sergei

Makarushka, Liubomyr, 176
Makarushka, Ostap, (**5**) *51*
Makovei, Osyp, 112, 157, 164, (**5**) *73*, (**6**) *170*, *210*
Makhovets', L., (**3**) *15*
Makovs'kyi, Vasyl', (**6**) *228*
Maksymchuk, Ivan O., (**6**) *63*, *138*
Maksymenko, Fedir P., *11*, *17*, (**1**) *1*, *57*, *83*, *85*, (**2**) *84*, (**4**) *78*
Maksymovych, Mykhailo, 115
Makukh, Ivan, 190, (**6**) *71*, (**7**) *51*
Malanchuk, Valentyn Iu., 197, (**2**) *101*, (**6**), *92* (**7**) 75, 78, (**9**) *16*, *17*
Malanchuk, Vyktoriia A.,151,(**6**) *130*,*171*
Maleczyńska, Ewa, *(***1**) *4*
Maleczyński, Karol, (**2**) *3*, *33*, (**4**) *15*
Malets, H.S., (**7**) *98*
Malinowski, Michael, (**6**) *181*
Malkin, Viktor A., 150, (**6**) *126*
Malyts'ka, Konstantyna, 157, (**6**) *174*
Mańkowski, Tadeusz, 88, (**2**) *33*, (**4**) *37*, *81*, *83*, (**10**) *76*
Mańteuffel, Tadeusz, (**10**) *1*
Marchenko, M.I., (**1**) *6*
Mardkowicz-Kokikow, Aleksander, 255, (**10**) *109*
Margoshes, Joseph, (**10**) *38*
Maria Theresa, 92, 94, 97, 101, 105, 228, 236, (**10**) *93*
Mark, Bernard, 233, (**10**) *8*
Mark, N., (**10**) *62*
Markov, Dmytro, 30, (**2**) *37*, (**7**) *29*
Markov, Osyp O., 150, (**1**) *77*, (**5**) *52*, (**6**) *125*
Markovits, Andrei S., (**5**) *60*, *72*, (**6**) *3*, *90*, *168*, (**10**) *24*, *38*
Markus, Vasyl, (**6**) *87*
Martínez Codó, Enrique, (**8**) *36*
Martiuk, Ivan, (**7**) *68*
Martovych, Les', 158, (**6**) *176*
Martovych, O., (**8**) *36*
Martynets', Volodymyr, 191, (**7**) *56*
Martyniuk, Ivan, (**2**) *100*
Martynowski, F.K., (**4**) *10*
Martyns'kyi, Apolinarii, (**6**) *12*
Marunchak, Mykhailo H., (**2**) *100*, (**6**) *87*
Marxist viewpoint, *see* Soviet Union, historiographical writings of
Mashotas, Volodymyr V., (**1**) *56*, (**7**) *103*
Maslo-soiuz, *see* Dairy Union
Maslov, Serhii I., 87, (**4**) *76*
Materialy i doslidzhennia z arkheolohiï Prykarpattia i Volyni, 47
Matiïv, Ivan, 73, (**4**) *9*
Matsiuk, O.Ia., (**4**) *77*, (**10**) *76*
Mattausch, Rudolf, (**6**) *43*
Matthews, Geoff, xvii
Matula, V., (**6**) *215*
Mauersberg, Stanisław, (**7**) *81*
Mavrodin, V.V., (**3**) *36*
Mayo, Olga K., xviii, (**1**) *99*
Mazovia, 65, (**4**) *19*
Mechitarist Library (Vienna), 245
Medvedyk, P.K., (**1**) *86*
Megas, Osyp, (**7**) *27*
Meisl, Joseph, 233, (**10**) *9*
Mejbaum, Venceslas, (**2**) *31*
Mękarski, Stefan, 42, (**2**) *108*
Mel'nichuk, Ia.S., (**10**) *88*
Mel'nychuk, Iurii S., (**6**) *177*, (**7**) *104*, *105*, *106*
Mel'nychuk, Petro, (**7**) *92*
Mel'nyk, Andrii, 211–212, (**8**) *25*; and Melnykites (*Mel'nykivtsi*), 212–213
Meltzer, Sh., (**10**) *56*
Memoirs, 9, 109, 118–121, 130, 150, 154,163,171, 172, 183, 191, 207, 237, 242, 252
Menczer, A., (**10**) *64*
Mendelsohn, Ezra, xviii, (**10**) *38*
Mennonites, (**10**) *105*
Mercenier, Feuillen, (**6**) *186*

Merkin, Zalman (Max Erik), (**10**) *41*
Miesięcznik Heraldyczny, 75
Milewski, Józef, (**6**) 48
Military history, see Polish-Ukrainian war; Revolutions/uprisings; Wars; World War I; World War II
Milkowicz, Wladimirus, see Myl'kovych, Volodymyr
Miłkowski, Zygmunt, (**6**) 65
Miller, Ivan S., 100, (**5**) 24, (**6**) 194
Ministry of Education and Religion (Warsaw), 199
Ministry of Religion and Education (Vienna), (**6**) 49
Minorities, xiii–xiv, 7, 224–255; Ukrainians (in Galicia) as, 130, 133, 141, (**1**) 47. See also Armenians; Germans; Jews; Karaites; Mennonites; Poles
Mirchuk, Petro, 191, 212, 219, (**7**) *57*, (**8**) *28*, *36*, (**9**) *4*, *5*, *7*
Mises, Ludwig von, 100, (5) *22*
Mishkinsky, Moshé, xviii
Missionary Congregation, *see* Archives, Vatican and Propaganda Fidei
Miziewicz, Stanisław, (**6**) *59*
Mlynchenko, Kuz'ma N., (**7**) *106*
Mochul's'kyi, Mykhailo, (**6**) *179*
Mohyl'nyts'kyi, Antin, 152, (**6**) *137*
Mohyl'nyts'kyi, Ivan, 110, (**5**) *49*, *65*, *73*
Mokhov, N.A., (**4**) *25*
Mokry, Włodzimierz, (**5**) *32*
Moldavia, 67, 68, 76
Mol'nar, Mykhailo, (**6**) *191*
Moloda Muza, 150, (**6**) *180*
Molodets'kyi, Volodymyr, (**8**) *39*
Molot, 144
Monasteries, 9, 12, 17, 84, 101, 105, (**1**) *43*, 82 (**4**) *62*, (**5**) *41*
Monchalovs'kyi, Osyp A., 30, (**2**) *37*, (**6**) *95*, *140*, *211*
Mongols, the, 52, 53, 59–60, (**3**) *43*
Moravcsik, Gyula, (**3**) *8*
Moravia, 48, 50, 96, 123
Morgensztern, Janina, (**10**) *14*
Moroz, Mykhailo O., 3, (**1**) *10*, *21*, (**6**) *145*, *154*
Moroz, O.N., (**6**) *154*
Morskoi, A. (V.I. Shtein), (**2**) *38*
Mortkowicz, J., (**2**) *35*
Moscow, 62, 68. *See also* Muscovy
Motuzka, M., (**7**) *96*
Motyl, Alexander J., xviii, 191, (**7**) *55*, *72*
Motylewicz, Jerzy, (**1**) *42*
Możdżeń, Stefan I., 147, (**6**) *112*
Mozil', Iurii, (**7**) *58*
Mroczko, Ksawery, (**2**) *89*
Mściwujewski, Mścisław, (**2**) *121*
Mshanets', 80, (**4**) *44*
Mudryi, Vasyl', 176, (**2**) *74*, *78*, *106*, (**6**) *115*, (**7**) *88*
Mudryk, Andrii, (**7**) *68*
Mukha, 68,76
Müller, Sepp, 250, (**10**) *89*, *91*, *95*, *98*
Müller-Brandenburg, (**6**) *242*
Mundare, Alberta, 19
Mundiak, Mariia M., (**6**) *189*, *191*
Murdzek, Benjamin P., (**6**) *85*
Murinov, I., (**2**) *38*
Muscovy, 55, 90, (**3**) *33*. *See also* Russian Empire
Museums, *see* Libraries and musuems
Mushynka, Mykola, (**1**) *20*, (**6**) *172*
Muzychka, Ivan, (**9**) *25*
Myczkowski, K., (**3**) *2*
Mykhailyk, P.P., (**7**) *71*
Mykolaievych, M., *see* Stakhiv, Matvii
Mykytas', V.L., (**6**) *173*
Myl'kovych, Volodymyr (Wladimirus Milkowicz), (**4**) *6*, *66*
Myshuha, Luka, (**6**) *87*

Myśliński, Jerzy, (**10**) *1*
Myśl Karaimski (**10**) *99*

Nadvirna, (**10**) *96*
Nahaievs'kyi, Izydor, 181, (**7**) *12*
Nahirnyi, Vasyl', 120, (**6**) *10*
Najdus, Walentyna, *101*, (**5**) *25*, (**6**) *16*, *82*, *90*
Nanovs'kyi, Ia.I., (**1**) *97*
Narizhyni, Symon, (**7**) *96*
Národní Museum (Prague), 19
Narodovtsi, *see* Populism
Nastasivs'kyi, M., (**6**) *87*
National Democractic party, *see* Ukrainian political parties
National Home (L'viv), 16, 17, 18, 36, 143, (**1**) *76*, *77*, *90*, (**2**) *71*
Nationalism, 95, 163, 178, 191, 192, 207, 222; and national autonomy, *see* Galicia; and national consciousness/identity, 57, 69, 81, 122, 142, 143, 153, 180, 202, 225, 227, 249; and "Ukrainian separatism" 29, 119, 143. *See also* Language/alphabet
Nationalization of industry, 210, 218. *See also* Socioeconomic structure
Nauchno-informatsionnyi biulleten' (later *Arkhivy Ukraïny*), 22–23
Nauchno-literaturnyi sbornik, 21
Naukovŷi (later *Lyteraturnŷi*) *sbornyk*, 21
Naumovych, Ivan G., 152, (**6**) *140*, *183*, *217*
Navrots'kyi, Volodymyr, 155, 163, (**6**) *163*, *204*
Nazarko, Irynei I., 25, (**1**) *17*, (**2**) *17*, *61*, (**7**) *91*
Nazarova, L.V., (**8**) *21*
Nazaruk, Osyp, (**6**) *243*, (**7**) *22*, *36*
Nechai, S.P., (**2**) *101*
Nechui-Levyts'kyi, Ivan, 165, (**6**) *214*
Němec, B., (**2**) *11*
Nemirovskii, Evgenii L., 87, 88, (**4**) *74*, *79*
Nesterets', M.M., (**8**) *5*
Nesterov, *see* Zhovkva
Nestorovych, Volodymyr, 193, (**7**) *68*
Nevrlý, Mikuláš, (**6**) *190*
Newspapers, *see* Press, the
New York Public Library, 19, (**1**) *99*
Niederle, Lubor, 49, (**3**) *12*
Niedziela, Zdzisław, 114, (**5**) *83*
Niemann, Hans, (**6**) *237*
Nikitin, S.A., (**6**) *42*
Nobility, *see* Socioeconomic structure
Nogha ha-Yareah, (**10**) *11*
Nomenclature, xv–xvii
Nossig, Alfred, 240, (**10**) *6*, *31*, *38*
Novovolyns'k, 45 (**2**) *132*
Novychenko, L.M., (**7**) *103*
Noy, Dov, (**10**) *49*
Nykyforchuk, Iurko, 10, (**1**) *50*
Nyzovyi, D.D., (**2**) *116*, (**8**) *18*

Obermayer-Marnach, Eva, (**2**) *10*
October Bolshevik Revolution, 33. *See also* Revolutions/uprisings
Oder valley, 48
Ohiienko, Ivan, 35, 87, (**4**) *76*, *79*, *80*
Ohloblyn, Oleksander P., (**1**) *1*, (**2**) *45*
Ohonovs'kyi, Omelian, 35, 108, 110, 149, 155, 163, (**2**) *62*, *63*, (**5**) *29*, *58*, *59*, *62*, *64*, (**6**) *136*, *142*, *155*, *158*, *160*, *168*, *169*, *201*
Ojczyzna, (**10**) *11*
Okhrymovych, Volodymyr, 122, 135, 157, (**6**) *18*, *69*, *72*, *112*, *171*, (**10**) *1*
Okunevs'kyi, Teofil, 163, (**6**) *203*
Old Ruthenians, xvi, 24, 108, 143, 145, 150, 163, 165, 166, 190, (**6**) *72*; domination of cultural life by, 151; views of, on Galicia, 29–30, (**6**) *95*
Old Slavonic, *see* Language/alphabet,

Church (Old) Slavonic
Oleksiuk, Mykhailo M., (**2**) *46*, (**7**) *80*, *102*
Olesnevych, Lev O., 138, (**6**) *84*, (**7**) *68*
Olesnyts'kyi, Ievhen, 120, (**6**) *10*, *61*
Oliinyk, L.V., (**1**) *6*
Oliinyk, Petro, (**7**) *16*
Olszak, Julian, (**2**) *110*
Olsztyn, 217
Omel'chenko, Hryhorii, (**5**) *77*
Omelianovych-Pavlenko, Mykhailo, (**7**) *18*
Onatsky, Eugene, (**6**) *87*
Onikiienko, V.V., (**2**) *24*
Opałek, Mieczysław, (**2**) *108*
Opolski, Władysław, 73
Oporets', (2) 113
Organization of Ukrainian Nationalists (OUN), 176, 178, 190–192, 193, 196, 205, 207, 208, 211–213, 219, (**7**) *56–58*, (**8**) *23–33*, (**9**) *7*
Orgelbrand, Samuel, (**2**) *10*
Oriavchyk, (**2**) *113*
Orłowicz, Mieczysław, (**2**) *26*, *111*
Ormian, Hayim, (**10**) *36*
Orthodox church, 34, 50, 53, 67, 81, (**4**) *50*, *58*; and cultural revival, xiii, 68, 78, 85; outlawed, 69; Russian encouragement/defense/restriction of, 165, 166, 167, 218, (**6**) *231*; and union with Rome, 61, 62, 69, 70, 76, 82–84, 218. *See also* Christianity; Religion(s)
Orthodox Church of the Assumption, 68
Orthography problem, (**6**) *104*. *See also* Language/alphabet
Orton, Lawrence D., (**1**) *8*
Oryshkevych, Petro, (**2**) *98*
Orzell, Laurence, (**7**) *39*
Osechyns'kyi, Volodymyr K., 119, 136, 169, (**1**) *6*, (**6**) *7*, *78*, *92*, *187*, *225*, (**7**) *45*
Osinski, Marjan, (**2**) *142*
Ossolineum (Ossoliński National Institute), 15, 16, 17, 18, 19, 35–36, 226, 245, (**1**) 74, 98, (**2**) *68–70*, (**10**) *1*, *76*
Ostaszewski-Barański, Kazimierz, 123, (**6**) *43*, *51*
Österreichische Nationalbibliothek, *see* Austria, National Library
Ostrih, 68
Ostrovskii, Grigorii S., 88, (**4**) *83*
Ottoman Empire, 92, 112
OUN, *see* Organization of Ukrainian Nationalists
Ovnanian, S., (**6**) *92*

''Pacification,'' 178, 191–193 (**7**) *48*, *63–66*
Padurra, Tomasz, 114
Painting, *see* Culture (art and architecture)
Pajączkowski, Franciszek, (**10**) *1*
Palatinate (Pfalz), 249, (**10**) *96*
Palestine, 230
Palii, Andrii, (**7**) *68*
Panchuk, M.I., (**7**) *75*
Panenko, I., (**7**) *3*
Paneyko, Basil, (**7**) *5*
Pan'kevych (Paňkevyč), Ivan, (**5**) *77*
Pan'kivs'kyi, Kost', 156, 164, (**6**) *167*, *208*
Pan'kivs'kyi, Kost' (son), 209, (**8**) *10*
Pannenkowa, Irena, (**6**) *48*, (**7**) *3*
Pan-Slavism, 112, 114, 166. *See also* ''Reunification''
Papée, Fryderyk, 42, (**2**) *108*, *114*, *136*
Papierzyńska-Turek, Mirosława, 190, (**7**) *52*
Paprocki, Stanisław J., (**7**) *4*, *53*
Paris Peace Conference, 32, 186, 187, (**7**) *30*, *37–39*

Parot'kin, I.V., (**8**) *38*
Partyka, Andrzej, 187, (**7**) *38*
Partyts'kyi, Omelian, 48–49, (**3**) *1*, *9* (**6**) *137*
Pashaeva, Nina M., 10, 127, (**1**) *6*, *49*, (**2**) *38*, *71*, (**6**) *42*
Pashuto, Vladimir T., 54, 58, 60, 62, (**1**) *2*, (**3**) *18*, *32*, *37*, *44*
Pasternak, Iaroslav, 5, 46, 50, 63, (**introd.**) *3*, (**1**) *25*, (**3**) *1*, *6*, *10*, *48*
Paszkiewicz, Henryk, 49, 56, 72, (**3**) *11*, *25*, (**4**) *7*
Pasznycki, Bazyli, (**2**) *97*
Patrylo, Isydor I., 9, (**1**) *43*, (**2**) *61*
Pauli, Żegota, 114
Pavents'kyi, Antin, (**2**) *79*
Pavliuk, I.S., (**6**) *92*, (**7**) *82*
Pavlov, A., 62, (**3**) *45*
Pavlyk, Mykhailo, 141–142, 156, 163, (**1**) *27*, (**6**) *95*, *145*, *166*, *197*, *200*, *201*, *203*, *205*, *206*
Pavlyk, O., (**1**) *15*, *50*
Pawiński, Adolf, (**10**) *82*
Pawlikowski Library, 16, (**1**) *98*
Pawłowski, Bronisław, (**5**) *15*, *16*
Pawłowski, Stanisław, (**10**) *3*
Pazdro, Zbigniew, 235, (**6**) *82*, (**10**) *16*
Pazyra, Stanisław, (**6**) *22*
Peasant and Workers Socialist Union (Sel-Rob), 198, (**7**) *75*, *78*, *80*
Peasantry, *see* Socioeconomic structure
Pelens'kyi, Ievhen Iu., 202, (**1**) *1*, (**6**) *175*, (**7**) *99*
Pelens'kyi, Iosyp (Józef Pełeński), (**4**) *83*
Pelesh, Iuliian, 4, 34, (**1**) *17*, (**2**) *58*
Pelipenko, Alexander, (**6**) *219*
Peremyshl', *see* Przemyśl
Peremyshliany, 229
Perestoroha, (**4**) *58*
Perfecky, George, 53, (**3**) *15*, *16*
Pergen, Anton, 96
Perl, Josef, 230, 239, (**10**) *36*
Perski, Jakub, (**10**) *18*
Pers'kyi, Stepan, *see* Shakh, Stepan
Persowski, Franciszek, 58, (**2**) *110*, (**3**) *30*, (**10**) *3*
Petliakov, Petro A., (**7**) *95*
Petrash, Osyp, 107, 110, (**5**) *55*, *58*, *62*, *64*
Petriv, I., (**9**) *17*
Petrov, Aleksei L., (**10**) *3*
Petrovych, Ivan *see* Kryp''iakevych, Ivan
Petrowicz, Gregory, 247, (**10**) *82*
Petrushevych, Antin S., 4, 61, 63, 70, 85–86, 96, 152, (**1**) *14*, *28*, *78*, (**3**) *14*, *42*, *44*, *47*, *50*, (**4**) *1*, *4*, *52*, *62*, *64*, *78*, (**5**) *5*, (**6**) *138*
Petrushevych, Ievhen, 168, 174, 175, 186, (**6**) *63*, (**7**) *31*, *34*
Petrushevych Museum, 16, (**1**) *77*
Petrushevych, Mykhailo, (**5**) *47*
Petrushevych, Stefan, 110, (**5**) *67*
Petrushko, V., (**9**) *18*
Petrykevych, Viktor, (**6**) *124*
Pflügl, Richard von, (**6**) *85*
Piątkowski, Kazimierz, (**7**) *9*
Piątkowski, Wiesław, (**9**) *11*
Picheta, Volodymyr, 32, (**2**) *45*
Pidhaitsi region, 40, (**2**) *99*
Pidhirtsi, (**2**) *87*
Pidpryhorshchuk, M.V., (**9**) *17*
Pieracki, Bronisław, 191, (**7**) *59*
Pieradzka, Krystyna, (**2**) *97*
Pietruski, Oktaw, (**4**) *5*
Pilat, T., (**6**) *16*
Pil'huk, Ivan I., (**5**) *51*, *87*
Piniński, Leon, 167
Piotrkowski, Ludwik, 246, (**10**) *79*
Piotrkowski, Stanisław, (**4**) *14*
Piotrowicz, W., (**7**) *94*
Piotrowski, J., (**2**) *87*
Pirozhenko, P. Kh., (**10**) *76*

Piskovyi, S., *see* Dashkevych, Iaroslav R.
Pląskowski, Tadeusz, (**9**) *11*
Plave, (**2**) *113*
Pletenets'kyi, Ielysei, 69
Plöchl, Willibald M., (**5**) *35*
Ploshchans'kyi, Venedykt A., 43, (**2**) *113*, (**4**) *62*, (**6**) *217*
Plotkina, P.B., (**1**) *68*
Pochaïv Monastery printshop, 88, 106, (**4**) *80*, (**5**) *46*
Pociej, Jan, (**4**) *53*
Podlachia, 189, (**4**) *19*
Podleski, Franciszek, (**6**) *65*, (**7**) *98*
Podlipský, Josef, (**5**) *87*
Podolia, 92, 229
Podolyns'kyi (Podolinskii), Serhii, (**6**) *93*
Podolyns'kyi, Vasyl' (W. Podoliński), (**6**) *28*
Pogodin, Aleksander L., (**2**) *38*
Pogodin, Mikhail P., 114, (**5**) *84*, *86*
Pohorecki, Feliks, (**1**) *74*, (**2**) **33**
Pohrebennyk, Fedir, (**6**) *170*, *176*
Pokos, L. V., (**2**) *38*
Pokuttia region, 70
Polaczkówna, Helena, (**4**) *40*
Polák, Václav, (**3**) *8*
Poland: archeological research in (**3**) *27*; archives of, 12, 13, 16, 19, 26, (**1**) *64*, *65*, *66*; Austrian Empire and, 117, 119, 225; bibliographies for, 7, 10; Communist party in, 198, 214, 217, (**7**) *72*; culture of, 31, 36, 67, 70, 81, 102, 225, 245, 249, (**4**) *56*, (**10**) *1*, (and Polish national revival) xiii, 226, 230; Galician/Ukrainian occupation and rule by, 25, 226, 233, 246, (before 1848) 12, 28, 31, 32, 50–61 passim, 65, 67–91, 92, 95–96, 98, 228, 235, 244, 249, (**5**) *16*, (1848–1918) 117, 119, 122, 128–129, 136, 169, (**6**) *224*, (interwar) 12, 160, 174–176, 178–202 passim, 231, 233, 253, (**7**) *97*, (post-World War II) 41, 217, 219–220; Hungary and, 27, 60–61, 65, 73; independence of, 127, 182, 225; Kingdom of, 65, 77, 94, 170, 227, 249; minorities in, 232–235, 238, 240, 246, 249, 252, 253; Parliament of, 189; partitions of, 70, 92, 94, 228; People's republic of, 220; and polonization, 70, 75, 78, 81, 102, 103, 109, 149, 160, 225 (*see also* Language/alphabet); revolutionary movements in, 98, 114, 117, 126, 134, 162, (**6**) *194* (*see also* Revolutions/uprisings); scholarship and writers of, 2, 22–29 passim, 37–43 passim, 55–58, 72–79 passim, 87–88, 96, 101, 104, 122–127 passim, 133, 137, 138, 161, 178–180, 182, 190, 191, 200, 201, 207, 213, 220, 225–227, (**3**) *27*,)**5**) *4*, (**7**) *4*, *83*, (**8**) *11*, *29*, (**9**) *11*, (Marxist view) 3, 91, 126, (on minorities other than Poles) 238, 246, 254, (Soviet view opposed to) 49, 56, 136, 178; -Soviet relations, 181, 187, 194, 231, (Polish-Soviet border, 1947) 217, (Polish-Soviet war, 1920) 188; trade with 59; -Ukrainian ethnographic boundary, 54, 57, 180, 227, (**10**) *3*; in World War I, 167, 169, 170–171, 227; in World War II and postwar, 205, 209, 211, 214, 217, 219–220, 231, 249
Poles (in Galicia), xiv, xv, 67, 70, 78, 81, 92, 96, 98, 100, 118, 122–135 passim, 169, 170–171, 224–227, (**10**)*1–4*
Polesie, *see* Polisia
Polianina, T.V., (**5**) *87*
Polians'kyi, Iurii, (**3**) *6*
Poliek, V., 23, (**2**) *7*
Polikarpenko, H., (**8**) *24*

Polish Historical Society, 21, 226, (**10**) *1*
Polish-Lithuanian Commonwealth, xiv, xv, 34, 55, 82, 92, 227, 252
Polish National Council (L'viv), (**6**) *42*
Polish Theater, 226, (**10**) *1*
Polish-Ukrainian war (1918–19), 175–175, 181, 182–184, 199, 231, (**7**) *16–19*
Polisia, 189
Poltava dialects, 145. *See also* Language/alphabet
Poltorats'kyi, O., (**8**) *7*
Polushkin, M.A., (**8**) *38*
Ponomarev, V.P., (**2**) *38*
Pope, the, *see* Roman Catholic church
Popov, B.M., (**2**) *132*
Popov, Nil A., (**5**) *69*, *84*
Popovych, Damaskyn, (**5**) *59*
Poppe, Andrzej, (**3**) *27*
Population: 18th-century, 92; growth of, 99, 137, 238; industrial, 140; minority (Polish, Jewish, German, Karaite), 225, 228, 229, 231, 238, 249, 252–253. *See also* Census(es); Emigration/immigration
Populism, 149, 162; Ukrainophile (*narodovtsi*), 138, 143, 153, 164
Porphyrogenitus, Constantine, (**3**) *8*
Potichnyj, Peter J., (**1**) *8*
Potocki, Andrzej, 135
Prague, 191, 200; Slav Congress in, 123, 124, 128
Prešov Region, (**1**) *20*
Press, the, 144–145, 161, 166, 178, 234, (**1**) *37–38* (**6**) *101–103*, (**7**) *67*; bibliographies and histories of, 7–8, 106, 222; censorship of, 102, 107, 113, 144, (**6**) *102*; Communist, 198; cultural revival and, 102, 116, 123, 142; Polish, 190; 226, (**10**) *1*; printshops and printing, 2, 35, 68, 69, 86–88, 106, 245, 247; scholarly journals, 21–23, 47, 192. *See also* Culture; Language/alphabet
Primary Chronicle, 50, 56
Printshops and printing, *see* Press, the
Prisoners of war, 184, (**6**) *234*
Pritsak, Omeljan, xviii, 254, (**1**) *12*, (**2**) *72*, (**10**) *103*
Prochaska, Antoni, 73, (**2**) *117*, *124*, *133*, *137*, (**4**) *5*, *8*, *14*, *23*, *42*, *48*, *56*, *95*
Proiektor, D.M., (**8**) *39*
Prokopchuk, Hryhorii, 160, (**2**) *106*, (**6**) *186*, (**7**) *93*
Prokopchyts', Evstakhii (I. Kołosowicz), (**6**) *28*
Propaganda Fidei, *see* archives, Vatican and Propaganda Fidei
Prosvita Society, 9, 37, 144, (**1**) *40*, (**2**) *74*, (**6**) *99*
Prószyński, Marceli, (**2**) *87*, (**7**) *8*
Protestantism, 109, 249. *See also* Religion(s)
Protests, *see* Revolutions/uprising; Strikes and protests
Prus, Edward, (**8**) *29*
Prussia, 92, 117, 250
Przemyśl (Peremyshl'), xv, 50, 52, 57, 230; archives in, 13, 72, (**1**) *66*, *99*; eparchies of, 18, (**1**) *92*, (**2**) *19*, (**4**) *61–63*; German control of, 207, 209, (**8**) *38*; guides to and studies of, 9, 41, 43, 64, 80, 234, 235, 243, (**1**) 42, (**2**) *102*, *110*, *111*, (**3**) *10*, *52*, (**4**) *45*, (**10**) *18*, *64*; Polish rule of, 217; as religious/cultural center, 25, 48, 67–68, 95, 102, 105, 146, (**6**) *109*; Russian capture of, 167, 168; as territorial unit, 65, (**2**) *113*, (**4**) *4*
Przewodnik Naukowy i Literacki, 22
Przeworsk, 72, 228
Przbysławski, Władysław, (**3**) *5*

Przysiecki, Feliks, 170, (**6**) *229*
Ptaszycki, Stanisław L., (**4**) *79*
Public Archives of Canada (Ottawa), 19
Pulnarowicz, Władysław, (**2**) *94*, (**4**) *20*
Pylypenko, Serhii, (**6**) *146*
Pypin, Aleksander N., 114, 150, (**2**) *63*, (**5**) *83*, (**6**) *129*
Pyrozhenko, P., (**5**) *21*
Pyvovarov, M., (**5**) *51*

Raciborski, Alexandre, (**6**) *65*
Radchenko, Volodymyr, (**7**) *105*
Radical party, *see* Ukrainian political parties
Radymno, 45, (**2**) *133*
Radzykevych, Volodymyr, (**6**) *162*
Radziejowski, Janusz, 198, (**7**) *45*, *77*, *78*
Raevskii, Mikhail F., 166, (**6**) *10*, *215*
Raffalovich, George (Bedwin Sands), (**6**) *227*
Rakovs'kyi, Ivan, (**2**) *9*
Rapacki, Władysław, (**6**) *16*
Rappoport, M.V., (**2**) *38*
Rapoport, Solomon J. (S. An-Ski), 230, (**10**) *28*
Rath, R. John, (**6**) *1*
Ratych, O.O., (**3**) *7*
Ratyńska, Barbara, (**7**) *40*
Rawita-Gawroński, Franciszek, *see* Gawroński, Franciszek Rawita
Rebet, Lev, (**7**) *58*, (**8**) *27*
Reboshapka, Ivan, (**1**) *20*
Red Army, 10, 32, 183, 188, 205, 207, 212–218 passim, (**8**) *14*
Red Rus' (*Chervona Rus'*/*Chervonaia Rus'*/Ruś Czerwona/Ziemia Ruska), xv, 65, 224, 228, 235. *See also* East(ern) Galicia; Galicia; Rus' palatinate
Red Russia, 232
Red Ukrainian Galician Army, 175
Redziński, Mieczysław, (**9**) *11*
Reference works, *see* Bibliographies; Encyclopedias and dictionaries; Statistical surveys; Yearbooks (*Zvity*)
Regional history, 38–41
Regula, Jan A., 198, (**7**) *77*
Řehoř, František, 161, (**6**) *189*
Reichenfelser, Heinz, (**10**) *97*
Reichstag, *Reichsrat*, *see* Austria/Austrian Empire
Reisen, Zalman, (**10**) *41*
Rej, Mikołaj, 226
Religion(s): and education, 38, 68, 95, 101–102, 104, 146, 148, 200, 249; equality of, 94; and religious art, *see* Culture; and religious identity, 122, 180. *See also* Armenian Rite Catholic church; Christianity; Church history; Greek Catholic (Uniate) church; Jews; Orthodox church; Protestantism; Roman Catholic church
"Reunification": Christian, *see* Roman Catholic church; of Galicia with Hungary, 28; of Rus' land with Russia, Soviet Union, 30, 32, 90, 114; of Ukrainian land and people, 33, 209, 215, (**1**) *54*, (**8**) *15*, *38*. *See also* Pan-Slavism
Reviziinyi Soiuz Ukraïns'kykh Kooperatyv, *see* Audit Union of Ukrainian Cooperatives
Revolutions/uprisings, 65, 90–91 188–189, 191, 194–197, 203, (**7**) *44*; 1490–1492 (peasant), 68, 76, (**4**) *25*; 1648 (Cossack), 69, 70, 78, 90, (**4**) *91–93*; 1830s and 1840s, 98, 100, 114, (**5**) *17*, *19 23*; 1848–1849, 28, 95, 116, 123–128, 142, 151, 159, 161, 162, (**5**) *19*, (**6**) *23–46*; 1863 (Polish), 117, 134, 162, (**6**) *70*, *194*; 1902 (peasant), 137, (**6**) *82*; 1905 (Russian), 141, (**6**) *91*, *92*; 1917 (Bolshevik), xvi, 33, 184, (**7**) *44*,

45; 1919 (''Drohobych armed revolt''), 188, (**7**) *43*. *See also* Brigand movement; Strikes and protests
Revyuk, Emil, (**7**) *64*
Řežábek, Jan, (**3**) *33*
Rhode, Gotthold, 58, 72, (**3**) *31*, (**4**) *6*
Ribbentrop-Molotov nonagression pact, 205, 207
Ridna Shkola, 199, 201, (**7**) *89*
Riga, Treaty of, 187, (**7**) *36*
Ringelbaum, E., (**10**) *13*
Ripets'kyi, Fedir I. (F.I.R.), 30, (**2**) *36*
Ripets'kyi, Stepan, 173, (**1**) *39*, (**6**) *243*, (**7**) *11*
Rivkin, Ellis, (**10**) *33*
Roback, Abraham, (**10**) *41*
''Robin Hoods,'' *see* Brigand movement
Robinson, Jacob, (**10**) *48*
Rocznik Przemyski, 22
Rocznik Towarzystwa Heraldycznego we Lwowie, 75
Rogowski, Jan, (**7**) *17*
Rohatyn, 68, 229, 243, (**10**) *65*
Roman (of Volhynia), 52, 60
Roman Catholic church, 68, 78, 101, 225–226, (**4**) *48*; archives of, 12, 14, 15, 33, 82, 105, (**1**) *67*, (**2**) *47–55*; and Christian unity/Union of Brest, 61, 62, 68–69, 70, 76, 81, 82–84, 218, 244, 247, (**2**) *55–58*, (**3**) *43*, *44*, (**4**) *56–59*, (**10**) *83*; Galician conversion to/ establishment of, 67, 70, 81, 83, 224; relations and negotiations with Vatican, 52, 62, (**3**) *32*, *43*, (**7**) *97*, (**9**) *25*. *See also Schematisma*, Roman Catholic dioceses
Romanchuk (Romanczuk), Iuliian, (**6**) *67*
Romanenchuk, Bohdan, 24, (**1**) *32*, (**2**) *15*, (**6**) *117*, *172*, (**7**) *86*
Romanovs'kyi, V., (**4**) *79*
Romanovych dynasty, 52–53, 65
Romanowicz, Tadeusz, (**6**) *16*
Romer, Eugeniusz, (**7**) *3*
Rosdolsky, Roman, *see* Rozdol's'kyi, Roman
Rosenfeld, Max, (**10**) *31*
Rossowski, Stanisław, (**6**) *229*
Rostyslav, and dynasty, 50, 52
Rothkirch, Leonhard von, (**6**) *241*
Rozdol's'kyi, Roman, 99, (**5**) *21*, (**6**) *44*
Rozenblit, I.M., (1) *68*
Rozheiovs'kyi, Teodor, (**6**) *28*
Rozhorche, (**2**) *113*
Rozwadowski, Jan, (**6**) *82*
Rubchak, Bohdan, (**5**) *180*
Rud', Mykyta P., 10–11 (**1**) *52*
Rudlovchak, Olena, (**5**) *64*
Rudnicki, Józef, 42, (**2**) *108*
Rudniev, V., (**8**) *7*
Rudnyts'ka, Milena, 211, (**8**) *22*, (**9**) *25*
Rudnytsky, Ivan L., xviii, 118, (**4**) *18*, (**6**) *3*
Rudnyts'kyi, Iaroslav B., (**introd.**) *3*, (**7**) *83*
Rudnyts'kyi, M., (**8**) *29*
Rudnyts'kyi, Stepan (S.R.), (**7**) *35*
Rudolf (of Austria-Hungary), 28
Rudovych, Ivan, 34, (**2**) *60*, (**4**) *56*
Rundstein, S., (**4**) *24*
Rurykovych dynasty, 50, 52
Rusalka dnîstrovaia, 102, 107
Ruś Czerwona, *see* Red Rus'
Rus'ka Besida, 144, (**6**) *99*
Rus'ka Besida Theater, 150
Rus'ka triitsa, *see* Rusyn Triad
Rus' land, *see* Red Rus'; Rus' palatinate
Rus' palatinate (*Województwo Ruskie*), xiv–xv, 65, 67, 73, 77, (**4**) *4*. *See also* Red Rus'
Rus' Primary Chronicle, *see* Primary Chronicle
Russian Empire, 92, 94, 95, 109, 142,

145, 185, 226; civil war in, 175; claims of, 28, 29, 30; Galician relations with, 112, 114, 115, 119, 122, 151, 165–167 (*see also* Russophiles); and Greek Catholic church, 168, 171, (**6**) *231*; occupation by, (1800s) 98, (**5**) *16*, (1914–15) 30, 117, 170, 230–231, 237, (**6**) *223, 227–231*; pogroms in, 229, 237; Polish revolt against, 117, 162 (*see also* Poland); and ''Russians'' as term for Ukrainians, xvi; in World War I, 167–172, (**6**) 237 (*see also* occupation by, *above*); writings of, on Galicia, 10, 30, 31. *See also* Soviet Union

Russian National party, 134, (**6**) *71*

Russian Revolution, *see* Revolutions/ uprisings

Russophiles, xvi, 133–134, 143, 151, 162–167 passim, 176, 185, 197, 202, (**6**) *67*, *95*, *96*, *97*, *184*, *219*, (**7**) *98*; and language, 145, 150; in World War I, 170, 184; writings by, 7, 24, 30, 40, 57, 95, 103, 107–110 passim, 119

Rusyn, Havryło, see Holovats'kyi, Iakiv

Rusyn(s): in Subcarpathian Rus', folklore on, (**1**) *20*; as term for Ukrainians, xvi

Rusyn Triad (*Rus'ka triitsa*), 102, 104, 106–110, 114

Ruthenian(s), 34, 179; ''invention'' of, 28, 123, 127; and ''Ruthenian terror,'' 185; use of term, xvi, 176

Ruthenian Council (Rus'kyi Sobor), 123, 127

Ruthenische Revue, 22

Rutkovych, Ivan, (**4**) *86*

Rutkowski, Mieczysław, (**2**) *3*

Rutkowski, Stanisław, (**7**) *17*

Rutkowski, T., 121, (**6**) *16*

Ruzanov, O.M., (**1**) *68*

Ruzhyts'kyi, E.I., (**1**) *69*

Rybakov, Boris, (**3**) *46*

Rybarski, R., (**4**) *46*

Rzepski, Stanisław, (**9**) *11*

Sabotage, 175, 176, 178. *See also* Strikes and protests

Sacher-Masoch, Leopold von, 96, (**5**) *8*

Sadan, D., (**10**) *69*

Sadovs'kyi, M., (**7**) *8*

Šafárik, Pavel Josef, 113, 114

Sahaidachnyi, Petro Konashevych, 69

St Barbara Church (Vienna), 104

St Basil the Great (monastic order), 9, 105, (**1**) *43*, *82* (**2**) *19*, (**4**) *62*, (**5**) *41*

St Cyril and Methodius Society, 149

St George Cathedral and St George Circle, 123, 159

St Gerhardt, Artur, (**5**) *14*

St Onufrius Basilian Monastery Library, 17

St Petersburg, 167

Salt exports, 52. *See also* Socioeconomic structure

Samarin, B.V., (**8**) *38*, *39*

Sambir, 14, 45, 64, 80, (**1**) *68*, (**2**) *134*, (**3**) *55*, (**4**) *46*

Sandomierz palatinate, 92

Sands, Bedwin (George Raffalovich), (**6**) *227*

Sanok, 39, 45, 72, 80, 226, 235, 243, (**2**) *135*, (**10**) *66*; as territorial unit, 65, (**2**) *88*, (**4**) *4*, *45*, *47*

San River and region, xiv, 40, 57, 94, 205, 210, 217, (**2**) *98*, (**10**) *3*, *18*; battle at, 167, 173, (**6**) *240*

Santifaller, Leo, (**2**) *10*

Sapieha, Adam, (**6**) *64*

Sapieha, Leon, 120, (**6**) *11*, *48*

Sardinia, 117

Saryusz-Zaleski, Wacław, (**6**) *89*
Satke, Władysław, (**2**) *92*
Savchenko, Fedir, 151, 166, (**5**) *88*, (**6**) *133*, *196*, *216*
Schall, Jacob, 233, (**10**) *8*, *26*, *45*, *100*
Schematisma (directories), 25, 97, 248; Armenian Catholic archdiocese, (**10**) *84*; Austro-Hungarian empire, (**5**) *10*, (**6**) *108*; Galicia, (**5**) *11*; Greek Catholic dioceses, (**2**) *19*; Roman Catholic dioceses, (**2**) *19*; St Basil the Great Monastic Order, (**2**) *19*
Schilling, Wladimir Singalewytsch von, (**6**) *68*
Schipper, Ignaz, 237, (**10**) *8*, *29*
Schmidt, Josef, (**10**) *96*
Schneider, Antoni, (**1**) *86*, (**2**) *20*
Schneider, Ludwig, 251, (**10**) *93*
Schnür-Pepłowski, Stanisław, 97, (**5**) *9*, (**6**) *128*, (**10**) *1*
Scholarly journals, *see* Press, the
Schorr, Joshua Heschel, 230
Schorr, Mojżesz, (**10**) *18*
Schreiber-Łuczyński, W., (**10**) *106*
Schutzman, N., (**10**) *59*
Seefeldt, Fritz, (**10**) *90*, *93*, *96*
Selians'kyi, Liubomyr, (**6**) *80*
Sel-Rob, *see* Peasant and Workers Socialist Union
Semaniuk, Nataliia V., (**6**) *178*
Sembratowycz, Roman, (**6**) *67*
Semko, S., (**7**) *100*
Sens, Brenda, xviii
Senytsia, Pavlo, (**7**) *85*
Separatism, *see* Nationalism
Serbs, 114
Serczyk, Władysław, (**6**) *120*
Serejski, Marian, (**10**) *1*
Seret River, 168
Serfdom, *see* Socioeconomic structure
Shadurs'kyi, M., (**4**) *59*
Shakh, Stepan (Stepan Pers'kyi), 108, (**2**) *74*, *97*, *106*, (**5**) *58*
Shalata, Mykhailo I., 108, (**5**) *58*
Shandruk, Pavlo, (**8**) *35*
Shankovs'kyi, Lev, 219, (**1**) *6*, (**7**) *18*, (**8**) *33*, *36*, (**9**) *6*
Shapovalov, I.I., (**7**) *106*
Sharanevych (Szaraniewicz), Izydor I., 4, 28, 54, 55, 59, 63, 76, 84, 85, 153, (**1**) *15*, *78*, (**2**) *67*, (**3**) *17*, *21*, *34*, *47*, *50*, (**4**) *17*, *59*, *67*, (**6**) *143*
Sharvit, E., (**10**) *66*
Sharych, Mykhail, (**6**) *220*
Shashkevych, Markiian, 107–108, (**5**) *52*, *53*, *55–59*
Shchurat, Stepan V., (**1**) *21*
Shchurat, Vasyl', 4–5, 112, 113, (**1**) *21*, (**5**) *38*, *79*, (**6**) *28*, *120*
Shchurovs'kyi, A., (**4**) *80*
Shelepets', Iosyf, (**1**) *20*
Sheliahin, D.O., (**9**) *13*
Shematyzm, *see Schematisma*
Sheptyts'ka, Sofiia z Fredriv, (**6**) *186*
Sheptyts'kyi, Andrei, 160, 168, 169, 171, 201, 209, 211, (**2**) *47*, (**6**) *184*, *185*, *186*, (**7**) *93*, (**8**) *12*
Sheptyts'kyi, Lev, 105
Shevchenko, Taras, 150, 162
Shevchenko Scientific Society, 17, 18, 36, 144, 164, (**1**) *91*, (**2**) *72*, (**6**) *212*
Shevchuk, Semen, (**7**) *5*
Shevelov, George Y., (**6**) *104*
Shlepakov, A.M., (**6**) *87*
Shmedes, K., (**2**) *20*
Shneider, Iuliia, *see* Kravchenko, Uliana
Shomer (Guardian of) Israel, (**10**) *38*
Shtein, V.I. (A. Morskoi), (**2**) *38*
Shukhevych, Roman, *see* Chuprynka, Taras

Shukhevych, Stepan, (**7**) *22*
Shukhevych, Volodymyr, 39, (**2**) *95*
Shumlians'kyi, Iosyf, (**4**) *63*
Shvydak, Oleh M., (**7**) *75*
Shymonovych, Ivan, 26, (**2**) *22*
Siarczyński, Franciszek, (**2**) *127*
Sich (Vienna), 149, (**6**) *120*
Sichyns'kyi, Denys, (**1**) *86*
Sichyns'kyi, Myroslav, 135, (**6**) *73*
Sichyns'kyi, Volodymyr (Vladimir Sičynśkyj), (**4**) *84*
Siegel, Stanisław, (**4**) *37*
Siegfried (Heinrich Czerwenzel), (**10**) *96*
Sigelman, J., (**10**) *73*
Sikora, Franciszek, (**3**) *52*
Silesia, 139, (**2**) *26*
Sil's'kyi Hospodar, *see* Agricultural Association
Singer, Isidor, (**10**) *9*
Šíp, František, (**7**) *23*
Sirenko, P.M., (**5**) *52*
Sirka, Ann, 147, (**6**) *110*
Sivers'ka, K., (**5**) *21*
Sivpolko, S., (**7**) *83*
Sizonenko, G.S., (**10**) *76*, *87*
Skaba, A.D., (**2**) *12*
Skalat, 244, (**10**) *67*
Skorski, Aleksander, (**6**) *119*
Skrokowski, Konstanty, (**6**) *224*
Skruten, L., (**1**) *82*
Skrypnyk, I.P., (**5**) *52*
Skrypnyk, K.I., (**9**) *17*
Skrypnyk, Mykola, 197, (**7**) *76*
Skrzypek, Józef, 58, 169, (**3**) *30*, (**6**) *224*
Skrzypek, Stanisław, (**7**) *4*
Skvarko, Zakhar, (**6**) *71*
Skyt Maniavs'kyi monastery, (**4**) *62*, *87*
Slav Congress (Prague), 123, 124, 128
Slavík, Václav, (**9**) *12*
Slavs, 165, 231; Galician relationship to, 29, 32, 48–49, 56–57, 104, 112–115, 143, 161–167. *See also* Pan-Slavism
Slavs'ke, (**2**) *113*
Slavutych, Iar, (**2**) *99*
Slipyi, Iosyf, 222–223, (**9**) *25*
Slovakia, 220, (**4**) *12*
Slovaks, 27, 113, 161
Slovanská knihovna (Prague), 19
Slovenia and Slovenians, 113, 209
Slovo, 166, (**6**) *216*, *217*
Slyvka, Iurii Iu., 181, (**7**) *13*, *75*
Smal'-Stots'kyi, Roman, (**6**) *157*
Smirnov, Mikhail, 55, (**3**) *22*, *32*, (**4**) *17*
Smishko, Markiian (Marcyan Śmiszko), (**3**) *2*, *10*
Smołka, Jan, (**1**) *66*, (**4**) *45*
Smolka, Stanisław, 29, 133, (**2**) *34*, (**6**) *64*
Smólski, G., (**10**) *106*
Smyrnov, *see* Smirnov, Mikhail
Sniatyn, 39, 248, (**2**) *89*, (**10**) *88*
Snihurs'kyi, Ivan, 105, 113
Sobieski, Zygmunt, (**8**) *11*
Sobin, Dimitry, (**7**) *30*
Sobiński, Stanisław, (**7**) *83*
Sochaniewicz, Stefan, (**1**) *61*, (**4**) *15*
Social class, *see* Socioeconomic structure
Social Democratic party, *see* Ukrainian political parties
Socialism, 136, 142, 153, 181, 184, 229, 230, 240
Socialist-Radical party, *see* Ukrainian political parties
Society for the Friends of Karaite History and Literature, (**10**) *99*
Socioeconomic structure, 78, 163; agrarian-based, 67, 75, 94, 99, 117, 125, 137, 139, 193, 194, 222; and class conflict, 32, 43, 59, 91 (*see also* Revolutions/uprisings); collectivization,

218, 222; cooperative movements, 116, 136, 138, 178, 193, 249; depression and, 194; and economic history, 71, 74, 79–80, 84, 97, 99–101, 121, 136–142, 193–195, 210, 237, 250 (*see also* Statistical surveys); and emigration, 237–238 (*see also* Emigration/immigration); feudal system, 52, 76, 79; industry, 77, 99, 100–101, 136, 139–141, 194, 195, 221, 225, (nationalization of) 210, 218; labor, 67, 139, 240 (*see also* Strikes and protests); land ownership and reform, 67, 78, 99, 136–137, 139–140, 209; minority status in, 229, 248; nobility, 67, 68, 70, 75–76, 78, 94, 246; peasantry, 37, 70, 82, 122, 123, 124, 159, 195, 208, 225, 228 (protests/uprisings by) 90, 100, 126, 186, 194, (socioeconomic conditions of) 71, 76, 99–100, 116, 119, 136–138; serfdom, 67, 68, 70, 76, 94, 95, 99, 100, 125, (abolished) 116, 123, 136, 137, ("economic") 137; trade, 52, 59, 67, 77, 78, 99, 101, 225, 244. *See also* Ukrainian political parties

Sofronenko, Kseniia A., (**3**) *36*

Sójka-Zielińska, Katarzyna, 137, (**6**) *81*

Sokal', 39, 45, 229, 244, (**2**) *90*, *136*, (**10**) *68*

Sokalski, Bronisław, (**2**) *90*

Sokhots'kyi, Izydor, 132, (**2**) *8*, (**6**) *63*

Sokolovs'ka, T.H., (**7**) *82*, (**8**) *20*, *21*, (**9**) *20*

Solchanyk, Roman, 196, (**7**) *72*

Solov'ev, Sergei, 55, (**3**) *23*

Sonevyts'kyi, Leonid C., (**4**) *61*, (**6**) *213*, (**7**) *39*

Sopotnicki, Józef, (**7**) *18*

Sosnovs'kyi, Mykhailo, (**7**) *62*

Southeastern Poland (*Polska Południowo-Wschodnia*), xvi

Soviet Galician Republic, *see* Galician Socialist Soviet Republic

Soviet Ukraine, 197, 199, 213, 222; Galicia as part of, 207, 208, 210, 217–218; recognizes Polish control of Galicia, 187; Ukrainianization policy in, 196, 217–218; writers and publications of, 71, 85, 91, 126, 137, 149, 153, 154, 184, 210

Soviet Union, xvi, 8, 14, 17; archeological research by, 47, 49; and the church, 34, 103–104, 169, 194, 201, 218, 222–223, 245, 247; foreign policy documents of, 166; Galician rule by, 12, 15, 16, 43, 119, 192, 207, 215, 217–218, 225, ("achievements" under) 210–211, 221–223; -Germany relations, 205, 207, 213, 249; interest of, in Galicia (interwar), 188–189; -Poland relations, 181, 187, 194, 231, (Polish-Soviet war, 1920) 188, (Polish-Soviet border, 1947) 217; in World War II, 205, 207–215, 217, 231, 249, (**8**) *37*. *See also* Red Army; Russian Empire

Soviet Union, historiographical writings of, 27, 38, 55, 74, 78, 79, 87, 89, 90, 100, 107, 109, 178, 194–195, 197, 200, 248; bibliographies of, 10–11; encyclopedias/dictionaries, 23–24, 41; Marxist perspective in, 2–3, 22, 32–33, 35, 103, 108, 119, 126, 140, 144, 196, 220 (and emphasis on class conflict) 32, 43, 59, 91; vs Polish view, 49, 56, 136, 169, 170–171, 181; revisionist views in, 42–43, 188; views of church in, 34, 62, 83, 103–104, 160, 171, 247; on World War II and

postwar, 207, 208, 210–211, 213, 218, 221–223. *See also* Soviet Ukraine
Sozans'kyi, Ivan, (**4**) *39*, (**6**) *24*, *45*, *158*
Spanovskii, Ia., (**2**) *38*
Spiš (Spisz), (**2**) *26*
Spivachevs'ka, Nina, (**1**) *37*
Spodarenko, I.V., (**2**) *132*
Sprawy Narodowościowe, 22, (**2**) *3*
Springer, Anton, (**6**) *27*
Śreniowski, Stanisław, (**4**) *14*
Sreznevs'kyi, Izmaïl, 115
Sribnyi, Fedir, 86, (**4**) *72*
Stadion, Franz, 123, 127, (**6**) *43*
Stadnicki, Kazimierz, (**4**) *48*
Stakhiv, Matvii (M. Mykolaievych), 119, 181, (**6**) *5*, *71*, *95*, (**7**) *11*
Stanymir, Osyp, (**7**) *22*
Stanyslaviv (Stanisławów, later Ivano-Frankivs'k), 8, 9, 12, 146, 160; minorities in, 229, 235, 244, 248, (**10**) *18*, *31*, *43*, *69*, *88*, *96*; as seat of government, 174; surveys of and guides to, 23, 25, 26, 39, 40, 41, 45, 235, 248, (**1**) *42*, *57*, (**2**) *24*, *91*, *99*, *113*, *138*, (**6**) *109*; as territorial unit, 176, 218, 225, 241. *See also* Ivano-Frankivs'k
Stara Ukraïna, 22
Starzyński, Stanisław, 38, (**2**) *82*
Staša, Josef, xviii
Stasiw, Myron, (**4**) *60*
Statistical guides and surveys, 11, 25–26, 96, 97–98, 118, 121–122, 136, 138, 146, 180, 221, 227, 232, (**2**) *18*, *19*, *20*, *111*, (**5**) *10*, *11*, (**6**) *14*, *16*, *17*, *18*, *76*, *108*, (**7**) *7*, *8*, (**9**) *13*, *14*, (**10**) *95*. See also *Schematisma*; Yearbooks
Statute of Kalisz (1264), 228
Stauropegial Brotherhood (later Institute), 17, 18, 21, 35, 68, 69, 85–86, 88, 106, 110, 143, (**1**) *78*, *86*, *88*, (**2**) *67*, (**4**) *64–72*, (**5**) *66*, (**6**) *99*
Stavrovs'kyi, Omelian, (**4**) *12*, *95*
Steblii, Fedir I., 100, (**1**) *54*, (**5**) *23*, (**6**) *28*, *39*, (**8**) *20*
Stefański, Stefan, (**2**) *135*
Stefanyk, Vasyl', 157, (**6**) *173*, (**7**) *99*
Stefanyk Library of the Academy of Sciences (L'viv), 15, 17, 18, (**1**) *84*, *94*
Steinberg, Mojżesz, (**10**) *18*
Stenographic records (of diet and parliamentary debates), 124, 131–132, 189, (**6**) *27*, *55–61*, (**7**) *47*, *48*
Stepaniv, Iaroslav, *see* Dashkevych, Iaroslav R.
Stepaniv, Olena, 42, (**2**) *107*
Stepovych, Andronyk, (**6**) *195*
Stesłowicz, Władysław, (**7**) *17*
Stets'ko, Iaroslav S., 211, 212, (**8**) *27*
Stöger, Michael, 236, (**10**) *21*
Stökl, Günther, (**1**) *1*, (**3**) *23*
Stone, Norman, (**6**) *237*
Stradch, (**2**) *113*
Streit, Leon, (**10**) *18*
Strel'skii, V.I., (**2**) *25*
Strepa, Jakob, 81
Strikes and protests, 90, 125, 133, 137, 141, 175, 181, 194. *See also* Revolutions/uprisings
Strizhkov, Iu.K., (**8**) *38*
Struk, Danylo S., (**6**) *173*
Struminskyj, Bohdan, (**1**) *99*
Stryi, 45, 146, 244, 249, (**2**) *137*, (**10**) *70*
Student Home (L'viv), 201
Student societies and activities, 133, 144, 149, 153, 162, 163, 198
Studium Ruthenum, 95, 101, 102, 104
Studyns'kyi, Kyrylo, 4, 104, 110, 113, 145, 151, 161, 164, (**1**) *13*, *19*, (**2**) *67*, *72*, (**4**) *85*, (**5**) *17*, *33*, *34*, *38*, *52*, *63*,

66, 69, 77, 78, 79, (**6**) *70, 101, 102, 105, 132, 159, 183, 189, 195, 197, 204, 210, 213*
Stupnicki, Hipolit, 26, (**2**) *20*
Stupnyts'kyi, Ivan, 159, (**6**) *183*
Styria, 167
Styr River and region, 56
Subcarpathia/Subcarpathian Rus', 31, 57, 61, 115, 125, 166, (**1**) *20,* (**2**) *38, 40. See also* Transcarpathia
Suchodolski, Bogdan, (**2**) *10*
Sudetenland, 249
Sudova Vyshnia, 72
Suffrage, *see* Elections
Sulimierski, Filip, (**2**) *21*
Sulimirski, Tadeusz, (**3**) *2*
Supreme Ruthenian Council (Holovna Rus'ka Rada), 123, 124, 125, 126, 128, (**6**) *24*
Supreme Ukrainian Council (Holovna Ukraïns'ka Rada), 168
Suski, J., (**7**) *8*
Svientsits'ka, Vira, (**4**) *86*
Svientsits'kyi, Ilarion S., 5, 16, 35, 37, 87, 115, 151, (**1**) *24, 76–78, 81, 93,* (**2**) *75,* (**4**) *76, 78, 87,* (**5**) *28, 85, 86,* (**6**) *131, 197, 217*
Svientsits'kyi, Pavlyn, 155, (**6**) *162*
Svieshnikov, Ivan K., (**3**) *7*
Sviezhyns'kyi, P.V., (**6**) *82*
Svistun, F.I., *see* Svystun, Pylyp
S'vit, 144, (**6**) *103*
Svitlynskii, Bohdan, (**6**) *228*
Svoboda, A., (**9**) *12*
Svobodová, K., (**9**) *12*
Svystun, Pylyp (F.I. Svistun), 95, 104, 119, (**introd.**) *4,* (**1**) *76, 77, 90,* (**4**) *1,* (**5**) *2, 26, 34, 47, 48, 67, 69, 79,* (**6**) *6, 24, 37, 51, 102, 134, 141, 183, 222*
Swiatłomir (H. Zaleski), (**6**) *114*
Świerczewski, Karol, 220
Sworakowski, Witold, (**2**) *3*
Symonenko, R.H., (**7**) *30*
Sysyn, Frank E., xviii, (**4**) *18,* (**5**) *60, 72,* (**6**) *3, 90, 168,* (**10**) *24, 38*
Szapszal, H. Seraja, 255
Szaraniewicz, *see* Sharanevych, Izydor I.
Szarłowski, A., (**2**) *91*
Szczecin, 217
Szczęśniak Antoni B., 213, (**8**) *29, 31,* (**9**) *11*
Szczęśniak, Bolesław, (**3**) *43*
Szelągowski, Adam, 58, (**3**) *30*
Szematyzm, see Schematisma
Szeptycka, *see* Sheptyts'ka, Sofiia z Fredriv
Szota, Wiesław Z., 213, (**8**) *31, 36,* (**9**) *11*
Szporluk, Roman, 222, (**9**) *22*
Sztendera, Jaroslaw, (**7**) *11*
Szujski, Józef, 133, (**2**) *33,* (**6**) *64*
Szwejgiert, Bolesław, (**9**) *11*
Szydelski, Stefan, (**4**) *48*
Szymonowic, Szymon, 226
Szyszman, Aleksander, 255, (**10**) *109*
Szyszman, Simon, 253, (**10**) *102*

Taffet, Gerszon, (**10**) *74*
Talerhof, 167, 170, (**6**) *228*
Tanty, Mieczysław, (**6**) *215*
Tarnavs'kyi, Myron, 183, (**7**) *20*
Tarnopol, *see* Ternopil'
Tarnovych, Iuliian (Iuliian Beskid), (**2**) *97,* (**7**) *86*
Tarnów, 168
Tarnowski, Stanisław, 29, 133, (**2**) *34,* (**6**) *64*
Tartakiv, 244, (**10**) *71*
Tartakower, Arich, (**10**) *30*
Tashkent Bolshevik party, 184

Tăslăuanu, Octavian C., (**6**) *238*

Tatars, the, 62, 65, 72, 227, 249, 252, (**4**) *27*, (**10**) *109*

Teacher's College and Gymnasium (Zalishchyky), 201, (**6**) *117*

Temnyts'kyi, Volodymyr (Voldemar Temnytsky), (**7**) *27*

Tenenbaum, Josef (Josef Bendow), (**10**) *27*, *28*, *31*, *43*

Terebeichyk, N.H., (**1**) *53*

Terebovlia (Trembowla), xv, 39, 40, 52, 64, (**2**) *93*, *99*, (**3**) *53*, (**10**) *16*

Tereshchuk, Petro, (**7**) *106*

Terlets'kyi (Terletsky), Markiian, (**2**) *78*

Terlets'kyi, Omelian, 35, 73, (**2**) *62*, *78*, (**3**) *24*, (**4**) *8*

Terlets'kyi, Ostap (Ivan Zanevych), 4, 100, 106–107, 110, 142, 143, 149, 156, (**1**) *18*, (**5**) *24*, *50*, *62*, *64*, (**6**) *96*, *123*, *163*, *164*

Ternavka, (**2**) *113*

Ternopil', xv, 12, 146, 168, 188, 229, 230, 244, (**1**) *57*; Russian occupation of, 98, 207, (**5**) *15*; as seat of government, 174, 175; siege of, 215; studies of and guides to, 26, 39, 41, 45, (**2**) *24*, *92*, *101*, *139*, (**10**) *36*, *72*; as territorial unit, 176, 218, 221, 225, 241, (**7**) *69*, (**9**) *14*; yearbooks, (**6**) *109*

Tershakovets', Mykhailo, 102, 113, (**1**) *13*, *19*, (**5**) *28*, *52*, *57*, *79*

Tesla, Ivan, (**6**) *87*

Tesliuk, M.M., (**7**) *74*

Theater, the, *see* Culture

Tichý, František, (**1**) *20*

Tikhomirov, I., 62, (**3**) *45*

Tiulina, H.V., (**1**) *68*

Tiutiunnyk, Iurko, (**7**) *22*

Tkachenko, V.A., (**1**) *18*

Tobiasz, Julian, (**8**) *37*

Tokarz, Wacław, 97, (**5**) *12*

Tomashivs'kyi, Stepan, 5, 90, 102, (**1**) *23*, (**2**) *43*, (**3**) *24*, (**4**) *61*, *88*, *91*, (**5**) *28*, (**7**) *5*

Tomaszewski, Jerzy, (**7**) *71*

Torosovič, Nikol, 244

Torzecki, Ryszard, 190, 213, (**7**) *52*, (**8**) *11*, *30*

Tovarysh, 144, (**6**) *103*

Trade, *see* Socioeconomic structure

Trakai (Troki), 252, 253

Transcarpathia, xvi, 218, (**4**) *12*. *See also* Subcarpathia/Subcarpathian Rus'

Transliteration, xvi–xvii. *See also* Language/alphabet

Transylvania, 27

Trembowla, *see* Terebovlia

Trofymuk, Stepan M., (**7**) *101*, *102*, *105*

Troitskii, S., (**2**) *38*

Troki (Trakai), 252, 253

Trubetskoi, Aleksander, 30, (**2**) *37*

Trusevych, Stepan M., (**6**) *47*

Trzebieński, Aleksander, (**4**) *48*

Trzynadlowski, Jan, 36, (**2**) *70*

Tsehel'nyk, Ia.Kh., (**7**) *102*

Tsehel's'kyi, L'ongin, 186, (**6**) *67*, *186*, (**7**) *32*

Tsehlyns'kyi, Hryhorii, (**6**) *57*, *128*

Tsehlyns'kyi, M.H., (**6**) *227*

Tselevych, Iuliian, 4, (**1**) *16*, (**4**) *62*, *95*

Tseniv, (**2**) *100*

Tsentrosoiuz, *see* Central Union

Tsiutsiura, Teodor Bohdan, (**6**) *52*

Ts'okh, Iosyf T., 198, (**1**) *38*, (**7**) *80*

Tsybko, O.H., (**7**) *42*, *71*, (**8**) *38*

Tučková, A., (**9**) *12*

Tudor, Stepan, 203, (**7**) *101*, *102*

Turkhol'ka, (**2**) *113*

Turaeva-Tserteli, E., (**2**) *38*

Turka, 39, 244, (**2**) *94*, (**6**) *109*, (**10**) *73*

Turkestan Soviet Republic, 184, (**7**) *25*
Turko-Mongolians, 255; and Turkic language, 253
Turks, the, 244
Turlejska, Maria, (**9**) *11*
Turska, Jadwiga, (**1**) *98*
Tverdokhlib, V.Iu., (**7**) *2*
Twardowski, Samuel, 226
Tyliszczak, Mikołaj, (**9**) *11*
Tyriava Sil'na, 45, (**2**) *140*
Tyrowicz, Marian, 97, (**1**) *4*, (**2**) *33*, (**5**) *9*
Tyshchyk, B.I., (**7**) *44*
Tyshyns'ka, Evstakhiia, 115, (**5**) *86*
Tys-Krokhmaliuk, Iurii, *see* Krokhmaliuk, Iurii Tys-Tysovets', (**2**) *113*
Tytov, T., (**6**) *181*

Uhniv region, 41, (**2**) *100*
Ujejski, Kornel, 226
Ukrainian Galician Army, 173, 175, 182–183, (**7**) *15*, *18–22*
Ukrainian Insurgent Army (Ukraïns'ka Povstans'ka Armiia, UPA), 212, 214, 217, 218–220, (**1**) *6*, (**8**) *36*, *37*, (**9**) *3–7*, *11*, *12*
Ukrainianization policy, *see* Soviet Ukraine
Ukrainian Military Organization (UVO), 175, 176, 190–191, 193, 211, (**7**) *56*
Ukrainian National Army, 214, (**8**) *35*
Ukrainian National Republic, 175, 184, 186
Ukrainian organizations and institutions; Academic Gymnasium, 200, (**6**) *117*; Art Museum, 19, (**1**) *97*; Central Committee (Cracow), 207, (**9**) *13*; Land Committee, 209, (**9**) *10*; National Council (1941), 209, (**8**) *10*; National Museum, 15, 17, 18, 37, (**1**) *81*, *93*, (**2**) *75*; Parliamentary Representation, 168, 171; Pedagogical Society, 199, (**7**) *89*; Supreme Liberation/Revolutionary Council (Ukraïnska Holovna Vyzvol'na Rada, UHVR, 1944), 217, 219, (**9**) *3*, *7*; Theological Scholarly Society, 201, (**7**) *90*
Ukrainian political parties, 116, 133, 134, 207, (**1**) *47*, (**7**) *49*; Catholic National, 176; National Democratic, 134, 176, (**6**) *71*; National Democratic Union (UNDO), 176, 178, 190, (**7**) *49*; Radical, 134, 190, (**6**) *71*; Social Democratic, 134, 142, 176, 190, (**6**) *71*; Socialist-Radical, 176, (**7**) *49*. *See also* Communist party
Ukrainian Sich Rifleman (Ukraïns'ki Sichovi Stril'tsi), 8–9, 168, 169, 173, 181, 182, 184, 211, (**1**) *39*, (**6**) *243*, (**7**) *18*
Ukrainian Soviet Socialist Republic, xvi, 11, 14, 33, 41, 194, 207, 217, 221, (**1**) *57*, *70*, (**9**) *13*
Ukrainische Rundschau, 22
Ukrainophiles, xvi, 103, 108, 109, 110, 144, 166; and language, 145; -Russophile animosity, 119, 143, 170, 202; in World War I, 167, 169. *See also* Nationalism; Populism
Ukrainskaia zhizn', 31
Ukraïns'ke literaturoznavstvo, 22
Ukraïns'kyi istorychnyi zhurnal, 22, (**2**) *5*
UNDO (National Democratic Union), *see* Ukrainian political parties
Undol'skii, Vukol M., 6, (**1**) *28*
Ungeheuer, Marjan, (**4**) *45*
Unger, Shabbetai, (**10**) *39*
Uniate movement, 69–70, 76, 81, 84, 245. *See also* Greek Catholic (Uniate) church; Roman Catholic church

Union for the Liberation of the Ukraine (Soiuz Vyzvolennia Ukraïny), 168, 171, (**6**) *234*
United States: emigration to, 137, 138–139, 229, 237, (**6**) *73*, *85–87*, (**10**) *30*, (and return from) 165; "imperialism" of, 188
Univ, 88, (**4**) *80*
University of L'viv, *see* L'viv, University of
UPA, *see* Ukrainian Insurgent Army
Urban history, 38, 41–45, 63–64, 71–72, 77–80, 81, 123, 243–244
Urbanitsch, Peter, (**6**) *1*, *3*
Ustiianovych, Kornylo N., 120, 155, (**6**) *10*, *161*
Ustiianovych, Mykola, 152, (**6**) *136*
Utrysko, Myron, (**2**) *96*
UVO, *see* Ukrainian Military Organization

Vahylevych, Ivan, 107, 108, 109, 112, 114, 115, (**5**) *53*, *60–62*, *84*, *88*
Vainbaun, O.H., (**1**) *58*
Vakhnianyn, Anatol', 120, (**6**) *10*, *47*
Vakulenko, Havriil S., (**8**) *37*
Vandůrek, Ladislav, (**9**) *12*
Varangians, 49
Varets'kyi, Vasyl' L., (**8**) *16*, *18*
Variahina, Vira D., (**8**) *37*
Vasil'ev, A.F., (**2**) *38*
Vasilevskii, L., (**6**) *19*
Vasiuta, I.K., (**7**) *71*
Vasyl'ev, Mykhailo, (**6**) *124*
Vasyl'kiv, O., 196
Vatican, the, *see* Roman Catholic church
Vavrik, Vasilii R., 7, 24, 107, 109, 110, (**1**) *15*, *32*, (**2**) *14*, (**5**) *55*, *62*, *64*, (**6**) *140*, (**7**) *24*
Vavryk, Mykhailo, (**1**) *43*, (**5**) *41*
Venkov, B.S., (**8**) *38*
Verbinskii, M.V., (**8**) *39*
Vergun, Dmitrii, 30, (**2**) *37*
Verkhrats'kyi, Ivan, 149, (**6**) *123*
Vernadsky, George, 60, (**3**) *37*
Versailles Treaty, 175
Veryha, Vasyl', (**1**) *6*, (**2**) *72*, (**6**) *117*, (**7**) *87*
Vesolovs'kyi, Iaroslav, (**6**) *74*
Vienna, 8, 96, 101, 106, 166, 238, (**6**) *117*, *156*; archives in, 15, 19, 245, (**1**) *71*; emigration to, 191, 231, 238, (**10**) *30*; Galician-Ukrainian leaders based in, 168, 171, 175, 186; imperial government at, *see* Austria/Austrian Empire
Vientskovskii, Dmitrii, (**6**) *182*
Vilnius, 109, 252, 253
Vincenz, Stanisław, (**10**) *43*
Vishnevskii, I.P., (**5**) *64*
Vistnyk, 192
Vîstnyk, 21
Vîstnyk, chasopys'...dlia Rusynov Avstrïiskoi dierzhavŷ (**6**) *101*
Vistula River region, 49, 57, 77, 92, 94
Vitoshyns'kyi, Ia., (**8**) *7*
Vitovs'kyi, Dmytro, 182
Vladimir-Suzdal, 62
Vlasenko, Vladlen P., (**7**) *103*
Vlasovs'kyi, Ivan, (**4**) *57*
Voinarovs'kyi, Tyt, 96, 120, (**5**) *3*, (**6**) *10*
Volhynia, 52, 57, 64, 65, 68, 86, 88, 92, 189, 252, 253, (**2**) *18*, *20*, (**10**) *91*, *97*; Communist movement in, (**7**) *72*. *See also* Galician-Volhynian principality
Volianiuk, M.M., (**6**) *92*
Voloboi, P.V., (**2**) *24*
Volodymyr, 50, 56, 57
Volodymyrko, 52
Voloshcha, (**2**) *113*

Volynets', Stepan, 132, (**2**) *8*, *74*, (**6**) *63*
Volyns'kyi, Petro K., (**5**) *51*
Von Guttry, A., (**2**) *29*
Vorobiova, T.O., (**1**) *42*
Vorobkevych, Ievhen, 34
Voskanian, N.A., (**10**) *80*
Voskresenskii, G.A., (**2**) *38*
Vozniak, Mykhailo, 103, 108, 112, 127, 151, 155, 164, (**5**) *29*, *43*, *46*, *57*, *58*, *62*, *64*, *65*, *73*, *74*, *87*, (**6**) *40*, *101*, *102*, *104*, *133*, *148*, *155*, *156*, *198*, *199*, *210*, *213*, *214*
Vradii, Nadezhda F., (**1**) *69*, (**10**) *76*
Vremennyk, 21, (**2**) *1*
Vrets'ona, Ievhen, (**9**) *8*
Vul'fson, E.S., (**6**) *19*
Vynar, *see* Wynar, Lubomyr R.
Vynnyky, (**2**) *100*
Vynnyts'kyi, Inokentii Ivan, (**4**) 62, 63
Vynnyts'kyi, Ivan, (**2**) *99*
Vyshens'kyi, Ivan, 69
Vyshyvanyi, Vasyl', *see* Wilhelm Franz Habsburg
Vytanovych, Illia, 32, 138, 193, (**6**) *84*, *163*, *167*, (**7**) *68*
Vytautas, 252
Vytvytsia, (**2**) *113*
Vytvyts'kyi, Sofron, 155, (**6**) *157*
Vytvyts'kyi, Stepan, 32

Wacław z Oleksa, *see* Zaleski, Wacław
Wagner, Viktor, (**10**) *97*
Wagner, W.A., (**4**) *41*
Waigel, Leopold, (**2**) *130*
Wakar, Włodzimierz, (**10**) *2*
Walach, Stanisław, (**9**) *11*
Wallachia, 67
Wandruska, Adam, (**6**) *1*, *3*
Wandycz, Piotr S., 118, (**6**) *3*
Wars, 52, 53, 78, 90, 188. *See also* Battle(s); Polish-Ukrainian war (1918-19); Revolutions/uprisings; World War I; World War II
Warsaw, xvi, 164, 199, 207; archival material in, 15, 190. *See also* Poland
Warsaw, Duchy of, 94
Warthegau (West Prussia), 250
Washburn, Stanley, (**6**) *237*
Wasilewski, Leon, 29, (**2**) *35*, (**7**) *4*
Wasiutyński, Bohdan, 238, (**10**) *32*
Wąsowicz, Michał, (**1**) *69*, (**4**) *37*, (**5**) *21*
Wasylewski, Stanisław, (**2**) *108*
Wawrzkowicz, Eugeniusz, 182, (**7**) *17*
Waxman, Meyer, 240, (**10**) *41*
Webersfeld, Edward, (**2**) *125*
Wein, Abraham, 232, (**10**) *7*
Weinloes, Israel, (**10**) *36*
Weinryb, Bernard D., 233, (**10**) *8*
Weisbrod, Avram, (**10**) *67*
Weissberg, Max, (**10**) *42*
Weliczker-Wells, Leon, (**10**) *47*
Welykyj, Athanasius G., 33, (**2**) *48–55*
Wenzel, Gusztáv, 60, (**3**) *38*
Wereszycki, Henryk, (**1**) *1*
Western Powers, *see* Allied Powers
Western Ukraine (*Zakhidna Ukraïna*), xvi, 2, 22, 35; People's Assembly of, 207
Western Ukrainian People's Republic (*Zakhidno-Ukraïns'ka Narodna Respublyka*), xvi, 174, 175, 185–188
White Croats, 48–50, 56, 57, (**3**) *8–12*
White Russians and White Russian Army, 175, 184, 186
Wiczkowski, Józef, (**2**) *108*
Widajewicz, Józef, 58, (**3**) *11*, *30*
Widmann, Karol, (**1**) *63*
Wiener, Leo, (**10**) *41*
Wierzbowski, T., (**10**) *12*
Wiesiołowski, Michał, 96, (**5**) *6*

Wikler, J., (**10**) *18*
Wilhelm, Franz, (**10**) *93*
Wilhelm Franz Habsburg (Vasyl' Vyshyvanyi), 169, 172, (**6**) *236*
Winiarski, Bohdan, (**6**) *20*, *54*
Winiarski, Ignacy, (**6**) *52*
Winiarz, Alojzy, (**1**) *62*, (**4**) *47*
Winter, Edward, (**6**) *150*
Wischnitzer, M., (**10**) *29*
Wisłocki, W.T., (**6**) *25*, *45*
Wisłok River, xiv, 94
Włodarski, Bronisław, 58, 61, (**1**) *4*, (**3**) *31*, *40*
Wójcik, Zbigniew, 15 (**1**), *71*
Województwo Ruskie, *see* Rus' palatinate
Wojnarowskyj, *see* Voinarovs'kyi, Tyt
Wojtanowicz, Elijasz, (**6**) *88*
Woliński, Janusz, 15, (**1**) *71*
Wondaś, A., (**2**) *127*
World Lemkos' Federation, 219
World War I, xiv, 9, 22, 26, 32, 117, 130, 134, 167–173, 184, 227, 230–231, 237
World War II, xvi, 11, 31, 33, 178, 205, 207–215, 217, 231, 233, 234, 242, 249–250
Worobkiewicz, Emmanuel-Eugen, (**2**) *60*
Wrocław, 15, 19, 36, 217, 245, (**1**) *98*, (**10**) *76*, *99*
Wschód, (**10**) *11*
Wurm, D., (**10**) *18*
Wurzbach, Constant von, (**2**) *10*
Wyka, Kazimierz, (**6**) *48*
Wynar, Lubomyr R., 165, (**4**) *76*, (**6**) *86*, *212*
Wynot, E., Jr, 190, (**7**) *54*
Wytrzens, Günther, (**6**) *156*

Yaremko, Michael, 31, (**2**) *39*
Yearbooks (*Zvity*), 146, (**2**) *81*, (**6**) *109*
Yiddish, *see* Language, Yiddish
Yl'nytskiï, Vasylii, *see* Il'nyts'kyi, Vasyl'
Young, Charles H., (**6**) *87*
Youth, *see* Student societies and activities

Zabokryts'kyi, I.Ia., (**9**) *20*
Zaborski, Tymon, 226
Žáček, Václav, 128, (**6**) *46*
Zachariasiewicz, Jan, 226
Zahaikevych, Bohdan, (**2**) *98*, *111*, (**3**) *10*, (**6**) *124*
Zahul, D., (**7**) *100*
Zaionchkovskii, A.M., (**6**) *237*
Zajączkowski, Ananiasz, 254, 255, (**10**) *101*, *109*
Zajączkowski, S., (**1**) *67*
Zajączkowski, Włodzimierz, (**10**) *103*
Zaklyns'kyi, Myron, (**7**) *16*
Zaklyns'kyi, Oleksii, 120, (**6**) *10*
Zaklyns'kyi, Roman, (**2**) *20*
Zakrzewski, Stanisław, (**4**) *7*
Zaks, Zofia, 187, 189, (**7**) *38*, *40*, *41*, *46*
Zaleski, H. (Swiatłomir), (**6**) *114*
Zaleski, Wacław (Wacław z Oleksa), 114, 127, (**6**) *43*
Zalishchyky, 201 (**2**) *100*, (**6**) *117*
Zalozets'kyi, Volodymyr (W. Zaloziecky), (**4**) *84*
Zalyns'kyi, Roman, (**2**) *20*
Zamkovyi, P.V., (**1**) *58*
Zamlyns'kyi, Volodymyr O., (**8**) *6*, *7*, *37*
Zanevych, Ivan, *see* Terlets'kyi, Ostap
Zap, Karel V., 96, 113, (**5**) *8*
Zapasko, Iakym, 87, (**4**) *76*, *78*, *79*
Zapletal, Florian, (**6**) *46*
Zaporozhian Cossacks, *see* Cossacks
Zapysky Chynu Sv. Vasyliia Velykoho, 22, (**2**) *4*
Zapysky Naukovoho tovarystva im. Shevchenka, 22

Zasans'kyi, V., (**9**) *18*
Zasenko, Oleksa, (**6**) *178*
Zavallia, (**2**) *113*
Zbarazh region, 40, 92, (**2**) *99*, (**6**) *109*
Zboriv, 45, (**2**) *141*
Zbruch River, xiv, 92, 168, 175
Zdan, *see* Zhdan, Mykhailo B.
Żegota, I. (I. Daszyński), (**6**) *64*
Żeleński, Władysław, (**7**) *59*
Zerov, Mykola, (**6**) *178*
Zhdan, Mykhailo B., 60, (**3**) *37*
Zhelekhovs'kyi, Iustyn, 120, 153, (**5**) *41*, (**6**) *10*, *141*
Zhilina, E., (**1**) *51*
Zholtkovs'kyi, Pavlo M., 89, (**4**) *81*, *85*
Zhovkva (Żółkiew), 45, 229, 244, 249, (**2**) *87*, *113*, *142*, (**10**) *74*
Zhuk, Andrii, (**7**) *67*, *68*
Zhuk, N., (**6**) *173*
Zhukov, T.I., (**7**) *71*
Zhupans'kyi, Ia.I., (**2**) *24*
Zhuravs'ka, I.Iu., (**6**) *190*
Zhyla, Volodymyr, (**2**) *99*
Zhytie i slovo, 21
Židlický, Václav, 112, (**5**) *75*
Zieduszucki, M.D., (**10**) 82
Zieliński, Konstanty, (**4**) *48*
Zieliński, Stanislaus, (**6**) *73*
Zielona Góra, 217
Ziemia Czerwieńska, 21
Ziemia Ruska, *see* Red Rus'
Zil'berman, Mark I., (**7**) *71*
Zilyns'kyi, Orest, 10, (**1**) *48*
Zinberg, Israel, 240, (**10**) *41*
Zionism, *see* Jews
Zlatoustovskii, B., (**1**) *51*
Zlenko, Petro, (**1**) *39*
Żółkiew, *see* Zhovkva
Zolochiv (Złoczów), 45, 228, 235, (**2**) *143*, (**10**) *18*
Zoria, 21
Zoria Halytska, 123, 144, (**6**) 101
Zschokke, Hermann, (**2**) *80*
Zuban', O.K., (**9**) *20*
Zubkovskii, V., (**6**) *19*
Zubryts'kyi, Denys, 4, 28, 29, 35, 42, 54, 57, 85, 111, 113, 114, (**1**) *13*, *86*, (**2**) *103*, (**3**) *19*, *20*, *28*, (**4**) *68*, *78*, (**5**) *69*, *74*, *79*, *84*, *86*
Zubryts'kyi, Mykhailo, (**1**) *92*, (**4**) *44*, (**5**) *28*, *39*
Zubyk, R., (**4**) *37*
Zucker, N., (**10**) *49*
Zvenyhorod, 52, 64, (**2**) *100*, *113*, (**3**) *51*
Zvity, *see* Yearbooks
Zwolska, Wanda, (**6**) *118*
Zyzanii, Lavrentii, 69

GALICIA
A HISTORICAL SURVEY AND BIBLIOGRAPHIC GUIDE

PAUL ROBERT MAGOCSI is Professor, Chair of Ukrainian Studies, at the University of Toronto

Galicia, an eastern European region that has been ruled by Poland, Austria, and the USSR at various times, has played an important and often crucial role in Ukrainian historical development. This is the first comprehensive bibliographic guide to its history.

The over-all arrangement is chronological and within that by theme. The book emphasizes political, socioeconomic, literary, linguistic, and archeological developments as they are recorded in fourteen languages. It contains more than 3000 references, 1000 notes, a detailed thematic and name index, and six maps which trace the historical development of Galicia.

Although Ukrainians have traditionally made up the largest part of Galicia's population, substantial minority populations of Poles, Germans, Armenians, Karaites, and most especially Jews have lived in the region at various times. The extensive literature on Galicia's Jews is brought together in this volume for the first time.

This volume is published in association with the Harvard Ukrainian Research Institute and the Canadian Institute of Ukrainian Studies. In 1982 it won Harvard University's Cenko Prize for the best work published in Ukrainian bibliography.

'This book is not only very timely ... but also a fine accomplishment in itself .... A careful check reveals that Dr. Magocsi hardly missed a title of crucial importance, and exactly this thoroughness enhances the value of the work.' Stephen M. Horeck, *American Historical Review*

'The volume represents an impressive achievement and ... is bound to remain an invaluable handbook for all students of central and east central European history.' Franz A.J. Szabo, *Slavic Review*

'In effect, this work is virtually a concise encyclopedia of the 'Galician problem' in the broadest sense of the word .... It is an excellent guide for all who are interested in any aspect of the historical territory known as eastern Galicia.' Benedykt Heydenkorn, *Kultura*

'It is much needed and will fill an important gap in knowledge.' Hugh Seton-Watson, *School of Slavonic and East European Studies, London*

'With meticulous scholarship and impressive subject expertise, this study guide presents a wealth of bibliographic information ... this work is an important contribution to Eastern European studies and is certain to stand users in excellent stead.' Paul L. Horecky, *Chief (ret.), Slavic and Central European Division, Library of Congress*